T0318303

THE ROUTLEDGE
HANDBOOK OF CRITICAL
FINANCE STUDIES

There has been an increasing interest in financial markets across sociology, history, anthropology, cultural studies, and related disciplines over the past decades, with particular intensity since the 2007–2008 crisis which prompted new analyses of the workings of financial markets and how "scandals of Wall Street" might have huge societal ramifications. The sociologically inclined landscape of finance studies is characterized by different more or less well-established homogeneous camps, with more micro-empirical, social studies of finance approaches on the one end of the spectrum and more theoretical, often neo-Marxist approaches, on the other.

Yet alternative approaches are also gaining traction, including work that emphasizes the cultural homologies and interconnections with finance as well as work that, more broadly, is both empirically rigorous and theoretically ambitious. Importantly, across these various approaches to finance, a growing body of literature is taking shape which engages finance in a critical manner.

The term "critical finance studies" nonetheless remains largely unfocused and undefined. Against this backdrop, the key rationales of *The Routledge Handbook of Critical Finance Studies* are firstly to provide a coherent notion of this emergent field and secondly to demonstrate its analytical usefulness across a wide range of central aspects of contemporary finance.

As such, the volume will offer a comprehensive guide to students and academics on the field of Finance and Critical Finance Studies, Heterodox Economics, Accounting, and related Management disciplines.

Christian Borch is Professor of Economic Sociology and Social Theory at the Copenhagen Business School, Denmark.

Robert Wosnitzer is Clinical Associate Professor of Management Communication at New York University Stern School of Business.

ROUTLEDGE INTERNATIONAL HANDBOOKS

For more information about this series, please visit: www.routledge.com/ Routledge-International-Handbooks/book-series/RIHAND

THE ROUTLEDGE HANDBOOK OF CRITICAL FINANCE STUDIES

*Edited by Christian Borch
and Robert Wosnitzer*

Routledge
Taylor & Francis Group
NEW YORK AND LONDON

First published 2021
by Routledge
52 Vanderbilt Avenue, New York, NY 10017

and by Routledge
2 Park Square, Milton Park, Abingdon, Oxon, OX14
4RN

*Routledge is an imprint of the Taylor & Francis Group, an
informa business*

Library of Congress Cataloging-in-Publication Data
A catalog record for this title has been requested

ISBN: 978-1-138-07981-6 (hbk)
ISBN: 978-1-315-11425-5 (ebk)

Typeset in Bembo
by codeMantra

CONTENTS

Contents

CONTRIBUTORS

Torsten Andreasen is a postdoctoral fellow affiliated with the collective research project "Finance Fiction: Financialization and Culture in the Early 21st Century" at the Department of Arts and Cultural Studies at the University of Copenhagen. His work currently focuses on the periodization of the correlation between literature and financial capital since 1980.

Christian Borch is Professor of Economic Sociology and Social Theory at the Copenhagen Business School, Denmark. He is the PI of the ERC-funded research project "Algorithmic Finance" (2017–2021), in which he examines the dynamics and consequences of the deployment of fully automated algorithms in financial markets. Christian is the author of several books, including *Social Avalanche: Crowds, Cities and Financial Markets* (Cambridge University Press, 2020).

Dick Bryan is Emeritus Professor of Political Economy at the University of Sydney, working on the changing role of households as objects of financial calculation. He is also the Chief Economist of the Economic Space Agency (ECSA), a cryptoeconomic startup company building a post-capitalist distributed token system which enables the valuation of output via its social contribution rather than its profitability.

Nathan Coombs is a lecturer in Economic Sociology in the School of Social and Political Science at the University of Edinburgh. His research focuses on post-crisis financial regulation, and he is a founding co-editor of the journal *Finance and Society*. His first book, *History and Event: From Marxism to Contemporary French Theory*, was published by Edinburgh University Press in 2015.

Rodrigo Fernandez is a postdoctoral scholar at the KU Leuven, and Associate Researcher at the Centre for Research on Multinational Corporations (SOMO) in Amsterdam. At the University of Leuven, he is participating in a project on the Real Estate-Financial Complex, investigating the relationship between finance and real estate developments across different national institutional models. At SOMO, he is researching the interface of corporate tax avoidance, tax havens, and shadow banking. In addition to books, book chapters, and reports, he has published in journals such as *Antipode, Competition and Change, Economic Geography, Economy and Society*, and *Socio-Economic Review*.

Clément Fontan is Professor of European economic policies at UCLouvain/ USL-B and a co-editor of the journal *Politique Européenne*. He is the co-author of *Do Central Banks Serve the People?* (Polity, 2018), and he has published extensively on central banking, financial ethics, and the Eurozone crisis in several journals and edited volumes.

Carolyn Hardin is Assistant Professor of media and culture and American studies at Miami University in Ohio. Her research uses cultural studies and political economy approaches to examine the relationship between culture and economy. She has written on the topics of neoliberalism, retirement investing, financial technology, and arbitrage, and her work has appeared in journals including *Cultural Studies, Journal of Cultural Economy*, and *American Quarterly*.

Julian Hartman is a PhD candidate researching in the role that universities play in the regional entrepreneurial ecosystem of Boston. After a brief corporate stint and an MBA, he became more interested in how business worked than how to work a business, and has been studying economic geography ever since.

David Harvie sells his labor-power to the University of Leicester, where he is Associate Professor of Finance and Political Economy and a member of the Centre for Philosophy and Political Economy. His research on social finance has been published in *Sociology, Historical Materialism, Environment and Planning A: Economy and Space, Journal of Urban Affairs*, and *Critical Perspectives on Accounting*. He is a co-editor of *Commoning with George Caffentzis and Silvia Federici* (Pluto Press, 2019).

Victoria Ivanova is a PhD candidate in Creative Technologies at the Centre for the Study of the Networked Image at London South Bank University.

Mark Kear is Assistant Professor in the School of Geography and Development at the University of Arizona. His research explores the variegated landscape of experimentation in the financial borderscapes of urban development, housing, and consumer finance. His most recent work can be found in *Urban Geography, Journal of Cultural Economy*, as well as *Economic Geography* and *Economy and Society*.

Martijn Konings is Professor of Political Economy and Social Theory at the University of Sydney. His publications include *The Development of American Finance* (2011), *The Emotional Logic of Capitalism* (2015), and *Capital and Time* (2018). He co-edits the Stanford University Press series *Currencies: New Thinking for Financial Times*, and he is the Editor-in-Chief of *Distinktion: Journal of Social Theory*. His current research is on the logics of asset-led inequality.

Mikkel Krause Frantzen is a postdoctoral fellow affiliated with the collective research project "Finance Fiction: Financialization and Culture in the Early 21st Century" at the Department of Arts and Cultural Studies at the University of Copenhagen. He is the author of *Going Nowhere, Slow* (Zero Books, 2019), and his current project centers around the finance fictions of the 1970s.

Ann-Christina Lange is a scholar of the sociology of finance. She currently works at the Innovation Centre Denmark in Tel Aviv and is affiliated with the ERC-funded research project "Algorithmic Finance" at the Copenhagen Business School. Her research focuses on high-frequency trading and social theory. Lange has been Assistant Professor at the Copenhagen Business School. Her recent work has been published in *Organization, Theory, Culture & Society,* and *Economy & Society.*

Louis Larue defended his PhD thesis in economics and philosophy entitled "Making sense of alternative currencies" at UCLouvain in 2019. He is now a postdoctoral researcher in financial ethics at Göteborg University, and his most recent published research is on Bitcoin and digital currencies.

Benjamin Lee is University Professor of Anthropology and Philosophy at the New School. He has served as Dean of the New School for Social Research and Provost of the university. He received a master's degree in Human Development and a PhD in anthropology from the University of Chicago. He is also a co-director with Dilip Gaonkar of the Center for Transcultural Studies in Chicago. A linguistic anthropologist by training, he was the author of *Talking Heads* and turned to the semiotics of finance. He is a co-author with Edward LiPuma of *Financial Derivatives and the Globalization of Risk* and co-editor with Randy Martin of *Derivatives and the Wealth of Societies*. He is presently working on a book about volatility with Ackbar Abbas and Emanuel Derman and is also currently working on a semiotic approach to the economics of cryptocurrencies.

Gerald Nestler is an artist and author who explores the "derivative condition" of social relations. As a part of this research, he aims to activate the semantic field of the term "resolution" as an alternative conception to transparency. Gerald graduated from the Academy of Fine Arts Vienna and holds a PhD from the Centre for Research Architecture, Goldsmith, University of London. To research finance from an artistic perspective he worked as a trader and broker.

In his practice, he combines theory and conversation with video, installation, performance, sound, and speech. Gerald has published widely on finance, technology, and art, including *Yx* (Schlebruegge.Editor, 2007); the *Kunstforum International* issues 200/201 on art and economy (ed. with Dieter Buchhart, 2010); *Forensis: The Architecture of Public Truth* (ed. by Forensic Architecture, Sternberg, 2014); *Making of Finance* (ed. with Armen Avanessian, Merve, 2015); and *Finance and Society* vol 2/2, "art and finance" (ed. with Suhail Malik, 2016).

Horacio Ortiz is Associate Professor at the Institute of Anthropology at School of Social Development at East China Normal University, Shanghai, China, and researcher at the Centre National de la Recherche Scientifique at IRISSO at the Université Paris-Dauphine, PSL University, Paris, France. He has published research on investment funds and stockbrokers in New York and Paris, on business schools and cross-border investment in Shanghai, as well as theoretical pieces on the anthropology and sociology of money and finance. He is the author of *Valeur financière et vérité. Une anthropologie politique de l'évaluation des entreprises cotées en bourse*, Presses de Sciences Po, Paris, 2014, and co-author of Muniesa et al., of *Capitalization: A cultural guide*, Presses des Mines, Paris, 2017. He is currently conducting research on digital payment systems in China.

José Ossandón is Associate Professor in the Department of Organization at the Copenhagen Business School. His current work focuses on new modes of economic knowledge produced to evaluate, repair, and govern market-based policy instruments, and on the encounters between financial firms' market devices and households' accounting and calculative practices.

Léna Pellandini-Simányi is Assistant Professor in the Institute of Marketing and Communication Management at the Università della Svizzera italiana, Switzerland. She received her PhD in Sociology from the London School of Economics and Political Science. She is author of the book *Consumption Norms and Everyday Ethics*, and her work has appeared in *Economy and Society*, *Sociology*, *Organization Studies*, and *Journal of Cultural Economy*, among others. Her research draws on market studies and economic sociology to look at how changing moralities and markets intersect. Her current projects focus on mortgage debt, the financialization of everyday life and responsibilization.

Alex Preda works at King's Business School at King's College London. He is the author of *Noise: Living and Trading in Electronic Finance* (University of Chicago Press 2017), among others.

Mike Rafferty is in the Department of Management at RMIT University, Melbourne, Australia. He currently researches issues of financialization as they relate to off-shore financial centers and the changing role of central banking in domestic and international finance and economy.

Adam Richard Rottinghaus is Assistant Professor of Media, Journalism and Film at Miami University in Oxford, Ohio, USA. He is a scholar/practitioner who conducts critical research on strategic communications and emerging technologies in work and consumer cultures. He has published in the *International Journal of Communication* and the *Journal of Cultural Economy*. For more than 15 years, he has been an award-winning graphic designer and art director specializing in print, web, and multimedia production, as well as marketing strategy and brand management in both retail and business-to-business contexts. He is working on a book manuscript that examines corporate power and marketing work culture inside the consumer electronics industry.

Daniel Scott Souleles is Associate Professor of Economic Anthropology at the Department of Management, Politics, and Philosophy at Copenhagen Business School. He studies finance, wealth, and inequality, and has done field work with Catholic Hermit Monks, Private Equity Investors, Employee Owned Companies, and on Computerized Stock Trading. His work has appeared in *Economic Anthropology, Economy and Society, Political and Legal Anthropology Review*, and *Critique of Anthropology*, among others. He is the author of *Songs of Profit, Songs of Loss: Private Equity, Wealth, and Inequality*, an ethnographic study of private equity investing (University of Nebraska Press, 2019).

Ekaterina Svetlova is Associate Professor in Accounting and Finance at the School of Business at the University of Leicester. Previously, she was a researcher and a lecturer at the University of Constance, Zeppelin University, and University of Basel. She also used to work as a portfolio manager and financial analyst in Frankfurt/Main, Germany. In 2018, she was appointed the leader of the Finance Hub of the ESRC Rebuilding Macroeconomics network at the National Institute of Economic and Social Research in London. She has published on themes such as economic sociology and social studies of finance. Her most recent books include *Financial Models and Society: Villains or Scapegoats?* (2018), *Chains of Finance: How Investment Management Is Shaped* (2017, with D.-L. Arjaliès, P. Grant, I. Hardie, and D. MacKenzie), and *Enacting Dismal Science: New Perspectives on the Performativity of Economics* (2016, with I. Boldyrev).

Yamina Tadjeddine is Full Professor of Economics at the Faculty of Law, Economics and Management at the Université de Lorraine, and Research Fellow Beta, UMR CNRS 7522. Her research focuses on financial practices and financial regulation. She is a founding member of the Social Studies of Finance Association (http://ssfa.free.fr/). She has published on financial economics and economic sociology of finance. She is the author of several books and has co-edited with I. Chambost and M. Lenglet, *The Making of Finance* (2019).

Bruno Tinel is Associate Professor at the Sorbonne School of Economics of the University of Paris 1 Panthéon-Sorbonne and a member of the Centre d'Economie de la Sorbonne (UMR 8174). His research is on the related transformations of both public finance and finance through history.

Frederik Tygstrup is Professor of comparative literature at the University of Copenhagen.

Jing Wang is Assistant Professor in Interactive Media Business at NYU, Shanghai. Jing studies the role of information and communication technologies in global finance. Her work has appeared in the *International Journal of Communication, Communication and the Public, Telecommunications Policy, The Political Economy of Communication*, and *The China Quarterly*. Jing has also been invited by the *China Business News* and the *China Global TV Network* to comment on Chinese fin-techs.

Angela Wigger is Associate Professor Global Political Economy at Radboud University, the Netherlands. Her current research focuses on the role of debt-led accumulation patterns in capitalist crises, crises responses, particularly in the field of competition and industrial policy and prefigurative forms of resistance. In addition to book chapters, she has co-authored *The Politics of European Competition Regulation: A Critical Political Economy Perspective* (Routledge, 2011, with H. Buch-Hansen), and published widely in journals such as *New Political Economy, New Political Science, Review of International Political Economy, Journal of Common Market Studies, Economy and Society, Globalizations*, and *Capital and Class*.

Robert Wosnitzer is Clinical Associate Professor of Management Communication at New York University Stern School of Business. His research focuses on financial cultures, social impact investing, and cryptocurrencies. He is a founding member of the Cultures of Finance Group at NYU's Institute for Public Knowledge, and holds an MA and PhD in Media, Culture and Communication from NYU Steinhardt. Prior to joining NYU, he traded and placed debt instruments with institutional clients for over a decade at firms including Lehman Brothers and Wells Fargo Capital Markets.

INTRODUCTION
What is Critical Finance Studies?

Christian Borch

Finance Feeding off of Critique

At a time when populism is sweeping the world and it is hard to escape the suspicion that this change in the political climate stems, in some significant measure, from the 2007–2008 financial crisis, the dubious practices it laid bare, the
immense economic effects it had, and the feeble political responses it provoked,
there are good reasons to call for a critical approach to finance. More precisely,
there is an urgent need to reconsider what might constitute a proper and effective critical engagement with finance. Certainly, there is no absence of critiques
of finance. However, the challenge is that finance and financial markets are
such complex structures that they often resemble quasi-autonomous phenomena that are obviously subjected to various forms of critique and regulation,
but nonetheless appear to neutralize any external pressure through multifarious
internal procedures. Indeed, it seems as if the German sociologist Niklas Luhmann's (1995a) lexicon of "operational closure" and "autopoesis" are suitable
categories with which to understand finance and financial markets: whatever
goes on in their environment matters only indirectly to them—namely, only as
filtered through their own internal logics. To illustrate this, just think of how,
on the one hand, a series of devastating critiques of questionable compensation
schemes were voiced in the aftermath of the 2007–2008 financial crisis, as these
schemes were widely believed to have fueled undue risk-taking practices, and
how, on the other hand, skyrocketing bonuses were nonetheless quickly rein-
troduced in this industry, as if no lessons had been learned from the build-up to
the crisis, neither morally nor in terms of incentivization.

While such an image of finance and financial markets leaves the impression
that critique is somewhat futile, a closer look suggests otherwise and inspires
some hope. Instead of a wholesale immunizing of itself against critical appraisal,

finance is better seen as entangled in a complex relationship with critique, in which critique and responses to it are an integral part of its *modus operandi*. For example, so-called high-frequency trading (HFT), in which the buying and selling of financial instruments are carried out by fully automated computer algorithms in a fraction of a second, emerged in part against a backdrop of a critique of former trading practices: the so-called specialists, i.e., human traders on the trading floors of, e.g., the New York Stock Exchange, allegedly mismanaged their privileges, giving rise to a call for less human-oriented markets (see also Ann-Christina Lange's chapter in this volume). This helped create the conditions for HFT. According to some observers, however, the computerized alternative to the human specialists has more in common with a Frankensteinian monster than with a genuine solution to the original problem—and so HFT is accused of replacing one set of problematic privileges with another, in that it supposedly transforms markets by establishing an elite of HFT firms that dominate an underbelly of exploited non-HFTs. This prompts critical calls for yet another reshaping of financial markets in a manner that eschews their alleged rigging under HFT (see, e.g., Budish et al., 2015; Lewis, 2014).

This is but one drop in a larger sea of examples of how critique is integral to finance. Indeed, critique has always been part and parcel of finance. Back in the 1890s, Max Weber articulated a strong critique of the ways in which German stock exchanges began catering to the public, thereby allowing alleged non-experts to participate in trading activity (Weber, 2000). This, Weber warned, writing, as an economist, could interfere in devastating ways with the positive economic functions provided by the exchanges. Similarly, it is an age-old trope that finance is deeply enmeshed in greed and speculative commotion, and that irrational behaviors can quickly escalate, with bubbles and crashes following in their wake (e.g. Mackay, 2002). In this sense, critique is immanent to finance and an integral part of its development, in that, as mentioned above, one type of critique might lead to developments that have unanticipated consequences, prompting new critiques and novel demands for change. Of course, none of this is unique to finance—it applies equally well to many other fields. But this almost dialectical relationship between finance and critique may nonetheless serve as a cautious reminder for critical studies of finance: critiques may be voiced for good reasons, but may also bring about changes, the negative effects of which might be worse than (or only marginally preferable to) the starting point. This is not meant to render critique impotent or irrelevant; rather, it merely indicates the complexity with which any serious critique must contend. Put differently, we consider easy critiques and "solutions"—such as a demand for a "revolution" or even the wholesale abandonment of finance—less appealing than critiques that attempt to address the internal complexity of their subject.

The aim of the present *Routledge Handbook of Critical Finance Studies* is to enter such critical terrain and subject finance to critical scrutiny. More than that, however, the *Handbook*'s objective is also to carve out a space for a new analytical approach or framework that might appropriately be called *critical finance studies*. This term already has some traction in the social sciences. With this volume, my co-editor, Robert Wosnitzer, and I hope to give the term a stronger anchoring and foundation, but also a firmer empirical commitment than has been the case in some past studies.

In this introduction, I will provide an overview of what we understand by critical finance studies. Rather than erecting strict boundaries that can then be vigorously policed, I will be preoccupied with outlining a critical gesture that we consider important and which will guide the contributions to this volume. As already alluded to, we particularly believe that critical finance studies should be firmly empirically based. Simply put, critique that is grounded in actual empirical work will be much more interesting—and also have more bite. I will develop the critical gesture in a somewhat roundabout manner, in that I will begin by briefly discussing how finance has been the object of increasing scrutiny by social scientists in recent decades, as well as what kinds of critique these types of analysis have generated. Against that backdrop, I will then present the contours of what we see as the alternative—or supplementary—approach, which we subsume under the label of critical finance studies.

I should note from the outset that, given the nature of the present volume, the aim is not to present a collection of chapters that all subscribe in a uniform fashion to one and the same type of critique, or which adopt an identical critical gesture. Rather, in keeping with our emphasis that a new type of critical finance studies is needed that takes seriously the empirical domain it critiques, it is to be expected that the different empirical topics covered in the *Handbook* will call for different critical modalities. I should also note that, while there is an emerging critical literature in (heterodox) financial economics, the *Handbook* speaks mainly to other social science audiences and types of literature, particularly those found in sociology and anthropology. This editorial decision is not meant to devalue the contributions of (critical or other) economists. Indeed, there may be considerable potential for cross-fertilizations across economic and non-economic approaches to finance—and in that spirit, some chapters are written either by or relate carefully to work by economists. However, in the *Handbook*, we have decided upon a more sociological and anthropological focus, in order to ensure stronger coherence between the chapters, and because we believe that existing sociological work on finance is marred by a certain fragmentation, with a differentiation into a number of semi-autonomous branches that are too rarely in dialogue with one another. While such fragmentation might be a result of a productive specialization, it is likely at some point to constitute an obstacle to progress in research. For that reason, the scholars invited to contribute to the *Handbook* represent different branches of sociological and anthropological thought. The idea is to plant the seeds for a new type of conversation in the social sciences, about how various forms of insights might be brought into fruitful contact with one another. In other words, one of our ambitions is that the different kinds of critique that the various chapters bring to the table will inspire future, as yet unanticipated, endeavors in critical finance studies.

It is also worth noting, before discussing the notion of critique, the kind(s) of finance in which we are interested. Much social science work on finance—whether it originates in economics, sociology, or anthropology—has focused attention on what one might call, as Liz McFall (2014: 10) does, "high finance," i.e., recognized financial institutions and actors (e.g., exchanges, traders, banks), as well as the things and notions that circulate within and among them (e.g., credit, risk, liquidity). What has attracted considerably less attention is "low finance," i.e., the "everyday, consumer" side of the coin (McFall, 2014: 10). However, in the light of discussions about financialization and the ways in which finance and financial concepts are increasingly being deployed and make their presence felt in fields beyond formal financial institutions—such as in everyday households—scholars have begun to take a greater interest in low finance. Here, the purpose is to better understand the many manifestations and implications of finance when examined from the point of view of people who do not work in the financial industry, but whose lives are nonetheless deeply impacted by the financial instruments that enter into their everyday affairs, be it in terms of consumption, insurance, debt, or credit (e.g. Langley, 2008; Martin, 2002; McFall, 2014). Of course, we might criticize the distinction between high and low finance as being too crude—in practice, as the financialization literature demonstrates, high and low are often entangled. And yet this distinction—which need not carry any moral valence—might serve a heuristic purpose, just as it might reflect the orientation of empirically minded researchers. Thus, the distinction between high and low finance nicely corresponds to the separation anthropologists make between studying up and studying sideways or down. While researchers investigating high finance are often confronted with exceptionally competent, highly technically skilled, and self-assured informants, those studying low finance are more likely to encounter informants who have a more external approach to the financial instruments that may penetrate their lives.

At the very least, this distinction between high and low demonstrates that finance is many things—and as such, it is to be expected that critical finance studies, too, is an empirically varied field. This obviously raises questions about which topics should be included in a handbook like the present one. Should it be topics that sanction the well-established interest in high finance, or should it be topics that push more toward a low finance reorientation? In this volume, we have decided to do both.

Finance in a Sociological Light

Recent decades have seen a surge in sociological and anthropological analyses of finance. Reflecting the fragmentation described earlier, it is possible to single out three traditions that, while they share certain inspirations and assumptions, can be treated distinctly. I realize that each of these traditions encompasses a great deal of internal complexity, that the various positions gathered under each umbrella category include many diverging emphases, and that some analyses of finance might not be easily assigned to any of these traditions at all. I nonetheless find it useful for the present purposes to gloss over such nuances and focus on the basic critical gestures that characterize each branch of theorization.

The first and oldest tradition goes by the name of *new economic sociology*. The central achievement of this tradition has been to examine all sorts of economic phenomena from a sociological perspective. More specifically, the shared ambition of this tradition, which gained momentum in the early 1980s, has been (a) to contrast economists' analyses of (and self-proclaimed hegemonic position in the study of) economic phenomena, by (b) demonstrating that (and how) economic life is tightly interwoven with social life. In other words, this tradition of especially US academics has strived to establish that economic phenomena can be treated analytically on a par with other social phenomena—in effect, dismantling any a priori distinction between economic and non-economic spheres (e.g., Granovetter, 1985). This analytical ambition amounts to a reversal of the Chicago economist and Nobel Laureate Gary Becker's attempt to deploy economic analysis in the study of phenomena that are not usually regarded as economic (e.g., Becker, 1968)—with each camp (sociologists versus economists) in effect pursuing their imperialistic endeavors from opposite sides. As this suggests, the primary critical gesture of the new economic sociology tradition has been aimed at prevailing economistic approaches and understandings, whereas financial practices themselves have received only secondary critical scrutiny, at least in the initial phases.

One illustration of how the primary target of critical analysis within the new economic sociology tradition has been constituted by economistic conceptions can be found in Wayne Baker's early work on the ways in which prices are formed on the trading floors of the Chicago Board Options Exchange in the pre-algorithmic era of inter-human trading (Baker, 1984a, 1984b). In contrast to an economistic notion that prices are formed on the basis of supply and demand, Baker argued that the interaction of human traders itself influences price-making and price volatility. Against that backdrop, Baker concluded, as his central critical impetus, "Students of the market should reevaluate the implicit assumptions of conventional economic and financial research in light of the findings presented here" (1984b: 124). He also suggested that his empirical work on floor trading ran "counter to some of the fundamental premises of microeconomic theory" (1984a: 803). While this was the central critical contribution of his study, he also pointed to some wider critical implications, including the need for exchanges and regulators to "investigate and ameliorate the detrimental effects caused by trading in large crowds" (1984a: 807).

A more elaborated critical attitude to financial practices is visible in Mitchel Abolafia's seminal study of trading floors in *Making Markets* (1996). The book opened with a discussion of how, in the early 1990s, Salomon Brothers, the then-dominant bond trading firm on Wall Street, had rigged the US Treasury bond market. Abolafia then embarked on a study of how such behavior could take place, and did so via a careful sociological investigation of how traders' individual pursuit of profit was embedded in particular normative orders and moral economies. While Abolafia's study clearly included a critical appraisal of actual market practices and their underlying sociological logics, the overall critical gesture once again targeted economistic conceptions of financial markets, which were rejected as presenting an "undersocialized view of markets" (1996: 189).

Finance merely constitutes one among many economic topics addressed by the new economic sociology tradition. By contrast, another and more recent branch of research, *social studies of finance*, deals with finance as its primary object of inquiry. Social studies of finance began as a broad sociological and anthropological interest in finance, but has subsequently evolved into a label for work that has a leaning towards science and technology studies (STS) and actor-network theory (ANT). Reflecting this inspiration, work within the social studies of finance tradition is usually characterized by an emphasis on the role of materiality and technological devices. This follows Bruno Latour's (2005: 76) "symmetry" dictum, according to which no a priori analytical asymmetry should be imposed between humans and non-humans. In this vein, Donald MacKenzie has carefully analyzed the ways in which price-making and liquidity in present-day HFT-dominated markets are closely intertwined with particular material technologies, such as fiber optics, microwaves, and the co-location of trading firms' servers in physical proximity to trading venues' matching engines (MacKenzie, 2017, 2018a; MacKenzie et al., 2012). Similarly, MacKenzie has been instrumental in showing how particular economic formulas—such as the Black-Scholes options pricing model—have had performative effects on the ways in which market participants approach and assess markets (e.g., MacKenzie, 2006). As MacKenzie argued in his seminal work *An Engine, Not a Camera* (2006), models are not passive representations (cameras) of markets; rather, they may well have performative effects (as engines) on these markets.

Reflecting its grounding in STS and ANT, one of the strong features of the social studies of finance literature is that it is based on rich empirical studies. Many of the investigations in this tradition are carried out on the basis of comprehensive qualitative empirical fieldwork (ethnography and interviews), one advantage of which is its ability to convey a sense of actual market practices. As mentioned, this interest in actual practices is combined with a focus on how such practices are co-shaped by technology, materiality, and models. However, even more pronounced than the economic sociology tradition is that the explicit critical drive of the social studies of finance work has been directed mainly at other scholarly positions, especially work that—at least according to proponents of social studies of finance—tends to neglect or give undue emphasis to the role of non-human entities. A broader critique of finance practices themselves is generally absent from the social studies of finance literature.[1]

Discussions of the lack of critical impetus in social studies of finance have primarily revolved around the notion of performativity, of which MacKenzie and Michel Callon are vital sponsors (e.g., Callon, 2007; MacKenzie, 2006). For example, Judith Butler has taken issue with Callon's suggestion that economic theories co-shape, in a performative manner, the economic reality they seek to describe and model. In particular, Butler is critical of Callon's view that "it is very important to abandon the critical position" of exiting sociological work (Callon, cited in Butler, 2010: 153). Her fear is "that this means abandoning any effort to evaluate and oppose those multivalent operations of capitalism that augment income disparities, presume the functional necessity of poverty, and thwart efforts to establish just forms for the redistribution of wealth" (2010: 153). Along similar lines, Paul du Gay (2010: 177) has argued that Callon's work is characterized by "a certain degree of political romanticism" or perhaps a forgetting of how politics works in practice. According to du Gay, "'the politics' that Callon refers to often appears to have more to do with the intellectual operation of certain sorts of theory than it does with the contingent practicalities of political activity and action" (2010: 177). A further kind of critical engagement with the social studies of finance literature can be found in attempts to provide its insights into the materiality of financial markets with a stronger notion of the social dynamics that are also at play in these markets. As argued in particular by scholars pursuing analyses of cultures of finance, there are aspects of financial markets that bring to the fore themes such as gift-giving, which call for a more distinctly anthropological analytical expertise (e.g., Lee & Martin, 2016).

While these critiques do not completely miss the mark, nor are they entirely justified. For example, it is not obvious why an analysis of the performativity of particular financial models could not entail a critical push toward highlighting problems associated with how finance is practiced. True, this may not engage more macro discussions of the role of, e.g., poverty and inequality—which are obviously important topics—but it need not imply that one assumes a non-critical stance just because one's attention is focused elsewhere. Indeed, Butler's response to Callon in particular might teach a broader lesson—namely, while the social studies approach to finance is often described as problematic because it is inherently apolitical, this critique is at times premature. There are two reasons for this.

The first, as I just pointed out, is that work that emphasizes the performative role of particular financial models can easily be critical (see also Ekaterina Svetlova's chapter in this volume for further discussion of this). MacKenzie has contributed significantly to demonstrating that such models may play a vital role for financial practices, and by extension for, e.g., price-making. To ignore the impact of such models—and how they are invented and propagated at, say, particular universities and business schools—is therefore to miss out on some of the key knowledge dimensions of finance. It should be obvious that finance cannot be reduced to a bunch of people engaged in profit-seeking behaviors; finance is also about the deployment of particular types of knowledge, and the emergence, dissemination, or waning popularity of such knowledge should be critically interrogated, as should the institutional contexts that influence how particular models may have performative effects (Svetlova, 2012, 2018). Taking up that baton, Robert Peckham (2013a, 2013b) offers important critical analyses of how, e.g., key market participants have deployed epidemiological vocabulary in recent years in order to make sense of financial markets and financial crises, but without in-depth reflection upon whether such vocabulary can be meaningfully transferred from one particular domain (population biology) to another (financial markets). As Peckham demonstrates in an essentially epistemological critique of this aspect of the present-day financial lexicon, there are clear limits to such conceptual transfers. Scholars such as Melinda Cooper (2011) and Paul Crosthwaite (2013) make a similar point in their critical examinations of the kind of naturalization of financial markets that might follow when finance is analyzed on the basis of a set of notions from the natural sciences. The point I wish to make is that to the extent that performativity discussions are embedded in such sociology of knowledge endeavors, nothing inherently prevents them from being critical—although, admittedly, in many performativity analyses, this explicit critical potential remains untapped.

However, such potential is realized in Marieke de Goede's writings. Inspired especially by Foucault's genealogical work, de Goede argues, "Understanding finance as a performative practice suggests that processes of knowledge and interpretation do not exist in addition to, or of secondary importance to, 'real' material financial structures, but are precisely *the way in which 'finance' materializes*" (2005: 7, original emphasis). While de Goede gives materiality a more discursive twist than social studies of finance scholars would likely appreciate, she demonstrates that discourses (including in the form of theories and models) can co-shape financial knowledge and practices—and that, given this performative ability, such discourses therefore call for critical scrutiny. "It is not just the case," she argues, "that financial knowledge is socially constructed, but the very *material structures* of the financial markets—including prices, costs, and capital—are discursively constituted and historically contingent" (2005: 7, original emphasis). It follows from this that excavating underlying discursive patterns and their historically contingent nature is driven by a clear critical ambition—namely, to dismantle the taken-for-grantedness and supposedly apolitical status of technical financial discourse. Furthermore, this type of work may challenge the explicit ideological embeddings of particular subsets of finance, and demonstrate that, contrary to that which is often taken for granted, their ideological commitments may be rather different from how they are typically portrayed. While not actively pursuing a Foucault-inspired approach, David Golumbia's analysis of the right-wing libertarian leanings of Bitcoin proponents is nonetheless a wonderful illustration of precisely this kind of approach (Golumbia, 2016).

The second reason why the usual critique of the allegedly non-critical stance of social studies of finance work is premature relates less to that framework itself and more to the proposed alternatives, which, I will argue, are often as problematic as that which they set out to replace, albeit for different reasons. To put it bluntly, when Butler evokes themes such as income disparity, the functional necessity of poverty, and the redistribution of wealth, she effectively conjures up a standard Marxist "critical theory" repertoire. This is entirely justifiable, but it is also the case that work within this critical-theory tradition is sometimes politically overdetermined, so that specific analyses appear to be driven more by a set of fixed political propositions than by an open analytical sensibility. In other words, such politically motivated studies often tend to quickly loosen the grip of (and interest in) the empirical world in order to advance a set of pre-defined political views. In the worst examples, this means that any empirical friction is disregarded, or conveniently subsumed into well-established, pre-set categories, leaving hardly any room for empirical surprise—which at times creates the sense that such analyses are in dire need of oxygen. One example of such an approach is Maurizio Lazzarato's ruminations over financial traders and their alleged "machinic subjectivity" (2014: 96–101), a form of subjectivity that Lazzarato decides to examine without *any* empirical substantiation. The problem with such work is that its lack of empirical foundation means that it offers little with which to understand and possibly critique modern finance. Even if critique may nonetheless be explicitly articulated in such work, it has no real bite—and it is certainly not likely to change finance for the better.

Lazzarato might be seen as an extreme representative of the third tradition I will discuss here, which consists of work that seeks to approach finance from an *explicitly critical* angle. Speaking of this as a "tradition" alongside new economic sociology and social studies of finance is perhaps to overstate the coherence and longevity of this strand of work. However, the work I refer to here has enough unifying elements to consider it as a whole. This tradition is based on Marxist inspirations—or at least subscribes to critical-theory tropes. Thomas Bay and Christophe Schinckus's "interdisciplinary manifesto" for critical finance studies (Bay & Schinckus, 2012) presents one outline of the commitments of such work. According to Bay and Schinckus, critical finance studies should aim at:

> deactivating the practice of finance [defined elsewhere in their manifesto as "turning means into ends"], rendering it inoperative, freeing it from its transcendental values, its predetermined purposes, its obligatory relationship to a specific end, pure ends included and try making it available for a new use. (2012: 3–4)

The strength of Marxist or critical-theory-inflected (including political economy) approaches to finance lies in their ability to point to the broader societal implications of finance, such as, *pace* Butler, how finance might be implicated in creating particular forms of social inequality (see, e.g., Godechot, 2012). Such works often also articulate critique in an immanent manner, in an attempt to unearth the inner systemic tensions of modern finance and the (potential crash or crisis-prone) dynamics they set in motion. While the former point in particular might be said to constitute an advantage over the social studies of finance tradition—which, by comparison, is often (deliberately) myopic in its analytical focus—this latter tradition generally has a stronger sense of the empirical micro details of finance. Another way of putting this is that while the Marxist/critical theory tradition clearly offers the most outspoken critique of finance (and not merely of other approaches, disciplines, or traditions), it is also the tradition that cares the least for the micro-empirical detail that informs new economic sociology and social studies of finance. One thing that tends to be disregarded in the Marxist/critical theory tradition—and in calls like the above for "rending finance inoperative"—is that finance need not be bad per se, and that people employed in finance are not inherently evil, despite the impression one occasionally gets from reading this literature.

Latour phrases this differently in his attack on conventional forms of critical theory: this type of work tends to put itself in a privileged position, by claiming to be able to detect the non-recognized illusions of the actors and the hidden patterns that guide their behaviors, including in ways that share some discomforting similarities with conspiracy theory (Latour, 2004). What is lacking from much critical theory is therefore, I repeat, a greater empirical sensibility—one that not only recognizes the possibility, for example, that actors may be well aware of their doings (and potential wrongdoings), but which also recognizes that finance fulfills important societal functions and serves particular purposes in the economy (Bush et al., 2012: 169). Admitting the social function of finance does not exclude thorny discussions about when finance, indeed, "is servant, not master, of the economy," to quote a *Financial Times* contribution about the legacy of the late Paul Volcker (Wolf, 2019). Nor does it exclude debates about overflow and excess, both of which are obvious targets of critique. The same goes for the unnerving indications that financial institutions nurture a dubious culture that privileges profit-seeking by any means, even if this entails active participation in large-scale money-laundering schemes, to pick a recent example.

Similarly, finance might be beneficial in some respects and less so in others. It might even be that the same financial practice can be assessed differently depending on which points of observation and benchmarks one uses. But these are precisely the empirical sensibilities toward which critical finance studies of the kind the *Handbook* proposes should be attuned. Let me therefore now try to crystallize, in a more positive fashion, some important dimensions of the kind of critical finance studies we envisage, and to which we hope this *Handbook* will contribute.

What, Then, Is Critical Finance Studies?

The brief—admittedly somewhat exaggerated—overview above identified a particular bias in each of the three traditions examined: the new economic sociology tradition suffers from an overdetermination to demarcate itself from economistic analyses, effectively reducing its critical impetus to how it serves this demarcation; the social studies of finance tradition suffers from critically engaging primarily with examinations that do not share its commitment to analyzing the role of non-humans; and Marxist/critical theory contributions tend to suffer from an asymmetric commitment to theoretical preconceptions of how finance works, at the expense of detailed micro-empirical analysis. Of course, each of these traditions has contributed important insights that can and should inform a novel critical agenda (and there are particular scholars from each of these traditions whose work resonates with what I will advocate below). Indeed, I wish to suggest that such a new critical finance studies agenda might take shape if specific elements from each of these traditions are brought together—and if these traditions are bridged in particular ways. In the following, I will provide the contours of such a critical approach.

Before getting to the positive formulations, however, we must address one further delimitation. As Martijn Konings has recently argued, it is hard, if not impossible, "to provide an objective set of criteria for what makes knowledge critical. A good critique is a performative achievement; we recognize it when we encounter it" (2018: 132). This is an echo of the types of attacks of critical theory-inflected approaches voiced by, e.g., Latour (2004) and Luhmann (1991). While I agree that it is indeed extremely difficult to establish objective criteria for critique, I nonetheless believe that it is possible to flesh out how a successful critical-performative achievement might look. In this spirit, the program for critical finance studies that we propose in this volume is committed to what might be called a new *principle of symmetry*—namely, an equal commitment to both empirical and theoretical works. We simply argue that there is a need for a critical approach to finance that is based on solid empirical understandings and sophisticated theoretical conceptualizations of its workings. The purpose of the empirical work is to ensure *familiarization* with particular dimensions of finance, whereas the purpose of the theoretical work is to achieve a *de-familiarization* of the understanding of these dimensions vis-à-vis the field's self-understanding, and to situate the analysis firmly in a social science context. This also means that while, e.g., ethnographic fieldwork is highly valuable for the empirical part, and while such fieldwork might inspire the use of emic terms, we argue for the relevance of sophisticated theoretical-conceptual work in order to create some distance to the field—a distance that can be seen as the condition for critical engagement, regardless of whether such critical engagement eventually approaches finance from an immanent or transcendental perspective.[2]

Before further specifying this, I fully recognize that we are proposing a rather broad and abstract notion of critique here, which, it could be objected, merely describes what some types of sociology have been doing for generations. Indeed, from Weber onward, scholars have combined empirical work with de-familiarizing concepts—without these scholars necessarily subscribing to an explicit notion of critique and/or without them being comfortable with labeling their work as critical or seeing it as advancing a critical agenda. So is the notion of critique as based on a principle of empirical-theoretical symmetry therefore simply a placeholder for rather standard modes of sociological work? In a sense, it could be, and we are fine with that. Our aim is not to reserve the critical gesture outlined above for a particular type of social science approach.

Rather, we simply suggest that this minimal conception is important when talking about critical work. We might add that, obviously, this minimal conception is likely to span a wide spectrum of incarnations. For example, it may be aligned with both lighter and heavier forms of traditional critique, i.e., with weaker or stronger assessments of financial practices and proposed remedies (see below).

It is equally important to note that there are certainly a range of ways in which such a double movement—a simultaneous commitment to empirical and theoretical-conceptual work—could be accomplished. The German philosopher Peter Sloterdijk suggests one such approach in his grand opus on "spheres." In it, Sloterdijk combines solid empirical work with strangely unfamiliar concepts, such as bubbles, globes, and foams—concepts invented in order to better understand the social, while at the same time resisting political appropriation (see especially Sloterdijk, 2004: 866). Another route is the one suggested by Paul Rabinow, according to whom it is advisable to theorize on the basis of a *"larger series of limited concepts"* (Rabinow, quoted in Roitman, 2014: 95, original emphasis). This would entail testing the de-familiarization capacity of various concepts, and replacing those that do not pass the test with new ones that may do. While such a strategy may require a lot of conceptual agility on part of the researcher, it has the advantage of being likely to circumvent the problem of lateral reason, as highlighted by scholars such as Bill Maurer (2005) and Annelise Riles (2000). Both have studied people who deploy vocabularies similar to those of the researchers, meaning that in such cases a critical vocabulary based on a de-familiarized lexicon does not exist. Rabinow's solution might be a pragmatic way out of this problem.

When it comes to the understanding of critique more specifically, I find it useful to build upon certain aspects of Foucault's notion. In a 1978 lecture entitled "What is Critique?," Foucault proposed an analytical agenda that examines (a) the processes of what he calls "governmentalization," i.e., the ways in which, from the sixteenth century on, Western Europe has engaged in reflections on how to govern, which gave rise to a veritable "art of governing men [*sic*]" in multiple arenas of life (1997: 27), and (b) how, in the same timespan, a parallel set of reflections emerged on "how not to be governed *like that*, by that, in the name of those principles, with such and such an objective in mind and by means of such procedures" (1997: 28, original emphasis). It is within this latter tradition that Foucault locates the rise of "the critical attitude," defined simply as "the art of not being governed quite so much" or, more precisely, *the art of not being governed thus* (1997: 28, 29). Historically, Foucault argues, this critical attitude has been differently bolstered, e.g., through legal reference to the "fundamental illegitimacy" of governing, by questioning the very authority of governing, and/or by querying and challenging "the politics of truth," which would mean "the movement by which the subject gives himself [*sic*] the right to question truth on its effects of power and question power on its discourses of truth" (1997: 30, 32).

Foucault's reflections on critique echo two points made earlier in this introduction. The first is that, in a similar vein to our opening remarks on finance and critique, he identifies an intimate historical relation between government and critique: the latter is integral to governmental practices (Lemke, 1997: 348; see also Lemke, 2011). This means that an obvious task for critical finance studies is to examine finance as a practice of government, i.e., as an attempt "to structure the possible field of action of others" (1982: 221), and to study the ways in which such exercise of governmental power develops in response to critique, be it from within or outside finance. This would amount to granting critique an immanent role in the organization and development of finance. An analytical endeavor of this sort could be aligned with Luc Boltanski's (2011) argument for moving from critical theory towards a pragmatic sociology of critique that attends to how actors—here, e.g., market participants—engage in critical judgment in their practical life (see also the chapters by Horacio Ortiz and José Ossandón in this volume).

The second connection is to de Goede's work. What de Goede does is precisely to take up the Foucauldian analytical interest in questioning "the politics of truth" by carefully examining how financial markets are discursively constituted and therefore, since they are historically shaped, changeable. The broader analytical task that emerges from this is the need to critically engage the various discursive elements of contemporary finance (be it "liquidity," "volatility," "speculation," "risk," "noise," or something else, see the chapters by Ortiz, Lee, Konings, Hardin and Rottinghaus, and Preda in this *Handbook*) that circulate as guiding concepts and (whose function and definitions) may be taken more or less for granted— without their genealogies and practical effects being fully understood (Langley, 2010). Put differently, the central analytical task that arises here is one that critically examines how a particular set of discourses performs a normative structure, one consisting of "truths" and benchmarks that guide certain practices within finance. Excavating such a normative structure is in keeping with Foucault:

> When I speak of critique I do not mean a work of destruction, of refusal and denial, but rather an investigative work that consists in suspending as far as possible the normative system which one refers to in order to test and evaluate it. (Foucault, cited in Lemke, 2011: 38)

While we see fruitful potential in pursuing critical finance studies on the basis of such Foucauldian lines, we should also note three ways in which we would suggest departing from Foucault. First, much of Foucault's work, including in relation to critique, centers on subjectivity and modes of subjectification. While questions of subjectivity are no doubt highly important, including in finance, we would argue for a broader conceptualization of critique: one that analyzes governmental practices in finance on multiple levels whenever relevant, i.e., not only on the level of subjectivity, but also in terms of collectivity, organization, and society.

Second, in response to the quote above, "suspending" the normative system need not entail a radical replacement. Rather, the idea is to temporarily analytically suspend its operations in order to reflect upon them, their limits, and their conditions of possibility. This latter dimension can also be aligned with the critical impetus behind Luhmann's work. Luhmann emphasized the analytical value of the so-called second-order observations, i.e., observations of how observers (such as market participants) observe, including the distinctions through which they observe (Luhmann, 1995b). What is gained from such an approach, Luhmann stressed, are insights into the epistemological foundations of observations, i.e., the very conditions on which observations are made. This includes insights into the blind spots that constitute observations: the unobserved distinctions behind any observation. Luhmann framed this approach as an alternative to standard critical-theory propositions, which are often guided instead by some a priori assumptions about how the world is organized—assumptions that are deployed as benchmarks for critique. By contrast, Luhmann conceived the second-order observation framework as a more empirically sensitive approach, which takes seriously how observers observe and then seeks to lay bare, in a critical manner, what these observers do not see—namely, their constitutive blind spots (Luhmann, 2002). Such an approach has been effectively deployed by, e.g., Janet Roitman (2014) in her critical examination of academic narratives of the 2007–2008 financial crisis and their blind spots. In his contribution to the *Handbook*, Konings similarly mobilizes Luhmann for a novel critical analysis (see also Konings, 2018; as well as Borch, 2016, 2020).

Third, we suggest departing from Foucault when it comes to the relative privileging of critique over suggested remedies for the subject of that critique. Foucault once famously remarked that:

> The necessity of reform mustn't be allowed to become a form of blackmail serving to limit, reduce or halt the exercise of criticism. Under no circumstances should one pay attention to those who tell one: "Don't criticize, since you're not capable of carrying out a reform." That's ministerial cabinet talk. Critique doesn't have to be the premise of a deduction which concludes: this then is what needs to be done. [...] It is a challenge directed to what is. (1991: 84)

Foucault's notion that critique need not entail a catalogue of solutions might have been legitimate in 1978 when this was formulated. However, this attitude looks increasingly unsatisfying in an era of populism, in which critique of the establishment thrives in the absence of genuine solutions. So, while Foucault is right that full-fledged solutions cannot always be derived from particular critiques, we believe that refusing to engage in discussions of practical solutions/interventions/changes can easily transform critique into a kind of laziness. It is too easy to blame this or that supposedly malign mechanism without offering some kind of practical response as a remedy. Therefore, in order to avoid cheap critiques and cheap moralizations, we suggest developing a critical finance studies approach that, through its empirical work, is indeed capable of combining critiques of finance with a pragmatic and practical sense of how, more concretely, dubious or problematic aspects can be alleviated.[3] This commitment parallels the critical ambition expressed by the urban geographer, Edward W. Soja, for whom critical work is characterized by "a commitment to producing knowledge not only for its own sake but more so for its practical usefulness in changing the world for the better" (Soja, 2000: xiv). The principle of symmetry described above, i.e., the dedication to both theoretical and empirical works, is, we believe, the best way to achieve such as goal.

As a final pointer for this critical gesture, and in continuation of earlier remarks, our suggestion for a new critical finance studies agenda does not entail a sweeping rejection of finance as such, nor does it amount to critiquing finance *en bloc*. Of course, certain systemic features may certainly invite critique, as Marxist approaches in particular stress. However, we would nonetheless argue for trying to strike a sensible balance between recognizing the functions that finance does serve (such as providing corporations with capital) with the types of—systemic or occasional—overflows, excesses, and injustices it creates. In a similar manner to how it is difficult, as per Konings, to say in advance what constitutes objective criteria for critique, so it is difficult to determine a priori when the correct balance has been struck between the functions of finance and its overflows and excesses. The goal here is not necessarily to try to establish that balance (although that would, of course, be a valuable objective), but simply to stress the need to operate with (or keep in mind) such a balance in critical analyses of finance. Just as Konings suggests that we recognize a good critique when we encounter it, so it might be said of critiques that strike the right balance—that they too have a certain performative dimension to them, as they are more likely to enter the dialectical economy of critique, change, and new critique I described in the beginning of this introduction.

As mentioned earlier, the reader should not expect all chapters in the *Handbook* to be full-fledged manifestations of the type of critical gesture I have tried to carve out here. We know that the scholars invited to contribute share at least some of the commitments outlined above, but we also recognize that some commitments may resonate more with some authors than with others. Nonetheless, what will hopefully be clear is that, when seen as a collective contribution, the various *Handbook* chapters indeed subscribe to the hallmarks we have identified for a new type of critical finance studies.

Overview of the Chapters

Needless to say, this *Handbook* is far from exhaustive in the topics it covers. We have selected a range of topics that we find important because they have attracted a lot of scholarly attention and/or because they constitute key dimensions of modern finance. Still, far from every relevant topic is covered.

For example, despite the significant impact of the 2007–2008 financial crisis, we decided not to devote an independent chapter to this or other financial crises (see instead, e.g., Kindleberger & Aliber, 2011; Mirowski, 2013; Tooze, 2018). That said, several chapters in the *Handbook* address the topic of financial crisis in various ways (see in particular the chapters by Konings; Hardin and Rottinghaus; Coombs; Wigger and Fernandez; Bryan, Harvie, Rafferty & Tinel; and Andreasen, Frantzen & Thygstrup). The same applies to austerity (e.g., Blyth, 2013; Schäfer & Streeck, 2013). While it does not receive a separate chapter, austerity is discussed in various contexts in the *Handbook* (see the chapter by Bryan, Harvie, Rafferty & Tinel, as well as the contribution by Hartman and Kear). More importantly, perhaps, the *Handbook* also does not contain a chapter on gender. This is not to suggest that gender is not a crucial component in critical finance studies. In fact, quite the opposite, and several scholars have detailed important ways in which gender matters to finance (e.g., Fisher, 2012; McDowell, 1997; 2010). Such work is exceptionally important, and we agree with Hartman and Kear that gender should be on the analytical radar—for example, the inequalities produced by finance often have gendered dimensions. We should also note that the *Handbook* has a clear geographical bias, in the sense that most of the topics it explores are examined primarily with a view to US and European contexts. However, some of the chapters cast the net wider (see, e.g., the chapters by Ossendón and Wang), while Hartman and Kear, in their chapter, examine the role of geography more specifically.

The *Handbook* is divided into three parts. The first part concerns "Key Concepts." The chapters in this part shed critical light on a set of important notions that populate finance discussions among both academics and market professionals. In the first chapter, Horacio Ortiz examines the concept of "liquidity." Rather than commit to one particular definition of liquidity, Ortiz critically scrutinizes various ways in which the notion of liquidity is mobilized in discussions about the workings of financial markets, by academics and practitioners alike. Drawing on an analytical approach that combines Foucauldian inspiration with anthropological and sociological insights, Ortiz lays bare the tensions that characterize the different uses of the concept of liquidity, as well as how the way in which it is used helps to establish and reinforce power relations. Indeed, while zeroing in on liquidity, Ortiz's analysis also makes a broader point: like other key finance terms, the analytical use of the notion of liquidity implies particular presuppositions that are anything but innocent; rather, they have all sorts of moral, technical, and political aspects. Shedding light on these aspects—as well as demonstrating the ways in which the use of the concept is embedded in particular social processes—is therefore an important task for critical finance studies.

In 1973, the Chicago Board Options Exchange was founded and the Black-Scholes options pricing model was first presented—two events that brought liquid options markets into being. In Chapter 2, Benjamin Lee discusses the context and broader implications of this, in effect shifting the focus from liquidity to volatility, which plays a key role in the Black-Scholes model via the latter's notion of implied volatility. While this chapter explores the same terrain as MacKenzie's analysis of the performativity of the Black-Scholes model, Lee's approach is different. In what may be interpreted as a critique of both financial economics and standard works within economic sociology, he argues that the rise of derivative finance—of which Black-Scholes is an exemplary model—can be seen as part of a larger cultural tectonic shift in the 1970s, in which volatility came to adopt a central position in social, cultural, and political life. In making this argument, Lee suggests that there are two sides to volatility—quantitative (associated with Black-Scholes and derivative finance) and qualitative (associated with affect and emotions). He further suggests that recent advances in behavioral economics, as well as ethnographic studies of traders, allow for a conceptualization that brings together the quantitative and qualitative dimensions of volatility, and in which trading is more akin to art, music, and sports than to rational decision-making.

Derivative finance is often seen as synonymous with speculative finance. In Chapter 3, Martijn Konings presents a rethinking of speculation. His central argument is that when political economists critique speculative finance, they often do so in a way that assumes a real economy from which the speculative domain detaches itself in perpetuity. Konings argues for a different conception that escapes this foundationalist viewpoint. His alternative consists of mobilizing Luhmann's notion of self-reference, arguing that financial markets, including their speculative aspects, should be seen as inherently self-referential. The central achievement of this move lies in the ways in which it redirects a critical approach to finance. Konings' analysis shows that if scholars take seriously the self-referential aspects of finance, this changes how regulation is conceived. In contrast to the foundationalist approach, according to which regulation is seen as external to markets, the self-referential perspective opens up for an understanding of financial regulation as embroiled in markets. The chapter then goes on to argue that this approach allows for a more precise account of the ways in which contemporary neoliberalism seeks to govern financial markets.

Chapter 4 addresses the topic of financial noise. Alex Preda shows how financial markets have been legitimized since the 1930s. He argues that a central political ambition in the struggle between socialism and capitalism was to demonstrate that markets are efficient, and thereby secure their widespread legitimacy. However, by scrutinizing the ways in which subsequent financial economists and behavioral economists conceive of markets, Preda shows that this claim of efficiency is undermined by the existence of financial noise—a phenomenon that Fisher Black, co-originator of the Black-Scholes model, described as a "structural ingredient of markets," i.e., something that cannot be completely eliminated. Indeed, Preda suggests that markets may in fact run on noise. Drawing on empirical studies of "noise" traders, who continue to lose money but nonetheless persist in markets, he further proposes that market participation may be driven by motivations other than profit maximization.

Together, these insights lead to a critical reconceptionalization of financial markets and their associated political agendas.

In Chapter 5, Carolyn Hardin and Adam Richard Rottinghaus critically examine the concepts of risk and arbitrage. Each of these concepts has important trajectories within financial economics, with risk serving as a measure of uncertainty, and arbitrage as the mechanism that ensures "the law of one price." However, Hardin and Rottinghaus conduct a critical genealogy of each concept to demonstrate that the neat conceptions that populate financial economics do not reflect reality. For example, they show that in the run-up to the 2007–2008 financial crisis, the risk assessments of credit rating agencies were seen as objective, as per text book accounts, whereas after the crisis hit, these agencies were quick to stress that they had only articulated "opinions." Indeed, in a case study of the financial crisis and, in particular, credit default swaps and collateralized debt obligation arbitrage, Hardin and Rottinghaus make clear that key assumptions in financial economics cannot be taken for granted, but must be carefully and critically deconstructed, in order to help lay bare the power relations they bring into being.

Having dissected a range of key finance concepts, the second part of the *Handbook* delves into "Central Actors and Institutions." In Chapter 6, the emphasis is on financial regulation. Nathan Coombs laments that critical studies of finance are often driven by an a priori suspicion of financial regulation that does not adequately consider its empirical complexities. Opening up a new horizon for the study of financial regulation, Coombs mobilizes insights from social studies of finance. In particular, he argues for taking seriously (a) the actors under study (in this instance, regulators), (b) the use and impact of financial models, and (c) attending to the ways in which macro and micro phenomena are interconnected, and in fact often collapse into one level. In his discussion of empirical domains such as HFT and the financial crisis, Coombs' central point is that, by adopting such an STS-inflected approach, a new type of empirically informed scholarship will emerge that is better suited to pinpointing the limitations of financial regulation and asking critical questions of it.

In Chapter 7, Clément Fontan and Louis Larue discuss central banking. Drawing on political economy, they argue that the prior independence of central banks—as reflected in the so-called Central Bank Independence template—was undermined by these banks' responses to the 2007–2008 financial crisis. Indeed, far from being neutral, objective, technocratic measures, the post-crisis interventions contributed to societal inequality, as they disproportionately benefited already wealthy people and institutions relative to the rest of society. In addition to demonstrating the uneven distributional effects of the power exercised by central banks—the low-finance effects of high-finance measures—Fontan and Larue present suggestions for alternative tools that would have more equal distributive effects. However, the authors also point out that, regardless of the tools deployed, there is always a need to critically interrogate and offset the powers of central banks.

In Chapter 8, Angela Wigger and Rodrigo Fernandez examine shadow banking and its relation to global debt. Shadow banking refers to credit intermediation by non-depository financial institutions—a system of credit provision that takes place in the shadow of the regular banking system. Drawing on historical materialism, Wigger and Fernandez argue that the expansion of shadow banking is closely tied to an overaccumulation of surplus capital, i.e., capital that cannot be absorbed in the production sphere and which then finds an outlet in shadow banking. They suggest that this overaccumulation of capital was the main cause behind the 2007–2008 crisis, and that shadow banking only exacerbated the problem, as it contributed to considerable debt creation. As well as detailing these processes, Wigger and Fernandez challenge the view that shadow banking spread in a kind of happenstance manner. Rather, they stress, active state involvement, in the form of regulation, has played a crucial role in the expansion of shadow banking.

In Chapter 9, Yamina Tadjeddine discusses financial intermediaries, with a particular focus on asset managers. The chapter's starting point is a critique of the ways in which neoclassical economics has traditionally understood capital markets—namely, as an encounter between, on the one hand, investors with financing capacities and, on the other, companies with financing needs. What this analytical schema fails to acknowledge is the role played by the myriad financial intermediaries (mutual funds, hedge funds, pension funds, etc.) that make up the chain of financial transactions. Tadjeddine sheds lights on these financial intermediaries, demonstrating their close relations to powerful circles in society and the ways in which they themselves exercise financial domination. Drawing upon fieldwork in an asset management company, the chapter details these points empirically and thereby proposes a richer picture of finance, which takes seriously the interior of important financial institutions.

In Chapter 10, Daniel Scott Souleles examines private equity, a part of finance that has received surprisingly little scholarly attention outside of economics. Based on a case study of a particular private equity deal, as well as extensive fieldwork on private equity companies, Souleles details the main mechanisms of private equity, which he sees as emblematic of present-day financial capitalism. Invoking Marcel Mauss's notion of the "total social fact," Souleles argues for an analysis of private equity that does not fall back upon narrow economic categories, but conceives of it within a larger comparative anthropological frame. According to Souleles, doing so prompts an investigation into who is involved in this type of activity, who benefits from it, and who suffers as a result. In other words, this comparative framework seeks to understand the ways in which private equity plays an active part in wealth distribution, including by creating new forms of inequality.

The following two chapters address more technical aspects of finance, which in various ways refer back to the features discussed in Coombs' chapter. In Chapter 11, Ekaterina Svetlova discusses financial models. Such models are ubiquitous—it is hard today to think of professional market participants who do not, directly or indirectly, rely on particular financial models. However, a range of theorizations have been applied to such models, and Svetlova differentiates between two main approaches. One is associated with early critical finance studies research with a critical-theory perspective. Central to this line of research was the observation that many financial models are unrealistic, and therefore, it is precisely the gap between models and reality that should be the target of the critique. An alternative approach is that of social studies of finance, which emphasizes the performativity of models. Returning to the discussions mentioned earlier in this introduction, Svetlova details the ways in which performativity theory shifts the analytical focus to the practice of finance professionals, and studies, in a bottom-up fashion, how these professionals use, develop, tweak, etc., financial models and how, in certain contexts, the use of the model ends up changing reality. Svetlova argues that this latter analytical approach carries its own substantial critical impetus.

In Chapter 12, Ann-Christina Lange digs into the field of HFT, a field also briefly touched upon in Svetlova's chapter. Firms specializing in this sort of trading are now central actors in financial markets. However, HFT is often accused of creating a rigged market and/or engaging in manipulative behaviors, such as the so-called spoofing. Drawing on fieldwork in the industry, Lange examines the backdrop to the rise of HFT and discusses its role in spoofing. She demonstrates that the interactive feedback loops between fully automated algorithms are a central feature of HFT. Lange argues that critical finance scholars need to take seriously this interactive dimension, as the emergent effects of interacting algorithms challenge established categories of liability and intentionality—categories that are important when regulators seek to show that firms are engaging in, e.g., spoofing.

The third part of the *Handbook* addresses a theme that has received considerable attention in recent years: financialization. However, instead of providing a general critical overview of the financialization debate (for this purpose, see Christophers, 2015; van der Zwan, 2014), the *Handbook* zeros in on some specific aspects pertaining to financialization. In Chapter 13, Dick Bryan, David Harvie, Mike Rafferty, and Bruno Tinel mobilize the analytical template of Randy Martin's "social logic of the derivative" in order to demonstrate that state responses to the 2007–2008 financial crisis incorporated a number of key derivative facets. This suggests that the state is deeply implicated in financialization processes—not just, in the indirect sense, that it creates structures that others can utilize in ways that position finance more centrally in society, but, more directly, that its interventions are characterized by a derivative logic. Specifically, the chapter shows that measures such as quantitative easing programs, "too big to fail" bailouts, and social impact bonds are all framed by the same logic. The critical spark of this analysis lies in its emphasis on how a cultural interpretation of derivative finance paves the way for a fresh, de-familiarized understanding of the ways in which states respond to crises.

In Chapter 14, Léna Pellandini-Simányi moves from the state level to a discussion of the financialization of everyday life. However, this shift in focus is not
meant to suggest that these two levels are disconnected. As Pellandini-Simányi
makes clear, the financialization of everyday life is closely tied to the rise of
neoliberal modes of government. The chapter delineates four distinct analytical
traditions that all provide valuable insights into the ways in which everyday
life has become financialized. These include Marxist and Foucauldian analyses,
cultural economic analyses, work inspired by social studies of finances, as well
as investigations that particularly emphasize the inequalities that come with
the financialization of everyday life. Pellandini-Simányi teases out the critical
potential of each of these traditions, demonstrating that while some of them
are explicitly normative, others are not, but that this does not imply a lack of
critical bite.

In Chapter 15, José Ossandón adds a further dimension to the discussion of
the financialization of everyday life by examining consumer credit and credit
assessment. Inspired by Boltanski's shift from a critical sociology to a sociology
of critique, Ossandón argues for a pragmatic sociology of credit that entails a focus on practices and an interest in the types of collectivity, or social formations,
that credit helps bring into being. The critical point of this analytical gesture is
to question one-sided analyses that see the financialization of everyday life as
purely exploitative and anti-social. Drawing on empirical studies of consumer
credit, Ossandón demonstrates that credit is also used by people to form new
collective ties. Attending to "low finance" in this way is therefore an important corrective to studies that primarily associate finance with "high finance"
dimensions.

The discussion of financialization continues in Chapter 16, in which Julian
Hartman and Mark Kear examine critical financial geography. The overall point
of Hartman and Kear's chapter is that finance always has a "where"—it unfolds
in particular spatial contexts—and analyzing the co-constitution of finance
and geography is key to understanding how finance works. In demonstrating
this point, the chapter focuses on the different geographies of financialization.
This includes the financialization of nature, of the city, and of daily life, all of
which—in spite of their particular geographic specificities—entail gendered,
racial, distributional, and other consequences. Further, Hartman and Kear discuss ways in which critical financial geography often needs to take into account
the law and legal dimensions. Just as finance is spatial, so is law—and it is
through such ties that particular, and surprising, connections emerge, which
bind together law, finance, and their geographies.

Chapter 17 combines a focus on financialization with a geographical emphasis on a non-Western context, as Jing Wang discusses the rise of fin-tech (the
financial use of digital technologies) in China. Wang's theoretical starting point
is performativity theory, but she broadens its scope in order to address wider
cultural and political aspects. Specifically, she details the ways in which a particular cultural and political context rendered fin-tech a popular phenomenon

in China. Politically, the Chinese government pushed for the marketization and financialization of society; culturally, fin-tech companies tapped into and further deepened this development, by marketizing their products as tools that could turn lay people into investors and put their savings into financial circulation. Like other chapters in the *Handbook*, the critical gist of Wang's analysis lies in its emphasis on the need to go beyond non-contextualized economistic approaches.

Giving further attention to particular cultural dimensions, the final two chapters add yet another layer to the financialization discussion. In Chapter 18, Torsten Andreasen, Mikkel Krause Frantzen, and Frederik Tygstrup examine finance fiction, i.e., the ways in which finance and its effects are represented in literature. The central point of this approach is to stress that finance extends into everyday life through more than merely the types of financial decisions that people face on a daily level. Literary fiction and its representations of finance contribute to the shaping of financial imaginaries, and thereby constitute more than "mere" representation. The chapter suggests that critical finance studies should include this fictional dimension, and demonstrates that literature has grappled with finance using different genres in different time periods. Specifically, the 1970s approached finance via the thriller; in the 1980s, finance fiction was characterized by a tension between realism and psychosis; and in the post-2008 crisis era, the predominant form of finance fiction seems to be the epic.

Finally, in Chapter 19, Victoria Ivanova and Gerald Nestler discuss the connections between art, markets, and finance. Artists often critique financial capitalism, laying bare its excesses and the forms of inequality that it produces and enhances. According to Ivanova and Nestler, the relationship between art and finance is one of art assuming a critical reflective modus. In addition to tracing the genealogy of this critical art paradigm, Ivanova and Nestler demonstrate its limitations—namely, that art in this category often itself ends up as a financial asset, as it enters the circuit it claims to critique. As a result, Ivanova and Nestler argue, a host of alternative art forms has emerged that seek to reconceptualize the relationship between art and finance, and which aim to avoid becoming a cog in the wheel. The central point of such artistic practices is that they do not see art and finance as separate domains, in which the former offers an external critique of the latter. Rather, art that belongs to this new paradigm instead places itself within the financial terrain, and seeks to critically express from within the ways in which finance operates.

We hope you will enjoy the chapters, individually and collectively, and that they will inspire new exciting work within critical finance studies.

Acknowledgments

I am grateful to Robert Wosnitzer for his work on the *Handbook*. Robert especially played an important part in the early phases of the editorial process. I am also grateful to José Ossandón for helpful comments on an earlier version of this introduction and to Jessica Modi and, in particular, Caitlin Welch for valuable editorial support.

Notes

1 More correctly, critiques of financial practices tend to be somewhat decoupled from the standard *scholarly* contributions. For example, MacKenzie's writings have been criticized for lacking critical edge, but such edge is clearly visible in his more popular articles on finance in the *London Review of Books* (e.g. MacKenzie, 2016). Also, in his recent scholarly work, MacKenzie argues for combining STS inspirations with political economy (MacKenzie, 2018b).
2 In this call to combine empirical and conceptual work, the point is not to denigrate the contributions by scholars whose work is purely (or almost purely) empirical or theoretical. A lot of rich analyses have been produced from either predominantly empirical or theoretical backgrounds, and there is certainly much to be gained from such work, including when it comes to pursuing the kind of critical agenda for which we are arguing. However, it is worth striving for a balance in which neither the empirical nor the theoretical part ends up playing second fiddle.
3 On this point, I depart from Konings, for whom the attempt to link critique with the question of "what is to be done?" "is to confer on it a responsibility that it is poorly equipped to handle, and to tempt it down the path of one foundationalism or another" (2018: 132). I believe that middle ways exist between tying critique to no solutions at all and winding up in a foundationalist position.

References

Abolafia, M. Y. (1996). *Making Markets: Opportunism and Restraint on Wall Street*. Cambridge, MA: Harvard University Press.

Baker, W. E. (1984a). "The social structure of a national securities market," *American Journal of Sociology* 89(4): 775–811.

Baker, W. E. (1984b). "Floor trading and crowd dynamics," in P. A. Adler and P. Adler (eds.), *The Social Dynamics of Financial Markets* (pp. 107–128). Greenwich, CT: Jai Press Inc.

Bay, T., & Schinckus, G. (2012). "Critical finance studies: An interdisciplinary manifesto," *Journal of Interdisciplinary Economics* 24(1): 1–6.

Becker, G. S. (1968). "Crime and punishment: An economic approach," *Journal of Political Economy* 76(2): 169–217.

Blyth, M. (2013). *Austerity: The History of a Dangerous Idea*. Oxford: Oxford University Press.

Boltanski, L. (2011). *On Critique: A Sociology of Emancipation*, trans. G. Elliott. Cambridge: Polity Press.

Borch, C. (2016). "High-frequency trading, algorithmic finance and the Flash Crash: Reflections on eventalization," *Economy and Society* 45(3–4): 350–378.

Borch, C. (2020). *Social Avalanche: Crowds, Cities and Financial Markets*. Cambridge: Cambridge University Press.

Budish, E., Cramton, P., & Shim, J. (2015). "The high-frequency trading arms race: Frequent batch auctions as a market design response," *The Quarterly Journal of Economics* 130(4): 1547–1621.

Bush, N., Martelli, P., & Roberts, K. (2012). "Failures of high reliability in finance," in P. Shrivastava and M. Statler (eds.), *Learning from the Global Financial Crisis: Creatively, Reliably, and Sustainably* (pp. 167–187). Stanford, CA: Stanford Business Press.

Butler, J. (2010). "Performative agency," *Journal of Cultural Economy* 3(2): 147–161.

Callon, M. (2007). "What does it mean to say that economics is performative?," in D. MacKenzie, F. Muniesa, and L. Siu (eds.), *Do Economists Make Markets? On the Performativity of Economics* (pp. 311–357). Princeton, NJ: Princeton University Press.

Christophers, B. (2015). "The limits to financialization," *Dialogues in Human Geography* 5(2): 183–200.

Cooper, M. (2011). "Complexity theory after the financial crisis: The death of neoliberalism or the triumph of Hayek?," *Journal of Cultural Economy* 4(4): 371–385.

Crosthwaite, P. (2013). "Animality and ideology in contemporary economic discourse: Taxonomizing homo economicus," *Journal of Cultural Economy* 6(1): 94–109.

de Goede, M. (2005). *Virtue, Fortune, and Faith: A Genealogy of Finance.* Minneapolis and London: University of Minnesota Press.

du Gay, P. (2010). "Performativities: Butler, callon and the moment of theory," *Journal of Cultural Economy* 3(2): 171–179.

Fisher, M. S. (2012). *Wall Street Women.* Durham and London: Duke University Press.

Foucault, M. (1982). "The subject and power," in H. L. Dreyfus and P. Rabinow (eds.), *Michel Foucault: Beyond Structuralism and Hermeneutics* (pp. 208–226). Chicago: University of Chicago Press.

Foucault, M. (1991). "Questions of method," in G. Burchell, C. Gordon, and P. Miller (eds.), *The Foucault Effect: Studies in Governmentality* (pp. 73–86). Chicago: University of Chicago Press.

Foucault, M. (1997). "What is critique?," in *The Politics of Truth* (pp. 23–82). New York, NY: Semiotext(e).

Godechot, O. (2012). "Is finance responsible for the rise in wage inequality in France?," *Socio-Economic Review* 10(3): 447–470.

Golumbia, D. (2016). *The Politics of Bitcoin: Software as Right-Wing Extremism.* Minneapolis: University of Minnesota Press.

Granovetter, M. (1985). "Economic action and social structure: The problem of embeddedness," *American Journal of Sociology* 91(3): 481–510.

Kindleberger, C. P., & Aliber, R. (2011). *Manias, Panics and Crashes: A History of Financial Crises.* Houndmills, Basingstoke: Palgrave Macmillan.

Konings, M. (2018). *Capital and Time: For a New Critique of Neoliberal Reason.* Stanford, CA: Stanford University Press.

Langley, P. (2008). *The Everyday Life of Global Finance: Saving and Borrowing in Anglo-America.* Oxford: Oxford University Press.

Langley, P. (2010). "The performance of liquidity in the subprime mortgage crisis," *New Political Economy* 15(1): 71–89.

Latour, B. (2004). "Why has critique run out of steam? From matters of fact to matters of concern," *Critical Inquiry* 30(2): 225–248.

Latour, B. (2005). *Reassembling the Social: An Introduction to Actor-Network-Theory.* Oxford: Oxford University Press.

Lazzarato, M. (2014). *Signs and Machines: Capitalism and the Production of Subjectivity*, trans. J. D. Jordan. New York: Semiotext(e).

Lee, B., & Martin, R. (eds.). (2016). *Derivatives and the Wealth of Societies.* Chicago and London: University of Chicago Press.

Lemke, T. (1997). *Eine Kritik Der Politischen Vernunft. Foucaults Analyse Der Modernen Gouvernementalität.* Hamburg and Berlin: Argument.

Lemke, T. (2011). "Critique and experience in Foucault," *Theory, Culture & Society* 28(4): 26–48.

Lewis, M. (2014). *Flash Boys: Cracking the Money Code.* London: Allen Lane.

Luhmann, N. (1991). "Am Ende Der Kritischen Soziologie," *Zeitschrift für Soziologie* 20(2): 147–152.

Luhmann, N. (1995a). *Social Systems*, trans. J. Bednarz, Jr. with D. Baecker. Stanford, CA: Stanford University Press.

Luhmann, N. (1995b). "The paradoxy of observing systems," *Cultural Critique* 31: 37–55.

Luhmann, N. (2002). "I see something you don't see," in N. Luhmann (ed.), *Theories of Distinction: Redescribing the Descriptions of Modernity* (pp. 187–193). Stanford, CA: Stanford University Press.

Mackay, C. (2002). *Extraordinary Popular Delusions and the Madness of Crowds*. New York, NY: MetroBooks.

MacKenzie, D. (2006). *An Engine, Not a Camera: How Financial Models Shape Markets*. Cambridge, MA: MIT Press.

MacKenzie, D. (2016). "Must do better," *London Review of Books* 38(9): 29.

MacKenzie, D. (2017). "Capital's geodesic: Chicago, New Jersey, and the material sociology of speed," in J. Wachman and N. Dodd (eds.), *The Sociology of Speed: Digital, Organizational, and Social Temporalities* (pp. 55–71). Oxford: Oxford University Press.

MacKenzie, D. (2018a). "Material signals: A historical sociology of high-frequency trading," *American Journal of Sociology* 123(6): 1635–1683.

MacKenzie, D. (2018b). "'Making,' 'taking' and the material political economy of algorithmic trading," *Economy and Society* 47(4): 501–523.

MacKenzie, D. et al. (2012). "Drilling through the Allegheny mountains: Liquidity, materiality and high-frequency trading," *Journal of Cultural Economy* 5(3): 279–296.

Martin, R. (2002). *Financialization of Daily Life*. Philadelphia, PA: Temple University Press.

Maurer, B. (2005). *Mutual Life, Limited: Islamic Banking, Alternative Currencies, Lateral Reason*. Princeton, NJ and Oxford: Princeton University Press.

McDowell, L. (1997). *Capital Culture: Gender at Work in the City*. Oxford: Blackwell.

McDowell, L. (2010). "Capital culture revisited: Sex, testosterone and the city," *International Journal of Urban and Regional Research* 34(3): 652–658.

McFall, L. (2014). *Devising Consumption: Cultural Economies of Insurance, Credit and Spending*. London and New York, NY: Routledge.

Mirowski, P. (2013). *Never Let a Serious Crisis Go to Waste: How Neoliberalism Survived the Financial Meltdown*. London and New York, NY: Verso.

Peckham, R. (2013a). "Contagion: Epidemiological models and financial crises," *Journal of Public Health* 36(1): 13–17.

Peckham, R. (2013b). "Economies of contagion: Financial crisis and pandemic," *Economy and Society* 42(2): 226–248.

Riles, A. (2000). *The Network inside Out*. Ann Arbor: University of Michigan Press.

Roitman, J. (2014). *Anti-Crisis*. Durham and London: Duke University Press.

Schäfer, A., & W. Streeck (eds.). 2013. *Politics in the Age of Austerity*. Cambridge: Polity.

Sloterdijk, P. (2004). *Sphären III. Schäume: Plurale Sphärologie*. Frankfurt am Main: Suhrkamp.

Soja, E. W. (2000). *Postmetropolis: Critical Studies of Cities and Regions*. Oxford: Blackwell.

Svetlova, E. (2012). "On the performative power of financial models," *Economy and Society* 41(3): 418–434.

Svetlova, E. (2018). *Financial Models and Society: Villains or Scapegoats?* Northampton, MA: Edward Elgar.

Tooze, A. (2018). *Crashed: How a Decade of Financial Crises Changed the World*. London: Allen Lane.

van der Zwan, N. (2014). "Making sense of financialization," *Socio-Economic Review* 12(1): 99–129.

Weber, M. (2000). "Stock and commodity exchanges ["Die Börse" (1894)]," *Theory and Society* 29(3): 305–338.

Wolf, M. (2019). "The legacy and lessons of Paul Volcker," *Financial Times*, December 11.

PART I

Key Concepts

1

LIQUIDITY

Horacio Ortiz

Introduction

The expression "liquidity" can be found in many analyses of money and finance, with very different meanings. Its definition is sometimes circumscribed to a limited set of practices, rules, and institutions, for example, when the purchase of low-rated financial securities by a central bank is described as a measure to enhance liquidity, or when a particular number, like the average volume of daily transactions on a particular financial asset, is termed as an indicator of the asset's liquidity. But the word can be used in more diffused ways, for instance, when the same said central bank claims it will act to avoid a general "liquidity crisis," without clarifying which assets, institutions, or particular transactions will be taken into account. Even when it seems to designate something very specific, the expression works nevertheless mainly as a metaphor that allows for associating a particular indicator, rule or practice, with more or less diffuse or contested moral and political meanings (Langley, 2015; MacKenzie et al., 2012; Pasanek & Polillo, 2011).

The purpose of this chapter is therefore to clarify the multiple meanings of the expression "liquidity" in the domain of finance, and some moral and political imaginaries of which it is a part. This implies a particular critical and reflexive stance. It is necessarily a critical move because it will show the limitations and presuppositions of the concept, which tend to be part of conflicting and normative practices. It is also reflexive, in the sense that instead of proposing a particular definition of the concept to solve its potential contradictions or limitations, the aim of this analysis is to leave these tensions open because this allows for understanding how they work in everyday practice, both among financial professionals and people responsible for monetary policy and among critical and non-critical scholars studying them.

The chapter's approach is based on the anthropology and the sociology of money and finance. The analysis will thus be focused on concrete practices at two analytical levels that can overlap: the use of the expression "liquidity" by financial professionals and regulators, and the practices that anthropologists, sociologists, and economists tend to describe or analyze in terms of liquidity. In the frame of this *Handbook*, the concept of liquidity must be approached through two partly different sets of questions: one concerning discussions about money in general, and another concerning the transaction of financial assets in what are often termed "financial markets." These issues are partly different because thinking of liquidity in theories of money implies the broad set of social relations in which money is implicated and produced, well beyond the frame of professional financial practices. At the same time, financial institutions play a central role in monetary practices at large, and are therefore always given important consideration in contemporary theories of money. Finally, the concept of liquidity is sometimes discussed exclusively as an organizational issue in segments of the financial industry. It is necessary to explore the relations between these different ways of problematizing the concept of liquidity in order to clarify under which particular theoretical presuppositions "liquidity" is defined as an object of analysis or as an analytic category.

Like many other concepts formalized in financial economics, liquidity can be considered to be both a normative ideal and a series of more or less connected observable phenomena. Many authors have suggested that these two aspects can mutually influence each other: if liquidity is defined as the possibility for any participant in a market to enter and exit, i.e., to buy and sell, without having a significant impact on prices, then liquidity breeds liquidity and illiquidity breeds illiquidity. Knowing that the market is liquid, participants may hold on to, buy or sell assets, following their random expectations. But if they think the market is or may become illiquid, they will probably not enter it, or have a tendency to exit, increasing its illiquidity. This narrative is sometimes mobilized by both social scientists and financial practitioners. It is, for instance, central in the "announcement effect" expected of some monetary policies, which aim at sustaining liquidity by claiming that they will apply concrete measures to do so, for instance, in moments of "capital flight." Within this understanding, the concept of liquidity seems to correspond to the kind of objects of analysis of "performativity" studies, which focus on how economic concepts are used to shape concrete practices. Some authors have nevertheless highlighted how, when this kind of analyses focus solely on what happens within "markets," they can lose the critical insights that come from questioning the concept of market itself as a complex result of a historical process of institution building marked by power relations (Butler, 2010; Cooper & Konings, 2016; Miller & Rose, 2010).

Within this broader critical outlook, many authors have analyzed concepts and practices that are fundamental for the multiple definitions of liquidity, inspired by Michel Foucault's focus on the relation between the establishment of institutions that crystallize power relations and the production of knowledge that legitimizes these relations in terms of truth claims that are epistemological, moral, and political (Foucault, 1976). Different definitions of money relate to different understandings of monetary policy and of the role of the state in the distribution of resources (Dodd, 2014; Hart, 1986), something that could be observed, for instance, in the regulatory debates concerning the financial turmoil of 2007–2008 (Brian & Rafferty, 2017; Langley, 2015). Similarly, different definitions of the financial industry imply different understandings of the production and circulation of financial assets by this social activity or group (Hart & Ortiz, 2014; Maurer, 2006, 2012). Using the word "liquidity" as an analytic concept to study monetary policy or the activities of the financial industry implies taking a position within these debates, accepting the presuppositions of a particular approach, and eschewing certain critical stances. The approach adopted in this chapter is thus not to use the concept as an analytic tool, but to explore some of the multiple ways in which it is defined by different approaches, which relate to broad social processes marked by power relations (de Goede, 2005; Langley, 2015).[1]

The following sections present a necessarily limited overview of the debates around the concept of liquidity, highlighting two sets of interrelated issues. The first concerns conceptions of liquidity developed in different theorizations of money and monetary policy. The second issue concerns conceptions of liquidity used in different analyses and theorizations of the financial industry. Since finance is usually problematized as an important part of the production and distribution of money in general, I will come back to the connection between these two issues in the concluding section.

Liquidity as a General Monetary Issue

This is of course not the place to recall the vast variety of theories of money and the combinations and controversies they allow for (see Dodd, 2014). In order to highlight some important debates about liquidity in these theories, I will organize them, somewhat arbitrarily, around three approaches: idealist, functionalist, and pragmatist (Ortiz, 2014a).

For theorists like Adam Smith and, in general, those who situate money as a tool developed out of the limitations of barter, money is a function of exchange (Smith, 1991). According to this approach, particular forms of money develop as a technical solution to needs that arise in particular forms of exchange: for instance, those that involve important volumes and very different objects and services. Marx's understanding of money can also be considered functionalist from this point of view: it appears as a necessary by-product of the relations of production (Marx, 2004). In both cases, money's circulation is determined by relations that initially existed without it, and functions as a representation of the value of what is exchanged, which is the best representation possible for Smith, and inevitably flawed for Marx (Foucault, 1966).

The liquidity of money is understood here as a technical aspect of exchanges. Money is in particular a fundamental tool to make exchanges faster, easier, and more extended, as an equalizer of the uses and products of labor. Part of contemporary monetary theory is inspired by this approach of money and liquidity, central in neoclassical economics and monetarism. From this point of view, monetary policy and financial regulation should be oriented at enhancing money's liquidity role (Rostock, 2011). Some contemporary Marxist approaches consider that this ideal of liquidity is realized in practice, as part of a historical shift in which financial value becomes the driver of production. This is the meaning that some authors give to the processes rendering social activities, and in particular labor relations and companies, "liquid," i.e., more amenable to short-term purchase and sale or to their conversion into money (see, for instance, Ho, 2009).[2] In some theorizations, "liquidity" becomes thus a main driver of new forms of exploitation through a financialized money form, so that critique should focus on liquidity in order to overthrow exploitation itself (Meister, 2016). In both cases, liquidity is considered an intrinsic characteristic of money, itself a function of other social relations: either that which is technically desirable to enhance the division of labor, production, and wealth, or a fetish which reinforces the liberal veil that covers exploitation in the capitalist mode of production.

Theorists like Simmel and Mauss, in different ways, insist on the moral, ideal nature of money. For Simmel, money allows for the freest individual expression of desire and at the same time renders this freedom absolutely dependent on the group of people who accept money as a means of exchange (Simmel, 2011). As an abstract equalizer of individual desires that best symbolizes the universal value of freedom, money allows for the global expansion of this dialectics. It is thus not a by-product of other human relations, but a main driver of them. Mauss defines money as any object allowing for the realization of the universal morality of hierarchical reciprocity observable in the obligation to give, receive, and give back (Mauss, 2016). Thus, money is a fundamental instantiation of the moral foundation of social relations, and it allows for the expansion of society by extending the moral obligations within and between groups, with the unification of humanity as its potential horizon. For both authors, the extension of exchange is thus the main driver of human development, understood in universalist moral and political terms. They highlight, in different ways, that this realization is always the product of multiple social conflicts that need to be studied in their specificity, in order to understand the concrete interdependencies, freedoms, and constrains that money allows for. In this complex process, the "liquid" character of money is a central constitutive component of the realization of humanity as a moral project.

Many approaches inspired by this holistic and idealist understanding of money have focused on the centrality of the state for the legitimacy and stability of monetary relations. From this perspective, monetary policy is part of the management of the social relations that constitute a social group often defined as a "nation" or a "people" (Aglietta & Orléan, 2002; Inhgam, 2004). In this context, liquidity acquires a different meaning. While it is the characteristic of money that allows for the transformation of social relations through distribution, it is also a danger for the community, for the same reasons that made it be praised by Simmel and Mauss: money's capacity to bridge social distinctions also threatens to destroy the monetary community by dissolving its borders. Keynes's analysis of economic activity stresses the idea that people tend to have a "liquidity preference" (Keynes, 1997: 166 ff.) that relates to Simmel's understanding of money desired in itself as a pure potential for the expression of the self (Simmel, 2011: 353–357). But from a macro perspective, Keynes's analysis of liquidity stresses the threat that this idea poses to the social group. The danger is not for him the dissolution of the community's borders, but the impact that liquidity can have on the group's internal relations, as it dissolves the responsibility that should come with the sense of belonging among its members:

> Of the maxims of orthodox finance none, surely, is more anti-social than the fetish of liquidity, the doctrine that it is a positive virtue on the part of investment institutions to concentrate their resources upon the holding of "liquid" securities. It forgets that there is no such thing as liquidity of investment for the community as a whole. (Keynes, 1997: 155)

For Keynes, liquidity, as an illusory idea, gives meaning to practices that in effect go against the fact that the social group is itself the foundation of money.

Many contemporary anthropologists and sociologists have developed analyses of money that situate its meanings and roles in particular and concrete practices (Dodd, 2014; Guyer, 2016; Hart & Ortiz, 2014; Zelizer, 2009). They eschew a general definition of money, and hence the moral and political presuppositions that come with it. The concept of liquidity is not considered as a necessary aspect of money. If it is an object of study at all, it is because the expression is used in concrete practices. We can observe this in two contemporary processes: the way in which financial regulation and central banking have defined the events of 2007–2008 as a liquidity crisis, and the way in which digital payment methods are considered as a technique to enhance liquidity.

De Goede's genealogical study of major financial concepts, such as "risk" and "market," shows that they are produced in a historical process of accumulation and transformation of narratives, operations, and methods of calculation (De Goede, 2005). In this process, they combine moral and political meanings that can be contradictory. The market as represented by an index thus combines positivistic uses of statistics, considered as a representation of natural laws, and moral and political presuppositions about the desirability of developing and investing in stock markets (see also MacKenzie, 2006; Preda, 2009). This highlights the multiple, often contradictory, historical processes that result in the elaboration of the major concepts with which monetary policy and financial regulation understand the activities of the financial industry. Studying the financial turmoil of 2007–2008, Langley (2015) proposes a similar treatment of the notion of liquidity. He shows that from a regulatory point of view, the events were initially termed a "liquidity crisis" in relation to particular understandings of the banking sector, of the role of central banks, and of some of their instruments, which partially relied on specific notions of financial markets. Enhancing open market operations and lending facilities for banks was thus the result of a complex combination of actors with partly conflicting interests, but also of multiple understandings and institutional tools and rules. These practices, understandings, tools, and negotiations that coalesced around a certain definition of which kind of "liquidity" defined the "crisis" were later considered insufficient to deal with and frame conceptually the events. The metaphor of "liquidity," with its emotional, moral, political, and technical aspects, was thus eventually overshadowed by other practices and imaginaries.

The development of digital payment systems based on mobile phones and smart phones in the last decade has often been problematized as a process enhancing the liquidity role that functionalist approaches attribute to money. This is particularly the case for payment systems such as M-Pesa in Kenya, adopted by millions of people, including segments of the population who lived until then not only without a bank account, but using relatively little cash. Bill Maurer's team's long-term analysis of these processes (Maurer, 2015; Maurer et al., 2013) has shown that indeed millions of people have entered circuits of exchange from which they were previously partly or totally excluded. These studies also describe how the integration of people into circuits of exchange by M-Pesa is based on very complex social networks and relations of power that contribute to establishing particular rules of trust, morality, and political legitimacy. This redefines social hierarchies and identities in ways that escape the imagination of functionalist and idealist approaches of money. How much the development of M-Pesa increases wealth among the poor who adopt it, or simply enmeshes them in new forms of domination, remains thus still to be seen. A parallel process has been the development of digital payment systems based on smartphones in China. Wechat Pay and Alipay were developed in the last few years, and are currently used by over 500 million people daily (see also Wang's chapter in this *Handbook*). They are connected to new forms of credit, as Alibaba and Tencent developed their own banks and financial services, and to governmental projects of surveillance and nudging through the development of a "social credit" system based on big data analysis (see Loubere, 2017 for a recent overview). This system ties the development of new forms of monetary relations to transformations in the meaning of citizenship, state, and nation, sustaining the centrality of the Chinese Communist Party at the particular crossroads of the commercial globalization of the Chinese territory and its closure through digital technologies. While payments are made easier and credit systems tied to them increase the capacity to transact, this "liquidity" is sustained by relations of forces in institutional settings with particular moral and political imaginaries, an assemblage that is at best only partially grasped by functionalist and idealist approaches of money.

Analyzing social relations as a series of market transactions, neoclassical economics takes up the idea that money is a medium of exchange, account, and store of value, and that finance is the exchange of money through time. Liquidity in the financial industry is thus a technical requirement for the socially optimal allocation of credit and of resources in general. Following a comparable view on money, some Marxian approaches see liquidity as a particularly destructive force, reinforcing relations of exploitation in the capitalist mode of production. From the idealist perspectives sketched above, the concrete workings of the financial industry must be replaced within the broader understanding of the roles of money in social relations. As enhancer of exchange and of the expansion of social interdependences, liquidity in financial markets may be understood as a step in the direction of human development along universal moral ideas. But for analyses that consider money as part of the ideas that contribute to constitute social groups and the stability of their hierarchies, liquidity in general, and the financial industry in particular, can, on the contrary, appear as a destructive or "anti-social" force. From a pragmatist perspective, it is important to understand how the concepts of "market," "efficiency," and "liquidity" are co-constitutive of particular social settings and relations of force. In all these cases, the meanings of liquidity can be technical, moral, and political, in contradictory, complementary or divergent ways.

As a monetary issue that concerns society at large problematized in terms of monetary policy or of the role of finance in society, the expression "liquidity" can have multiple, sometimes contradictory meanings, which can be normative, descriptive, or both. In concrete practice, as the last "liquidity crisis" shows, these meanings can be combined and transformed, in relation to particular institutions, understandings and negotiations that shift over time. Using the concept of liquidity as an analytic category implies accepting the limitations imposed by these theoretical presuppositions, which are moral, political, and technical.

Liquidity as an Organizational Issue in the Financial Industry

The concept of liquidity is also used with a narrower analytic scope in several social science studies that analyze the financial industry as a social space organized a series of "markets." The definitions of liquidity depend here closely on those of "market" and tend to be connected, in one way or another, to an often critical discussion of the conceptions of financial markets and market liquidity formalized in neoclassical economics. These approaches usually offer an important critique of some of the main assumptions of financial regulation, financial economics, and financial practitioners about what happens in the financial industry. Yet, accepting the terms of neoclassical economics as the main frame for discussion may limit the critical import of some of these approaches. It is therefore important to recall the understanding of financial markets and liquidity in neoclassical economics and in standardized professional financial methodologies in order to situate the terms of these debates.

In most jurisdictions, the exchange of stocks, bonds, and other financial securities by companies such as investment funds, insurance companies, and banks, accompanied by brokerage houses and rating agencies, is problematized and regulated by mobilizing a general conceptual frame based on neoclassical economics (Abdelal, 2007; Aglietta & Rebérioux, 2004; Krippner, 2011). According to this frame, these employees and institutions operate in order to constitute markets where investment is carried out from the point of view of investors seeking to maximize returns and limit risks. The interests of investors are concretely defined by standardized formulas and procedures, established historically in a circulation of people and ideas between regulatory, academic, and professional milieus (MacKenzie, 2006; Whitley, 1986). Liquidity is here defined and problematized as a characteristic of the transactions between these professionals. From a theoretical point of view, liquidity is considered a fundamental aspect of well-functioning markets, and hence defined as a series of requirements allowing for market efficiency, such as the possibility of any individual investor to enter and exit the market with any volume of transaction and without having an impact on prices. From a normative perspective, regulators seek to secure particular practices and possibilities defined as liquidity. A typical measure is the establishment of "circuit-breaker" rules, which usually imply that trading of a stock stops for a short time if the price falls by 10% within a trading day, and which may lead to stopping all trading for the day after a certain threshold. This measure is supposed to stem potential panics, which can become "liquidity" crises according to the idea that illiquidity breeds illiquidity, described above.

In the formalizations of financial economics and in the methodologies and rationales mobilized in professional financial practice, liquidity refers to a series of concepts that relate to the stylized notion of a perfectly working market that stands at the basis of market efficiency. This generic definition becomes specified in partly disconnected indicators and practices that give more limited definitions of "liquidity." From the point of view of practitioners, liquidity can be defined by multiple indicators that are used in their official attempts to maximize returns and limit risks, often with the aim of determining what is called a "liquidity risk." These can be, for instance, bid-ask spreads, volumes, and number of trades, the relation between any of these indicators and some measure of volatility, among others. Price itself can be considered an indicator of liquidity, when it is considered to reflect what is called a "liquidity premium." In financial economics, liquidity is closely connected to the idea that the amount of exchanges and the volumes exchanged are big and continuous enough so that any individual buyer or seller can enter or exit the market without having an impact on price. Decrease in bid-ask spreads is thus understood as an increase of liquidity and efficiency in price discovery. In all these cases, liquidity is conceived as a characteristic of the practices of the financial industry, themselves defined as exchanges in financial markets, with the moral and political horizon of market efficiency as a condition for the optimal allocation of social resources.

We can use an analysis of high-frequency trading (HFT) published by the CFA Institute, a major professional organization representing the financial industry in the United States, as a telling example of how a similar understanding of liquidity is shared in financial economics and in the financial industry (CFA Institute, 2015).[3] Some influential authors in financial economics consider HFT as beneficial for liquidity and market quality because of the increase in volumes exchanged and the reduction of bid-ask spreads (Brogaard et al., 2014; Hendershott et al., 2011).[4] Taking up this academic literature, the CFA report distinguishes three indicators of "liquidity" (CFA Institute, 2015: 4–14 for what follows): "market breadth," defined by the bid-ask spread, where the smallest spread indicates higher liquidity; "market depth," defined by the quantities offered for purchase and sale; and market "resilience," indicating the capacity to "absorb" orders without the price being affected. These indicators are partly related. Higher volumes on both sides of the trade (bid and ask) will tend to reduce the margins gained by intermediaries, and imply a higher "resilience" in relation to individual trades. But all these measures are relative. What may count as high volumes at one point in time may be an indicator of a shallow market at another. Also, the report considers that the development of "dark" markets and HFT has changed the understanding of liquidity. On the one hand, automated trade orders of HFT increases the number of trades, something that is supposed to be beneficial for liquidity. On the other hand, HFT occurring on dark markets has access to both the information internalized in these exchanges and the information available on "lit" markets such as the New York Stock Exchange and Nasdaq. HFT is thus more informed than market-makers on lit markets, adversely affecting the informational quality of prices and liquidity defined in terms of volumes and bid-ask spreads in the latter. The fragmentation of exchanges, supposed to be beneficial to liquidity because it frees transactions from a monopoly of rules, can then lead to negative consequences for liquidity itself. Thus, the author of the CFA report concludes by stressing the difficulty to determine, technically, whether HFT has an overall positive or negative impact on liquidity.

This example is interesting because it explores core issues concerning liquidity raised in the financial industry, according to the main theoretical frame of neoclassical economics, which deems liquidity a central component of market efficiency and therefore inherently beneficial for the social allocation of resources. It is also interesting for our discussion because it raises many of the issues addressed by critical finance studies, well beyond the case of HFT. We can highlight three main issues: the idea that liquidity is based on homogeneous information shared by all participants, the idea that liquidity is based on participants' attempts to maximize returns to the detriment of other participants, and the idea that financial markets are neutral institutions serving exchange for all participants equally and therefore serving society at large.

Concerning the notion of information in the discussion of liquidity, the sociological analyses of the processes of knowledge production are used to critique the natural character of liquidity presupposed in neoclassical analyses and in financial regulation and practice. In a very influential paper, Carruthers and Stinchcombe (1999) take up a stylized definition of liquidity defined as continuous trading with market-makers who agree on a single price for a single commodity. The authors show that these conditions have been attained historically in very different ways, by the conscious effort of the state in the case of US mortgages, and by a concourse of unintended consequences in the case of English stock markets. In both cases, the authors show that the homogenization of the assets exchanged, central in the production of liquidity, is the result of social practices that cannot be taken for granted as a natural condition of exchange. The definition of what an asset is and how it should be valued and exchanged, which stands at the core of what would count as "information" about it, is thus a very particular institutional construct that may fail in many occasions. Pitluck (2014) analyzes how particular productions of knowledge and narratives about the distinction between "foreign" and "domestic" investors are central in the constitution of "herds" in Malaysia's stock markets. The way "information" is constituted creates clusters of knowledge that are not bridged by the fact that each participant knows what the others know, but that are stabilized around sociological processes of institution and identity formation.

The rise of HFT in recent years, as the CFA report quoted above shows, has brought new elements into the debates about liquidity in finance, which have been taken up by the social sciences (Lange et al., 2016). MacKenzie et al. (2012) show that HFT creates a technological and geographical competition, as proximity to exchanges increases the speed, measured in milliseconds, with which automated HFT algorithms access information about bid-ask prices and respond to them. Kilometers of cable and computing capacity make a relevant difference in terms of monetary returns. This implies a direct inequality between the participants who have access to these technologies and locations and those who do not. The authors highlight the importance of moral discourses about "fairness" in these debates. They follow thus Fabian Muniesa's study of how the way in which a price is determined in automated exchanges impacts heavily the way returns are distributed between sectors of the financial industry, which makes negotiations about what kind of algorithms are going to be used a discussion framed in the moral and political terms of the idea of market efficiency and price fairness and accuracy formalized in neoclassical economics (Muniesa, 2000, 2007). The political injunction to establish and secure liquid markets as a condition for market efficiency and the optimal allocation of resources it is supposed to allow for is thus mobilized by different sectors to push for particular technical decisions that play with the different indicators of "liquidity" and the interpretations they allow for. These studies show that "information" is thus an institutional production, specific to particular social processes and technological possibilities, far from a general idea of objective knowledge shared equally by all participants.[5]

A second series of questions concerns the idea that liquidity depends on the activities of participants whose sole rationale is return maximization as defined by the standardized methods and formulas used in the financial industry and usually formalized in financial economics. Authors studying traders have highlighted that their practices vary greatly, in relation to particular forms of organization and training. Abolafia (1996) has thus stressed the importance of both formal and informal sets of rules regulating competitive relations between traders. While these professionals are explicitly pitched against each other, they also develop forms of communication and unwritten rules that contribute to the stability of the group as a profession with a particular position within the circulation of money in the financial industry. Thus, some trades or ways of trading may be oriented towards collaborative group building and not only towards individual short-term gain. Godechot's analysis of traders' negotiations concerning the distribution of bonuses also highlights the importance of competition, collaboration, and hierarchy between professions and desks within and between companies in the elaboration and legitimization of particular investment strategies, that impact bid-ask spreads or investment in particular assets or asset classes (Godechot, 2001, 2016). Zaloom's study describes the stringent and ongoing bodily and emotional discipline that traders undergo in their workplace (Zaloom, 2006). She shows that the application of methods of speculation, which are supposed to sustain and thrive in liquid markets, is the never fully achieved result of constant peer pressure, organizational rules, and traders' construction of professional identities that are sometimes at odds with their non-professional lives.

These studies show that the forms of calculation and the concrete actions of purchase and sale standardized in the financial industry are multiple and contradictory, and cannot be subsumed under a single coherent narrative (Muniesa et al., 2017; Ortiz, 2014b). In order to understand what strategies and calculations lead to a particular bid-ask spread, to particular volumes being exchanged at a point in time, or to the participation or not of certain financial institutions in the exchange of a certain asset or asset class, one needs to take into account the way in which fees and bonuses are negotiated within and between companies, as well as the relations of cooperation, hierarchy, and competition among employees, professions, and companies (Arjaliès et al., 2017). These studies show that the figure of the investor presupposed in neoclassical economics and in standardized professional financial methodologies is not embodied in a particular person or actor, but is disseminated, in multiple and often contradictory instantiations, in the practice of financial employees, where it is co-constituted with their personal careers and labor relations. These studies thus undermine the presuppositions about the rationales of investment that stand at the basis of neoclassical economics' understanding of liquidity in financial markets.

A third issue that is central in the discussions about liquidity concerns the organization of exchanges, sometimes approached through the expression "market structure." Focus on stock exchanges often corresponds to the presupposition that they most closely resemble the ideal of free markets elaborated in neoclassical economics. But empirical analyses of stock exchanges, and the fact that many other financial assets are exchanged in varying forms of over-the-counter transactions render the picture much more complex. Baker (1986) attributed different forms of price formation to different organizations of markets, in particular concerning the number of participants and the volumes exchanged. As the CFA report quoted above and the studies on HFT remind, the development of the so-called "dark-pools" has changed the idea that stock markets are unified transparent venues where all participants meet on equal terms. Yet, "dark-pools" are themselves developed partly according to the narrative of liquidity, as they would allow for big institutions to conduct large-scale transactions without impacting other markets. The moral and political narratives of liquidity organize part of these tensions, without solving them (Arjaliès et al., 2017). Lemoine's analysis of the sale of sovereign bonds by the French government to the banks that resell them in the so-called "secondary market" shows how political calculations and relations of forces are central in exchanges that bring together a limited amount of powerful actors (Lemoine, 2013, 2016). This echoes the slow temporality and complex negotiations observed in the purchase of asset-backed securities and the sale of tranches of collateralized debt-obligations studied in Ortiz (2014c). These studies show that the relations of exchange established in the financial industry do not result from the encounter of maximizing investors in open arenas where they all share equally available information. They are rather the result of complex commercial relations between employees, professions, and companies, within the bureaucratic setting of the financial industry, in which activities are standardized according to contracts and regulations that strongly limit the possibilities for action and that raise important social and legal barriers against non-participants (Clark, 2000; Montagne, 2006). These analyses thus highlight the political character and the analytical limitations of the imaginary of "market" and "market structure" with which neoclassical economics and financial professionals and regulators tend to problematize liquidity.

Critical social studies of exchange practices in the financial industry show the concrete social processes, institutional arrangements, and technological conditions of bid-ask spreads, volumes of trading, and strategies of investment in particular assets or asset classes. They clarify the complex production of shared forms of knowledge labeled as "information," the multiplicity of processes whereby professionals buy or sell, and the many institutional arrangements of exchange that can lead to very different distributions of money. Analyzing these processes following neoclassical economics' ideas about finance being organized in markets where liquidity would depend on market structure and information availability means asking a very limited set of questions and accepting the political presupposition that market efficiency leads to a socially optimal allocation of resources. The critical studies that retain certain concepts of "market," "market structure," and "liquidity" to study the organization of the financial industry may encounter some of the limitations imposed by this frame of analysis, and exposed by the studies that integrate the stabilization of these concepts as part of the historical constitution of financial institutions and the concrete relations of power of which they are part in the present.

Conclusion

This chapter has shown that different theories of money can offer divergent understandings of "liquidity." In functionalist approaches of money, liquidity tends to be defined as a function and enhancer of social practices of exchange that drive the production and circulation of money. This is the case both when it is desired as a fundamental condition for an optimal allocation of resources by neoclassical economics, and when it is accused of being a driver of further exploitation by Marxian approaches. In idealist approaches, money's capacity to bridge and expand society and the morality of interdependence and individual freedom may give liquidity a positive meaning. Yet, some authors following this initial approach consider, on the contrary, that liquidity, as an illusion of extreme individual freedom, can also be detrimental to the social group on which money itself is based. Pragmatist approaches of money require avoiding an initial moral or political appraisal of liquidity, and show instead how its technical, moral, and political meanings can be multifarious and mobilized differently in different situations.

The analysis of liquidity in the financial industry is usually framed in academic production, in financial regulation, and by actors of the financial industry themselves, in the terms of neoclassical economics. Liquidity is considered a fundamental feature of market efficiency that policy is expected to protect and enhance. Critical studies of finance show that what is thereby designated as liquidity corresponds to multiple social processes, where information, operations of purchase and sale, and the rules of exchange all result from power relations with long and complex histories. These processes do not correspond to the idealization of rational actors and free markets that plays both normative and descriptive roles in neoclassical economics. These studies are thus powerful tools to problematize mainstream narratives and practices with which the distributive role of the financial industry tends to be legitimized in many jurisdictions across the globe. Yet, analyses that focus on a critique of the concepts of neoclassical economics, such as information, trading rationality, or market structure, may be limited by the terms of neoclassical economics itself. This is probably also the case for Marxist analyses that consider that the liquidity presupposed in neoclassical economics corresponds to an observable and fundamental reality, eschewing other understandings of money from discussions about the distribution of resources. While they delegitimize mainstream discourses about finance, these studies may run the risk of also conveying the idea that these discourses must remain the main frame of discussion.

Idealist approaches of money allow for exploring the role of the financial industry going beyond the organization of markets according to the narrative of market efficiency, and taking into account other power relations and legitimizing discourses that contribute to the constitution of social groups. They allow for understanding monetary policy and the financial industry as part of political processes, where multiple social groups and social activities are both in competition and interdependence, within social hierarchies that are legitimized with imaginaries that are technical, moral, political, and religious, among others. Yet, their universalist and holistic presuppositions may in turn have difficulty accounting for the multiplicity of relations established through practices of the financial industry that go across groups and within groups without forming new collective identities or shared interest.

Pragmatist approaches of money provide tools to situate the concept of liquidity in observable practices in the financial industry, staying attentive to the many ways in which it makes sense for those who use it in specific social relations. While these approaches may not have a common normative stance, studies influenced by Foucault's or Marx's critique of power relations tend to elaborate a critique of the financial industry as a series of activities, institutions, and narratives that produce inequality and social hierarchies according to truth claims that the analysis tends to relativize historically and socially. These studies thereby politicize the practices of money in general, as well as those of the financial industry in particular, multiplying the entry points for reflexive critique. The concept of liquidity, with its multiple meanings, appears thus as part of particular political imaginaries about the fairness of the distribution of resources. Like other concepts used in the financial industry and in monetary policy, such as "investors," "markets," "risk," and even "crisis," adopting it as an analytic category may frame the discussion within the limits of these imaginaries. Analyzing it as part of the meanings that actors give to their practice, and not using it as an analytic category, may therefore contribute to a more productive critical stance.

Acknowledgments

I thank Christian Borch and Robert Wosnitzer for their very helpful comments on the first draft of this chapter, as well as Marc Lenglet for his initial suggestions. All errors are of course mine.

Notes

1 Jefferis (2018), on the contrary, proposes to use the concept of "liquidity" as an analytic category, equating it more or less with the notion of "exchange," which may make it slightly redundant if not confusing.
2 For the limits of the concepts of "financialization" and "neoliberalism" to analyze these processes, see, respectively, van der Zwan (2014) and Venugopal (2015).
3 This chapter only evokes HFT as an example of current discussions about liquidity in financial economics and in the financial industry. For a deeper and broader analysis of HFT, see Ann Christina Lange's chapter in this *Handbook*

4 Using the same concepts and presuppositions about market efficiency, with other sets of data, the Deutsche Bundesbank arrives at the opposite conclusion (Deutsche Bundesbank, 2016).
5 Studying this issue, the sociology of knowledge has offered fundamental critiques of financial economics, and within it the studies of the "performativity" of economics have produced a particularly consistent research program (Callon & Muniesa, 2003).

References

Abdelal, R. (2007). *Capital Rules: The Construction of Global Finance*. Cambridge, MA: Harvard University Press.
Abolafia, M. (1996). *Making Markets: Opportunism and Restraint on Wall Street*. Cambridge, MA: Harvard University Press.
Aglietta, M., & Orléan, A. (2002). *La monnaie entre violence et confiance*. Paris: Editions Odile Jacob.
Aglietta, M., & Rebérioux, A. (2004). *Dérives du capitalisme financier*. Paris: Albin Michel.
Arjaliès, D.-L., Grant, P., Hardie, I., MacKenzie, D., & Svetlova, E. (2017). *Chains of Finance: How Investment Management is Shaped*. Oxford: Oxford University Press.
Baker, W. E. (1986). "Floor trading and crowd dynamics," in P. Adler (ed.), *The Social Dynamics of Financial Markets* (pp. 107–128). Greenwich, CT: JAI Press Inc.
Brian, D., & Rafferty, M. (2017). "Reframing austerity: Financial morality, savings and securitization," *Journal of Cultural Economy* 10(4): 339–355.
Brogaard, J., Hendershott, T., & Riordan, R. (2014). "High frequency trading and price discovery," *The Review of Financial Studies* 27(8): 2267–2306.
Butler, J. (2010). "Performative agency," *Journal of Cultural Economy* 3(2): 147–161.
Callon, M., & Muniesa, F. (2003). "Les marchés économiques comme dispositifs collectifs de calcul," *Réseaux* 122: 189–233.
Carruthers, B., & Stinchcombe, A. L. (1999). "The social structure of liquidity: Flexibility, markets, and states," *Theory and Society* 28: 353–382.
CFA Institute. (2015, August). *Liquidity in Equity Markets: Characteristics, Dynamics, and Implications for Market Quality*. Retrieved from https://www.cfainstitute.org/en/advocacy/policy-positions/liquidity-in-equity-markets-characteristics-dynamics-and-implications-for-market-quality
Clark, G. L. (2000). *Pension Fund Capitalism*. Oxford: Oxford University Press.
Cooper, M., & Konings, M. (2016). "Pragmatics of money and finance: Beyond performativity and fundamental value," *Journal of Cultural Economy* 9(1): 1–4.
De Goede, M. (2005). *Virtue, Fortune and Faith: A Genealogy of Finance*. Minneapolis and London: University of Minnesota Press.
Deutsche Bundesbank. (2016, October). "Significance and impact of high-frequency trading in the German capital market," *Deutsche Bundesbank Monthly Report* 37.
Dodd, N. (2014). *The Social Life of Money*. Princeton, NJ: Princeton University Press.
Foucault, M. (1966). *Les mots et les choses*. Paris: Editions Gallimard.
Foucault, M. (1976). *Histoire de la sexualité 1. La volonté de savoir*. Paris: Editions Gallimard.
Godechot, O. (2001). *Les Traders. Essai de sociologie des marchés financiers*. Paris: Editions La Découverte.
Godechot, O. (2016). *Wages, Bonuses and Appropriation of Profit in the Financial Industry: The Working Rich*. London: Routledge.
Guyer, J. I. (2016). *Legacies, Logics, Logistics: Essays in the Anthropology of the Platform Economy*. Chicago, IL and London: The University of Chicago Press.
Hart, K. (1986). "Heads or tails? The two sides of the coin," *Man* (N.S.) 21: 637–656.
Hart, K., & Ortiz, H. (2014). "The anthropology of money and finance: Between ethnography and world history," *Annual Review of Anthropology* 43: 465–482.

Hendershott, T., Jones, A., & Menkveld, J. C. (2011). "Does algorithmic trading improve liquidity?," *The Journal of Finance* 64(1): 1–33.

Ho, K. (2009). *Liquidated: An Ethnography of Wall Street*. Durham and London: Duke University Press.

Ingham, G. (2004). *The Nature of Money*. Cambridge: Polity Press.

Jefferis, C. (2018). "Financial performativity as evidence of immanence: The phenomenology of liquidity crisis in contemporary markets for risk," *Journal of Cultural Economy* 11(4): 291–302.

Keynes, J. M. (1936/1997). *The General Theory of Employment, Interest and Money*. New York, NY: Prometheus Books.

Krippner, G. R. (2011). *Capitalizing on Crisis: The Political Origins of the Rise of Finance*. Cambridge, MA: Harvard University Press.

Lange, A.-C., Lenglet, M., & Seyfert, R. (2016). "Cultures of high-frequency trading: Mapping the landscapes of algorithmic developments in contemporary financial markets," *Economy and Society* 45(2): 149–165.

Langley, P. (2015). *Liquidity Lost: The Governance of the Financial Crisis*. Oxford: Oxford University Press.

Lemoine, B. (2013). "Les 'dealers' de la dette souveraine. Politique des transactions entre banque et Etats dans la grande distribution des emprunts français," *Sociétés Contemporaines* 2013(4): 59–88.

Lemoine, B. (2016). *L'ordre de la dette. Enquête sur les infortunes de l'état et la prospérité du marché*. Paris: Editions La Découverte.

Loubere, N. (2017). "China's internet finance boom and tyrannies of inclusion," *China Perspectives* 4: 9–18.

MacKenzie, D. (2006). *An Engine, not a Camera: How Financial Models Shape Markets*. Cambridge, MA: The MIT Press.

MacKenzie, D., Beunza, D., Millo, Y., & Pardo-Guerra, J.-P. (2012). "Drilling through the Allegheny mountains," *Journal of Cultural Economy* 5(3): 279–296.

Marx, K. (1872/2004). *Capital: A Critique of Political Economy Vol. 1*, trans. Ben Fowkes. London: Penguin Books.

Maurer, B. (2006). "The anthropology of money," *Annual Review of Anthropology* 35(2): 1–22.

Maurer, B. (2012). "Finance 2.0," in J. C. Carrier (ed.) *A Handbook of Economic Anthropology*, Second Edition (pp. 183–201). Cheltenham: Edward Elgar.

Maurer, B. (2015). *How Would You Like to Pay? How Technology Is Changing the Future of Money*. Durham and London: Duke University Press.

Maurer, B., Nelms, T. C., & Rea, S. C. (2013). "'Bridges to Cash': Channeling agency in mobile money," *Journal of the Royal Anthropological Institute (N.S.)* 19: 52–74.

Mauss, M. (1924/2016). *The Gift*, trans. J. Guyer. Chicago, IL: The University of Chicago Press.

Meister, R. (2016). "Liquidity," in B. Lee and R. Martin (eds.), *Derivatives and the Wealth of Societies* (pp. 143–173). Chicago, IL and London: The University of Chicago Press.

Miller, P., & Rose, N. (2010). "Political power beyond the state: Problematics of government," *British Journal of Sociology* 61(1): 271–303.

Montagne, S. (2006). *Les Fonds de Pension. Entre protection sociale et spéculation financière*. Paris: Editions Odile Jacob.

Muniesa, F. (2000). "Un robot walrasien. Cotation électronique et justesse de la découverte des prix," *Politix* 13(52): 121–154.

Muniesa, F. (2007). "Market technologies and the pragmatics of prices," *Economy and Society* 36(3): 377–395.

Muniesa, F., Doganova, L., Ortiz, H., Pina-Stranger, Á., Paterson, F., Bourgoin, A., Ehrenstein, V., Juven, P.-A., Pontille, D., Saraç-Lesavre, B., & Yon, G. (2017). *Capitalization: A Cultural Guide*. Paris: Presses des Mines.

Ortiz, H. (2014a). "Funcionalismo, idealismo y pragmatismo: dilemas sobre el dinero en las ciencias sociales," *Perspectivas: Revista de Análisis de Economía, Comercio y Negocios Internacionales* 8(1): 135–154.

Ortiz, H. (2014b). "The limits of financial imagination: Free investors, efficient markets and crisis," *American Anthropologist* 116(1): 38–50.

Ortiz, H. (2014c) *Valeur financière et vérité. Enquête d'anthropologie politique sur l'évaluation des entreprises cotées en bourse.* Paris: Presses de Science Po.

Pasanek, B., & Polillo, S. (2011). "After the crash, beyond liquidity," *Journal of Cultural Economy* 4(3): 231–238.

Pitluck, A. Z. (2014). "Watching foreigners: How counterparties enable herds, crowds, and generate liquidity in financial markets," *Socio-Economic Review* 12: 5–31.

Preda, A. (2009). *Framing Finance: The Boundaries of Markets and Modern Capitalism.* Chicago, IL and London: The University of Chicago Press.

Rostock, H. (2011). "Parallel journeys," *Journal of Cultural Economy* 4(3): 255–283.

Simmel, G. (1900/2011). *The Philosophy of Money*, trans. D. Frisby. London: Routledge.

Smith, A. (1776/1991). *An Inquiry into the Nature and Causes of the Wealth of Nations.* New York, NY: Prometheus Books.

Van der Zwan, N. (2014). "Making sense of financialization," *Socio-Economic Review* 12: 99–129.

Venugopal, R. (2015). "Neoliberalism as concept," *Economy and Society* 44(2): 165–187.

Whitley, R. (1986). "The transformation of business finance into financial economics: The roles of academic expansion and changes in U.S. capital markets," *Accounting, Organizations and Society* 11(2): 171–192.

Zaloom, C. (2006). *Out of the Pits: Traders and Technology from Chicago to London.* Chicago, IL and London: The University of Chicago Press.

Zelizer, V. (2009). *Economic Lives: How Culture Shapes the Economy.* Princeton, NJ and Oxford: Princeton University Press.

2
VOLATILITY

Benjamin Lee

Introduction

On February 5, 2018, the S&P 500 and Dow Jones Industrial Average had their largest single day point declines ever as a much-anticipated correction hit the stock market, which then quickly recovered. Yet unlike previous market crashes, the media focused almost as much on the VIX (Volatility Index) as it did on stock markets, proclaiming that volatility was back as the VIX more than doubled. Since the VIX had been unprecedentedly quiet for over two years, some commentators noted that the markets had finally caught up to the cultural and political volatility of the Trump administration.

What does this public manifestation of the VIX signify? There is a quantitative aspect of the public reaction. The VIX is the implied volatility of the S&P 500; it is managed and calculated by the Chicago Board Options Exchange (CBOE) and calculated using the Black-Scholes equation. The CBOE created the VIX in 1993 and began selling options on it a decade later. But there is also a qualitative dimension to the story that is tied to social affect and emotion. The VIX remained a relatively obscure market index until it became known as the "fear gauge," and the recent newspaper headlines showed that both dimensions of volatility have captured the popular imagination.

If we dig a bit further into the history of the VIX and the CBOE, it turns out that they are emblematic of the history of derivative finance from its origins to its present popularity. The CBOE was founded in 1973, the same year as the publication of the Black-Scholes equation, the crown jewel of finance. From its inception, the CBOE was clouded in controversy because options were considered gambling and thus illegal. Milton Friedman helped carry the day by arguing that since the Black-Scholes equation was formally identical to a heat transfer equation in physics, options trading was scientific and not gambling!

Twenty-five years later in the midst of the Great Moderation that derivative finance would help usher in, Alan Greenspan would argue for a deregulation of over-the-counter derivatives that would consolidate their role in the rise of neoliberalism and eventually trigger the Great Recession and Obama's decision to bail out the banks. Neoliberalism and derivative finance were mutually imbricated from the very beginning. Neoliberal policies deregulated derivatives while the explosive growth of derivative finance created a new finance-driven global order. This culminated in the 2016 election that pitted a prudent neoliberal risk manager against a self-acknowledged master of volatility. His election and subsequent trade policies signal the end of a neoliberalism that began with Thatcher and Reagan, was consolidated under Clinton, and continued through the Bush and Obama administrations. In a pairing that might seem surprising at first, Trump and the public ascension of the VIX signal that volatility is now the sign of the times.

We can see both the financial and social senses in the etymology of volatility. "Volatilis" derives from the Latin "volare" (to fly), and in its earliest uses means "fleeting, transitory," with undertones of rapid unpredictable changes as in the flight of birds (in Middle English "volatiles" refers to winged creatures such as birds or butterflies). It was first applied to birds, then gases, and later to people and things, and is now used to describe changes of intensity in everything from the weather to moods and dispositions. Yet despite its semantic variability, volatility now seems to be applied to changes of two broad classes of phenomena: those that can be measured, such as the weather or stock prices, and those that cannot, such as affects and emotions. But what do these "quantitative and qualitative" uses of volatility have in common besides that they are both ascribable to intensities and their changes? We can think of temperatures and affects as increasing or decreasing and psychophysics seeks to correlate the extensive and intensive dimensions of sensations, but there seems to be an irreducible gap between quantitative and qualitative "modulations of intensity"—it's hard to say "I'm two and half times angrier now" except as a rhetorical gesture. On the other hand, risk is both quantifiable and affect-laden. Can the quantitative and qualitative dimensions of volatility be reconciled?

What Is Quantitative Volatility?

Although it is now a commonplace to say that we are living in an age of volatility, it is not clear what that means. Is it just a feeling of accelerated change or does it express something deeper and more profound? How is volatility different from risk and uncertainty? High volatility seems to go hand in hand with unpredictableness; the resulting uncertainty would seem to increase the sense of risk (see also the chapter by Hardin and Rottinghaus in this *Handbook*). Modern portfolio theory, which sought to maximize return and minimize risk, represented volatility as the standard deviation of stock prices. It was the square root of the variance, which was the expected value of squared deviations from the mean, and was designed to measure the magnitude or spread of prices around a mean; the squaring was to ensure that positive and negative differences didn't offset each other. But even the financial treatment of volatility highlights two overlapping problems that will affect our general understanding of volatility. The first is captured in this quote from Paul Wilmott, a well-known "quant":

> Actual volatility is a measure of the amount of randomness in a financial quantity at any point in time. It's what Desmond Fitzgerald calls the "bouncy, bouncy." It's difficult to measure, and even harder to forecast but it's one of the main inputs into option-pricing models... It's difficult to measure since it is defined mathematically via standard deviations, which requires historical data to calculate. Yet actual volatility is not a historical quantity but an instantaneous one. (Wilmott, 2009: 162)

What financial analysts want is instantaneous randomness, but the standard approaches involve a calculation of a mean from historical data. The historical time is the "empty homogenous" time of classical physics, clocks, and calendars in which all events are supposed to take place as opposed to the indexical or real-time of the event of trading in which time flows from the future through the present and into the past. But the instantaneous time of the event leads to the second problem: how do you distinguish the volatility, which would measure the spread of alternatives from what actually happens, from the actual change that occurs? All you can observe is the actual change (i.e., the stock price goes up or down two dollars), but the instantaneous randomness/volatility is a range around that change computed from a historical average, i.e., meaning that it isn't instantaneous. What is the ontological status of the counterfactual alternatives?

Derivative finance would tackle these problems with the development of the Black-Scholes model for pricing options. In order to price an option on an underlying stock, you need to continuously neutralize directional risks as the price of the underlying changes; this combination of "delta-hedging" and "dynamic replication" will allow access to the upside ("convexity") of volatility, and the cost of the hedge will turn out to be the price of the option. At the same time, one could bypass computing a historical average for the standard deviation and get closer to the "bouncy-bouncy"; once option markets became sufficiently liquid and transparent, people began taking the market prices of options and inserting them into the formula, run it backwards, and then obtain the market's estimate of the future volatility of the underlying stock, what became known as the "implied volatility." Delta-hedging and dynamic replication were the key breakthroughs in the Black-Scholes model; implied volatility is now the dominant measure of volatility—the VIX is the implied volatility of the S&P 500.

In derivative finance, the model for stock price movements is taken from the "random" behavior of Brownian movement; stock prices are assumed to follow a lognormal path, which was Louis Bachelier's insight in 1900 and remains as one of the foundations of options pricing theory. In 1905, Einstein was able to link the macroscopic random motion of pollen particles to their constant microscopic bombardment by water molecules, establishing the existence of an atomic level of physical phenomena. Originally applied to the seemingly random movement of pollen particles suspended in water, Brownian motion was extended to gases (dust particles in air) and then to stock prices, completing a movement from physical (pollen particles) to mental things (stock prices) (see also the chapter by Ortiz in this *Handbook*). The Black-Scholes model for pricing options, which is the foundation of derivative finance, is formally equivalent to the diffusion equation in physics.

The randomness of the diffusion process also fit the connection between information and stock prices that was developing in finance in the late 1960s. Fischer Black and Myron Scholes created their options model in the early 1970s at the University of Chicago (Robert Merton was at M.I.T.) when Eugene Fama was also developing the efficient market hypothesis, which stated that stock prices followed a random walk because the information that trading relied upon arrived randomly on the market. Since the continuous time limit case of a random walk is a Brownian motion, stock prices were also thought to follow Brownian motion (more specifically, geometric Brownian motion in which the varying quantities are the logarithms of stock prices) with traders replacing pollen particles and information replacing water molecules.

Geometric Brownian motion has mathematical properties that are of special interest to quants: it is not only fractal but also a martingale and Markovian. Although there are different definitions of what a fractal is (some mathematical, others influenced by fractal art and design), they converge on the idea of irregularities that are self-similar at different scales, such as frost crystals, coastlines, or certain tree structures.[1] Fractals are "jagged" patterns which when magnified reveal no new structural details but rather a repeating "self-similar" structure at different levels of perspective. Because of their jagged structure, fractals are "nowhere differentiable" and can't be handled by standard integral calculus, which applies only to smooth functions; a new type of "stochastic calculus" (Ito's calculus) had to be developed in order to deal with the non-smoothness of Brownian motion. The jaggedness of Brownian motion is the random movement of pollen particles or stock prices in which any segment has the same formal properties as the whole—producing what at first seems a contradiction in terms, regularities out of randomness. If one "zooms in" and "blows up" any segment of a Brownian motion, it will have the same jagged shape as the larger segment—self-similar at different scales.

The mathematical analysis of geometric Brownian motion divides it into two components: a predictable linear drift component and an unpredictable random component. The following equation describes a small change in the price of the stock as a function of drift and random components: the change in stock price (dS) is a function of time (t), two constants representing the expected rate of return of stock, μ, and its volatility or standard deviation, σ, and a Brownian process (B_t):

$$d\left(S_t\right) = \mu S_t dt + \sigma S_t dB_t$$
$$[\text{drift}] + [\text{random}]$$

The diffusion process describes the behavior of a stock but its option should have the same volatility. The relation of an option to its underlying stock was mathematically thought of as a function on the underlying stock price behavior. The drift was linear and could be handled by standard calculus. The problem was how to model the random component of the Brownian movement. An option is the right but not the obligation to buy (a call) or sell (a put) a stock at a fixed price at a determinate future date. For example, a call option on Apple stock might have a strike price of $100 90 days in the future. If the price at expiration is above $100, then the profit is the stock price minus $100; in our example, if Apple stock is at $110 at expiration, the profit is $10 (minus the price of the call). If the price is below $100, then the buyer would simply not exercise his or her option. This asymmetry between a potentially unlimited upside and a maximum downside of $0 produces the convexity of an option: it measures the value of "optionality"—"time and the right to choose" is worth paying for (Derman, 2016: 199).

While the option's payoffs are known at expiration, the value of the option will change between when it is purchased and expiration. Unlike laws in physics, which are supposed to be timeless, the price of an option depends on the stock's behavior at a future date and then is "read" backward to the present; its value has to be "discounted" to the present moment. Although one knows what the profit or loss is at expiration for every stock price, the price before expiration depends on the unpredictable behavior of the stock, which is suspect to market factors. This is the fundamental insight of the "efficient market hypothesis." Since information arrives randomly on the market, and such information influences trading, stock prices reflect this random behavior and follow geometric Brownian motion.

The great insight of Black and Scholes is that if one could systematically eliminate the drift and random components of stock price movements, one would be left with the equivalent of the risk-free interest rate, i.e., the price of simply holding money in a non-volatile financial instrument such as a treasury bill. The basic idea behind Black-Scholes is how to convert the risky and volatile behavior of stock prices into that of a risk-free instrument. The trick is to neutralize or "hedge away" the directional stock price movements so that the portfolio consisting of an option and a proportional short position in the stock will become riskless, i.e., earn the riskless rate of interest. Black-Scholes showed how to make new financial instruments (an option) out of existing ones (the underlying stock) and quickly became the principle of innovation that drove the explosive growth in derivative finance. In "How We Came Up with the Options Formula" (1989), Fischer Black describes the process of dynamic replication in which the delta-hedge is reset each time the stock price changes as the core of Black-Scholes:

> Suppose there is a formula that tells how the value of a call option depends on the price of the underlying stock, the exercise price and the maturity of the option, and the interest rate.
>
> Such a formula will tell us, among other things, how much the option value changes when the stock price changes by a small amount within a short time. Suppose that the option goes up about $.50 when the stock goes down $1.00. Then you can create a hedged position by going short two option contracts and long one round lot of stock.
>
> Such a position will be close to riskless. For small moves in the stock in the short run, your losses on one side will be mostly offset by gains on the other side. If the stock goes up, you will lose on the option but make it up on the stock. If the stock goes down, you will lose on the stock but make it up on the option.
>
> At first, you create a hedged position by going short two options and long one stock. As the stock price changes, and as the option approaches maturity, the ratio of option to stock needed to maintain a close-to-riskless hedge will change. To maintain a neutral hedge, you will have to change your position in the stock, your position in the option, or both.
>
> As the hedged position will be close to riskless, it should return an amount equal to the short-term interest rate on close-to-riskless securities. This one principle gives us the option formula. It turns out that there is only one formula for the value of an option that has the property that the return on hedged position of option and stock is always equal to short-term interest rate. (Black, 1989: 4)

Although there are several ways of deriving the Black-Scholes equation there are two basic principles from which Black-Scholes can be derived. The first is that no one will pay for avoidable risks (i.e., risks that you can get rid of), and the second is that securities that have the same future payoffs must have the same present price otherwise investors would buy the cheaper one and sell the more expensive one, earning a riskless profit. If we return to the differential equation describing stock price movements as having drift and random components:

$$\mathrm{d}\left(S_t\right) = \mu S_t \mathrm{d} + \sigma S_t \mathrm{d}B_t$$

The drift component $\mu S_t dt$ is linear, smooth, and continuous while the random Brownian component is also continuous but non-smooth and jagged. One of the properties of Brownian motion is that any portion or segment has the same formal properties of the whole, so that even an infinitesimally small segment still has a jagged non-smooth appearance, making standard calculus inapplicable. The result is that although $\mu S_t dt$ is treatable by traditional calculus, the

Brownian portion $\sigma S_t dB_t$ requires stochastic calculus that can handle its non-smooth or jagged behavior. The standard Riemann-Stieltjes integral calculates the value of an integral as the limit of the sum of the areas of rectangles as they become infinitesimally small.

Taking the limit of progressively narrower rectangles presupposes that the function is smooth and continuous. Since geometric Brownian motion is fractal "all the way down," its "jaggedness" will continue even as the rectangles become narrower; there is no limit that the sum approaches. Ito's lemma provides a stochastic calculus methodology for calculating that limit by using the normal distribution; for the above function, the corresponding stochastic partial differential equation given by Ito's lemma is:

$$dF_t = \frac{\partial F}{\partial S_t} d(S_t) + \frac{\partial F}{\partial t} dt + \frac{1}{2}\sigma_t^2 \frac{\partial^2 F}{\partial S_t^2} dt$$

The appearance of our original function $d(S_t)$ shows that any function that takes an Ito process as its object and has the same variables is itself an Ito process with linear (drift) and stochastic components (random); it's basis for the fractal self-similarity of geometric Brownian motion. Substituting $\mu S_t dt + \sigma S_t dB_t$ for $d(S_t)$, we get the following function, which is again divided into drift and random components:

$$dF_t = \underbrace{\left(\mu S_t \frac{\partial F}{\partial S_t} + \frac{\partial F}{\partial t} + \frac{1}{2}\sigma_t^2 \frac{\partial^2 F}{\partial S_t^2} \right) dt}_{\text{drift}} + \underbrace{\sigma_t S_t \frac{\partial F}{\partial S_t} dB_t}_{\text{random}}$$

Since options are functions on stocks, an equation can be written using the same variables that commensurate the option function with the stock price function; for example, the call function is a function of the prices of its underlying stock and the resulting call function will also have drift and random components.

We can similarly derive the Black–Scholes differential equation for an option ("V" replaces "F" in the above formula) by creating a replicating portfolio in which the random $\left(\sigma_t S_t \frac{\partial F}{\partial S_t} dB_t \right)$ and expected return $\left(\mu S_t \frac{\partial F}{\partial S_t} \right)$ components are neutralized via delta-hedging; the only unknowns are the volatility and risk-free rate, which is often assumed to be given by US treasury bonds.

$$\frac{\partial V}{\partial t} + \frac{1}{2}\sigma^2 S^2 \frac{\partial^2 V}{\partial S^2} + rS\frac{\partial V}{\partial S} - rV = 0$$

1   $\frac{\partial V}{\partial t}$= time decay, how much the option value (V) changes if the stock price doesn't change (t = time);

2 $\dfrac{1}{2}\sigma^2 S^2 \dfrac{\partial^2 V}{\partial S^2}$= convexity term, how much a hedged position makes on the average from stock moves; V = option price, σ = volatility of the stock, S = stock price;

3 $rS\dfrac{\partial V}{\partial S}$= drift term allowing for the growth in the stock at the risk-free rate, r;

4 $-rV$ = the discounting term, since the payoff is received at expiration but you are valuing the option now. (Wilmott, 2009, 130–131)

The key term here is (2), the convexity term, which refers to a "hedged position" that Black earlier described as the fundamental breakthrough of derivative pricing and contains the ideas of delta-hedging and dynamic replication. If we go back to the equation for the call option, the trick is to convert the random portion into a linear drift-like component by hedging out all directional risk, which gives the risk-free rate of interest. Convexity is a mathematical measure ("Jensen's inequality") of the asymmetry of the payoffs—the maximum upside for a call is unlimited while the maximum loss is the price of the option. It is the value that optionality confers by having an expiration date and a strike price— it's the upside of optionality, reflecting the insight that "time and the right to choose are worth money." In the standard mathematics of portfolio theory, the expected return of a stock is the mean price movement adjusted for some time period, usually a year; graphically it is represented by a straight line and is a first derivative. Convexity is a second derivative compared to the linearity of the standard expected return calculations in portfolio theory. It is measured by $\dfrac{\partial^2 V}{\partial S^2}$, the second derivative or the change in the option price given a change in "delta," which is how much the option price changes with a change in the stock price (the first derivative), i.e., how much the option price changes with a change in delta.

Delta-hedging and dynamic replication are written into the "grammar" of Black-Scholes; calculating the option price depends on hedging and replicating until the expiration date of the option, with each step in the price process dependent only on the previous one in a potentially un-ending process of dynamic replication. Black-Scholes shows that if you want to access and price volatility, you need to hedge out or neutralize directional risk; as the asset price changes, you need to continuously reset the hedge ("delta-hedging") in a process ("dynamic replication") that only ends at the expiration or "death" of the option. In the case of Black-Scholes, delta-hedging shrinks the "volatility spread" to the riskless-rate of interest because all directional risk has been eliminated.

After the discovery of the Black-Scholes model and the founding of the Chicago Options Exchange, options trading increased so dramatically that there was a fairly robust distribution of options at different strike prices and

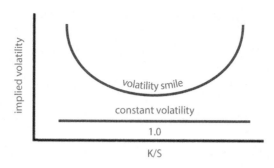

Figure 2.1 Volatility smile.

expirations. With the establishment of liquid options markets (see also the chapter by Ortiz in this *Handbook*), one could then calculate the "implied volatility" of the underlying stock and the corresponding hedge ratio by inserting the market price of the option into an inverted Black–Scholes equation, and calculate the "implied" volatility of the underlying stock. It was considered to be the market's estimate of the future volatility of the stock. Since it's a prediction, it's not quite the "bouncy-bouncy" and there will be a "realized volatility" with which it can be compared. But it moves closer to the instantaneous volatility of trading because the resulting implied volatility is not a historical average but the volatility calculated from the most recent market price.

The assumption of Black–Scholes is that volatility is constant. However, the calculation of implied volatilities revealed that options on the same stock with the same expiration dates but different strike prices might vary; the resulting graph resembles a smile, sneer, or grimace rather than the straight line that constant volatility would imply. Figure 2.1 plots the implied volatilities against K/S, the ratio of the option strike price to the stock price.

The smile indicates that implied volatility contradicts the basic assumption of the model used to calculate it: instead of being constant, volatility varies. One of the ways to deal with the smile is to assume that volatility is itself volatile or stochastic. If volatility is a measure of the spread of stock prices, then the spread itself is constantly changing, producing the smile. There is general acceptance of the smile and that volatility is not constant; much of the work in derivative finance is developing alternative models using refinements such as stochastic volatility or incorporating jumps.

What Is Qualitative Volatility?

The distinction in finance between instantaneous randomness and historical volatility touches upon two competing notions of time: the empty homogeneous time of classical physics in which all events were supposed to take place (presupposed by historical volatility) and the indexical time (the instantaneous time of trading) in which the relations between events generated a sense of past, present, and future. It was the philosopher Henri Bergson who would bring volatility and indexical time together in his notion of "duration." In *Matter and Memory* (1911) he formulated a notion of "qualitative multiplicity," which he saw as opposed to the quantitative multiplicities of mathematics and science. For Bergson, everything was in motion and the problem was to create an image out of the experience of that initial volatility:

> Matter thus resolves itself into numberless vibrations, all linked together in uninterrupted continuity, all bound up with each other, and traveling in every direction like shivers through an immense body. In short, try first to connect together the discontinuous objects of daily experience; then, resolve the motionless continuity of their qualities into vibrations on the spot, which are moving in place; finally, fix your attention on these movements, by abstracting from the divisible space which underlies them and considering only their mobility (that undivided act which our consciousness becomes aware of in our own movements); you will thus obtain a vision of matter fatiguing perhaps for your imagination, but pure, and freed from all that the exigencies of life compel you to add to in external perception.–Now bring back consciousness, and with it the exigencies of life: at long, very long, intervals, and by as many leaps over enormous periods of the inner history of things, quasi-instantaneous views will be taken, views which this time are bound to be pictorial, and of which the more vivid colours will condense an infinity of elementary repetitions and changes. In just the same way the multitudinous successive positions of a runner are contracted into a single symbolic attitude, which our eyes perceive, which art reproduces, and which becomes for us all the image of a man running. (Bergson, 1911: 277)

While the trajectory of derivative finance has been to start with the mathematics of Black-Scholes and then try to capture the instantaneous randomness of the event of trading, Bergson starts from the other extreme, from the changing intensities of affects, emotions, and psychological processes before any sense of quantitative measure or comparison. These different "flows" meet perception like notes in a melody, and unfold as a "heterogeneous multiplicity" in which part and whole are constantly reconstituting their relations. Duration—the flow of time into past, present, and future—is a qualitative multiplicity in which "several conscious states are organized into a whole, permeate one another, gradually gain a richer content" (Bergson, 1910: 122). We experience affects such as joy or sorrow as flows of changing intensities whose complex modulations Bergson described in passages that would inspire writers as diverse as Wallace Stevens, Willa Cather, and Marcel Proust (Bergson's cousin-in-law), as in this famous description of "an obscure desire" that starts as a "feeble intensity" and becomes an all-enveloping "deep passion":

> For example, an obscure desire gradually becomes a deep passion. Now, you will see that the feeble intensity of this desire consisted at first in

its appearing to be isolated and, as it were, foreign to the remainder of your inner life. But little by little it permeates a larger number of psychic elements, tingeing them, so to speak, with its own colour and lo! your outlook on the whole of your surroundings seems now to have changed radically. How do you become aware of a deep passion, once it has taken hold of you, if not by perceiving that the same objects no longer impress you in the same manner? All your sensations and all your ideas seem to brighten up: it is like childhood back again. We experience something of the kind in certain dreams, in which we do not imagine anything out of the ordinary, and yet through which there resounds an indescribable note of originality. (Bergson 1910: 8)

Bergson then describes intensity as facing two directions, one towards the inner flow of duration and the other towards external measurement and comparison:

The idea of intensity is thus situated at the junction of two streams, one of which brings us the idea of extensive magnitude from without, while the other brings us from within, in fact from the very depths of consciousness, the image of an inner multiplicity. Now, the point is to determine in what the latter image consists, whether it is the same as that of number, or whether it is quite different from it. (Bergson, 1910: 73)

Bergson's answer to his own question was that quantitative multiplicities were an objectification of qualitative multiplicities. He argued that the concept of number presupposed an image of a collection of objects in space; enumerating a flock of sheep involved each sheep being treated as spatially distinct yet combined in a common space. Counting abstracts from the particularity of the sheep (their location in time and space, their size and coloring, etc.) and the consequent quantification involves a homogenization of the heterogeneous qualities of the individual sheep. Spatialization had a "corrupting" influence on our understanding of creativity and freedom:

For, if the confusion of quality with quantity were confined to each of the phenomena of consciousness taken separately, it would give rise to obscurities, as we have just seen, rather than to problems. But by invading the series of our psychic states, by introducing space into our perception of duration, it corrupts at its very source our feeling of outer and inner change, of movement, and of freedom. Hence the paradoxes of the Eleatics, hence the problem of free will. We shall insist rather on the second point; but instead of seeking to solve the question, we shall show the mistake of those who ask it. (Bergson, 1910: 73–74)

The reference to the Eleatics is to Zeno's paradox, which some feel is solved by the development of the infinitesimal in calculus; the reference to the problem of free will is to Kant, who according to Bergson mistakenly placed space along with time and causality as the basic categories of the understanding. According to Bergson, the introduction of space into our perception of time is a fundamental mistake that haunts philosophy from its classical origins to the present.

Bergson championed the qualitative exploration of subjectivity and linked it to his notion of duration, the indexical flow of time between past, present, and future. Through the work of Giles Deleuze, Bergson and Spinoza have become two of the most important philosophical influences on the development of contemporary affect theory. In the translation of Deleuze and Guattari's *Mille Plateaux,* Brian Massumi gives a highly influential definition of affect as "an ability to affect and be affected" (Massumi in Deleuze & Guattari, 1987: xvi), which he attributes to Spinoza. In his contemporaneous discussion of Bergson's "major theses on time" (Deleuze, 1985: 82) in his cinema books, Deleuze draws together Bergson's treatment of time with Spinoza's analysis of affect "it was initially the affect, that which we experience in time; then time itself, pure virtuality which divides itself in two as affector and affected, 'the affection of self by self,' as definition of time" (Deleuze, 1985: 83). In 1995, Massumi would publish *The Autonomy of Affect*, which explicitly used Spinoza, Bergson, and Deleuze to create the theoretical parameters for affect theory. Much of its subsequent development took the affective pulsebeat of neoliberalism as it developed through the Great Moderation until the financial crisis of 2007–2008, which was the same time as the explosive development of derivative finance (and according to Piketty, growing wealth inequality). The arc of affect theory's fascination with neoliberalism starts with Ronald Reagan (analyzed in *The Autonomy of Affect*) and extends to Lauren Berlant's recent and highly influential *Cruel Optimism* (Berlant, 2011), which gives us a glimpse of the affective dynamics of neoliberalism as they enter the age of Trump.

Most affect theorists, however, did not pay much attention to the imbrication of neoliberalism with derivative finance. Perhaps this was because Marxist scholars saw finance as "fictitious capital"; the most influential Marxist analysis was probably David Harvey's 1990 explanation of the development of postmodernism as stemming from "time-space compression" caused by the increased turnover of capital in the wake of the collapse of Fordist manufacturing. Whatever the importance of volatility was in finance, it couldn't be a new source of value, which remained tied to labor.

However, there was an unexplored potential connection between affect theory and derivative finance in the unlikely person of Giles Deleuze. In his earlier writings on language, Deleuze was already interested in Markov chains and their combination of structure and randomness as a critique of Chomsky's rule-governed transformational grammar. In *Mille Plateaux*, there is an informed discussion of the work of Benoit Mandelbrot on fractals; Mandelbrot was an early advisor to Eugene Fama of efficient market fame, and as a Polytechnique graduate and French PhD he was fluent in French and regularly lectured in Paris on fractal geometry; Deleuze and Lacan were rumored to have attended his seminars.

Deleuze's discussion of fractals occurs in the penultimate chapter of *Mille Plateaux*, which focuses on the social implications of Riemann's distinction between smooth and striated spaces, especially for art and music. He sees Bergson as translating Riemann's distinction into two types of multiplicity, "one qualitative and fusional, continuous, the other numerical and homogenous, discrete" (Deleuze, 1987: 484), which is first presented in Bergson's *Time and Free Will* but Deleuze saw as underlying all his work, even his debates with Einstein about time and relativity. Deleuze even goes so far as to identify striated spaces with whole number Hausdorff dimensions (a measure of roughness) and smooth spaces with fractional (fractal) dimensions.

Although there is no evidence that Deleuze followed the developments in derivative finance (he might have heard about the fractal analysis of stock prices from Mandelbrot), the discovery of the Black-Scholes model for pricing options would inaugurate a new era in the quantitative exploration of volatility. In the Black-Scholes equation, the price of an option derived from the volatility of the underlying stock; in order to access that volatility and price it, you needed to get rid of all directional risk, not dissimilar to Deleuze's thesis that in order for cinema to represent the qualitative volatility of thought and affect one needed to neutralize the "sensori-motor" directionality of action-based cinematic narration. The publication of the Black-Scholes equation for pricing options would provide a way of making new financial instruments out of old and catalyze the development of derivatives—it became the principle of financial innovation as markets sought new instruments to transfer and distribute risk. And yet, it all started with Brownian motion as the origins of quantitative finance could be traced to Bachelier's insight in 1900 that stock prices on the Paris Bourse seemed to follow Brownian motion, which some 70 years later would be the basic presupposition of the efficient market hypothesis and the Black-Scholes equation.

The Affect of Finance

The marginalization of affect in derivative finance is a product of its history. The Chicago Options Exchange was founded in the same year as the publication of the Black-Scholes model, 1973, and since Black-Scholes was a version of the diffusion equation, it's not surprising that the first generation of quants thought they were inventing a "physics of finance." Buttressed by the axiomization of expected utility in Von Neumann and Morgenstern's *Theory of Games and Economic Behavior* (1972), portfolio theory and then derivative finance adopted decision-making under uncertainty as the framework for analyzing strategic action; the "belief-desire" model in the philosophy of action became the dominant model for subjectivity and absorbed affect into an expanded notion of preferences, which in order to be rational, had to follow the axioms of expected utility. But as the history of financial crises shows, people don't always behave rationally. Von Neumann and Morgenstern's four axioms (completeness, transitivity, independence of lotteries, and continuity of lotteries) formalize expected utility theory, which states that rational decision-making under uncertainty will maximize expected utility. By providing an axiomization for expected utility, Von Neumann and Morgenstern also provided the framework for the formalization of the belief-desire model, which was carried out by a variety of philosophers the most note-worthy of whom was Donald Davidson, one of the most influential analytic philosophers of the late twentieth century. His first book was on decision theory with Patrick Suppes and Sidney Siegel (Davidson et al., 1957), and he applied its methodology to the philosophy of action and language. The belief-desire model is still the dominant one in the philosophy of action, and utility maximization was the basis for Gary Becker's extension of economic principles to social issues (1964); it deeply influenced moral philosophy as both John Rawls' *A Theory of Justice* (1971) and Robert Nozick's *Anarchy, State, and Utopia* (1974) were heavily indebted to game theory. Expected utility was also the basis for modern portfolio theory; two chapters of Harry Markowitz's *Portfolio Selection: Efficient Diversification of Investments* (1959) are devoted to expected utility and one to "probability beliefs."

The significance of a *Theory of Games and Economic Behavior* is that it formalizes the belief-desire model of action and decision-making that is still dominant in economics and the social sciences. This model combines a logical analysis of the linguistic encoding of speaking, thinking, and feeling shared across most European languages with a mathematical treatment of preferences that results in the thesis that utility maximizing is the basic form of rationality. Even behavioral economics, which is often seen as giving a more rigorous framework for Keynes's famous comment about "animal spirits," presupposes utility maximization as providing the standard from which deviancies can be measured; Tversky and Kahneman's classic paper "Prospect Theory: An Analysis of Decision Under Risk" is self-described as presenting "several classes of choice problems in which preferences systematically violate the axioms of expected utility theory" (1979: 263).

The dominant model for the last 60 years in economics and finance has been the confluence of the axiomization of expected utility by Von Neumann and Morgenstern and the belief-desire model in the philosophy of action. Although the origins of the belief-desire model in analytic philosophy could be traced back to the logician Gottlob Frege, Von Neumann and Morgenstern's use of expected utility theory to analyze strategic interactions provided a framework for the formal investigation of subjectivity that would quickly spread not only to the philosophy of action, but also to ethics, the philosophy of language, and, of course, economics and finance. Part of its success was that Frege's work analyzed the logical behavior of intentionality as encoded in European languages in verbs of speaking, thinking, and feeling, thereby establishing a connection to what might be called our everyday "folk-theory" of subjectivity; the theory seemed to be grounded in everyday discourse. This confluence set off an explosion of research in the 1950s and 1960s designed to ascertain whether people acted in accordance with the dictates of expected utility theory; the exceptions gave birth to the work of Tversky and Kahneman, who turned them into the now booming field of behavioral economics and finance.

The effect of the combination of the Fregean approach to subjectivity and expected utility theory was to focus on the relationship of beliefs and desires to the exclusion of affects and emotions; since these also took propositional complements ("I am angry that...," "I fear that...") they were treated like other propositional attitudes. The belief-desire model "regimented" subjectivity to make it compatible with decision-making, leaving the qualitative side of volatility unexplored even as it expanded our repertoire of quantitative tools to measure and manage risk, uncertainty, and volatility. As the empirical research grew about when and where people did or did not obey expected utility theory, Tversky and Kahneman designed a series of very ingenious verbal experiments in which they discovered that there were systematic ways in which people did not behave "rationally." Although they presupposed the belief-desire model in which people were "punctual" decision-makers, they saw everyday reasoning as based upon heuristics, framing, or affective biases. However, the basic belief-desire model remained dominant until Daniel Kahneman's *Thinking, Fast and Slow* (2011), which introduced what might be called a "flow" model of affect that contrasted with the punctual decision-making of the belief-desire model. Kahneman bundled his and Tversky's research along with affective and unconscious biases into "System 1" thinking, which was supposed to contrast with the punctual rational decision-making of "System 2" thinking. However, Kahneman did not give an account of the dynamics of affect and the qualitative side of volatility, which will take us back to Frege and the foundations of the belief-desire model.

The Intensionality of Intentionality

Frege's analysis of propositional attitudes such as "know" or "believe" would shape future work on the extension/intension distinction in analytic philosophy, which would be extended to other philosophically important contexts such as indexicality and modality; the sense and reference distinction turned out to be of paramount philosophical importance because it highlighted the problem of identity. An *extensional* context was one in which terms referring to the same object could be co-substituted without a change in the truth value of the expression of which they were parts; contexts in which co-substitution of identities fails are *intensional*. "Intersubstitutability salve veritate" is a fundamental property of mathematics, logic, and science: "1+3," "2+2," and "4" can be substituted for one another in any mathematical expression without changing its truth value. Frege's counter-example to extensionality was that of the "Morning Star" and the "Evening Star," which both refer to the planet Venus. If the "Morning Star" is the brightest object in the morning sky and the "Evening Star" is the brightest object in the evening sky, the sentence "Galileo believes that the Evening Star is the brightest object in the morning sky" can be false because Galileo didn't know that the Morning Star=the Evening Star. Verbs of speaking, thinking, and feeling that take propositional complements are logically "intensional"; the "that"-clause signals that what follows is a representation or proposition, suggesting that there is a representational component to all psychological states. The "intensionality of intentionality" became the logical hallmark of subjectivity, as extensionality is that of mathematics and science.

What Frege discovered was that there were contexts in which intersubstitutability salve veritate failed because of reference shift. However, failure of intersubstitutability is not restricted to subjectivity. Linguistic indexicals such as deictics ("this," "that") are intensional because their referents shift with the moment of speaking; these include the first and second person pronouns, deictics, honorifics, and time in the form of tense and aspect. Tense presupposes the moment of speaking, and each speech event presupposes its own time reference, which shifts from utterance to utterance; since past and future tenses presuppose the present moment of speaking, linguistic time is intensional and not extensional as calendar time is. But surprisingly modal contexts of necessity and possibility are also logically intensional: if it is true that "9=number of planets," the sentence "It is necessarily true that the numbers of planets is 9" could be false because the solar system might not have evolved that way.

The logical property of intensionality applies to verbs of thinking, feeling, and speaking, including performatives and became the logical sign of subjectivity. What these verbs share is that they can take propositional complements introduced by subordinating conjunctions—"that" in English, "dass" in German, or "que" in French. These include "mental state verbs" such as propositional attitudes such as "believe" ("I believe that..."), or "know" ("I know that...") and pro-attitudes such as "want" ("I want that...") or "desire" ("I desire that..."); mental activity verbs such as "decide" ("I decide that..."), "recognize" ("I recognize that as..."), or "judge" ("I judge that..."); and performative verbs of speaking such as "promise" ("I promise that...") or "order" ("I order that..."). From these three classes of verbs—mental state, mental activity, and performatives—we can uncover a "family resemblance" that crosscuts subjectivity and moves from mental states > mental activities > performative actions, i.e., an agent chooses (mental activity) from his beliefs and desires (mental states) to perform some action (performatives).

In the ensuing articulation of the belief-desire model, the most important intensional states were belief, desire, and intention. Focusing on the representational component of these expressions, Searle (1985) would propose that the various propositional attitudes differed in their "direction of fit"; beliefs had a representation to world fit—a belief was false if it didn't match the world—and desires had a world to representation direction of fit—a desire was unfulfilled if the world wasn't changed to match the desire. An action resulted from the chiasmus produced by intentional states with opposite directions of fit.

Although pieces of the belief-desire model were in place before Von Neumann and Morgenstern (Frege's "Sense and Reference" appears in 1892), the axiomization of expected utility provides the bridge between the logical analysis of subjectivity and a formal account of rationality as utility maximization. The breakthrough is in Von Neumann and Morgenstern's ingenious use of lotteries to pry apart beliefs about the likelihood of outcomes and peoples' preferences or desires for them; the result is to give a quantitative treatment of preferences that goes beyond simple ordinal scaling by preserving relative differences in intensity and is compatible with ratio-scaled monetary outcomes.

Expected utilities are numerical representations of preferences. Von Neumann and Morgenstern specify four axioms that such preferences must follow in order for them to be represented as expected utilities. The first two axioms are completeness and transitivity, and the other two concern lotteries. Lotteries commensurate beliefs about the likelihood of outcomes and the strength of desires or preferences, transforming the ordinal ranking of preferences into a ratio scale of numerically proportional differences. For example, if outcome A is preferred to B, and B to C, one can construct an ordinal scale of A>B>C but any quantitative measure that reproduces the ordering is possible. Their solution is to introduce a choice between receiving B for sure and a lottery between A and C where the probability of receiving A is p and receiving C is $1 - p$. As p changes from 1 (100% certain to get A) to 0 (certain to get C) there will be a point where the decision-maker is indifferent between the certain outcome B and the lottery involving A and C. As p changes from 1 (A) to 0 (C), the preference will change from choosing the lottery between A and C to choosing B. If that point is $p = 1/2$, then we can create a scale of $1>1/2>0$ that represents the translation of these preferences into expected utilities.

Von Neumann and Morgenstern's axiomization occurs in the first chapter of a 600-page book about strategic games. It was immediately picked up by analytic philosophers because it fit the logical trend in the philosophy of action introduced by Frege's analysis of sense and reference and yet could be used to explain human behavior, at least in the form of strategic games such as poker; it seemed to herald the beginning of a formal philosophy of action and subjectivity. Donald Davidson was one of the first to import these insights into philosophy and use it for analyzing action and interpretation. *Decision-Making: An Experimental Approach* was an analysis and experimental test of whether people followed Neumann-Morgenstern expected utility theory—under what circumstances would expected utility theory be considered psychologically accurate. For example, building upon the Von Neumann-Morgenstern lottery approach, Davidson asks that if you start with people's choices, how do you distinguish his subjective beliefs about likelihoods from his values (i.e., desires)? Davidson proposes a second lottery ("gamble") to disentangle subjective probabilities from subjective utility, i.e., beliefs from desires:

> I am struck by the analogy with a well-known problem in decision theory. Suppose an agent is indifferent between getting $5.00, and

a gamble that offers him $11.00 if a coin comes up heads, and $0.00 if it comes up tails. We might explain (i.e., "interpret") his indifference by supposing that money has a diminishing marginal utility for him: $5.00 is midway on his subjective value scale between $0.00 and $11.00. We arrive at this by assuming the gamble is worth the sum of the values of the possible outcomes as tempered by their likelihoods. In this case, we assume that heads and tails are equally likely.

Unfortunately there is an equally plausible alternative explanation: since $5.00 obviously isn't midway in utility between $0.00 and $ 11.00, the agent must believe tails are more likely to come up than heads; if he thought heads and tails equally probable, he would certainly prefer the gamble, which would then be equal to a straight offer of $5.50.

If you have the choices and either the probabilities or the preferences, you can figure out what is missing. But if all you have is the action, how can you distinguish beliefs about likelihoods from preferences (desires)? Davidson proposes extending Von Neumann and Morgenstern's use of lotteries to give an empirically verifiable quantitative account of beliefs and desires:

Suppose that there are two alternatives, getting $11.00 and getting $0.00, and that there is an event E such that the agent is indifferent between the following two gambles: Gamble One—if E happens the agent receives $11.00; if E fails to happen he gets $0.00. Gamble Two—if E happens he gets $0.00; if E fails to happen he gets $11.00. The agent's indifference between the gambles shows that he must judge that E is as likely to happen as not. For if he thought E more likely to occur than not, he would prefer the first gamble which promises him $11.00 if E occurs, and if he thought E more likely not to occur than to occur he would prefer the second gamble which pairs E's non-occurrence with $11.00. This solves, for decision theory, the problem of how to separate out subjective probability from subjective utility, for once an event like E is discovered, it is possible to scale other values, and then to determine the subjective probabilities of all events. (Davidson, 1984: 145)

Davidson and other researchers at that time tried to show that such an empirically verifiable quantitative account of beliefs and desires could explain intentional action. Building upon this work, in a path-breaking article "Actions, Reasons, and Causes" (1980), Davidson argues that a pairing of the requisite beliefs and desires can be a causal reason for an action; this would translate expected utility theory into an empirically verifiable psychological model of beliefs and desires. This went against a highly influential view attributed to Wittgenstein that reasons are not causes for actions; intentional explanations make it understandable what has been done and why (the "point" of an action), but do not constitute causal explanations. Davidson rebutted these arguments by insisting that intentions were explanatory in both hermeneutic and causal senses. Both beliefs and desires are logically intensional and are states that differ in their direction of fit. Weighing one's beliefs and desires, one makes a decision that forms an intention that then brings about the desired action. Since beliefs and desires contain representational states, they are causally effective through the choices one makes, i.e., *this* action will bring about what I desire *now*. Intensional states such as belief and desire became causally effective because one chooses among them to make an "all-out judgment" (i.e., intention) that is both the reason and cause for an action; one has effectively traversed the underlying structure of our folk-model of subjectivity: from mental states (beliefs and desires)>mental activities (choices or decisions)> performative actions. Reasons for actions become quantifiable combinations of beliefs and desires which could also causally explain actions; the belief-desire model thus provided a causal explanation of action and would link subjectivity to action and interpretation.

Davidson would expand the expected utility/game theoretic approach to the philosophy of interpretation and meaning, reinforcing the interest in analytic philosophy to provide more abstract solutions to problems of intensionality. At the same time, the belief-desire model and decision-making under uncertainty became the dominant framework for subjectivity in quantitative finance. Since belief and desire were at the core of expected utility theory, other affects were relegated to whatever Keynes meant by "animal spirits," i.e., why people disobeyed expected utility theory, which would open the way for Tversky and Kahneman.

Where Quantitative and Qualitative Meet

Lying outside of behavioral economics emphasis on heuristics and framing, there is of course the media's focus on the affective excesses of Wall Street, which intersects with affect theory's interest in popular culture. Works such as *Wall Street, Liars' Poker, The Bonfire of Vanities, The Wolf of Wall Street, Billions,* and even (or especially) *American Psycho* focus on the speculative greed and excesses of finance capitalism and neoliberalism. Yet both finance and affect theory skirt Bergson's challenge: does the volatility that you can measure have anything to do with the volatility that you can feel? Caitlin Zaloom, an anthropologist who worked in the open-outcry pits of the Chicago Commodities Exchange, writes that in trading moments of decision-making "ride" upon the ebb and flow of socially shared affects:

> Traders speak of their best trading moments in ways that make them sound like mystical engagements. They need to abandon self-consciousness to gain full access to the market's interior and use discipline to block outside contexts from their conscious thoughts and to enhance their abilities to read, interpret, and ultimately merge with the market. Traders often speak of being "in the zone" or of a "flow"

experience. In the zone, economic judgments and actions seem to come without effort from the instincts of the trader. The market and the trader merge, giving him special access to the natural rhythms of financial fluctuations. (Zaloom, 2006: 135)

Elie Ayache, a former market-maker and developer of options software, puts affect right at the heart of options trading:

Through the dynamic delta-hedging and the anxiety that it generates (Will I execute it right? When to rebalance it, etc.), the market-maker penetrated the market. He penetrated its volatility and he could now feel it in his guts. In a word, he became a *dynamic trader.* He now understood – not conceptually, but through his senses, through his body – the inexorability of time decay, the pains and joys of convexity. (Ayache, 2008: 36)

"Delta-hedging," "time decay," and "convexity" are technical terms that refer to different aspects of the Black-Scholes formula for pricing options. In the act of trading each of these quantitative terms is associated with particular affects—"anxiety," "inexorability," "pains and joys"—that are felt by the trader "in his guts." Trading brings together a quantitative dimension compatible with the expected utility theory and a qualitative dimension that is more describable in terms of the ebb and flow of affective intensities rather than any form of decision-making. Ayache's description portrays market-making not in terms of rational decision-making but in affective terms that would fit extreme sports, a not surprising choice as traders often describe trading as "surfing the volatility wave." Trading is less like a decision-making process than a "flow" experience that is shared among expert practitioners such as musicians, dancers, athletes, and traders.

Both Ayache and Zaloom's descriptions point to a different dimension of trading than the decision-making model dominant in economic and financial analysis. Because of Von Neumann and Morgenstern, expected utility theory was seen as the framework for the analysis of interaction, as their explorations of game theory created the area of inquiry known as "decision-making under uncertainty." The core of this model is decision-making, and the belief-desire-intention model becomes the framework to analyze both action and communication. However, the primacy given to desire, preferences, utilities, and the causal explanation of action has sidelined the discussion of other affects and emotions. Indeed, the repeated references by traders to "surfing volatility" or being "in the zone" suggest a "flow" or "wave" model for affects and emotions that interacts with the "punctual" decision-making model of game theory.

Zaloom's use of "flow" refers to the work of the psychologist Mihaly Csikszentmihalyi on creativity (1990), which Daniel Kahneman also mentions in *Thinking, Fast and Slow,* which is an overview of the field of behavioral economics that he and Amos Tversky founded in their search for why people didn't behave rationally in accordance with expected utility theory. In a variety of ingenious experiments, Tversky and Kahneman presented people with verbal problems and developed a variety of convincing explanations for why people didn't behave "rationally" (maximize utility), opening up a new field which it was hoped could explain the gyrations of the market in panic selling and "irrational exuberance." The development of behavioral economics started out with a growing collection of heuristics and frames but in his best-selling *Thinking, Fast and Slow*, Kahneman consolidated them into what he called "System 1 thinking"; whereas System 2 thinking was "reflective" decision-making under uncertainty, System 1 thinking included everything from the maxims of prospect theory to affects. In real life, System 1 thinking predominates with System 2 intervening when something goes wrong or the situation became cognitively taxing. "Flow" occurs when there is effortless concentration on the task at hand with loss of the sense of time and thus combines the "effortlessness" of System 1 with the concentration characteristic of System 2; flow creates an affectual bridge between Systems 1 and 2.

But what Kahneman doesn't mention is that "flow" was the product of an optimal modulation of a volatility spread, which hints that the surfing metaphors may be more than analogical. Looking at the peak experiences of artists and athletes, Csikszentmihalyi suggested that "being in the zone" occurs when there is an optimal alignment of goals and abilities, which people describe as being completely absorbed by the task at hand so that time seems to stand still. In such experiences, an affectual tension-field is set up between one's aspirations and abilities; the resulting affective modulation is a delicate dance between discouragement when goals and aspirations overwhelm abilities or boredom when the task setting is insufficiently challenging. The idea of a tension-field or "spread" between goals and abilities intersects with Bergson and Deleuze's insights that affectual changes are the modulation of intensities before any comparative judgment—one can become qualitatively angrier and angrier without any quantitative sense of how much angrier one has become. Affects are constantly changing but their volatility does not follow the discrete-time punctuation of decision-making, but the wave-like flow of indexicalized continuous time, or what the philosopher Henri Bergson would call "duration." Flow is the psychological modulation of duration.

A flow model for the qualitative dimension of volatility introduces what is missing from the belief-desire model of decision-making under uncertainty: the flow of affect. Behavioral economics focuses on "heuristics" and "framing" but makes little mention of "sensibilities" or concepts such as ethos and spirit that were central, for example, to Weber's account of capitalism. Flow models would also be compatible with Bourdieu's "habitus," which arose out of his studies of the "flow of gifts" in pre-capitalist ritualized exchange (Bourdieu, 1977); the "habitus" consisted of pre-cognitive sensibilities embodied in complex affects such as the "sense of honor" or *nif* among the Kabyle or what Goffman (1967) would call "face." Thaler and Sunstein's "nudges" (2009) are part of what they call the non reflective "Automatic System of Thinking"

(Thaler & Sunstein, 2009: 19) but could also be considered as pre-cognitive directional indices for managing the "flow" of interaction.

While behavioral economics has not investigated the dynamics of affect and emotions, analytic philosophers soon discovered several other contexts that were logically intensional in addition to subjectivity. Two of the most important were time and modality, both of which have a connection to volatility. Modality includes the idea of counterfactuality—what could have been otherwise or what could have happened instead of what did. Counterfactuality is built into the problem of volatility in the idea of a "spread" of alternatives; for example, each of the alternatives to the actual price is a counterfactual possibility to what actually happened. But perhaps the most intriguing connection is between the qualitative dimensions of affect/volatility and time, especially the phenomenon of tense. Linguistic time is calibrated to the moment of speaking, and thus, time reference shifts with every speech event. The past and future are defined in terms of their relation to the "now" of speaking, and thus, Bergson's duration is the indexical flow of time between present, past, and future. The time of mathematics and classical physics does not distinguish between past, present, and future; it is an extensional "calendar" time in which all events are supposed to take place, rather than a time defined by event of speaking and shifting with every utterance. Zaloom and Ayache's examples anchor market-making in the indexical flow of time. Affect, time, and volatility meet in the act of trading.

The Intensities of Time

In "The Perception of Time, Risk, and Return during Periods of Speculation" (2002), Emanuel Derman proposes that trading may presuppose an event-based or indexical time instead of the abstract calendar time presupposed by finance and Black-Scholes. He calls it "tic-time," which is based upon the intensity of trading—in periods of intense trading, traders try to keep up with one another, noting the "action" around them; traders count "tics," i.e., trading opportunities, and the expected return is measured in units of tic-time, the amount of expected return per tic (not per second, as might be the case for calendar time). Tic-time is tied to trading events as they unfold in indexical time; it's this "flow" that traders experience as they surf the volatility wave. Derman captures this move to the indexical and the intensional by readjusting the time differential in the formula from which Black-Scholes will be derived:

$$dS_i/S_i = \mu_i dt + \sigma_i dZ_i$$
(calendar time)
$$dS_i/S_i = M_i d\tau_i + \Sigma_i dW_i$$
(tic-time)

The first formula says that a small change in the price of a stock is the sum of drift and Brownian components measured in calendar time. The second formula adjusts d*t* to an intrinsic time differential $d\tau_i$. $d\tau_i$ represents an infinitesimal increment in the intrinsic time τ_i that measures the rate at which trading opportunities for stock$_i$ pass; it counts the intensity of indexical trading events. The symbol M_i represents the expected return of stock$_i$ per unit of its intrinsic time and Σ_i denotes the stock's volatility measured in intrinsic time, as given by the square root of the variance of the stock's returns per unit of intrinsic time. The stock's *trading frequency* is the number of intrinsic time ticks for a given stock per calendar second—the trading frequency is a translation of tic-time which is dimensionless into ratio-scaled calendar time. For people who trade in intrinsic time, the calendar time between ticks is irrelevant and the only thing that matters is the number of ticks that pass by and the risk and return per tick. Derman hypothesizes "that short-term stock speculators expect returns proportional to the *temperature* of a stock, where temperature is defined as the product of the stock's traditional volatility and the square root of its trading frequency" (Derman, 2002: 282, original emphasis). The temperature of a stock is equal to "$\sigma_i\sqrt{v_i}$," where "σi" is the volatility of the stock in calendar time and "v_i" is its trading frequency and "provides a measure of the perceived speculative riskiness of the stock in terms of how it influences expected return" (Derman, 2002: 291). Replacing calendar time with intrinsic or tic-time, Derman derives the traditional Sharpe Capital Assets Pricing Model (CAPM), suggesting that it is possible to rethink much of finance in terms of intrinsic rather than calendar time. Whereas calendar time is "a universal, stock-independent measure," intrinsic time is tied to the frequency of trading or the time between trading opportunities; it measures the *indexical intensity* of trading in real time. Derman then constructs two different expected return and volatility measures, one based on calendar time and the other intrinsic time, and then uses the latter to explain the evolution of market bubbles. This suggests a temporal evolution in the use of Black-Scholes. At the time of its initial discovery, since it was known to be formally equivalent to the heat equation, Black-Scholes was seen as part of a potential "physics of finance" and like any other physics equation, operated in "calendar time." The development of calibration, implied volatility, and tic-time pushes the use of Black-Scholes into the real-time of the market in which the quantitative dimension of volatility meets its qualitative counterpart in the intensity of trading; the two dimensions are neatly caught in the representation of temperature as "$\sigma_i\sqrt{v_i}$" (calendar time volatility multiplied by the square root of trading frequency or intensity). Although finance has emphasized the quantitative dimension of volatility, it is precisely its mathematical rigor and constant falsification in practice that allows us to see what lies outside of it. Behavioral finance systematically explores the exceptions to expected utility theory but then moves beyond a punctual model of decision-making to discover what lies beyond it: a flow model of affect grounded in a different sense of time closer to that of art (see also the chapter by Ivanova and Nestler in this *Handbook*), music, and even sports.

Conclusion

In the early 1990s, two books came out that pointed to the early 1970s as signaling transformations in Western society that can now be seen with hindsight as involving volatility. Ulrich Beck's *Risk Society* (1992) describes the risk and uncertainties produced by modernization itself as opposed to natural catastrophes such as earthquakes or hurricanes. David Harvey's *The Condition of Postmodernity* (1990) focused on the rise of postmodernism, especially its fascination with fragmentation and transitoriness. Beck's book does not explicitly mention volatility, and he explains the rise of risk society by "reflexive modernization" brought about by the economic and social pressures of globalization. Harvey explains the rise of postmodernism in terms of the pressures of economic globalization; flexible accumulation spearheaded by the Asian Tigers dismantles the Fordist economy in the United States, releasing an economic volatility that has a direct effect on culture. The ensuing cultural volatility is explained in terms of the time-space compression that flexible accumulation introduces by accelerating the turnover time of capital. If we combine their insights, a conceptual matrix of risk, uncertainty, and volatility emerges at the same time as the beginnings of derivative finance and develops throughout the rise of neoliberalism, and if the VIX incident of February 5, 2018, is an index, continues with growing strength through the present. Despite their differences (Beck insisted that risk society was intellectually independent of postmodernism), however, both describe volatility as an effect of other forces ("reflexive modernization" and "flexible accumulation" both of which have their roots in globalization) rather than a constitutive force on its own terms.

But what is the status of volatility in a digital age? The early 1970s that Beck and Harvey write about antedate the internet, whose development takes off commercially in the mid-1990s. In *Thinking, Fast and Slow*, Kahneman discusses a variety of research on public value judgments, including Lichenstein and Slovic's work (2006) on affect heuristics and Sunstein and Kuran on availability cascades, which are affectively charged "self-reinforcing processes of collective belief formation" (Sunstein & Kuran, 2007: 683), which produce "irrationalities" that undermine traditional public sphere values. Although their original pioneering work was done on incidents that antedate the rise of the internet (the Love Canal Affair in 1979 and the Alar Scare in 1989), the basic mechanisms of affect and availability heuristics are seen as applying to contemporary public debates. However, the focus on psychological mechanisms leaves unanswered whether the ubiquitous rise of digital technologies introduces a new level of complexity into the analysis of public value formation, especially in the light of Benedict Anderson's (1983) claim of the print-mediated origins of the public sphere and nation-state. Although there may continue to be availability cascades in contemporary public discourse that follow what might be called a "media transmission and debate" model of the public sphere, there also seem to be new forms of volatility introduced by digital technologies, returning us to where we started: the VIX and our contemporary culture and politics of volatility.

As Vilem Flusser pointed out in his prescient *Towards a Philosophy of Photography* (1983), the pixelated digital image contains within it an ontology whose immanent potential we have just begun to unravel. In its on and off structure of pixels, a digital image (what Flusser called a "technical image") becomes the perfect vehicle for representing and transmitting the random structure of information. In information theory, information is the presence of regularity in randomness ("noise") tempered by redundancy. The first time a regularity appears out of a background of noise, it conveys a lot of information but as the signal repeats, its informativeness decreases. The on-off structure of pixels acts as a binary code that allows the programming of any computable function. Randomness, volatility, information, and computation are thus at the heart of what might be called an "information ontology" whose core is the "technical image." Such images not only represent and calculate volatility (the continuous time calculation of the VIX would not be possible without the computer), but they make possible the representation and transmission of technical images.

With the development of efficient market theory, the stock market enters the digital information age not only as one of the original sources of big data but also as the dominant way of understanding the relation between information and volatility. Efficient market theory considers the market as an information processor even as CNBC begins to turn global time into market time, as indicated by the stock ticker that would appear at the bottom of its viewers' television screens (CNBC is founded in 1989). Everything becomes calibrated to a 24-hour market-time clock in which all events across the world took place; as commentators would say, "the market is always open somewhere." If we add the efficient market hypothesis that information arrives randomly and that some information distributions have a fractal or semi-fractal structure (like Brownian motion), then we are in the realm of chaos theory in which small differences can have huge effects (the so-called "butterfly effects": a butterfly flapping its wings causes a hurricane in Texas) because certain dynamic systems are especially sensitive to initial conditions that recursively build as time unfolds. Even though such systems are deterministic, prediction becomes impossible because of the range (i.e., volatility) or spread between outcomes; from similar starting points, such dynamic systems end up incommensurably different. Media and internet technologies have increased the "turnover" time of information so the fractal butterfly effects become increasingly commonplace; the overflow of "availability cascades" become the norm rather than the exception.

Imagine Ayache's description of market-makers on the Paris Bourse transferred to modern VIX traders. Traders are receiving digital images of implied volatilities on their Bloomberg machines, which also broadcast the latest news updates. Information from several different sources is coming in randomly, and then an announcement is that Trump is going to double the embargo on

Chinese goods because he has heard that Xi Jinping has dared him "to bring it on." But Trump himself is watching several right-wing media programs at once, and he's exposed to the similar conditions of randomness of information as the traders on the VIX. Digital technologies make possible the representation and transmission of information about volatility. But their representation and transmission contribute to the randomness that they represent and transmit and this is all being constantly updated in real-time. The traders notice the blips in implied volatilities and immediately wonder what is going on as they shift from calendar time to tic-time and have to decide whether and when to enter the market, which if it produces a large enough panic Trump will have to address it on the media, initiating a new cycle of volatility. It's volatility all the way up and down, and that's increasingly the state of the world as digital technologies draw us into each other's living and bedrooms.

Note

1   This wavering is caught in Mandelbrot's definitions of a fractal (Mandelbrot is considered to be the father of fractal geometry). In 1982 Mandelbrot gave a tentative definition of a fractal as "a set of which the Hausdorff-Besicovitch dimension exceeds the topological dimension," but by 1986 he had simplified it to "A fractal is a shape made of parts similar to the whole in some way" (Feder, 1988: 11).

References

Anderson, B. (1983). *Imagined Communities*. London: Verso.

Ayache, E. (2008, June). "I am a creator." *Wilmott Magazine*, pp. 36–46.

Bachelier, L. (1900). "Theory of speculation," trans. D. May. *Annales scientifiques de l'Ecole Normale Superieure* 3(17): 21–86.

Beck, U. (1992). *Risk Society: Towards a New Modernity*. London: Sage Publications.

Becker, G. (1964). *Human Capital: A Theoretical and Empirical Analysis, with Special Reference to Education*. Chicago, IL: The University of Chicago Press.

Bergson, H. (1910). *Time and Free Will*, trans. F. L. Pogson. London: George Allen and Unwin.

Bergson, H. (1911). *Matter and Memory*, trans. by N. M. Paul and W. S. Palmer. London: George Allen and Unwin.

Berlant, L. (2011). *Cruel Optimism*. Durham: Duke University Press.

Black, F. (1989). "How we came up with the option formula," *Journal of Portfolio Management* 15(2): 4–8.

Bourdieu, P. (1977). *Outline of a Theory of Practice*. Cambridge: Cambridge University Press.

Csikszentmihalyi, M. (1990). *Flow: The Psychology of Optimal Experience*. New York, NY: Harper.

Davidson, D. (1980). "Action, reasons, and causes," in D. Davidson (ed.), *Essays on Actions and Events* (pp. 3–19). Oxford: Clarendon Press.

Davidson, D. (1984). "Belief and the basis of meaning," in E. Lepore (ed.), *Truth and Interpretation* (pp. 141–154). Oxford: Clarendon Press.

Davidson, D., Suppes, P., & Siegel, S. (1957). *Decision-making: An Experimental Approach*. Stanford, CA: Stanford University Press.

Deleuze, G. (1985). *Cinema 2: The Time Image*. Minneapolis: The Athlone Press.

Deleuze, G., & Guattari, F. (1987). *A Thousand Plateaus: Capitalism and Schizophrenia*, trans. B. Massumi. Minneapolis: University of Minnesota Press.

Derman, E. (2002). "The perception of time, risk, and return during periods of speculation," *Quantitative Finance* 2: 282–296.

Derman, E. (2016). "Remarks on financial models," in B. Lee and R. Martin (eds.), *Derivatives and the Wealth of Societies*. Chicago: University of Chicago Press.

Feder, J. (1988). *Fractals*. New York, NY: Plenum Press.

Flusser, V. (1983). *Towards A Philosophy of Photography*. Princeton, NJ: Princeton University Press.

Frege, G. (1892). "Über Sinn und Bedeutung," in M. Black in Geach and Black (eds. and trans.), Zeitschrift für Philosophie und philosophische Kritik, 100: 25–50; translated as 'On Sense and Reference', 1980, 56–78. Oxford: Blackwell.

Goffman, E. (1967). *Interaction Ritual*. New York, NY: Anchor Books.

Harvey, D. (1990). *The Condition of Postmodernity*. London: Blackwell.

Kahneman, D. (2011). *Thinking, Fast and Slow*. New York: Farrar, Straus and Giroux.

Lichenstein, S., & Slovic, P. (eds.). (2006). *The Construction of Preference*. Cambridge: Cambridge University Press.

Markowitz, H. (1959). *Portfolio Selection: Efficient Diversification of Investments*. New Haven, CT: Yale University Press.

Massumi, B. (1995). "The autonomy of affect," *Cultural Critique* 31, The Politics of Systems and Environments, Part II: 83–109.

Nozick, R. (1974). *Anarchy, State, and Utopia*. New York, NY: Basic Books.

Rawls, J. (1971). *A Theory of Justice*. Cambridge: Harvard University Press.

Searle, J. R. (1985). *Expression and Meaning: Studies in the Theory of Speech Acts*. Cambridge: Cambridge University Press.

Sunstein, C., & Kuran, T. (2007). *Availability Cascades and Risk Regulation*, John M. Olin Program in Law and Economics Working Paper No. 364.

Thaler, R., & Sunstein, C. (2009). *Nudge: Improving Decisions about Health, Wealth, and Happiness*. New York, NY: Penguin.

Tversky, A., & Kahneman, D. (1979). "Prospect theory: An analysis of decision under risk," *Econometrica* 47(2): 263–292.

Von Neumann, J., & Morgenstern, O. (1972). *Theory of Games and Economic Behavior*. Princeton, NJ: Princeton University Press.

Wilmott, P. (2009). *Frequently Asked Questions in Finance*. Chichester: John Wiley & Sons.

Zaloom, C. (2006). *Out of the Pits*. Chicago, IL: University of Chicago Press.

3

SPECULATION

Martijn Konings

Introduction

Speculation has always been a central focus of the critique of finance—so much so that the rejection of speculation has become emblematic of what it means to offer a critical perspective on finance. What I consider to the paradigmatic critique of finance takes finance to task for its tendency to generate unstable bubbles of fictitious value that are not rooted in real value or solid economic foundations. It sees finance not as governed by neutral imperatives of efficiency and equilibrating mechanisms, but rather as driven by what Keynes called "animal spirits," irrational bets on the future that are not warranted by fundamental values. On such readings, the attribution of self-stabilizing and self-correcting properties to financial markets is rooted in an inability to recognize the problem of the recurrent character of the speculative impulse and the instability that necessarily results. This paradigmatic critique is increasingly often formulated through Polanyi's understanding of the process of market "disembedding." It rejects the notion that markets can be self-regulating: through speculative trends, they tend to become disembedded from their environment in ways that are unsustainable and give rise to the need to restore limits and foundations.

This chapter formulates a critique of this general orientation of the critique of financial capital. It bears emphasizing that my target here is the critique of speculation precisely in its paradigmatic character. After all, there are plenty of financial practices of which we would be unable to understand the problematic effects if we did not have an appreciation of the role of speculative forces. Currency speculation by hedge funds and subprime credit extended by predatory mortage lenders are cases in point, and large literatures exist on these topics that clarify the role of speculative practices in producing inequality and instability at the global and national level. Nor is this to deny the possibility of local manifestations of irrational speculation that can easily be called as such: there have been plenty of instances in history where the unsustainably speculative character of a particular set of prices was perfectly obvious, even to the participants who are all waiting to get out at the right time. The problem that I am concerned with arises when the critique of speculation becomes detached from such empirical investigations and comes to feature as a general theoretical point. This also means that I am using the term "speculation" in a way that isn't meant to be overly technical and that shades over into its more philosophical uses. For instance, I will rely on a re-reading of Hyman Minsky's work to develop my argument, but I am here more interested in his observation that any economic investment is speculative than in his more technical classification of speculative financing structures—and in this way it serves as a useful bridge between economic and broader, more philosophically inclined perspectives on speculation. In other words, the critique of financial capital cannot be rooted in a rejection of speculation.

At the heart of the critique of speculation is a distinction between real and fictitious value: speculation is seen to generate financial forms that lack substance and whose claim to value is fake and illusory. In the terms of contemporary social theory, the critique of speculation is premised on a substantivist or foundationalist conception of value. This line of thinking has entailed a particular understanding of regulation and governance, which is focused primarily on the possibility of restraining or regulating speculative forces. In this way, a materialist foundationalism is often complemented by an idealist perspective on the nature of public authority: mechanisms of governance tend to be understood as standing in an external relation to finance, as standing above rather than being embroiled in the dynamics of economic life.

The problem with the paradigmatic critique of finance is also empirical: its inability to account for the fact that a history of the secular expansion of credit runs right through the history of financial volatility. At each point in history, there is a common-sense plausibility to the idea that the amount of speculative credit has become excessive, unsustainable when considered in relation to the productive capacity of economic life. But it has proved extremely difficult to operationalize this idea and to specify the point at which speculative credit becomes unsustainable. Capitalist finance enjoys a stellar track record of disproving predictions of collapse (Konings, 2011). In the introductory chapter of this volume, Borch notes the paradoxical resilience of financial systems: their ability to survive economic and political events (such as the crisis of 2007–2008 and the widespread critique of the role of finance in contemporary society that emerged during the following decade and is still in full force) that might have been expected to take the wind out of their sails.

When seen from a broad historical perspective, it needs to be acknowledged that any attempt to legislate standards of value or to specify foundations has been disrupted by actors pushing for the promissory character of credit to be extended beyond existing definitions and parameters, and by financial innovations that open up new ways to make claims on the future through the creation of credit. To put this differently, the role of speculation in the making of the present state of capitalism is only comprehensible if we understand it as part of a self-referential logic. The paradigmatic critique of finance rejects that idea altogether: its point is precisely that finance is not self-referential, that capital does not have autonomous powers of self-multiplication. To think otherwise, it is argued, reflects a lack of critical insight, an inability to see through the ideological self-justifications and fantasies (such as the efficient market hypothesis) of orthodox economics. In this chapter I want to argue that we should acknowledge the self-referential character of finance and that it is possible to approach this in a critical way.

The critique of speculation has most currency in political economy (Keen, 2017; Streeck, 2014). But to foreground it as having a paradigmatic status, as I do here, is to emphasize that its influence extends well beyond those fields. This suggests a slightly different point of entry than that adopted by Borch, who emphasizes that there exist various avenues for articulating finance and critique. That is certainly true, and I agree about the vital importance of the new resources that he highlights, which are prominently represented in this volume. But I wonder if our existing habits of thought prevent us from deploying these resources to the fullest possible extent. Thus, whereas the introductory chapter outlined a number of (very sensible) methodological parameters for the emerging field of critical finance studies, I wonder if we need to do some additional preliminary work to address the blockages that prevent us from working with these to develop more productive lines of critique.

Once we move out of the field of political economy, the hold of the paradigmatic critique of finance as I have outlined it in the above is certainly more ambiguous and tenuous. New perspectives on finance in the social sciences and humanities in particular have tended to adopt a different style of analysis: refusing to take an external, strongly normative or judgmental point of view, they take more seriously the way financial actors themselves understand and narrate their practices. I agree with Borch that there is nothing inherently non-critical about such an approach—indeed, the shift from external to immanent forms of critique is a necessary move in the attempt to revitalize the project of critique. But I nonetheless feel it is important to recognize that, in practice, these new perspectives have often been less interested in renewing than moving "beyond" critique (Latour, 2014). Thus, whereas the paradigmatic critique of finance entirely rejects the self-image of finance as irrational, new scholarship has at times displayed a somewhat exaggerated fascination with the way financial actors view and model their own practices (e.g., Lépinay, 2011; Mackenzie, 2006; cf. Cooper & Konings, 2015).

That is certainly not meant as a blanket judgment, nor to deny that many scholars working in new approaches to finance are critical of the way finance operates. But it is not clear that the field has been able to translate theoretical innovations into a compelling new approach to critique. In particular, despite its rejection of foundationalist modes of thinking, it has had considerable difficulty theorizing the self-referentiality of finance from a critical perspective. That is why—to the extent that it has been unwilling to go along with the post-critique trend—it has been susceptible to relapsing into the more established narratives furnished by the paradigmatic critique of finance. Critique has continued to center on the idea that there is something excessive about finance, that its speculative dynamics fail to respect limits and foundations.

That our conceptual intuitions have been primed in a way that is not easily bypassed is suggested by the travails of one of the key concepts in the conceptual armature of critical finance studies—performativity. The latter concept is central to the field's ambitions to move beyond foundationalist assumptions and, on the face of things, would appear to be a decisive move in providing a critical perspective on self-referentiality, allowing us to understand speculation not as a wilful disregard of ontological value foundations but as the temporally situated logic whereby values are constructed in a world that lacks pre-existing ontological foundations. Performativity implies a different approach to the speculative dimension of economic life: speculation is not primarily seen as a dysfunctional deviation from fundamental values but rather taken as a normal aspect of modern economic life, as reflecting the absence of foundational certainties and the impossibility of eradicating risk. Economic action by its very nature engages uncertainty; it is inherently anticipatory and forward-looking. This means that speculations are constitutive and potentially productive: they are not simply right or wrong predictions about the future, but they can provoke the future, bring into being the economic reality that they project (Adkins, 2018; Muniesa, 2014).

This represents an important shift in perspective. But its implications have yet to be pursued in ways that challenge the paradigmatic critique of speculation. The performativity theme has been pursued primarily at the micro- and meso-level, often through the empirical or ethnographic exploration of risk practices, and its implications for broader questions of order and system-level dynamics have remained highly uncertain. It could of course be argued that this simply reflects a different thematic focus. To some extent that may be the case, but there are nonetheless good reasons to think that there is something about the way the performativity question has been framed that limits its critical reach. Here we can follow Butler's (2010) concern that the performativity literature has at times been prone to returning to idealist conceptions of social constitution as a primarily discursive process. Seen from this angle, it is useful to situate performativity as part of a wider constructivist turn, one that has had a major impact on the political economy literature as well, and to emphasize the difficulty that this constructivist turn has had in escaping from the gravitational forces of Kantian idealism.

This chapter argues that the problematics of "construction" and "performance" can be usefully reframed in terms of Niklas Luhmann's understanding of self-reference. Luhmann's radical-constructivist understanding of self-referential constitution militates against any attempt to fall back on notions of construction as a linear process governed by the rational logic of discursive legitimation. This is then used to offer a new perspective on Hyman Minsky's work. In political economy and beyond, Minsky is known as a critic of financial speculation and excessive levels of debt, who looked to the state to impose restrictive regulations on these dynamics. This chapter suggests that Minsky's work can be read in a very different way: for Minsky *all* investments were to some degree speculative in the sense that their market price does not reflect an underlying fundamental value but is shaped by the interactive logic of valuation. Minsky was closer to the Keynes who likened the dynamics of valuation to those of a beauty contest than the Keynes who became an iconic thinker of financial repression.

This also means that his work contains a more subtle understanding of financial governance than has so far been recognized. His commentary on the monetary policy situation of the 1970s shows that he understood all too well that the state simply did not possess the kind institutional independence that might have enabled it to curtail speculative financial processes. He viewed the problems as stemming precisely from the fact that the central bank was unable to extricate its operations from the logic of the financial system itself. This analysis of the 1970s bore striking resemblance to Hayek's critique of what he termed "rational constructivism," which argues that it is essentially impossible for public authority to rise above the economic logic of risk and uncertainty and to occupy an external, neutral point of view from which to govern. But whereas Minsky seemed to have taken his own analysis as cause for despair about the possibility of returning to a well-functioning economy, Hayek's neoliberalism saw a clear way out of the problem. For him, the problem was the belief in the possibility of social engineering that progressive liberalism had entertained in the first place, and the solution was accordingly seen to consist in the active repudiation of irrational fantasies of rational construction and a more committed embrace of the necessity of contingency. Hayek enjoins the economic subject to view speculation as a productive impulse—not simply in a narrowly economic respect but as the only road to social order in general—and to actively engage it.

The Hayek connection is relevant because it is a way to give specific content to the notion that the governance of contemporary finance is of a "neoliberal" character. The question of neoliberalism has been hotly debated in recent years, and along with this growing interest has arisen a prominent position that bears out the post-critique stance and rejects the concept as essentializing, empirically vacuous, and therefore redundant (Venugopal, 2015). This response may be understandable in view of the tendency in much of the neoliberalism literature to frame its emergence in terms of the specific initiatives and ideas of discrete actors and organizations (Mirowski, 2013), but if fails to engage Foucault's (2008/1979) argument that neoliberalism involves a more diffuse form of governmental reason, an imaginary of order that is not reducible to specific ideas or interests (Brown, 2015). Distancing itself from perspectives that view neoliberalism as primarily involving the capture of public institutions and discourses by financial elites, the chapter argues that the importance of neoliberal reason consists in the changing ways in which public authority has aligned its operation with the speculative logic of the financial system.

Persistent Foundationalism

The prominence of the critique of speculation and the appeal to ontological value foundations that it makes would seem to suggest that the critique of foundationalism has altogether bypassed political economy scholarship. But the opposite is in fact the case: the critique of economic determinism and essentialism is one of its central concerns, and the idea that economic life is "constructed" is at the core of a great deal of political economy work (Blyth, 2002; Widmaier, 2016). The central idea of such work is to reject the assumption of "the economy" as a self-contained, monolithic entity and to emphasize the way it has been constituted through historical processes. Some authors focus primarily on the role of ideas, others on cultural norms, and still others on formal political institutions (see Abdelal et al., 2010 for a representative collection). But what is important for our purposes here is that this literature by and large understands the process of "construction," that is, the relation between the constructive force and what is being constructed, on a model of linear causation. In other words, constructivist political economy has taken the form of an intentionalist (or rational) constructivism, which assumes acts of construction to be self-transparent and views ideas and norms as working in largely predictable ways (cf. Bucher, 2014; Palan, 2000).

Assessed by such an idealist conception of construction, much of human life is of course not constructed, and a great deal of political economy scholarship has accordingly continued to resist the idea that social life is constructed "all the way down." As a result, the constructivist political economy literature has come to revolve around the need to "balance" ideal and material factors, that is, the need to combine an emphasis on constructedness with an acknowledgment of an external reality of hard facts. This has tended to undermine the distinctiveness of the approach, and when it comes to empirical research the constructivist turn in political economy has often assumed the guise of a somewhat conventional mixed-methods perspective—what has been termed "analytical eclecticism" (Sil & Katzenstein, 2010).

Of course, constructivist scholars would readily reject the idea that they remain attached to a version of foundationalism. A common line of defense here is to reduce the problem of foundationalism to the problems with Marxist materialism (in particular the labor theory of value). At work here is what may be termed a Kantian leap, which takes the critique of material necessity and the rediscovery of contingency as the occasion for a return to an idealist essentialism. It reinstates an instrumental perspective on knowledge, which abstracts precisely from the constitutive effects of observation and substitutes for this an idealist emphasis on the causal importance of norms and ideas (e.g., Abdelal et al., 2009). This often relapses into a materialist foundationalism of its own:

assessments of the stability of social life are profoundly shaped by the contrast between speculative finance and the "real economy," and by a tendency to take the manufacturing economy of the Fordist era as a normative point of reference.

Scholars working in critical studies of finance have drawn on actor-network theory to develop the problematic of construction in different ways. Key here has been the theme of performativity (Callon et al., 2007; Mackenzie, 2006), which has aimed at a more radical break with foundationalist assumptions. The concept serves both as a means to underscore the contingent, constructed character of institutions and identities, and as a means to understand how they achieve whatever degree of coherence they enjoy. The dependence on iterative enactment makes entities inherently fragile, but it also introduces a ritualistic element into the dynamics of their constitution. The central ambition of performativity scholarship has thus been to move beyond a traditional epistemological problematic, and to think of measures and forms as immanent yet productive: they are performative both in the sense that they need to be performed (have no independent existence) and in the sense that they do something (they alter something in the existing state of affairs).

For all the promise that this idea holds when it comes to bringing speculation into the heart of thinking about economic life, the performativity literature has displayed a notable tendency to be drawn back into a more idealist perspective (Butler, 2010; Cooper & Konings, 2015). There has remained a marked conceptual gap between performativity as a means to highlight the contingent nature of social facts and human institutions, on the one hand, and analyses of the constitutive powers of performativity, on the other. It is often precisely the history, context, or micro-level operation of the felicitous speech act that is insufficiently specified—meaning that its normative force is not so much accounted for but rather relied upon as an explanation (Bryan et al., 2012).

In order to understand the logic at work here, it is useful to briefly trace the way in which actor-network theory has moved from its original province—social studies of science—into the study of money and finance. Founded on a definite anti-Kantianism, actor-network theory has always been highly suspicious of traditional notions of representation and rejects the idea that the patterning of associations is regulated by external principles. By viewing questions of signification and reference in terms of the topological dynamics of networks, it seeks to take the magic out of meaning and signification. Along such lines, actor-network theory has tended to think of itself as a "material semiotics" (Law, 2009: 142) or as "an empirical version of poststructuralism" (Law, 2009: 145). According to Latour, it is the failure to carefully follow the material processes through which identities are constructed that leads into the dead-end of representational theory—what he refers to as a "salto mortale" (Latour, 1999: 74, quoting William James), the Kantian leap from the material actuality of things to an idealism of symbols and language.

But as actor-network theorists have moved into the study of finance, they have found it very difficult to avoid that very Kantian leap. This is evident in

Callon's prominent work, which has evolved from a material semiotics (Callon, 1986) to a framework that views economic logics as effects of epistemic devices and economic theories (Callon, 1998). The way in which the ideational dimension is brought back suggests that it was never properly accounted for in the basic framework of actor-network theory—that semiotics was never convincingly integrated into materialism without leaving a remainder, and that the poststructuralist dimension was never convincingly rendered intelligible in empirical terms. If actor-network theory's initial reluctance to engage with imaginaries and fictions was motivated by a concern to avoid traditional metaphysics and representational idealism, this all too readily morphed into a somewhat dismissive attitude towards questions of observation and reflexivity. But questions regarding the status and role of human knowledge are not so easily displaced. Latour's "irreductionist" project (1988) seeks to offer a clean solution to the problem of the epistemic moment, and this can plausibly be seen as its own kind of reductionism. Paradoxes that are sidelined too quickly have a way of making themselves felt in unexpected ways and at inconvenient times, and, as the travails of actor-network theory into the study of finance have made clear, can lead to a somewhat unstable back-and-forth between materialism and idealism.

Speculation and Self-Reference: A Luhmannian Perspective

To cut through this problem, we might follow Esposito's (2013) Luhmannian attempt to reconstruct the performativity problematic in terms of the logic of self-reference. For Luhmann, there is no way to truly know whether the nature of things is essentially mind or matter. Any attempt to "solve" the question through a particular theoretical formulation is likely to end up in a back-and-forth between materialism and idealism, reifying each in turn and so reproducing rather than productively engaging the paradoxical character of the problem. The ability of an assemblage to relate to itself is an inescapably paradoxical affair: reflexivity involves the continuous breaching of the bounds of immanence without ever attaining a transcendental position. This makes Luhmann's brand of constructivism "radical": the process through which an identity is assembled never generates a consciousness that can comprehend itself in a transparent manner and can know itself objectively. A Luhmannian problematic thus starts from an acknowledgment that traditional problematics of realism and idealism cannot be resolved on their own terms—that whatever side we take on such issues, we will always be left with a remainder, a part of our experience that is not accounted for. Instead, it treats the paradoxical character of self-reference as a clue to how systems are constructed and operate (Esposito, 1996).

Like the performativity concept, Luhmann's notion of self-reference is marked by a certain duality. In its minimal sense, it denotes "mere" self-referentiality, the ability of a system to recognize itself as a complex assemblage of contingent connections and to register its dependence on the ongoing enactment of that relational configuration (Luhmann, 2013: 44). In its maximal sense, self-referentiality denotes the way in which systems reproduce themselves through their own operations, that is, the emergence of "autopoietic" capacities (Luhmann, 2013: 77). But whereas performativity scholarship tends to be characterized by a strong disconnect between its minimal and maximal senses (performativity understood as a condition of contingency, on the one hand, and as an operation that overcomes that contingency, on the other), this is not the case with Luhmann's idea of self-reference: the system's recognition and engagement of contingency always remains the driving force of dynamics of self-organization and social construction (Borch, 2011). A system is always under pressure to do something, to select from among the myriad connections possible (Luhmann, 2002: 160). Incapable of transcending its own point of view and unable to get an objective perspective on what it needs, it must speculate, make decisions without having all relevant knowledge. A system's Gödelian inability to transcend its own premises and its Münchhausenesque ability to set itself in motion are always different sides of the same self-referential coin.

At its root, the speculative character of life derives from the fact that the act of observation cannot observe itself. The classic image here is that of the eye that cannot see itself, and the constitutive blind spot this indicates is central to Luhmann's work (Luhmann, 2013: 103, 114; Moeller, 2006: 73). A system's machinery of seeing can be extremely sophisticated, but it cannot observe the totality of its own operations in real-time and it cannot therefore ever fully predict or comprehensively control the effects of its own functioning. System reproduction always generates novelty and complexity that the system cannot anticipate or symbolize through those very capacities (Luhmann, 2013: 105). Every attempt to self-reproduce is therefore speculative, beset by an irreducible element of uncertainty that cannot be neutralized as a matter of principle. Crucially, however, it's not just that my relationship to the world is characterized by uncertainty; it's also that the world, made up of other actors, responds to this fact, which is something that I know and must also respond to. The world is composed of observers who observe other observers, and our speculations need to constantly adjust as they seek to size up and locate a moving target: "Speculation takes its cue from speculation" (Luhmann, 2002: 184). This dynamic entails a rapid multiplication of sources of contingency: the world is not just contingent, but often highly volatile. Luhmann's work is essentially an extended meditation on the question of how double contingency generates more or less stable (but never static) forms of organization from within its own logic, in the absence of an external engineer making clean, surgical interventions.

Luhmann's conception of double contingency corresponds closely to Orléan's (1989) economic logic of specularity, which expresses the idea that speculation is not a process whereby we guess at foundational values (although that is how we may rationalize our speculations) but rather a process whereby we position ourselves vis-à-vis the speculative investments made by others. This refers to a Keynesian tradition of thought that has always been highly critical of mainstream ideas of perfect information and equilibrium. Post-Keynesian theory in particular, which has sought to rescue Keynes's thought from its incorporation into mainstream economics, has argued that orthodoxy's exclusive focus on quantifiable risk ignores the importance of real, incalculable uncertainty (Davidson, 2002). But to separate uncertainty from calculable risk in this way is itself highly problematic. Such an approach relies on an understanding of probability as positive knowledge about the future rather than as a means to handle our lack of such knowledge (Esposito, 2007), and it views uncertainty as an external limit to statistical probability rather than as something that is always already at play in the engagement of risk (Kessler, 2009). We may recall here Keynes's famous comment about value being like a beauty contest. Although this drives at a notion of specularity, in practice it is almost always referred to in support of arguments that contrast the self-referentiality and groundlessness of speculative finance to the rational kind of finance that serves the production of real value. Genuine uncertainty is thus taken to indicate the point at which economic action becomes irrational, driven by speculations rather than real value. The upshot has been an inability to systematically foreground the problematic of economy as the question of how order emerges through contingency.

Minsky as Postfoundational Theorist

Hyman Minsky's work can be read as offering a penetrating analysis of that problematic. Of course, Minsky is widely known as the quintessential post-Keynesian critic of speculation, and the notion of the "Minsky moment" is nowadays widely used to refer to the moment when an unstable structure of speculative fictions begins to unravel. That interpretation is closely bound up with a strong emphasis on his characterization of financing structures, attributing instability to the move away from hedge financing (seen as grounded in the real value of material production), and the growing reliance on increasingly speculative (and eventually "Ponzi") financing structures (see Minsky, 1977). Such readings are by no means without textual support but they are certainly one-sided. Minsky was acutely aware that all investments were to some degree speculative in the sense that their success or failure would only be determined in an unknown future: "the essence of capitalism is that units have to take positions in an uncertain world" (Minsky, 1980: 515). Uncertainty is at the heart of the problem of economy: if the future could simply be discounted, all economic questions would be trivial.

The logic of banking is central to Minsky's account of how the dynamic of interacting speculative positions generates economic order. A bank is an institution that enjoys no special foresight and does not escape risk, but is positioned in such a way that its promises come to function as a standard (that is, a more or less stable currency), conferring on it a distinctive infrastructural importance. Of course, the endogenous origins of money (as arising out of dynamics of credit and debt) is a well-rehearsed theme in heterodox economics, but such arguments have never been able to divorce themselves from the more general idea that financial stability is at its core dependent on external interventions to suppress speculative impulses and return market dynamics to conformity with underlying values (e.g., Wray, 2015). For Minsky, however, this is to miss the point about endogeneity and represents a misleading way to think about financial governance (cf. Mehrling, 2000): there is no clear dividing line between practices of banking and their governance, no qualitative break between the endogenous logic of specularity and the governance of that logic. The banking crises that are so central to capitalist development usually trigger new forms of banking: when confidence in a particular currency falters, the response is typically a scramble to prop up that particular measure by integrating it in a wider pattern of banking. Financial crises have historically been a motor behind processes of financial integration and the emergence of national currencies.

Central banking does not represent a means of exogenous regulation: even if it is charged with a public purpose, in terms of its basic operations it is itself a form of banking. When a bank comes under pressure, the response is never an across-the-board credit contraction: large borrowers, too-big-to-fail constituents, are the last to experience the contraction of credit and can count on the most accommodation. Central banking similarly responds to the particular topological properties exhibited by financial networks, that is, the existence of financial nodal points and the possibility that their failure will take down wider social structures. The central bank responds to strains in the financial operations that connect it to other banks as these make themselves apparent in the payments system. The process of financial management can accordingly appear remarkably banal: when failure threatens, there is little to be done other than to fortify the key nodes of the payments system by providing them with additional credit and forms of insurance. The central bank's ability to safeguard the integrity of the system as a whole is centrally predicated on its capacity for risk shifting, the selective socialization of risk. A too-big-to-fail logic based on backstopping and bailout is thus a core feature of capitalist financial management, which is something that Minsky understood very well and led him to be highly skeptical towards claims of discretionary precision management made on behalf of modern monetary policy. As he put it, "Unless the economy is such that depression-inducing financial instability would occur from time to time in the absence of Federal Reserve intervention, the Federal Reserve System is largely superfluous" (Minsky, 2008/1996: 49).

Here we can link to older debates in the history of economic thought. Following Mehrling (1999), we should read Minsky not so much as a post-Keynesian who insisted on the role of true uncertainty as a limit to economic rationality, but rather by placing him in a distinctive tradition of thinking about the nature of central banking that saw the lender-of-last resort function as the essence of financial governance (Bagehot, 1873; Hawtrey, 1932; Thornton, 1802). As long as questions of central banking have been on the political agenda, commentators have sought to provide rules and criteria to ensure that its policies would observe fundamental values and so forestall the need for morally objectionable too-big-to-fail interventions. Such proposals have often assumed the form of some variation on Hume's quantity theory of money (which asserts the possibility of defining money from a neutral, external point of view and legislating limits to its creation) or Smith's concern to anchor credit creation in an objective distinction of real and fictitious forms of credit. However, as Thornton already pointed out, the logic of risk is not easily contained within the parameters of a specific doctrine (Mints, 1945: 52). He viewed speculative credit as playing its own constructive role, facilitating productive events that otherwise might not have materialized. He was well aware that the flipside of this productive non-neutrality of bank credit was the instability that it caused, and he placed great emphasis on the role of the central bank in the stabilization of the banking system. Thornton's appreciation of importance of the central bank's lender-of-last-resort function was thus motivated by a concern that it is not in fact possible to exogenously regulate the dynamics finance in a way that brings them in line with fundamental values.

Rethinking Financial Governance

Whereas political economy scholars typically view the Glass-Steagall prohibition on stock market speculation by commercial banks as key to the stability of the post-New Deal financial system, for Minsky this played only a secondary role. He thought of the New Deal reforms rather as representing a way to adjust and expand the lender-of-last-resort function (which had failed to prevent American and global capitalism from sliding into the interwar crisis)—that is, to make it operate more preventatively, to extend its scope, and to make it less dependent on the discretion of Federal Reserve policy-makers. Key here was deposit insurance, which was crucial in taking away the rationale behind bank runs by removing the rationale behind bank runs and so functioned as an integral part of the central banking function (Minsky, 1982: 144; 2008/1986: 52). The government-sponsored enterprises similarly functioned as permanently available sources of liquidity, while practices of financial policy-making became increasingly oriented to stabilizing the payments system by preventing liquidity bottlenecks. From the 1930s to early 1950s the effects of this were greatly magnified by the Federal Reserve's support for the market in government debt (Gaines, 1962). In other words, the New Deal reforms created what has come to be known as an extensive "financial safety net" for the banking system (Schwartz, 1987).

This configuration of financial institutions transformed financial dynamics in significant ways, and the early post-war period saw no major instability or meltdowns (Minsky, 2008/1986: 50). But the result was a permanent inflationary pressure (Minsky, 2008/1986: 17). As Minsky put it, "instead of a financial crisis and a deep depression being separated by decades, threats of crisis and deep depression occur every few years; instead of a realized deep depression, we now have chronic inflation" (2008/1986: 106). This created a distinctive set of governance challenges: although the post-war Federal Reserve viewed managing inflation as one of its main tasks, it was essentially counteracting the pressure that the New Deal arrangements had built into the system at large (Burns, 1979). Whenever the Fed sought to constrain banks' capacities for credit creation, the result was a rapid growth of new forms of banking outside the existing regulatory framework—what has recently come to be known as a "shadow banking system," much of which could draw on these facilities (for a discussion of shadow banking, see the chapter by Wigger and Fernandez in this *Handbook*). Minsky (1957) was one of the first to note this trend and viewed it as a forceful reminder that, pretenses of precision notwithstanding, the basic operational rationality of financial management consisted in last-resort lending and the provision of insurance. The accuracy of this assessment was borne out by the course of financial management during the 1960s and 1970s: even as regulators were increasingly concerned about inflation, they saw no alternative to accommodating the financial practices that were responsible for the problem (Mayer, 1999). During the 1970s, as it became clear that even economic stagnation would not slow down inflation, the Federal Reserve increasingly came to understand the problem as one that was sustained at basic operational levels of financial management.

The dilemmas of financial governance became even more pronounced as it became clear that uninsured shadow banking meant a return to dynamics of financial leveraging and deleveraging that entailed significant system-level risk and therefore would need a response. Extending insurance arrangements to the capital markets was not a viable option for both political and economic reasons, and so a future of ad hoc bailouts seemed to be in the offing. Minsky seemed to feel that there was no real way out of this predicament: absent a major overhaul of American capitalism, there seemed to be no way for the American state to escape the kind of awkward dynamic in which was constitutively embroiled. These feelings were to some extent shared by Arthur Burns, Federal Reserve Chairman for most of the decade. In a 1979 speech entitled "The Anguish of Central Banking," he complained that the Federal Reserve could simply not conquer inflation without generating a range of intolerable side effects (Burns, 1979: 16). It just did not find itself in a position that permitted it to access clean policy solutions, and so the previous decade "monetary policy came to be governed by the principle of undernourishing the inflationary process while still accommodating a good part of the pressures in the marketplace" (Burns, 1979: 16).

Burns concluded that "fairly drastic therapy will be needed to turn inflationary psychology around" (Burns, 1979: 24). Such therapy came soon after he left, in the guise of the turn to monetarism initiated by Paul Volcker. Monetarist doctrine can be viewed as a modern incarnation of Hume's quantity theory: to ensure that money functions in its neutral capacity, it proposes that the central bank maintains strict institutional control over the quantity of its creation (Friedman, 1956). Volcker was skeptical about its merits as an economic theory and never believed that the creation of money could be exogenously controlled (Silber, 2012). He was well aware that the state's lending and insurance functions were an integral part of the endogenous process whereby the dollar was constituted as a stable measure and were for that reason indispensable infrastructure. But at the same time he saw the role of the state as a problem insofar as it contributed to inflation. He looked to monetarism not as a means to enforce an external limit on the financial system, but as a means to affect expectations (cf. Holmes, 2013; Kaplan, 2003). He took it as a rhetorical device, as a way for the state to productively engage—rather than just accommodate—the endogenous dynamics of banking.

In other words, Volcker perceived the problem as one of how financial governance might change the way it related to a process in which it was constitutively implicated and could not simply extricate itself from. We might say that he engaged a Hayekian problematic—how is ordering possible if there is no political agency that can place itself outside of the logic of risk and speculation? Hayek's work contains a radical-constructivist problematic, which addresses the question of how steering is possible in the context of an endogenously driven logic that rules out sovereign decisions and exogenous interventions (Cooper, 2011; Kessler, 2013). Although he referred explicitly to systems and complexity theory only later and occasionally (e.g., Hayek, 1967: 22–42), his work substantively became organized around the problematic of economic self-organization from the time he formulated his critique of socialist planning as a critique of rational constructivism (1937). In this way, Hayek's thinking foregrounded a problematic that led a more subterranean life in other strands of neoliberalism—how the awareness of the limits of rational constructivism could be internalized into practices of ordering and governing.

My point here is not to stress the practical role of neoliberal intellectuals like Hayek in shaping monetary policy-making. Rather, I am foregrounding Hayek's work to suggest a specific perspective on the contours of a neoliberal rationality of governance, an issue that has received considerable attention in the wake of the publication of Foucault's lectures at the Collège de France (Brown, 2015). At the core of the understanding of neoliberalism that Foucault advanced in his later work is the idea that it does not involve a simple revival of classic liberalism (e.g., 2008/1979: 118, 131, 147): whereas classic liberalism simply demanded space for the utilitarian logic of market exchange to unfold, neoliberalism embraces a speculative orientation towards the future as an organizing principle. The modern subject is centrally driven by a security dispositif, but its attempts to deal with challenges and threats never transcend the condition of risk and the need to speculate (de Goede, 2012).

When this logic comes fully into its own, the pressure to make decisions amidst uncertainty poses a challenge to any clear-cut distinctions between defensive and offensive moves. This notion has been helpfully elaborated by François Ewald, who suggests that the development of risk governance can be understood in terms of a transition from defensive orientations that are primarily concerned with organizing insurance to more purposely proactive orientations that work on "an ethic of the necessary decision in a context of uncertainty" (Ewald, 2002: 294). Whereas the former employ the logic of the normal distribution, the latter push into areas of risk that challenge meaningful actuarial calculation. With specific respect to modern financial governance, we can note that even though it has always involved the alignment of governmental operations with the logic of risk, until well into the twentieth century this had a rather passive and reactive orientation, accommodating rather than using the dynamics of speculation. It is here that neoliberalism intervenes, insisting that governance should proactively engage the speculative dimension of economic life.

The way in which neoliberalism has brought speculation into the heart of governmental rationality means that it has come to function on what the critical security studies literature has referred to as a logic of preemption (de Goede, 2008; Massumi, 2007; for an attempt to extend the relevance of this concept to economics questions, see Opitz & Tellmann, 2015), a paradoxical practice that fully blurs the distinction between prevention and activation. Preemptive reason can be understood as an operationalization of the dispositif that Hayek insisted was the only possible way to produce order through contingency: it is characterized by a reflexive awareness of its own speculative foundations and a willingness to move beyond a naïve doctrine of prevention. Even as it presents itself as eliminating threats and obstacles to security, its modus operandi and ordering capacity is predicated on the possibility of activating and engaging new sources of contingency, proactively enforcing adjustment by allowing crises and instability to play a productive role. Neoliberalism thus signifies the movement of governmental rationality from a logic of anticipation and prevention to one of speculative preemption: it goes beyond a generic concern with the future to embrace an orientation to the pragmatic uses of instability, uncertainty, and crisis (Ewald, 2002: 294).

Neoliberal Reason

Neoliberal policies have often been oriented not to the prevention of failure but rather to its preemption—in the dual sense of the word, both activating it and forestalling its most serious consequences. Volcker saw the American financial system heading for decline (reflected in the growing reluctance of foreigners to hold dollars), and he acted on this awareness preemptively, by triggering a potentially productive crisis: the turn to monetarism was meant to provoke, driven by the intuition that a sudden policy turn could activate some of the financial system's endogenously situated ordering mechanisms. Volcker's move was offensively speculative—motivated not by a clear perception of the outcome of his moves but by an intuition of their productive, ordering potential. Far from the Federal Reserve making external interventions, it aggressively engaged the banking mechanisms of money production, creating new sources of uncertainty in hopes of stabilizing the financial standard.

What was not in itself surprising was the rapid expansion of shadow banking that followed the policy turn: that was precisely why in the past the Federal Reserve had held back from contractionary policies or quickly reversed them. The Volcker speculation consisted precisely in the wager that the instability caused by the Fed's persistence with those policies would set in motion wider processes of adjustment. The Volcker shock restored the value of the dollar not by enforcing an external quantitative limit on the creation of credit but by activating some of the financial system's key self-organizing mechanisms. The extent to which the success of the monetarist turn was contingent on wider adjustments was illustrated by Volcker's (2000) own admission that the Reagan administration's confrontation with organized labor had been crucial to the conquest of inflation (cf. Axilrod, 2011: 99). And that was only one element in a wide-ranging set of policies that accelerated the destruction of the secure employment contracts of Fordism (Lazzarato, 2009; Martin, 2002).

Even as neoliberal restructuring brought down inflation and alleviated external pressure on the dollar, these developments were accompanied by significant financial volatility and a series of bank failures. The 1980s saw a series of bailouts of systemically important institutions, which fostered expectations regarding the way the American state would handle such events in the future (Stern & Feldman, 2004). Sufficiently large and interconnected financial institutions increasingly did business in the expectation that if their speculations went sour, the state would step in to alleviate their payments constraints. Although this amounted to an insurance regime for the shadow banking system, it did not fan inflation because it remained informal and so could operate much more selectively than blanket deposit insurance (Panitch & Gindin, 2012: 179). If it was certainly recognized that this exacerbated moral hazard issues (that bailout interventions sustain and reinforce the very practices that brought on the need for them), this reflected not a moment of governmental irrationality but the fact that neoliberalism's preemptive rationality undermines any hard-and-fast distinction between problems and solutions.

This new institutional configuration facilitated a further reorientation of financial governance, as the ability of banks to create credit outside of the central bank's regulatory capacity was no longer the source of anxiety that it had been before. The Federal Reserve now began to use interest rate to proactively relieve liquidity pressures on large financial institutions (Ferguson & Johnson, 2010; Watson, 2014); it enhanced insurance for the key nodes of the payments system; and the growth of the government-sponsored enterprises and the infrastructure of securitization techniques supported had similar effects. The new approach that emerged recognized that crises were likely to continue to occur periodically and that the use of bailouts could not be ruled out and that the aim should be to manage their application and minimize their undesirable side effects. As Golub et al. (2015: 657) put it, during the neoliberal era the Federal Reserve increasingly focused on "post-hoc interventionism," aiming to improve its ability to contain the effects of a crisis after it occurs. Panitch and

Gindin (2012: 266) capture this development in terms of a shift of concern from "failure prevention" to "failure containment." Among Federal Reserve insiders this became known as the "mop up after" strategy (Blinder & Reis, 2005).

It is crucial here to recognize that, as Ewald emphasizes (e.g., 2002: 285), the transition to preemptive modes of governance should not be understood as a clean replacement of one principle with another: the speculative orientation of neoliberal governance always articulates with the continued operation of normalizing forces and the principle of insurance. The neoliberal concern to provoke the future is complemented by a reactionary moment that manifests itself fully when uncertainty threatens to tip over into failure. At such times, society has no option but to fortify the nodal points of financial interconnectedness, historically generated patterns of leverage and power. During the financial crisis sovereignty became highly speculative, investing itself in assets whose value was fundamentally in doubt; but at the very same time its policies were grounded in the widespread (if resentful) recognition that it was simply doing what had to be done. The future simply imposes itself, albeit in the shape of the past. As Massumi (2005: 6) puts it: "The before-after seizes the present. The future-past colonizes the present." The logic of preemption now manifests itself in yet a third sense, as a foreclosure on the future. And yet, bailouts do not simply stabilize the system in a straightforward way or effect a return to foundations. Bailouts are themselves highly speculative interventions that involve a great deal of dislocation and demand a response, rekindling the preemptive rationality even as they make apparent its contradictions.

Conclusion

By identifying the logic of preemption, this chaper has tried to suggest a way in which an immanent critique of contemporary finance may be formulated. The paradigmatic critique is preoccupied with the irrational character and ontological incoherence of speculation, and it looks to public institutions, conceived as acting in independence from the rationality of capital, to suppress this. The approach developed in this chapter has emphasized the constitutive, generative character of financial speculation and the internal logic of the processes that it sets in motion, and it has developed a perspective on public institutions as fully imbricated with speculative financial processes. It has also argued that this is particularly important when it comes to the assessment of neoliberalism: the paradigmatic critique of finance has been unable to recognize or engage the distinctive rationality of neoliberal governance, which is grounded in a recognition of the limits of rational-constructivist conceptions of authority and cognizant of the need to activate contingency.

Of course, many would wonder whether this kind of immanent critique is really a critique at all. When seen from a certain angle, this chapter has enlisted Luhmann's systems theory and an unknown version of Minsky to develop a Hegelian dialectic of speculative capital, which depicts contradictions and obstacles as limits that are overcome each time and move the rule of capital to a more totalizing level of social control—aided and abetted by that institution (the state) in which progressives of all stripes continue to invest so much of their political hope. It would be easy to disavow this point. But my sense is in fact that such an emphasis on the secular expansion of promissory connections through the very contradictions that those connections generate needs to be part of any viable critique. If there is one thing that the past decades have taught us, it's that so many of the things that we thought would be clear limits to the growth of capital have only become the kind of negativities or irritations that drive the system of capitalism's self-referential expansion. That should have been the occasion not for a retreat from thinking about capital, but fertile ground for elaborating the post-foundational insight about the inherent impossibility of accessing an objective, external position that allows for the objective identification of limits.

The real mistake here would be to conflate this point about the secularizing thrust of capitalist development with a more normative assessment about progress in history. I am here following a particular line of theorizing about Hegelian dialectics (Cole, 2014; Malabou, 2004; Rose, 2009/1981): trying to rescue it from its wholesale rejection by poststructuralist thought, these contributions have sought to re-appropriate dialectics not as a theory of historical progress but as a this-worldly analysis of the rationality of history-making. My supplement to this line of thought—driven by my specific political economy orientation—is the need to bring the "system" back in, thereby positioning Luhmann in relation to the legacy of Hegel and Marx. The dialectic describes how determinate entities emerge and systemic logics operate in a world without foundations.

Not to include this appreciation of the secular self-expansion of capital would simply be to hold on to the fantasy that we may be able to find an outside position, a set of external criteria against which we can assess the existing state of affairs and which offer solid ground for our political interventions. This is indeed the kind of critique that has run out of steam, as Latour (2004) has correctly noted. But the very fact that the disavowal of totalizing dynamics and an affirmation of pluralism has become the signature move of postfoundational theory means that it has not in fact broken with the terms of the problematic that gave rise to that critique in the first place. And this typically manifests itself when people start contemplating the thorny reality of capital.

Latour's own work stands as a prime example of how postfoundational theory has come to dance around the suppressed awareness of capital. In one of the more revealing instances, towards the end of his recent *An Inquiry into Modes of Existence*, he identifies it as the central obstacle to a more plural world that modernity might have delivered:

> By identifying technological innovations [TEC], the splendors of works of art [FIC], the objectivity of the sciences [REF], political autonomy [POL], respect for legal linkages [LAW], the appeal of the living God [REL], they would have glowed in the world like one of the

most beautiful, most durable, most fruitful civilizations of all. Proud of themselves, they would have had no burden weighing them down, crushing them like Atlas, like Sisyphus, like Prometheus, all those tragic giants. But they went on to invent something else: the continent of *The Economy*. (Latour, 2013: 379)

Elsewhere he notes that the economy is "an infinite and boundless domain totally indifferent to terrestrial existence and the very notion of limits, and entirely self-centered and self-governed" (Latour, 2014: 6). Crucially, however, these totalizing tendencies noted here have no place in Latour's work taken as a whole—they are truly incompatible with his pragmatic ontology, and so they end up being treated as a manifestation of plain irrationality, denounced in a spirit of moralistic lament that is entirely in keeping with the paradigmatic critique of finance. The endpoint of Latour's thinking, then, is exactly the kind of critical stance that he has done more than anyone else to discredit.

If the post-critical impulse does not escape capital's field of gravity, that by itself might be taken as a starting point of sorts. That is to say, we might consider abandoning our preoccupation with the possibility of accessing an objectively grounded critique that can be positively formulated and start with an acknowledgment that the existing world provides no ready-made set of procedures or instruments that permit its deconstruction. The fact that we are caught in a strange, self-referential loop means that any attempts to move against the systemic logic of capital have a deeply aporetic character. In this sense, the kind of critical theory that Luhmann's postfoundational systems theory implies is perhaps not too far from a negative dialectics, which seeks to disrupt the immunitarian logic of capital that while fully recognizing its historical reality and its totalizing dynamic. "Universal history must be construed and denied" (Adorno, 1973/1966: 320). The task of critique is not to discursively disavow systemness in order to facilitate a soothing faith in unviable practical solutions; instead, the task of critique is deeply contradictory, namely to "[t]o use the strength of the subject to break through the fallacy of constitutive subjectivity" (Adorno, 1973/1966: xx)—how to change the course of history without being able to identify in a positive way the blind spots on which the historical process currently feeds.

The question here is of course what it might mean to "deny" universal history. Adorno gave us little to go on in this respect: as Rose (2014/1978) points out, his work over time tended towards a performative and indulgent hyper-consciousness of the impossibility of a positive, objectively grounded critique. But it seems to me that there is no way around returning to the place of impossibility indicated by Adorno, and an embrace of the critical attitude that he felt was entailed by this—one that aims to reframe our understanding and experience of the world and recognizes that practical interventions skipping this step are likely to leave intact or fuel the universal history they are hoping to adjust or subvert. No attempt to interrupt the immunitarian logic of capital is likely to do much unless it starts with a recognition of our own implication in it.

Acknowledgments

Many thanks to Christian Borch and Robert Wosnitzer for their help with and feedback on this chapter. This chapter draws on materials previously published in *Distinktion: Journal of Social Theory* ("How finance is governed: Reconnecting cultural and political economy," 19(2): 135–151), and I gratefully acknowledge permission to reproduce these materials here.

References

Abdelal, R., Blyth, M., & Parsons, C. (eds.). (2010). *Constructing the International Economy*. Ithaca, NY: Cornell University Press.

Abdelal, R., Herrera, Y. M., Johnston, A. I., & McDermott, R. (eds.). (2009). *Measuring Identity: A Guide for Social Scientists*. Cambridge: Cambridge University Press.

Adkins, L. (2018). *The Time of Money*. Stanford, CA: Stanford University Press.

Adorno, T. W. (1973 [1966]). *Negative Dialectics*. New York, NY: Continuum.

Axilrod, S. H. (2011). *Inside the Fed. Monetary Policy and Its Management, Martin through Greenspan to Bernanke*. Cambridge, MA: MIT Press.

Bagehot, W. (1873). *Lombard Street: A Description of the Money Market*. New York, NY: Scribner, Armstrong & Co.

Blinder, A. S., & Reis, R. (2005, August 25–27). "Understanding the greenspan standard," paper presented at the Federal Reserve Bank of Kansas City symposium, *The Greenspan Era: Lessons for the Future*. Jackson Hole, Wyoming.

Blyth, M. (2002). *Great Transformations. Economic Ideas and Institutional Change in the Twentieth Century*. Cambridge: Cambridge University Press.

Borch, C. (2011). *Niklas Luhmann*. New York, NY: Routledge.

Brown, W. (2015). *Undoing the Demos: Neoliberalism's Stealth Revolution*. New York, NY: Zone.

Bryan, D., Martin, R., Montgomerie, J., & Williams, K. (2012). "An important failure: Knowledge limits and the financial crisis," *Economy and Society* 41(3): 299–315.

Bucher, B. (2014). "Acting abstractions: Metaphors, narrative structures, and the eclipse of agency," *European Journal of International Relations* 20(3): 742–765.

Burns, A. F. (1979). "The anguish of central banking," *1979 Per Jacobsson Lecture*, Belgrade.

Butler, J. (2010). "Performative agency," *Journal of Cultural Economy* 3(2): 147–161.

Callon, M. (1986). "Some elements of a sociology of translation: Domestication of the scallops and the fishermen of St Brieuc Bay," in J. Law (ed.) *Power, Action and Belief: A New Sociology of Knowledge* (pp. 196–233). London: Rouledge.

Callon, M. (1998). "Introduction: The embeddedness of economic markets in economics," in M. Callon (ed.), *The Laws of the Markets* (pp. 1–57). Oxford: Blackwell.

Callon, M., Millo, Y., & Muniesa, F. (eds.). (2007). *Market Devices*. Oxford: Blackwell.

Cole, A. (2014). *The Birth of Theory*. Chicago, IL: University of Chicago Press.

Cooper, M. (2011). "Complexity theory after the financial crisis," *Journal of Cultural Economy* 4(4): 371–385.

Cooper, M., & Konings, M. (2015). "Contingency and foundation: Rethinking money, debt and finance after the crisis," *South Atlantic Quarterly* 114(2): 239–250.

Davidson, P. (2002). *Financial Markets, Money, and the Real World*. Cheltenham: Edward Elgar.

Esposito, E. (1996). "Observing interpretation: A sociological view of hermeneutics," *MLN* 111(3): 593–619.

Esposito, E. (2007). *Die Fiktion Der Wahrscheinlichen Realität*. Frankfurt am Main: Suhrkamp.

Esposito, E. (2013). "The structures of uncertainty: Performativity and unpredictability in economic operations," *Economy and Society* 42(1): 102–129.

Ewald, F. (2002). "The return of Descartes's Malicious demon: An outline of a philosophy of precaution," in T. Baker and J. Simon (eds.), *Embracing Risk: The Changing Culture of Insurance and Responsibility* (pp. 273–301). Chicago, IL: University of Chicago Press.

Ferguson, T., & Johnson, R. (2010). "Too big to bail: The "Paulson put," US presidential politics, and the global financial meltdown," in M. Konings (ed.), *The Great Credit Crash* (pp. 119–169). London/New York, NY: Verso.

Foucault, M. (2008). *The Birth of Biopolitics*. New York, NY: Palgrave. (Original work published in 1979).

Friedman, M. (1956). "The quantity theory of Money—a restatement," in M. Friedman (ed.), *Studies in the Quantity Theory of Money* (pp. 3–21). Chicago, IL: University of Chicago Press.

Gaines, T. C. (1962). *Techniques of Treasury Debt Management*. New York, NY: Free Press of Glencoe.

de Goede, M. (2008). "The politics of preemption and the war on terror in Europe," *European Journal of International Relations* 14(1): 161–185.

de Goede, M. (2012). *Speculative Security: The Politics of Pursuing Terrorist Monies*. Minneapolis: University of Minnesota Press.

Golub, S., Kaya, A., & Reay, M. (2015). "What were they thinking? The federal reserve in the run-up to the 2008 financial crisis," *Review of International Political Economy* 22(4): 657–692.

Hawtrey, R. G. (1932). *The Art of Central Banking*. London: Longmans, Green and Co.

Hayek, F. (1937). "Economics and knowledge," *Economica* 4(13): 33–54.

Hayek, F. (1967). *Studies in Philosophy, Politics and Economics*. London: Routledge & Kegan Paul.

Holmes, D. R. (2013). *Economy of Words: Communicative Imperatives in Central Banks*. Chicago, IL: University of Chicago Press.

Kaplan, M. (2003). "Iconomics: The rhetoric of speculation," *Public Culture* 15(3): 477–493.

Keen, S.(2017). *Can We Avoid Another Financial Crisis?* Cambridge: Polity.

Kessler, O. (2009). "Towards an economic sociology of the subprime crisis?," *Economic Sociology_The European Electronic Newsletter* 10(2): 11–16.

Kessler, O. (2013). "Sleeping with the enemy? On Hayek, constructivist thought, and the current economic crisis," *Review of International Studies* 38(2): 275–299.

Konings, M. (2011). *The Development of American Finance*. New York, NY: Cambridge University Press.

Latour, B. (1988). *The Pasteurization of France*. Cambridge, MA: Harvard University Press.

Latour, B. (1999). *Pandora's Hope. Essays on the Reality of Science Studies*. Cambridge, MA: Harvard University Press.

Latour, B. (2004). "Why has critique run out of steam? From matters of fact to matters of concern," *Critical Inquiry* 30(2): 225–248.

Latour, B. (2013). *An Inquiry into Modes of Existence. An Anthropology of the Moderns*. Cambridge: Harvard University Press.

Latour, B. (2014). *On Some of the Affects of Capitalism*, Lecture given at the Royal Academy, Copenhagen, February 26.

Law, J. (2009). "Actor network theory and material semiotics," in B. S. Turner (ed.), *The New Blackwell Companion to Social Theory* (pp. 141–158). Oxford: Wiley.

Lazzarato, M. (2009). "Neoliberalism in action: Inequality, insecurity and the reconstitution of the social," *Theory, Culture & Society* 26(6): 109–133.

Lépinay, V. A.(2011). *Codes of Finance: Engineering Derivatives in a Global Bank.* Princeton, NJ: Princeton University Press.

Luhmann, N. (2002). *Risk. A Sociological Theory.* New York, NY: Routledge.

Luhmann, N. (2013). *Introduction to Systems Theory.* Cambridge: Polity.

Mackenzie, D. (2006). *An Engine, Not a Camera: How Financial Models Shape Markets.* Cambridge, MA: MIT Press.

Malabou, C. (2004). *The Future of Hegel: Plasticity, Temporality and Dialectic.* New York, NY: Routledge.

Martin, R. (2002). *Financialization of Daily Life.* Philadelphia, PA: Temple University Press.

Massumi, B. (2005). "The future birth of the affective fact," *Conference Proceedings: Genealogies of Biopolitics*: 1–12.

Massumi, B. (2007). "Potential politics and the primacy of preemption," *Theory and Event* 10(2). doi: 10.1353/tae.2007.0066.

Mayer, T. (1999). *Monetary Policy and the Great Inflation in the United States: The Federal Reserve and the Failure of Macroeconomic Policy, 1965–79.* Cheltenham/Northamption, MA: Edward Elgar Publishing.

Mehrling, P. (1999). "The vision of Hyman P. Minsky," *Journal of Economic Behavior & Organization* 39(2): 129–158.

Mehrling, P. (2000). "The state as financial intermediary," *Journal of Economic Issues* 34(2): 365–368.

Minsky, H. P. (1957). "Central banking and money market changes," *Quarterly Journal of Economics* 71(2): 171–187.

Minsky, H. P. (1977). "The financial instability hypothesis: An interpretation of Keynes and an alternative to 'standard' theory," *Challenge* (March-April): 20–27.

Minsky, H. P. (1980). "Capitalist financial processes and the instability of capitalism," *Journal of Economic Issues* 14(2): 505–523.

Minsky, H. P. (1982). *Can "It" Happen Again?* New York, NY: M.E. Sharpe.

Minsky, H. P. (2008). *Stabilizing an Unstable Economy.* New York, NY: McGraw Hill. (Original work published 1986).

Mints, L. W. (1945). *A History of Banking Theory in Great Britain and the United States.* Chicago, IL: University of Chicago Press.

Mirowski, P. (2013). *Never Let a Serious Crisis Go to Waste: How Neoliberalism Survived the Financial Meltdown.* London: Verso.

Moeller, H.-G. (2006). *Luhmann Explained: From Souls to Systems.* Chicago, IL: Open Court.

Muniesa, F. (2014). *The Provoked Economy: Economic Reality and the Performative Turn.* Abingdon: Routledge.

Opitz, S., & Tellmann, U. (2015). "Future emergencies: Temporal politics in law and economy," *Theory, Culture & Society* 32(2): 107–129.

Orléan, A. (1989). "Mimetic contagion and speculative bubbles," *Theory and Decision* 27(1–2): 63–92.

Palan, R. (2000). "A world of their making: An evaluation of the constructivist critique in international relations," *Review of International Studies* 26(4): 575–598.

Panitch, L., & Gindin, S. (2012). *The Making of Global Capitalism: The Political Economy of American Empire.* London/New York, NY: Verso.

Paudyn, B. (2015). "The struggle to perform the political economy of creditworthiness: European Union governance of credit ratings through risk," *Journal of Cultural Economy* 8(6): 655–672.

Rose, G. (2009 [1981]). *Hegel Contra Sociology.* London: Verso.

Rose, G. (2014 [1978]). *The Melancholy Science: An Introduction to the Thought of Theodor W. Adorno.* London: Verso.

Schwartz, A. J. (1987). "The lender of last resort and the federal safety net," *Journal of Financial Services Research* 1(1): 1–17.Sil, R., & Katzenstein, P. J. (eds.). (2010). *Beyond Paradigms: Analytic Eclecticism in the Study of World Politics.* New York, NY: Palgrave.

Silber, W. L. (2012). *Volcker: The Triumph of Persistence.* New York, NY: Bloomsbury.

Stern, G. H., & Feldman, R. J. (2004). *Too Big to Fail: The Hazards of Bank Bailouts.* Washington, DC: Brookings Institution Press.

Streeck, W. (2014). *Buying Time: The Delayed Crisis of Democratic Capitalism.* London/New York, NY: Verso.

Thornton, H. (1965 [1802]). *An Enquiry into the Nature and Effects of the Paper Credit of Great Britain.* New York, NY: Augustus M. Kelley.

Venugopal, R. (2015). "Neoliberalism as concept," *Economy and Society* 44(2): 165–187.

Volcker, P. A. (2000, September 26). *Interview.* Commanding Heights, PBS. Retrieved from http://www.pbs.org/wgbh/commandingheights/shared/minitext/int_paulvolcker.html.

Watson, M. (2014). "Re-establishing what went wrong before: The greenspan put as macroeconomic modellers' new normal," *Journal of Critical Globalisation Studies* 7: 80–101.

Widmaier, W. (2016). *Economic Ideas in Political Time: The Rise and Fall of Economic Orders from the Progressive Era to the Global Financial Crisis.* Cambridge: Cambridge University Press.

Wray, L. R. (2015). *Why Minsky Matters: An Introduction to the Work of a Maverick Economist.* Princeton, NJ: Princeton University Press.

4

FINANCIAL NOISE

Alex Preda

Introduction

There are probably few academic terms that, over the last three or four decades, have had a career as broad and successful as "noise." Across the natural and social sciences, the humanities, and literary fiction,[1] to mention but a few, "noise" has been a constant presence, albeit with varying meanings and implications. It is not my aim here to provide an analytical overview of how this term has been used across all social science disciplines, or to undertake a philosophical reflection upon it; this has been recently and effectively done elsewhere (Malaspina, 2018). Rather, I will zoom in from the start on the implications of this term for financial economics and on the extent to which it can support a program of research in the sociology of finance. Why noise in finance, though? There are several good reasons for this: in finance, noise is seen as a fundamental concept, and yet many would like to see it set aside. It has generated hundreds of research papers and yet, it is still largely seen as an unsolved issue. It is both a conceptual and an empirical puzzle, with significant consequences for how we conceive markets.

As for sociology, and especially the sociology of financial markets, they have been rather disinterested in noise. This is neither a significant concept, nor part of the analytical toolkit of economic sociology, nor part of any sociological tradition. It does not play any role in the sociological conceptualization of markets, including here financial markets. The contrast couldn't be greater with the significant role noise plays in multiple varieties of finance theory (e.g., behavioral finance, mainstream financial economics, market microstructure), and in the ways financial markets are conceptualized. Therefore, it is not unreasonable to start by investigating the financial concept of noise and explore not only its sociological relevance, but also the ways in which the sociology of financial markets can incorporate it, or at least address issues that are relevant to it.

Noise, Efficiency, and Competition

Financial economics has felt the impact of "noise" in more than one way; a quick search in academic databases reveals that over the past decades hundreds of papers on "noise" have been published in academic finance journals. Over the past two decades, the number of academic disciplines dealing with financial markets has multiplied; at the same time, we have seen a diversification of approaches within the disciplines themselves. "Noise" is credited by some financial economists with having contributed substantially both to the multiplication and to the internal diversification of disciplines.

I mean this by the following: while 20 years ago finance was taught primarily in business schools and in economics departments under the umbrella of financial economics, nowadays we see finance taught in mathematics and in physics departments as well, under the terms financial mathematics, computational finance, or econophysics. This, among others, has led to an institutional landscape where research and teaching on financial markets are located across schools of social and natural sciences, comprising, among others, financial economics, market microstructure, behavioral finance, and econophysics (see also Preda, 2017). Within each of these, we encounter distinct understandings of "noise," which sometimes are parallel to each other. "Distinct understandings" means in this context not only different concepts of, but also distinct methodologies and techniques of analyzing noise. Sometimes, noise is more a scheme of thought than a concept. If anything, the advent of "big data"—that is, the availability of large datasets of financial transactions and the application of computer and data-analytical methods—has increased the relevance of noise, as well as increasing the term's complexity.

What, then, is noise in financial markets? If we are to follow Cécile Malaspina (2018: 119), we need to distinguish among noise as a concept, as a scheme of thought, and as a common understanding. To start with the latter meaning, a common understanding of noise would be that of (more or less random) disturbances, or disruptions of an otherwise regular process (such as a social interaction), or which can create annoyance. This common understanding is present not just in everyday conversations, but also in social science papers, where noise is seen as disturbances which mask an underlying pattern (e.g., Macy & Tsvetkova, 2015: 307). Noise as a concept is related to the *statistical* notion of information, to information entropy, and to the degrees of choice and uncertainty. These statistical notions, however, are discursively translated across disciplines (without necessarily translating their formal expressions as well), a process which has led to the emergence of various schemes of thought, including in finance (Malaspina, 2018: 18).

It is the latter realm that is relevant in the present context. The idea that in financial markets prices both incorporate and reveal information (making markets efficient) had been formulated in the 1960s by Paul Samuelson and Eugene Fama, respectively, as a reaction to empirical studies showing the random character of variations in stock prices (Delcey, 2019) (if stock prices vary at random, then there is not much use having stock analysts, a stance that had already been expressed in the 1930s).

Information had already been made into a core economic concept earlier: starting in the 1930s, in relationship to debates about centralized planning and socialist economies, some economists (including F. A. Hayek) argued that what is allocated within economic processes is not primarily goods and services, but information (Mirowski & Nik-khah, 2017: 63). The efforts of the Cowles commission to systematically collect economic data at national level lent credence to supporters of the economic concept of information in the United States. As the center of the debates relocated from Europe to the United States, and particularly to Chicago in the 1950s, an extension of the concept of information to financial markets will have appeared to some as a natural next step. We have to note, though, that the centrality of the economic concept of information crystallized within debates around a particular political project—socialism—and around the superiority of a capitalist market system with competition and efficiency at its core. This is relevant with respect to the broader significance of financial noise.

The notion that stock prices incorporate information points to supposedly rational, analytical processes through which investors take decisions based on (numerical) data available to them, decisions which in their turn lead to transactions being conducted at specific prices. The assumption of rational, analytical decision-making processes serves both as a heuristic device and as a blackbox: as a heuristic device, in the sense that it guides the analysis of the linkages between various types of financial data (for instance, between company earnings and stock prices). It is at the same time a blackbox, in the sense that such analytical processes are assumed, rather than investigated in detail. This assumption blacks out the constructed character of many types of price data in financial markets, data which require various layers of processing and are not the direct outcome of transactions (e.g., closing prices).

Separately from each other, Paul Samuelson and Eugene Fama argued that the random movement of stock prices was consistent with the latter incorporating information, and therefore with market efficiency. That markets are efficient was among others a way of reformulating the notion of competition, which had plagued economics for a long time. (Why should competition be, at societal level, better than other organizational principles?[2]) In earlier drafts of his paper on efficient markets, Eugene Fama had operated with the assumption of two categories of traders, loosely modeled on the real life distinction between fundamental and technical analysts, and argued that the former are superior to the latter. Later, this changed to the notion that a majority of market actors are rational profit maximizers competing among them, and it is this competition that makes markets efficient (Delcey, 2019). If information is efficiently incorporated into stock prices, these will converge toward fundamental value (confirming thus the superiority of fundamental analysts and of traders acting on fundamental information). At the same time, information is efficiently in-corporated into prices because the majority of market actors are rational profit maximizers competing with each other—that is, racing toward obtaining information and acting on it.

In the 1970s, some financial economists realized that there were a number of issues with this account. First, one would need to spell out how specifically information is incorporated into prices. Is this a social interaction process, or is it a purely cognitive one, taking place at individual level? One could easily make the argument that nobody takes decisions in complete isolation, but bringing social interactions into the game would threaten the notions of efficiency and of profit maximizers.

Second, and at least as important, if information is costly—which it is—then it pays for some traders not to spend much effort searching for it, knowing that other traders have it. Since prices will incorporate this information in the end, traders who are not willing to spend effort (or money, or any other resources) for it will ultimately have the same information as traders who do spend resources on it. This takes away any incentive for traders to spend resources on obtaining information. In the end, transactions will stop—and markets with them. Assuming that all traders are informed means that markets will not work. Assuming that some traders are informed and some are not does not solve the problem, because the uninformed traders will observe the informed ones and will ultimately have the same information.

The idea of an information-driven, efficient system of transactions that should be a paragon of the virtues of competition becomes thus self-defeating. The solution, provided by Sanford Grossman in the mid-1970s, was to postu-late two necessary classes of market actors: informed and noise traders (Dow & Gorton, 2006: 2).[3] It goes without saying that postulating two classes of market actors is a heuristic device for avoiding the conundrums of a model of financial markets grounded in information, but which does not say much about how this information is acquired, or how social interactions might affect it. In later studies, we encounter more elaborate devices building on this, which postulate the existence of three, and not just two classes (e.g., informed, uninformed, and noise traders as in Bloomfield et al., 2009). Noise as a heuristic device though does not preclude the legitimate question, who such traders might be—and indeed financial economists have raised it repeatedly. Being a heuristic device, noise traders are not seen as a fixed social category either—which does not pre-clude the question who they might be as a social category (albeit not necessarily a fixed one). With that, noise is seen not as a transient phenomenon, but as a necessity in financial markets. Black, in his well-known presidential address to the American Finance Association from 1985, called it a structural ingredient of markets.

Let's now take a step back and consider this argumentative scaffolding in its entirety, in a broader perspective: what appears as an untestable proposition and acknowledged as untestable by its very proponents (the efficient incorporation of information into prices—e.g., Fama, 1970: 384) can also be seen as a political project of legitimation (one does not need to make too great an effort for that). After all, the integration of information into the arsenal of key economic concepts was started as part of a political project. If financial markets (as a nearly ideal market format) are efficient, then capitalism as a specific economic order must be efficient too. Financial markets had long struggled to gain legitimacy by offering audiences various rhetorical constructs—patriotism, prosperity for all, and even heroism (e.g., Fraser, 2009; Ott, 2011). The argument about financial markets as (efficient) distributors of information only added to this discursive panoply, and in a decisive way. The projection of a popular capitalism, or a capitalism for all—a projection that, perhaps, ironically, reached its apogee in the 1990s—rests, to a large extent, on the assumption that information is distributed efficiently to all market players. This is a political argument as well as an assumption allowing us to model a set of probabilistic equations.

Of course, some might argue that focusing on information being incorporated into prices leaves a lot of aspects out, aspects that might be deemed as very significant. What is more troubling, though, is that the notion of noise seems to undermine the legitimacy of financial markets in a more radical way: not only that the said markets do not distribute information efficiently, but they also necessarily require some participants to stay in the market *while* losing money. It is hard to see how the rhetoric of capitalism for all (through investments) can square with admitting noise as a structural ingredient.

Noise as a Structural Ingredient in Markets

How do we conceive thus of noise as being a structural ingredient in markets, and what are the implications? And how could the legitimacy of markets be salvaged while still accepting such an uncomfortable, yet necessary notion? I should emphasize again that, up to this point, information and noise are not treated as statistical concepts, but as schemes of thought.

Financial economists have tried at least two ways of doing this, with different, yet interrelated implications. One is to conceive noise as manifesting itself in the flow of buy and sell orders containing price and volume data—in other words, in the order book. Instead of treating the latter as fully informational, we treat it as a mix of noise and information, a mix that can be subject to statistical analysis. We should note here that this is a key aspect of the market microstructure approach (Dow & Gorton, 2006: 3), and that it allows shifting from a notion of noise as a scheme of thought to a statistical concept of noise. Yet, this approach does not tell us *why* noise is a structural ingredient—it just tells us that it is a permanent feature and that it is analyzable. Evidence of the persistence and ubiquity of noise in the order flow is not an explanatory substitute for its necessity.

The other way of looking at noise as a structural ingredient in markets is by asking the question, who are these traders? In this case, the investigation is redirected from the order flow to the market actors placing these orders. The above question, which is acknowledged by financial economists as essential, can be reformulated in several ways. Before getting to that point, however, we need to state why it is essential. It is so because we would expect lesser traders either to get informed (that is, to learn) or, in time, to be weeded out of the market. In other words, either they get better and start making money, or they keep losing money and exit the market. In either scenario, we get back to a situation where markets will have to stop, because there are no noise traders anymore.

Therefore, the question "who are these traders?" shouldn't be answered primarily in terms of their demographic profiles, but in terms of what keeps them in the market while they keep losing money. This does not mean that trading decisions cannot vary according to demographic profiles. It means framing the question either in terms of motivation or in terms of cognitive biases impacting the decision-making of noise traders. As Dow and Gorton (2006: 3) put it: "If the uninformed noise traders could at least buy the market portfolio, then they could earn the average return on the market. But, in fact they are not allowed to buy the market portfolio. That is their root problem" (Noise traders cannot buy the market portfolio because that would mean earning the average market return, whereas by definition they, as a category of market participants, lose money).

Behavioral approaches identify biases—that is, departures from idealized standards of judgment and decision-making (standards assumed by the concepts of efficient markets and of utility maximization) as an explanatory mechanism for the existence of noise trading.[4] Noise in markets is unavoidable because biases are unavoidable (this shifts the focus from noise being a structural ingredient, or a necessity, to noise being unfortunate, yet unavoidable). Biases related to attention, confidence, reaction to information, imitation, or attitudes toward loss and risk should be seen as noise generators (accounting for why prices deviate from intrinsic value) and should explain why traders persist in markets. Seen in the terms of the legitimacy project I have discussed, above, this would translate approximately along the following lines: (efficient) financial markets for all could work very well, were it not for some unfortunate cognitive deficiencies which produce anomalies and make unsuccessful traders persist in the market.

The challenges faced by behavioral explanations of this kind are as follows: (1) they apply equally to professional and to non-professional market actors. That means, even if they might differ in magnitude between professional and amateur traders, they will be encountered in both categories of actors. In this sense, everybody is more or less a noise trader (in this case, information becomes the exception, rather than the rule in markets). This would ultimately undermine confidence in a professional class of market actors, assumed to be capable of systematically identifying and acting upon information. (2) In order to avoid difficulties of this kind, behavioral finance research asserts that market actors are capable of rectifying or reducing their biases, at least up to a certain extent, through learning processes. If learning processes reduce biases, however (albeit not at the same rate), then in the end there will be no noise traders in the market. (3) The number of biases that can be directly investigated by analyses of real market transactions, and of the order flow, is relatively small. While there is a considerable body of experimental research documenting cognitive biases in economic decision-making, the number of biases documented by analyzing the order flow is smaller. This has consequences with respect to opportunities for empirically showing that it is biases that, in the long run, keep noise traders in the market and make thus the latter possible. The implication of such a stance, however, is that (financial) markets are not paragons of rationality but rather very problematic arrangements for conducting transactions (they perpetrate cognitive limitations).[5] Another implication is that, in the end, not even professional market groups are free of biases, which cannot be completely eliminated by learning.

The alternative is to examine the motivations of traders: in other words, instead of (or perhaps in addition to) assuming cognitive biases, we should look at what keeps traders in the market in spite of losses. A significant assumption financial economics operates with is that traders are in the market in order to "make money"—in other words, their motives are homogeneous,[6] even if their knowledge and skills might not be. Noise traders directly contradict this assumption, because their primary goals in trading might be other than making a profit. If this is so, it undermines both the assumption of efficiency and the assumption that the value of financial markets resides in providing and distributing capital (e.g., Goetzmann, 2016). If one's primary goal is not profit, capital is distributed efficiently—if and when it is—rather by accident than systematically. This, however, was one of the main rationales for promoting the project of an efficient capitalism from the 1930s onward. If financial markets do not systematically distribute capital efficiently and cannot provide prosperity for all, then what justifies them?

Any transactional arrangement that keeps (some) participants losing as a necessary condition of its existence appears as problematic at least. As I have argued above, ascribing losses to cognitive biases does not make things much better, because it implies that markets simply reproduce cognitive limitations, allowing at least some participants to exploit them. Neither efficiency nor knowledge are improved if this were the case.

At this point, we should stop and ask: what empirical evidence do we have that investors and traders lose money *and* stay in the market? At least with respect to individual investors[7] in North American and Western European markets, the evidence that they are not *consistently* making a profit is substantial and present in the majority of studies over decades (e.g., Linnainmaa, 2011; Mahani & Bernhardt, 2007; Seru et al., 2009). And yet they are persistent. Survival studies show that individual investors stay in the market in spite of them not making any consistent profit (Hayley & Marsh, 2016). This raises the possibility that the motivations of market actors might not be homogeneous, and that the profit motive is not the universal driver for market activities.[8] While this has been acknowledged earlier as theoretically fundamental, one of the consequences of heterogeneity is, simply put, that financial markets are also necessarily something else than (more or less efficient) allocators of capital (e.g., Dow & Gorton, 2006: 4)—and that perhaps they are primarily something else. The attempts to tackle the conceptual shortcomings of an information-based approach to finance by introducing the notion of noise actually provide an opportunity for re-conceptualizing markets from the groundup—that is, from the level of interactions.

Financial Markets as "Something Else"

To be clear, the arguments I have laid out in the previous pages are not a view merely parallel to the basic assumptions of finance theory: they are a view necessarily emerging from the attempts to tackle the conundrums of these assumptions. Ultimately, they lay bare the failure of the efficiency project—that is, of the attempt to legitimize markets on grounds of information. And we should keep in mind here that the efficiency project is inextricably tied to the popular capitalism project.

While laying bare this failure, the above arguments also open the possibility for a sociology of financial markets that does not treat social psychological factors, or market interactions as additional variables to the utility or the profit function. First, this view departs from stances such as "markets are also social institutions" (the hostile worlds view—e.g., Zelizer, 2011: 174) or "markets are embedded in social institutions" (the embeddedness view—e.g., Granovetter, 1985; Krippner & Alvarez, 2007). It avoids both the separation between economic and social features of transactions, and the treatment of social features as subordinated to the economic—that is, as factors that might impact to a certain extent the profit motive, but do not in any way challenge the primacy of the latter. Second, it opens up the avenues for an empirical research program into markets that can illuminate both the dynamics of keeping noise in the market—and therefore perpetrating the latter—and market transactions as forms of social action. I will deal now with these aspects one by one.

More often than not, persistence in the market in the face of losses has been attributed to cognitive biases that may be more pronounced among individual traders than among institutional ones (nevertheless, they are present in both). Attributing more pronounced cognitive biases to individual investors dovetails with the view (widespread among financial economists) that it is actually they, the individual investors, who are "noise." This, however, does not change the terms of the problem—quite the contrary. If we look at the variation across financial markets, we see that not all of them conform to the Western European and North American model of a dominance of institutional investors. Asian financial markets, for instance, have substantial proportions of individual investors—in some cases, they provide more than half of the equity market value (e.g., Chen, 2014: 3). This means that we encounter instances of markets where what is considered "noise" is dominant. To exaggerate—but only slightly—we have markets running on noise, and not on information.

This variation points to the fact that transactions can be organized in different ways. To what extent are these ways conducive to a longer survival in the market? In other words, instead of assuming that actors stay in the market because of their own cognitive deficiencies, we can ask to what extent different modes of market organization are conducive to different rates of survival, perpetrating thus noise. With respect to institutional traders, we know that institutional and organizational factors such as the incentive structure or performance benchmarking trigger imitative behavior, contributing thus to longer market survival even when the performance is only average or negative (e.g., Bikchandani & Sharma, 2000; Boyson, 2010; Dasgupta & Prat, 2008) (as long as a large enough group of traders have similar performances, they will survive in the market).

With respect to individual traders, we have more recently learned, among others, that the integration of social media with trading platforms changes trader behavior. Traders using social media tend to stay longer in the market (potentially accumulating losses) compared with traders who do not use social media (Tong et al., 2018). They imitate each other more, and imitation is substantially more stable over long periods of time (Gemayel & Preda, 2018a). Traders using social media also act under a scopic regime—they observe each other in real time—and therefore will use their transactions as status signals in their competitions to attract followers (Gemayel & Preda, 2018b). The empirical evidence we have points to the fact that the ways in which transactions are organized, the ways in which traders can observe each other or not, the ways in which they communicate with each other, the information they have about each other impact their survival in the market, in spite of a vast majority of them not making any consistent profits.

This questions not only the homogeneity of the profit motive as a given, but also the notion that noise is produced (almost exclusively) by inherently human psychological factors, factors which can be more or less mitigated. Noise is produced (to varying degrees) by the very organization of markets, and by the ways in which specific features allowing for interaction and communication are part and parcel of this organization. The serious doubts about the ubiquity of the profit motive—and I should emphasize here that such doubts are not formulated merely as an external critique, but emerge from the analysis of cold, hard financial data—forcefully lead one to the question: what good is it an arrangement which necessarily makes some participants lose money? Some might argue that losing is punishment for cognitive deficiencies, or the price paid for learning. However, societies do not treat markets as correctional or educational arrangements—they treat them as allocative ones.

This makes possible a turn from the allocative to the social—a social that is not just a series of variables added to the profit function. If financial markets are not, or not exclusively the allocative arrangements many have claimed them to be, what else are they then?

This turn can be translated into a series of topics that cut across the sociology of finance and behavioral finance,[9] and that can be made into more systematic research programs. These topics are significant for the way in which we conceive of financial markets as social institutions, and for a broader sociological concept of markets. Among them are the following: (1) strategic interactions and relationality, (2) reciprocal observations and their effects in markets, (3) motivational logics of trading.

First, we see strategic interactions as intrinsic to (financial) markets. However, strategic interactions do not exclude, but rather require relationality. That markets are webs of social interactions and relationships has been argued by economic sociologists for a long time. More often than not, this argument has been specified either by emphasizing the role of social networks as being constitutive of markets (e.g., White, 2002), or by highlighting how market transactions are conditioned by non-transactional social relationships (e.g., Zelizer, 2011). Both have tended to underemphasize the strategic character of market interactions, in which parties engage in moves with fateful implications for each other (Goffman, 1969: 201). Yet, such interactions do not preclude, but rather require collaborative efforts and relationships. They can require displays to third parties and can have devoted audiences, oftentimes supported by social networks. Therefore, attention to non-transactional relationships and social networks does not automatically require neglecting strategic interactions. Since these latter intrinsically require expression moves (such as deceptions), which can be seen as a source of noise, we can investigate whether and how the latter is made possible by and organized along specific social relationships.

Second, as sociologists of finance have repeatedly emphasized, the electronic format of transactions changes an apparently minor, yet key organizational feature: interactions are primarily anchored in temporal, not in physical co-presence (Knorr Cetina, 2009). This opens up for participants to reciprocally observe each other's actions (and features, such as financial performance, or trades) in real time, irrespective of whether they are physically co-located or not (e.g., Heimer & Simon, 2015). A scopic system emerges (Knorr Cetina, 2003), which might change the behavior of participants (Gemayel & Preda, 2018b). Therefore, we should investigate whether and how scopic systems contribute to noise in markets. This aspect has a broader relevance, since we know now, from several studies, that the usage of social media induces behavioral changes. We know, for instance, how it changes dating behavior or political behavior (e.g., Bail et al., 2018; Ong & Wang, 2015)—it is important against this background to investigate how it changes financial behavior.

The third topic is motivational logics. As I have argued above, the general assumption of finance scholars (including here sociologists of finance) has been that actors engaging in market transactions do it for money. For financial economists, this assumption of homogeneity of motives plays a crucial role. For sociologists of finance, it is something which should not be assumed as a given or left uninvestigated. Motivational logics can be very diverse; they can emerge out of (or be formed by) webs of social relationships and by interactions (such as strategic interactions, among others). A proper, systematic, and thorough investigation of such motivational logics in relationship to noise is very much needed.

Overall, we lack a systematic research program on noise that should investigate *both* its presence and its causes in different types of markets and under various transaction formats. To remember, the paradox of noise is not that investors lose money consistently, but that they lose money consistently *and* stay in the market. We have plenty of empirical evidence about individual investors and traders, but we have little evidence about how institutional traders and investors across various markets are noise traders too. Conceptually speaking, noise should not be limited to individual traders. Yet, we lack a systematic research program on institutional noise across types of markets, such as foreign exchange, equity, fixed income, or derivatives markets, and across types of traders.

Financial markets are varied not only with respect to the type of instruments they deal in, but also with respect to their participants and with respect to how transactions are organized. At a very fundamental level, we can talk about three kinds of variations here: in the object of transaction, in their participants, and in their organization (variations in transaction technologies could be seen as pertaining to organizational variation). A research program on noise would inherently have descriptive and comparative components, in the sense of investigating levels and characteristics of noise across market variations. This means examining close-up not only Western financial markets, where institutional traders dominate, but also markets where individual traders and investors have a substantial presence. The distinction we often encounter in financial economics, between developing and developed markets, does not fully overlap with the variations I am talking about: we encounter, for instance, fully developed, sophisticated financial markets with a substantial presence of individual investors (Japan, Hong Kong, and Taiwan are cases in point here). At a very basic, descriptive level, we should investigate the differences in noise levels between individual and institutional traders in relationships to how transactions are organized and conducted, to the technologies used, to the organization of the financial industry, or to how flows of capital are captured, among others.

Furthermore, we know very little about the causes of noise. We are still not able to provide fully convincing explanations of why noise happens, even less so when we take into account variations across markets. Without such explanations, our understanding of financial markets will remain limited. Until now, the causes of noise have been grouped under two rubrics: cognitive biases and organizational factors, such as the incentive structure in the mutual fund industry. Yet, the cognitive bias explanation works only against the assumption of a perfectly rational model of decision-making, and accounts for why market actors lose money, not necessarily for why they lose *and* stay in the market—which is the real noise problem. Moreover, learning processes in trading—perhaps one of the most intensely investigated topics in behavioral finance over the past years—may reduce, but not eliminate losses (e.g., Hayley & Marsh, 2016).

Organizational factors, including here technology, have not been investigated systematically either. We know little about how the dynamics of professional careers in markets relate to noise; how the technological dynamics of markets impact noise (although there are strong indications that it does); how status seeking processes and status inequalities relate to noise.[10] All these are sociological topics awaiting investigation.

One additional aspect, highly relevant to such a research program, is as follows: if we accept that markets run on noise, then it becomes critical that capital flows are continuously channeled into them. We should not assume this process to be either automatic or self-evident. Capturing capital flows implies effort; it implies active searches for money that can be made into capital; and it implies a process of capture, in the sense of creating commitments—as in committing this money to a particular form of capital, namely trading capital. Yet, we know very little about the concrete, practical transformations of money into capital, even if they seem to be essential for markets running on noise.

More often than not, (behavioral) economists have approached such transformations from the perspective of choice-making, as intrinsic to decisions: how do investors decide whether to invest savings in, say, real estate versus equities? What biases make their decisions less than optimal, and what nudges do they need in order to go in the right direction?

If such an approach were to be centered on maximizing the utility of one choice versus the other, it would neglect not only the whole series of necessary transformations making such choices possible (money would have to be moved from the category of savings into that of investment), but also the fact that choices themselves do not take place in a void: decision-makers do not merely face alternatives passively put before them by disinterested third parties, but active attempts to capture capital. Such attempts can include appeals to self-determination and agentic powers, but also promises of future returns, or representations of financial transactions as fun and entertaining. They can also include harnessing personal relationships and social networks in the process of transforming savings into capital and then capturing parts of this as financial capital. We know little about these processes, and we know little about the ways in which they shape not only decisions to invest in markets, but also decisions within markets.

Recent sociological investigations have emphasized that transforming money into capital is a complex social process irreducible to any given number of biases and nudges. Various groups and institutions intervene in this process, a crucial aspect of which is impression management (e.g., Arjaliès et al., 2017). Mobilizing capital flows requires that such groups (e.g., fund managers, analysts, strategists) interact constantly with relevant audiences, putting a (needless to say, attractive) face to financial decision-making: work in financial markets is always facework too (Goffman, 1967). In a certain sense, this dovetails with the historical argument about the rhetorical force of "popular capitalism" through investing, a force which, at its roots, is intimately related to the political project of legitimizing financial markets through efficiency. We need, however, more detailed, fine-grained investigations of how this facework is performed, and how capital groups target, establish relationships with, and capture specific audiences. This, too, is part of the noise project.

This leaves one final question open: to what extent, and how, does a research program focused on noise contribute to a sociological understanding of financial markets, and especially to one focused on the interaction order of markets? To what extent can we build a sociological concept of financial markets that is not limited to seeing them as (admittedly inefficient) allocation mechanisms, or as institutional framings that constrain action? If we are to admit the study of the interaction order as intrinsic to the sociological enterprise, and if we are to admit that studying market transactions can bring insights into the properties and dynamics of this order, then we should not avoid concepts such as action and agency in the study of decision-making and of transactions. We should also not avoid investigating the multi-layered character of agency, together with the organizational conditions under which such layers are reshuffled and agency can become problematic.

This may sound all too abstract, but let me give here two tentative examples of how this can be pursued further. The first example is that of cryptocurrency markets: here, institutional constraints are low, in the sense that regulation and legal definitions of cryptocurrencies as financial instruments are emerging only now. Definitions of cryptocurrencies are not clear-cut, and they are contradictory: are cryptos more like equities, or more like currencies, or more like derivative instruments? In practice, cryptocurrencies are subject to hybrid uses, in the sense that they are being used for payments in physical and online locations, but also traded in ways similar to financial assets. Constraints are low also in the sense that decision-making by traditional financial institutions, such as central banks announcements, seems to have little impact on trading decisions in cryptocurrency markets. At the same time, technological constraints are high, in the sense that market transactions depend on rules, protocols, and languages specific to a technological ecosystem. These rules, protocols, and languages shape possibilities for action, without eliminating the agency of market participants, and without eliminating strategic interactions, including here possibilities of deceit. They shape the identities of market actors too, as well as the procedures through which such identities are reciprocally acknowledged, and mutual obligations brought into relationships to such acknowledgments. Given this, we can study the conditions under which a specific organization of strategic interactions might keep participants in transactions while consistent monetary rewards are absent. In other words, we can investigate how specific interaction ecosystems bind participants to them in spite of exit possibilities at any given time. A relatively close analogy would be that with the situation depicted in Louis Buñuel's 1962 film *The Exterminating Angel*, where participants in a set of dinner interactions which turn oppressive do not leave, even if they do not enjoy the dinner interactions, and even if they are free to do so at any time.

The second example concerns agency in market interactions. Sociologically speaking, agency has been defined as the willingness to take problematic and consequential courses of action (Goffman, 1967). In relationship to market transactions, this willingness has been understood as being driven by what economists call utility maximization. In its turn, utility has been understood in terms of one's wealth—that is, in monetary terms (Burton & Shah, 2013). Simply put, players engage in market transactions in order to maximize their wealth but, being risk averse, they would prefer certain over uncertain returns. It is only because returns on risk-free assets are too low that they engage in transactions with an uncertain outcome, or in combinations of investments with varying degrees of risk. A crucial difference between the sociological definition of action and the economic understanding of the same (making a choice is intrinsic to action) is that this latter sees utility, and especially monetary utility, as coextensive with "willingness to engage." This reduces agency to the pursuit of utility maximization, whereas in the sociological understanding this willingness is neither reduced to utilitarian motives nor reduced to a prior motivation (i.e., prior to the interaction). Increasingly, behavioral economists and finance scholars have come to acknowledge that, in financial markets, there can be more than just one utility (e.g., Konana & Balasubramanian, 2005). But willingness to take problematic and consequential chances shouldn't be reduced to a motivation acquired prior to the act of taking chances. It can as well be something that crystallizes first in this act. We might want to investigate then willingness rather than a priori motivations, and see whether and how such willingness, when co-evolving with interactions, keeps participants in action, in spite of them not deriving any consistent monetary gains from transactions. This is a point similar with the one made in the previous example: investigating how specific, costly interaction formats keep participants in, and not against their will, but because such interactions co-generate willingness.

The examples I have given above take various kinds of financial markets and transactions, as occasions for investigating the properties of the interaction order, and as conceptualizing markets as types of interaction formats. While departing from the understanding of markets as efficient allocation mechanisms (a view behavioral economists increasingly repudiate), such a conceptualization opens the way for a dialogue with behavioral finance, both in the sense of incorporating insights from the latter and of addressing behavioral puzzles with sociological means.

Conclusion

More often than not, the sociology of financial markets has sought to develop research programs in contradistinction to approaches coming from financial economics or from behavioral finance. This explains why concepts seen as central in the latter play no role or only a minor one in sociological approaches. The arguments I have laid above follow a different route, in that they stay close to concepts from financial economics and to the empirical puzzles associated with them. This makes possible formulating a sociological research program not as an alternative to, but as something necessarily arising from the empirical puzzles of finance.

This does not mean that such a program is not critical—quite the contrary. It fully acknowledges that the conceptualization of financial markets around information is intimately linked to a political project with broader implications. It does not accept uncritically and unconditionally the legitimacy of this project. It does not take concepts from financial economics as self-evident—it takes them as occasions for sociological investigations. However, instead of an external critique—one which would ignore, brush aside, or simply reject the empirical puzzles of finance, it takes them as a starting point and occasion for developing an internalist, bottom-up critical approach—that is, one grounded in the study of market interactions.

In this perspective, noise, which at best has been neglected in the sociology of markets, acquires a completely different significance. It makes us address empirical, puzzling discoveries—why do traders lose money and stay in the market?—and, at the same time, it opens up ways of rethinking (financial) markets as something else than allocation mechanisms or systems of transactions. What this "something else" is remains to be discovered through empirical investigations. In other words, a research program on noise should be unashamedly empirical and discovery-oriented.

This empirical orientation goes hand in hand with the program's emphasis on variation in markets. It acknowledges the inherent limits of privileging what I would call here the "Western model" of financial markets, characterized by the dominance of institutional actors, a model that is the result of particular historical evolutions. As I have argued above, we came to see more and more than not all developed financial markets follow this model. Significant, global marketplaces seem to run on noise, in the sense of a substantial participation of non-institutional actors. At the same time, new marketplaces emerge, in fashions that do not entirely fit institutional understandings—markets in cryptocurrencies are a case in point. A sociology of global finance will have to acknowledge such variations and take them as the starting point when embarking on a program of empirical discoveries.

Notes

1 For "noise" in cultural history, see Attali (1985); for the history of music, see Ross (2009); for literary fiction, see DeLillo (1985); for political science, see Silver (2013).
2 In the nineteenth century, before the advent of neoclassical economics that inaugurated a formal treatment of price equilibrium and a heuristic understanding of the notion of competition, political economists had difficulties in conceptualizing the latter: if competition was akin with haggling in town markets, then why didn't it lead to price convergence—that is, to equilibrium (Dennis, 1975: 180, 186; Stigler, 1957)? Competition was seen as a key organizational principle for economic

transactions, and, increasingly, as a general organizational principle for society. Empirical observations of market competition were, however, noisy, in the sense that they didn't support such a principle.

3   The relationship between noise in markets and competition is unclear: does noise foster competition or not? The search for information in markets is understood as a competitive one. Yet, the existence of noise traders, which is a necessity if markets are to work, introduces disincentives to compete (e.g., Dridi & Germain, 2009), as well as distortions, since noise traders do not interpret information rationally (e.g., Cipriani & Guarino, 2005). At the same time, the notion of competition, similarly with that of noise traders, is a heuristic device for modeling price equilibrium and is not understood as a particular interaction format, as a particular set of institutions, or as a particular form of irrationality.

4   Some behavioral approaches focus explicitly on the existence of noise traders as the main conceptual challenge requiring an empirical analysis of judgmental imperfections, with regard to the model of perfect cognition (e.g., Burton & Shah, 2013; Hirshleifer, 2015). At the same time, behavioral economists try to explain how deviations from perfect cognition—that is, biases—can lead traders to make profits and thus survive in the market (e.g., Hirshleifer & Luo, 2001).

5   The existence of cognitive limitations undermines the view of markets as (superior) discovery mechanisms for unexploited opportunities and for innovating discovery procedures (e.g., Hayek, 2002: 18–19).

6   Homogeneity of motives is one of the key assumptions of rationality in financial markets: traders, irrespective of their degree of skill and information, are driven by the same profit motives. This assumption is maintained even under the premise of heterogeneous expectations among traders, caused by asymmetric or incomplete information (e.g., Biais et al., 2010; Grundy & Kim, 2002; Patton & Timmerman, 2010). It is the dominant, if not the exclusive presence of the profit motive that makes markets what they are, namely efficient allocators of capital (e.g., Brine & Poovey, 2017: 314; Goetzmann, 2016: 480). However, if the traders' motivations are heterogeneous—that is, pertaining to drivers other than profit—then an information-based account of markets becomes problematic indeed.

7   I should emphasize here that while individual investors are regularly associated with noise, the latter is not exclusively associated with individual investors. Fund managers can be noise traders as well (e.g., Hughen & McDonald, 2005). In behavioral terms, individual traders are understood as having less skills and more cognitive biases than institutional traders. But if noise traders can be both individual and institutional actors, the assumption of a gap in cognitive biases along the lines of individual versus institutional actors becomes problematic.

8   Note here that this profit motive can be expressed either as "I want money" or as "I need money." The difference is that the latter expression opens the way for postulating the existence of occasional traders, who are assumed to be uninformed or less informed because they do not act constantly. Nevertheless, this does not mean that such traders will be driven out of the market by their failure to obtain the money they need.

9   It is to be noted here that behavioral finance has started recently moving away from the study of cognitive biases to that of social interactions and their impact on decision-making in markets, a move that has been called "social finance" (Hirshleifer, 2015). Irrespective of whether one wants to see this as a step towards partial integration or not, or as a sign of the sociology of finance being heard, there are topics of investigations that speak to both disciplines.

10 It is relevant here that a good number of empirical studies have addressed the opposite of noise, namely whether it is possible to make money and stay in the market.

Usually, these studies focus on "alpha"—that is, on whether we can identify fund managers or traders who consistently make money (e.g., Levich & Pojarliev, 2012). Some of these studies have tried to compare "alpha" in financial markets with "alpha" in private equity (e.g., Buchner, 2014; Fan et al., 2013): their implication is that markets are not necessarily the most efficient way of allocating capital. Of course, we can view the finance studies on alpha both as symptomatic for a culture of status seeking in markets and as symptomatic for the skepticism about financial markets as being driven by information. Either way, the search for alpha can be seen as mirroring the problem of noise in markets.

References

Arjaliès, D.-L. et al. (2017). *Chains of Finance. How Investment Management Is Shaped.* Oxford: Oxford University Press.

Attali, J. (1985). *Noise: The Political Economy of Music.* Minneapolis: University of Minnesota Press.

Bail, C. A., Argyle, L., Brown, T., Bumpus, J., Chen, H., Hunzaker, M. F., & Volfovsky, A. (2018). "Exposure to opposing views can increase political polarization: Evidence from a large-scale field experiment on social media." doi: 10.31235/osf.io/4ygux.

Biais, B., Bossaerts, P., & Spatt, C. (2010). "Equilibrium asset pricing and portfolio choice under asymmetric information," *Review of Financial Studies* 23(4): 1503–1543.

Bikchandani, S., & Sharma, S. (2000). "Herd behavior in financial markets," *IMF Staff Papers* 47(3): 279–310.

Bloomfield, R., O'Hara, M., & Saar, G. (2009). "How noise trading affects markets. An experimental analysis," *Review of Financial Studies* 6(1): 2275–2302.

Boyson, N. M. (2010). "Implicit incentives and reputational herding by hedge fund managers," *Journal of Empirical Finance* 17(3): 283–299.

Brine, K. R., & Poovey, M. (2017). *Finance in America: An Unfinished Story.* Chicago, IL: The University of Chicago Press.

Buchner, A. (2014). *The Alpha and Beta of Private Equity Investments.* Working paper. University of Passau.

Burton, E., & Shah, S. (2013). *Behavioral Finance: Understanding the Social, Cognitive, and Economic Debates.* New York, NY: Wiley.

Chen, Y.-H. (2014). *Stock Trading and Daily Life: Lay Stock Investors in Taiwan.* PhD Thesis, University of Edinburgh.

Cipriani, M., & Guarino, A. (2005). "Noise trading in a laboratory financial market. A maximum likelihood approach," *Journal of the European Economic Association* 3(2–3): 315–321.

Dasgupta, A., & Prat, A. (2008). "Information aggregation in financial markets with career concerns," *Journal of Economic Theory* 143(1): 83–113.

Delcey, T. (2019). "Samuelson vs. Fama on the efficient market hypothesis. The point of view of expertise," *Oeconomia* 9(1): 37–58.

DeLillo, D. (1985). *White Noise.* New York, NY: Viking.

Dennis, K. (1975). *"Competition" in Economic Thought.* PhD thesis, St. John's College, Oxford.

Dow, J., & Gorton, G. (2006). *Noise Traders.* NBER. Working paper 12256.

Dridi, R., & Germain, L. (2009). "Noise and competition in strategic oligopoly," *Journal of Financial Intermediation* 18(2): 311–327.

Fama, E. (1970). "Efficient capital markets: A review of theory and empirical work," *Journal of Finance* 25(2): 383–417.

Fan, F. J., Fleming, G., & Warren, G. (2013). "The alpha, beta, and consistency of private equity reported returns," *The Journal of Private Equity* 16(4). 21–30.

Fraser, S. (2009). *Wall Street. America's Dream Palace.* New Haven, CT: Yale University Press.

Gemayel, R., & Preda, A. (2018a). "Does a scopic regime produce conformism? Herding behavior among trade leaders on social trading platforms," *European Journal of Finance* 24(14): 1144–1175.

Gemayel, R., & Preda, A. (2018b). "Does a scopic regime erode the disposition effect? Evidence from a social trading platform," *Journal of Economic Behavior and Organization* 154: 175–190.

Goetzmann, W. N. (2016). *Money Changes Everything. How Finance Made Civilization Possible.* Princeton, NJ: Princeton University Press.

Goffman, E. (1967). *The Interaction Ritual: Essays on Face-To-Face Behavior.* New York, NY: Pantheon.

Goffman, E. (1969). *Strategic Interaction.* Philadelphia, PA: University of Pennsylvania Press.

Granovetter, M. (1985). "Economic action and social structure: The problem of embeddedness," *American Journal of Sociology* 91(3): 481–510.

Grundy, B. D., & Kim, Y. (2002). "Stock market volatility in a heterogeneous information economy," *Journal of Financial and Quantitative Analysis* 37(1): 1–27.

Hayek, F. A. (2002). "Competition as a discovery procedure," *Quarterly Journal of Austrian Economics* 5(3): 9–23.

Hayley, S., & Marsh, I. (2016). "What do fx retail traders learn?," *Journal of International Money and Finance* 64: 16–38.

Heimer, R., & Simon, D. (2015). *Facebook Finance: How Social Interaction Propagates Active Investing.* Working Paper. Federal Reserve Bank of Cleveland. Retrieved from https://ssrn.com/abstract=2021935.

Hirshleifer, D. (2015). "Behavioral finance," *Annual Review of Financial Economics* 7: 133–159.

Hirshleifer, D., & Luo, G. Y. (2001). "On the survival of overconfident traders in a competitive securities market," *Journal of Financial Markets* 4(1): 73–84.

Hughen, J. C., & McDonald, C. (2005). "Who are the noise traders?," *Journal of Financial Research* 28(2): 281–298.

Knorr Cetina, K. (2003). "From pipes to scopes: The flow architecture of financial markets," *Distinktion* 7: 7–30.

Knorr Cetina, K. (2009). "The synthetic interaction: Interactionism for a global world," *Symbolic Interaction* 31(2): 61–87.

Konana, P., & Balasubramanian, S. (2005). "The socio-economic-psychological model of technology adoption and usage. An application to online investing," *Decision Support Systems* 39: 505–524.

Krippner, G., & Alvarez, A. (2007). "Embeddedness and the intellectual projects of economic sociology," *Annual Review of Sociology* 33: 219–240.

Levich, R. M., & Pojarliev, M. (2012). "Active currency management Part II. Is there skill or alpha in currency investing?," in J. James, I. Marsh, and L. Sarno (eds.), *Handbook of Exchange Rates* (pp. 471–501). New York, NY: Wiley.

Linnainmaa, J. T. (2011). "Why do (some) households trade so much?," *The Review of Financial Studies* 24(5): 1630–1666.

Macy, M., & Tsvetkova, M. (2015). "The signal importance of noise," *Sociological Methods and Research* 44(2): 306–328.

Mahani, R., & Bernhardt, D. (2007). "Financial speculators' underperformance. Learning, self-selection and endogenous liquidity," *Journal of Finance* 62(3): 1313–1340.

Malaspina, C. (2018). *An Epistemology of Noise.* London: Bloomsbury.

Patton, A. J., & Timmerman, A. (2010). "Why do forecasters disagree? Lessons from the term structure of cross-sectional dispersion," *Journal of Monetary Economics* 57(7): 803–820.

Mirowski, P., & Nik-khah, E. (2017). *The Knowledge We Have Lost in Information: The History of Economics in Modern Information.* Oxford and New York, NY: Oxford University Press.

Ong, D., & Wang, J. (2015). "Income attraction: An online dating field experiment," *Journal of Economic Behavior & Organization* 111: 13–22.

Ott, J. (2011). *When Wall Street Met Main Street: The Quest for an Investor Democracy.* Cambridge, MA: Harvard University Press.

Preda, A. (2017). "The sciences of finance, their boundaries, their values," in E. Ippoliti and P. Chen (eds.), *Methods and Finance: A Unifying View on Finance, Mathematics and Philosophy* (pp. 151–168). Berlin: Springer.

Ross, A. (2009). *The Rest Is Noise: Listening to the Twentieth Century.* New York, NY: Harper.

Seru, A., Shumway, T., & Stoffman, N. (2009). "Learning by trading," *The Review of Financial Studies* 23(2): 705–739.

Silver, N. (2013). *The Signal and the Noise: The Art and Science of Prediction.* New York, NY: Penguin.

Stigler, G. (1957). "Perfect competition, historically contemplated," *Journal of Political Economy* 65(1): 1–17.

Tong, X., Preda, A., & McFaull, A. (2018). *The Cost of Sociability: Why Do Sociable Investors Persist in the Market While Making Losses?* Working paper. King's College London.

White, H. (2002). *Markets from Networks: Socioeconomic Models of Production.* Princeton, NJ: Princeton University Press.

Zelizer, V. (2011). *Economic Lives: How Culture Shapes the Economy.* Princeton, NJ: Princeton University Press.

5

RISK AND ARBITRAGE

Carolyn Hardin and Adam Richard Rottinghaus

Introduction

Risk is a deceptively tricky concept in finance. On the one hand, the smooth functioning of everything from consumer credit cards to international currency markets depends on the measurement and modeling of risk. On the other hand, risk is a supposed quantification of uncertain future possibilities. The tension between uncertainty and the need for actionable, meaningful, and tangible—in a word, objective—assessments of uncertainty defines risk in contemporary financial practices. In the traditional sense, risk is the potential deviation from expected rates of investment return. Investors need some idea of what that deviation might be in order to make rational investment decisions. As one textbook explains:

> Naturally, if all else could be held equal, investors would prefer investments with the highest expected return. However, the no-free-lunch rule tells us that all else cannot be held equal. If you want higher expected returns, you will have to pay a price in terms of accepting higher investment risk. (Bodie et al., 2008: 10)

Exactly what that price should be can only be known if risk can be measured.

Yet, despite financial practitioners best efforts to measure, manage, and profit from uncertain possibilities, time and again events escape "objective" risk modeling parameters, leading to the so-called "market failures" and financial crises.[1] The objectivity of risk is not based on the reliability of measuring it, but rather on assumptions stemming from 70 years of increasing quantification in financial theory and practice. In what follows, we tell that history, challenge the objectivity of risk, and explain different approaches to analyzing the effects of its objectification.

The other subject of this chapter, arbitrage, is a similarly problematic term. The standard definition of arbitrage is the buying and selling of equivalent, but mispriced, securities. One business school textbook describes arbitrage as:

> simultaneously buying the asset where it is cheap and selling it where it is expensive. In the process, [arbitrageurs] will bid up the price where it is low and force it down where it is high until the arbitrage opportunity is eliminated. (Bodie et al., 2008: 325)

From this perspective, price discrepancies are a market inefficiency and arbitrage increases market efficiency by bringing prices into parity.

However, as we demonstrate below, arbitrage is not a benevolent public service provided by financial traders to make markets efficient, but a structuring principle of financial profit making. An 1892 article in the *New York Times* declared, "it is alleged that probably three-fourths of all the business done at the Exchange is transacted through arbitrage houses" (1892). In 2014, Mark Blyth, a professor of political economy at Brown University, quoted an eerily similar statistic to a reporter:

> A funny thing about these very big banks… they make 70% of their profits through trading, basically swapping bits of paper with each other for arbitrage gains, none of which arguably adds to anything except global liquidity and doesn't really do much for real investment. (Woolf, 2014)

Despite more than a century of technological change, geopolitical reorganization, and expanding scope of financial influence across social and cultural life, arbitrage has consistently accounted for more than two-thirds of financial profit making! Such a startling continuity should force financial theory to come to terms with the fact that arbitrage is not the result of momentary errors in market efficiency. Arbitrage is a standard profit making practice in finance today, which—it turns out—depends upon precisely the taken-for-granted quantification of risk.

Borch notes in the introduction to this *Handbook* that a key aim of critical finance theory is to challenge accepted narratives, rather than analyze financial practices on the terms practitioners or economists set. He writes:

> The broader analytical task that emerges from this is the need to critically engage the various discursive elements of contemporary finance (be it "liquidity," "volatility," "speculation," "risk," "noise," or something else […]) that circulate as guiding concepts and (whose function and definitions) may be taken more or less for granted—without their genealogies and practical effects being fully understood. (2020: 13)

This chapter pushes critical finance scholars to rethink and retheorize risk and arbitrage. When one assumes that risk is objective or that arbitrage brings prices into parity and eliminates inefficiency, it is easy to miss the mechanisms of profit and functions of power constituted through these financial practices. By interrogating these taken-for-granted premises at the core of finance, critical finance studies can produce knowledge necessary to reshape the understanding *and* practice of finance.

We begin by tracing the current financial economic understanding of arbitrage in relation to the "Law of One Price." We then offer a brief genealogy of risk in financial and critical theory. We conclude with a case study on credit default swaps (CDS) before the financial crisis in order to demonstrate the limitations of treating risk as an object and arbitrage as a guarantor of efficiency. In doing so, we aim to open new space for critical finance theorists to analyze risk and arbitrage without the taken-for-granted assumptions about what risk is or what arbitrage does.

The Law of One Price

There is only one "law" given in finance textbooks—the Law of One Price— also called the "fundamental theorem of financial economics." The Law states, "if two assets are equivalent in all economically relevant respects, then they should have the same market prices" (Bodie et al., 2008: 325). In other words, securities that have the same risk profile and expected return are equivalent in all economically relevant aspects and must therefore have the same prices. This may seem self-evident, but of course similar or even the same goods trade at different prices in different markets for any number of contextual reasons. More obvious examples of this are evident in the consumer context, such as buying a Coke at the grocery store versus buying one at Disneyland. But in financial markets, the Law of One Price characterizes such a disparity as a "mispricing," or an error in efficiency that must be corrected for markets to properly function. What's more, a good deal of financial labor is expended developing and applying models to determine security equivalence. Beunza, Hardie, and MacKenzie explain that "the 'similarity' of financial assets is always in a sense theory-dependent" (2006: 24). According to the Law of One Price, such efforts would then reveal securities that should have the same price, but currently do not.

The fact that such "mispricings" both exist and must be revealed by the "theory-dependent" labor of financial analysts makes clear that the Law of One Price does not always, or even frequently, hold. The Law of One Price is not a law in the scientific sense, i.e., a fact of nature that has been confirmed by repeated observation. Instead, it is more like the juridical laws of nation-states. It requires enforcement. As textbooks explain the logic, when traders notice a mispricing, they are quick to buy the cheap asset and short the expensive one.[2] Traders will undertake this deal because it nets a profit from the difference between the disparate prices. A further assumption is that with enough time and trade volume, the forces of supply and demand will raise the price of the cheap asset that traders want to buy, and lower the price of the expensive asset that traders prefer to sell. Eventually, this will bring the prices of these economically equivalent assets together at a point of parity, i.e., the "one price" of the Law of One Price. Arbitrage is the financial practice of buying and selling equivalent assets with unequal prices.

There are two main forms of arbitrage: buying and selling the *same* good and buying and selling *equivalent* goods. The former is epitomized in high-frequency trading, in which traders use advantages of speed gained through proprietary fiber-optic lines, microwave networks, or even lasers to buy stocks they believe will soon rise in price and then sell them back for a tidy profit. The trading takes place over extremely small intervals in time and can involve buy first or sell first strategies depending on the direction of anticipated price fluctuations. Firms expend considerable resources to be able to trade faster than other firms because this kind of arbitrage provides enormous profit opportunities—though these opportunities are eliminated as other firms catch up (Hardin & Rottinghaus, 2015; see also the chapter by Lange in this *Handbook*).

The buying and selling of equivalent goods is a bit more interesting, in that it is more thoroughly "theory-dependent" (Beunza et al., 2006). Complex risk and return models establish comparative baselines for asset equivalency. The best example of this form of arbitrage involves "call options"—contracts that grant the buyer an option to buy a set number of stocks at or before an expiration date (see also the chapter by Lee in this *Handbook*). According to the Black-Scholes-Merton (BSM) options pricing formula, the price of a call option can be replicated by borrowing at the risk-free rate of interest and buying a precise portion of the underlying stock. This "replicating portfolio" must then have the same price as the call option (Hull, 2011). If it does not, investors could buy the replicating portfolio and sell call options, netting a profit.

The proof of the Law of One Price is not the consistent adherence of prices to the principle, but the ways in which traders enforce it precisely when it does not hold. As one textbook puts it, "The Law of One Price is enforced by arbitrageurs: if they observe violation of the law, they will engage in arbitrage activity [...] until the arbitrage opportunity is eliminated" (Bodie et al., 2008: 325). The arbitrage opportunity is eliminated when the excess supply of the expensive asset and the excess demand for the cheap asset force their prices to converge. The history of options markets bears out this point. Before the introduction of the BSM formula, options did not have consistent prices. After its introduction, arbitrageurs did precisely the arbitrage explained above, bringing the price of the options and their replicating portfolios into parity (MacKenzie, 2006).

Arbitrage is therefore framed as something of a public service, and arbitrageurs as friendly police officers. When prices get out of whack, benevolent traders show up and police them back into parity, assuring that all traders pay the same price for economically equivalent assets. In fact, arbitrageurs deploy exactly this argument in practice. Hirokazu Miyazaki writes that when index arbitrage came under scrutiny as a possible cause of the 1990 stock crash in

Japan, "Sekai arbitrageurs [...] asserted that arbitrage performed the important economic function of linking the cash and futures markets so that investors might use the futures markets for hedging" (Miyazaki, 2007: 404).[3] Without arbitrageurs enforcing the sole law of finance, even hedging one's investments would be impossible. Thank goodness for their sacrifice!

Arbitrage is, in this interpretation, the mechanism which theoretically ensures that markets fully reflect all available information, i.e., are efficient (Fama, 1970). This interpretation of arbitrage is not only espoused in financial economics and by arbitrageurs themselves, but is also replicated in social scientific work on the subject. In the first decade of the 2000s, social studies of finance (SSF) came to focus emphatically on arbitrage as an object of study. The opening movement of this era was Donald MacKenzie's (2003) study of arbitrage trading at Long-Term Capital Management (LTCM). MacKenzie focuses on the "performative" aspect of arbitrage—on the supply and demand mechanism of buying low and selling high that should push disparate prices towards one another. Mackenzie defends the dominant interpretation of arbitrage in his analysis of LTCM, which lost more than $2 billion in 1998 because its trades failed to make prices converge. He claims that the arbitrage trade would have worked except that social problems—specifically a "flight to quality" triggered by the Russian debt default and imitation by other traders—intervened (MacKenzie, 2003: 352). MacKenzie explains that LTCM's arbitrage trades were meant to converge over time, but that the default triggered investors to buy Treasury bonds (the "flight to quality") which made LTCM's arbitrage positions diverge instead. In addition, the widening spreads caused other firms who had imitated LTCM's trades to panic and liquidate their positions, widening spreads even more. MacKenzie claims that if LTCM had maintained their positions long enough—and other investors and regulators had acted rationally—the two legs of the trade would have converged and LTCM would have made a profit. What prevented this efficient process was "'social' risks from patterns of interaction within the financial markets, rather than shocks from the 'real economy' or from events" (MacKenzie, 2003: 373). He therefore takes the economic definition of arbitrage for granted and only qualifies it by suggesting that sociological processes may sometimes interfere.

Ian Hardie more straightforwardly defends "the place of arbitrage within efficient markets theory" (Hardie, 2004: 244). He even goes so far as to reject MacKenzie's and other sociologists' use of the term arbitrage because they include trades that do not strictly conform to the arbitrage conditions outlined in economic textbooks. In 2006, Daniel Beunza collaborated with MacKenzie and Hardie to advance a new project for economic sociology, which they term "material sociology of arbitrage." In setting up the project, they claimed that "arbitrage constitutes markets" by bringing prices in different markets into parity at a "world price" (Beunza et al., 2006: 722–723). In sum, they characterize arbitrage as a benevolent financial practice that polices prices in accordance with the Law of One Price.

What is left unexamined by this interpretation of arbitrage is the stakes of the trade for those who undertake it—profit. In standard definitions of arbitrage, the only mention of profit is in reference to the theoretical condition that arbitrage is only actually arbitrage if it produces "riskless profit" (Billingsly, 2006). The condition of risklessness relies upon the financial notion that risk is the necessary correlate of return. Profit is measured as the return available on an investment or the increase in the value of a position. Risk is the probability that a given position will pay off, or not, and is thus a measure of potential variability in expected return. High-risk investments must promise higher returns to "compensate" investors for the possibility that no return will be captured at all. In other words, risk and return should be positively correlated according to financial economics. It appears as common sense that people who are willing to take on more risk would only do so if there is a potentially greater reward on the other side. No guts, no glory.

Arbitrage is the exception to this rule in that it offers a profit based not on risk-taking, but simply on finding an error in efficiency—a mispricing of two equivalent assets that the market has accidentally allowed to exist. So, while the correlation of risk and return is a basic underlying principle of finance, arbitrage is the exception that proves the rule. It provides riskless profit because it shouldn't exist at all. In finance theory, arbitrage only ever exists due to a sort of glitch in the matrix, a momentary error in market efficiency that must— and will—be immediately corrected by traders. However, history shows that arbitrage is not a fleeting, marginal aspect to financial trading, but the central form of financial profit making that firms pay dearly to engage in (Hardin & Rottinghaus, 2015). In short, arbitrage is not occasionally found and exploited, but invested in and nurtured. The dominant narrative of arbitrage is, then, at best a partial tale. Therefore, understanding how arbitrage is made possible becomes an important question for critical investigations of finance. Arbitrage of equivalent securities depends on identifying securities that have equivalent risks and returns; therefore, risk must necessarily be an objectively measurable feature of securities for arbitrage to be possible. In other words, arbitrage depends on risk being a knowable, objective fact. Risk's existence as such has an important historical origin story, to which we now turn.

A Brief Geneology of Financial Risk

If risk is the probability that actual return will deviate from expectations, then attempting to adequately measure it is a slippery practice. The mathematical notion of probability was built on models of pure chance, like the toss of a coin, or drawing a particular number out of a sequence (Bernstein, 1996). But measuring financial risk means measuring the future probability of human behavior, as it is human decisions that, in the aggregate, produce fluctuations in financial asset prices. As centuries of financial bubbles and crises have taught us, this kind of prediction is much trickier. And in fact, the history of the concept of risk within finance shows that it is only very recently, and due to some very dubious human decisions, that we have come to see financial risk as measurable at all.

Prior to the late 1950s, the academic discipline of finance taught a "mix of common sense, judgment, and tradition that had strikingly little to do with economics" (Fox, 2009: 78). During this time, analysts evaluated the risk of firms, but in a qualitative and broad manner. Further, the idea that risk could be attenuated through diversification (holding a group of different stocks rather than just one) was acknowledged in investment guides but not explicitly modeled or calculated.[4] The seismic shift towards mathematization in finance mid-century utterly transformed the notion of risk within financial theory. In their ground-breaking book, *Theory of Games and Economic Behavior* (1944), John von Neumann and Oskar Morgenstern produced a set of rules that showed that individuals will make choices by maximizing the utility they expect to receive from a given gamble. This notion of "expected utility" produced the first formal mathematical explanation of the concept of risk. For von Neumann and Morgenstern, risk was the *subjective* probabilities individuals assign to potential outcomes. Individuals' expected utility was modulated by their attitude toward risk, not by an objective measurement of it.

Harry Markowitz extended this notion of expected utility to investment decisions in his 1955 PhD dissertation. Markowitz decided to use historical figures to estimate both expected return and risk. For the former, he used the historical mean of a stock's return. For the latter, he defined those formerly subjective probabilities (or "risk") as the historical variance of the stock's price. Markowitz used these assumptions to produce what might be considered the first financial economic theory of how to select an "efficient" portfolio of stocks. Markowitz claimed that an optimal portfolio could be constructed knowing only the expected return (mean) and risk (variance) of each security available for selection. With this information, portfolios could be calculated to offer the best return for any given level of risk (Rubenstein, 2006).

Instead of assessing any number of possible indications of the risks a company faced, or investors' subjective attitudes towards risk, Markowitz's approach meant one could simply analyze the historical record of a stock's price. Assuming that the past performance alone could be an adequate measure to produce an optimal portfolio is remarkably unrealistic. Yet, it was necessary for transforming a seemingly incalculable multiplicity of subjective, individual investor judgments into fixed mathematical and statistical results. It is important to note the dramatic slippage that occurred between von Neumann and Morgenstern's original subjective probabilities and the now "objective" and measurable variance of past stock performance. That slippage between subjective probabilities and rigorous mathematical formulae "objectively" measuring stock variance set the concept of risk on a path to becoming both fundamental to financial economics and utterly taken-for-granted.

The objectified form of risk pioneered in Markowitz's portfolio selection was further enshrined in mathematical finance through the Capital Assets Pricing

Model (CAPM). Developed in the mid-1960s, the CAPM is "the centerpiece of modern financial economics" (MacKenzie, 2006: 279). The formula assumes that the optimal portfolio selection suggested by Markowitz is undertaken by all investors. According to the CAPM, the return that can be expected on any stock is equal to the return of the entire market (or representative index such as the S&P 500) multiplied by a risk factor specific to each stock, known as "beta." Following Markowitz, beta is calculated using historical variance as the measure of risk, further solidifying the notion that risk was objective and measurable.

Risk found its full objective status in the BSM options pricing formula developed in 1973. The formula defines the price of an option as a function of the current stock price, the "strike" price of the option (the price at which the option can be exercised), the "risk-free" interest rate (the rate on the safest borrowing, such as US Treasury bonds), the time to expiration of the option, and the volatility (the historical standard deviation or square root of historical variance) of the underlying stock (Bodie et al., 2008). The price given by BSM was constructed relative to observable variables in the present with one exception: the volatility, or risk, term.

Present stock volatility is a paradoxical notion, albeit one derived from modern calculus (see also Lee's chapter in this *Handbook*). Volatility is a measure of change over time, so measuring it at a particular instant would seem to be impossible. Change requires at least two moments in time over which a distinction can be mapped. Differential calculus, however, purports to measure instantaneous change. The mathematical derivative (as opposed to the financial kind) is precisely the rate of change at an instant—or the slope of a continuous curve at one point. Indeed, Robert Merton's proof of BSM used stochastic calculus. However, unlike measuring the slope of a continuous curve that has already been drawn, measuring the instantaneous volatility of a stock is different, because the future arc of the stock's price hasn't already been drawn. Thus, instantaneous volatility would seem to be a measure of stock price change in the next moment in the future, i.e., a true prediction of risk at the next moment in time.

As explained above, when the BSM was first published, the prices of options didn't conform to the formula, but within three years of the original publication, they consistently did. Latané and Rendleman suggested that those market prices could actually be plugged into the formula so that the volatility term could be solved for rather than using standard deviation as an input (Latané & Rendleman, 1976). This "implied volatility" term gives an instantaneous, rather than historical, "measurement" of the riskiness of the stock. The convention for traders became, and remains, to quote the implied volatility rather than the option prices. When the BSM is solved for the volatility term, past variance of the stock is not an input. Instead, the volatility term is read off the other variables in the equation. BSM thus offers a measure of risk in the present, without appeal to past variance or subjective analysis of possible futures. Rather than a term that must be approximated using past data, volatility or risk becomes the mathematical result of the BSM formula, an empirical fact that doesn't require grounding in the past, only the cold hard numbers of the formula. In short, BSM completed the objectification of risk.[5]

After BSM, the taken-for-grantedness of risk has come to play a fundamental role in financial markets, particularly through the role of risk measurements in regulation. For example, the Basel Accord on international banking standards sets minimum capital requirements.[6] The Accord relies on accepted risk measurement techniques, particularly those used by external credit rating agencies. Agency credit ratings from the big three—Moody's, S&P, and Fitch—are standard measures of risk in Basel, but also in Securities and Exchange Commission regulations and in internal guidance for large institutional investors like pension funds (Benmelech & Dlogosz, 2009). However, in testimony before Congress after the financial crisis, executives of these agencies asserted over and over again that their ratings were mere "opinions" (Ferguson, 2010). Herein lies the paradox of measuring financial risk. When the rubber meets the proverbial legal road—and liability for such measurements is on the line—their squishiness, their subjectivity, and their true impossibility are quickly remembered. Yet, supposedly objective risk measurements are necessary inputs for traders to assess and undertake arbitrage in equivalent securities.

Risk's becoming objective hasn't been limited to financial discourse. One of the most prominent treatments of risk outside of finance is Ulrich Beck's *Risk Society* (1992/2008). In it, Beck argues that industrial era wealth production was an outcome of mitigating the risks associated with meeting society's material needs. However, post-industrial modernization ultimately inverted the relationship between wealth production and risk production. A "risk society" no longer produces wealth through the mitigation of material risk, but instead produces material risk through its means of wealth production. According to Beck, risk societies are more individualized in cultural, political, and economic organization and therefore more indifferent to the ways in which the individual is subject to an increasing array of new global threats to their life and livelihood.

The notion of risk as the statistically verifiable threat of danger embedded in Beck's work is influential in critiques of postmodernity that see neoliberalism as, at least in part, shifting risk from large, stable entities that can best handle it (governments, large corporations) to individual citizen-worker-consumers whose lives are rendered precarious by the transfer (Clarke, 2010; Hacker, 2008; Hardin, 2014; Langley, 2008). Critics claim that the free market ideologies of individual responsibility and self-management are covers for this risk shift. This notion of risk undoubtedly flows to some degree from the financial definition of risk as an objective measure of potential loss, but also, interestingly, the term comes to stand in for large-scale shifts in power relations within society between unions, corporations, governments, and individuals. The recourse to describe these shifts as "risk transfer" may itself be evidence of the power of the notion of objective risk. The term is so taken-for-granted that it is a more convincing frame to understand political and economic change than, say, an accounting of the legislative and legal unwinding of the liberal Fordist compromise and welfare state.

A more specific notion of financial risk shows up in sociological, anthropological, political economic, and cultural analyses of finance. MacKenzie characterizes risk as a material fact made meaningful within social systems through specific mechanisms of knowledge production. In "The Credit Crisis as a Problem in the Sociology of Knowledge," he addresses the question of "whether and how those risks were taken into account in the evaluation of ABS, CDOs and ABS CDOs" (MacKenzie, 2011: 1781). MacKenzie's argument assumes that if knowledge production is correct, risk can be accurately measured, priced, and exchanged. In short, the problem in measuring risk is the ways in which it is made meaningful to key actors, not with the ostensibly objective measurement itself (MacKenzie, 2011). Similarly, Caitlin Zaloom frames the logic that risk equals reward as a "social fact" in order to examine the ways in which "risk taking" animates the temporal and spatial organization of financial markets (Zaloom, 2004). MacKenzie's and Zaloom's studies offer granular examinations of the daily, social practices of risk measurement and risk taking, but in so doing, they—like financial economists and regulators—take risk as an already existing material reality.

Ivan Ascher (2016) and Dan Bouk (2015) examine risk calculation, prediction, and commodification in terms of its larger social implications. Bouk's history of life insurance examines the intersection of actuarial insurance calculation and medical practices around the turn of the twentiethth century. For Bouk, their entanglement marks a key turning point in the expansion of corporate power through risk commodification in everyday life (Bouk, 2015). Ascher's *Portfolio Society* (2016) asks, "What kind of world transforms risk into a commodity?" He argues that the predictive risk calculations in the late twentieth century and the resultant commodification lead to a unique development in capitalism, in which "capital's relation to its own future (and hence everyone's relation to the future) is itself mediated by financial markets" (Ascher, 2016: 24). Ascher's key contribution is to draw attention to risk calculation as a primary exercise of capitalist power mediating future possibilities and practice beyond the scope of financial markets. Both Ascher and Bouk theorize on the grounds that risk is a commodity, and elide the implicit objectivity as "the thing" that is brought into social exchange through capitalist practice.

Risk, calculation, and management are also central concerns to Foucauldian theories of governmentality and discourse. From that perspective, risk is a specific kind of discourse that organizes and orders a range self-governance and management practices. For example, Paul Langley resituates risk within everyday calculative practices of savings and borrowing. Citing Mitchell Dean (1999: 177) he declares, "There is no such thing as risk in reality" (Langley, 2008: 26). Rather than seeing risk as a material fact that finance measures and circulates, Langley examines the ways in which everyday financial practices are not "reducible to state-based legitimation of speculative forms of 'risky' accumulation" (Langley, 2008: 10). Francois Ewald examines the ways in which risk and insurance are techniques of political, economic, and social management. For Ewald, insurance produces risk as a discourse of calculability by ordering future potentiality into distributed economic arrangements among a population (Ewald, 1991). Thus, the Foucauldian approach to risk sees it as a discourse which orders and enables practices, thus avoiding the implicit objectivity while accounting for risk's effectivity.

By viewing risk as a discourse that organizes power relations in society, Foucauldian scholars avoid reinforcing the objectivity of risk that financial economics has constructed. As opposed to analyses that treat risk as a fact, they focus on the effects of taking risk for granted. This is a welcome intervention in critical finance studies. But even this fails to untangle the complex tension between uncertainty and objectivity that the concept of risk produces within financial markets.

The first incarnation of financial risk, in the work of von Neumann and Morgenstern, was subjective because any given gamble is uncertain, and individuals could necessarily only guess at the potential outcome. The slippages from individual subjective guesses to historical measurements of variance and then instantaneous implied volatility made the notion of risk within financial economics more and more objective, but they did nothing to change the uncertainty of the unfolding of future events. Even after nearly 70 years of quantitative financial economics, the greatest financial crisis since the Great Depression was an utter surprise to most market participants and regulators. In other words, *we are no better at assessing risk for having objectified it.*

Risk is a necessarily and inescapably paradoxical concept. On the one hand, despite years of measurement and modeling, risk remains a stubbornly intractable calculation, a social fact that refuses to materialize once and for all. On the other hand, it animates much financial activity. It is the most determining factor in calculating return. It is the thing that will determine if an investment is made. Objective measurements of risk designed to establish security equivalency are required for many forms of arbitrage. Risk makes profit possible, but we know that measuring risk isn't actually possible! Risk is the emperor's new clothes, the reason for the party, and yet, utterly unassessable. Far from accepting its objectivity, critical scholarship on risk should ask: how is its taken-for-grantedness secured through material practices in financial markets? And, what does taking its objectivity for granted produce?

In what follows we examine a case study to illustrate such an analysis. We turn to the CDS market in the run-up to the 2007–2008 market crash in order to show the ways in which risk is not a measurable "fact" but instead a discourse and set of practices which create the condition of possibility for profit through arbitrage in subprime mortgage-backed securities (MBS). The case study is an attempt to provide critical distance between the assumptions about risk that anchor traders' practices and the material infrastructures, cultural contexts, and discourses which constitute financial markets in practice.

Case Study: Credit Default Swaps and CDO Arbitrage

In this section, we focus on the ways in which traders and regulators produced and perpetuated a narrative of the "insuranceness" of CDS, despite their use in speculation and arbitrage profit making. The insuranceness of CDS was a key factor in objectifying the risk of MBS and other debt securities. Thus, in our estimation, it was a necessary precondition for arbitrage to take place. We are not suggesting that measurements of risk were simply manipulated from their "true" dimensions in order for greedy traders to profit. Instead, material and social practices aimed at establishing the possibility that risk is measurable made the enormous profit from arbitrage in mortgage-backed debt securities possible. In other words, it was the process of objectifying risk, not any particular measurement of it, that mattered.

A 2008 *New York Times* article matter-of-factly introduces the then relatively foreign and esoteric financial derivatives known as credit default swaps. Gretchen Morgenson gives a definition that is contradictory, referring to the instruments as both insurance and speculative investments. She writes, "these insurance contracts, known as C.D.S.'s, allow investors to bet on a company's health or hedge against possible default by an issuer whose debt they hold" (2008). How can a financial instrument function as insurance (meant to guard against possible loss) and speculative investment (meant to bet on future events)? This question goes to the heart of a tension between the profit making that CDS actually enable and the presumption that risk can be fully accounted for in the prices of CDS. Morgenson's article typifies what we will call the *insurance discourse* of CDS, which is trotted out with remarkable consistency anytime one introduces and explains how CDS function (Ferguson, 2010; Hull, 2011; McKay, 2015; Morgenson, 2008; Tett, 2009).

In this framework, when a company takes a loan or issues bonds there is a possibility that it will default or fail to pay back the loan. Banks who make loans and investors who purchase bonds run the risk of default, and if they want to avoid that potential risk, they can purchase insurance against it in the form of CDS. Negotiated between independent counterparties, in the so-called over-the-counter (OTC) or non-exchange traded market, a CDS exchanges a small monthly fee from the protection buyer for payment of face value of the loan or bond by the protection seller if default occurs.

CDS certainly operate with an insurance-like logic in the sense that, like health or life insurance, a smaller fee (premium) is paid so that the protection seller agrees to pay out a larger amount in the event that a loss (illness or death) occurs. When they were first developed in the mid-1990s by JP Morgan (in a primitive format known as BISTRO), CDS were in fact meant to transfer the risk of default of large corporate loans made by banks to other parties (particularly investors) willing to accept that risk for a small periodic fee (Freeman, 2009; Tett, 2009). The origination of CDS in corporate debt—where firms are subject to regulatory scrutiny and it was relatively easy to model the factors impacting their ability to repay loans—lent credence to the assumption that CDS functioned as insurance.

The insuranceness of CDS was accepted by regulators and solidified when those regulators allowed banks to reduce their cash reserves (capital requirements) for loans whose default risk had been swapped (Tett, 2009). For loans held outright on a bank's balance sheet, Basel I (effective in the United States from 1992 to 2008, the heyday of CDS) required 8% of the loan to be held in cash in the case of default (Getter, 2012). The cash could not be used by banks to make additional profitable transactions such as speculative investments. When regulators accepted the premise that CDS was insurance that effectively removed the risk of default from the bank, it allowed banks to reduce their regulatory capital proportionally for any loans on which CDS were purchased (Goodman, 2002; Tett, 2009). In effect, regulators endorsed the insuranceness of CDS by agreeing that they removed risk.

However, CDS were not actually regulated like insurance. Only a few years after CDS became a regular part of the growing OTC derivatives market, the Commodity Futures Modernization Act (CFMA) legally excluded CDS from government regulation. CFMA set CDS outside of the reserve capital requirements that must be met by insurance companies for products like life and health insurance (Morgan, 2010). Therefore, while CDS were being accepted by regulators as insurance products that could make investors whole in the case of default, issuers of CDS didn't have to prove to those same regulators that they themselves had even a fraction of the capital to pay out in those cases. This would become a leading driver of the financial crisis when mass defaults on MBS lead swarms of CDS buyers to line up for default payments from firms like AIG, who had issued CDS on over $400 billion worth of debt (Davidson, 2008).

However, before the crisis, the insurance discourse of CDS—reinforced as it was by commentators and regulators—allowed CDS prices to become a shorthand for risk among traders. Regulators accepted that CDS accurately reflected the risk of default because they assumed that CDS counterparties would work hard to make sure that the agreed upon price of protecting against possible default of a loan accurately represented the actual risk of default. If the CDS protection buyer allowed risk to be estimated too high, they would pay too much for protection. If the seller allowed the risk to be estimated too low, they wouldn't be compensated enough for carrying the risk. By looking out for their own interests—echoes of the Smithian utopia purely intentional—CDS counterparties would agree to the best possible estimate of default risk crystallized in the price of the CDS. This logic of the insurance discourse echoes the efficient market hypothesis and the ability of markets to distribute information and thus correctly price securities.

There are a number of indications that the insurance discourse didn't fully fit the everyday uses of CDS. First, there was a proliferation of CDS contracts written between parties neither of whom owned the underlying debt—particularly MBS—on which they were based. Since regulators treated CDS as OTC derivatives, there was never a requirement that one needed to own the securities on which they purchased "insurance." As a consequence, for every CDS purchased as insurance by those with a stake in the underlying mortgage-backed security before the crisis, there were several iterations of CDS speculating on the possibility of default (Angelides et al., 2011). This has been described as purchasing insurance on a home you don't own and then hoping it will burn down (or actually doing the burning yourself in some cases) (Morgenson & Story, 2009).

Economists rightly point out that this speculative function of CDS contradicted its insuranceness as counterparties to uncollateralized CDS don't have "skin in the game" (Acharya et al., 2009). Worse, without skin in the game, traders benefited from amplifying—rather than distributing or reducing—the risk pool. The assumption that CDS contracts were insurance, and therefore proxies for collateralized debt obligation (CDO) risk, ignores any potential market pressure on CDS prices from such speculators.

Second, we are now able to see, ex post facto, that the prices of CDS in the run-up to the crisis did not represent the riskiness of the subprime MBS that would eventually be called "toxic assets" (MacKenzie, 2011, 2012; Salmon, 2009). The standard logic of CDS would indicate that the riskier the underlying investment (such as subprime MBS), the higher the cost of "insuring" against its default. Risky subprime securities should have been costly to protect via CDS, and while they were more expensive to insure than prime, "conforming" loans, they were not nearly expensive enough to withstand the eventual housing crash. Already in 2006, foreclosure rates were rising and the *New York Times* publicly warned that a subprime foreclosure crisis was coming (Nixon, 2006). Yet the cost to insure subprime MBS and subprime CDOs with CDS didn't even begin to rise until mid-2007 (Tett, Bond & Leitner). It was clear that CDS prices were not predicting the crash, but rather trailing the news of it, meaning that far from offering the ex-ante protection of a well-underwritten insurance product, CDS were badly out of sync with reality even as it unfolded.

While CDS may not, therefore, have been a functional proxy for the risk of subprime MBS as an insurance product, they did enable and legitimate profit making for traders in the form of arbitrage. In the early 2000s, firms began to use risky, subprime MBS to make new securitized debt products call collateralized debt obligations (CDOs). There was high demand for securities that paid a high return and were also highly rated (i.e., low risk) by the credit rating agencies. AAA MBS fit that bill, but the lower rated, riskier MBS were harder to sell. Firms began to buy up these riskier pieces and securitize them into an entirely new debt offering, or CDO. For reasons we will soon address, the majority of those CDO deals were given the safest AAA rating, making them easy to sell in the secondary market to investors looking for safe, high-yield securities

The purpose of these deals is evident in the name given to the majority of them: the so-called "arbitrage CDOs" became an increasingly popular profit making strategy in the late 1990s and 2000s. With arbitrage CDOs, the risky, high-yield subprime MBS making up the collateral pool paid more than the resulting debt securities sold to investors, meaning that the securitizing firm made a profit merely from buying the collateral pool, repackaging it, and selling it back to investors (Kothari, 2006). CDS enabled and then turbo-charged this form of arbitrage profit making. First, CDO arbitrage required that the low-rated collateral be transformed into a highly rated debt offering. Investors were only interested in debt with AAA ratings, and yet the collateral in MBS-backed CDOs carried an average rating of BB (Covey et al., 2006). The "alchemy" of pooling together risky MBS and producing a new issue of AAA debt was achieved by the use of a particular default correlation formula by credit rating agencies (Benmelech & Dlogosz, 2009). The input to this formula that supposedly captured the probability of correlated default in the collateral pool was CDS prices—the very indicators that the insurance discourse of CDS held up as risk proxies (Salmon, 2009). Without CDS prices to estimate correlated default, ratings agencies wouldn't have been able to certify CDOs as AAA, and then the profit from arbitrage CDOs would not have been possible.

Second, also in the early 2000s securitizers began using CDS to create "synthetic CDOs," CDOs that weren't constructed by buying up risky MBS, but rather by selling CDS on MBS that the firm itself did not own. Based on the assumption that CDS accurately priced the risk of default on underlying securities, the securitizing firm could sell investors a tranched portion of CDS premiums, rather than the actual MBS themselves, producing an equivalent security to arbitrage. Synthetic arbitrage CDOs reduced the amount of capital needed to make a CDO arbitrage profit, and thus became even more popular than cash CDOs (Goodman, 2002).

The insurance discourse of CDS and its solidification in regulations, formulae, and material practices in financial markets enabled arbitrage to take place not as an accident of inefficiency, but as an accomplishment of a system whose goal was arbitrage profit making. Like other forms of risk measurement in finance, such as variance and implied volatility, CDS were taken to be objective reflections of market risk. The default on billions of dollars' worth of MBS and CDOs, which had—with the help of CDS prices in default correlation models—been rated as AAA in the crisis, revealed the nakedness of the emperor in this case. When accepted as insurance and enshrined in ratings-generating formulas as proxies for risk, CDS offered a felicitous mechanism for enabling arbitrage profit. Arbitrage was possible not because CDS prices somehow accurately represented objective risk, but because of the collective affirmation that CDS price *could* represent risk.

Conclusion

In this chapter, we provided a brief history and introduction to the critical study of risk and arbitrage in finance. In tracing these specific lineages of thought, our aim has been to draw attention to the treatments, problematics, and stakes of the ways in which risk and arbitrage are studied. In doing so, we have also cautioned that critical scholars of finance must be careful not to reproduce taken-for-granted assumptions about what they are or what they do. The pressing needs to deconstruct taken-for-granted financial logics such as "the greater the risk, the greater the reward" and "arbitrage generates riskless profit" are only two examples which exemplify this concern.

We have also, though perhaps less explicitly, indicated the need to continue to develop scholarship in the porous boundaries between disciplinary distinctions among methods, theories, and objects. Dogmatic adherence to known constructs—such as the source of value or the Law of One Price—can inhibit critical analyses of the rapidly changing conditions of contemporary financial practices. Moreover, scholars must continue to develop theorizations that transgress traditional financial boundaries which bracket everyday consumer practices from those of global institutions. Langley's (2008) *The Everyday Life of Global Finance* is a prime example of this kind of work. We need more of it.

Critical theorizations of risk and arbitrage are skeptical of dogma, attuned to power relations, and open to finding surprising results. Risk is not always (or ever) measured in mathematical formulae. Arbitrage does not always make markets more efficient. Finance is the place where these two elements—risk and arbitrage—form, devolve, and reform as contingent discourses, practices, and relations of power and profit. Critical finance studies must chronicle their story without presuming in advance to know the ending.

Notes

1 Commentators have made much of the so-called "fat tails" and "black swans," both of which are ways to conceptualize events (price changes, defaults, crises, etc.) that occur more frequently than economic models might suggest. In other words, they are indications that not all is right in risk modeling in finance (Fox, 2009: 133; see also Taleb, 2007).
2 Shorting is defined as borrowing a security in order to sell it, as opposed to selling a security already owned.
3 Hedging is a practice central to modern finance. Unlike traditional investing in which a stock or investment is purchased and held over time, professional trading at investment banks and hedge funds requires both taking positions, whether long (buying) or short (selling), and then hedging them by entering into positions that to some degree mitigate the risk that adverse price movements will significantly impact that trader. US Treasuries are typical hedging instruments for bond traders (Wosnitzer, 2014). Stock index futures may serve as a hedging instrument for traders who own a portfolio of stocks. If the portfolio loses a great deal of value, executing a futures contract sold before the crash would make up for at least some of the loss.
4 For example, Frank Knight famously defined risk as uncertainty that could be "reduced [...] by grouping cases" (Knight, 1921).
5 BSM transforms risk from a representation of past variance into something like an index in Peirce's sense. Implied volatility seems to be a fact, something that is not approximate or representative, but an output that is entirely objective. Implied volatility thus more fully obscures the constructedness of the notion of risk than previous approximations. We owe this insight to Robert Wosnitzer.

6 Capital requirements are the amount of reserves that banks and investment firms need to keep on hand to cover losses.

References

Acharya, V. V., Brenner, M., Engle, R. F., Lynch, A. W., & Richardson, M. (2009). "Derivatives: The ultimate financial innovation," in V. V. Acharya and M. Richardson (eds.), *Restoring Financial Stability: How to Repair a Failed System.* Hoboken, NJ: John Wiley & Sons.

Angelides, P., Thomas, B., Born, B., Holtz-Eakin, D., Georgiou, B., Murren, H. H., Graham, B., Thompson, J. W., Hennessy, K., & Wallison, P. J. (2011). *The Financial Crisis Inquiry Report: Final Report of the National Commision on the Causes of the Financial and Economic Crisis in the United States.* Washington, DC: United States Federal Government.

Ascher, I. (2016). *Portfolio Society: On the Capitalist Mode of Prediction.* Brooklyn, NY: Zone Books.

Beck, U. (2008). *Risk Society: Towards a New Modernity,* trans. M. Ritter. London: SAGE Publications. (Original work published 1992).

Benmelech, E., & Dlogosz, J. (2009). "The alchemy of CDO credit ratings," *Journal of Monetary Economics* 56(2): 617–634.

Bernstein, P. L. (1996). *Against the Gods: The Remarkable Story of Risk.* New York, NY: Wiley.

Beunza, D., Hardie, I., & MacKenzie, D. (2006). "A price is a social thing: Towards a material sociology of arbitrage," *Organization Studies* 27(5): 721–745. doi: 10.1177/0170840606065923.

Billingsly, R. S. (2006). *Understanding Arbitrage: An Intuitive Approach to Investment Analysis.* Upper Saddle River, NJ: Wharton School Publishing.

Bodie, Z., Kane, A., & Marcus, A. J. (2008). *Investments* (8th ed.). Boston, MA: Mcgraw-Hill.

Borch, C. (2020). "Introduction: What is Critical Finance Studies," in C. Borch and R. Wosnitzer (eds), *The Routledge Handbook of Critical Finance Studies* (pp. 1–25). London and New York: Routledge.

Bouk, D. (2015). *How Our Days Became Numbered: Risk and the Rise of the Statistical Individual.* Chicago, IL: University of Chicago Press.

Clarke, J. (2010). "Of crises and conjunctures: The problem of the present," *Journal of Communication Inquiry* 34(4): 337–354.

Covey, D., Koss, M., Mago, A., Vaidya, J., Zola, B., Sabarwal, R., Kazarian, D., Mingelgrin, D., Risa, S., Huang, V., Brav, O., & Ciampini, G. (2006). "ABS CDOs – A primer," in *Lehman Brothers: Fixed Income, U.S. Securitized Products Research.* New York: Lehman Brothers.

Davidson, A. (2008, September 18). "How AIG fell apart." *Reuters.* Retrieved from https://www.reuters.com/article/us-how-aig-fell-apart-idUSMAR85972720080918.

Dean, M. (1999). *Governmentality: Power and Rule in Modern Society.* Thousand Oaks, CA: Sage Publications.

Ewald, F. (1991). "Insurance and risk," in G. Burchell, C. Gordon and P. Miller (eds.), *The Foucault Effect.* Chicago, IL: University of Chicago Press.

Fama, E. F. (1970). "Efficient capital markets: A review of theory and empirical work," *The Journal of Finance* 25(2): 383–417.

Ferguson, C., & Marrs, A. (Producers), and Ferguson, C. (Director). (2010). *Inside Job* [Motion Picture]. United States of America: Sony Pictures Classics.

Fox, J. (2009). *The Myth of the Rational Market: A History of Risk, Reward, and Delusion on Wall Street.* New York, NY: HarperBusiness.

Freeman, J. (2009, May 13). "The credit crisis and its creation: An out-of-control free market or one distorted by regulation." *The Wall Street Journal*. Retrieved from https://www.wsj.com/articles/SB124217981370213553.

Gardner, D., Kleiner, J., Milchan, A., & Pitt. B. (Producers), & McKay, A. (Director). (2015). *The Big Short* [Motion Picture]. United States of America: Paramount Pictures.

Getter, D. E. (2012, November 14). *U.S. Implementation of the Basel Capital Regulatory Framework*. Library of Congress, Washington, DC: Congressional Research Service.

Goodman, L. S. (2002). "Synthetic CDOs: An introduction," *The Journal of Derivatives* 9(3): 60–72.

Hacker, J. S. (2008). *The Great Risk Shift: The New Economic Insecurity and the Decline of the American Dream*. Oxford: Oxford University Press.

Hardie, I. (2004). "'The sociology of arbitrage': A comment on MacKenzie," *Economy and Society* 33(2): 239–254.

Hardin, C. (2014). "Neoliberal temporality: Time-sense and the shift from pensions to 401(k)s," *American Quarterly* 66(1): 95–118.

Hardin, C., & Rottinghaus, A. R. (2015). "Introducing a cultural approach to technology in finance," *Journal of Cultural Economy* 8(5): 547–563.

Hull, J. C. (2011). *Options, Futures, and Other Derivatives* (8th ed.). Upper Saddle River, NJ: Pearson College.

Knight, F. H. (1921). *Risk, Uncertainty and Profit*. New York, NY: Hart, Schaffner and Marx.

Kothari, V. (2006). *Securitization: The Financial Instrument of the Future*. Hoboken, NJ: John Wiley & Sons.

Langley, P. (2008). *The Everyday Life of Global Finance: Saving and Borrowing in Anglo-America*. New York, NY: Oxford University Press.

Latané, H. A., & Rendleman, R. J. (1976). "Standard deviations of stock prive ratios implied in option prices," *The Journal of Finance* 31(2): 369–381.

MacKenzie, D. (2003). "Long-term capital management and the sociology of arbitrage," *Economy and Society* 32(3): 349–380.

MacKenzie, D. (2011). "The credit crisis as a problem in the sociology of knowledge," *American Journal of Sociology* 116(6): 1778–1841.

MacKenzie, D. (2012). "Knowledge production in financial markets: Credit default swaps, the ABX and the subprime crisis," *Economy and Society* 41(3): 335–359.

MacKenzie, D. A. (2006). *An Engine, Not a Camera: How Financial Models Shape Markets*. Cambridge, MA and London: MIT Press.

Miyazaki, H. (2007). "Between arbitrage and speculation: An economy of felief and doubt," *Economy and Society* 36(3): 396–415.

Morgan, G. (2010). "Legitimacy in financial markets: Credit default swaps in the current crisis," *Socio-Economic Review* 8: 17–45.

Morgenson, G. (2008, July 6). "A window in a smoky market." *The New York Times*, pp. BU1–BU2.

Morgenson, G., & Story, L. (2009, December 23). "Banks bundled bad debt, bet against it and won." *The New York Times*, p. A1.

N/A. (1892). "Arbitrage business." *The New York Times*, p. 9.

Nixon, R. (2006, December 20). "Study predicts foreclosure for 1 in 5 subprime loans." *The New York Times*, p. C4.

Rubenstein, M. (2006). *A History of the Theory of Investments: My Annotated Bibliography*. Hoboken, NJ: John Wiley & Sons.

Salmon, F. (2009, February 23). "Recipe for disaster: The formula that killed wall street." *Wired*. Retrieved from https://www.wired.com/2009/02/wp-quant/.

Taleb, N. N. (2007). *The Black Swan: The Impact of the Highly Improbable*. New York, NY: Random House.

Tett, G. (2009). *Fool's Gold: How the Bold Dream of a Small Tribe at J.P. Morgan Was Corrupted by Wall Street Greed and Unleashed a Catastrophe*. New York, NY: Free Press.

Von Neumann, J., & Morgenstern, O. (1944). *Theory of Games and Economic Behavior*. Princeton, NJ: Princeton University Press.

Woolf, C. (2014, May 20). Credit Suisse pleads guilty to tax crime charges. But is anyone going to jail? *Public Radio International*.

Wosnitzer, R. (2014). *Desk, Firm, God, Country: Proprietary Trading and the Speculative Ethos of Financialism*. PhD: Media, Culture, and Communication, New York University (3624594).

Zaloom, C. (2004). "The productive life of risk," *Cultural Anthropology* 19(3): 365–390.

PART II

Central Actors and Institutions

6

FINANCIAL REGULATION

Nathan Coombs

Introduction

Much like finance itself, critical thinkers tend to be suspicious of its regulation. Sometimes for good reason. From the saving and loans scandals of the 1980s to the failure to act over LIBOR interest rate fixing, regulators have far from a flawless track record. Indeed, if every financial failure is in some senses a regulatory failure, then it is not surprising that after the near-collapse of the financial system in the 2007–2008 crisis, many asked: where were the central banks and securities authorities who were meant to be keeping us safe? "Asleep at the wheel" was the kneejerk response of those frustrated by their inertia. Yet as it became clear that regulators not only failed to anticipate risks but had, over the past decade, ushered in many of the changes responsible for amplifying those risks,[1] explanatory efforts shifted from the "how" to the "why." Stigler's (1971) idea of regulatory capture, focused on the revolving door between financial firms and government, assumed a central role in making sense of the previous decade's deregulatory drive (Baker, 2010; Carpenter & Moss, 2014; Johnson & Kwak, 2010). Subtler forms of cultural, cognitive, and intellectual capture were also proposed (Kang, 2014; Kwak, 2014). In these accounts, regulators didn't need to be dominated by the financial sector to betray the public interest; they were lulled into complacency by free-market orthodoxy and the veneration of efficient markets, rational expectations, and the mathematical "innovations" which, it was believed, had distributed risk safely throughout the financial system (FSA, 2009; see also the chapter by Hardin and Rottinghaus in this *Handbook*).

Other analyses, predominantly from policy-setting institutions, honed in on regulators' lack of knowledge. Failures of banking supervision, information gaps about derivatives markets, and a poor understanding of the endogenous instabilities of the financial system were presented as a problem of regulators hitting an epistemological impasse with the tools at their disposal (BCBS, 2009; IMF & FSB, 2009). In the years since, attempts to break through the impasse have been multifaceted: from work by the new US Office for Financial Research, to attempts to measure systemic risk, to increased data collection by regulatory authorities. These knowledge augmentation efforts, often justified in reference to the post-crisis "macroprudential" agenda (a concern with systemic risk in the financial system as a whole), have been recognized by scholars, but with steadily diminishing levels of enthusiasm. In part, that is because many were expecting more sweeping changes in the wake of the crisis (Helleiner, 2014). Those who have addressed regulators' new knowledge practices and policy tools have often been no less critical, focusing on the difficulties of governing complex and reflexively adaptive markets (Dorn, 2012a; Riles, 2013; Stellinga & Mügge, 2017). Disappointment and fatalism have become default scholarly registers.

This chapter argues for a different approach which it calls the social studies of financial regulation. The pseudo-neologism takes its inspiration from the social studies of finance (SSF): a branch of economic sociology which, since the early 2000s, has applied the methodological tools of anthropology and science and technology studies to research on financial markets. With its roots in Michel Callon's (1998; Callon et al., 2007) ideas about how economics performs the economy, as well as the attention to "non-human actors" licensed by actor-network theory (ANT; Latour, 2005; Law & Hassard, 1999), SSF's distinctive methodological contribution concerns its attention to corporeal embodiment, technical infrastructures, and distributed cognition (MacKenzie, 2008: Chapter 2). In keeping with these foci, some of the field's famous studies include the "global microstructures" of screen-based trading (Knorr Cetina & Bruegger, 2002); the performativity of the Black-Scholes options pricing formula (MacKenzie, 2006; MacKenzie & Millo, 2003); the role of securitization in the credit crisis (MacKenzie, 2011; MacKenzie & Spears, 2014b; Poon, 2009); and financial automation and high-frequency trading (HFT; Borch & Lange, 2017; MacKenzie, 2017; MacKenzie et al., 2012; MacKenzie & Pardo-Guerra, 2014).

Regulation is never far away in this line of work, nor could it be given that financial products are themselves "synthetic bundles of law and measurement" (Thiemann & Lepoutre, 2017: 1776). Nevertheless, given the constitutive role of regulation in the evolution of markets, a number of authors have questioned why the field has not paid more attention to regulatory technologies (Coombs, 2016, 2017; Langley, 2015; Lenglet, 2011; Williams, 2009). The limited contact with wider debates about regulation in other parts of the academy could also be noted, whether that be ideational shifts (Baker, 2013; Blyth, 2002), structural power (Woll, 2016), or supervisory compliance strategies (Baldwin & Black, 2008). Whatever the reasons for the absence of dialogue, this chapter argues that SSF can provide a sound methodological basis for interrogating financial regulation if adapted to the regulatory object of study. Below, the proposed adaptations are distilled into three lessons, which provide a set of guiding methodological principles for a social studies of financial regulation building upon the field's science studies origins.

These lessons might strike readers as out-of-place in a volume dedicated to critical finance studies. If the take-home message of this chapter is the need to understand the motivations, tools, and cultures of regulators and regulation before criticizing their perceiving failings, does this not imply a less critical, or even acritical, approach? Some might draw that conclusion. Certainly, the SSF has a history of frustrating critics with its reluctance to "get political." But as Borch writes in this volume's introduction, critique resting on conviction rather than a firm empirical basis is likely to prove a blunt instrument. Or, in Mehrling's (2017: 3) emphatic words: "If we want change, we need to anchor our ideas in reality, which is to say in the logic that is expressed, in practice, in the [financial] system as it operates today." Extending that insight to the regulatory sphere, it is not enough to speak in generalizations determined by political or social theories. Even limited engagement with regulators does much to dispel that idea that they are uniformly captured or laboring under the impression that their big data sets afford them omniscient knowledge. One will find as much critique of regulatory practices from within the regulatory community as in the academic literature. Paradoxically, then, the contention of this chapter is that by suspending some of the usual critical scholarly reflexes, at least temporarily, a social studies of financial regulation can not only discern instances of regulatory success, but also tease out more powerful critiques of its failings and limitations.

Lesson 1: Listen to the Actors

Bruno Latour's (2005) injunction to "follow the actors" might not, at first, seem a promising basis for researching financial regulation. Methodological advice that has proven so productive in the laboratory setting, where the researcher is granted unfettered access to the social construction of scientific knowledge, has no obvious counterpart in the secretive worlds of central banking, securities regulation, and transnational standard-setting. While there has been a drive over recent decades for regulators to make greater efforts at public engagement, the sensitivity of regulatory activities in the financial field limits the potential for ethnography and constrains the scope for frank exchanges in an interview setting. Unlike private-sector financial practitioners, who can be surprisingly open about divulging their practices, when pushed on their agenda regulators will usually defer to publically available policy documents.

Nevertheless, even if it not possible to follow the actors in a classically Latourian sense, approaching the regulatory field with humility will allow researchers to listen to the actors and appreciate the significance of what they *do* have the freedom to say. That is particularly the case in the post-crisis era in which the "frontier quality" (Moloney et al., 2015: 2) of financial regulation presents researchers with an opportunity for studying innovation under conditions of epistemic uncertainty. For researchers willing to shelve their assumptions and follow regulators into their own problem set, exploring the practical metaphysics of their work, there is much to be gained by attempting to understand what it is that they are doing and attempting to achieve. Full immersion in that frontier space will allow researchers to better appreciate the disconnections between existing scholarly research and the aims, means, and ends of regulatory practices.

To use an example from my own research (Coombs, 2020), following the financial crisis, stress testing emerged as one of the key ways that regulators sought to improve the resilience of banks. In contrast to the backward-looking modeling practices that were important for determining the state of banks' balance sheets prior to the crisis, post-crisis regulatory stress tests involve the regulatory authority crafting a hypothetical macroeconomic crisis and asking the private banks to simulate how their balance sheets stand up in the scenario. For example, regulators might craft a crisis scenario in which unemployment rises sharply, mortgage defaults increase, and share prices crash, with the aim to see if banks are capable of remaining solvent and supplying credit to the economy. What happens then depends upon the jurisdiction in question, but in the United States, the consequences of poor performance are potentially severe. Failing the test can result in sanctions where the Federal Reserve prevent banks from undertaking planned dividend payments or share buybacks.

Given that stress testing is one of regulators' most powerful levers of control over financial firms today, it is surprising that the practice has attracted so little academic attention. Political economists, sensing a "Minsky moment" with the post-crisis "macroprudential ideational shift" (Baker, 2013), have catalogued the ways in which regulations have proven insufficiently counter-cyclical (Underhill, 2015). Langley (2013) sees in the crisis-era stress tests as a shift away from probabilistic risk governance towards anticipatory, enactment-based knowledge; but he has not explored the practice's continued role as a fixture of post-crisis banking supervision. Policy literature fares little better. Goldstein's (2017) book, *Banking's Final Exam*, while ostensibly about stress testing, in fact focuses on how capital is measured in the baseline, non-stressed scenario. The result is a significant lacuna in the scholarship. What stress testing is seeking to achieve, what knowledge the exercises furnish, and what changes the practice is effecting are questions yet to be posed satisfactorily. Is stress testing a form of anticipatory governance? Or is it about reforming banks' risk management and organizational cultures? Or is it simply about driving higher capitalization across the banking sector? It is this lesson's contention that a good first step towards answering these questions would be to ask the regulators and firms implementing the tests—and listen attentively to their answers.

Another example. As documented by a string of high-profile exposes in the popular press (Lewis, 2014; Patterson, 2012), financial markets have become increasingly automated since the early 1990s. With the colocation of trading firms' servers next to exchanges' data centers, the use of short but sophisticated arbitrage algorithms, and the development of high-speed communications networks, trading has accelerated towards sub-perceptual milli- and micro-second speeds. In recent years, a nascent sociological literature has emerged on this HFT. Its historical sociology, the subjectivity and emotions of HF traders, and the material political economy of the technical infrastructure have all proven productive areas of research (Borch & Lange, 2017; MacKenzie, 2017; MacKenzie & Pardo-Guerra, 2014; see also Lange's chapter in this *Handbook*). Inevitably, given concerns prompted by events such as the 2010 "Flash Crash" (in which algorithmic trading was implicated in the Dow Jones crashing by 9% in a matter of minutes), there has also been much interest in the HFT's regulatory implications, generally from one of two interconnected angles. First is concern with speed. Does the velocity of HFT pose hitherto unprecedented challenges for market governance (Angel, 2014)? Second is interest in the consequences of automation. Does the fact that it is now algorithms executing the majority of trades mean that it is necessary to rethink the regulatory regime's human-centric conception of agency (Kirilenko & Lo, 2013; Lenglet, 2011)?

These are important questions. However, here again, it is necessary to contrast scholarly reflections with policies and practices. For when one examines regulations directed at automated trading,[2] their emphases are more prosaic; the focus is on improving the testing of automated trading systems and providing trade surveillance departments with better means to monitor the market. When I conducted research on the German High-Frequency Trading Act, the regulators I spoke to dismissed speed or post-human agency as having anything to do with the Act's motivations (Coombs, 2016). The Act's requirement that trading firms label (tag) their algorithms with a numerical code was instead a response to the difficulties trade surveillance officers were experiencing in interpreting market events with only trader IDs to identify the different strategies at play. These practical concerns made the implementation of the Act's algorithm-tagging rule no less vexed. The rule's novelty required regulators to pose acutely philosophical problems: what individuates an algorithm? Where does one algorithm begin and another stop? Should an algorithm be defined with respect to code or its strategy?

How regulators answered these questions by building upon the expertise of market participants ultimately proved a case study in "meta-regulation" (Gilad, 2010) rather than speaking directly to scholars' concerns about the movement into the algorithmic age. The disconnect is, to some extent, inevitable. As argued by Ziewitz (2016), as a result of growing interest in algorithms across the humanities and social sciences, "algorithm" has come to function as a "figure" or "sensitizing concept," channeling diverse concerns about computation, automation, and control. Indeterminacy is not necessarily a problem; polyvalent concepts can be productive; they allow academics to pose the big questions that might otherwise get lost in the minutiae of concrete practices. What the social studies of financial regulation can do, by listening to how regulators are tackling problems pragmatically, is conceptually regulate such discussions and rein in their speculative excesses.

To be clear, this lesson's suggestion to listen to regulatory actors does not just mean to interview them in person (even if desirable). Listening can be as mundane an act as reading, in an unprejudiced way, their reports, speeches, and analyses. For if one approaches regulation with the attitude sometimes found in certain strands of political economy or critical sociology, convinced that regulators are failing and determined to find out why, then the answers to the inquiry will likely be pre-determined by the questions. Neither is disdain for "technocrats" conducive to understanding their motivations and operational constraints. There is a beautiful passage in Annelise Riles' (2011) book, *Collateral Knowledge*, which sends a countervailing message to those who would cast technocrats as little more than the shadowy vehicles for elite conspiracies. She recalls discussions with a systems-builder at the Bank of Japan developing a real-time settlement system for derivatives trading in the late 1990s. Although the system unwound prior regulatory interventions and curbed the central bank's role in economic coordination, it was not conceived by the actors involved in the project as neoliberal capitulation. Rather, giving the banks what they wanted, in the historical context of the time, was invested with a utopian spirit of improvement and modernization. Riles reflects poignantly on the political ambivalence and imaginative subjectivity of the technocratic spirit:

> Technocratic thought goes hand in hand with dreams: dreaming is an act setting itself apart from the world as it is lived today. It is a small-scale, personal utopianism, predicated on a distance between the world as other see it and the world as it could be. (Riles, 2011: 140)

It is, I propose, the task of researchers to take seriously these small acts of dreaming and utopian vision. By its nature, financial regulation is rarely a transformative project. More often than not, its technocratic remit precludes the grand ambitions which excite social scientists. This lesson's call to listen to the actors means to make attempts at closing that gap; to learn to appreciate the incremental improvements regulators are seeking, and evaluating their successes or failures on those terms.

Lesson 2: Models Matter

The second lesson will be familiar to those who have followed the development of SSF since the early 2000s. An innovation of the field has been to encourage focus on the mathematical models and technical details of financial practices, breaking down the division of labor between financial economics and the (broader) social sciences (on financial models, see also Svetlova's chapter in this *Handbook*). From the tradition's pragmatist perspective, modeling is seen not as aiming for objective truth, but rather as a cultural practice aiming to generate useful results (Millo & MacKenzie, 2009), to provoke "reality as effectuation" (Muniesa, 2014: 16). Callon (1998) is widely credited with setting in motion this strand of thought when he theorized how economics, in the act of measurement, does not represent the economy, but remakes it in its image. MacKenzie and Millo's (2003) study of the Black-Scholes-Merton (BSM) option pricing formula takes the insight a step further. Arguing that Callon's understanding of performativity assumed a frictionless account of how economic measurement effectuates economic change, MacKenzie and Millo instead show the contingent, cultural work by traders on the Chicago Board Options Exchange necessary for the BSM model's predictions to converge with actual market prices. Thus, their study demonstrates not that models have intrinsically transformative powers, but rather that the conversion of ideas into material practices is a fragile process. For every model's success, there is a model that fails to realize its theoretical promise.

Other investigations which demonstrate the fruitfulness of a technical orientation focus on the 2007–2009 financial crisis. In contrast to popular representations of the crisis as the result of a private-sector run rampant, a common theme of sociological scholarship is to stress the unintended consequences of the US government's efforts to extend credit for home ownership after the Great Depression (Poon, 2009). Even the instrument so centrally involved in the crisis, the "mortgage-backed security" (MBS)—where a pool of mortgage loans are packaged into a bond paying a fixed income to investors—emerged in the 1970s to help fund new mortgages through the government-sponsored enterprises, Fannie Mae and Freddie Mac. Fligstein and Goldstein (2010; Goldstein & Fligstein, 2017) show that while in its initial stages, the introduction of MBS encouraged fragmentation in the mortgage market with the infamous "originate to distribute" model, by the 2000s banks began to vertically integrate the securitization value chain in order to capture its lucrative fees. Major US banks became heavily invested in issuing loans for new mortgages, securitizing and selling those loans, and also retaining a significant number for themselves. Due to pressure to keep the supply chain fed with new loans for mortgage securitization, from 2003 banks moved into the "non-conventional" mortgage market: namely, subprime and non-conforming loans. The "collateralized debt obligation" (CDO), an instrument structurally similar to MBS but with its origins in corporate loan market, played a crucial role in feeding the machine by enabling the repackaging of risky BBB-rated MBS tranches into apparently safe AAA-rated MBS-CDO (a CDO with MBS as its underlying assets).

MacKenzie's (2011) study puts under a microscope the models used to financially engineer MBS-CDO and explains how they could have caused so much damage without assuming coordinated malfeasance in the financial sector. In contrast to Fligstein and Goldstein's focus on industrial control *within* firms, MacKenzie's explanatory focus rests with the "clusters of evaluation practices" (MacKenzie, 2011: 1782) or "evaluation cultures" (MacKenzie & Spears, 2014b: 395) spanning *across* different banks and credit rating agencies. At the center of the story is the emergence of the parallel evaluation culture in the 1990s for assessing the risk of CDO. Driven by advances in mathematical modeling,

CDO, unlike MBS, were evaluated using the family of Gaussian copula models designed to quantify the correlation in the risk of default of the underlying asset pool. On MacKenzie's account, it was the independent evaluation cultures of MBS and CDO, and their eventual combination in the MBS-CDO, that led to arbitrage opportunities being exploited systematically and risks heightened. However, as MacKenzie and Spears (2014a) note, this does not mean that CDO quants employed Gaussian copula models in ignorance of their limitations; some were skeptical about them from the beginning. What emerges is a sense of the power and opacity-generating properties of financial models without reducing their users to "model dopes" (MacKenzie & Spears, 2014a: 419; see also Beunza & Stark, 2012; Svetlova, 2012). Models provide a useful communicative and calculative medium that cuts across institutions, but can also prove dangerous by creating organizational blind spots that lead to risks being overlooked.

For researchers sympathetic to SSF, it should be clear that models matter. The point of this lesson is that bringing these sensibilities to bear in studying the regulatory sphere holds untapped potential for opening up new avenues for social scientific analysis. A brief survey of the existing literature explains why. Within political science, work on regulation has historically operated at a certain level of abstraction from the details of regulatory practices. The focus has been on the shifting balance of power between states, the role played by transnational technical networks, and the tension between global soft-law and state sovereignty (e.g. Helleiner & Pagliari, 2011; Young, 2014). In the limited sociological work on financial regulation, the public/private dichotomy has done equivalent heavy-lifting. Public regulation is associated with state control and a degree of (at least potential) democratic determination; private regulation, by contrast, is associated with a self-regulatory regime which precludes democratic determination of the decision-making process (Carruthers, 2015; Dorn, 2012b, 2015, 2016). Insofar as insistence on the distinction between public and private is a response to laudatory theorization of multi-level governance that became popular in the 1990s, it serves as a necessary corrective for placing control back at the center of the scholarly analysis. On the other hand, it is in danger of missing the significance of the emergence of the Black-Scholes world of financial risk management (Coombs & van der Heide, 2020; Millo & MacKenzie, 2009). In the same way that MacKenzie's notion of "evaluation cultures" draws attention to practices that cut across financial institutions, so too does it point to the limits of an understanding of financial governance divided into discrete public and private spheres.

The best example is provided by the evolution of international capital regulation. In brief, a bank's capital is the size of its assets (such as its loans) minus its liabilities (such as the debt it takes on to fund those loans). The capital ratio, perhaps the most important metric in banking regulation, is a measure of the quality of this capital. It places secure capital (such as a bank's retained earnings) on the numerator, and divides that by the risk-sensitive capital (such as the bank's loans) in the denominator. The idea is that the higher a bank's capital ratio is, the more resilient the bank will be to loan defaults or adverse market movements during an economic crisis (the most accessible introduction to the subject is Admati & Hellwig, 2013).

The origins of the Basel Accord, the first international bank capital standard, go back to the early 1980s. The desire for a global definition of capital and capital ratio standard was motivated by a perceived global decline in bank capital at the time (Goodhart, 2011: Chapter 6). The result was a tortuous negotiating process between states and their central banks giving rise to the 1988 Accord, Basel I, which settled upon an 8% capital to risk-weighted assets standard and a risk bucket methodology assigning different types of credit risk to a limited number of categories. For example, OECD sovereign bonds were awarded a risk weight of 0%, whereas equities received a weight of 100%. Going into the 1990s, the Basel Committee then began work on expanding capital requirements to include interest rate risk and market risk. Impressed with the modeling going on in banks, grounded in academic financial theory, the expansion of the standards culminated in the 1997 Market Risk Amendment, which allowed banks to utilize their internal Value-at-Risk (VaR) models for determining the regulatory capital necessary to cover the risk in their trading book. Basel II went further with the introduction of an advanced internal ratings-based approach, allowing banks to also calculate themselves the regulatory capital needed to cover their credit risk. The discretion this afforded to banks' risk managers is widely credited with encouraging the decline in bank capitalization in the run-up to the 2007–2009 financial crisis. In its aftermath, Basel III, agreed upon in 2010–2011, responded with increased capital ratio requirements, a stricter definition of capital, and counter-cyclical provisions.

There are a number of ways to analyze the policy evolution. A standard political economy approach would be to refract the events through the prism of great power rivalry: an interpretation with clear saliency in the run-up to the first Basel Accord.[3] Dorn's sociological approach, by contrast, sees a shifting balance between public and private actors, with Basel I as public-private regulation, Basel II as private-public regulation, and Basel III as an ambiguous move back towards public-private regulation (Dorn, 2012b). A social studies of financial regulation might, however, take an alternative approach. This would involve tracing the role played by the "no-arbitrage" evaluation culture (MacKenzie and Spears, 2014a) in shaping the internal modeling provisions of the Market Risk Amendment and Basel II. With close attention to the historical sociology of these modeling practices, the approach would trace the practices' sociological and material dynamics, and how they cut across and ideationally infused both public and private spheres (Coombs and van der Heide, 2020). The aim is to see how risk management, and its attendant technologies, ended up exerting its own dynamics and path dependencies in financial regulation (for another example of such analysis, see Lockwood, 2015).

If the idea of evaluation cultures can shed light on the policy evolution, it remains less clear if performativity is an appropriate concept through which to analyze regulation. After all, regulatory models are explicitly prescriptive and to say that when they are implemented they have "performed" their function is not to say anything that could not be said with simpler language. One way in which the idea of performativity might prove relevant is in analyzing the unintended consequences of regulatory interventions. For example, I have argued that although the German HFT Act's algorithm-tagging rule was intended primarily to help trade surveillance departments, the rule's implementation has led to beneficial cultural changes within trading firms through opening up their algorithmic black boxes to scrutiny (Coombs, 2016). Another way that the concept has been put to work is in understanding the difficulties faced by regulators. In a series of articles addressing post-crisis developments from credit rating reform to macroprudential policies, Stellinga (2019, 2020; Stellinga & Mügge, 2017) argues that while regulators don't think expressly in terms of performativity, they do recognize that markets have reflexive, adaptive, and complex dynamics which militate against attempts at market control. From this perspective, it is not necessary to see regulators as captured or ideologically aligned with financial interests to explain their timidity.

In sum, a social studies of financial regulation recognizes that models matter. The models addressed in this lesson derive from the Black-Scholes genealogy of risk management which the majority of work in SSF focuses on, but "model" in the regulatory domain can be interpreted in a more catholic sense. Even the original Basel I risk bucket methodology was a model of sorts, albeit one at odds with the computationally complex form of modeling pioneered in banks. And yet, the approach I am suggesting should not stop at recognizing that models matter. By drilling down into their fine details, scholars should seek to interrogate their origins, the problems they are addressing, and the effects they have. How to do so is the subject of lesson 3.

Lesson 3: Discover the Macro in the Micro

The question of the link between the micro and the macro has theoretical antecedents dating as far back as classical philosophy and metaphysics (Alexander & Giesen, 1987). Within sociology, the micro-macro divide has typically pivoted on whether the structural constraints of society, institutions, and economic systems are decisive, or whether individual or small group acts of interaction, interpretation, and sense-making should be the focus for empirical investigation. There have been countless attempts at synthesizing these perspectives, but ANT has arguably championed the most radical perspective by arguing that there is no way that we can know "*a priori* that macro-actors are bigger than or superior to micro-actors" (Callon & Latour, 2015: 280). ANT questions the assumption that the designations "macro" or "micro" map on to objectively larger or smaller units of analysis, with different methodological tools being appropriate to address them. As an alternative, it proposes that both "levels" are the result of unstable translations that researchers need to map out. The implication for the study of financial markets, according to MacKenzie (2008: 33), is we should be suspicious of fixed scales of analysis dividing up small, "micro" phenomena such as technical devices and interpersonal interactions from large, "macro" phenomena such as capitalism, globalization, and so on.

Knorr Cetina and Bruegger (2002) provide a convincing application of this approach in their theorization of foreign exchange (FX) markets as "global microstructures" in which "face-to-screen" interaction and "response-presence-based conversation" sustain the transnational order. In contrast to economic sociology's tendency to theorize away the specificities of market types, they argue that the non-intermediary trading culture of FX markets lessens the significance of organizations in their coordination. Instead, understanding these markets requires attention to the part played by individual traders who are granted freedom to take positions depending upon their own judgment. The shift in emphasis not only directs attention to traders' screen-based coordination activities, but can also, Knorr Cetina and Bruegger claim, explain the readiness of banks to locate their operations in global financial centers rather than remaining close to traditional industrial production centers. A "small," micro observation about the idiosyncrasies of market coordination speaks to a "large," macro question about financial geography.

Another study that bridges the micro-macro divide is MacKenzie's (2011) aforementioned analysis of the global financial crisis. To recall, this locates a contributing factor in the divergent evaluation cultures of MBS and CDO which allowed the benefits of diversification to be illegitimately reaped twice in the construction of MBS-CDO. One of MacKenzie's most provocative claims—provocative because some have argued that it depoliticizes the financial crisis by reducing it to a technical error (Engelen et al., 2011)—is that in extending the use of CDO from corporate loans to mortgages, a lack of historical data, and a desire to maintain consistency with existing practices led to a correlation factor of 0.3 being arbitrarily adopted. The choice was a fateful one, since if banks and credit rating agencies had opted for a higher correlation of, for example, 0.8, then it would not have been possible to construct profitable arbitrage CDO. Thus can a seemingly innocuous technical decision help to explain the roots of the credit crisis. Yet, as MacKenzie stresses, this micro finding is not a substitute for macro analyses; it is intended to complement them by drawing attention to how the technical substratum bisects the systemic dimensions of the crisis.

If the idea of discovering the macro in the micro is firmly enshrined in SSF, how might such an approach be extended to financial regulation? There are at least two potential ways. The first concerns the sociology of classification. As the rich science studies literature on standards and their stories has shown, seemingly slight definitional and classification issues are important objects of analysis in the history of knowledge (Bowker & Star, 1999). Some of the best work in the field focuses on cases of biological classification and their large effects on institutional structures, funding mechanisms, and discursive constructions that build up around the contested "object." For example, viruses have proven persistently difficult objects to classify, falling between the cracks of life and non-life, and these classification dilemmas have caused institutional impediments to scientific progress in this area.

In finance, classification dilemmas for regulators can have similarly large-scale effects. One striking example is recent work on the historical sociology of HFT. Seeking to account for how it is possible that HF algorithms can predict prices, MacKenzie (2018) identifies an important predictive signal transmitted between the Chicago futures markets and stock trading in New York. The "futures lead" arises because regulatory rules governing futures trading allow greater leverage than with equities. MacKenzie traces the origins of the divergent rules to the creation of the Commodity Futures Trading Commission (CFTC) in 1974. The addition of "twenty carefully chosen words to the long list of commodities" determining the agency's mandate—namely "and all services, rights, and interests in which contracts for future delivery are presently or in the future dealt in"—was decisive for creating a permanent jurisdictional demarcation between the CFTC and the Securities and Exchange Commission (MacKenzie, 2018: 1657). The historically contingent "micro" feature of the agencies' remits and their differing rules on leverage is responsible for the establishment of a vast technological infrastructure of fibre optic cables and microwave paths for HFT between Chicago and New York.

A study by Funk and Hirschman (2014) further underlines the importance of such categorical regulatory distinctions. By tracing the history of interest rate and FX swaps from the early 1980s, they argue that financial innovations create problems for regulators and opportunities for private-sector firms. Because regulators use categories to "filter and make sense of the people, organizations, and products they oversee" (Funk & Hirschman, 2014: 670), innovations that do not fit into those categories can be deeply destabilizing. Other studies have shown how market actors actively lobby against the classification of their products so as to evade regulation (Weiss & Huault, 2016).

Of course, regulation does not begin and end with the classification decisions of public actors. A second way to discover the macro in the micro concerns how regulatory rules and models are implemented by the firms themselves. Here, there is an excellent opportunity to explore the under-documented interpretative work of compliance officers. Compliance officers have an organizationally ambiguous role, being on the payroll of firms but tasked with the para-regulatory function of ensuring that their firm upholds the rules. That task is often far from straightforward (Lenglet, 2012). With the details of rules often indeterminate, compliance officers have to exercise interpretative discretion in determining how regulatory "rules and models are reshaped during their implementation" (Schneiberg & Bartley, 2008: 49). For example, in the implementation of the German HFT Act, it was the way that the "parameter" of an algorithm was left undefined that opened the door to a multiplicity of interpretations by different trading firms. The result was that some firms were tagging only a handful of algorithms, with others labeling thousands per year (Coombs, 2016). Such findings can potentially speak to questions about the efficacy of regulatory knowledge. As Thiemann and Lepoutre (2017) demonstrate in their comparative study of the evolution of shadow banking markets in Germany, the Netherlands, and France, divergences in the decade preceding the crisis were a result of "creative compliance" by financial firms. The extent of firms' creative compliance in these countries was a function of the structural embeddedness of national regulators in wider interpretative communities. For example, the French regulator, being deeply embedded in the operations of firms, was able to know both what they were doing and to exercise discretionary power to clamp down on practices they considered as stretching the rules too far.

Conclusion

More than two decades on from Callon's (1998) provocative claim that the economy is embedded in economics, SSF insights have been picked up by the wider scholarly community. However, the diffusion of the field's methodological principles into work on financial regulation remains in its infancy. Although conceding that ethnographic fieldwork faces distinct challenges in the regulatory sphere, this chapter argues that SSF's theoretical ideas and sensibilities can help open up the black boxes of this secretive policy domain. The chapter's unifying idea is that to do so, it is necessary to reject the fatalism that colors so much scholarly commentary on financial regulation. Even if, as many authors argue, the post-crisis macroprudential policy shift has proven disappointing, does that mean that all we need to do is conduct post-mortems on its unrealized promises? Or are there fresh insights to be gained by fine-grained empirical research on the regulatory innovations that it has made possible? What new frontiers might we discover if we allow the frame of reference to shift?

Critically, if the social studies of financial regulation is seen as a sensibility more than a fixed conceptual or methodological toolbox, then it is not "owned" by sociology. It is inevitable that political scientists feel more of an impulse to "get political," but that does not mean critique needs to be driven by negativity, or a desire to denounce. Nor does it mean that to be sociological means to aspire to rigorously value-free analysis. Today, scholars recognize that there is no need for new academic "microtribes" (Alvesson et al., 2017) and are embracing "post-disciplinary" approaches (Samman et al., 2015) regardless of the disciplines' different emphases and dispositional norms. This chapter has sought to embrace that spirit. Any discipline or field can adopt the principles I have laid out and take them in whichever direction they see fit. And they should. An uncharted frontier awaits.

Notes

1 Commonly identified regulatory efforts contributing to the crisis include the following: the 1999 Gramm–Leach–Bliley Act which repealed most of the provisions in the 1933 Glass-Steagall Act dividing commercial from investment banking in the United States, and the 2004 Basel II capital regulations which allowed banks to utilize their own internal models for calculating their regulatory capital.

2 These include the European Union's second Markets in Financial Instruments Directive, the German High-Frequency Trading Act, and the Commodities and Futures Trading Commission's proposed Regulation Automated Trading.
3 The interaction between global rule-making with national-level interpretation has also been identified by the international political economy literature as a driver of regulatory arbitrage in shadow banking before the crisis (Thiemann, 2014).

References

Admati, A., & Hellwig, M. (2013). *The Bankers' New Clothes*. Princeton, NJ: Princeton University Press.

Alexander, J. C., & Giesen, B. (1987). "From reduction to linkage: The long view of the micro-macro debate," in J. C. Alexander, B. Giesen, R. Munch, and N. J. Smelser (eds.), *The Micro-Macro Link* (pp. 1–42). Berkeley: University of California Press.

Alvesson, M., Gabriel, Y., & Paulsen, R. (2017). *Return to Meaning: A Social Science with Something to Say*. New York, NY: Oxford University Press.

Angel, J. J. (2014). "When finance meets physics: The impact of the speed of light on financial markets and their regulation," *Financial Review* 49(2): 271–281.

Baker, A. (2010). "Restraining regulatory capture? Anglo-America, crisis politics and trajectories of change in global financial governance," *International Affairs* 86(3): 647–663.

Baker, A. (2013). "The new political economy of the macro-prudential ideational shift," *New Political Economy* 18(1): 112–139.

Baldwin, R., & Black, J. (2008). "Really responsive regulation," *The Modern Law Review* 71(1): 59–94.

Basel Committee on Banking Supervision (BCBS). (2009). *Principles for Sound Stress Testing Practices and Supervision*. Basel: Bank for International Settlements.

Beunza, D., & Stark, D. (2012). "From dissonance to resonance: Cognitive interdependence in quantitative finance," *Economy and Society* 41(3): 383–417.

Blyth, M. (2002). *Great Transformations: Economic Ideas and Institutional Change in the Twentieth Century*. Cambridge: Cambridge University Press.

Borch, C., & Lange, A.-C. (2017). "High-frequency trader subjectivity: Emotional attachment and discipline in an era of algorithms," *Socio-Economic Review* 15(2): 283–306.

Bowker, G. C., & Star, S. L. (1999). *Sorting Things Out: Classification and Its Consequences*. Cambridge, MA: MIT Press.

Callon, M. (1998). "Introduction: The embededness of economic markets within economic theory," in M. Callon (ed.), *The Laws of the Markets* (pp. 1–57). Oxford and Malden, MA: Blackwell Publishers.

Callon, M., & Latour, B. (2015). "Unscrewing the Big Leviathan: How actors macrostructure reality and how sociologists help them to do so," in K. Knorr-Cetina and A. V. Cicourel (eds.), *Advances in Social Theory and Methodology: Toward an Integration of Micro- and Macro-sociologies* (pp. 277–303). London and New York, NY: Routledge.

Callon, M., MacKenzie, D., Muniesa, F., & Sui, L. (eds.). (2007). "What does it mean to say that economics is performative?," in *Do Economists Make Markets? On the Performativity of Economics* (pp. 311–357). Princeton, NJ: Princeton University Press.

Carpenter, D. P., & Moss, D. A. (2014). *Preventing Regulatory Capture: Special Interest Influence and How to Limit It*. New York, NY: Cambridge University Press.

Carruthers, B. G. (2015). "Economy and law: Old paradigms and new markets," in N. Dodd and P. Aspers (eds.), *Re-Imagining Economic Sociology* (pp. 127–146). Oxford: Oxford University Press.

Coombs, N. (2016). "What is an algorithm? Financial regulation in the era of high-frequency trading," *Economy and Society* 42(5): 278–302.

Coombs, N. (2017). "Macroprudential versus monetary blueprints for financial reform," *Journal of Cultural Economy* 10(2): 207–216.

Coombs, N. (2020). "What do stress tests test? Experimentation, demonstration, and the sociotechnical performance of regulatory science," *The British Journal of Sociology* 71(3): 520–536.

Coombs, N., & van der Heide, A. (2020). "Financialization as mathematization: The calculative and regulatory consequences of risk management," in P. Mader, D. Mertens, and N. van der Zwan (eds.), *The Routledge International Handbook of Financialization* (pp. 358–368). Abingdon: Routledge.

Dorn, N. (2012a). "Knowing markets: Would less be more?," *Economy and Society* 41(3): 316–334.

Dorn, N. (2012b). "Render unto Caesar: EU financial market regulation meets political accountability," *Journal of European Integration*, 34(3): 205–221.

Dorn, N. (2015). *Democracy and Diversity in Financial Market Regulation*. Abingdon: Routledge.

Dorn, N. (2016). "Introduction: Questions asked," in N. Dorn (ed.), *Controlling Capital: Public and Private Regulation of Financial Markets* (pp. 1–18). Abingdon: Routledge.

Engelen, E., Erturk, I., Froud, J., Johal, S., Leaver, A., Moran, M., Nilsson, A., & Williams, K. (2011). *After the Great Complacence: Financial Crisis and the Politics of Reform*. Oxford: Oxford University Press.

Financial Services Authority (FSA). (2009). *The Turner Review: A Regulatory Response to the Global Banking Crisis*. London: Financial Services Authority.

Fligstein, N., & Goldstein, A. (2010). "The anatomy of the mortgage securitization crisis," in M. Lounsbury and P. M. Hirsch (eds.), *Markets on Trial: The Economic Sociology of the U.S. Financial Crisis* (pp. 27–68). Bingley: Emerald Group Publishing.

Funk, R. J., & Hirschman, D. (2014). "Derivatives and deregulation, financial innovation and the demise of Glass–Steagall," *Administrative Science Quarterly* 59(4): 669–704.

Gilad, S. (2010). "It runs in the family: Meta-regulation and its siblings," *Regulation & Governance* 4(4): 485–506.

Goldstein, A., & Fligstein, N. (2017). "Financial markets as production markets: The industrial roots of the mortgage meltdown," *Socio-Economic Review* 15(3): 483–510.

Goldstein, M. (2017). *Banking's Final Exam: Stress Testing and Bank-Capital Reform*. Washington, DC: Peterson Institute for International Economics.

Goodhart, C. (2011). *The Basel Committee on Banking Supervision: A History of the Early Years 1974–1997*. Cambridge: Cambridge University Press.

Helleiner, E. (2014). *The Status Quo Crisis: Global Financial Governance after the 2008 Meltdown*. New York, NY: Oxford University Press.

Helleiner, E., & Pagliari, S. (2011). "The end of an era in international financial regulation? A postcrisis research agenda," *International Organization* 65(1): 169–200.

International Monetary Fund (IMF) and Financial Stability Board (FSB). (2009). *The Financial Crisis and Information Gaps: Report to the G-20 Finance Ministers and Central Bank Governors*. New York: International Monetary Fund.

Johnson, S., & Kwak, J. (2010). *13 Bankers: The Wall Street Takeover and the Next Financial Meltdown*. New York, NY: Pantheon Books.

Kang, M. (2014). "The politics of bank bailout in Japan: A cognitive capture and leadership view," *The Pacific Review* 27(2): 193–215.

Kirilenko, A. A., & Lo, A. W. (2013). "Moore's law versus Murphy's law: Algorithmic trading and its discontents," *The Journal of Economic Perspectives* 27(2): 51–72.

Knorr Cetina, K., & Bruegger, U. (2002). "Global microstructures: The virtual societies of financial markets," *American Journal of Sociology* 107(4): 905–950.

Kwak, J. (2014). "Cultural capture and the financial crisis," in D. Carpenter and D. A. Moss (eds.), *Preventing Regulatory Capture: Special Interest Influence and How to Limit It* (pp. 71–98). New York, NY: Cambridge University Press.

Langley, P. (2013). "Anticipating uncertainty, reviving risk? On the stress testing of finance in crisis," *Economy and Society* 42(1): 51–73.

Langley, P. (2015). *Liquidity Lost: The Governance of the Global Financial Crisis.* Oxford: Oxford University Press.

Latour, B. (2005). *Reassembling the Social: An Introduction to Actor-Network Theory.* Oxford: Oxford University Press.

Law, J., & Hassard, J. (1999). *Actor Network Theory and After.* Malden, MA and Oxford: Wiley-Blackwell.

Lenglet, M. (2011). "Conflicting codes and codings: How algorithmic trading is reshaping financial regulation," *Theory, Culture & Society* 28(6): 44–66.

Lenglet, M. (2012). "Ambivalence and ambiguity: The interpretative role of compliance officers," in I. Huault and C. Richard (eds.), *Finance: The Discreet Regulator: How Financial Activities Shape and Transform the World* (pp. 59–84). Houndmills: Palgrave Macmillan.

Lewis, M. (2014). *Flash Boys: Cracking the Money Code.* London: Allen Lane.

Lockwood, E. (2015). "Predicting the unpredictable: Value-at-risk, performativity, and the politics of financial uncertainty," *Review of International Political Economy* 22(4): 719–756.

MacKenzie, D. (2006). *An Engine, Not a Camera: How Financial Models Shape Markets.* Cambridge, MA: MIT Press.

MacKenzie, D. (2008). *Material Markets: How Economic Agents Are Constructed.* Oxford: Oxford University Press.

MacKenzie, D. (2011). "The credit crisis as a problem in the sociology of knowledge," *American Journal of Sociology* 116(6): 1778–1841.

MacKenzie, D. (2017). "A material political economy: Automated trading desk and price prediction in high-frequency trading," *Social Studies of Science* 47(2): 172–194.

MacKenzie, D. (2018). "Material signals: A historical sociology of high-frequency trading," *American Journal of Sociology* 123(6): 1635–1683.

MacKenzie, D., Beunza, D., Millo, Y., & Pardo-Guerra, J. P. (2012). "Drilling through the Allegheny mountains," *Journal of Cultural Economy* 5(3): 279–296.

MacKenzie, D., & Millo, Y. (2003). "Constructing a market, performing theory: The historical sociology of a financial derivatives exchange," *American Journal of Sociology* 109(1): 107–145.

MacKenzie, D., & Pardo-Guerra, J. P. (2014). "Insurgent capitalism: Island, bricolage and the re-making of finance," *Economy and Society* 43(2): 153–182.

MacKenzie, D., & Spears, T. (2014a). "'A device for being able to book P&L': The organizational embedding of the Gaussian copula," *Social Studies of Science* 44(3): 418–440.

MacKenzie, D., & Spears, T. (2014b). "'The formula that killed Wall Street': The Gaussian copula and modelling practices in investment banking," *Social Studies of Science* 44(3): 393–417.

Millo, Y., & MacKenzie, D. (2009). "The usefulness of inaccurate models: Towards an understanding of the emergence of financial risk management," *Accounting, Organizations and Society* 34(5): 638–653.

Moloney, N., Ferran, E., & Payne, J. (2015). "Introduction," in N. Moloney, E. Ferran, and J. Payne (eds.), *The Oxford Handbook of Financial Regulation* (2nd ed., pp. 1–10). Oxford: Oxford University Press.

Muniesa, F. (2014). *The Provoked Economy: Economic Reality and the Performative Turn.* London: Routledge.

Patterson, S. (2012). *Dark Pools: The Rise of A. I. Trading Machines and the Looming Threat to Wall Street*. New York, NY: Random House.

Poon, M. (2009). "From new deal institutions to capital markets: Commercial consumer risk scores and the making of subprime mortgage finance," *Accounting, Organizations and Society* 34(5): 654–674.

Riles, A. (2011). *Collateral Knowledge: Legal Reasoning in the Global Financial Markets*. Chicago, IL: The University of Chicago Press.

Riles, A. (2013). "Market collaboration: Finance, culture, and ethnography after neo-liberalism," *American Anthropologist* 115(4): 555–569.

Samman, A., Coombs, N., & Cameron, A. (2015). "For a post-disciplinary study of finance and society," *Finance and Society* 1(1): 1–5.

Schneiberg, M., & Bartley, T. (2008). "Organizations, regulation, and economic behavior: Regulatory dynamics and forms from the nineteenth to twenty-first century," *Annual Review of Law and Social Science* 4(1): 31–61.

Stellinga, B. (2019). "Why performativity limits credit rating reform," *Finance and Society* 5(1): 20–41.

Stellinga, B. (2020). "The open-endedness of macroprudential policy. Endogenous risks as an obstacle to countercyclical financial regulation," *Business and Politics* 22(1): 224–251.

Stellinga, B., & Mügge, D. (2017). "The regulator's conundrum. How market reflexivity limits fundamental financial reform," *Review of International Political Economy* 24(3): 393–423.

Stigler, G. J. (1971). "The theory of economic regulation," *The Bell Journal of Economics and Management Science* 2(1): 3–21.

Svetlova, E. (2012). "On the performative power of financial models," *Economy and Society* 41(3): 418–434.

Thiemann, M. (2014). "In the shadow of Basel: How competitive politics bred the crisis," *Review of International Political Economy* 21(6): 1203–1239.

Thiemann, M., & Lepoutre, J. (2017). "Stitched on the edge: Rule evasion, embedded regulators, and the evolution of markets," *American Journal of Sociology* 122(6): 1775–1821.

Underhill, G. R. D. (2015). "The emerging post-crisis financial architecture: The path-dependency of ideational adverse selection," *The British Journal of Politics and International Relations* 17(3): 461–493.

Weiss, H. R., & Huault, I. (2016). "Business as usual in financial markets? The creation of incommensurables as institutional maintenance work," *Organization Studies* 37(7): 991–1015.

Williams, J. W. (2009). "Envisioning financial disorder: Financial surveillance and the securities industry," *Economy and Society* 38(3): 460–491.

Woll, C. (2016). "Politics in the interest of capital: A not-so-organized combat," *Politics & Society* 44(3): 373–391.

Young, K. (2014). "The politics of global financial regulation," in T. Oatley and W. K. Winecoff (eds.), *Handbook of the International Political Economy of Monetary Relations* (pp. 304–326). Cheltenham/Northampton, MA: Edward Elgar Publishing.

Ziewitz, M. (2016). "Governing algorithms: Myth, mess, and methods," *Science, Technology, & Human Values* 41(1): 3–16.

7

CENTRAL BANKING

Clément Fontan and Louis Larue

Introduction

Before the 2007–2008 global financial crisis, the vast majority of social scientists were not paying much attention to the politics of central banking, despite the fact that, since their creation, central banks have been pivotal institutions between private financial institutions and public authorities (Singleton, 2010). During the past decades, central banks acquired considerable independence from public officials under the Central Bank Independence (CBI) template (McNamara, 2002). Governments justified their decisions to delegate monetary competences by relying on a narrow conception of monetary policy, in which central bankers should only seek to control inflation and ignore the implications of their policies on other economic issues such as financial stability or wealth inequalities (Issing et al., 2001; Marcussen, 2009). Heterodox economists and critical political economists opposed this view by declaring that monetary policy is fundamentally political as it deals with complicated policy trade-offs, which generates winners and losers (Epstein & Gintis, 1995; Forder, 2005). However, until 2007, their concerns were very marginal and remained at the fringes of the political debate. The vast majority of policy-makers, economists, and central bankers themselves agreed on the fact that the CBI template was the optimal institutional arrangement between fiscal and monetary authorities.

However, the changing role of central banks since the crisis has reversed the situation. Indeed, in face of the risks associated with an implosion of the financial system, central banks moved away from their traditional inflation-targeting framework and started to implement systemic unconventional monetary instruments in order to stabilize large interconnected financial systems and, later on, to revive growth (Goodhart et al., 2014). For the sake of simplicity, let us say that these unconventional instruments unfold in two categories: an extension

154

of regular liquidity offers in terms of maturity, volume, and collateral range, on the one hand, and straight purchases of securities on secondary markets (the so-called Quantitative Easing (QE) programs), on the other hand. This change of role has inflated central banks' balance sheets by five times for the Federal Reserve and the European Central Bank (ECB) and by ten times for the Bank of England between 2007 and 2019 (Potter & Smets, 2019).

In addition to these changes in monetary policy, central banks have also obtained or gained back prudential supervisory competences, which they were deprived from since the end of the 1990s (McPhilemy, 2016). In the case of the ECB, it also exerted coercive pressures on Eurozone economic reforms through the conditionality of its financial interventions and its participation in the so-called "Troika," which included the European Commission and the International Monetary Fund and supervises the implementation of these reforms (Fontan, 2018).

This shifting role led to a (re)politicization of central banking: the salience of monetary issues rose in the public debate, it created new political cleavages and new policy watchers appeared (Best, 2016; Tesche, 2019). This repoliticization worries central bankers, who see it as a threat for their independence (Goodhart & Lastra, 2018). Indeed, when independent regulatory agencies extend the remit of their power, political authorities often seek to regain control and reduce their level of autonomy (Elgie, 2002). Recent examples include Donald Trump's Twitter attacks against the Federal Reserve Chair, Jay Powell, and the German backlash against the asset purchases and the negative interest rates implemented by the ECB.

Conversely, central bankers try to neutralize repoliticization and these efforts influence the design of their policies. In fact, independent regulatory agencies often pursue "reputational strategies" in order to maintain or extend their level of autonomy (Carpenter, 2010). Central bankers often seek to subsume their new unconventional monetary tools under the pre-crisis justifications of their independence (Van't Klooster & Fontan, 2019). By emphasizing continuity, they keep decisions on new monetary instruments in the domain of their expert judgments, and thereby outside the domain of democratic politics (Hay, 2007; Johnson et al., 2019). These strategies were successful to the extent that, until today, no major central bank has suffered a significant loss of independence. In parallel, there is still a very high consensus among economists in favor of the status-quo (Dietsch et al., 2018: Chapter 4). However, this pretense to continuity obfuscates the fact that new monetary tools come with significant distributive consequences, whose costs might outweigh their benefits (Fontan et al., 2016).

In this chapter, we review how the (critical) political economy literature has scrutinized the evolving role of central banks this last decade and we debunk central banks' pretense to continuity. Since monetary policy has been successfully scientized in the last decades, this critical perspective asks to pay equal attention to the "real-world" monetary policy developments and to the scientific debates on these developments. We remain, however, agnostic on the performativity of scientific knowledge on central bank operations.

We focus on two lines of criticism that are central to the inquiry developed in this *Handbook of Critical Finance Studies*.[1] First, we examine how financial power shapes central banks' unconventional policy to the benefit of private finance. Second, we review how these "high-finance" struggles affect "low-finance," that is, what are the distributive effects of post-crisis monetary policy on firms and households? Finally, we examine current debates on alternative monetary tools, which could potentially fare better than current monetary arrangements in distributive, ecological, and democratic terms.

In what follows, we analyze the pre-crisis CBI template that informs the practices and rhetoric of central bankers to this day ("The Era of CBI") and the heterodox criticism against this model ("The Heterodox Criticism of CBI"). Then, we explain how financial power shapes central banks' unconventional monetary operations ("Financial Power"), outline the distributive implications of unconventional monetary policies ("The Distributive Dimension of Unconventional Monetary Policy"), and expose debates on future monetary arrangements ("After the Crisis: Which Alternative Monetary Policy Instruments?").

The Era of CBI

Central banks are public institutions that have the monopoly over the issuance of legal tender. They are not the sole creators of money: the greatest part of the money supply is made of the sum of all credits issued by private banks (McLeay et al., 2014). However, central banks' money has a special privilege that makes them pivotal regulatory institutions within the state-finance nexus: all other kinds of money are promises redeemable in central banks' money (Pistor, 2013). This privilege gives central banks the capacity to achieve two policy objectives that are crucial for the functioning of financialized capitalist systems: price stability and financial stability (Goodhart, 2011).

While these two objectives remained constant throughout their history, central banks were also assigned other roles, which fluctuate in time and space. For example, the US Federal Reserve is tasked with the mission of pursuing full employment. Some central banks, especially in non-Western countries, aim at maintaining a stable exchange rate and support national developmental policies (Campiglio et al., 2018). In the same vein, Western central banks were also backing up domestic credit policies in the aftermath of the Second World War until the advent of the CBI era (Monnet, 2018). Historically, the extent of objectives granted to central banks is correlated with their degree of independence: the higher the degree of independence of central banks, the smaller their set of goals, and vice versa.

The CBI template swept around the world in the late 1980s. Its main premises were that central banks should remain politically independent and that their main task was to maintain low inflation. The theoretical sources of CBI are rooted in the context of the inflationary 1970s in industrialized countries. Since established Keynesian theories seemed unable to explain the inflationary pressures of the time (De Vroey, 2016), other schools of thought started to gain preeminence in the macro-economic debate. The so-called new classical macroeconomics were very influential in the build-up of the CBI template (Barro & Gordon, 1983; Kydland & Prescott, 1977; Lucas, 1972). The core issue identified by these theories is the "time-inconsistency problem," which relates to the lack of credibility of elected officials when they announce that they are committed to fight inflation. Since market participants believe that elected officials cannot resist manipulating the money supply, they adapt their expectations and price future inflation in their investment decisions, which, in turn, generate inflation pressures.

The policy upshot is to reinforce the credibility of central banks' anti-inflationary stance by isolating them from political pressures and removing incentives that might distract them from their price stability objective. Kydland and Prescott (1977) proposed to adopt strict monetary rules to anchor credibility, but their proposal was quickly dismissed following rule-based policy failures (Kaldor, 1985). Rogoff's (1985) proposal was much more successful because it made anti-inflationary credibility compatible with flexible policy-making. His solution consists in appointing a "conservative" central banker who is significantly more biased against inflation than other policy-makers are, so as to minimize the risk of letting central banks engage in expansionary and inflationary policies.

The CBI template constitutes an important exemption to the majoritarian rule in liberal democracies. According to its proponents, its legitimacy depends on two important features. The first feature is that central banks have only one policy objective: price stability, and one tool to achieve it: the setting of short-term interest rates. That goal is "narrow": it does not require policy measures beyond the technical operations required to reach the inflation target. Second, that goal can easily be operationalized and monitored by tracking changes in the price index. Low inflation can, therefore, serve as an objective and narrow guide for central banks' actions. In practice, from the 1980s onward, the vast majority of central banks converged on a very similar pattern of practices to reach their objectives (Borio, 2011). In the pre-2007 era, central banks usually determined a target rate, and then aimed at maintaining that rate thanks to open market operations (OMO), in which liquidity is provided in the form of central banks reserves to commercial banks at a certain interest rate against collateral for a short time. In that framework, central banks have only an indirect influence on real economic variables: private banks form the channels of transmission of central bank monetary policy and allocate credit to households and firms.

The second feature that justifies the CBI framework is that the pursuit of price stability by central banks does not have major distributive consequences (Ingham, 2004). This implies that central bankers can treat monetary policy as "neutral," in at least two senses. First, in line with what monetarists have claimed since the 1960s (Friedman, 1968), most central bankers generally adhere to the view that monetary policy does not have any long-term effect on macroeconomic variables, except for inflation. Changes in "real" variables (such as worker productivity) affect the economy in the long run, but "monetary" variables do not. Hence, price stability was considered as a precondition for the successful pursuit of other objectives rather than a variable that can be manipulated for distributive purposes. Second, OMOs were supposed to have a neutral impact on the relative prices of financial assets and, thus, to avoid interferences in the price formation process among market participants (market neutrality).

In sum, under the CBI template, central bank operations were broadly perceived as apolitical (Marcussen, 2009); the goal to attain was narrow and consensual and the technical means to achieve it unproblematic. Crucially, this perception also forms the justifications for the very high level of independence given to central bankers.

The Heterodox Criticism of CBI

Against this consensus, heterodox scholars constantly claimed that monetary policy is utterly political and they tried to debunk the myths underlying the CBI framework (Aglietta & Orléan, 1998).

First, even if the aims of monetary policy are narrow, fulfilling these aims give rise to important trade-offs (Forder, 1998). For instance, the aims of price stability and full-employment often come at odds with each other, as fast-growing economic systems may generate inflationary pressures. Moreover, the beneficial nature of price stability cannot be assessed in isolation from other economic phenomena or from outside specific political contexts. For instance, in the post-war period, West Germany experienced both low inflation and low unemployment rates thanks to its economic model based on good export competitiveness and strong institutional coordination between the Bundesbank and powerful trade unions (Hall & Franzese, 1998). However, following the creation of the Eurozone, the imitation of the German price stability model was less beneficial for other European countries where wage coordination and export performance are weaker (e.g., Spain, Italy, France, Greece, and Portugal).

Second, monetary policy, even before 2007, has distributional effects. Indeed, low inflation tends to benefit creditors, at the expense of debtors. Compared to other groups, owners of financial assets have benefited from a disproportionate increase in their wealth since the early 1980s, which marked the starting point of the financialization of the economy (Epstein, 2005). This is the result of financial deregulation and high real interest rates, which stemmed from conservative inflation-targeting monetary policies. Some central bankers have acknowledged that monetary policy can generate these distributional impacts (Fontan et al., 2016: 15). However, they generally dismiss the relevance of these effects by framing them as the unintended, small, and unavoidable consequences of monetary policy, which, according to them, could be addressed with fiscal policy (Fontan et al., 2016: 16–17).

Third, the independence of central banks from political actors does not mean that central banks are independent from financial markets. Indeed, the financialization of the economy, which has accelerated since the 1980s, meant that financial intermediaries (on financial intermediaries, see also the chapter by Tadjeddine in this *Handbook*) raised in importance and gained increased powers to influence their regulators, including central bankers. Adolph's (2013) seminal research documents several cases of former central bankers moving to private institutions at the end of their careers, or of private bankers getting appointed in high-profile positions in central banks. The troubling conclusion is that those passing through these revolving doors are more likely to take decisions in favor of the private financial sector, which amplifies the risks of "regulatory capture."

In short, from the 1990s until the 2007–2008 financial crisis, the CBI framework reigned (almost) unchallenged. The overall consensus was that central banking was mostly concerned about technicalities, and that its main purpose was to maintain low inflation. It was believed that the financialization of the economy was conducive to financial stability and that monetary policy had no effect on the distribution of wealth and income. However, the next two sections show that the 2007 financial crisis has put a serious blow to these conceptions and has shaken the pre-crisis consensus. In fact, the discrepancy between the stability of the CBI paradigm and the changing role of central banks since the crisis is a major research agenda for critical finance studies.

Financial Power

The CBI framework might have successfully isolated central bankers from political pressures but failed at identifying another source of influence: financial power. Beyond the issue of regulatory capture (cf. the previous section), scholars have identified two sources of power wielded by the financial sector over central banks: (1) structural power and (2) infrastructural power.

Financial *structural power* derives from the central role played by financial institutions in our economies (Culpepper & Reinke, 2014). When banks become too-big-to-fail (TBTF) during the financialization process, it is much more likely that public authorities will bail them out in the case of financial difficulties (Woll, 2014). The awareness that policymakers' hands are tied creates a problem of moral hazard, since banks have an incentive to grow to the point that they become TBTF. In fact, Federal Reserve insiders acknowledged in 2004 that reputational and economic costs linked to the failure of a TBTF institution would be so high that they would have no choice but to bail out insolvent banks, even though it would trigger a moral hazard problem (Stern & Feldman, 2004).

Arguably, the liquidity offered to insolvent institutions in the early stages of the crisis and the systemic unconventional monetary tools implemented later on confirmed that, when central banks are faced with a trade-off between short-term financial stability and long-term financial stability, they tend to favor the former (Jacobs & King, 2016; Kalaitzake, 2019). In turn, these interventions transformed central banks into "bad banks," to the extent that they swapped liquidity against risky assets previously owned by commercial banks (Cour-Thimann, 2013). Moreover, banks did not use this favorable situation to recapitalize and consolidate their balance-sheets to be more resilient when the next financial crisis hits (Brunnermeier & Sannikov, 2016). Rather, the discrepancy between the post-crisis weak economic growth and market euphoria suggests that financial operators did not make any fundamental changes to their risky behaviors (Admati & Hellwig, 2014; Turner, 2016).

Considering that the economic and social consequences of the 2007 market meltdown would have been more severe without the swiftness and the scope of central bank interventions, moral hazard could be considered as a small price to pay (Eichengreen, 2014). However, in this case, we would expect central bankers and other political authorities to support stricter financial regulation and deleveraging of the financial sector to prevent similar scenarios in the future. Yet, financial regulation reforms did not meaningfully limit the problematic financial activities that led to the crisis (Helleiner, 2014; Thiemann et al., 2018). The first research results on the role played by central banks in these reforms show that, far from advocating stricter rules, they have advocated further financialization of the banking sector (Conti-Brown, 2016: 160; Gabor & Vestergaard, 2018; Kalaitzake, 2019). We argue that financial structural power partly explains this regulatory neglect.

Commercial banks wield *infrastructural power*, i.e., they exert control over the transmission channels of monetary policy (Braun, 2018). In the words of Braun, these channels of transmission are "infrastructural entanglements" which makes central bankers dependent on bankers to steer the economy. Scholars have explored how central banks' depoliticization strategies ignited commercial banks' infrastructural power before the crisis on both sides of the Atlantic (Braun, 2018; Krippner, 2012; Walter & Wansleben, 2019). Now, they study how this leverage led to the protection and promotion of problematic market activities by central bankers and their lack of control over the use of the liquidity provided to financial operators since the crisis.

After Lehman Brothers' bankruptcy, the Fed, the BoE, and the ECB injected massive amounts of liquidity to stabilize problematic segments of financial markets propelled by the 1990s financial innovation and deregulation, such as repo and securitization markets (Braun, 2016; Gabor & Ban, 2016; Krippner, 2012). In fact, since the crisis, central banks became "market-makers of last-resort": they now provide safe assets to market participants who use them as collateral in repo market operations (Mehrling, 2010).[2] Moreover, the ECB came to rely so much on the smooth functioning of repo markets for the transmission of its monetary policy that it successfully opposed their inclusion into the EU financial transactions' tax proposal (Gabor, 2016; Kalaitzake, 2017). Moreover, the ECB and the BoE have also been at the forefront of the EU authorities' efforts to revive securitization markets under the Capital Market Union proposal (see *Competition and Change*, special issue 2018, 22(2)). In other words, central bankers have actively defended and promoted problematic market activities that led to the crisis because the transmission of their monetary policy came to rely on their smooth functioning.

The issue is that there is a huge discrepancy between the amounts of liquidity injected by central banks in the financial markets and their impact on economic performance (Turner, 2016). This is because commercial banks exploit their leverage to use the liquidity provided by central banks for purposes other than providing credit to economic agents (such as either investing in exiting assets or derivatives or engaging in share buybacks). Political economy research on the conditionality attached to monetary instruments has shown that central bankers fail to control the use of their liquidity (Dietsch et al., 2018: Chapter 3). For example, as no conditionality was attached to the initial ECB Long-Term Refinancing Operations (LTRO), banks engaged in trade activities that are problematic from the point of view of central bank policy objectives: they borrowed liquidity at 1% to purchase risk-free sovereign bonds with higher interest rates and pocketed the difference. When some form of conditionality on the use of liquidity was introduced (Targeted (T)LTRO), banks were reluctant to participate in these operations, and the ECB quickly gave up its attempt to control the use of its liquidity (Fontan, 2018).

In the same vein, the latest ECB monetary policy innovation combines TLTRO with the creation of a two-tier system[3] on bank reserves. This allows "dual interest rates" in which central banks set an interest rate for bank lending, which is lower than the interest rate paid by banks on their reserves held at the central bank. Hence, "dual interest rates" raise the net interest income of the private financial sector: the ECB "pays" banks to pursue lending (Mackintosh, 2019). Like with its other unconventional tools, the ECB justifies these very generous conditions for the private banking sector with the argument that such advantages are necessary to incentivize banks to lend more to firms and households (European Central Bank, 2019).

In sum, isolating central banks from political pressures does not solve the issue of their independence towards financial market interests. Quite the contrary, the answer of independent central banks to the financial crisis has exposed that their policies are, at least to some extent, influenced by the structural and infrastructural power wielded by financial institutions. Studying financial power over central banks offers vibrant research perspectives to analyze recent developments within the state-high finance nexus (Strange, 1986). Moreover, since the crisis, central banks became key policy actors in national and supranational financial reforms thanks to their epistemic authority (Omarova, 2018). From this perspective, analyzing their research production on financial regulation might add a new piece to the puzzle of lackluster post-crisis financial regulation (on financial regulation, see also the chapter by Coombs in this *Handbook*).

The Distributive Dimension of Unconventional Monetary Policy

The analysis of financial power sheds lights on how central bank operations are impacted by the preferences of market players in the high finance circles. Studying the distributive effects of central banks' unconventional policies helps to understand how financial power impacts low finance, that is, wealth distribution at the household/firms level. In fact, the criticism addressed by heterodox scholars against the "neutral monetary policy" assumption underlying the CBI framework (cf. "The Heterodox Criticism of CBI" section) must be renewed in line with the shift in the instrumentation of monetary policy since the crisis. While we know that the bias displayed by conservative central bankers in favor of price stability has advantaged the owners of financial capital over other economic agents, does unconventional monetary policy generate winners and losers?

Central bankers claim that their asset purchase programs do not have significant distributive effects. In fact, they recognize that their purchases have direct inegalitarian effects: when central banks purchase sovereign bonds, this pushes up the value of those bonds – and affects other market segments too as it fosters demand for corporate bonds and equities. Since the households that hold financial assets are concentrated at the top end of the wealth distribution, asset purchases make rich people even richer (Bell et al., 2012). However, central bankers claim that this is not the end of the story just yet. Asset purchases also trigger indirect effects: they help to revive growth and, thus, boost employment and wages, which mostly help the modest households. In turn, the combined effects of direct and indirect channels on households' wealth depend on the composition and the distribution of financial assets and debts among households (Colciago et al., 2019: 23).

ECB economists claim that, in the case of asset purchases conducted in the Eurozone since 2015, indirect effects outweigh direct effects and they conclude that ECB asset purchases have actually decreased wealth inequality (Ampudia et al., 2018: 33; Lenza & Slacalek, 2018). Can we trust this in-house ECB research and extrapolate that, in general, asset purchases have helped to decrease inequalities? Since these are the only studies (to our knowledge) to make such strong claim on the egalitarian effects of asset purchases, it is important to discuss them to make our larger point about the distributive dimension of unconventional monetary policy. Fontan et al. (2019) found four reasons to be doubtful about these results, and we introduce a fifth argument, which tackles the market neutrality issue.

First, a recent literature review of the Heterogeneous Agents New Keynesian (HANK) models[4] gives a much more nuanced view than the research produced by the ECB (Colciago et al., 2019). After identifying four direct channels of transmission of unconventional tools and two indirect ones, this literature review notices that most of the research has considered these channels in isolation and that the research results of these studies contradict each other. The authors conclude that the existing empirical evidence on the distributive effects of monetary policy is mixed: effects vary according to the channel under study, the examined monetary tool, and the economic structure of the country and households. In other words, contrary to the conclusions of the ECB researchers who considers only two channels of distribution, it is impossible to estimate precisely the distributive effects of unconventional monetary policy until HANK models incorporate direct and indirect channels of transmission of monetary policy simultaneously rather than in isolation.

Second, there are solid reasons to have doubts about the capacity of HANK models to deliver robust estimations of the distributive effects of unconventional monetary policy. Indeed, the distinction between direct and indirect effects indicates that the former is easier to measure than the latter. While direct effects have, without doubt, inflated financial asset prices, causal links between asset purchases and the stimulation of economic growth are much harder to track down. For example, a recent study has shown that the identification strategy used in Lenza & Slacalek (2018) is invalid (Elbourne & Ji, 2019). Indeed, these authors have substituted the values attached to the ECB monetary policy in the model by random numbers but reached similar results. If macroeconomic changes associated with monetary policy were robust, results with random numbers should have been different from the ones used in the ECB's studies.

Third, the measurement of wealth inequalities is problematic. For example, by using the national wealth-to-national income ratio as a proxy for wealth inequalities rather than the Gini index,[5] Fuller et al. (2019) found that rising house prices, which is an effect of asset purchases, has inegalitarian effects. By contrast, in conventional central banks models, it is assumed that rising house prices help to decrease wealth inequalities, which are measured with the Gini index. Moreover, the measurement of inequalities in the monetary economics literature does not really correspond to common perceptions of inequalities. This discrepancy is exemplified in the left panel of Figure 7.1, which replicates a simulation of the impact of ECB purchases on wealth inequalities (Ampudia et al., 2018: fig. 4).

According to the authors, the fact that the lowest quintile experiences the fastest wealth growth in percentage among the whole population is an indicator of the egalitarian effects of asset purchases. Yet, the representation of the data in percentage hides huge disparities of variation in monetary values. The right panel of Figure 7.1 shows it well: 2.5% of 1,100€ barely amounts to 30€ of additional wealth for the poorest quintile while the median wealth for the richest quintile is augmented by more than 5,000€. While these evolutions would be associated with a slight decline in the Gini index, it would take more than 350 years for the net rise in median income of the lowest quintile to exceed the higher quintile.

Fourth, this study and other central banks' researchers do not consider alternative counterfactual scenarios seriously enough. While central bankers often repeat that asset purchases might have inegalitarian effects, they underline that

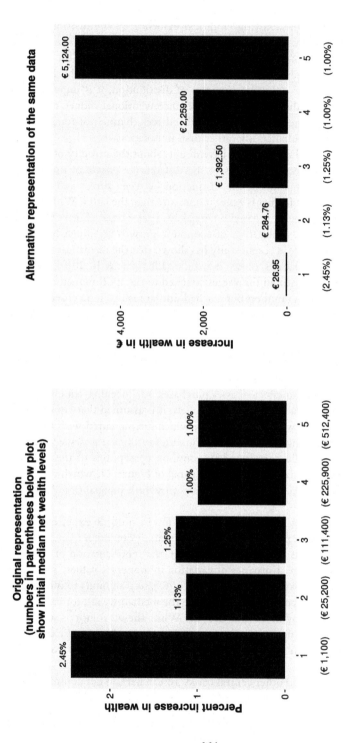

Figure 7.1 Two dissenting views on the distributive effects of asset purchases (Fontan et al., 2019, p.11).

the lack of implementation of these instruments would have brought even worst distributive outcomes since poor households suffer the most during recessions (Fontan et al., 2016: 18). Asset purchases were arguably a better policy option than doing nothing. However, it does not preclude alternative monetary tools that would fare better than QE in distributive or environmental terms. We turn to these alternatives in our next and last section.

Last but not least, central banks do not only purchase sovereign bonds: many of them intervene now on corporate securities markets[6] (Van't Klooster & Fontan, 2019). Central bankers claim that these interventions are "market neutral," that is, they do not distort relative prices of financial assets. To implement market neutrality, central bankers mirror investment funds' business models as they follow a passive neutral strategy, which consists in purchasing a basket of securities that is representative of the market universe. While central bankers seem to be successful in not distorting prices within the corporate securities markets, their purchases create clear winners and losers. Winners include the firms with a large exposure to the corporate securities markets whose securities are directly purchased by central banks, that is, big multinational firms with a large carbon footprint (Matikainen et al., 2017). Conversely, losers are small and medium enterprises (SMEs), which do not have the financial capacities to emit bonds.

In sum, unconventional monetary policies have distributive consequences. While it is still difficult to identify winners and losers of these policies, preliminary research indicates that owners of financial assets and multinational firms with a large carbon footprint are part of the former group while households and SMEs are part of the latter group. In the light of these indications, it is easy to understand why central bankers fear for their legitimacy. However, rather than trying to hide these facts by claiming that their interventions are neutral, central bankers should acknowledge these inescapable consequences and look for policy instruments that could deliver better outcomes.

After the Crisis: Which Alternative Monetary Policy Instruments?

In this section, we review several alternative instruments that, according to their proponents, might weaken financial power and lead to better distributive outcomes. Most notably, these proposals illustrate how the current framework within which central banks navigate might have become obsolete.

One of them is the so-called "helicopter money" proposal, in which central banks would credit citizens' account directly, rather than going through financial intermediaries. Born as a thought experiment by Milton Friedman (1968), the idea was later revived by NGOs and left-wing elected officials in the aftermath of the global financial crisis. Muellbauer (2014), an academic and think-tank researcher, argues in favor of providing "all workers and pensioners" with a 500€ payment from the ECB, using their social security number or the electoral register to identify them. In the non-academic world, this policy has sometimes been called "QE for the people" to highlight its appeal in comparison with the QE programs in the United States and Europe (e.g., van Lerven, 2016).

The main rationale given to that proposal (Blyth & Lonergan, 2014; Buiter, 2014; Muellbauer, 2014) is that, in economies suffering from a lack of spending, giving money directly to people (instead of buying bonds) would help to revive growth or help stop a recession. According to Muellbauer (2014), this effect is expected to be larger in economies where people are relatively more cash-poor (e.g., Portugal or Spain) than in economies, such as Germany, where people have already constituted large amounts of savings.

The helicopter money proposal suggests that, for central banks to have significant effects on the post-crisis economy, they might need to get rid of the CBI framework and the regular channels of transmission of monetary policy. However, with helicopter money, private banks would still hold a central place within the financial system, since money would be credited on citizens' bank accounts. As the 2007–2008 financial crisis has shown, the important weight of private banks in the economy creates a moral hazard problem and helicopter money would not help to decrease financial power (see "Financial Power" section).

Central Bank Digital Currencies (CBDC) could provide a useful tool for central banks to bypass the private sector while allowing them to implement unconventional monetary policies, such as the helicopter money proposal. In fact, today, central bankers seriously consider implementing CBDC. CBDC would be labeled in a national currency (euro, dollar, sterling pound...) and would, in most scenarios, amount to giving access to central bank balance sheet to a larger public (Barrdear & Kumhof, 2016; Bordo & Levin, 2017; Broadbent, 2016; Dyson & Hodgson, 2016). In practice, each citizen would have an account, labeled in CBDC, either directly at the central bank or indirectly through specific agencies. In any case, the money would stay at the central bank, and be legally its money, even if accredited financial intermediaries could provide access to these accounts to the public. Citizens and firms would be able to exchange their money held in cash or on their bank account against CBDC.

The implementation of CBDC on a large scale has the potential to reduce dramatically financial power. Contrary to the "simple" helicopter money proposal, CBDC would allow central banks to credit citizens' accounts directly without necessarily resorting to banking intermediaries (Engert & Fung, 2017: 6). CBDC could also help alleviate financial structural power, by making private banks less vital for the economy. Citizens could opt for holding their savings on central banks' accounts, which, by definition, would be much safer than commercial banks' accounts (Broadbent, 2016; Dyson & Hodgson, 2016: 9–10). Moreover, the introduction of CBDC would decrease banks' infrastructural power by offering an alternative payment system that is not managed by the private banking sector.

Both proposals would be in line with the dynamics unfolding in central banking since the 2007 financial crisis. In short, these dynamics have consisted in giving greater powers to central banks while looking for ways to circumvent the damaging effects of financial power. Yet, the increased powers of central banks have not come with stricter political controls (Adolph, 2018; Högenauer & Howarth, 2016; Jones & Matthijs, 2019). Without significant changes in the current central banking framework, the helicopter money and CBDC proposals would aggravate this problem: central bankers would have access to household and firms financial data, and they would take decisions with even more profound distributive consequences than current unconventional monetary policy.

One way forward to increase their legitimacy would be to adapt their mandate, by putting more weight on the distributional or environmental impact of their (unconventional) policies (Fontan et al., 2016; Van't Klooster, 2018). Alternatively, greater cooperation between monetary and fiscal authorities does not necessarily involve mandate change: central banks could increase their purchases of public investment banks, respect ethical or environmental criteria defined by the parliament when purchasing bonds, or form tier committees with fiscal authorities to set allocative targets (Ryan-Collins & Van Lerven, 2018). From this perspective, the current central banks' frameworks in South-East Asia and the former mandates of Western central banks during the 1950s offer glimpses of how monetary policy could contribute more directly to the fight against climate change and inequalities (Campiglio et al., 2018; Monnet, 2018).

Concluding Remarks

Between the 1990s and the 2007–2008 financial crisis, central banking followed a specific template, which, by historical standards, has narrowed down the objectives of monetary policy to price stability and isolated central banks from political pressures to an unprecedented degree (Singleton, 2010). While heterodox scholars maintained that central banks were inherently political institutions, the CBI template reached a very high level of consensus among policy-makers and economists and it led to an effective depoliticization of monetary issues (Marcussen, 2009). The 2007 financial crisis changed this state of affairs, since it fragilized central assumptions of the CBI model (such as the neglect of financial stability). Moreover, the unconventional monetary instruments implemented by central banks have been much more controversial than the regular pre-2007 interest rates policies (Goodhart et al., 2014).

In this chapter, we have identified two critical research agendas, which offer stimulating perspectives on how to grasp the power dynamics at play in this new era of central banking. On the one hand, there is a new stream of political economy literature, which untangles the state-finance nexus by analyzing the role played by central banks in the stabilization of hypertrophied and fragile financial systems. This analysis of "high finance" power games reveals that private banks were able to wield structural and infrastructural power over central banks and, thus, have influenced the formulation of unconventional monetary policy in their favor.

On the other hand, to understand how these "high finance" power struggles impact "low finance," we have reviewed the most recent macro-economic research on the distributive implications of asset purchases. While acknowledging the mixed empirical results of this stream of research, we are very critical of the in-house ECB research claiming that asset purchases have helped to decrease inequalities. On the contrary, rich households and multinational firms with large carbon footprint seem to be the obvious winners of unconventional policies, while gains by poorer households and SMEs are less obvious.

Finally, in the light of all the drawbacks of the unconventional monetary policy developed under the CBI framework, we have explored two potential reforms that are gaining traction in the public debate: helicopter money and CBDC. These proposals have an obvious ethical appeal but they could reinforce the unchecked gain of power of central banks since the crisis. In sum, future research in critical finance studies should pay specific attention to the widening gap between the gain of new powers by central bankers and their resilient high level of protection against political interferences.

Notes

1 In this chapter, we had to exclude other significant topics of interest on central banking. Yet, we encourage readers to pay attention to the international dimension of the monetary system, which is fraught by the discretionary politics of the Federal Reserve (Sahasrabuddhe, 2019) or to the ideational research aiming at opening the "black-box" of central banks' decision-making (Ferrara, 2019; Golub et al., 2015).
2 This evolving role mirrors the changing structure of financial systems where collateral-based repo operations became the main source of financing for banks and other financial intermediaries (Gabor, 2016).
3 A two-tier system exempts part of commercial banks reserves held at the central bank from negative rates.
4 HANK models differ from the Representative Agents New Keynesian (RANK) models that were used before the crisis in that they allow modeling various consumption responses of households to monetary policy changes (Kaplan et al., 2018).
5 The Gini index is the most common measure to track wealth inequality.
6 The ECB, the Bank of England, and the Swiss National Bank are three good examples.

References

Admati, A., & Hellwig, M. (2014). *The Bankers' New Clothes: What's Wrong with Banking and What to Do About it.* Princeton, NJ: Princeton University Press.
Adolph, C. (2013). *Bankers, Bureaucrats, and Central Bank Politics: The Myth of Neutrality.* Cambridge: Cambridge University Press.
Adolph, C. (2018). "The missing politics of central banks," *Political Science & Politics* 51(4): 737–742.
Aglietta, M., & Orléan, A. (eds.). (1998). *La monnaie souveraine.* Paris: Odile Jacob.
Ampudia, M., Georgarakos, D., Slacalek, J., Tristani, O., Vermeulen, P., & Violante, G. (2018). *Monetary Policy and Household Inequality.* Discussion Papers No. 2170, ECB Working Paper Series. Frankfurt am Main: European Central Bank.

Barrdear, J., & Kumhof, M. (2016). *The Macroeconomics of Central Bank Issued Digital Currencies*. Staff Working Paper No. 605. Retrieved from http://www.bankofengland. co.uk/research/Pages/workingpapers/2016/swp605.aspx.

Barro, R. J., & Gordon, D. B. (1983). "Rules, discretion and reputation in a model of monetary policy," *Journal of Monetary Economics* 12(1): 101–121.

Bell, V., Joyce, M., Liu, Z., & Young, C. (2012). "The distributional effects of asset purchases," *Bank of England Quarterly Bulletin*, Q3/2012.

Best, J. (2016). "Rethinking central bank accountability in uncertain times," *Ethics & International Affairs* 30(2): 215–232.

Blyth, M., & Lonergan, E. (2014). "Print less but transfer more: Why central banks should give money directly to the people," *Foreign Affairs* 93(5): 98–109.

Bordo, M. D., & Levin, A. T. (2017). *Central Bank Digital Currency and the Future of Monetary Policy*. Working Paper No. 23711. Washington, DC: National Bureau of Economic Research.

Borio, C. (2011). *Central Banking Post-Crisis: What Compass for Uncharted Waters?* BIS Working Paper No. 353. Retrieved from https://ideas.repec.org/p/bis/biswps/353. html.

Braun, B. (2016). "From performativity to political economy: Index investing, ETFs and asset manager capitalism," *New Political Economy* 21(3): 257–273.

Braun, B. (2018). "Central banking and the infrastructural power of finance: The case of ECB support for repo and securitization markets," *Socio-Economic Review*, forthcoming.

Broadbent, B. (2016). *Central Banks and Digital Currencies*. Speech at the London School of Economics, London. Retrieved from http://www.bankofengland.co.uk/ publications/Documents/speeches/2016/speech886.pdf.

Brunnermeier, M. K., & Sannikov, Y. (2016). *The I Theory of Money*. NBER Working Paper No. 22533. National Bureau of Economic Research.

Buiter, W. H. (2014). "The simple analytics of helicopter money: Why it works — always," *Economics: The Open-Access, Open-Assessment E-Journal* 8(2014–28): 1–45. doi: 10/gfq93g.

Campiglio, E., Dafermos, Y., Monnin, P., Ryan-Collins, J., Schotten, G., & Tanaka, M. (2018). "Climate change challenges for central banks and financial regulators," *Nature Climate Change* 8(6): 462–468.

Carpenter, D. P. (2010). *Reputation and Power: Organizational image and pharmaceutical regulation at the FDA*. Princeton, NJ: Princeton University Press.

Colciago, A., Samarina, A., & de Haan, J. (2019). "Central bank policies and income and wealth inequality: A survey," *Journal of Economic Surveys* 33(4): 1–33.

Conti-Brown, P. (2016). *The Power and Independence of the Federal Reserve*. Princeton, NJ: Princeton University Press.

Cour-Thimann, P. (2013). "Monetary policy and redistribution: Information from central bank balance sheets in the Euro area and the US," *Review of Economics* 64: 293–324.

Culpepper, P. D., & Reinke, R. (2014). "Structural power and bank bailouts in the United Kingdom and the United States," *Politics & Society* 42: 427–454.

De Vroey, M. (2016). *A History of Macroeconomics from Keynes to Lucas and Beyond*. Cambridge: Cambridge University Press.

Dietsch, P., Claveau, F., & Fontan, C. (2018). *Do Central Banks Serve The People?* Cambridge: Polity.

Dyson, B., & Hodgson, G. (2016). *Digital Cash: Why Central Banks Should Start Issuing Electronic Money*. London: Positive Money.

Eichengreen, B. (2014). *Hall of Mirrors: The Great Depression, the Great Recession, and the Uses-and Misuses-of History*. Oxford: Oxford University Press.

Elbourne, A., & Ji, K. (2019). *Do SVARs Identify Unconventional Monetary Policy Shocks?* CBP Discussion Papers. Retrieved from https://www.cpb.nl/sites/default/files/omnidownload/CPB-Discussion-Paper-391-Do-SVARs-identify-unconventional-monetary-policy-shocks.pdf.

Elgie, R. (2002). "The politics of the European Central Bank: Principal-agent theory and the democratic deficit," *Journal of European Public Policy* 9(2): 186–200.

Engert, W., & Fung, B. (2017). *Central Bank Digital Currency: Motivations and Implications*, No. 16. Retrieved from https://www.bankofcanada.ca/2017/11/staff-discussion-paper-2017-16/.

Epstein, G. A. (ed.). (2005). *Financialization and the World Economy.* Cheltenham: Edward Elgar.

Epstein, G. A., & Gintis, H. M. (eds.). (1995). *Macroeconomic Policy after the Conservative Era: Studies in Investment, Saving and Finance.* Cambridge: Cambridge University Press.

European Central Bank. (2019, September 12). *ECB Introduces Two-Tier System for Remunerating Excess Liquidity Holdings.* [Press release]. Retrieved from https://www.ecb.europa.eu/press/pr/date/2019/html/ecb.pr190912_2~a0b47cd62a.en.html.

Ferrara, F. M. (2019). "The battle of ideas on the Euro crisis: Evidence from ECB inter-meetingspeeches,"*JournalofEuropeanPublicPolicy.*doi:10.1080/13501763.2019.1670231

Fontan, C. (2018). "Frankfurt's double standard: The politics of the European Central Bank during the Eurozone crisis," *Cambridge Review of International Affairs* 31(2): 162–182.

Fontan, C., Claveau, F., & Dietsch, P. (2016). "Central banking and inequalities: Taking off the blinders," *Politics, Philosophy & Economics* 15(4): 319–357.

Fontan, C., Dietsch, P., & Claveau, F. (2019). "Les banques centrales et la justice sociale," *Éthique Publique* 21(2). doi:10.4000/ethiquepublique.4856

Forder, J. (1998). "The case for an independent European Central Bank: A reassessment of evidence and sources," *European Journal of Political Economy* 14(1): 53–71.

Forder, J. (2005). "Why is central bank independence so widely approved?" *Journal of Economic Issues* 39(4): 843–865.

Friedman, M. (1968). "The role of monetary policy," *American Economic Review* 58: 1–17.

Fuller, G. W., Johnston, A., & Regan, A. (2019). "Housing prices and wealth inequality in Western Europe," *West European Politics*, forthcoming. doi: 10.1080/01402382.2018.1561054.

Gabor, D. (2016). "A step too far? The European financial transactions tax on shadow banking," *Journal of European Public Policy* 23(6): 925–945.

Gabor, D., & Ban, C. (2016). "Banking on bonds: The new links between states and markets," *JCMS: Journal of Common Market Studies* 54(3): 617–635.

Gabor, D., & Vestergaard, J. (2018). "Chasing unicorns: The European single safe asset project," *Competition & Change* 22(2): 139–164.

Golub, S., Kaya, A., & Reay, M. (2015). "What were they thinking? The Federal Reserve in the run-up to the 2008 financial crisis," *Review of International Political Economy* 22: 657–692.

Goodhart, C. A. E. (2011). "The changing role of central banks," *Financial History Review* 18(2): 135–154.

Goodhart, C. A. E., Gabor, D., Vestergaard, J., & Ertürk, I. (2014). *Central Banking at a Crossroads: Europe and Beyond.* London: Anthem Press.

Goodhart, C. A. E., & Lastra, R. (2018). "Populism and central bank independence," *Open Economies Review* 29(1): 49–68.

Hall, P. A., & Franzese, R. J. (1998). "Mixed signals: Central bank independence, coordinated wage bargaining, and European Monetary Union," *International Organization* 52(3): 505–535.

Hay, C. (2007). *Why We Hate Politics*. Cambridge: Polity.

Helleiner, E. (2014). *The Status Quo Crisis: Global Financial Governance after the 2008 Meltdown*. Oxford: Oxford University Press.

Högenauer, A.-L., & Howarth, D. (2016). "Unconventional monetary policies and the European Central Bank's problematic democratic legitimacy," *Zeitschrift Für Öffentliches Recht* 71(2): 1–24.

Ingham, G. (2004). *The Nature of Money*. Cambridge: Polity.

Issing, O., Gaspar, V., Angeloni, I., & Tristani, O. (2001). *Monetary Policy in the Euro Area: Strategy and Decision Making at the European Central Bank*. Cambridge: Cambridge University Press.

Jacobs, L. R., & King, D. S. (2016). *Fed Power: How Finance Wins*. Oxford: Oxford University Press.

Johnson, J., Arel-Bundock, V., & Portniaguine, V. (2019). "Adding rooms onto a house we love: Central banking after the global financial crisis," *Public Administration*, 97(3): 546–560.

Jones, E., & Matthijs, M., (2019). "Rethinking central-bank independence," *Journal of Democracy*, 30(2): 127–141.

Kalaitzake, M. (2017). "Death by a thousand cuts? Financial political power and the case of the European Financial Transaction Tax," *New Political Economy* 22: 709–726.

Kalaitzake, M. (2019). "Central Banking and financial political power: An investigation into the European Central Bank," *Competition & Change* 23: 221–244.

Kaldor, N. (1985). "How monetarism failed," *Challenge* 28: 4–13.

Kaplan, G., Moll, B., & Violante, G. L. (2018). "Monetary policy according to HANK," *American Economic Review* 108: 697–743.

Krippner, G. R. (2012). *Capitalizing on Crisis: The Political Origins of the Rise of Finance*. Cambridge, MA: Harvard University Press.

Kydland, F. E., & Prescott, E. C. (1977). "Rules rather than discretion: The inconsistency of optimal plans," *Journal of Political Economy* 85: 473–491.

Lenza, M., & Slacalek, J. (2018). *How Does Monetary Policy Affect Income and Wealth Inequality? Evidence from Quantitative Easing in the Euro Area*. ECB Working Paper No. 2190. Frankfurt am Main: European Central Bank.

Lucas, R. E. (1972). "Expectations and the neutrality of money," *Journal of Economic Theory* 4: 103–124.

Mackintosh, J. (2019, September 17). *A New Central Bank Approach: Pay Banks to Lend*. Retrieved from https://www.wsj.com/articles/a-new-central-bank-approach-pay-banks-to-lend-11568721602.

Marcussen, M. (2009). "Scientization of central banking: The politics of a-politicization," in K. Dyson and M. Marcussen (eds.), *Central Banks in the Age of the Euro: Europeanization, Convergence, and Power* (pp. 373–390). Oxford: Oxford University Press.

Matikainen, S., Campiglio, E., & Zenghelis, D. (2017). *Policy Brief: The Climate Impact of Quantitative Easing*. London: Grantham Research Institute.

McLeay, M., Radia, A., & Thomas, R. (2014). "Money creation in the modern economy," *Bank of England Quarterly Bulletin*, 2014 (Q1): 1–14.

McNamara, K. (2002). "Rational fictions: Central bank independence and the social logic of delegation," *West European Politics* 25(1): 47–76.

McPhilemy, S. (2016). "Integrating macro-prudential policy: Central banks as the 'third force' in EU financial reform," *West European Politics* 39(3): 526–544.

Mehrling, P. (2010). *The New Lombard Street: How the Fed Became the Dealer of Last Resort*. Princeton, NJ: Princeton University Press.

Monnet, E. (2018). *Controlling Credit: Central Banking and the Planned Economy in Postwar France, 1948–1973*. Cambridge: Cambridge University Press.

Muellbauer, J. (2014, December 23). "Combatting Eurozone deflation: QE for the people". Retrieved 23 September 2019 from https://voxeu.org/article/combatting-eurozone-deflation-qe-people.

Omarova, S. T. (2018). *Central Banks, Systemic Risk and Financial Sector Structural Reform.* SSRN Scholarly Paper No. ID 3099621. Rochester, NY: Social Science Research Network.

Pistor, K. (2013). "A legal theory of finance," *Journal of Comparative Economics* 41: 315–330.

Potter, S. & Smets, F. (2019). *Unconventional Monetary Policy Tools: A Cross-Country Analysis.* CGFS Papers, No. 63. Basel: Bank for International Settlements.

Rogoff, K. (1985). "The optimal degree of commitment to an intermediate monetary target," *Quarterly Journal of Economics* 100: 1169–1189.

Ryan-Collins, J., & Van Lerven, F. (2018). *Bringing the Helicopter to Ground: A Historical Review of Fiscal-Monetary Coordination to Support Economic Growth in the 20th Century.* IIPP Working Paper No. 2018-08. Retrieved from https://www.ucl.ac.uk/bartlett/public-purpose/node/887/.

Sahasrabuddhe, A. (2019). "Drawing the line: The politics of federal currency swaps in the global financial crisis," *Review of International Political Economy* 26: 461–489.

Singleton, J. (2010). *Central Banking in the Twentieth Century.* Cambridge: Cambridge University Press.

Stern, G. H., & Feldman, R. J. (2004). *Too Big to Fail: The Hazards of Bank Bailouts.* Washington, DC: Brookings Institution Press.

Strange, S. (1986). *States and Markets.* London: Continuum.

Tesche, T. (2019). "Instrumentalizing EMU's democratic deficit: The ECB's unconventional accountability measures during the eurozone crisis," *Journal of European Integration* 41(4): 447–463.

Thiemann, M., Birk, M., & Friedrich, J. (2018). "Much ado about nothing? Macroprudential ideas and the post-crisis regulation of shadow banking," *Kölner Zeitschrift Für Soziologie und Sozialpsychologie* 70(1): 259–286.

Turner, A. (2016). *Between Debt and the Devil: Money, Credit, and Fixing Global Finance.* Princeton, NJ: Princeton University Press.

Van Lerven, F. (2016). *A Guide to Public Money Creation: Outlining the Alternatives to Quantitative Easing.* Retrieved from http://positivemoney.org/2016/04/our-new-guide-to-public-money-creation/.

Van't Klooster, J. (2018). "Democracy and the European Central Bank's emergency powers," *Midwest Studies In Philosophy* 42(1): 270–293.

Van't Klooster, J., & Fontan, C. (2019). "The myth of market neutrality: A comparative study of the European Central Bank's and the Swiss National Bank's corporate security purchases," *New Political Economy,* forthcoming. doi: 10.1080/13563467.2019.1657077.

Walter, T., & Wansleben, L. (2019). "How central bankers learned to love financialization: The Fed, the Bank, and the enlisting of unfettered markets in the conduct of monetary policy," *Socio-Economic Review,* forthcoming. doi: 10.1093/ser/mwz011.

Woll, C. (2014). *The Power of Inaction: Bank Bailouts in Comparison.* Ithaca, NY: Cornell University Press.

8

SHADOW BANKING AND THE RISE OF GLOBAL DEBT

Angela Wigger and Rodrigo Fernandez

The Intellectual and Social Context of Shadow Banking: An Introduction

Shadow banking has formed part of the global financial system for quite some time but only received academic and popular attention in the wake of the 2008 crisis. Paul McCulley (2009), Executive Director of PIMCO, short for Pacific Investment Management Company, coined the term in a speech in 2007 at the Kansas City Federal Reserve Bank in Jackson Hole, Wyoming, when he referred to credit intermediation by non-depository financial institutions, or the so-called non-banks or quasi-banks that operate in the shadow of regular banks. Shadow banking comprises a system of institutionalized lending structures between borrowers and lenders that interconnect across various jurisdictions and markets, involving a diverse array of cash-wealthy individuals or corporations with high savings, investment banks, structured investment vehicles, asset management firms, hedge and/or private equity funds, or other financial holding corporations, insurance companies, mutual funds, or pension funds (for an overview of different conceptualizations, see Helgadóttir, 2016).

Credit provision outside the regular banking system has existed for centuries, but the scale and level of institutionalization of shadow banking today is historically unmatched. Shadow banking has increased both before and after the 2008 crisis erupted, and is likely to increase further in the near future. The systemic dimension of shadow banking is crucial. Shadow banking entails more than an aggregate of atomized financial players that are randomly scattered around the world. Hence, to speak of "shadow banks" would be a misnomer, even though the term is occasionally used (see Bayoumi, 2017). Shadow banking assets are disproportionately concentrated in offshore financial centers (OFCs) and tax havens. Shadow banking is sometimes also referred to as a "market-based credit system," but "market-based" is equally misleading as it suggests that conventional banks operate outside of markets. Importantly, shadow banking is not something separate or in parallel to the core banking system (Turner, 2012). Large systemic banks in advanced economies in particular are deeply intertwined with shadow banking. Not only have they been among the main designers of the shadow banking system, they often also operate as powerful nodes in sponsoring or owning non-banks, thereby making use of a diverse set of legal entities, or they are involved in activities like broking or underwriting different shadow banking activities. Moreover, as will be shown in this chapter, the systemic nature of shadow banking is also foregrounded in its role of absorbing and processing an abundance of liquid capital searching for yield outside the realm of production. Shadow banking channels this liquidity into collateralized debt instruments, consisting of all sorts of debt but mostly sovereign debt and asset-backed securities such as mortgages, and provides a machinery that allows for trading large quantities of these debt instruments on a daily basis. By moving debt off balance sheet, regular banks, often large systemic banks, tap into liquid financial markets and thereby improve their liquidity basis, which then serves as leverage for the issuance of new debt. Thus, on the one hand, shadow banking offers a profitable outlet for liquid financial capital, and, on the other hand, provides several mechanisms for large systemic banks to exploit leverage opportunities beyond domestic deposits or liquidity requirements, and manufacture new credit, and thus debt, as part of their profit base. Shadow banking, in other words, both depends on and facilitates debt-led accumulation structures.

The bulk of academic contributions on shadow banking has long exclusively stemmed from scholars located in the field of economics and law, who considered financial intermediation outside conventional banking structures an integral part of a modern and innovative financial system and praised it for creating new possibilities for cheap credit (see, e.g., Aitken & Singh, 2010). Much emphasis was given to the fact that shadow banking allowed for matching demand and supply for credit *efficiently* (FSB, 2011, 2012). No doubt, this literature produced very astute and detailed insights into the mechanics of shadow banking, the players, and instruments involved. However, this literature did not further question, discredit, or problematize shadow banking but instead saw it as a welcome mechanism to mitigate financial risks through a wide spread. Most of the analyses were also rather narrow, utterly economistic and mostly descriptive, lacking a theoretically informed explanation for the emergence and rise of shadow banking, albeit most analyses were pervaded by an implicit rationalist and/or institutionalist theoretical undercurrent. With the bankruptcy of Lehman Brothers in September 2008, an US investment bank deeply entangled with shadow banking, more critical scholarly accounts on shadow banking made their inroads, mostly from the field of political economy. In particular when the Group of Twenty (G20) meetings in 2010 in Seoul and 2011 in Cannes declared shadow banking a nefarious and shadowy practice, and a breeding ground for financial instability, a range of scholars challenged the mainstream understanding that shadow banking would perform an efficient brokerage role in matching demand and supply. Shadow banking was even seen as the root cause for why the global financial crisis of 2008 erupted (Bengtsson, 2013; Gorton & Metrick, 2010; Kessler & Wilhelm, 2013; Lysandrou & Nesve-tailova, 2015; Mehrling, 2011; Nesvetailova, 2015; Palan & Nesvetailova, 2013; Pozsar, 2014; Rixen, 2013; Thiemann, 2014). The fact that the activities by non-depository banks fell off the radar of state regulation was particularly high-lighted as the reason for the crisis, basically assuming that had shadow banking only been regulated and supervised effectively, there would be no crisis today.

This post-2008 literature on shadow banking forms part of the wider critical finance literature that has gained increasing prominence with the unfolding of the 2008 crisis, which is also testified by this *Handbook*. More critical accounts on shadow banking are certainly to be welcomed. Indeed, who wouldn't want to be critical about a financial system that has completely run out of proportion and caused a major economic downturn, affecting the lives of millions of peo-ple, while many financial players are back with double-digit windfall profits? Challenging scientific orthodoxies and taken-for-granted knowledge, posing new questions, and reopening established intellectual terrains is an academic virtue, but is it enough to justify the label "critical"? There is a risk that the prefix "critical" is used inflationary and downgraded to a posh synonym for criticizing only (Sayer, 2009: 768; Wigger & Horn, 2016). We observe that most of the literature on shadow banking is merely *empirically critical* and lacks a critical theoretical understanding of the broader ontology of capitalism and the dynamics of its continued reproduction, as well as the role of the state in facil-itating shadow banking (see, for example, Bengtsson, 2013; Helgadóttir, 2016; Lysandrou & Nesvetailova, 2015; Murau, 2017; Nesvetailova, 2015; Palan & Nesvetailova, 2013; Rixen, 2013; Thiemann, 2014). As a result, shadow bank-ing is still treated as an atomistic field, cut off from broader societal develop-ments, while financialized capitalism and the systemic dependency on debt-led accumulation structures is either ignored or mentioned in passing only. At the same time, critical scholars, whether Marxists or scholars with critical the-ory inflected contributions, hitherto have paid only scant attention to shadow banking (exceptions are Bryan et al., 2016; Fernandez & Wigger, 2016). This is quite unfortunate as this branch of literature brings with it critical theory and generally draws on an in-depth and comprehensive theorization of the role of finance in capitalism, its crises, and the state and its role in making it possible for society at large to absorb ever more debt (see for example Harvey, 2006, 2010, 2011; Hudson, 2012; Lapavitsas, 2013). As outlined by Christian Borch in the introduction to this *Handbook*, the strength of Marxist and Marxist-inspired literatures lies in their ability to point to broader societal ramifications and the creation of new forms of social inequality through debt and debt creation.

Drawing on a historical materialist understanding, this chapter seeks to go be-yond merely empirically critical work and locate shadow banking into the broader whole, notably the structural and recurring problem of overaccumulation, also defined as the capital absorption problem, which has led to growing cash pools searching for yield. According to this view, the inability of capital to reproduce itself through investments in the sphere of production is seen as the root cause for the crisis, and thus not shadow banking in the first place. Shadow banking rather provides a temporary outlet for overaccumulated surplus capital to be reinvested profitably. This does however not mean that shadow banking is not linked to the crisis. Shadow banking is integral to debt creation. In fact, we are living in times that total debt is increasing to an extent that conventional banking does not allow for. A crisis erupts whenever the accumulation of debt is getting too much out of sync with the accumulation of capital (see Harvey, 2011).

The chapter is structured as follows: before linking the shadow banking to the structural problem of overaccumulation, major developments and dimensions of shadow banking are outlined. "The Intellectual and Social Context of Shadow Banking: An Introduction" section takes stock of the expansion and spatio-temporal concentration of shadow banking in OFCs and points to the politics of how shadow banking is being measured. In parallel, the section traces the unprecedented growth of global debt, which, as will be argued later, is linked to the expansion of shadow banking. "The Expansion of Shadow Banking alongside the Expansion of Debt" section addresses the ostensible absence of state agency that is commonly referred to as the reason why shadow banking triggered the 2008 crisis. It will be shown that state regulatory apparatuses have been indispensable for the emergence and growth of shadow banking in various ways, and most notably through the establishment of OFCs and tax havens, as well as related conduit structures, which have come to underpin today's shadow banking system. "The Recurring Problem of Overaccumulation and Neoliberal Solutions" section reconvenes structure and agency by identifying the recurring problem of overaccumulation and more than 30 years of neoliberal governance as the reason for why financial markets over-leveraged, and have grown out of proportion relative to the real production economy, thereby working out the particular role of shadow banking in causing the crisis. The conclusions recapitulate the main arguments and go beyond existing work by suggesting future research avenues that hitherto have not yet been addressed.

The Expansion of Shadow Banking alongside the Expansion of Debt

Shadow banking has expanded dramatically both before and after the 2008 crisis, and is often argued to account for roughly half of the current global banking system. The Financial Stability Board (FSB), established in 2008 by the G20, among others for the purpose of measuring and monitoring shadow banking, estimated that the overall size of shadow banking assets has risen from US$26 trillion in 2002 to US$71 trillion in 2012, which is almost a threefold expansion in a decade (FSB, 2017). Measuring shadow banking activities is however not unequivocal and disputes on what accounts as a shadow banking surface regularly.

The rationale of the FSB's first annual "Global Shadow Banking Monitoring Report" initially was to "cast the net wide." Accordingly, shadow banking was broadly defined as "financial intermediation by non-banks" and included broad range of actors, including pension funds, insurers, and numerous other financial institutions (OFIs), as well as a vast range of activities, products, and markets. On this basis, the critical role of mailbox companies or special purpose entities (SPEs) in producing, channeling, and processing shadow bank assets was exposed, which pointed to the spatial concentration of shadow banking assets in OFCs and tax havens (see Fernandez, 2014; Fernandez & Wigger, 2016; see more on this in the next section). The method of casting the net wide soon became heavily politicized, most notably by jurisdictions that revealed an extremely high concentration of shadow banking, like the Netherlands, one of the world's largest tax havens if measured in capital flows. After criticism of the Dutch central bank, the FSB changed its methodology and adopted a three-layered representation of non-bank finance, "non-bank" understood as financial assets that were not on a bank's balance sheet. The three layers unfold like a Matryoshka, the nested Russian doll: the largest category is called MUNFI, short for Monitoring Universe of Non-bank Financial Intermediation, which is an aggregate of all categories of non-bank finance; the second category forms part of MUNFI and is titled "other financial institutions" (OFIs), while the third and inner layer is categorized as "shadow banking: narrow definition" (FSB, 2018; see Figure 8.1). When the FSB was still committed to "casting the net wide," the category OFIs included hedge funds, SPEs, money market funds, broker dealers, collective investment vehicles, captive investment vehicles, structured investment vehicles, real estate investment trusts and various types of "other unidentified" (FSB, 2018: 14). Arguably, the category was messy. The FSB subsequently broke down the category into "shadow banking: narrowly defined" and "regular OFIs," distinguishing between OFIs that primarily deal with credit intermediation with financial institutions, on the one hand, and OFIs that engage in other financial activities, such as managing intra-company flows, debt, and profits of transnational corporations (TNCs), on the other. However, with the new category "shadow banking: narrowly defined," the scope of shadow banking was artificially reduced because it excluded the vast array of mailbox activities used by financial and non-financial corporations to organize cash flows and shift profits to low tax jurisdictions. The narrow definition of shadow banking thus can be argued to reflect merely the tip of iceberg. Among others, the new category misconstrues the actual size and expansion of shadow banking as it ignores that non-financial corporations themselves have built up growing cash pools and become important players in the shadow banking system themselves (Fernandez & Hendrikse, 2015). In this sense, the original OFI category has been much more encompassing. Moreover, by nesting the category in the larger MUNFI category, institutional investors that engage with OFIs can no longer be identified. Nonetheless, the category MUNFI consisting of an aggregate of insurance corporations, pension funds, and OFIs is probably the best indicator to assess the size and growth of shadow banking. As can be seen in Figure 8.1 and Table 8.1, the assets of MUNFI have increased from US$59 trillion in 2002 to US$160 trillion in 2016.

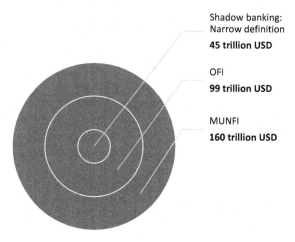

Shadow banking:
Narrow definition
45 trillion USD

OFI
99 trillion USD

MUNFI
160 trillion USD

Figure 8.1   Measuring shadow banking.
Source: FSB (2018).

Table 8.1 Total Financial Assets of Financial Intermediaries in USD trillion

	Banks	Central Banks	Public Financial Institutions	Insurance Corporations	Pension Funds	Other Financial Intermediaries
2002	51.9	4.7	11.2	14.7	11.9	32.6
2003	54.5	5.0	11.4	17.1	13.2	36.3
2004	60.1	5.6	11.3	19.0	14.4	40.4
2005	70.6	6.5	11.8	19.7	15.9	46.7
2006	76.7	7.0	11.9	21.9	17.2	53.6
2007	88.4	8.4	12.6	24.0	18.1	61.6
2008	104.2	12.4	13.1	18.2	18.2	58.0
2009	101.0	12.6	13.3	19.8	19.9	59.8
2010	105.9	13.9	12.9	21.2	21.8	64.0
2011	114.3	16.9	13.0	21.9	22.8	65.6
2012	117.9	18.6	13.3	23.5	24.5	71.8
2013	118.9	19.6	13.8	24.7	26.4	78.5
2014	125.8	21.4	14.3	26.7	28.0	87.5
2015	128.9	23.3	15.0	27.5	29.1	92.5
2016	137.8	26.2	16.0	29.1	31.0	100.0

Source: FSB (2018)

Shadow banking has expanded in a highly uneven fashion, and often in correspondence with the size and pace of growth of a country's banking system (see Table 8.1). Shadow banking has long been considered to be merely a US phenomenon (see Pozsar et al., 2010). Indeed, in the United States, shadow banking has overtaken conventional banking, and the United States hosts not only the world's largest economy but also the largest share of global shadow banking activity. Yet, the US share of global shadow banking is "only" 40%, followed by the Eurozone with about 20% (FSB, 2017: 48). In Europe, shadow banking is disproportionately concentrated in the United Kingdom (29%) (European Commission, 2012: 11). Most of the literature also focused on London as Europe's main hub for shadow banking (Palan, 1999; Palan & Nesvetailova, 2013), and the tax avoidance opportunities offered by the historical debris of the British Empire and its offshore interconnections (Maurer, 2008). Comparatively less attention has been paid to Luxembourg, the Netherlands, and Ireland, which account for, respectively, 17%, 15%, and 8% of global shadow banking (European Commission, 2012: 11), all countries with tax havens and OFCs. Interestingly, the largest Eurozone economies are relatively small players in shadow banking, with Germany and France accounting for a mere 7% and Italy for 4% (European Commission, 2012: 11). Shadow banking in Europe is however likely to expand further in the future alongside the envisaged Capital Markets Union (CMU) in the context of the European Union (EU). The European Commission's plans for the CMU aim at inducing a structural shift towards the US model of market-based finance, where non-bank alternatives alongside bond funding prevail over bank loans (see for more, Braun & Hübner, 2018; Engelen & Glasmacher, 2018; Epstein & Rhodes, 2018; Gabor & Vestergaard, 2018; Mertens & Thiemann, 2018). Most of the shadow banking literature has focused on the Global North. Yet, shadow banking has been on the rise in China as well. In 2017, Chinese shadow banking assets accounted for an estimated US$9.6 trillion, which renders China the world's third largest shadow banking hub after the United States and the EU (FSB, 2018: 16).

The expansion of shadow banking parallels the expansion global debt creation. Ever since the crisis hit in 2008, overall global debt levels, including public, corporate, and private household debt, have increased to a historically unprecedented level. In 2007, overall global debt was estimated at US$142 trillion, equivalent to 269% of world GDP (McKinsey & Company, 2015). At the end of the first quarter of 2018, overall global debt was estimated at US$247 trillion, equivalent to 318% of world GDP (IIF, 2018). In other words, global debt is more than three times the size of the global economy, and more than twice the size of the debt of 1915 and 1935 (based on credit-to-GDP data from 1870 to 2010) (Jordà et al., 2014). Debt growth outpaces global GDP growth, and most of the major economies have higher debt levels relative to their GDP than they did in 2007, while China's debt has quadrupled since the financial bubble burst in 2007 (IMF, 2018). As the pace of debt creation cannot be maintained endlessly, the expansion of debt, *inter alia* facilitated by shadow banking, bears the prospect of a crisis far more dramatic than what we have witnessed hitherto.

The (Non-)Regulation of Shadow Banking Revisited

When the 2008 crisis erupted in the form of a heightened liquidity shortage ("credit crunch") and the threat of insolvency of major financial institutions, first in the United States and shortly afterward also in Europe, Paul Krugman, economist and influential commentator, blamed shadow banking for being the root cause for the crisis and thereby referred to the absence of government backstops that usually ensure the resilience of the conventional banking sector (Krugman, 2009). Subsequently, also other scholars started to assign the reasons for the crisis to the non-regulation or the lenient regulation of shadow banking, or the presence of regulatory loopholes, as well as absence of effective coordination mechanisms between international and domestic levels of regulation. With the exception of the occasional post-Keynesian approach (Nesvetailova, 2015), most of this literature draws on rationalist institutionalist approaches, which highlight explanations such as inter-state competition to attract capital, the role of regulatory arbitrage or cognitive capture, or combinations thereof (Lysandrou & Nesvetailova, 2015; Rixen, 2013; Thiemann, 2014). Accordingly, either states have been "captured" by rent-seeking financial actors shopping for the most lenient jurisdiction (Lysandrou & Nesvetailova, 2015; Rixen, 2013; Thiemann, 2014), or states have been "blinded" by epistemic communities about self-regulating markets (Gabor, 2016a), or they have simply suffered from outright myopia (Kessler & Wilhelm, 2013).

Regulatory loopholes or the absence of direct governance mechanisms seem to suggest that shadow banking exists in a legal vacuum outside the reach of the state. Regulators are however deeply embedded in shadow banking in various ways (see also Coombs's chapter in this *Handbook*). To begin with, financial markets, including shadow banking, are constructed by law. Financial assets are after all contractual commitments that are legally enforceable through courts. While most of the literature would agree with this, the absence of the state within shadow banking tends to be ascribed to the fact that it lacks the prudential government backstops of conventional banks regarding capital requirements and liquidity buffers, trading rules, and safety nets, such as deposit insurances and bank bailouts by governments in case of a credit crunch or bankruptcies. Indeed, shadow banking is more unstable than conventional banking: it has no depository basis and hence no deposit insurance, and in the absence of liquidity requirements, it builds on far higher leverage, and thus higher risk-taking. However, one should not forget that licensed private institutional creditors, such as conventional banks, are also unstable. Conventional banks also make use of leverage when issuing credit on the basis of saving deposits and thereby create debt and eventually money *ex nihilo*, *de novo* merely by writing down fictitious capital on the borrower's account (Sgambati, 2016). Banks speculate that not all deposit holders will withdraw their money at once, but in case of a liquidity shortage, a so-called bank run can be fatal, and as bank runs easily spread from one bank to another, they can cause a financial meltdown.

Shadow banking involves maturity or liquidity transformations similar to conventional banking; yet, while conventional banking offsets long-term loans through short-term liabilities like deposits, maturity transformations within shadow banking concern short-term liquid liabilities, usually drawn from money-market funds or hedge funds (basically different sorts of investors with cash that is not invested productively elsewhere), which are then used for buying long-term illiquid assets, such as high-grade fixed-income products (bonds) and a variety of structured asset-backed papers held by banks, which are in need for money. Shadow banking manufactures, often together with the conventional banking system, various forms of tradable pooled-debt instruments that can be sold to investors, and thus moved off a bank's balance sheet. There are two ways through which conventional banks and other financial entities can make use of the non-deposit-based liquidity investors. The first concerns repo market transactions, involving repurchasing agreements: banks borrow cash on a short-term basis by selling safe assets (collateral, such as government bonds) alongside an agreement to repurchase the asset at a later stage for a fixed yet higher price, basically an equivalent to an interest rate. The agreement to repurchase is then called a repo. Repo markets have existed for decades; yet, in the run-up of the crisis, repo transactions expanded massively, thereby providing cash-rich investors with a profitable outlet and enabled banks and other financial entities with an access to quick cash (for an overview on the expansion of repo markets, and the role of central banks in repo markets, see Gabor, 2016b). Another mechanism through which banks tapped into non-deposit-based liquidity is securitization, which entails that long-term debt (illiquid contracts that otherwise would have stayed on the banks' balance sheet as a long-term assets) is being repackaged and bundled into securities (short-term debt instruments) that can be bought by cash-rich lenders. Through this practice, conventional banks could move the maturity of the loan to the present—hence, without having to wait until the loan matured. The space created on the balance sheet and the new liquidity base obtained through the sale then served as leverage to issue new loans. Hence, through securitizing loans, conventional banks could exploit the shadow banking system to issue new loans, which then are again securitized and sold in return for liquid cash, and so forth. Securitization was primarily based on mortgage debt, and increased massively alongside inflating residential real estate prices. Very often, securitized loans were not fully removed from the banks' balance sheets but stored on special purpose vehicles owned by the bank (see Acharya et al., 2013). Thereby, securities could be sold and resold to investors many times over. Banks guaranteed the payment of interests or a fee, but kept the risks; yet, thereby they could span the leverage of single assets several times, leading to leverage ratios of sometimes over 1:30. Through borrowing from OFIs and over-leveraging, the banking sector has become more indebted than any other economic sector (Turner, 2015: 24). As collaterals can lose their value quickly, lenders can get impatient, and borrowing through shadow banking can dry up very quickly, causing severe financial distress for the over-leveraged conventional banking sector, which is what has happened in 2008.

A range of scholars, institutions, and governments have pointed to the dangers of securitization, and the recycling of debt through selling and reselling debt to investors multiple times (Adrian & Shin, 2010; Brunnermeier, 2009; Gabor & Ban, 2016; Gorton & Metrick, 2012). Nonetheless, also here states, or emerging state apparatuses like the EU, play a facilitating role. The European Commission, the executive body of the EU equipped with the sole right to initiate new legislative proposals, is determined to revive the securitization market by establishing the CMU. The European Commission has proclaimed non-bank credit intermediation no longer as a cause of but a solution to the current crisis, arguing that shadow banking "performs important functions in the financial system" as it creates "additional sources of funding" and offers "investors alternatives to bank deposits" (European Commission, 2012, 2015). The EU project of the CMU is testimony to the successes booked by the financial sector to recover the tarnished reputation of shadow banking.

The continued role of state regulatory infrastructures in facilitating shadow banking can also be revealed when considering that shadow banking did not spread randomly as some authors seem to suggest (see, for example, Thiemann, 2014) but instead nested itself in OFCs and tax havens (see Fernandez & Wigger, 2016; Palan, 1999; 2002; Palan & Nesvetailova, 2013; Rixen, 2013). OFCs can be defined as "a country or jurisdiction that provides financial services to non-residents on a scale that is incommensurate with the size and the financing of its domestic economy" (Zoromé, 2007). While non-financial corporations have settled in OFCs since the 1950s for tax avoidance purposes, financial corporations followed from the 1990s onward. Most of the literature on OFCs has not prominently discussed shadow banking however (Donaghy & Clarke, 2003; Maurer, 2008; Picciotto, 1999; Roberts, 1994, 1995; Wójcik, 2013), while the literature on shadow banking has mostly focused on first-tier financial centers like New York or London, thereby ignoring OFCs. However, shadow banking links first-tier financial centers to offshore jurisdictions according to a particular hierarchy and functional differentiation. OFCs are not separate, stand-alone hubs but part of a wider hierarchical network. They form critical outposts in the circulation of financial capital, often routing large capital flows through different OFCs which offer complimentary services, rather than being in competition with each other. Estimates suggest that today about half of the global stock of money passes through OFCs (Palan & Nesvetailova, 2013: 1). The spatial condensation and the various functional differences of OFCs are being facilitated and thus continuously reproduced by state regulation. This can include legal prerequisites for easy incorporation, generous tax laws, and exemptions, as well as the conclusion of bilateral tax or investment agreements with other jurisdictions that make it attractive for financial and non-financial corporations to be incorporated in particular OFCs. Moreover, OFCs generally tend to host a highly specialized professional services industry with consultants, marketing experts, lawyers, accountants, and tax avoidance experts, offering tailor-made services to all sorts of corporations.

Setting up trusts and investment vehicles, the so-called special purpose entities (SPEs), are core activities of the professional service industry. SPEs are complex legal constructs that operate as pass-through entities for shifting profits and eroding tax bases (see also OECD, 2013), and mostly come without employees, rental contracts, or ownership of real estate, and hence without major operational costs (Maurer, 2008; Palan, 2002; Palan et al., 2010; Wójcik, 2013). SPEs can be wholly owned subsidiaries or form part of a more complex and opaque ownership structure, serving the purpose of removing activities such as risky debt from the parent company's balance sheet. Financial players involved in shadow banking often draw on a wide range of SPEs scattered across many jurisdictions. As Nesvetailova (2015: 3) put it, behind the facade of banking conglomerates, "there is a plethora of entities, transactions and quasi-legal cells, many of which are 'orphaned' from the visible part of the bank by complex legal and financial operations [...]." Frequently, the core business of SPEs is group financing and holding activities of assets and liabilities in other countries, which is why SPEs generally have little or no physical presence in host jurisdictions (OECD, 2013). Nesvetailova (2015: 432) distinguishes three types of SPEs in the shadow banking industry: bank-owned SPEs that transform bank loans into securities; structured investment vehicles sponsored by commercial banks or investments that transform securities into collateralized debt obligations (CDOs); and conduits owned or sponsored by regular banks.

To recapitulate, shadow banking did not expand in an unregulated environment off the radar of states but has been made possible through the permissive state regulatory apparatus in various ways. As the next section demonstrates, in order to understand the expansion of shadow banking and its particular nexus with the crisis, we need to go beyond facilitating state institutional explanations and understand the recurring structural problem of overaccumulation.

The Recurring Problem of Overaccumulation and Neoliberal Solutions

Critical political economy approaches situate capitalist crises not in the absence of state regulation but in the recurring structural problem of overaccumulation, which refers to the lack of attractive possibilities to reinvest past profits (surplus capital) in the production sphere at a particular historical juncture and location (Clarke, 2001; Harvey, 2006, 2010). Whenever surplus capital cannot be recapitalized and thus reactivated in the realm of production, alternative outlets need to be found, as capital needs to circulate or die (Harvey, 2014: 73). Possible outlets can be investments in land or nature, real estate or mergers, and acquisitions or investments in financial markets, the so-called sphere of capital circulation. Investments in the financial circuit can become more profitable than existing structures of capital accumulation, such as trade, commodity, and service production, leading to a situation in which the financial circuit of capital, notably, through the extension of debt, comes to prevail (see also Krippner, 2011: 27–28). Or as Marx (1847/1975: 134–135) observed almost 170 years ago, there "are even phases in the life of modern nations when everybody is seized with a sort of craze for making profit without producing." Financial capital can attain ephemeral value through the mere circulation of capital: the faster financial capital moves, such as in a speculative frenzy, the higher the yields (Harvey, 2010: 41; Lapavitsas, 2013: 264). Shadow banking is testimony to this by offering a system that makes it possible to trade all sorts of debt instruments, in the form of packaging illiquid assets such as loans to be sold to investors several times over, thereby facilitating the extension of credit, and its flipside, debt, far beyond the conventional banking system.

Credit and its flipside, debt, as a circulating form of fictitious capital, is not rooted in what has already been produced but instead lays a claim to the appropriation of a portion of the production of future surplus value, thereby linking the present to the future. Whenever the financial sector is unregulated and thus, scarcity of finance capital is (temporarily) offset by permissive regulation, claims to future surplus production can be made infinitely, at least in theory (Wigger, 2018). Debt-led accumulation can only temporarily solve some of the paradoxes of capital accumulation, and thus not be a long-term solution to the problem of chronic overaccumulation. With a growing global balance sheet with ever more debt, on the one hand, and debt claims accumulated by capital owners, on the other hand, the realization of debt repayment is being pushed ever further into the future. A crisis emerges when it becomes apparent through defaults and bankruptcies that debt cannot be serviced, or as Harvey (2011) put, the accumulation of capital and the accumulation of debt get too much out of sync. Financial crises are thus never detached from the production sphere but rooted in the real economy and its inability to produce actual surplus.

Most of the literature on shadow banking has ignored overaccumulation and debt-led accumulation structures as the reason for the crisis (an exception is Bryan et al., 2016). In contrast, critical political economy literatures (broadly defined) have provided excellent insights on debt-led accumulation (see, for example, Crouch, 2009; Soederberg, 2014; Stockhammer, 2004). While this literature generally does not account for the specific role of shadow banking in facilitating excessive credit/debt, it demonstrates well the fundamental shift away from regulated Keynesian-type of macroeconomic demand management of post-war economies towards a more supply-side-oriented neoliberal approach, and it is here where shadow banking needs to be located. The rise of shadow banking epitomizes the transformation that started with the great stagflation crisis of the 1970s, which was indeed a crisis of overaccumulation: when the long wave of post-war Fordist growth came to a halt, markets in the advanced economies were saturated; production grew faster than demand, leading to overcapacity in manufacturing sectors and eventually a major profit squeeze and sharp decreases in output and exports. Once inflation-based Keynesian interventions proved unsuccessful to deal with overaccumulation, neoliberal policies were adopted in the hope of restoring corporate profits. Market barriers of all sorts were dismantled; corporate taxes reduced; labor markets flexibilized; wages repressed; and, in addition to a monetarist focus of keeping inflation low, financial markets were deregulated and lending standards relaxed. In addition, the clear-cut financial architecture centered on national banks and national capital markets of the Bretton Woods era was rescaled into a scattered landscape of a broad range of cross-border intermediation channels, linking the offshore world to the first-tier financial centers.

Neoliberal policies implied that less surplus from the production sphere had to be redistributed and that ever more capital was freed for the circulation sphere. To give but a few examples: the decline of the wage share of GDP from 64% in 1980 to 54% in 2002 translated into an annual transfer of 10% of global GDP from labor to capital (UNCTAD, 2013: 14). The reduction of the average OECD corporate income tax rate from 49% in 1981 to 27% in 2007 culminated in a growing corporate "savings glut" from the 2000s onward (OECD Tax Database; The Economist, 2005). Corporations in advanced economies transformed from net borrowers in the 1970s (with up to 15% per year), into net savers from 2000 onward, hoarding financial assets at a rate of 3% of GDP in G7 countries per year (IMF, 2006: 135). The OECD estimated that, in 2011, corporate savings in the range of US$1.7 trillion were stashed in OFCs (OECD, 2013: 68). The global "savings glut" expanded further alongside large current account surpluses in emerging markets and oil-producing economies, which were channeled into sovereign wealth funds. The assets of institutional investors almost quadrupled in the period from 2001 to 2013, from US$26 trillion to 97 trillion (OECD, 2016), while Quantitative Easing (QE) by central banks added another US$12 trillion in from 2008 to 2018 (Fernandez et al., 2018: 23), and one might add to this the growing reserves of the super-rich: private-wealth management topped US$42 trillion in 2011 (TheCityUK, 2012: 1).

Alongside saturated markets, lingering overcapacity, and slowly growing aggregate demand—investments in the real economy stagnated. New profitable outlets were found in the circulation sphere. As safe assets to invest in, the so-called high-quality collaterals, typically sovereign bonds or mortgage-backed assets, became increasingly scarce (Moreira & Savov, 2017), shadow banking fabricated new assets and provided an opportunity to offload overaccumulated surplus capital profitably. Notably, debt instruments often based on residential real estate assets, provided the collateral for the "rentier" or "money-dealing" fraction of capital seeking profitable investment. Shadow banking thus created non-productive forms of capital valorization through the mere circulation of finance capital, and thus offered a "financial fix," analogous to Harvey's (1985) notion of a "spatial fix": a machinery for overaccumulated capital to invest profitably into these debt instruments. Shadow banking not only absorbed overaccumulated liquid surplus capital but also became a central node in the spiral of further debt creation. Conventional banks were offloading a growing pool of tradable debt when tapping into a diverse set of funding structures other than deposits, including interbank-borrowing and borrowing from outside the banking sector, such as through money-market funds or repo markets, and using it as a leverage to extended credit. Shadow banking enabled the liquidity of conventional banks necessary to pump out ever more debt in the form of fictitious paper claims to future wealth. Or as Nesvetailova (2015: 447) poignantly put it, shadow banking created an "overcrowded future" by offering an "infrastructure for mining, enhancing and shifting debt and its related products into the future." Consequently, shadow banking should not be understood as the root causes of the crisis, but rather as a temporary solution.

Shadow banking will continue to increase as long as the wider economy can take on more debt, which is premised on the state regulatory framework facilitating ever higher levels of indebtedness and disciplining debt servicing. Against the backdrop of declining wages, and the dismantling of traditional welfare state provisions, which implies that public services (previously free of charge) have to be pursued with private money, people resort to debt not for hedonistic lifestyle reasons but to ensure the material conditions of existence (see Graeber, 2011; Langley, 2008). Debt provided through easily available consumer credit—be it in the form of credit cards, store cards, "buy now, pay later" offers, high-street bank loans, current account overdrafts—in addition, the growth of more flexible and diverse forms of mortgage finance has become key to stabilize demand. The current build-up of debt is untenable in the long-run, and the risk of defaults increases, and therewith the risk of a financial crisis that is far bigger than the 2008 crisis. Similar bailouts of the financial sector on the basis of taxpayers' money will be not only politically unfeasible and also de facto impossible. While the destruction of the bloated financial sector might be desirable, it will most certainly be accompanied by fierce social struggles and major repercussions for the distribution of wealth.

In Conclusion: Possible Future Directions in Research on Shadow Banking

This chapter took stock of the shadow banking literature and discussions that have emerged in the aftermath of the 2008 crisis and sought to demonstrate the role of shadow banking absorbing overaccumulated surplus capital, on the one hand, and facilitating the extension of credit and its flipside, debt, far beyond conventional banking system, on the other hand. As a corrective to studies that have identified the absence of the state in shadow banking as a reason for why the crisis erupted, it has been argued here that states, and state regulation, have been and continue to be a constant and constitutive element in the expansion and reproduction of capital in general, and shadow banking in particular, whether through enforcing financial contracts, creating OFCs and tax havens, or policies that make it possible for society at large to become ever more indebted. Research that links shadow banking to

OFCs is relatively scarce, however. We know very little about the specialized work division and complementary shadow banking practices among different offshore financial hubs that serve as complimentary steppingstones. More research is needed on the statecraft that reproduces the rescaled financial architecture of the offshore world and the financial core, and on the variegated nature of different types of shell structures designed by the network of professional service providers, such as lawyers, accountants, trusts, and fiduciary services, as well as the web of dealers, fund managers, and customers in the prime financial centers of New York and London.

Furthermore, what has not been addressed in this chapter and in most of the literature on shadow banking is the role of states in lubricating liquid capital markets through massive QE programs. Central banks in the advanced industrial core have acted as buyers of last resort since the eruption of the 2007/2008 crisis. Notably, in the direct aftermath of the financial crisis, the United States adopted a purchasing program to stabilize markets for securitized assets and to keep financial institutions afloat, all deeply involved in shadow banking transactions. Soon after, also the central banks of the Eurozone, the United Kingdom, Japan, and Switzerland unleashed QE programs; yet, the character of QE changed. While the initial aim was "portfolio rebalancing," the purpose gradually transformed into stimulating financial institutions to substitute safe assets, such as public debt, high-grade corporate bonds, and mortgage-backed securities with cash which central banks created in the process (Fernandez et al., 2018). By moving safe high-quality collaterals of financial institutions onto the balance sheet of central banks, safe assets to invest in decreased and the appetite for more risky assets by MUNFI-type of financial players increased (Fernandez et al., 2018). In other words, against the backdrop of scarcity of high-quality collaterals, shadow banking is likely to expand even more in the future. Arguably, the long-term effects of the QE statecraft on shadow banking still remain to be seen; yet, we can currently observe inflating bubbles across different sets of assets on stock markets, real estate, and corporate bond markets, as well as massive investments in the debt of the so-called emerging markets. Thus, we would encourage critical finance researchers to locate the expansion of shadow banking into the broader context of market liquidity, consisting of overaccumulated surplus capital that is not being invested in the production sphere, and to research the wider state-financial market nexus, notably by investigating the effects of QE in the vast expansion of shadow banking.

References

Acharya, V. V., Schnabl, P., & Suarez, G. (2013). "Securitization without risk transfer," *Journal of Financial Economics* 107(3): 515–536.

Adrian, T., & Shin, H. S. (2010). "Liquidity and leverage," *Journal of Financial Intermediation* 19(3): 418–437.

Aitken, J., & Singh, M. (2010). "The (sizable) role of rehypothecation in the shadow banking system," *IMF Working Paper* 10/172. Retrieved from https://www.imf.org/en/Publications/WP/Issues/2016/12/31/The-Sizable-Role-of-Rehypothecation-in-the-Shadow-Banking-System-24075.

Bayoumi, T. (2017). *Unfinished Business: The Unexplored Causes of the Financial Crisis and the Lessons Yet to Be Learned.* New Haven, CT: Yale University Press.

Bengtsson, E. (2013). "Shadow banking and financial stability: European money market funds in the global financial crisis," *Journal of International Money and Finance* 32 (February): 579–594.

Braun, B., & Hübner, M. (2018). "Fiscal fault, financial fix? Capital Markets Union and the quest for macroeconomic stabilization in the euro area," *Competition & Change* 22(2): 117–138.

Brunnermeier, M. K. (2009). "Deciphering the liquidity and credit crunch 2007–2008," *Journal of Economic Perspectives 23*(1): 77–100.

Bryan, D., Rafferty, M., & Wigan, D. (2016). "Politics, time and space in the era of shadow banking," *Review of International Political Economy* 23(6): 941–966.

TheCityUK. (2012). "Fund management." Retrieved from https://www. Thecityuk.com.

Clarke, S. (2001). "Class struggle and the global overaccumulation of capital," in R. Albritton, M. Itoh, R. Westra, and A. Zuege (eds.), *Phases of Capitalist Development: Boom, Crises and Globalizations* (pp. 57–76). Basingstoke: Palgrave.

Crouch, C. (2009). "Privatised keynesianism: An unacknowledged policy regime," *British Journal of Politics and International Politics* 19(2): 263–275.

Donaghy, M., & Clarke, M. (2003). "Are offshore financial centres the product of global markets? A sociological response," *Economy and Society* 32(3): 381–409.

The Economist. (2005, July 7). "The corporate saving glut." Retrieved from http://www.economist.com/node/ 4154491.

Engelen, E., & Glasmacher, A. (2018). "The waiting game: How securitization became the solution for the growth problem of the Eurozone," *Competition & Change* 22(2): 165–183.

Epstein, R., & Rhodes, M. (2018). "From governance to government: Banking union, capital markets union and the new EU," *Competition & Change* 22(2): 205–224.

European Commission. (2012). "Non-bank financial institutions: Assessment of their impact on the stability of the financial system," *Economic Papers* 427, November. Brussels: European Commission.

European Commission. (2015). "Action plan on building a capital markets union," COM/2015/0468. Brussels: European Commission.

Fernandez, R. (2014). "Schaduwbankieren en belastingontwijking: Een obscuur Nederlands tafereel," September, Amsterdam: SOMO.

Fernandez, R., Bortz, P., & Zeolla, N. (2018). "The politics of quantitative easing: A critical assessment of the harmful impact of European monetary policy on developing countries," June, Amsterdam: SOMO.

Fernandez, R., & Hendrikse, R. (2015). "Rich corporations and poor societies: The financialisation of Apple," October, Amsterdam: SOMO.

Fernandez, R., & Wigger, A. (2016). "Lehman brothers in the Dutch Offshore Financial Centre: The role of shadow banking in increasing leverage and facilitating debt," *Economy and Society* 45(3–4): 407–430.

FSB. (2011, April 11). "Shadow banking: Scoping the issues. A background note of the financial stability board," *Consultation Documents.* April, Basel: FSB.

FSB. (2012, November 18). "Global shadow banking," *Monitoring Report 2012.* November, Basel: FSB.

FSB. (2017). "Global shadow banking monitoring report 2016." Retrieved from http://www.fsb.org/wp-content/uploads/global-shadow-banking-monitoring-report-2016.pdf.

FSB. (2018). "Global shadow banking monitoring report 2017." Retrieved from http://www.fsb.org/wp-content/uploads/P050318-1.pdf.

Gabor, D. (2016a). "A step too far? The European financial transactions tax on shadow banking," *Journal of European Public Policy* 23(6). 925–945.

Gabor, D. (2016b). "The (impossible) repo trinity: the political economy of repo markets," *Review of International Political Economy* 23(6): 967–1000.

Gabor, D., & Ban, C. (2016). "Banking on bonds: The new links between states and markets," *Journal of Common Market Studies* 54(3): 617–635.

Gabor, D., & Vestergaard, J. (2018). "Chasing unicorns: The European single safe asset project," *Competition & Change* 22(2): 139–164.

Gorton, G., & Metrick, A. (2010). "Regulating the shadow banking system," *Brookings Papers on Economic Activity* Fall(2010): 261–312.

Gorton, G., & Metrick, A. (2012). "Securitized banking and the run on repo," *Journal of Financial Economics* 104(3): 425–451.

Graeber, D. (2011). *Debt: The First 5000 Years*. New York, NY: Melville House.

Harvey, D. (1985). *The Urbanization of Capital: Studies in the History and Theory of Capitalist Urbanization*. Oxford: Blackwell.

Harvey, D. (2006). *Limits to Capital*. New York, NY: Verso.

Harvey, D. (2010). *The Enigma of Capital and the Crises of Capitalism*. London: Profile Books.

Harvey, D. (2011). "The vote to end capitalism," Retrieved from http://davidharvey.org/2011/07/the-vote-to-end-capitalism/#more-929.

Harvey, D. (2014). *Seventeen Contradictions and the End of Capitalism*. London: Profile Books Ltd.

Helgadóttir, O. (2016). "Banking upside down: The implicit politics of shadow banking expertise," *Review of International Political Economy* 23(6): 915–940.

Hudson, M. (2012). *The Bubble and Beyond: Fictitious Capital, Debt Deflation and Global Crisis*. Dresden: ISLET.

IIF. (2018). *Global Debt Monitor – July 2018*. Retrieved from https://www.iif.com/publication/global-debt-monitor/global-debt-monitor-july-2018.

IMF. (2006). Awash with cash: Why are corporate savings so high? Retrieved from https://www.imf.org/external/pubs/ft/ weo/2006/01/pdf/c4.pdf.

IMF. (2018, April). *Fiscal Monitor: Capitalizing on Good Times*. New York, NY: International Monetary Fund.

Jordà, O., Schularick, M., & Taylor, A. M. (2014). "The great mortgaging: Housing finance, crises, and business cycles," *NBER Working Paper* 20501. Cambridge, MA: National Bureau of Economic Research.

Kessler, O., & Wilhelm, B. (2013). "Financialisation and the three utopias of shadow banking," *Competition and Change* 17(3): 248–264.

Krippner, G. R. (2011). *Capitalizing on Crisis: The Political Origins of the Rise of Finance*. Cambridge, MA: Harvard University Press.

Krugman, P. (2009, June 18). "Out of the shadows," *New York Times*. Retrieved from https://www.nytimes.com/2009/06/19/opinion/19krugman.html.

Langley, P. (2008). *The Everyday Life of Global Finance: Saving and borrowing in Anglo-America*. Oxford: Oxford University Press.

Lapavitsas, C. (2013). *Profiting Without Producing: How Finance Exploits Us All*. New York, NY: Verso.

Lysandrou, L., & Nesvetailova, A. (2015). "The role of shadow banking entities in the financial crisis: A disaggregated view," *Review of International Political Economy* 22(2): 257–279.

Marx, K. (1847/1975). *The Poverty of Philosophy*. Moscow: Progress Publishers.

Maurer, B. (2008). "Re-regulating offshore finance?," *Geography Compass* 2(1): 155–175.

McCulley, P. (2009). *The Shadow Banking System and Hyman Minsky's Economic Journey* (Global Central Bank Focus May, PIMCO). Newport Beach, CA: PIMCO.

McKinsey and Company. (2015). *Debt and (Not Much) Deleveraging*. London: McKinsey Global Institute.

Mehrling, R. (2011), *The New Lombard Street: How the Fed Became the Dealer of Last Resort*. Princeton, NJ: Princeton University Press.

Mertens, D., & Thiemann, M. (2018). "Market-based but state-led: The role of public development banks in shaping market-based finance in the European Union," *Competition & Change* 22(2): 184–204.

Moreira, A., & Savov, A. (2017). "The macroeconomics of shadow banking," *Journal of Finance* 72(6): 2381–2432.

Murau, S. (2017). "Shadow money and the public money supply: The impact of the 2007–2009 financial crisis on the monetary system," *Review of International Political Economy* 24(5): 802–838.

Nesvetailova, A. (2015). "A crisis of the overcrowded future: Shadow banking and the political economy of financial innovation," *New Political Economy* 20(3): 431–453.

OECD. (2013). *Addressing Base Erosion and Profit Shifting.* Paris: OECD.

OECD. (2016). *Institutional Investors' Assets and Liabilities.* Paris: OECD.

Palan, R. (1999). "Offshore and the structural enablement of sovereignty," in M. Hampton and J. Abbott (eds.), *Offshore Finance Centers and Tax Havens: The Rise of Global Capital* (pp. 18–42). Basingstoke: Palgrave Macmillan.

Palan, R. (2002). "Tax havens and the commercialization of state sovereignty," *International Organization* 56(1): 151–176.

Palan, R., Murphy, R., & Chavagneux, C. (2010). *Tax Havens: How Globalization Really Works.* Ithaca, NY: Cornell University Press.

Palan, R., & Nesvetailova, A. (2013). "The governance of the black holes of the world economy: Shadow banking and offshore finance," *CITYPERC Working Paper Series* 2013/03. London: City University.

Picciotto, S. (1999). "Offshore: The state as legal fiction," in M. P. Hampton and J. Abbott (eds.), *Offshore Finance Centres and Tax Havens: The Rise of Global Capital* (pp. 43–79). Basingstoke: Palgrave Macmillan.

Pozsar, Z., Adrian, T., & Ashcraft, A. (2010). "Shadow Banking", Staff Report No. 458. New York: Federal Reserve Bank of New York.

Pozsar, Z. (2014). "Shadow banking: The money view," *The Office of Financial Research Working Paper Series* 14-4. Washington, DC: US Treasury Department.

Rixen, T. (2013). "Why reregulation after the crisis is feeble: Shadow banking, offshore financial centres, and jurisdictional competition," *Regulation & Governance* 7(4): 435–459.

Roberts, S. (1994). "Fictitious capital, fictitious spaces: The geography of offshore financial flows," in S. Corbridge, R. Martin, and N. Thrift (eds.), *Money, Power and Space* (pp. 91–115). Oxford: Blackwell.

Roberts, S. (1995). "Small place, big money: The Cayman Islands and the international financial system," *Economic Geography* 71(3): 237–256.

Sayer, A. (2009). "Who's afraid of critical social science?," *Current Sociology* 57(6): 767–786.

Sgambati, S. (2016). "Rethinking banking: Debt discounting and the making of modern money as liquidity," *New Political Economy* 21(3): 274–290.

Soederberg, S. (2014). *Debtfare States and the Poverty Industry: Money, Discipline and the Surplus Population.* New York, NY: Routledge.

Stockhammer, E. (2004). "Financialization and the slowdown of accumulation," *Cambridge Journal of Economics* 28(5): 719–741.

Thiemann, M. (2014). "In the shadow of Basel: How competitive politics bred the crisis," *Review of International Political Economy* 21(6): 1203–1239.

Turner, A. (2012, March 14). "Shadow banking and financial instability," speech at Cass Business School. Retrieved from http://www.fsa.gov.uk/static/pubs/ speeches/ 0314-at.pdf.

Turner, A. (2015). *Between Debt and the Devil: Money, Credit and Fixing Global Finance.* Princeton, NJ: Princeton University Press.

UNCTAD. (2013). *Trade and Development Report 2013*. Retrieved from http://unctad.org/en/PublicationsLibrary/tdr2013_en.pdf.

Wigger, A. (2018). "Understanding the competition-crisis nexus: Revisiting US capitalist crises," *Rethinking Marxism* 29(4): 556–573.

Wigger, A., & Horn, L. (2016). "Taking critical ontology seriously. Implications for Political Science methodology," in H. Keman and J. Woldendorp (eds.), *Handbook of Research Methods and Applications in Political Science*. Cheltenham: Edward Elgar.

Wójcik, D. (2013). "Where governance fails: Advanced business services and the offshore world," *Progress in Human Geography* 37(3): 330–347.

Zoromé, A. (2007). "Concept of offshore financial centers: In search of an operational definition," *IMF Working Paper* 07/87. Washington, DC: International Monetary Fund.

9

FINANCIAL INTERMEDIARIES

Yamina Tadjeddine

Introduction

Classical financial theory ignores the existence of financial intermediaries. In neoclassical micro-economics, the capital market brings together agents with financing capacity—investors—and agents with financing needs—companies. Thanks to the private information they possess, the latter on the productive potential of the company, the former on the marginal productivity of their investment, the trade can take place. In the Asset Pricing Theory approach, only financial securities are considered, these being defined through two statistical dimensions: their risk and their return. The resulting optimum portfolio depends on these parameters as well as on the investor's degree of risk aversion. Once again, there is no need to seek the services of an intermediary. Naturally, in macro-economics, we find the same absence. Hicks (1974) contrasts the intermediated economy with the market economy where investors purchase their securities directly from issuers. The bank is distinguished by its inevitable presence in the transformation of deposits into loans.

This naturalized vision of finance could not be further removed from reality: the financial security only exists because of the presence of systems and organizations that give it its attributes (liquidity, status), take care of its distribution (via market institutions, distributors, advisors) and ensure its price history can be traced. For financial institutions existed before securities (Carruthers & Stinchcombe, 1999). It is these institutions and not securities themselves that have driven the development of finance. Without them, without their reputation, without the trust the community places in them, securities would not circulate since investors would not buy them. This chapter therefore proposes to take a critical look at these financial institutions, which are too often invisible and overlooked, and whose nature, function, and legitimacy remain a mystery to the layman.

This issue is particularly relevant in today's world, where the number of financial intermediaries is constantly growing. The space occupied by shadow banking is emblematic of this proliferation: the historical banking relationship involving only one intermediary, the bank, has been replaced by myriad contracts, organizations, and actors. In one recent study (FSB, 2015) the number of intermediaries between the household and the investor in a loan securitization was estimated at an average of 40. This lengthening of the chain is also particularly striking in the wealth management world. The figure of the individual speculator buying and selling securities on his own is now outmoded. Today the investment of individual savings and, even more so, regulated savings (pensions, insurance, different forms of profit sharing) involves numerous intermediaries: pension funds, asset management companies, financial advisors, depositories, brokers, etc.

Another singular feature of these invisible actors is their diverse nature (Lenglet & Gialdini, 2014). An intermediary is generally an organization associated with a legal category such as an asset management company or a stock exchange intermediary. It may also be a new activity that does not yet have its own specific legal category and is defined with respect to existing categories. This is the case for fintech companies and shadow banking entities (on these topics, see the chapters in this *Handbook* by Wang and Wigger & Fernandez, respectively). But sometimes an intermediary has no legal personality; it is just a tool or an algorithm. Muniesa (2007) studied the essential role played by the algorithm in setting closing prices and order books in the organization of financial trading.

Financial intermediaries can be classified based on their official economic function:

- Some are tasked with implementing buy or sell orders. They include finding brokers, market-makers, clearing houses, and stock exchanges. In economics, this is the field of finance microstructures.
- Some are involved in the investment of savings for third parties: asset management, mutual funds, pension funds, trusts, financial advisors, depositories, compilers, hedge funds, private equity organizations, and financial analysts.
- Others deal in corporate financing, the organization of primary issues of securities: investment banks, M&A services, securities services, and rating agencies.
- Some are involved in the setting up of over-the-counter (OTC) contracts for the transfer of risks (structured investment vehicles (SIVs), special purpose vehicles (SPVs)), and the setting up of swaps and other derivatives.
- Finally, all too often we forget to include intermediaries involved in public finance in this list.

Some of these functions are associated with independent entities, as is often the case in the United States. In Continental Europe, they are typically subsidiaries of banking and insurance groups, which often have a number of different subsidiaries covering the full spectrum of banking and financial activities.

I propose first of all to review the discourse that legitimizes financial intermediaries through economic theory. The angle adopted is a resolutely micro-economic one, starting with the initial theory of financial intermediation put forward by Gurley and Shaw (1956). In the second part, I will present some socio-politically inspired approaches that highlight the appearance of financial intermediaries through the possibility of legitimizing the capture of economic rents. This aspect, which appears in many recent works focusing on the financialization of the economy, emphasizes the link between financial institutions and certain forms of political domination. Finally, the third part will present some of my own work in the field of social studies of finance which are based on observational field research and which explore the socio-economic nature of financial intermediation. I will concentrate particularly on one field: asset management companies. My contribution will be critical as it proposes to de-naturalize the financial world and to stress the extent to which the dominant paradigm denies the social and political uniqueness of financial intermediation.

The Micro-Economic Legitimization of Financial Intermediation

This first part presents the theoretical motives put forward to justify the micro-economic role of financial intermediaries. Three registers are cited: transaction and information costs, liquidity creation, and innovation.

Financial Intermediaries Linked to Transaction Costs and Information Asymmetries

Financial intermediaries made their entrance into the closed world of actors theorized by economics with the work of Gurley and Shaw (1956, 1960). Although these contributions were the subject of some criticism, they still constitute the benchmark on the question of financial intermediation today. The authors place themselves in the context of a perfect market in the presence of agents with financing capacity (investors) and agents with financing needs (companies). The former could buy the securities issued by the latter directly. And yet they prefer to do so through organizations whose function is to buy the securities issued by primary issuers (companies, states) and to sell their own securities or debts to investors, pocketing a margin consisting of the difference between the return on the primary securities and the yield paid to the holders of their securities, known as secondary securities. The financial intermediary is therefore defined as a device that transforms the substance of securities into other securities. This transformation may be of deposits into loans for banks or of financial securities into shares for mutual funds. This transaction does not eliminate the financial risk, but instead mutualizes it: rather than being borne by one investor alone, it is spread between the different contributors (depositors, subscribers, shareholders) in proportion to their contribution.

If the investor rationally chooses to go through a costly intermediary, it is because he or she can benefit from the latter's expertise to reduce market-access and information costs and take advantage of mutualized management of the savings, offering economies of scale. The intermediary secures the financial transaction by reducing information asymmetry and therefore the risk of making bad choices when selecting securities. This last argument is particularly effective in the case of asset management. It was already being used as an advertising pitch when the first investment trust was launched, the Foreign and Colonial Government Trust created by R. Flemming in 1868, which attracted almost 75,000 investors (Cassis, 1994).

Gurley and Shaw's model was the first legitimization of financial intermediaries as trading facilitators in a context marked by asymmetrical information and the presence of transaction costs. It led to a vast body of micro-economic literature that defined the financial intermediary only in terms of his or her informational role. Later research would clarify this function by distinguishing banks, where the information produced remains private, from financial intermediaries, where the information is disclosed (Diamond, 1984). This first justification perfectly fits organizations producing financial knowledge, such as financial analysts who publish recommendations on companies, and rating agencies who assess issuer default risk.

Financial Intermediaries and Liquidity

Economists have difficulty perceiving the eminently social construction of the markets and the contribution of organizations to their smooth operation. And yet certain financial intermediaries are conditioning the very existence of these markets. In particular, they are behind the genesis of the essential quality of securities: liquidity. This refers to the possibility that any holder of a security has of selling it at any time without causing a drastic change in its price (on liquidity, see also Ortiz's chapter in this *Handbook*). Keynes (1936: Chapter 12) was the first economist to emphasize the importance of this singularity in the genesis and development of financial activities. However, he does not really detail all the concrete processes involved in the transformation of a fixed asset—the company—into liquid securities. This quality has not been studied in any greater detail in micro-economics, which assumes it to be natural. It has been left to sociologists, Carruthers and Stinchcombe (1999), to look into how a security becomes liquid, drawing on its financial history. They showed that liquidity is a product of conventions whose origins are closely linked to intermediaries. Socio-economics therefore attributes another, no doubt even more essential role to financial intermediaries. Benetti and Cartelier (1980) had already proposed to look more closely at these invisible conventions that micro-economics ignores and which are nevertheless necessary. They use the nomenclature hypothesis to explain how even before the famous pure and perfect competition hypotheses—atomicity, homogeneity, mobility, transparency—it was possible to quietly overlook these conventions. Carruthers and Stinchcombe concern themselves more particularly with the historical and social processes that have contributed to the establishment of a continuous market and above all to the homogenization of the financial security. In particular, they study the role of market-makers. They are interested in market-makers because they act as wholesalers in securities, holding them in stock to enable individuals to buy and sell them whenever they please. Market-makers orient clients' choices based on the securities they have in their portfolio. The possibility of trading a new security also requires being aware of these characteristics and therefore being able to assign it to a public asset class with recognized qualities. Institutions will draw on their reputation and their know-how to give such a security intelligible qualities and to present it to the investor in such a way as to arouse his or her interest and incite him or her to buy it. Ortiz (2014) studied the discourse used by hedge fund managers to attract investors and emphasizes precisely this importance of classification and the types of images used to persuade investors. The influence of financial analyses on individual decisions is just as illustrative (see Chambost, 2018). Financial intermediaries are therefore at the very source of the existence of a financial security and its marketing.

Financial Intermediaries and Financial Innovations

One strong criticism leveled at Gurley and Shaw's model concerns the importance given to transaction costs in their theoretical demonstration. In fact, these costs have fallen hugely as the finance world has changed. The computerization of financial transactions and the financial markets has reduced the costs of connecting co-traders and the costs of transferring ownership rights. In addition, individuals now have real-time access to the same information as professionals. It could therefore have been expected that certain intermediaries would disappear and their numbers fall. Paradoxically, what we have witnessed is a proliferation of financial intermediaries. Allen and Santomero (2001) provided an explanation: intermediaries develop in response to financial innovations. This justification of the genesis of intermediaries had already been proposed by Hyman Minsky. As the financialization of the economy has been accompanied by an acceleration in financial innovations, in particular in the derivatives sector, a logical concomitant increase in the number of intermediaries has occurred. The current sophistication of derivatives and the development of more complex markets such as the securitized products market requires skills that are rare and specific, forming niches in which these new intermediaries can position themselves. Under these conditions, the *raison d'être* of these institutions is purely endogenous and has legitimacy only in the presence of financial innovations. This tells us something quite edifying about the period we are living in: financial intermediaries would seem only to exist because there are financial innovations and these financial innovations justify the existence of excess profit in the Schumpeterian tradition. It is then easy to understand the motivation currently behind the financial sector's constant innovation and the financial hypertrophy that has resulted.

Financial Intermediaries as Actors in the Process of Financialization

The first part of this chapter was intended to give an understanding of the micro-economic role of financial intermediaries without pre-empting any conclusions on the overall effect. I will now look at the influence exerted by these intermediaries on the economic system and on society more generally. This is a theme that is widely dealt with in works on the financialization process (Epstein, 2005; Krippner, 2011, Van der Zwan, 2014). Here, more generally, it is the question of the domination of finance that is addressed.

Financial Intermediaries and Political Power

I will begin here with an economist-historian known for his work on the international monetary system and who is not spontaneously associated with the critical finance movement: Marc Flandreau. And yet, his last book, *Anthropologists in the Stock Exchange: A Financial History of Victorian Science* (2016), will serve as the basis for my introduction to this second part. Flandreau's aim is to understand the dynamics of financial domination in the Victorian period (1837–1901). His starting point for this is a surprising discovery: the presence of influential financiers, members of the Bondholders Committee, in the ranks of the learned societies (such as the Royal Geographical Society, the Anthropological Society, and the Ethnological Society). This frequent occurrence is no mere coincidence, but evidence of the importance for financiers of being in the structures of power to ensure a regular income. The committees in question (Council of Foreign Bondholders founded in 1868, then the Corporation of Foreign Bondholders in 1873) were made up of affluent figures. On the London market for foreign debt issued by companies, states, or colonies of the British Empire, they played an essential role in the success of an issue. When a Committee supported an issue, it publicized it by organizing meetings and placing chapters in the newspapers. They also acted as advisors to the British Foreign Office. Their influence was essential in the financial sphere since they were orienting savings through the information they provided and creating liquidity. They were therefore financial intermediaries essential to the smooth operation of the London market.

Now let us look at their reasons for joining the learned societies. These societies organized meetings where explorers who had discovered remote regions came to talk about their travels. They also funded "scientific" missions to explore new territories. It is immediately obvious what the interest was for a nineteenth-century financier in attending these meetings and being able to orient the sources of financing: it enabled them to acquire private information on the economic potential of these distant lands, as well as on their political and social organization. This insider information enabled them to formulate their advice on new issues, but also to enter into contact with local elites in order—for a consideration—to help them with the issuing process. Here we find an illustration of the informational role of the financial intermediary in a context marked by high transaction costs. These committees gave them a scientific legitimacy enabling them to recommend or advise against investing in certain companies and certain states. They were even able to persuade market opinion to buy certain bonds and then persuade them to do the very opposite, as was the case, for instance, with the Honduran railways before and after May 1872. But, and this is the crux of Flandreau's theory, this presence in the learned societies was not limited to an informational function. Above all, it gave them a scientific legitimacy enabling them to intervene in the political and diplomatic spheres. Flandreau illustrates this with several examples, including the military expedition carried out against the Emperor Tewodros II of Abyssinia in 1868. This decision was made by the newly appointed Prime Minister Benjamin Disraeli in order to free some British hostages. The Anthropological Society openly supported Benjamin Disraeli and the need for an intervention in Abyssinia against John Russell (Foreign Secretary (1859–1865), then Prime Minister (1866–1868)).

This link between financial intermediaries and central political power is also perceptible in their historical location. I have explored the location of management companies in France (Tadjeddine, 2010) and in Paris (Tadjeddine, 2018b). The Parisian history includes a financial component that expands with the centralization of economic power in the capital. A financial industry was established very early in the economic and political heart of the city. As early as the twelfth century, money changing and lending activities were going on the Pont au Change bridge that links the royal castle on the Île de la Cité with the economic districts along the right bank of the Seine. Afterward financial activities moved to the right bank, to Palais Royal then Rue Quincampoix, where the frenetic episode involving the shares of the Banque Royale took place between 1716 and 1720. The location of banking and finance activities in Paris became permanent at the end of the nineteenth century and lasted until the middle of the 1990s. Jobs in finance are concentrated in the wealthy *arrondissements* on the right bank—around the Bourse (stock exchange), the Opéra, and the Champs Elysées—close to the centers of French political power, and where the press and large corporations set up their headquarters at the end of the nineteenth century. This concentration in the economic and political heart of a country is a permanent feature in finance, which can be explained by the very nature of the financial service, which is linked to information, trust, currency, and power.

This influence of financial and banking intermediaries on power is now largely documented through the socio-political analysis of lobbies. Studying organizations from a critical angle means exposing the power of finance resulting from the different pillars making up this activity: control of wealth and membership of elites. It is obvious that financial intermediaries have direct access to means of payment whose channels of circulation they control. This control, combined with knowledge of tax and regulatory arbitrage, enables them to divert revenues. And they can do so all the more easily given that as they all belong to the same social networks, meaning opportunities to meet are frequent and discreet. Once they have won over the politicians, the lobbyists will be able to orient public choices in order to legitimize a tax and regulatory system that guarantees them a regular income and enables them to avoid too great a degree of public scrutiny (Seabrooke, 2006). Although this capture of the political is not new, it is today proving to be a salient feature of our societies, and political power appears to be relatively powerless to counteract this influence and lacking the will to act on the continuing increase in economic and social inequalities induced. The scandals relating to tax havens are particularly emblematic of this powerlessness, even when the misappropriation is being committed by well-known organizations and people (Palan et al., 2013).

A study of the intermediaries in public finance is also highly instructive in understanding the connections between the space where political power is exerted and that of the financial intermediaries. A recent book by Lemoine (2016) follows the recent history of the French Treasury and describes how the logic of government debt came into being with new intermediaries and new pressures on the French state. We are currently working with Nicolas Pinsard on the public offices that were created in France in 1467 by Louis XI and which would become, over the centuries, powerful financial intermediaries controlling the levying of taxes, but also the main royal creditors from the reign of Louis XIV onward (Pinsard & Tadjeddine, 2019). Today, the financialization of public finances constitutes a particularly active sector in terms of financial innovations and therefore the appearance of new financial intermediaries. This has led to the existence in France of public-private partnerships and structured loans. These are niches that have become particularly attractive as the state is seen as a "good payer" and therefore a safe bet, which has attracted all sorts of speculators, including "vulture funds." These mainly American funds buy up distressed public debt and then sue the debtor states for the full value of the debt. Argentina, Peru, Zambia, and the Democratic Republic of Congo have been victims of this kind of attack where the creditor's rights generally take precedence over the general interests of the society concerned.

Financial Intermediaries and Economic Rent

With financialization, society has become an exceptional field for observing the macro-economic and social effects of the development of financial activity and the proliferation of financial intermediaries. Economists have been working for about 20 years to quantify the scale of the ongoing process of financialization.

To do so they have drawn on national accounting data, measuring the relative weight of financial intermediaries in the production of wealth or in payroll figures (Philippon & Resheff, 2013), in the distribution of economic rent (Duménil & Lévy, 2001), and in the rise in social and spatial inequalities (Godechot, 2013). This work has allowed the reality of financial domination to be assessed.

It is important to complete this work with a more qualitative perspective in order to grasp how financial logic and financial intermediaries are penetrating not only businesses, but also areas such as art, justice, education, urban planning, agriculture, healthcare, and sport. For these financial intermediaries will impose their evaluation models, their codes, their images, their worldview, their legitimacy, and in the end their rent. Financialization can indeed be understood as a process of preemption by financial actors of the hoped-for future revenues produced by economic and social actors (companies, public bodies, prisons, hospitals, states, etc.). Economic and social producers become tied to these promises of future revenues, which force them to achieve performance targets, bear the associated risks and, where necessary, implement the choices necessary for their achievement. Chambost (2013) illustrates this process with the case of the arrival of a private equity fund in the capital of a clinic, showing how it leads to the flexibilization of work and the individualization of pay in order to achieve profitability targets set by financial investors (on private equity, see also Souleles's chapter in this *Handbook*).

Studying a Financial Intermediary from the Angle of Socio-Economics: Management Companies

Figure 9.1 offers a schematic overview of these organizations: intermediaries in the true sense of the word are shown in the middle (sovereign investment funds, mutual funds, pension funds, insurance companies, hedge funds, private equity). They receive money from governments, households, and companies who trust them to manage their investments (pension funds and insurance firms, primarily). They are therefore responsible for selecting securities on the regulated markets (shares, money liabilities), OTC markets, or directly with non-listed companies. While the activities of mutual funds, pension funds, and insurance companies are subject to regulations which require them to hold primarily regulated securities, hedge funds are free to invest in all available segments. Private equity firms prioritize investments in non-listed companies.[1]

For those with savings, asset management proposes to turn to the expertise of an intermediary—the fund manager—in order to build up a portfolio of financial securities. The fund manager is considered to have a greater understanding of those entities issuing financial securities (governments, corporations) and of how the market works. He or she is also expected to have privileged access to information and rumors, and is therefore better informed as to how best to yield profit from capital. It is this enhanced knowledge concerning opportunities for

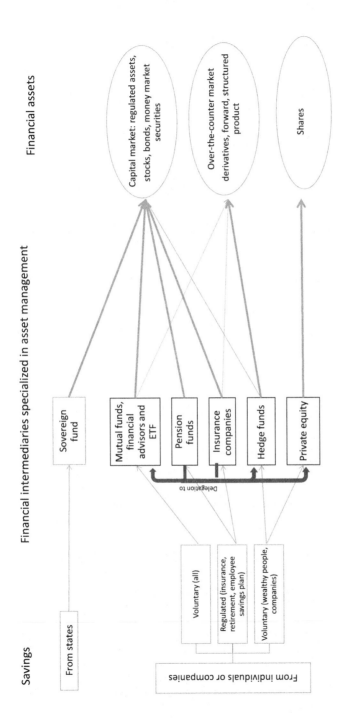

Figure 9.1 Financial intermediaries: from savings to financial portfolios.

speculative profit that justifies his or her fees. Appealing to the services of a fund manager means the saver can expect a higher profit than what he or she would have achieved without this mediation.

From the perspective of a canonical economic interpretation, a direct connection should exist between the quality of the service provided by the manager—namely the judicious selection of securities to include in a portfolio—and the capital yields paid out to the saver. The issue of the quality of financial services would therefore be resolved. Yet, the financial reality is marked by the uncertainty of price variations: financial hazard is not Gaussian, it follows more complex processes which render its prediction impossible both in the short and long term. As a result, speculative profit achieved over the short term is above all the result of good luck or of a bad turn. It provides little information regarding the value of the service provided by the manager and furthermore makes it impossible to determine his or her prospective ability to attain the same returns. This informational deficiency both ex ante and ex post creates suspicion and market failures (Akerlof, 1970). Nevertheless, in practice, the trade undoubtedly takes place as certain arrangements like signals or reputation are employed to resolve the market failure. The existence of such arrangements was revealed through socio-economic research examining the quality of services by Eymard-Duvernay (1989), Gadrey (2004), and Karpik (1989). Ortiz (2005) additionally proposed to assimilate these various socio-economic studies, in order to understand the nature of the relationship between fund manager and broker. He shows how the personalization of the trades leads to the existence of various modes of qualification. I pursue this pathway within this section, basing my work upon another type of relationship (between sales personnel and institutional investors).

This section therefore proposes to examine the service produced by an asset management company. I first succinctly describe the activity of fund management delegation that takes place between institutional investors and asset management corporations. I then focus on the quality of the financial service. The financial relationship cannot singularly be reduced to the returns yielded; rather, it is built through a collection of social and political arrangements that I discuss at the end.

The Relation between Institutional Investor and Asset Management Companies

Asset management companies provide the service of portfolio management. In France, conducting fund management activities for third-party accounts is regulated by the AMF, Autorité des marchés financières (the Financial Market Authority). According to a report on third-party account management published in 2012 by the AMF, in this same year there existed a total of 604 asset management companies which between them handled 2,867 billion Euros. However, this elevated figure obscures a major imbalance: the subsidiary of large insurance and banking groups manage practically 90% of the assets (AMF, 2012). I have monitored the case of one management firm, the subsidiary of a private Belgian bank, which declared in April 2013 that it had under its management 2.6 billion Euros worth of assets. This private bank employs around a hundred employees and offers its services to private individuals, though also and more importantly to institutional investors. We were able to observe the work of the person responsible for customer relations with their institutional clients. The observation consisted of regular encounters with this person, within their firm, for over more than a year, in addition to the consultation of numerous commercial documents (prospectus presenting the company's products, contracts, calls for tender, reports).

The main institutional investors in France are insurance companies, private health insurance firms, pension funds, associations, and foundations. The origin of funds could be private savings or regulated capital (insurance reserves or retirement funds), the management of which is controlled by public rules. In France, 69% of managed assets are from institutional investors. Consequently, the relationship between institutional investor and asset management company is at the very core of current financial capitalism (Aglietta & Rigot, 2009). Certain institutional investors own the subsidiaries of fund management firms and hence invest their funds within them. This is the case with several insurance firms (AXA with AXA IM), but also with a number of private health insurance firms (EGAMO is a subsidiary of MGEN) and some social organisms (Pro BTP Finance). Institutional investors can also choose to invest with an external service provider, such as the private Belgian bank that I was able to observe. The service may be carried out in various juridical forms: share subscriptions for UCITS (undertakings for collective investment in transferable securities) or trust. It is common that institutional investors turn at the same time towards various competing internal and external service providers. Decisions concerning the delegation of fund management involve numerous internal actors (financial directors, executive officers, lawyers, follow-up committees, etc.), but also external consultants who will be tasked with selecting the management firms. The representative for the management firm is generally the salesperson responsible for canvassing new clients and fulfilling their expectations.

The Nature of the Financial Service

Within the collective management market, the client (here the institutional investor) must choose a producer (the manager). The production in this trade is the portfolio yield. This yield is furthermore the only market signal received by the client, yet it is impossible to infer from it the true quality of the manager.

We thus find ourselves confronted with a key debate within the informational economic theory, which concerns the consumer's knowledge about the quality of the provided service. Three types of services have been identified in economic literature. In the first instance, Nelson (1970) proposes to distinguish between services for which the quality can be discerned ex ante ("search goods") and services for which the quality will only be known once consumed ("experience goods"). Darby and Karni (1973) have added a third category, "credence goods," covering those services for which it is impossible even ex post to discern the quality. Yet none of these three categories are applicable to the circumstances of financial services due to the presence of financial uncertainty. The knowledge of past yields is not reliable enough to distinguish good managers either ex ante or ex post. The financial service therefore cannot be classified as either a search good or an experience good. Neither is it, on the other hand, a credence good in which the agent is able to use the information asymmetry in an opportunistic way to maximize his or her own interest. The existence of financial uncertainty harms equally the client (who may lose their money) and the portfolio manager (whose hard work may go unrecognized).

The financial service thus falls under the definition of a unique good, also known as "singularities" (Karpik, 2007). The challenge of the trade is to overcome this lack of information by establishing a personal relationship based on the co-production of a service. To this end, the protagonists must back up the commercial relation with measures that they will eventually define over time and which will allow the financial service to be qualified, framed, and monitored.

The Arrangements Required for Trading and Legitimizing Financial Services

Financial services cannot merely be summarized as a simple market exchange, as they involve a personal relationship that engages the co-exchangers. As such, it is not only the yield that is bought, and which must be taken into consideration by the client and the seller, but also a collection of practices, knowledge, rules, symbols, and feelings which will bind together the protagonists (Ortiz, 2005). These non-commercial and co-constructed arrangements are precisely what constitute the essence of the financial trade. In these conditions, the characterization of the good or bad manager, as well as any impending sanction, is dependent upon the nature of the relationship founded. We propose to illustrate this unique aspect of the financial service through three arrangements thus observed: membership with symbolic social networks (a personal arrangement, according to Karpik, 2007); the standardization of practices involving the use of predefined styles, benchmarks, and classifications (impersonal, significant or formal arrangements, again according to Karpik, 2007); and finally framework agreement (the contrat-cadre, according to Eymard-Duvernay, 1994).

Personal Arrangements

Historically, calling upon a specialist to manage one's private fortune relied heavily upon the individual and personal trust built up between two protagonists

Personal knowledge, belonging to shared social networks, or having family in common reassured the saver with regard to the correct moral standards of the person who was responsible for investing his or her savings. The commercial agreement is made possible thanks to the individuals' embeddedness in social structures that bring with them moral guarantees concerning the fund manager's good will. The commercial conclusion is nothing more than the outcome of these weak ties which initially allowed the seller and the client to enter into contact and to establish a connection across the long term. Any knowledge of embezzlement would give rise to social rupture, with the manager being banned from the group, and as a consequence commercial rupture would ensue. The research of Pinçon and Pinçon-Charlot (1998) has demonstrated the importance of private clubs within upper-class society and in particular within the financial sphere. Individuals who belong to the same social networks (Freemasons, clubs, and religious communities) or who share similar activities (hunting, mountaineering) encourage trust. Also, finance has for a long time used this symbolic capital in order to persuade clients to place their trust in them when it comes to investing their assets (Tadjeddine, 2018b). An address bears with it a reputation, a guarantee communicated via the symbolic nature globally associated with certain neighborhoods. Pinçon and Pinçon-Charlot (2007) speak of the "spatial signature." The social and symbolic capital associated with a territory due to the history of its occupants is transferred to any entities domiciled within that location.

Nevertheless, following the current liberalization of society in which values such as transparency, avoiding conflict of interest, and short-term competition dominate, this "personal" form which relies on reciprocity, informality, and opacity has been denounced. At present, it is impossible for the financial director of a private health fund, for example, to justify his or her choice of portfolio management uniquely on the basis of pre-existing social connections. Despite all this, weak ties still remain essential to building connections between actors. A salesperson is only valuable as long as the names in his or her address book are influential and loyal. As such, the salesperson whom I observed had maintained a number of relations over several decades, even though the individual in question had changed companies several times.

Impersonal, Significant, and Formal Arrangements

The second grouping assembles together arrangements which aim to homogenize and characterize practices by establishing a reference point for judging and comparing the services provided (Vatin, 2009). As such, the service bought is no longer idiosyncratic, but can be compared to others which are equivalent in order to evaluate the fund manager's skills in the light of his or her peers. Moreover, the relationship is no longer strictly personal but involves the existence of recognized evaluation agencies. In asset management, this movement towards professional standardization during the 1980s was based on classical financial theory following the naturalization of "benchmarks," and later in response to practitioners via the creation of a professional practices rating.

Traditional asset management developed in reference to the evaluation model of financial assets: the CAPM—Capital Asset Price Model. This model enabled a reference portfolio composed of a sample of assets that account for the global evolution of a market to be established. The market index thus acquired scientific legitimacy and naturalization, and ever since all financial centers have been equipped with one or several indexes (the CAC40 in Paris, S&P500 in New York, etc.). Global, ethical, sector, and mandatory indexes were developed in the wake. These indexes were defined and built by market firms responsible for listing and pairing together orders (such as Euronext) or financial companies (such as Standard & Poor's). The success of these indexes resulted for the most part from the fact that they provided a publicly accessible referent, which allowed the yield of a portfolio built up by the manager to be compared with the reference portfolio.

The existence of indexes also allowed portfolio management to become standardized. From the beginning of the 2000s, a new financial product, created and developed in the United States during the 1990s, the Exchange Traded Fund (ETF) appeared in France. These products automatically reproduce the index, without involving any expert input from the fund manager. They were subject to an extremely strong buying craze, notably among institutional investors, who subsequently bought into an industrialized product (Gadrey, 2004), for which the yield remains risky yet perfectly correlated with the market index. As such the ETF enables any uncertainty concerning the quality of the manager to be eliminated and maintains only financial uncertainty. With the arrival of ETF, the financial intermediary is summed to a standardized contract associated with an algorithm.

There exists a second impersonal arrangement: classification by asset management style. The domination of passive index management signaled the death-knell for manager expertise, as all that was deemed necessary to obtain an optimal yield was a basket of "scientifically" defined securities. From the 1980s, several professionals in asset management and financial econometricians discussed and wrote about the fact that certain managers who developed strategies for selecting securities, regularly and considerably obtained higher yields than those theoretically predicted (Aaron et al., 2005). This observation directly challenges the thesis of information efficiency, though it grants scientific legitimacy to employing a fund manager. Upon this basis, three strategies for securities selection gained prominence among both clients and practitioners: the sector, growth, and value styles. The sector or geographical style aims to select securities in relation to their activity sector or geographical zone. The growth style consists of selecting companies that are predicted to experience high growth rates. The value style favors unlisted companies, abnormally affordable, and predicted to undergo a hike in prices.

The categories unite together homogeneous practices in that they are all based on similar strategies for selecting securities. Allocation in one or the other of these categories can take place via public information, through studies carried out by specialized companies or by the manager declaring their preferred style.

These categories are currently employed as often by managers to explain their strategy, as they are by clients to choose. They contribute towards standardizing practices by obliging managers to qualify their strategy through pre-determined categories. Consequently, the UCITS funds of the private Belgian bank are presented within the prospectus of the AMF, as they similarly are directly to clients, in accordance with whichever dominant style the manager happens to choose. Nevertheless, this categorizing process leaves a wide berth of choice within a selection of securities, which explains the possibility of differentiated yields. Ratings based on styles are created, and the quality of the manager is judged in the light of these categories.

The "Contract-Cadre" or Framework Agreement

The final grouping is concerned with contractual arrangements which explain and frame the production process. These arrangements were put into place during the 1990s in the United States and later on in France, during the shift towards the judicialization of society. They were initiated by institutional investors to counterbalance the power held by asset managers in the delegation relationship. An initial set of rules enacted ex ante by the client or by an external consultant outlines the preferences and expectations of the institutional investor on the subject of funds investment. Two methods exist: either these rules are published during calls-for-tender and are communicated to the highest number of people possible, or they are communicated during individual encounters with select firms, and in this case we refer to due diligence. The management firm, if it wishes to trade with the client, must fulfill these expectations by answering detailed questionnaires about its practices concerning the selection of securities, its management style, its reference indexes, its risk management, its staff members, its internal organization, its clients, performances, etc. It is only after having answered all these questions that the commercial relationship can begin through the competitive comparison of the various responses given by the managers. A selection and listing takes place on the basis of the responses given. Using this base, the client chooses one or several asset companies. It informs some of the non-selected firms that they may have an opportunity of being selected at a later date, if they change certain elements within their proposed service. Consequently, a historical account takes place which allows for the behavioral evolution of firms to be monitored. Once the selection is concluded, a contract then binds together the institutional investor and the chosen manager.

Strictly speaking, this commercial contract contains two elements: the first details the expectations of the client in terms of the management (market sectors, management styles, risks, reference indexes, and the freedom regarding this index, i.e., "tracking error"); the second outlines a set of rules targeted at reducing any moral hazard by framing the practices and obliging the manager to pass on regular information via reporting and during meetings. The information communicated explains the motivations behind the selection of securities, the reasons for the performances attained, and the future directions. As such the institutional investor frames the work of the manager and obliges him or her to regularly disclose information. The manager's opportunism is much lower, and the portfolio yield represents nothing more than a lone indicator among many others.

Conclusion

This chapter on financial intermediaries has attempted to provide an overview of the contributions of a critical approach to finance with the aim of understanding the role of these intermediaries in the economic system but also in society overall. The work presented here draws on a variety of disciplines: economics, sociology, anthropology, political science, and management. This interdisciplinarity allows us to grasp the reality of finance in its economic, social, and political unity. The use of empirical methods allows us to deconstruct the financial object, virtually naturalized by economics, and to free ourselves of the presuppositions concerning it. This enables us to think differently about financial intermediaries and the practices, social interactions, and structures that make up finance. As a result, finance is no longer addressed only from the dominant angle of trade—as proposed by orthodox economics—but from a much wider perspective, in which finance is viewed as a veritable place, field, and system of production. Here we have chosen to look at finance on a particular observation scale: that of organizations. But other scales are possible: techniques, people, and institutions. These observation scales are all legitimate and can contribute, together and separately, to understanding how finance works when taken as a whole (see also Chambost et al., 2018).

Note

1 The following builds on Tadjeddine (2018a).

References

Aaron, C., Bilon, I., Galanti, S., & Tadjeddine, Y. (2005). "Les styles de gestion de portefeuille existent-ils?," *Revue d'Economie Financière* 81: 171–188.
Aglietta, M., & Rigot, S. (2009). *Crise et Rénovation de la Finance*. Paris: Odile Jacob.
Allen, F., & Santomero, A. M. (2001). "What do financial intermediaries do?," *Journal of Banking and Finance* 25(2): 271–294.
Akerlof, G. A. (1970). "The market for "lemons": Quality, uncertainty and the market mechanism," *Quarterly Journal of Economics* 84(3): 488–500.
Autorité des Marchés Financiers. (2012). *Rapport annuel sur la gestion d'actifs pour le compte de tiers en 2012*. Paris: AMF.

Benetti, C., & Cartelier, J. (1980). "L'hypothèse de nomenclature," in C. Benetti & J. Cartelier (eds.), *Marchands, salariat et capitalistes* (pp. 94–123). Paris: La Découverte.

Carruthers, B. G., & Stinchcombe, A. L. (1999). "The social structure of liquidity: Flexibility, markets, and states," *Theory and Society* 28(3): 353–382.

Cassis, Y. (1994). *City Bankers 1890–1914*. Cambridge: Cambridge University Press.

Chambost, I. (2013). "De la finance au travail. Sur les traces des dispositifs de financiarisation," *La nouvelle revue du travail* 3.

Chambost, I. (2018). "The role of financial analysts in the social construction of financial value," in I. Chambost, M. Lenglet & Y. Tadjeddine (eds.), *The making of finance perspectives from the social sciences* (pp. 37–43). New York: Routledge.

Chambost, I., Lenglet, M., & Tadjeddine Y. (eds.). (2018). *The making of finance perspectives from the social sciences*. New York: Routledge.

Darby, M. R., & Karni, E. (1973). "Free competition and the optimal amount of fraud," *Journal of Law and Economics* 16(1): 67–88.

Diamond, D. W. (1984). "Financial intermediation and delegated monitoring," *The Review of Economic Studies* 51(3): 393–414.

Duménil, G., & Lévy, D. (2001). "Costs and benefits of neoliberalism: A class analysis," *Review of International Political Economy* 8(4) 578–607.

Epstein, G. A. (Ed.). (2005). *Financialization and the world economy*. Cheltenham: Edward Elgar Publishing.

Eymard-Duvernay, F. (1989). "Conventions de qualité et formes de coordination," *Revue économique* 40(2): 329–359.

Eymard-Duvernay, F. (1994). "Coordination par l'entreprise et qualité des biens," in A. Orléan (éd.), *Analyse économique des conventions* (pp. 307–334). Paris: PUF.

Flandreau, M. (2016). *Anthropologists in the Stock Exchange: A Financial History of Victorian Science*. London and Chicago, IL: The University of Chicago Press.

FSB. (2015). *Global Shadow Banking Monitoring Report* 2015. Basel: Financial Stability Board.

Gadrey, J. (2004). *Socio-économie des services*. Paris: La Découverte.

Godechot, O. (2013). "Financiarisation et fractures socio-spatiales," *L'Année sociologique* 63(1): 17–50.

Gurley, J. G., & Shaw, E. S. (1956). "Financial intermediaries and the saving-investment process," *The Journal of Finance* 11(2): 257–276.

Gurley, J. G., & Shaw, E. S. (1960). *Money in a Theory of Finance*. Washington, DC: Brookings Institution.

Hicks, J. (1974). "Capital controversies: Ancient and modern," *The American Economic Review* 64(2): 307–316.

Karpik, L. (1989). "L'économie de la qualité," *Revue française de sociologie* 3(2): 187–210.

Karpik, L. (2007). *L'économie des singularités*. Paris, Gallimard.

Keynes, J. M. (1936). *The General Theory of Employment, Interest and Money*. New York, NY: Prometheus Books.

Krippner G. (2011). *Capitalizing on Crisis: The Political Origins of the Rise of Finance*. Cambridge, MA: Harvard University Press.

Lemoine, B. (2016). *L'ordre de la dette: Enquête sur les infortunes de l'État et la prospérité du marché*. Paris: La Découverte.

Lenglet, M., & Gialdini, L. (2014). "Opérateurs de marché," in F. Tannery, A.-C. Martinet, T. Hafsi, & J.-P. Denis (eds.), *Encyclopédie de la stratégie* (pp. 855–866). Paris: Vuibert.

Muniesa, F. (2007). "Market technologies and the pragmatics of prices," *Economy and Society* 36(3): 377–395.

Nelson, P. (1970). "Information and consumer behavior," *Journal of Political Economy* 78(2): 311–329.

Ortiz, H. (2005). "Évaluer, apprécier: les relations entre *brokers* et gérants de fonds d'investissement," *Économie rurale* 286–287: 56–70.

Ortiz, H. (2014). "The limits of financial imagination: Free investors, efficient markets, and crisis," *American Anthropologist* 116(1): 38–50.

Palan, R., Murphy, R., & Chavagneux, C. (2013). *Tax Havens: How Globalization Really Works*. Ithaca, NY: Cornell University Press.

Philippon, T., & Resheff, A. (2013). "An international look at the growth of modern finance," *Journal of Economic Perspectives* 27(2): 73–96.

Pinçon, M., & Pinçon-Charlot, M. (1998). *Les Rothschild, une famille bien ordonnée*. Paris: La Dispute.

Pinçon, M., & Pinçon-Charlot, M. (2007). *Sociologie de la Bourgeoisie*. Paris: La Découverte.

Pinsard, N., & Tadjeddine, Y. (2019). "L'édit de la paulette 1604: la marchéisation des finances royales," *Revue d'économie financière* 135(3): 273–280.

Seabrooke, L. (2006). *The Social Sources of Financial Power: Domestic Legitimacy and International Financial Orders*. Ithaca, NY: Cornell University Press.

Tadjeddine, Y. (2010). "An address in Mayfair or Vendôme: Spatial rationality of hedge funds," *Banker & Markets and Investors* 107: 45–54.

Tadjeddine Y. (2018a). "Financial services – a collection of arrangements," in I. Chambost, M. Lenglet & Y. Tadjeddine (eds.), *The making of finance perspectives from the social sciences* (pp. 17–23). New York: Routledge.

Tadjeddine Y. (2018b). "Territories of finance – the Parisian case," in I. Chambost, M. Lenglet & Y. Tadjeddine (eds.), *The making of finance perspectives from the social sciences* (pp. 127–134). New York: Routledge.

Van der Zwan, N. (2014). "Making sense of financialization," *Socio-Economy Review* 12(1): 99–129.

Vatin, F. (eds.). (2009). *Évaluer et valoriser. Une sociologie économique de la mesure*. Toulouse: Presses Universitaires du Mirail.

10
PRIVATE EQUITY

Daniel Scott Souleles

Sing, O' Muse, of Corporate Woe, and of Pensions Unfulfilled[1]

There's an urban legend, common enough in the United States that the good people at Snopes.com[2] have had to debunk it: that Twinkies, yellow sponge cakes with a white cream filling made by Hostess Brands, ubiquitous in grocery stores and gas stations nationwide, are unperishable and will last forever (Snopes.com, 2012). Twinkies could withstand a nuclear war and even the cockroaches that survive the ensuing fallout.

Obviously, this isn't true.

Twinkies, in their current incarnation, have a shelf-life of around 65 days (Harwell, 2016). While this is far longer than any pastry you'd make at home, it is a bit short of eternity. More than anything, I suspect this tall-Twinkie-tale gets at the relationship that some people can have with the food of their childhood, as well as the stuff that makes up the taken-for-granted boundaries of their lives. Of course, Twinkies would, could, should survive forever, or, at least, always be around. I had them. My parents had them. Why wouldn't my kids, and their kids, and the cockroaches that inherit the earth also have them? But, for around nine months, between November 2012 and July 2013, Twinkies disappeared from American shelves.

The actual weeks when Twinkies went out of stock led to mourning, melancholy, and lamentation from journalists and consumers alike. To take one example, *The Statesman Journal* from Salem, Oregon reported that, "The announcement that Hostess Brands, Inc. is going out of business has prompted a full parking lot and a line throughout the local Wonder Hostess Thrift Store on Portland Road." *The Statesman Journal* goes on to profile Sonja Bahr, who drove some distance to buy $105 dollars-worth of Hostess baked-goods (enough for around 25 boxes of Twinkies). The Wonder Hostess Store explained the closure on their website, saying, "We are sorry to announce that Hostess Brands, Inc. has been forced by a Baker's Union strike to shut down all operations and sell all company assets" (Pallone, 2012).

Cathy Jett in the *McClatchy-Tribune Business News*, to take another example, wrote an article called "So Long, Sweet Twinks," and quoted a number of people from towns a-ways South of Washington D.C.: "It's the food you grew up with as a kid. It's what your mother threw in your lunchbox," said Art Williams as he and his wife filled their shopping cart. "It's pretty sad," added Joanne Williams, who had shopped at the outlet for bread, rolls, and cakes for more than 20 years on her way home from work at Mary Washington Hospital, "I feel Sorry for all the people losing their jobs" (2012).

The panic, ultimately, was unwarranted; Twinkies returned to shelves. Still, the attentive reader may have noted some conflict in accounting for the half-baked hoarding: Hostess blamed their closing, bankruptcy, and liquidation on an intransigent union. And Joanne Williams shed a tear for those losing their jobs. These allusions are the frosting on the cake of a tumultuous 20 years that Hostess and their Twinkies endured: 2 bankruptcies, 18,500 firings, a revolving door of CEOs, exorbitant executive bonuses, union-led strikes, abandoned pensions, consumer panic, and tying it all together, pushing much of the action were a sequence of private equity (PE) buyout deals, deals that are nowhere present in consumer's casual reflection on Twinkies' fate. In turn, the recent history of the Twinkie offers a good entry point to explain what PE is; show how it works, what it does, and how it touches so many facets of people's lives; as well as explain a bit about the scholarship that has tracked its rise. More pragmatically, it will explain how the machinations of financiers, PE investors in this case, can make something, a small and meaningful part of people's lives like the Twinkies vanish and then reappear according to a logic completely divorced from everyday life and experience.

PE companies are firms of finance people who pool other people's money into "funds," and use those funds and even more borrowed money to buy, manage, and sell other companies as investments. Though a relatively new form of investment that has only existed since the end of the 1970s (Appelbaum & Batt, 2014), as of 2015 there were around 5,800 PE firms that managed around US$3.8 trillion in assets and were responsible for around 3,423 buyout deals (Elvin, 2015: 7, 16, 96), which is perhaps around 20% of all company buying that happens in a given year (see also Klier, 2008: 1).[3]

In what follows I'll elaborate on the Hostess/Twinkies case to explain how PE works and offer an approach to understanding PE deals that draws from an account of PE deals as total social facts. Then I'll compare this to other ways of knowing about PE investors drawn from other anthropologists, sociologists, historians, journalists, and financial economists. I'll close by making an argument that PE is a prototypical process of financialized capitalism, and can best be understood by historically informed anthropological analysis.

Given that my blood sugar has plummeted over the few prior paragraphs, it's probably proper to pivot back to the Twinkie...

Of Put-Upon Hard-Working People, and of Greedy CEOs

As I noted above, even the most cursory accounting for the Hostess Twinkie saga, bankruptcy, mass firings, fire-sale, and rebirth, gestures towards the various groups of people and property that played a role in the bankruptcy, dissolution, purchase, and ultimate restructuring of Hostess. This observation is both key to my suggestion of how to understand PE deals and is drawn from the theorizing of David Graeber. In a 2013 article called "It is value that brings universes into being," Graeber says that we might see society "as an arena for the realization of value" (2013: 226) and that societies might be "imagined as a kind of game where the players are vying to accumulate some form of 'Capital,' but that at the same time there is a kind of higher level game of dominance, subordination, and autonomy" (2013: 228). I take Graeber's observation as an invitation to inventory the value projects that the various groups involved in Hostess had, as well as to suggest what sort of pattern for value conflict and resolution a PE deal sets, what sort of game everyone is playing. Below, I will suggest that PE deals look like total social facts as typified by Marcel Mauss (2000/1925) and that this has ramifications for understanding the distribution of wealth, poverty, and work that PE deals create and allocate. First, though, to the players and their prerogatives:

Starting from the inside out, from those closest to the Twinkies, we'll first meet the 18,500 or so people who actually made Hostess run on a day to day basis, prior, of course, to the November 2012 dissolution. They worked in hot bakeries, operating on an industrial scale, and worked driving and delivering all manner of baked treats and breads to a nation-wide network of Hostess shops and outside stores that sold the goods that rose at Hostess. This workforce was spread across 36 bakeries, 565 distribution centers, and at 570 bakery outlet stores (Devaney, 2012). Moreover, this workforce was heavily organized—there were 372 collective bargaining agreements (Mufson, 2012), across a number of unions, two of the largest being the Teamsters who represented 7,500 souls (Webb, 2012), and the Bakery, Confectionary, Tobacco Workers and Grain Millers Union who represented 5,000 (Giegerich, 2012). Keep in mind, aggregate union membership in the United States's private sector is around 7 percent. (Dunn & Walker, 2016)

As Hostess slid into its second bankruptcy, the various union employees bore wounds from their first encounter with company-wide insolvency. Specifically, in order to keep Hostess alive, workers forewent nearly US$1 billion in pension contributions. Reporter Steven Mufson has this to say about one of the union presidents:

Frank Hurt, President of the Bakery, Confectionery, Tobacco Workers & Grain Millers International Union [...] blamed management. He said executives launched a deli-style bread that "was just a loser from Day One."

He said they starved the advertising budget. And he said that the union had been compliant, freezing wages for four or five years as the number of workers fell. As for the pension plan, which is owed $944 million, Hurt said Hostess has not made a payment to the fund since July. "I have to tell you, Wall Streeters don't give a damn about people. Zero. They could (sic) care less," Hurt said. "That's what's wrong with this country." (2012)

For Hurt and his union, Hostess was mismanaged, making suspect product decisions, failing to advertise adequately, and neglecting worker's pensions. His account gets at a larger sense of frustration and mistrust workers had for Hostess's management. Note, too, the conflation of Wall Street with corporate management. This will be important in a few paragraphs.

As we might expect, management saw things differently. Here is Mufson reporting on Brian J. Driscoll, the CEO of Hostess Brands:

There was plenty of finger-pointing on Wednesday. In the bankruptcy filing, Brian J. Driscoll, chief executive of Hostess Brands, blamed its failure on "restrictive" labor rules and legacy pension burdens. He lamented that the company had 372 collective-bargaining agreements with a dozen unions and that Hostess paid $103 million a year to employees" pension funds. He said the Teamsters' contract rules required different workers for making bread and cake deliveries and limited flexibility to serve small outlets.

Bankruptcy, the company said, offers another chance to "reengineer," [or] overhaul its union accords and shed pension liabilities. "The Company's current cost structure is not competitive," the company said in a statement. And that, "combined with the economic downturn and a more difficult competitive landscape" prompted the need for a reorganization. (2012)

For management, management isn't the problem; overpaid, unreasonable union employees are the problem. The reporter, Mufson, goes on to arbitrate, though, saying, "Hostess lost $250 million in the less than three years since it emerged from its previous bankruptcy. That means it would have lost money without any pension costs at all" (Mufson, 2012).

So far, we have a typical labor/management dispute. Labor thinks management is doing a bad job and underpaying them; management thinks the opposite. However, we're missing a third, crucial party: PE investors, who were around every step of the way over the last 20 years. Instead of just management and labor, we actually have owners, management, and labor. Moreover, PE's role in all this is only possible due to shifts in the relative importance of financiers in business more generally and the changes in the legal and societal treatment of corporations that allow for PE, the legal agents of a pooled-investment fund, to act and be treated like owners of a company like Hostess.

In the United States, as corporations became larger and more frequently traded on stock exchanges, particularly in the later part of the nineteenth and early parts of the twentieth century, the question of who controlled a corporation arose. Berle and Means (1991/1932), in their book *The Modern Corporation and Private Property*, observe that due to public listing on stock exchanges, owners became increasingly distant and hypothetical from the companies they legally owned a share of, and, in turn, managers became more powerful. Berle and Means went on to suggest that, to counteract the weakness of ownership, some form of voting rights should be given to shareholders of corporations. Running parallel with these sorts of trends and further shaping corporate structure and governance were US federal anti-trust laws, which, through the mid-twentieth century encouraged the growth of large, diversified conglomerates whose divisions existed in competitive markets instead of vertically or horizontally integrated concerns (Fligstein, 1990).

Collectively these trends point towards a situation in the mid-1970s in which many large publicly traded American companies were made up of dissimilar business units and run according to the imperatives of relatively autonomous managers. At least, this was the situation that held in corporate and investor America until the economic turmoil of the 1970s hit; everything from stagnant wage growth, spiking commodity prices, and to rising unemployment suggested that something was rotten with how America did business, leaving space for both new understandings of corporations and new ways to rearrange them to make money.

Ideologically there was a shift away from thinking about firms as owing something to the nation, or to their workers, or to the communities in which they operated, toward simple mercenary profit. Diversified conglomerate firms were doing too many things at once, needed to be stripped down and simplified, and accountable to their owners. This change in perspective came from economists like Michael C. Jensen and William H. Meckling, who in 1976 suggested that "most organizations are simply legal fictions which serve as a nexus for a set of contracting relationships among individuals" (1976: 310), and that those individuals have "divisible residual claims on the assets and cash flows of the organization" (1976: 311). Another economist, a famous one, Milton Friedman published essays with titles like "The Social Responsibility of Business Is to Increase Its Profits" (1970), in place like the *New York Times*. Taken together, these sorts of polemical statements set the atmosphere and provided a number of interpretive frames that eased the policy shifts that allowed for the rise of PE investment firms.

From a more concrete point of view, the sagging profitability of a number of publicly traded firms provided a space for "take-over" investors to do "buy-outs" of companies, taking control by buying a majority of stock and then making operational and financial changes to a company. These early takeovers were often engineered by current and former investment bankers who knew both how to take control of a company and how to use the company to borrow money to either pay out shareholders or invest in the company, often leading a company to have more wealth than it appeared to on paper (and ultimately more debt than a previous generation of corporate executives thought was healthy).

The innovation they used, formerly known as "bootstrapping," laterally called a "leveraged buyout," was to have a corporation borrow money to buy itself from existing owners, carry debt, but be held and managed by the PE firm as an investment. The PE firm never had any accountability to creditors (that was the responsibility of the corporate entity they invested in), though it could stand to lose the amount of money it had put up to borrow a larger amount. PE firms would use similar borrowing practices across the course of their ownership tenure to take more money out of a company, often as investment profit, and put more debt on a given company. Elaborating much further on the early days of PE defies the constraints of this chapter. So, for a more detailed account of the rise of PE see Baker and Smith (1998); for an exemplary account of some financiers' transition from investment banking to managing a PE fund see Anders (1992) or Carey and Morris (2012); for a sense of the public perception of early PE deals see Smith (1976), Hirsch (1986), or Burrough and Helyar (1990); for an updated account of PE's interaction with management and the companies they invest in, see Appelbaum and Batt (2014); and for how destructive and disruptive PE deals can be see Holland (1989) or Faludi (1990).

These takeovers were often in the service of pension and other investment funds. In the late 1970s there were regulatory changes to the interpretation of the laws governing pension investments in the United States that allowed these funds to invest in alternative investment categories (alternative to stocks and bonds) and permitted them to put their money with PE managers (Lerner, 2000). Beyond pension funds, often university endowments, sovereign wealth funds, wealthy families, and insurance companies will all invest in PE (see, e.g., Elvin, 2015: 76ff.). In a basic way, much of the social infrastructure of the United States is funded by PE and other interest- or dividend-bearing financial investments. This is typical of a larger shift from productive, manufacturing work as being what creates most wealth in the United States to investing, interest, and debt creating a proportionately larger share of wealth (Krippner, 2011; see also Clark, 2000). The upshot of all of this for the workers and managers at Hostess is that the desire of PE investors is what ends up patterning ownership decisions. Moreover, there were actually several PE firms seeking to turn a profit selling nostalgia and cream filling.

After Hostess's first bankruptcy, a New York-based PE firm, Ripplewood Holdings, bought a controlling share of Hostess (Hamilton, 2012). Lest the above lead you to think that PE investment is one-dimensional, here is Andrew Ross Sorkin on Ripplewood's ultimately unsuccessful plans for Hostess:

> Ripplewood, which was founded by Timothy C. Collins, a major Democratic donor, is expected to lose most, if not all, of the $130 million or so it invested in Hostess. The Company's lenders led by Silver Point Capital and Monarch Alternative Capital, are not expected to fare well either.

The behind the scenes tale of Hostess and Ripplewood may be the opposite of a project to buy it, strip it and flip it. When Mr. Collins originally looked at Hostess, he was trying to make investments in troubled companies with union workers. He was convinced that he could work with labor organizations to turn around iconic American businesses, and he hoped Hostess would become a model for similar deals. (2012)

Despite high aspirations to heal a union-heavy company, Ripplewood seems to have made some classic PE decisions that teed up Hostess for its second bankruptcy in 2012.

First, coming out of bankruptcy, the PE transaction itself added about US$200 million in debt to the company, bringing its total to US$670 million. Second, Ripplewood charged Hostess management and consulting fees. Third, executive and managerial salaries seemed to double or triple, all while senior management churned, running through six CEOs in ten years (McGregor, 2012; Sorkin, 2012). All this happened while Hostess made no substantive changes to its product offering, operational structure, or labor agreements. Ripplewood basically failed to fix Hostess, and perhaps accelerated things by doing what PE typically does: increasing debt, raising their and managerial compensation, and churning through highly paid executive management, leading to work-place demoralization and the sensation of working in an investment as opposed to a company.

The failure, too, of a relatively union friendly PE firm set the stage for a second bankruptcy, and the PE firms Apollo Global Management, LLC, and Metropoulos & Co. to take control of a number of parts of Hostess in the course of a bankruptcy proceeding that saw the firing of most of the company's workers and the returning of the Twinkie to America's larder.

Apollo and Metropoulos were a different sort of PE firms from Ripplewood. PE firms generally have one of a few genres of strategies that they use to make money (though, they're often blended in practice). In the early days, PE firms could make money financially—buying a company, borrowing a lot of money to distribute to investors, and then paying down the debt via currently existing cash flows. This mode of PE ownership is increasingly implausible as competitive pricing of companies has increasingly included this sort of financial maneuver in the cost of buying. It no longer pays to manipulate a company only with financial engineering, to simply load it up with debt to pay dividends and fees. By contrast, there are a large number of growth strategies—these entail taking a company and investing in a product line, productive capacity, research, or even buying rival companies all with the idea of allowing a company to grow larger and more profitable. Then there are "distressed" investors, PE funds that seek out companies in and around bankruptcy with serious financial and operational problems. Distressed (pejoratively, "vulture") investors hope to buy these companies at bargain prices and then either fix the company or assemble a wholly new company from failed company parts and then sell that as an investment.

Whereas Ripplewood seemed committed to leaving Hostess intact—unions, pensions, and all—and managing their way out of distress, Metropoulos and Apollo intervened in the course of bankruptcy to buy a number of Hostess's parts, shed of union pension obligations and all employees, and reassembled a much smaller Hostess, designed to deliver Twinkies and other sweet, long-lived baked goods, as cheaply and quickly as possible. Moreover, Metropoulos had an expertise in working with well-known consumer brands like Hostess.

To do all this, Apollo and Metropoulos spent US$410 million to buy the Hostess brand, a number of pastry products (Twinkiers, Ho Hos, Ding Dongs, and Donettes, among numerous others), as well as five bakeries and their assorted equipment (PR Newswire, 2013). Recall, prior to bankruptcy, Hostess had 36 bakeries in total. Moreover, bankruptcy proceedings allowed Metropoulos and Apollo to discard all outstanding pension debts and obligations, as well as union contracts, starting over with a clean labor slate. By 2016, the *New York Times* could observe that "In 2012, Hostess had about 8,000 employees and eight bakeries dedicated exclusively to snack cakes. Six other plants produced at least some desserts. Today, the new Hostess has only three plants and 1,200 workers" (Corkery & Protess, 2016).[4]

Beyond having fewer workers and fewer bakeries, the newly constituted Hostess was able to turn their temporary absence into a marketing coup, advertising Twinkies return as "the sweetest comeback in the history of ever" (Corkery & Protess, 2016). The *New York Times* went on:

> Nowhere was it sweeter, perhaps, then at the investment firms Apollo Global Management and Metropoulos & Company, which spent $186 million in cash [the rest was borrowed] to buy some of Hostess's snack cake bakeries and brands in early 2013. Less than four years later, they sold the company in a deal that valued Hostess at $2.3 billion. Apollo and Metropoulos have now reaped a return totaling 13 times their original cash investment. (Corkery & Protess, 2016)

Apollo and Metropoulos's success gets at both the ways people in their society tend to think about businesses, and the ways that they do not. When a company is sold, the price is often some reflection of the amount of money it generates over some number of years. To give one example, when I did my own field work with PE investors (Souleles, 2019), I would often hear that a rough thumbnail price for a company would be three to six times the amount of free cash it has coming in a given year. On Hostess Brands Inc.'s 2017 form 10-K,[5] its EBITDA, or one measure of free cash flow, was US$230.2 million. Put another way, the company could buy itself in ten years, at a price of US$2.3 billion. Put another way, in five years the company is capable of paying back all of its old pension debt.

The point about pension debt is important. US bankruptcy laws allow the disposition of pension debt. US bankruptcy laws allow Apollo and Metropoulos to take brands made valuable by decades of unionized labor, discard paying a pension, and then profit from those brands.

> Bankruptcy judges have broad powers to determine who gets paid and how much. Stockholders—the owners—are generally wiped out, although not always. Management sometimes continues collecting big salaries and bonuses [they did in this case] [...] The most controversial feature of the latest round of bankruptcies is that Hostess, Kodak and AMR want to use bankruptcy to relieve them of their pension promises. Under Chapter 11, retirees in line for pensions are considered unsecured creditors—at the bottom of the list of who gets paid. Labor contracts can be voided, too, giving companies a break from union work rules. What angers many union workers and leaders is that executives may give themselves separate retirement plans that are honored. (Asbury Park Press, 2012)

Taken together, this is more or less what happened with Hostess's bankruptcy. Executives continued to take bonuses; a federal judge in bankruptcy court voided union contracts; and that same federal judge in bankruptcy court absolved future buyers of Hostess's various brands of pension obligations.

Labor, management, financial capitalism, and the agents of the state all make up the core players in a PE deal. At one step removed are surrounding communities, who cope with the trauma of layoffs rippling through their social and economic world. Nowhere are their voices present in Apollo and Metropoulos' management's, or the bankruptcy court's plans. Then at one further remove are the consumers of Hostess products, who, as the top of this chapter suggested, simply pined for their pastries and read no great political import in why their treats went away or why they returned. No one talks about PE management. The closest we come is the union's generic reference to "Wall Street." And in the final outer ring, are the journalists, writing the first draft of history, recording and analyzing in real time. Journalists have no direct power or say in the process, and are nominally simply reporting. But they also sketch, in a fragmented way, the various players in this social drama and allow an analyst and researcher like me to cobble together a narrative, and, perhaps, interpret it.

Of Silly Rambling Theories, and Things Mostly of the Mind

As I suggested above, PE deals have been happening predictably and regularly since the late 1970s. They're repetitive and have a pattern. Because of this, I find it useful to reach into anthropological theory, and claim them as an instance of a "total social fact," both because I think this phenomenon describes the way that people and things move around, and also because this sort of theorization allows me to compare a relatively recent social phenomenon to other times and places, so that it doesn't seem as strange or incomprehensible as it might.

"The total social fact" comes from Marcell Mauss's 1925 *Essai sur le Don*, often translated in English as just *The Gift* (Mauss, 2000/1925). Mauss suggests that there is a phenomenon, a way of exchanging and rearranging people and possessions, that draws and gathers the totality of a society in, and then sends it all back out rearranged (Wendling, 2010). In *The Gift*, Mauss identifies a few instances of total social facts—Northwest Coast potlatch feasts and the Kula exchange in the Trobriand Islands are two of the most famous anthropological examples. He points out how social status and exchange relationships are overlapping within systems of exchange, and how they mutually constitute and point to one another. Social status and standing both structure a total social fact and provide the key to understand the why of income, wealth, and peoples' distribution across a social landscape.

In the PE deal, we have the rearrangement of people, their jobs, the places those jobs happen, and the wealth that work creates, all moved around according to the imperatives of financial ownership. In this case, Apollo and Metropoulos bought de-unionized and de-pensioned pieces of a former company that had made its way through bankruptcy. They had the wealth, the legitimate ideas, and the backing of the state to do so. They revamped the company, took a tremendous amount of money out for owners and investors, and now run a business that employs a fraction of its former headcount.

All told, the story of PE is twofold: (1) it's about the values of PE investors, specifically how they think companies should operate as compared to all the other people who exist in and around businesses, and (2) the way in which ideologies of corporations and the rule of law that privilege shareholding owners above all other groups is allowed to carry the day. This concern, too, provides a bridge to understanding the broader ways that financiers control the distribution of wealth in their societies.

Closest to PE investors might be the work of investment bankers as portrayed by Karen Ho (2009). Investment bankers though also involved in the buying and selling of companies like PE investors are essentially middle-men. They give advice to people buying and selling businesses, and they often sell shares created in an IPO or sell debt created in bond offerings, all to finance deals. Whereas PE investors often seek to make operational changes to companies and typically control them for several years, investment bankers make money by the transaction. In Ho's telling, this leads them to value short-term churn over any sort of restructuring. They wouldn't likely care what happened to Hostess, Inc. one way or the other after helping out with a deal. Though, given their interstitial position in the world of financing, what they think is important in a company can often structure the terms of transactions and set the boundaries of what is possible when companies change hands, all according to a far more "short-term" logic than that of PE investing.

Continuing in the direction of shorter time horizons are various forms of stock traders (e.g., Borch, 2016; Miyazaki, 2013; Zaloom, 2006). One feature of the world that Hostess and Apollo inhabit is that control over businesses is reduced to an often tradable, transferrable fraction of company equity called a stock or a share. These equity stakes circulate in public on various stock markets and exchanges, at several removes from the actual underlying company. In this way traders are able to treat shares as investments or even wagers and gambling risks at incredibly high speeds. None of this is innocent, either. Both the rise or fall of stock price and the trades and "deals" at the core of stock trading affect the worth of a company and its ability to get capital investments. The circulation, speculation, and trading that stock investors participate in has serious material consequences for the underlying companies, despite stock traders rarely having any sort of first-hand familiarity with the businesses they trade. Their transactions are highly abstracted deals that rearrange the social world according to the logic and imperatives of highly liquid, speculative markets.

At another end of the time/value spectrum sits long-term investors such as family investment offices (Marcus, 1992). These sorts of offices buy and hold, potentially forever. They simply exist to maintain and expand the intergenerational wealth of a family. In this version of investing, the PE fund never sells an asset but simply takes money out of it. The business is subsumed under the imperative of transferring wealth to owners, in perpetuity. Of course, owners need not have anything to do with the company and the people who generate money for them.

It's this comparative frame, this ability to assess a social scene and see in aggregate how wealth moves around, and see who is ignored and why and according to what measure of wealth and value, that this comparative anthropological approach to PE offers. It also offers a bridge to a few comparative theories of social inequality. Archaeologists have suggested that one way that inequality is perpetuated in society is by means of controlling the methods for recording and thereby codifying what is valuable (Flannery & Marcus, 2012; Scott, 2017). The passion play of PE as total social fact shows how many different ways we might understand a company (by the lights of consumers, or unions, or managers, or even financiers), and how investment logic ultimately wins and sets the terms of social rearrangement. That is the value that counts.

More generally too, theorists of deep human history and the social patterns that seem to emerge over the species life of homo sapiens have suggested that "bottlenecking" of people and resources is a persistent phenomenon (Earle et al., 2011). Put another way, it seems that fairly regularly human groups encounter both natural and human-made (though the distinction is not always clear) bottlenecks which limit the number of people who have access to resources. In this way, we might see PE setting a sort of human-made bottleneck around having access to the resources that Hostess's ability to make snack cakes provides. Their bottleneck is the business plan they create which has no pensions, dramatically fewer workers and plants, and thereby closes out the majority of people and protections that were at Hostess prior to its second bankruptcy. Adopting a comparative anthropological frame of analysis for PE both allows the analyst to understand the larger social impact of PE deals, and how they're similar and different to both other financial deals and other instances of inequality.

It's also what's missing from much research that comes out of business schools, and from departments and journals of finance or economics. More than anything, this research rarely offers any sort of interpretation of the social significance of PE, what it means and why, and how it does what it does. Insofar as these questions are attempted, they are addressed in the abstract, reductive, and numerical language of financial economics or cost accounting. These approaches can be useful additions to a larger comparative research agenda, and occasionally supply interesting data-sets, but are often unimaginatively blindered. Several early articles in the *Journal of Financial Economics* and *The American Economic Review* (Jensen, 1989; Kaplan, 1989a, 1989b; Zimmerman, 2015) typify this mode of scholarship, arguing that specific types of buyouts are good because they fix the problems of wayward managerial agents, or that the companies simply make more money due to creative tax maneuvering or the sort of "operational" efficiencies an owner like Apollo would pursue, as though these were the only relevant standards of informed analysis (Foley, 2006).

More usefully, though, are articles that, though narrowly and numerically conceived, can fill out a more detailed picture of PE. One such paper is Braun et al.'s (2016; see also Phalippou, 2014) suggestion that contemporary PE has competed itself to a point where there are fewer structural advantages to investing in PE, one can no longer make purely financial plays, and that past investment performance does not seem to predict future investment performance. PE, in this telling, and after examining the profitability in 13,523 investments across 865 buyout funds, has become just another asset class. While this is a helpful perspective, to make any interpretive use of this sort of scholarship, one has to have a larger historical frame that understands the rise and fall of industries and financialized modes of making money that seem to come at particular capitalist crises. Without this, it's just some more interesting facts about PE.

One other minor genre of PE scholarship that is of use to contextualize PE, is that which comes from business history. Darek Klonowski's (2011) book *Private Equity in Poland: Winning leadership in emerging markets* illustrates the state level, institutional framework necessary to allow businesses to be bought as investment and managed by financiers. Too, this sort of scholarship reinforces the point made in the Hostess saga that a key part of the deal process is the state enforcing bankruptcy and private property laws against the interest of thousands of wayward workers.

Of Bottlenecks, Accounting Tricks, and Stuff That Takes Up Time

The above section is meant to give a sense of how identifying deals as total social facts allows the analyst both to trace out the dynamics of financialized capitalism (Who buys what? Who rearranges what? And according to whose ideas?), and to understand why its profits get allocated the way they do. Moreover, it's meant to show some of the shortcomings and uses of more narrow scholarship on PE. In short, the rearrangement of people and wealth that happens in a total social fact occurs according to the logic of those with power to arbitrate what is valuable in a given society. Sometimes they compete with each other (Beidelman, 1989), and other times, as in the case of Apollo and Metropoulos they collaborate to consolidate their class advantage. The key to all of this, though, is how PE investors see companies as investments, as reducible to numbers and abstractions, and as entities that take on debt and disgorge profit, and the people that work in them as incidental human capital, and how this understanding wins the day.

Often in the course of my own field-work, I would attend industry conferences. These meetings were my only opportunities to see the heads of the largest firms, live and in person, taking questions. In February of 2014, I and around 1,000 of my closest friends got to see Leon Black, the founder of Apollo, speak about Hostess. He sat on a raised stage, with a mic and a spotlight, wearing a suit, and he answered questions. When asked about Hostess, here are my notes on what he said:

> Hostess Twinkies was a unique situation. Here you had a brand that is up there in terms of recognition—like McDonald's and Coca Cola—it had a good revenue line, but it's margins had been squeezed to death via some union issues that the company had been battling for many years. Some debt, but the real issue with Hostess was margin squeeze.
>
> In the margin you have perishables and non-perishables. Bread is a perishable. You have to have your bakeries near your final distribution outlets and it has to get there very quickly or it's gone in a few days. It needs special types of transportation; and it costs a lot. Non-perishables have a 3-6-month shelf life and don't need the same costs.
>
> The company found itself in a situation where union said non-perishables had to be treated like perishables and the company wasn't making it. They finally said unless we change this we have to file for bankruptcy. The union wouldn't agree to that. So, the company filed for bankruptcy. I wasn't involved in any of that.
>
> Once it went into bankruptcy, the court mandated that legacy contracts go away. In bankruptcy, our partner, Dean Metropoulos, who spent a career in successful food companies (Vlasic, Pabst, Bumblebee Tuna), we were basically able to cherry pick five or six of the plants dealing with the nonperishables and not have to deal with all the extra costs of the perishables and the extra transportation costs.
>
> Once the court blessed our buying those pieces of the company, we got the great brands (Hostess, Ring Dings), we were able to get them back on the selves after about four months, once the court blessed the deal. I think we have the best of both worlds now. We have the great brands; we have the revenues; but the costs are much less. That, I think was a unique opportunity.

In his telling, unions wanting their pension paid is "margin squeeze." Moreover, the company battles the union, as though it were some external entity instead of the overwhelming majority of the people working at Hostess. We don't hear anything about the past PE managers. We don't hear anything about executive churn. And we don't hear anything about why 18,000 people stopped trusting those that ran their company. We hear about "margin-squeeze."

When we hear about the value of Hostess's brand, we don't hear about who created it, and we have no conversation about who should profit from its worth. These are all foregone conclusions. We don't hear about communities that had perishable bakeries, or what someone should do about an insolvent pension. Insofar as we hear about regular people, they're only consumers. They're those that are happy to get their Twinkies, a ravenous horde maddened by nostalgia's impossible desires. Like the ghosts that seek investment returns, they hunger, feast, and are never full.

Notes

1 The interpretive argument I'm developing here is a simplified, condensed version of the argument I develop in a book, an ethnography of private equity investors (Souleles, 2019). Here, I am taking for granted the majority of the empirical work that bolsters my analytic scheme.
2 Snopes.com is a website that researches urban legends, often debunking them.
3 Arjaliès et al. give another way to make sense of private equity's significance: They note that by the end of 2012 there were around US$87 trillion dollars under investment management, which is nearly equivalent to a year's global GDP, and around 40% of the world's financial assets. Private equity would account for about 4% of all the money that is invested (2017: 1). To understand the effect that private equity has, though, I think it's important to keep in mind the other measure of significance—the fact that somewhere around 20% of all companies that are bought and sold go through a private equity transaction, and that private equity deals, as in the case of Hostess and Twinkie often take on the form of a larger social drama in which basic questions of who should get rich, who should have a job, and what sort of work a country should do gets played out in real time in the context of a private equity deal. (Still, US$3.8 trillion is a lot of money; only four countries have a higher GDP, and that's IF you count the EU as a country...)
4 I know that in the paragraph above it says that Apollo and Metropoulos bought five bakeries and this block quote say they have three plants. In the course of their new ownership tenure, Apollo and Metropoulos closed some facilities.
5 An annual financial and business report that publicly traded US firms have to submit to the Securities and Exchange Commission.

References

Anders, G. (1992). *Merchants of Debt: KKR and the Mortgaging of American Business*. New York, NY: Basic Books.
Appelbaum, E., & Batt, R. (2014). *Private Equity at Work: When Wall Street Manages Main Street*. New York, NY: Russell Sage Foundation.
Arjaliès, D. L., Grant, P., Hardie, I., MacKenzie, D., & Svetlova, E. (2017). *Chains of Finance: How Investment Management Is Shaped*. Oxford: Oxford University Press.

Asbury Park Press. (2012, February 8). "Bankruptcy can be a reprieve for some," *Asbury Park Press*, 7.

Baker, G., & Smith, G. D. (1998). *The New Financial Capitalists: Kohlberg, Kravis Roberts and the Creation of Corporate Value*. Cambridge: Cambridge University Press.

Beidelman, T. O. (1989). "Agonistic exchange: Homeric reciprocity and the heritage of Simmel and Mauss," *Cultural Anthropology* 4(3): 227–259.

Berle, A. A., & Means, G. C. (1991/1932). *The Modern Corporation and Private Property*. Piscataway, NJ: Transaction Publishers.

Borch, C. (2016). "High-frequency trading, algorithmic finance and the flash crash: Reflections on eventalization," *Economy and Society* 45(3–4): 350–378.

Braun, R., Jenkinson, T., & Stoff, I. (2016). "How persistent is private equity performance? Evidence from deal-level data," *Journal of Financial Economics* 123: 273–291.

Burrough, B., & Helyar, J. (1990). *Barbarians at the Gate: The Fall of RJR Nabisco*. New York, NY: Harper and Row.

Carey, D., & Morris, J. E. (2012). *King of Capital: The Remarkable Rise and Fall, and Rise Again of Steve Schwarzman and Blackstone*. New York, NY: Currency.

Clark, G. (2000). *Pension Fund Capitalism*. Oxford: Oxford University Press.

Corkery, M., & Protess, B. (2016, December 11). "How the Twinkie made the superrich even richer," *New York Times* (Late Edition, East Coast), A.1.

Devaney, T. (2012, January 11). "Bankruptcy filing no 'Ho Ho' for Twinkies maker," *McClatchy-Tribune Business News*.

Dunn, M., & Walker, J. (2016). "Union membership in the United States." U.S. Bureau of Labor Statistics—Spotlight on Statistics" (website). https://www.bls.gov/spotlight/2016/union-membership-in-the-united-states/pdf/union-membership-in-the-united-states.pdf. Accessed April 1, 2018.

Earle, T., Gamble, C., & Poinar, H. (2011). "Chapter 8: Migration," in A. Shyrock and D. L. Smail (eds.), *Deep History: The Architecture of Past and Present* (pp. 191–218). Berkeley: University of California Press.

Elvin, C. (ed.) (2015). *2015 Preqin Global Private Equity & Venture Capital Report*. New York, NY: Preqin.

Faludi, S. C. (1990, May 16). "The reckoning, the reckoning: Safeway LBO yields vast profits buy exacts a heavy human toll—The 80's-style-buy-out left some employees jobless, stress-ridden, distraught—owner KKR hails efficiency," *The Wall Street Journal*, A.1.

Flannery, K., & Marcus, J. (2012). *The Creation of Inequality: How Our Prehistoric Ancestors Set the Stage for Monarchy, Slavery, and Empire*. Cambridge, MA: Harvard University Press.

Fligstein, N. (1990). *The Transformation of Corporate Control*. Cambridge, MA: Harvard University Press.

Foley, D. K. (2006). *Adam's Fallacy: A Guide to Economic Thinking*. Cambridge, MA: The Bellknap Press of Harvard University.

Friedman, M. (1970, September 13). "The social responsibility of business is to increase its profits," *The New York Times*, SM.17.

Giegerich, S. (2012, September 14). "Teamsters accept hostess concessions," *McClatchy-Tribune Business News*.

Graeber, D. (2013). "It is value that brings universes into being," *HAU: Journal of Ethnographic Theory* 3(2): 219–243.

Hamilton, W. (2012, January 12). "Cupboard is again bare for Hostess," *Los Angeles Times*, B.1.

Harwell, D. (2016, July 6). "Hostess brands is back with a vengence," *The Washington Post*, A.12.

Hirsch, P. M. (1986). "From ambushes to golden parachutes: Corporate takeovers as an instance of cultural framing and institutional integration," *American Journal of Sociology* 91: 800–837.

Ho, K. (2009). *Liquidated an Ethnography of Wall Street*. Durham, NC: Durham University Press.

Holland, M. (1989). *When the Machine Stopped: A Cautionary Tale from Industrial America*. Boston, MA: Harvard Business School Press.

Hostess Brands, Inc. (2017). "United States securities and exchange commission: Form 10-K" Retrieved from http://www.hostessbrands.com/phoenix.zhtml?c=254431&p=irol-sec#15487575. Accessed March 27, 2018.

Jensen, M. C. (1989). "Agency costs of free cash flow, corporate finance, and takeovers," *The American Economic Review* 76(2): 323–329.

Jensen, M. C., & Meckling, W. H. (1976). "Theory of the firm: Managerial behavior, agency cost, and ownership structure," *Journal of Financial Economics* 3: 305–360.

Jett, C. (2012, November 17). "So long, sweet Twinkies," *McClatchy-Tribune Business News*.

Kaplan, S. (1989a). "The effects of management buyouts on operating performance and value," *Journal of Financial Economics* 24: 217–254.

Kaplan, S. (1989b). "Management buyouts: Evidence on taxes as a source of value," *The Journal of Finance* 44(3): 611–632.

Klier, D. O. (2008). *Managing Diversified Portfolios: What Multi-Business Firms can Learn from Private Equity*. Heidelberg: Physica-Verlag.

Klownowski, D. (2011). *Private Equity in Poland: Winning Leadership in Emerging Markets*. New York, NY: Palgrave.

Krippner, G. (2011). *Capitalizing on Crisis: The Political Origins of the Rise of Finance*. Cambridge, MA: Harvard University Press.

Lerner, J. (2000). *Venture Capital & Private Equity: A Casebook*. New York, NY: John Wiley & Sons, Inc.

Marcus, G. E. (1992). *Lives in Trust: The Fortunes of Dynastic Families in Late Twentieth-Century America*. Boulder, CO: Westview Press.

Mauss, M. (2000). *The Gift: The Form and Reason for Exchange in Archaic Society*, trans. W. D. Halls. New York, NY: W.W. Norton & Company. (Original work published 1925).

McGregor, J. (2012, November 17). "Why didn't Hostess workers believe the threats?," *The Washington Post*.

Miyazaki, H. (2013). *Arbitraging Japan*. Berkeley, CA: University of California Press.

Mufson, S. (2012, January 12). "Hostess files for bankruptcy," *The Washington Post*, A.12.

Pallone, C. (2012, November 16). "Residents swarm Salem Hostess store as company announces closure," *Statesman Journal* Salem, OR.

Phalippou, L. (2014). "Performance of buyout funds revisited?," *Review of Finance* 18: 189–218.

P. R. Newswire. (2013, March 12). "Hostess Brands Selects Apollo Global Management and Metropoulos & Co. as Winning Bidder for Majority of Snack Cake Business, Including Twinkies®."

Scott, J. C. (2017). *Against the Grain: A Deep History of the Earliest States*. New Haven, CT: Yale University Press.

Smith, A. (1976). *The Money Game*. New York, NY: Vintage Books.

Snopes.com. (2012). "Forever Twinkies: Do hostess Twinkies have an indefinite shelf life," *Snopes.com* (website). Retrieved from https://www.snopes.com/fact-check/forever-twinkies/. Accessed March 19, 2018.

Sorkin, A. R. (2012, November 20). "Private equity and hostess stumbling together," *New York Times* (late edition, East Coast), B.1.

Souleles, D. S. (2019). *Songs of Profit, Songs of Loss: Private Equity, Wealth and Inequality*. Lincoln, NE: The University of Nebraska Press.

Webb, S. (2012, January 25). "Focus: Why US baker hostess went stale," *Just-Food Global News*.

Wendling, T. (2010). "Us et abus de la notion de fait social total," *Revue du Mauss* 36: 87–99. Retrieved from https://www.cairn.info/revue-du-mauss-2010-2-page-87.htm. Accessed January 20, 2016.

Zaloom, C. (2006), *Out of the Pits*. Chicago, IL: University of Chicago Press.

Zimmerman, J. L. (2015). "The role of accounting in the twenty-first century firm," *Accounting and Business Research* 45(4): 485–509.

11

FINANCIAL MODELS

Ekaterina Svetlova

Introduction

In the aftermath of the 2008 crisis, financial models have been heavily criticized for being dangerous and not sufficiently helping people to make sound investment decisions. Models were accused of causing the turmoil or, at least, of failing to give advance warning. The arguments behind these accusations are familiar: financial models are abstract and unworldly constructs so that their users are predestined to be misguided. Thus, the argument goes, as insufficient models became widespread tools for decision-making in financial markets, the vast majority of market participants were seduced by their mathematical sophistication and blindly followed them towards alleged safety. Financial models "behaved badly" while confusing "illusion with reality" (as the title of the book written by the famous quant turned publicist and educator Emanuel Derman (2011) suggests). The general problem related to this blindness was discussed as the so-called "model-based herding": markets might start to move in resonance, and such a development could threaten their stability, causing bubbles and crashes as we partly observed in 2008.

Furthermore, the more recent severe stock market corrections have again raised the question of how dangerous financial calculative technologies are for markets' stability and whether humans are losing control. Nasdaq CEO Adena Friedman said on CNBC that "humans are definitely in charge of the decisions in the market" and that "the algorithms are written basically on the back of a human decision." At the same time, CNBC quoted influential banking analyst Dick Bove who claimed that "the United States equity markets have been captured by out-of-control technological investment systems."

Thus, mathematical models and algorithms turned out to be at the epicenter of critical debates about finance and its societal implications. However, in order to better evaluate this debate, we have to ask *What does it mean to be critical?* This question has been prominently addressed in the field of critical management studies (Fournier & Grey, 2000), not in the field of critical finance though. From my point of view, there are two understandings of "being critical" that have transpired in finance studies so far (see also Curran, 2018).

One refers to criticizing *finance as a body of knowledge*, as a science involved in developing and spreading unrealistic models that are detached from the complex reality of economic life and thus prone to provide a misleading advice. While focusing primarily on the issue of "truth" and representation as well as the epistemological standards of assessing financial models, this critical finance perspective has perceived the problems associated with financial modeling from the position of philosophy of social sciences. This approach was at the origin of what I call the "strong" critical finance perspective discussed in the introduction to this *Handbook* as "an explicitly strong angle" (Bay & Schinckus, 2012; Frankfurter et al., 1994; McGoun, 1993, 1997). Importantly, building upon the "critical theory" (e.g., Horkheimer, 1982[1937]), the proponents of this position took the "ideological" or even "political" standpoint in the critical debate on finance. They claimed that the false assumptions implied in financial modeling are never value-neutral, and that finance is always enmeshed with social and political power and thus contributes to inequality, unjust risk distribution, market crashes, etc.

The other approach—as pursued, for example, by social studies of finance (SSF)—takes a different, more subtle, stance on "being critical." It shifted the attention from how financial models fail to adequately represent the economic reality to how they are used and shape (or perform) reality. For some observers, e.g., Mirowski and Nik-Khah (2007) and Curran (2018), this move lacks any critical "bite" and rather downplays the essential role of economists and financial theorists in facilitating (or neglecting) major economic instabilities and inequalities. Furthermore, while understanding performativity as an interventional account of financial science ("models and theories shape reality"), some detractors of the SSF wonder why scientists do not interfere with market practices more actively and do not clearly pursue a critical, i.e., ideological, agenda, during those interventions, as the concept of *critical performativity* (Alvesson & Spicer, 2012; Spicer et al., 2009) suggests.

What is often missed in this debate is that the theoretical and methodological move carried out by the SSF scholars was more profound than just the shift from representation to performativity. It was a move to investigate *finance as a practical field*, not (just) as science, and to focus on market practitioners such as traders, security analysts, hedge fund managers, and merger arbitragers. The financial market professionals, next to financial mathematicians at universities and business schools, became important subjects of the intensive empirical investigations. Thus, what the SSF brought to attention is that financial models travel both ways—from academia to markets and back—and are used not because they give market professionals true knowledge about markets (or "reality"), but because they fulfill other, non-epistemic functions: they help users to make or legitimize decisions, present themselves as experts, communicate with each other, etc. Though slow (due to their origin in the STS and sociology of knowledge), the SSF re-shifted its focus from knowledge production to acting sensibly and decision-making under market uncertainty as central activities in which models are involved and represent just one, though important aspect. For the SSF, financial market practitioners are not "F9 model monkeys" (Tett & Thal Larsen, 2005) who uncritically adopt models imported from academia and ignore their deficiencies but pragmatic users who combine models with judgments, emotions, narratives, etc., in order to make financial decisions.

In this context, "being critical" means to question the traditional functional and representational view of finance and to aim for better, i.e., deeper understanding of financial practices and their interplay with models and theories. For me, this approach subscribes rather to "critical thinking" (akin to "Socratic questioning") that implies scrutinizing the mainstream ideas, not taking them for granted, comparing theory to observations, and forming judgment while being guided by practice (e.g., Beyer, 1995). The main trait of this bottom-up critical position is that its proponents don't patronize practitioners but take their views and procedures seriously. By doing so, the SSF scholars "complicate" the link between models and reality. They don't know in advance what they will say at the end of their analysis, whereas the top-down "ideology" always knows what it claims. "Critical thinking" is not about naming and criticizing phenomena but about understanding how these phenomena come about giving the investigation a subtle critical gesture. There is a difference between *critical as political* and *critical as analytical* that has never been seriously thematized with respect to finance, and maybe this chapter and the *Handbook* more generally will get it off the ground.

In this contribution, I will juxtapose the views of the "strong" critical finance and SSF on financial models, compare their conclusions, and, based on this comparison, identify some promising directions for the future critical discussion. Primarily, in my view, the potential of *politics of performativity* (Boldyrev & Svetlova, 2016: 10) should be explored in-depth in order to understand the potential of the interventional and more generally the critical approach to finance.

"Strong" Critical Finance: Still Waiting for the Last Finance Professor

Though the discussion about unrealistic and useless models in finance that accelerated after the crisis of 2008 might have appeared refreshing and radical to some financial market observers, it was certainly not new for the "strong" critical finance scholars. Already in the 1990s, when "strong" critical finance made its first steps, the critique of financial theory and models was at the core of their debate. One of the initial meetings of the group—the roundtable at the

Financial Management Association (Frankfurter et al., 1994)—devoted most of its time to the discussion of the gap between the established financial models such as the Capital Asset Pricing Model (CAPM), the Efficient Market Hypothesis (EMH), and the Modigliani and Miller model, and the real-life phenomena that can be observed in markets. The roundtable participants criticized financial modeling for its reliance solely on the assumptions of utility maximization, calculable risk, perfect competition, and frictionless markets. The critical finance scholars focused on what models *cannot* explain or which aspects of reality they unjustifiably exclude. For example, the neoclassical Miller and Modigliani model does not account for the abnormal profitability of some corporate investment opportunities and ignores the possibility of companies' bankruptcy (Frankfurter et al., 1994: 178f.); such models, so the critical finance scholars argued, cannot explain real people's behavior.

This gap between models and reality was conceptualized by the Frankfurter et al. circle as "hyperfinance," the finance namely that lost any touch with economic reality and just refers to nothing but itself (McGoun, 1997). Based on Baudrillard's work, financial theories and models were considered to be *simulacra*, namely copies of reality that became completely detached from the original and thus actually stopped being even copies (McGoun, 1997; Schinckus, 2008).

For the "strong" critical finance proponents, a good example of *simulacrum* is the theory of "fair" value. According to the established finance theory, the "fair" value is a correct, or true, value of a company based on its "fundamentals" and thus, the "fair" estimate of what the asset is worth today and how much investors should be ready to pay for this asset, assuming that markets are efficient; the price, or what an investor effectively pays when buying a security, might deviate from the intrinsic value but always fluctuates around it (Koller et al., 2010: 337). For McGoun (1997), however, the "fair" value is a useless concept, a simulacrum with no anchor in the corporate reality because investors cannot determine the "fair" value due to the uncertainty of future cash flows; thus, stock prices don't have anything to do with corporations' fundamentals and fluctuate widely. Thus, for "strong" critical finance, financial markets are a self-referential postmodern game where people primarily speculate and trade for the sake of trading without real purpose, causing the fluctuations that cannot be captured by the existing financial theory. Keasey and Hudson (2007) labeled the mainstream finance a "house without windows," and Frankfurter (2006) notoriously wrote about the EMH and the CAPM as "blind" religion and ideology.

Thus, the "strong" critical finance debate about financial models has been clearly of philosophical nature and addressed the question about the relation between models and reality as one about the nature of knowledge in finance: *How can financial models produce knowledge despite their unrealistic assumptions, insufficient forecasting power, untrue representations, and other epistemological flaws?* The criticism in this context meant blaming models for being imperfect and proclaiming them useless due to their non-conformity with "reality." The future of financial theory and modeling was painted as doom and gloom:

> I see the finance field going down cointegration paths and GARCH [Generalized AutoRegressive Conditional Heteroscedasticity] and ARCH [AutoRegressive Conditional Heteroscedasticity] and garbage model trails and coming eventually to a very untimely end in a dark alley in St. Louis, because there will be nothing left. There will be this one person with a few bags of belongings and dirty hair, who will say, "I am the last finance professor." But nobody will pay him anymore, because everyone realizes that what he did was silly. (Frankfurter et al., 1994: 100)

Though posing important critical questions about the epistemic value(s) of financial models, the critical finance unfortunately missed the opportunity to bridge its discussion with the extensive work in philosophy of science and STS on *modeling as a scientific activity*. The philosophical and STS literature has been explicitly concerned with the question of how models help to acquire scientific knowledge about real-world phenomena (target systems); at the same time, *financial* models have never been at the core of their attention. Still, the philosophical debate about models as representations (Giere, 1988, 2010; van Fraassen, 1980), the idealization, and de-idealization accounts (Cartwright, 1989, 1999; Mäki, 2009; Morgan & Knuuttila, 2012), particularly a prolonged discussion about the unrealistic assumptions of economic models and the poor correspondence of these models with the target system (Hausman, 1992; Reiss, 2012), could have stimulated and enriched the critical debate about financial models initiated by the "strong" school, especially the debate on the link between models and reality as well as on the "truth" issue.

It is particularly interesting that some philosophers have claimed that models can be useful even if they do not expose any direct connections to the real world. Accounts of models such as credible worlds (Sugden, 2000), parables (Cartwright, 2008), fictions (Frigg, 2010; Godfrey-Smith, 2009), and make-believe (Toon, 2012) suggest that models are not created by observing a target system and stripping out complicating factors ("idealization") but by imagining a model world that could be true and thus allowing for meaningful communication and understanding of essential relationships between parameters. These concepts correspond to McGoun's (2003) suggestion to see the CAPM and the Black-Scholes option pricing model not as positive or normative models but as metaphors, or "useful frameworks", that rather serve as rhetorical devices and not as scientific explanation tools. Again, the cross-fertilization between philosophy of science and financial economics might have helped to develop an interesting account of financial models as instruments of *fictional truth* (cross-referring to Beckert's (2016) concept of fictional expectations).

At the same time, the "strong" critical finance scholars could not help but open their discussion to sociology of financial markets. They started to pose the question why models that are completely detached from reality have been strongly influential in *the academic world*, even received Nobel prices (e.g., the CAPM in 1990), in other words, why we still have not seen the impoverished last finance professor yet. They pointed out that the reasons might be "sociological" or "cultural," e.g., the scientization and quantification of finance in academia, particularly in business schools, and claimed the necessity to "undertake research on the process of research itself" (McGoun, 1993: 174) without seriously following this empirical program.

With regard to *the practice of markets*, the "strong" school made an interesting observation that investment professionals are rather skeptical about the "unrealistic" models and thus reluctant to apply them in their practice (e.g., McGoun, 1993 on CAPM) as models don't "survive contact with the real world" (Coleman, 2014). Based on interviews with fund managers, Coleman claimed that financial theories and models don't play an important role in the professional investors' decision-making. The reasons for the denial are manifold: (a) false assumptions (e.g., risk-return trade-off, market efficiency, rational expectations, and "fair" asset pricing) that are not supported by empirical tests and (b) the unavailability of the relevant data. Thus, when relying on models, financial decision-makers fear to lose sight of the markets while sitting in "the house without windows."

In sum, the critical finance researchers pointed out to some important critical issues related to financial modeling and formulated the promising research program that they missed to fully implement. The "strong" critical tradition suggested that finance should open itself towards a variety of new topics and disciplines, e.g., philosophy, ethics, and art (Bay & Schinckus, 2012), and pay attention to broader social implications of finance and contextualize finance within society, markets, and organizations. Importantly, in order to understand the "notoriety" of unrealistic financial models in academia and practice of markets, the critical finance scholars envisaged the application of qualitative methods of empirical research (Bettner et al., 1994; Frankfurter et al., 1994). Coleman (2014: 235) suggested that the first step towards the new financial paradigm would be bridging the gap between models and reality "by setting out the actual behavior of markets, investors and managers."

At the same time, the critical finance scholars seldom carried out any significant empirical work despite proclaiming its necessity. They rather directed their efforts towards the replacement of one dogma (classical finance) by the other ideology, e.g., the Marx-inspired criticism of wealth maximization, the casino capitalism, the too loose control of markets and capital, the uneven distribution of financial resources, etc. They envisaged the radical, politically engaged program (akin to the "critical theory") and proposed the theory of fair markets (Frankfurter, 2006) as a very general alternative to the CAPM/EMH paradigm. Curiously though, the most important points of their program, for example, interdisciplinarity and devotion to the deep empirical research were taken up and put into life by the SSF to which I turn now.

SSF: Power and Failure of Financial Models

The SSF is an emerging interdisciplinary field that applies the findings and the methodological apparatus of various social sciences (sociology, anthropology, geography, political economy, etc.) to the analysis of financial markets. A significant effort of the SSF scholars has been dedicated to the critical analysis of how modern economic life is shaped by mathematical models. The "critical" in the SSF context is rather understood as careful bottom-up questioning of the status quo while paying particular attention to the practice of markets where financial models are applied. Let me highlight some important SSF insights that are crucial for the critical debate on modeling.

Taking Practitioners Seriously

The SSF scholars demonstrated that the academics-practitioners gap is not as strongly pronounced in financial modeling as in other disciplines. Finance has been traditionally characterized by the striking proximity and entwinement of theory and practice. Financial models have constantly traveled between, or simultaneously "inhabited," two worlds: academia and the financial industry. Indeed, some models such as the Black-Scholes model were created at universities and then adapted in the practice of markets. However, today, it is not seldom that models are developed by practitioners. This trend became especially distinctive in the last decade of the twentieth century, when many academics trained in mathematics and physics were hired by investment banks as "quants" or financial engineers (Patterson, 2010), and was re-enforced now with the development of high-frequency trading or HFT (on high-frequency trading, see also Lange's chapter in this *Handbook*). Financial modeling today is a constantly revolving process between science and practice the borders of which are nearly non-existent.

These insights led the SSF scholars to recognize the prominence of practitioners in financial modeling. As the primary goal of financial market participants is not to acquire knowledge but to make decisions, it is dissatisfactory to consider their practices as purely "epistemic," science-centred practices. Whereas scientists can live in the "small" world of their idealized models and work with models that are caricatures of reality or just "credible worlds" (Spears, 2014), practitioners need models that guide them through the world and enable them to decide and act. Model use in practice of markets principally differs from scientific modeling. Financial market participants understand their decision-making as a constant process of discovery where "equipment matters" (MacKenzie, 2009: 13).

The SSF rejects both the over-calculative and under-calculative views on modeling in markets (Beunza & Garud, 2007). Whereas the so-called over-calculative position suggests that blind applications of formal financial models dominate the markets constantly rendering them at the edge of an imminent disaster, the under-calculative view, on the contrary, considers calculations and modeling to be useless or unimportant as financial agents rely primarily on social resources such as norms, institutions, and networks. But how can we claim that investment professionals—such as Coleman (2014) suggests—completely ignore or neglect models when the latter have become important and ubiquitous tools in all fields of financial markets? In today's financial world, to model or not to model is not the question.

Thus, the SSF has striven to develop a third—integrative—view of financial markets and modeling. For example, analyzing the use of models by merger arbitrageurs, Beunza and Stark (2012) provide an empirical example of model use as the interdependence between the social and the calculative. The authors claim that no aspects—neither social (mimesis, networks, institutions) nor calculative (models)—should be neglected when explaining decision-making in financial markets. Rather, the calculative, social, and technical aspects should be simultaneously taken into consideration. The analysis of this "collectively constructed calculative technology" (Beunza & Garud, 2007: 19) has become the key programmatic issue of the SSF and represents their critical stance.

Performativity, Counter-Performativity, and the Indeterminacy of Model Effects

Taking the integrative view as point of departure, the SSF developed a distinct account of the relationship between models and "reality," namely the account of performativity. According to the performativity concept, the relationship between financial models and economic reality is understood not as passive (representation), but as active. Financial models have effects: they influence or even constitute what they aim to represent.

The careful analysis of these effects—and herewith of the link between models and reality—is an important critical gesture of the SSF. The critical stance of the performativity concept becomes particularly obvious if one avoids its simplistic reading. Indeed, performativity was often understood as the one-way travel of theoretical financial models into the realm of markets without any contingencies and "problematicness" behind this travel and its effects (Curran, 2018). However, the performativity scholars rather strive to understand and show empirically how economic phenomena and events come about and how they are shaped by financial modeling and technology. By doing so, they explicitly highlight the non-deterministic character of those processes.

This non-determinism is important for the "critical" finance discussion for two reasons. First, it allows performativity theory to criticize the mainstream approach to economics (Esposito, 2013: 108) bringing to the fore the contingency of market participants' expectations, the reflexivity of their behavior, and the radical uncertainty of markets, the issues namely that are widely neglected by the mainstream economic theory. Second, the performativity concept provides a nuanced answer to one of the central "critical" questions about modern financial markets: *How endangered and "crisis-prone" are they?* As already indicated, the common discussion of financial crises claims that the widespread thoughtless use of models creates specific risks that are relevant for the markets as a whole, namely model herding. Those risks are described in the literature as "second-order dangers" (Holzer & Millo, 2005), "model risk" (Esposito, 2013), or "resonance" (Beunza & Stark, 2012), and relate to a distinct new form of interdependence among market participants which is mediated by models. The performativity scholars, however, do not focus on blaming models or markets but show in careful empirical analysis how model-based actions can provoke—or avoid—herding.

The non-deterministic character of performativity—and thus of models' effects on markets—is emphasized in two SSF concepts: *cultures of model use* and *counter-performativity.*

First, in my book *Financial Models and Society* (Svetlova, 2018), I demonstrate how indeterminant performative effects unfold in the multifaceted interplay between users and models in the practice of markets or flexible *cultures of model use.* Investors might apply their formal tools but ignore the tools' recommendations in the very process of decision-making or, relying on own judgments, narratives, emotions, social observations of the others, etc., "overlay" the decisions models prescribe. Furthermore, financial analysts frequently use their dividend cash flow (DCF) models as "opinion proclaimers," i.e., they apply models to express their pre-formed opinions about the market or a security; in other words, financial analysts play with parameters and numbers in the model until the model fits the subjective "fair" price or the users' subjective views more generally. Qualitative "overlay" and opinions' representation do not mean that the valuation process is completely detached from reality of markets as the "strong" critical finance suggests. On the contrary, the SSF empirical findings demonstrate how valuation is anchored in the reality by means of models. The empirical accounts rather point out that, in many cases, financial models do not provide direct prescriptions for decisions, and, therefore, the link between models, decision-making, and market events is not as straightforward as the ongoing critique of financial models indicates. We find large "pockets" where human judgment and stories are as important as the complicated formulas and algorithms, and their interplay produces uncertainties and unforeseen consequences for financial decision-makers. Generally, performativity analysis contributes to better understanding of the uncertain nature of economic events and critically questions probabilistic calculus and rationality of agents which are at the core of mainstream economics.

The second concept that points to the indeterminacy and ambiguous character of models' effects is *counter-performativity.* Models may create a reality that they describe but, at the same time, can be counter-performative producing as well:

a very particular form of misfire, of unsuccessful framing, when the use of a mathematical model does not simply fail to produce a reality (e.g., market results) that is consistent with the model, but actively undermines the postulates of the model. The use of a model, in other words, can itself create phenomena at odds with the model. (Bamford & MacKenzie, 2018: 100)

Those misfires can appear, on the one hand, when performative "felicity conditions" are not fulfilled (MacKenzie, 2007: 70). As witnesses and a priest must be present at the wedding ceremony in order to "bring about" husband and wife, the Black-Scholes model in the 1970s—in order to produce effects—had to acquire sufficient authority to warrant users' beliefs, possess sufficient cognitive simplicity, and be publicly available and supported by an appropriate technology so that a sufficient number of market participants could start to use it. If all those conditions were not fulfilled, the Black-Scholes model might have failed to create the billion-scale option market. Also, when circumstances changed in 1987, the model produced counter-performative effects: its use created "skewed" patterns of implied volatility that contradicted the straight line posited by the model (Bamford & MacKenzie, 2018).

On the other hand, more generally, the misfires are intrinsic to every performative process: "[B]reakdown is constitutive of performativity (performativity never fully achieves its effect, and so in this sense 'fails' all the time)" (Butler, 2010: 158). Performativity is closely related to performance, or staging, that is, by its very nature, devoid of any planning and control; artistic performances are unique and unrepeatable—and thus to some extent always unpredictable and surprising. There are no pre-defined circumstances in which a performance succeeds. Financial models participate in financial markets' performances as communicative tools, persuasion devices, and props for "scientific" and "objective" knowledge helping to feign (or perform) investment decisions as rational and legitim. Those theatrical acts of persuasion and convincing staging—like performances in a real theatre—might not be liked or "believed" by audiences and thus fail, or misfire, at any moment. In this sense, models might produce unintended or unexpected results. This proposition can be best illustrated using the example of herding.

Herding, Anti-Herding, and Financial Markets Stability

The widespread use of similar models might lead to herding. Beunza and Stark (2012) demonstrate, for example, in their account of reflexive modeling that, while constantly observing and backing out the spread plot that represents the market consensus, merger arbitragers might lock themselves into the thinking of the market and connect themselves to other financial actors. Hence, individual errors, interlocked in the process of model application, might be amplified and produce resonance of decisions.

Because models become themselves a part of the very phenomena they describe and their use and effects are constantly observed by other market participants, models unintentionally co-produce unwanted (or "critically" questionable) market phenomena, e.g., the misestimation of market risks in the case of the Long-Term Capital Management (Holzer & Millo, 2005), the GE-Honeywell merger failure (Beunza & Stark, 2012), "the correlation crisis" and faulty valuation of structured products prior to financial crisis (MacKenzie, 2011), or the drastic price fall in August 2007 due to "quant quake" (Tett & Gangahar, 2007).

Still, in normal times, the individual(ized) applications of financial models might produce dissonance, i.e., the divergence of opinions among market participants (Beunza & Stark, 2012). The analysis of *cultures of model use* as well as the *counter-performativity* account supports this view and relativizes the fear of an imminent market collapse due to blind usage of identical models: *the anti-herding tendencies* can be created in the process of model use.

As every decision implies the "undoing" of models, there is always a moment of flexibility in financial decision-making. The empirical patterns of model application demonstrate that, while using models to structure decisions, observe markets, or express opinions, investment professionals are free to follow or not follow the model prescriptions, to suspend or "game" them. There are many individually fashioned styles of using one and the same model. For example, the DCF can be applied by fund managers to anchor and communicate decisions, by investors to "reverse engineer" the market, and by financial analysts to express their judgment. Exactly because the styles of model use differ, there is no way that the different users manipulate models absolutely identically and derive the same results. Various strategies of "model overlay" and "opinion proclamation" can be applied by market participants to disagree with the market or, at least, to question the market's views. Thus, the various strategies of model use give rise to forces that counteract herding tendencies. *Cultures of model use* do not automatically promote a particular behavior in financial markets but can re-enforce disagreement. Also, the counter-performativity account highlights that models can produce unexpected results.

Recently, Borch (2016) stressed that we have to take into consideration the further technological aspect of markets: the algorithms. He claimed that, due to the increased importance of algorithms in financial markets, the herding tendencies have further amplified. He questioned Beunza and Stark's (2012) and my view that model use frequently generates dissonance and claimed that the interdependences we observe in the HFT segment are interdependences among algorithms, and that human oversight and human control generally play a lesser role in the modern financial markets. Still, the emotional interference of traders with their algorithms cannot be damped completely (Borch & Lange, 2017).

This discussion of *who is in control of markets* is at the core of the "critical" dispute about modern finance and its technology. The nuanced analyses of model use produced in the SSF allow to lead an evidence-based discussion on the issue and not to jump to pre-formed conclusions or adhere to blaming. As already said, the SSF critical approach is akin to "critical thinking" that does not accuse financial market practitioners of being thoughtless and blind but takes their views seriously as a point of departure for a balanced reality-rooted analysis of financial practices.

Furthermore, the SSF does not produce simple recipes. From their point of view, the traditional solutions for improving financial market stability, e.g., to "conquer" models as an evil, to ban them and go back to "intuition" (Derman, 2011) and "common sense" (Triana, 2011), or to generally apply "fewer" models as the "strong" critical finance suggests, seem to be off target. First, given their ubiquitous use, it is unrealistic to eliminate models and algorithms from modern markets. Second, models as such do not represent a danger because in fact they do not dictate decisions; they are always combined with judgment, emotions, and tacit knowledge in the practice of their use. The problem is not about the re-introduction of human judgment into the nearly fully automated and formalized markets. We can hardly find a model or an algorithm used without a human component at one or the other stage: social and organizational elements are constantly "folded" into a market (Muniesa, 2007). These observations relativize the accusations of the "strong" critical finance proponents towards financial models as being disconnected from the real world; rather, models are *always* connected to markets through fulfilling various non-epistemic functions in the practice of their use (e.g., Millo & MacKenzie, 2009; Svetlova, 2018); those non-epistemic connections and effects should be analyzed in more empirical details.

Thus, if the goal of critical finance is to understand how to arrive at the "better," i.e., more stable and less crisis-prone markets, the SSF suggests focusing on an in-depth analysis of various "qualculative" practices (Cochoy, 2008) and the modi of differently combining human judgment and modeling. The cultures of model use in a merger arbitrage department take different forms than those that they take in an HFT company or in asset management. Critical finance should avoid generalizations and investigate these practices in their own right. The governability of modern markets depends on the proper understanding of cultures of model use and counter-performativity which simultaneously produce order and disorder, resonance and dissonance. A "restorative regulation"—understood as the correction of purely technical malfunctioning of markets (Engelen et al., 2012)—can hardly be applied to financial markets understood as socio-technical agencements.

Some Thoughts on Future Research

At the core of the critical finance studies seems to be the issue of *politics of performativity* (Boldyrev & Svetlova, 2016; also Cabantous et al., 2016): *How being analytical does not preclude being political and vice versa?* This might continue to be the central question for the future research in the field.

I think that the more nuanced approach to performativity presented in this chapter suggests some directions. It clearly rejects the "simplified" reading of Callon's (1998) and MacKenzie's work as one implying "the conflation of economic models with economic reality" (Curran, 2018: 493) in a quasi-automatic way and thus neglecting the central critical issue with regard to models: they are false and misleading and thus a significant factor of market turmoils.

Performativity studies in my understanding do not ignore the gap between models and reality but suggest that financial market participants close this gap *in situ* of markets, in the process of model construction and model use by means of narratives, interpretations, pragmatically addressing various audiences, pre-formulating the anticipated model results, etc. Financial models are constantly connected to the markets in current decision-making situations; they calculate but are also suspended, confirmed, or questioned with regard to their results in those immediate, real-time connections to the market. They might succeed but might also produce the unexpected and unintended effects that undermine their own predictions. In other words, there are many—often unforeseen—ways of how they change the economic world and financial markets.

These insights rather call not for performativity being generally "more critical" but for more analytical rethinking of the concept, its theoretical value, and political consequences. First of all, as already mentioned, performativity theory might enrich the mainstream economics by clarifying the social nature of radical uncertainty and critically analyzing such phenomena as market fluctuations and herding, asset valuation, risk-taking in banks and corporations, as well as credit ratings.

Furthermore, the performativity studies might want to clearer acknowledge that, while moving into the realm of markets or even being created directly in banks, asset management, or HFT companies, financial models and algorithms find themselves in an explicitly non-epistemic context. Thus, the performativity debate should be less about "epistemic cultures" or "knowledge cultures." While analyzing practitioners' decision-making as searching for productive methods to simultaneously calculate and suspend calculations, we are not merely talking about "the other kind of knowledge," the specific "tacit knowledge," or "know-how," but about a process where knowledge produced by models is just one component of real actions as immediate involvements with the complex, constantly evolving world. Financial models are applied as not purely epistemic devices in the practice of financial markets; thus, their examination from the critical finance perspective should take this issue into consideration and ask: *which non-epistemic functions do models fulfill and with which effects?*

Such an investigation opens up to multiple contingencies and counter-performative effects that are implied in the situational bridging the gap between models and markets and pays attention to materiality and processuality of financial markets. The performativity studies can show how models' influence in non-epistemic contexts is mediated by the institutional environment, fictional (and often ideological) narratives, political interests, and the power of the involved actors. Thus, bridging the gap between models and reality is often about "the struggles of performation," a series of collective efforts to create and sustain certain realities based on one's vision that does not have anything to do with academic knowledge. It is also about "the political engineering of sociomaterial agencements that are constituted within and across organizations, institutions and markets" (Cabantous et al., 2016: 3). Those struggles can be uncovered and analyzed in critical finance studies as *politics of performativity*.

Obviously, this analysis is not inherently apolitical as it reveals special powers that mediate between academia, markets, and society. However, it is less judging and interventional and aims to awake the interest of practitioners and invites the latter to reflect on their practice. In accordance with Curran, this program could allow for "developing a critical approach to social science as both a body of knowledge *and* a series of social and political processes that constantly reshape social and material life in often unexpected ways" (2018: 494) overcoming the juxtaposition of being *critical as political* and *critical as analytical*.

References

Alvesson, M., & Spicer, A. (2012). "Critical leadership studies: The case for critical performativity," *Human Relations* 65(3): 367–390.

Bamford, A., & MacKenzie, D. (2018). "Counterperformativity," *New Left Review* 113: 97–121.

Bay, T., & Schinckus, C. (2012). "Critical finance studies: An interdisciplinary manifesto," *Journal of Interdisciplinary Economics* 24(1): 1–6.

Beckert, J. (2016). *Imagined Futures: Fictional Expectations and Capitalist Dynamics.* Cambridge, MA: Harvard University Press.

Bettner, M. S., Robinson, C. & McGoun, E. (1994). "The case for qualitative research in finance," *International Review of Financial Analysis* 3(1): 1–18.

Beunza, D., & Garud, R. (2007). "Calculators, lemmings or frame-makers? The intermediary role of securities analysts," *Sociological Review* 55(s2): 13–39.

Beunza, D., & Stark, D. (2012). "From dissonance to resonance: Cognitive interdependence in quantitative finance," *Economy and Society* 41(3): 383–417.

Beyer, B. K. (1995). *Critical Thinking.* Bloomington, IN: Phi Delta Kappa Educational Foundation.

Boldyrev I., & Svetlova, E. (2016). "After the turn: How the performativity of economics matters," in I. Boldyrev and E. Svetlova (eds.), *Enacting Dismal Science: New Perspectives on the Performativity of Economics* (pp. 1–27). New York, NY: Palgrave Macmillan.

Borch, C. (2016). "High-frequency trading, algorithmic finance and the flash crash: Reflections on eventalization," *Economy and Society* 45(3–4): 350–378.

Borch, C., & Lange, A.-C. (2017). "Market sociality: Mirowski, Shiller and the tension between mimetic and anti-mimetic market features," *Cambridge Journal of Economics* 41(4): 1197–1212.

Butler, J. (2010). "Performative agency," *Journal of Cultural Economy* 3 (2): 147–161.

Cabantous, L., Gond, J.-P., Harding, N., & Learmonth, M. (2016). "Critical essay: Reconsidering critical performativity," *Human Relations* 69(2): 197–213.

Callon, M. (1998). "Introduction: The embeddedness of economic markets in economics," in M. Callon (ed.), *The Laws of the Market* (pp. 1–57). Oxford, MA: Blackwell.

Cartwright, N. (1989). *Nature's Capacities and Their Measurement.* Oxford: Oxford University Press.

Cartwright, N. (1999). *The Dappled World: A Study of the Boundaries of Science.* Cambridge: Cambridge University Press.

Cartwright, N. (2008). "Models: Parables vs fables," *Insights* 1(11): 2–10.

Cochoy, F. (2008). "Calculation, qualculation, calqulation: Shopping cart arithmetic, equipped cognition and the clustered consumer," *Marketing Theory* 8 (1): 15–44.

Coleman, L. (2014). "Why finance theory fails to survive contact with the real world: A fund manager perspective," *Critical Perspectives on Accounting* 25: 226–236.

Curran, D. (2018). "From performativity to representation as intervention: Rethinking the 2008 financial crisis and the recent history of social science," *Journal for the Theory of Social Behaviour* 48(4): 492–510.

Derman, E. (2011). *Models. Behaving. Badly: Why Confusing Illusion with Reality Can Lead to Disaster, on Wall Street and in Life.* New York, NY: John Wiley & Sons.

Engelen, E., Ertürk, I., Froud, J., Johal, S., Leaver, A., Moran, M., & Williams, K. (2012). "Misrule of experts? The financial crisis as elite debacle," *Economy and Society* 41(3): 360–382.

Esposito, E. (2013). "The structures of uncertainty: Performativity and unpredictability in economic operations," *Economy and Society* 42(1): 102–129.

Fournier, V., & Grey, C. (2000). "At the critical moment: Conditions and prospects for critical management studies," *Human Relations* 53(1): 7–32.

Frankfurter, G. (2006). "The Theory of Fair Markets (TFM): Toward a new finance paradigm," *International Review of Financial Analysis* 15(2): 130–144.

Frankfurter, G. M., Carleton, W, Gordon, M., Horrigan, J., McGoun, E., Philippatos, G., & Robinson, C. (1994). "The methodology of finance: A round table discussion," *International Review of Financial Analysis* 3(3): 173–207.

Frigg, R. (2010). "Models and fiction," *Synthese* 172 (2): 251–268.

Giere, R. N. (1988). *Explaining Science.* Chicago, IL: University of Chicago Press.

Giere, R. N. (2010). "An agent-based conception of models and scientific representation," *Synthese* 772(2): 269–281.

Godfrey-Smith, P. (2009). "Models and fictions in science," *Philosophical Studies* 143(1): 101–116.

Hausman, D. (1992). *The Inexact and Separate Science of Economics.* Cambridge: Cambridge University Press.

Holzer, B., & Millo, Y. (2005). "From risks to second-order dangers in financial markets: Unintended consequences of risk management systems," *New Political Economy* 10 (2): 223–245.

Horkheimer, M. (1982[1937]). "Traditional and critical theory," in M. Horkheimer (ed.), *Critical Theory: Selected Essays* (pp. 188–243). New York, NY: Continuum.

Keasey, K., & Hudson, R. (2007). "Finance theory: A house without windows," *Critical Perspectives on Accounting* 18(8): 932–951.

Koller, T., Goedhart, M., & Wessels, D. (2010). *Valuation: Measuring and Managing the Value of Companies.* Hoboken, NJ: John Wiley & Sons.

MacKenzie, D. (2007). "Is economics performative? Option theory and the construction of derivatives markets," in D. MacKenzie, F. Muniesa, and L. Siu (eds.), *Do Economists Make Markets? On the Performativity of Economics* (pp. 54–86). Princeton, NJ: Princeton University Press.

MacKenzie, D. (2009). *Material Markets: How Economic Agents Are Constructed.* Oxford: Oxford University Press.

MacKenzie, D. (2011). "The credit crisis as a problem in the sociology of knowledge," *American Journal of Sociology* 116(6): 1778–1841.

Mäki, U. (2009). "Missing the world: Models as isolations and credible surrogate systems," *Erkenntnis* 70(1): 29–43.

McGoun, E. (1993). "The CAPM: A Nobel failure," *Critical Perspectives on Accounting* 4(2): 155–177.

McGoun, E. (1997). "Hyperreal finance," *Critical Perspectives on Accounting* 8(1–2): 97–122.

McGoun, E. (2003). "Financial models as metaphors," *International Review of Financial Analysis* 12(4): 421–433.

Millo, Y., & MacKenzie, D. (2009). "The usefulness of inaccurate models: Towards an understanding of the emergence of financial risk management," *Accounting, Organizations and Society* 34(5): 638–653.

Mirowski, P., & Nik-Khah, E. (2007). "Markets made flesh: Performativity and a problem in science studies, augmented with consideration of the FCC auctions," in D. MacKenzie, F. Muniesa, and L. Siu (eds.), *Do Economists Make Markets? On the Performativity of Economics* (pp. 190–224). Princeton, NJ: Princeton University Press.

Morgan, M. S., & Knuuttila, T. (2012). "Models and modelling in economics," in U. Mäki (ed.), *Philosophy of Economics: Handbook of the Philosophy of Science* (pp. 49–87). Amsterdam: Elsevier Science.

Muniesa, F. (2007). "Market technologies and the pragmatics of prices," *Economy and Society* 36(3): 377–395.

Patterson, S. (2010). *The Quants: How a New Breed of Math Whizzes Conquered Wall Street and Nearly Destroyed It*. New York, NY: Crown Business.

Reiss, J. (2012). "The explanation paradox," *Journal of Economic Methodology* 19(1): 43–62.

Schinckus, C. (2008). "The financial simulacrum: The consequences of the symbolization and the computerization of the financial market," *The Journal of Socio-Economics* 37(3): 1076–1089.

Spears, T. C. (2014). *Engineering Value, Engineering Risk: What Derivatives Quants Know and What Their Models Do*. PhD dissertation, University of Edinburgh.

Spicer, A., Alvesson, M., & Kärreman, D. (2009). "Critical performativity: The unfinished business of critical management studies," *Human Relations* 62(4): 537–560.

Sugden, R. (2000). "Credible worlds: the status of theoretical models in economics," *Journal of Economic Methodology* 7(1): 1–31.

Svetlova, E. (2018). *Financial Models and Society: Villains or Scapegoats?* Cheltenham: Edward Elgar Publishing.

Tett, G., & Thal Larsen, P. (2005). "Market faith goes out the window as the 'model monkeys' lose track of reality," *Financial Times*, May 20.

Tett, G., & Gangahar, A. (2007). "System error: Why computer models proved unequal to market turmoil," *Financial Times*, August 15, p. 7.

Toon, A. (2012). *Models as Make-Believe: Imagination, Fiction, and Scientific Representation*. Basingstoke: Palgrave Macmillan.

Triana, P. (2011). *The Number That Killed Us: A Story of Modern Banking, Flawed Mathematics, and a Big Financial Crisis*. New York, NY: John Wiley & Sons.

van Fraassen, B. C. (1980). *The Scientific Image*. Oxford: Clarendon Press.

12

HIGH-FREQUENCY TRADING

Ann-Christina Lange

Introduction

The arrest of the British trader Navinder Singh Sarao has occupied a lot of space in the trading world and in the public news (Ford, 2016). Sarao was fighting extradition to the United States after he was criminally charged with *spoofing* in stock index futures. In November 2016 the trader pleaded guilty of market manipulation using automated computer programs to issue fake orders and thereby manipulate the market to move in his favor. His manipulative act was said to have caused the extreme market behavior on May 6, 2010, known as the Flash Crash, in which nearly one trillion dollars evaporated within a few minutes (CFTC, 2015a, 2015b).

Recently, a few other cases have come into public attention. In 2016 the US trader Michael Coscia was sentenced to three years in prison. He was found guilty of disrupting financial markets in the same manner as Sarao (Meyer, 2016). Coscia was making profits by flooding futures markets with small orders at millisecond intervals, fast enough to cancel them before they get executed but slow enough to trick other traders' expectations about future prices.

Exchanges, regulators, and prosecutors have sharpened their focus on spoofing in recent years due to increased concerns over erratic behavior in increasingly high-speed automated markets. At the same time, financial experts in a wish for a "fair" marketplace call for a new critical agenda. Some critics claim that high-frequency trading (HFT) and the innovations supporting it create a two-tier market due to speed advantage, which means that high-frequency traders access market information faster than others (Haldane, 2011). Michael Lewis (2014a, 2014b) has in his bestselling book *Flash Boys* even denounced a situation in which rigged markets are now unable to perform their function in the economy. He claims that high-frequency traders are able to trade in front of and thereby exploit ordinary investors.

Due to this critique and the increase in spoofing charges the regulators are now looking into the nature of HFT and its regulatory landscape (cf. Barlyn & Ajmera, 2016). As such, the recent debate on fairness and the charges against the "spoofers" amount to a much broader issue—the good and bad of HFT. As Juan Pablo Pardo-Guerra (2016) notes "spoofing has become a particular notable object of contention for regulators and market participants alike." Spoofing is being portrayed as a new kind of crime committed by "bad" HFTs who contemplate sophisticated scams (Meyer, 2016). A specific assumption about the social world and its relation to objects is implicated in such an understanding of the financial world. Regulators read the incentives of single traders (taken to be a sovereign self-sufficient human in control of his or her algorithmic devices) and look for motivations in order to judge whether a crime was committed (e.g., Dragos & Wilkins, 2014: 162; Seyfert, 2016: 272). High-frequency traders are being charged with accusations of *intentionally* manipulating the markets to act in their favor—a scam that is seen to create systematic failures like the Flash Crash. Fairness, systematic failure (increased erratic behavior), and market manipulation are not separate issues but very much related in the debate about HFT, what it is and how regulators deal with it.

However, the Flash Crash and its relation to the act of spoofing raises more fundamental questions about the relation between the trader and his or her machine, and the risks that accrue to this new system of high-speed algorithmic finance. As Donald MacKenzie notes in response to the charges against Mr. Sarao: "It is very striking if a single trader, operating on his own, could constitute so much of one of the world's most important markets" (MacKenzie, 2015). In fact, MacKenzie (2019) has, in other writings, suggested that the consequences of HFT should be understood in terms of the "interaction order" that emerges between high-speed automated algorithms interacting in the market. Due to the development of HFT, the financial markets are increasingly composed of interacting agents (algorithms) acting and responding to one another at a time scale that far surpasses human perception.[1]

HFT algorithms are designed to move in and out of positions in fractions of a second to earn a penny or less, a practice that can be repeated more than million times a day. The technological advancement seems to suggest a mode of social interaction that exceeds the human senses. In order to critically engage with HFT, scholars have argued that it is paramount to understand this interactional order and its very mode of operation by investigating how traders act and think in practice (MacKenzie, 2019; see also Borch's introduction to this *Handbook*). This chapter contributes to show what a sociological approach to HFT might offer in relation to the accusations posed against HFT and, more importantly, to validate the call for a new critical agenda taking the social interaction between algorithms into consideration.

The aim of this chapter is not to qualify HFT in a normative manner as a practice that is either moral or immoral, legitimate or illegitimate, personal or impersonal, but rather to understand the underlying conditions or code of conduct that are at stake in HFT—and how these matter for the kinds of critique that can be raised against HFT as a practice.

Accordingly, this chapter provides an (historical) overview of the market microstructure and regulatory changes that gave rise to the development toward HFT and subsequently its critique. In providing this overview, the chapter captures recent insights from the sociological literature on HFT, arguing that critique ought to bring into view the actual practices of HFT and take into account how HFT traders and programmers conceive of market dynamics. Also, the chapter gives an updated view on the status of HFT and the intelligence of automated trading systems in relation to how these are presented in more popular accounts.

The structure of this chapter is as follows. The next section briefly reviews the concept of high-frequency trading and traces the way in which HFT came into being. The chapter continues with a description of the algorithmic practices of HFT as put forward by scholars from the sociology of finance tradition (based on empirical evidence from inside HFT practices), and then offers some thoughts on the future scope of HFT. The chapter ends with a brief conclusion on implications for critique.

Contextualizing HFT

The transformation of the practice of finance that made fully automated trading and HFT possible has been fostered by technological innovation, on the one hand, and new regulations, on the other. At the center of this are the automation of the financial exchanges and the development of the electronic order book, which is an electronic file that shows the bids and offers that have not yet been executed (Castelle et al., 2016).[2] Most accounts of this development in the sociology of finance focus on the radical shift since the 1990s (Castelle et al., 2016; MacKenzie et al., 2012). Manuel Castelle et al. (2016) note that in 1998 the US Securities and Exchange Commission (SEC) introduced the Regulation Alternative Trading Systems, which authorized alternative trading systems known as Electronic Communication Networks (ECNs) as either exchanges or broker-dealers. The intention was to restrict the monopoly that the New York Stock Exchange (NYSE) and NASDAQ had gained by automating their order-matching systems.

NASDAQ has been electronic since 1971 where it introduced an electronic quotation system via which competing market makers could trade securities (Hanson & Hall, 2012). In 1976, the NYSE introduced its Designated Order Turnaround system, allowing for the electronic transmission of orders to buy and sell securities (Burr, 2014). This gave rise to trading strategies, which exploited the spread (the difference between the best offer to sell and the best bid to buy) between the S&P 500 equity index and the futures market. In the 1990s, with the introduction of ECNs, more computer systems were developed to facilitate the entry and execution of orders electronically via the use of algorithms and the practice of exploiting the spread between correlated financial products became widespread across different financial markets. The ECNs were competing broker-dealer systems and provided direct market access and eliminated the need for brokerage firms to facilitate trading. According to Bogdan Dragos and Inigo Wilkins (2014: 166), ECNs contributed to "impersonal efficiency, automation, transparency and higher speeds of execution," which changed the way in which exchanges, brokers, and dealers compete. Due to the legitimization of ECNs, it became possible to trade without human intervention, in an anonymous manner and with lower trading costs.

However, HFT also evolved as a response to regulatory changes described by another body of literature in the sociology of finance (e.g., Coombs, 2016; Lenglet, 2011). Such accounts present the rise of HFT as a direct effect of the enactment of a set of US rules known as Regulation National Market System (Reg NMS). These were passed by the SEC in 2005 and fully enacted in 2007 in order to strengthen the US equity market. In part, Reg NMS was a direct response to a problematization of the behavior of specialists and locals, who used to serve as market makers (meaning that if there are insufficient buyers or sellers, they maintain order flow by trading with their own capital). Such specialists, at least at the NYSE, guarded access to the order book (MacKenzie, 2018: 12). MacKenzie et al. (2012: 283) note that electronic trading was perceived as fairer than older forms of trading where external participants had to place orders via the specialists who often had economic interests of their own.

In 2004, a specific case brought attention to this problem. A group of NYSE specialists were accused of not maintaining a fair market. Against this backdrop, Reg NMS aimed to secure fair competition and decrease the discretionary power of specialists (Lewis, 2014a: 96; MacKenzie et al., 2012: 283). In doing so, the regulators found inspiration in the electronically centralized quotations of NASDAQ to propose a "central market system" (later to be known as "national market system" or NMS). The existing centralized quotation systems made it possible to imagine a National Market System as a central limit order book (MacKenzie, 2018; Pardo-Guerra, 2016). This resulted in an updated rule prohibiting "trade-throughs," i.e., the execution of trades at prices outside of the national best bid and offer (NBBO). By emphasizing the need for immediate and automatic order execution at the NBBO, Reg NMS not only targeted the discretionary power of specialists; in effect, it enabled ultra-fast market participants to exploit price discrepancies (caused by a time delay) between different exchanges. This will be explained in further detail below.

MacKenzie (2019) describes more recent factors, which might also have contributed to the rise of HFT. In 2001, US stock exchanges were permitted to quote prices in decimals instead of fractions in order to increase liquidity. This move is known as decimalization, and is widely acknowledged to have affected the overall functioning of financial markets, as it reduced the minimum tick size or spread from one-eighth of a dollar to one cent (Castelle et al., 2016; MacKenzie, 2019; MacKenzie et al., 2012). This further decreased the importance of specialists on the exchanges and eventually led to a vast increase in algorithmic trading. In this new and more liquid market structure, the institutional traders were splitting up orders executed by algorithms in order to reduce their market impact and to execute trades faster and at better prices (Burr, 2014; Lenglet, 2011).

These institutional and regulatory changes all acted as catalysts for the increase of very fast, ultra-low-latency techniques, such as the use of high-speed computer programs for the execution of orders with a high level of frequency. Several of these techniques exploit the market fragmentation where multiple exchanges compete in the same security. Castelle et al. (2016) note with reference to Lee (2002) that the competition between exchanges led to increased payment for order flow, i.e., exchanges give a rebate to those "makers" submitting standing limit orders, and added a fee to "takers" executing market orders or marketable limit orders. Castelle et al. (2016) also point out that the developments described above would not in themselves lead to the kind of automation that we see today if it were not for the behavior and adaptation of the traders that make use of such new technologies. They draw attention to Caitlin Zaloom's (2006) study of how the electronic order book motivated traders who used to manually place their order (by clicking their mouse) to enter deals by automated trading systems. Zaloom describes how the traders embraced the new technologies that gave them the means to catch opportunities of exploiting time delay and to systematically control their trading strategies.[3] It was now possible to perform simultaneous matching in multiple contracts. The traders could benefit from the electronic technologies via computerized algorithmic software directly linked to the exchanges. Trading could now be done automatically based on the parameters of the algorithms at a much faster speed than their competitors. MacKenzie et al. (2012) further discuss the materiality of algorithmic trading that, in their view, give significance to special location and to physical phenomena such as the speed of light. They highlight HFT as the center of a controversy where issues of materiality are interwoven with new questions of legitimacy, particularly fairness in the financial markets.

The increased use of high-speed algorithms and the trading strategies has led the regulators to define this as a practice with its own definition. The SEC defines high-frequency traders as "professional traders acting in a proprietary capacity that engage in strategies that generate a large number of trades on a daily basis" (Securities and Exchange Commission, 2010: 45). A working group under another US regulatory body, the Commodity Futures Trading Commission (CFTC), has proposed a broader definition that focuses more on the trading activity itself than on those engaged in it:

High frequency trading is a form of automated trading that employs:

(a) algorithms for decision making, order initiation, generation, routing, or execution, for each individual transaction without human direction;
(b) low-latency technology that is designed to minimize response times, including proximity and colocation services;

(c) high speed connections to markets for order entry; and

(d) high rates of orders or quotes submitted. (CFTC, 2012)

Following the definitions by the SEC and CFTC, HFT is both defined as a specific organizational practice, proprietary trading, and as a specific use of technological tools to execute trading strategies.[4]

HFT Algorithms and Interactive Feedback Loops

High-frequency trading comprises a range of different trading strategies made possible by the use of automated algorithms and high-speed electronic exchange systems including the maker-taker fees. Some of these strategies are more or less aggressive in their trading behavior. Common denominators of such strategies include reducing latency (the time taken from issuing an order algorithmically until it is executed at the exchange), receiving information without delay, and being ahead of the rest of the market (Lange et al., 2016; MacKenzie et al., 2012).

Based on empirical observations and interviews, scholars from the field of sociology of finance have described the most common HFT strategies. They can be divided into three basic types all of which rely on exploiting time delay—to buy or to sell before the competitors.

In the first case, high-frequency traders exploit the price differences between exchanges and profit from correlation. They speculate on being faster than the price move between two highly correlated financial instruments. Also, they speculate on the correlation between different financial products, which means that if the price of one stock moves up or down it is very likely that another, related stock will do the same. It might be that they are traded with the same index and have the same probability of following the price moves of the whole index or that they are dependent upon the same factor, such as oil prices or political initiatives (Lange, 2017; MacKenzie et al., 2012). For instance, the algorithm buys government bonds traded at the NYSE and futures traded at the Security Futures Exchange in Chicago (OCX). There is a 13-millisecond delay in the transmission of data from New York City to Chicago. This delay creates arbitrage opportunities of exploiting the price discrepancies between US Treasury bonds traded at the NYSE and futures traded at the OCX. When the price of a government bond on the NYSE and its corresponding futures contract at OCX are out of sync, the algorithm would buy the less expensive one and sell it on the more expensive market. This is often characterized as spreading by high-frequency traders (e.g., Lange, 2015), which is exactly the idea about profiting from the time delay between different exchanges.

A second type of strategy is known among high-frequency traders as scalping. This type of strategy exploits upcoming price differences in the value of one asset across different trading venues. Jacob Arnoldi describes this kind of strategy in further detail. He correctly writes that:

One way of determining price changes is by monitoring, and responding, to the order flow at exchanges before that information is disseminated at other exchanges. This is possible if algos can monitor and respond to orders placed in the exchange system milliseconds before others. (2016: 6)

The third and least controversial strategy is market making where the algorithm seeks to quote bids and offers in the same instrument and makes the market buy and sell according to certain basic rules. This type is explained to be a rather passive strategy since the algorithms are in fact doing nothing but waiting for the order to come in and act upon that information (MacKenzie, 2019). This strategy leans on order-book depth asymmetry, say if there are more buyers than sellers, or vice versa. The algorithm posts orders on the best bid/offer and flips to the other side to capture the spread. In this case the high-frequency trader does not act as a buyer or seller but acts more like a middleman who makes the buyer and seller meet—the role previously fulfilled by specialists described above (Lange, 2016; MacKenzie, 2019; MacKenzie et al., 2012).

The most important issue for high-frequency traders is in their own words "to be on the top of the order book." The main advantage of HFT is the combination of speed and processing power. Access to market data is paramount for all of the strategies defined above. In an article in the *London Review of Books,* MacKenzie (2014) has described the use of fiber-optic cables and how microwave technology is being developed at extreme costs to facilitate the execution of HFT strategies. The goal is to achieve the shortest distance and thereby transmission time when issuing an order. Others have pointed to how high-frequency traders achieve special access to the exchanges data feeds and make use of special order types (for a description of the use of order types, see Bodek, 2013; Lange, 2017; Pardo-Guerra, 2016). Special deals and rebates are being offered by the exchanges in order to attract high-frequency traders to execute more deals on their exchange, as HFTs offer huge order flow and make the market more liquid, i.e., there is always someone on the other side of a trade (MacKenzie et al., 2012: 285). Arnoldi (2016) mentions the use of raw data feeds where ask and bid prices are being offered 30 milliseconds before they are routed and thereby become visible on the electronic platform. Another practice is colocation services where high-frequency traders place their servers inside the exchange to be as close to its matching engine as possible to reduce the distance and thereby time it takes to execute an order (MacKenzie et al., 2012: 286).

This development shows that HFT strategies have more to do with order placement and less with price forecasting—and is highly dependent upon queue positioning—to be at the top of the order book. High-frequency traders may execute a huge amount of orders every second but might only earn a fraction of a penny on each. They would not hold inventory overnight—the average holding time (i.e., the time they actually own a financial product) is often about ten seconds. The logic of HFT is about mitigating the risk of keeping and holding inventory. All this means that the traders need a rebate from the exchanges trading fees that they normally charge per trade executed to be able to make a profit from their strategies. This is the maker-taker model explained above.

What is specific for HFT algorithms (in contrast to other trading practices using slower algorithmic tools) is that they are quite simple in order to be fast. They react in similar ways given the limited input they are able to process. HFT algorithms cannot predict market movements beyond the three to five tick points from which they aim to profit. In fact, the signal processing is not so much an effect of a pre-programmed strategy or highly complex mathematical models. The dimension that is considered highly proprietary is not the strategies but the technology that is involved in reducing latency. Most HFT firms develop their trading systems in-house in order to optimize execution time (e.g., Lange, 2016). Again, HFT profit lies less in a pre-programmed strategy or highly complex mathematical models, and more in optimizing order execution with the use of sophisticated black-box technology. In what follows I will give an example from some of my observations among high-frequency traders to explain the inside functioning and operation of high-frequency traders' black-box systems.

The HFT black-box system is, among other things, composed of different strategies and algorithms. The strategies configure the algorithms (spreader, market maker, or scalping) and define the kind of order it sends to the order book (i.e., how long it should stay in the order book before getting canceled, the amount it quotes, etc.). Whether that order is "filled" (i.e., executed) or not is information that informs the next strategy and is sent back to the black box. The reason for such a complex system is again speed and execution time. A high-frequency trader I interviewed in Chicago 2016 explained that they do not have time to wait for the data feeds update as it is too slow compared to other traders:

> We don't have to wait for the data feeds update to come in, which is too slow if someone is putting in a huge bunch of orders all at once. You know, we might be literally raising our orders versus their orders at the exchange, who is going to be executed sooner. So we don't have time to wait for the exchange to send out their data feed updates.

One important strategy to obtain market data before others is to execute a huge amount of orders with the purpose of detecting how other traders might react to certain market moves. A high-frequency trader I interviewed in New York in 2014 said, "you read other algorithms. The information that is retrieved is fed back to the algo that would issue the next order in response to this information."[5]

They do so by constantly issuing and canceling orders to be in front of the price move that they aim to profit from. In the case of scalping, a high-frequency trader I followed for six weeks in his New York office said that he would design his algorithms to exploit slower market actors:

> What you do [in scalping] is making markets. So you are offering and bidding competitively on one exchange. That way when someone pays the spread, when someone buys the offer or sells the bid, they are first to know because they got filled. If they are part of that sell or buy, they find out immediately and that gives them the time-jump to go on to the next exchange and if they sold they can buy on that exchange and make profit on the difference.

The trader from Chicago also explained that:

> The fact that I am participating on the market gives me time to speed-jump because the information were a fill and that preempts market data significantly [...] and when you receive that fill, that's what triggers your next orders essentially, to these other exchanges.

Basically, high-frequency traders' black boxes are designed in a fashion where adaptive feedback loops are placed centrally. The strategy is designed to determine from the position change how to react. It will send out another quote based on its previous interaction in the market. An order is conditioned by the previous ones and by the ways in which the algorithms adapted to the market information that that order produced (if it got filled or rejected). This means that the traders issue orders and when that order is filled, some of the black box's other algorithms would react to the price information. Every action is defined by a fixed set of rules, which transforms themselves according to the action of others. In fact, each algorithm not only computes the desired answers to a given problem, it feeds back and informs the internal operations of the trading system, which, in turn, "speaks" and interacts with other trading systems operating in the market.

This interaction is taken even further, as the traders explained that they would force a trigger by putting orders in the market that were never intended to get executed. They put in quotes to trigger responses. One trader has explained the use of what he called "shield quotes" where he quotes a few ticks behind in a certain market. He explained that:

> If that quote get filled we know that someone has placed a big order because, you know, if there are twenty orders ahead of us in the last data feeds update and we got filled that means that twenty of the other orders got filled at the same time.

High-frequency traders issue a huge amount of quotes, often with the intention of not getting the quotes executed. Orders are issued with the only hope of providing essential information of how the markets are moving. It would be impossible for the traders to achieve this information in a computer lab. HFT is a system characterized less by a linear set of instructions controlled by the programmer and more by a multiplicity of interacting algorithms. Back-testing or simulation models are problematic for most of these algorithms. Traders strive to base their assumptions on real-time price moves adjusted to adaptive market behavior. Achieving information before the exchanges' data feed updates can only be done with real orders.

By quoting the market in real-time, the algorithms create the signals upon which they also react. Borch (2017: 8) describes this in Foucauldian terms arguing that HFT algorithms are engaged in "conduct of conduct" when they seek to structure the possible field of action of others by deploying strategies that effectively change the market environment in which other algorithms are operating. MacKenzie emphasizes this point by showing that traders claim to attend to writing algorithms that, when reading the order book, are able to distinguish "real" orders from the fake orders being canceled before they are executed. In this case the signals produced by issuing quotes are signs that indicate when the algorithms need to pull a quote. High-frequency traders make anticipation on the basis of the order-book dynamics, and try to affect the anticipation other market participants have of the order-book dynamics. MacKenzie points this out with reference to Goffmann's notion of interaction order:

> Among the things an algorithm does in automated trading is to have material effects on the behaviour of other algorithms; reciprocally, their behaviour influences what *it* does. The ensemble of such effects is what I mean by the "interaction order of algorithms." (MacKenzie, 2019: 42, original emphasis)

Beyond Human Intentionality

As the empirical material demonstrates, spoofing is not a single strategy deployed by some high-frequency traders. Rather it seems to be a fundamental technique used to read the market in combination with all different sorts of other HFT strategies (with or without the intention to manipulate other traders' trading behavior). In the end, there is no "real" difference between a "fake" spoof order and an order that is executed to read the market. Pardo-Guerra describes the case when:

> the trader could have orders on both sides of the market to benefit from the spread. A more aggressive trader could enter and submit more aggressive orders that then interact with the other side of the defendant's orders. Seeing those aggressive orders, the defendant concludes the market is moving, cancels his orders, and submits orders on both sides of the new market price. (2016: 18–19)

The empirical examples show that a range of HFT strategies exist which aim at "sniffing" out hidden liquidity and other market changes that are generally considered legitimate strategies. Spoofing is presented by the high-frequency traders as a way to read the market, an observational technology that in fact informs HFT strategies. Orders are executed to detect information about other algorithms' trading behavior.

Suddenly we see that practices that used to be illegal become possible (without regulatory intervention) due to the invention of new technological devices. A new reality has taken over the regulatory approach for how to evaluate if markets are being manipulated or not.

The empirical material suggests that high-frequency traders are reading the market as a collective result of non-international interacting agents. HFT black-box trading tools demonstrate a probabilistic system that connects and seeks to determine the behavior of one algorithm to the behavior of others. In this way, the underlying asset is used as a price indicator and not considered a "real" good (investment object). An asset is not considered a future entity but a present indicator of a correlation, in the case of spreading, a signal defining opportunities of arbitrage. The interaction order in HFT is not concerned with determining expectations about a future price move based on the expectations of other traders (and possibly hope for a correspondence to the future reality of the price), but simply with acting upon other algorithms' behavior from reading the order book. The order of the interaction is not determined by human intentionality but is a consequence of the qualitative features of HFT algorithms, i.e., they are programmed to read the order book by issuing and canceling orders (Borch & Lange, 2017; Lange, 2015). This interconnectedness of algorithms testifies to the fact that HFT algorithms might at an aggregated level affect or amplify larger market moves like the Flash Crash, which at the same time render significant interventions by isolated human traders (like Mr. Sarao) less likely.

Such a conclusion raises a range of important questions in relation to formulating a critical approach toward HFT: Who is liable for a market-wide crash when caused by interacting algorithms? Is it the traders who pre-programmed the algorithms to interact with other algorithms? The exchanges that cater for the high-frequency traders? Is it the traders who developed the strategy to execute orders without human intervention? Or the programmers who wrote the code?

Conclusion: A "New" Critical Agenda

Due to the specific features of automated trading in general and HFT in particular we need to ask ourselves: What is the critical in critical finance when dealing with interactive trading algorithms? The answers to such questions are difficult when algorithms interact and change their behavior based on this interaction. Algorithms no longer represent a neutral device isolated in space and time operating as faithful "delegates" on behalf of a human trader (Mackenzie, 2019: 55).

This chapter took the case of spoofing as its point of departure to illustrate the status and need for a new critical agenda on how to engage with the financial market. The sociological literature on market microstructure (the automation of exchanges and the invention of the order book) together with the observations and interviews conducted with high-frequency traders paints a clear picture. The use of "spoofing techniques" is tied to the occurrence of the limit order book described above and the anonymity of the trading algorithms. The literature shows, ironically, that it was the regulatory framework that was created from debates regarding competitions and fairness that promoted the code of conduct for the use of spoofing—an unintended side effect. From a regulatory point of view, law categorizes spoofing as an activity that distorts true prices through calculated deception and manipulation (Pardo-Guerra, 2016: 12). What to a regulator's mind differentiates a real trade from the fictitious or manipulative one is the intent of whoever originated the trade or its underlying automated trading system.

The considerations presented in this chapter—taking the non-intentional interacting order between algorithms into account—turn existing conceptions of what is fair on its head, calling for an entirely new critical agenda. The use of high-speed algorithms and their interactional features created a profitable loophole for technologically advanced trading firms with the ability to operate if not legally than at least under the radar in areas that were previously considered as inappropriate by the industry itself. Spoofing is now a fundamental mode of operation and not an immoral act that the regulators can attribute to one single individual. The Flash Crash is just one manifestation of this practice. Scholars have shown that smaller crashes are taking place on a regular basis without anyone knowing the consequences of such irregular market behavior (Johnson et al., 2012). I have pointed toward a few critical questions that need to be studied further and for which a new critique of finance needs to be developed. The ability to extract profit from local interactions and the global robustness of the financial system is a tension that is as much of political as it is of sociological interest and one that needs to be studied further perhaps with different tools. This has consequences for how we might understand the regulation of HFT, and the possibility of holding non-intentional actors such as interacting algorithms accountable for their actions.

Notes

1 Others have emphasized the unintentional "butterfly effect" that Mr. Sarao's trading strategy might have affected as contributing to the Flash Crash (Foresight, 2012: 71–72; Sornette & von der Becke, 2011).
2 For an elaboration of the automation of financial exchanges, see Muniesa (2007) and Pardo-Guerra (2011).
3 For a more detailed description of the transition from the open-outcry trading pit to high-frequency trading, see Borch et al. (2015) and Borch and Lange (2017).
4 It is such infrastructures that Pardo-Guerra (2016: 11) argues play an important role in spoofing. For a more in-depth review of the regulatory issues of algo-trading, see Lenglet (2011) and Coombs (2016).
5 In this chapter, I make use of the empirical data I collected between 2014 and 2016 as part of the "Crowd Dynamics in Financial Markets" research project at Copenhagen Business School. The methods and use of the data have been explained elsewhere (see Beverungen & Lange, 2018; Borch & Lange, 2017; Lange 2016, 2017).

References

Arnoldi, J. (2016). "Computer algorithms, market manipulation and the institutional-ization of high-frequency trading," *Theory, Culture and Society* 33(1): 29–52.

Barlyn, S. & Ajmera, A. (2016, January 5). "Wall St. Watchdog homes in on high-frequency trades to combat spoofing," *Reuters, Business News.*

Beverungen, A. & Lange, A-C. (2018). "Cognition in high-frequency trading: The costs of consciousness and the limits of automation," *Theory, Culture and Society* 35(6): 75–95.

Bodek, H. (2013). *The Problem of High Frequency Trading: Collected Writings on High Frequency Trading & Stock Market Structure Reform.* New York, NY: Decimus Capital Markets.

Borch, C. (2017). "Algorithmic finance and (limits to) governmentality: On Foucault and high-frequency trading," *Le Foucaldien* 3(1): 1–17.

Borch, C., Hansen, K. B. & Lange, A-C. (2015). "Markets, bodies, and rhythms: A rhythmanalysis of financial markets from open-outcry trading to high-frequency trading," *Environment and Planning D: Society and Space* 33(6): 1080–1097.

Borch, C. & Lange, A.-C. (2017). "High-frequency trader subjectivity: Emotional attachment and discipline in an era of algorithms," *Socio-Economic Review* 15(2): 283–306.

Burr, A. C. (2014). "Cancelling the order: How high frequency traders are disrupting the derivatives market, and what the regulators can do to stop them." Retrieved from http://works.bepress.com/andrew_burr/1 (Accessed 1 December 2014).

Castelle M., Millo, Y., Beunza, D., & Lubin, D. C. (2016). "Where do electronic markets come from? Regulation and the transformation of financial exchanges," *Economy and Society* 45(2): 166–200.

CFTC. (2012). Sub-Committee on Automated and High Frequency Trading, Working Group 1, Presentation to the TAC. Retrieved from http://www.cftc.gov/ucm/groups/public/@newsroom/documents/file/tac103012_wg1.pdf on December 1, 2014.

CFTC. (2015a). "Criminal complaint, United States of America vs. Navinder Singh Sarao, AO 91 (Rev.11/11). Washington, DC: CFTC & SEC.

CFTC. (2015b). "United States of America vs. Nav Sarao Futures Limited PLC and Navinder Singh Sarao: Appendix to Plaintiff's motion for statutory restraining order containing declarations and exhibits," *Case: 1:15-cv-03398.* Washington, DC: CFTC & SEC.

Coombs, N. (2016). "What is an algorithm? Financial regulation in the era of high-frequency trading," *Economy and Society* 45(2): 279–303.

Dragos, B., & Wilkins, I. (2014). "An ecological/evolutionary perspective on high-frequency trading," *Journal of Sustainable Finance and Investment* 4(2): 161–175.

Ford, J. (2016, November 12). "'Spoofing' case highlights perils of automated trading," *Financial Times.*

Foresight. (2012). "The future of computer trading in financial markets, Final Project Report, London, The Government Office for Science." Retrieved from https://www.gov.uk/government/uploads/system/uploads/attachment_data/file/289431/12-1086-future-of-computer-trading-in-financial-markets-report.pdf.

Haldane, A. (2011). "The race to zero." [Speech]. *The Bank of England.* Retrieved from https://www.bis.org/review/r110720a.pdf.

Hanson, T. A., & Hall, J. R. (2012). "Statistical arbitrage trading strategies and high frequency trading." Retrieved from SSRN: http://ssrn.com/abstract=2147012.

Johnson, N., Zhao, G., Hunsader, E., & Meng, J. (2012). "Financial black swans driven by ultrafast machine ecology." doi: 10.2139/ssrn.2003874.

Lange, A-C. (2015). *Crowding of Adaptive Strategies: Swarm Theory and High-Frequency Trading*. Copenhagen: unpublished manuscript.

Lange, A-C. (2016). "Organizational ignorance: An ethnographic study of high-frequency trading," *Economy and Society* 45(2): 230–250.

Lange, A-C. (2017). "The noisy motions of instruments: The performative space of high-frequency trading," in T. Beyes, M. Leeker, and I. Schipper (eds.), *Performing the Digital: Performance Studies and Performances in Digital Cultures* (pp. 101–116). Bielefeld: Transcript Verlag.

Lange, A-C., Lenglet, M., & Seyfert, R. (2016). "Cultures of high-frequency trading: Mapping the landscape of algorithmic developments in contemporary financial markets," *Economy and Society* 45(2): 149–165.

Lee, R. (2002). "The future of securities exchanges," in R. E. Litan & R. Herring (eds.), *Brookings-Wharton Papers on Financial Services: 2002* (pp. 1–33). Washington, DC: Brookings Institution Press.

Lenglet, M. (2011). "Conflicting codes and codings: How algorithmic trading is reshaping financial regulation," *Theory, Culture and Society* 28(6): 44–66.

Lewis, M. (2014a). *Flash Boys: A Wall Street Revolt*. New York: Allen Lane.

Lewis, M. (2014b, March 31). "The wolf hunters of wall street," *New York Times*.

Mackenzie, D. (2014). "Be grateful for drizzle," *London Review of Books* 36(17): 27–30.

MacKenzie, D. (2015). "On 'spoofing'," *London Review of Books* 37(10). Available online: https://www.lrb.co.uk/the-paper/v37/n10/donald-mackenzie/on-spoofing

MacKenzie, D. (2018). "Material signals: A historical sociology of high-frequency trading," *American Journal of Sociology* 123(6): 1–49.

MacKenzie, D. (2019). "How algorithms interact: Goffman's interaction order in automated trading," *Theory, Culture and Society* 36(2): 39–59.

MacKenzie, D., Beunza, D., Millo, Y., & Pardo-Guerra, J. P. (2012). "Drilling through the Allegheny Mountains: Liquidity, materiality and high-frequency trading," *Journal of Cultural Economy* 5(3): 279–296.

Meyer, G. (2016, July 14). "US trader guilty of 'spoofing' sentenced to three years in prison," *Financial Times*.

Muniesa, F. (2007). "Market technologies and the pragmatics of prices," *Economy and Society* 36(3): 377–395.

Pardo-Guerra, J. P. (2011). "The automated house: The digitalization of the London stock exchange, 1955–1990," in B. Bátiz-Lazo, J. C. Maixé-Altés, and P. Thomes (eds.), *Technological Innovation in Retail Finance: International Historical Perspectives* (pp. 197–220). New York, NY: Routledge.

Pardo-Guerra, J. P. (2016). *What is a 'Real' Transaction? The Infrastructural Moralities of Spoofing in High-Frequency Trading*. San Diego: unpublished manuscript.

Securities and Exchange Commission. (2010). *Concept Release on Equity Market Structure*. Washington, DC: The Securities and Exchange Commission.

Seyfert, R. (2016). "Bugs, predations or manipulations? Incompatible epistemic regimes of high-frequency trading," *Economy and Society* 45(2): 251–277.

Sornette, D., & von der Becke, S. (2011). "Crashes and high frequency trading: An evaluation of risks posed by high-speed algorithmic trading," *Zurich: Swiss Finance Institute. Research Paper Series* No.11-63.

Zaloom, C. (2006). *Out of the Pits: Traders and Technology from Chicago to London*. Chicago, IL: University of Chicago Press.

PART III

Financialization

13

THE FINANCIALIZED STATE

Dick Bryan, David Harvie, Mike Rafferty and Bruno Tinel

Introduction: Leverage, Liquidity and Social Derivatives

The term "financialization" is becoming an increasingly popular concept to describe many recent changes in economic and social organization and processes. But there is no generally accepted definition of the concept, partly because different definitions focus on different developments. For some, financialization is about finance-as-industry growing larger in its share of GDP or profitability. For others, it is about the growing power of finance in corporate decision-making via shareholder value. Financialization is also invoked to explain the growing need not only for households to borrow for everyday living, especially housing, but also for university education and basic consumption. A newer frontier in this research is addressing changes involving those occurring "inside" financial markets and institutions and in the design of financial products (Bryan & Rafferty, 2017).

Less attention has been given to the spread of financial logics into areas beyond those conventionally depicted as "finance," such as the new agendas of risk shifting and risk management of households and associated social policy. This chapter explores the spread of financial logics into the state—such that many aspects of state policy are being "financialized." Currently depicted by reference to over-arching processes of "neo-liberalism," "financialization" can mean many things in relation to the state. These meanings include: fiscal agendas of austerity; the sale of state-owned assets; the imposition of commercial criteria on assets and activities that remain within the state; as well as policies that subsidize and advance the political power of financial institutions.

Such developments are not uniform within or across nation-states; nor is there a telos to the process of state financialization. But within the literature on the state and financialization there is little attention to states' increasing strategic use of financial ways of thinking in policy formation, especially through concepts such as leverage[1] and liquidity[2] (Bryan & Rafferty, 2014, 2017, 2018; Martin, 2002).

It is not that the concepts of leverage and liquidity are themselves absent in contemporary analysis of states and policy. Indeed, any engagement with debt, for instance, is necessarily about leverage, and any discussion about central banking necessarily invokes issues of liquidity. Our concern is that engagement with leverage and liquidity is too often incidental, and not pursued as a key feature of state financialization. Our proposition, therefore, is that leverage and liquidity form a broader logic identifying how the financial role of states is transforming.

Our objective, however, is not to offer yet another formal restatement of the role of the state, as if states are reducible to delineated roles. It is to identify an emerging range of leveraged state positions to build the proposition that apparently discrete policy changes in the aftermath of the global financial crisis of 2007–2008, often simply depicted by reference to "neo-liberalism," can be seen to involve the strategic management of leverage and liquidity and embed a logic of financial derivatives. The irony is that state policies designed to combat the crash of derivative markets in 2007 and 2008 are in effect deploying derivative structures and techniques.

Randy Martin (2015) has coined the term "the derivative form" or a "derivative logic" (in parallel with Marx's value form and logic of capital). Martin uses the heuristic of derivatives to help understand changes in social organization, from cultural processes, to university governance, to military strategy in the "war against terror." The essence of this analysis is the identification that the derivative involves two things: leverage (purchasing a large risk exposure on a small outlay) and decomposing things we have generally thought of as a whole into a range of attributes. In financial markets, the objective is to break down an equity or a loan or a portfolio into its elemental and different risks, so that each of these risks might be priced and traded discretely. Extended to the social world, there is recognition that this same decomposition of "things" to their constituent risks and managing those risks is a driver of change, even if these risks are not traded in formal markets. Here we are also invoking what Randy Martin (2014: 190) depicted as the "social logic of derivatives":

> Derivatives give form to that contradictory relation between the move to money as such, and the moves deeper into social materiality and interdependence. Unpacking derivatives, not simply as a technical device of finance, but as a key to the social logics and relations that inhere in the current conjuncture of capital, will address three cardinal riddles of finance. First, what does financial dominance mean for an understanding of how capitalism works (or doesn't); second, what historical difference does this prevalence of finance make; and third, how to understand the social and political implications of the preponderance of financial debt?

In this chapter, we explore this derivative logic by developing three key propositions. They all concern the way in which changes in leverage and liquidity are blurring conventional categories. In a nutshell, we argue that the social logic of the derivative, which is permeating the state, is changing and even erasing earlier distinctions between: (i) the state and financial markets; (ii) what were formally thought to be discrete state activities—namely, monetary and fiscal policy; and (iii) community or social policy and finance. To be clear, we do not claim that this logic has erased these distinctions completely but only that there is a trend in this direction. And, to reiterate, nor do we claim that these trends are the same everywhere or that they are occurring everywhere. We illustrate our argument with examples of policies, especially those prevalent in the United States and, to a lesser extent, the United Kingdom.

Financial Derivatives: A Brief Background

A derivative logic needs a brief explanation, for by now we should understand that they are more than devices of leveraged gambling. A derivative gives exposure to an attribute of market performance (generally via a price change, but it could be in a variety of indices) of an asset without (necessarily) involving ownership of the underlying asset. Derivatives are traded in order to take a range of risk positions (hedge/speculation, long/short) on an unknown future. The leverage comes from the fact that it is far cheaper to purchase a derivative on an asset than to own the asset itself. Hence for an expenditure equal to the price of an asset, it is possible to acquire large multiples of derivative exposure. The wins are many multiples more than for the owner of the underlying asset; but so often too are the losses.[3]

It is further useful to explain the two basic types of derivative instrument that underpin our analysis: *put options* and *call options*. Put options give their holder the right to sell an asset at a certain price at a certain time or over a certain time period. Call options give their holder the right to buy an asset at a certain price or over a certain time period. The put option trades falling prices or values; the call option rising prices or values. Because these contracts are generally settled in cash, not via the transfer of ownership of the underlying asset, there is no need to own the asset against which the options have been purchased.

Normally in explanations of derivatives, the underlying asset is assumed to be a commodity—for example, steel or coffee beans—or a financial asset—for example, a certain quantity of yen or euros, or a "basket" of shares. If the "spot price" of steel or yen rises above the "strike price" of a call option linked to steel or yen, then the holder of this option will exercise it, making a "profit" on the difference between the spot and strike prices *minus* the premium or price they paid for the option. The seller of the call option, who received the premium but who must sell the asset (in this case steel/yen) at a price below that in the spot market, makes an equivalent loss.

But this derivative logic is not restricted to the products traded in standard derivative exchanges. It is present, under another name, in daily life. For example (and one we return to shortly), medical and other forms of insurance take the financial form of call options. The option's seller is the insurer, its buyer the insured person or household; the "underlying asset" of uncertain future value is the cost of medical treatment arising from some "event" (ill-health). If the insured person remains healthy then the cost of medical treatment, i.e., the value of the underlying asset, is zero: the option, in effect, is not exercised. But in the event that medical treatment is required, then the underlying's value rises with the cost of this treatment: in other words, the option is exercised. The price of the option is the insurance premium and, as with "textbook" examples (where the underlying is steel or coffee or currency), this price/premium will likely be higher the more likely is the option to be exercised—i.e., the higher the likelihood of medical treatment being required.

With this brief background, we can look at a range of prevalent, post-crisis financial policy positions.

Quantitative Easing

The process of Quantitative Easing (QE) that followed the global financial crisis in many advanced capitalist countries is perhaps the most expensive and expansive post-crisis policy. QE involved states buying assets of unknown and often dubious quality so as to ensure liquidity in financial markets. In the US version of QE, these dubious assets typically related to a housing investment; in the European version, such assets were typically bank loans. The assets were then held on the states' books, and cash was returned to the seller.

The effect was to provide capital markets with put options: the capacity to put risks (and risky assets) back onto the state. In the midst of crisis, the state bought financial assets at full, pre-crisis value, in the knowledge that their market price was likely to fall. By selling these assets to the state, financial institutions didn't have to write down the assets' value; but as the assets were not subsequently sold by the state, their value was never written down: the state's loss on the put options was never recorded (rather they were treated as contingent claims). The "price" paid by the banks for the acquisition of these put options was the guarantee that they would maintain liquidity in financial markets.

QE is not just option-like in its financial structure, but its particular form also had significant but neglected consequences, which are best understood through the lens of options. In the United States, QE targeted debt markets and derivative markets in almost equal measure. The targeting of debt markets via the purchase of Treasury bonds is familiar. But the US Federal Reserve also targeted derivative products; specifically, mortgage-backed securities. Mortgage-backed securities (MBS) are derivatives because their owner holds exposure to an income stream (a bundle of monthly mortgage repayments) but no ownership of either the mortgages themselves, or the "underlying" properties (houses). It is this derivative nature of MBS that made (and makes) them so vulnerable to crashing. A QE policy involving the large-scale purchase of MBS is no less a leveraged, derivative position held by the Federal Reserve.

But QE lasted longer than the purchase of so-called toxic assets: QE rapidly evolved into a more pervasive policy to re-build asset market "confidence" (prices). In the United States, the Federal Reserve's argument for QE was initially about reflating the mortgage-backed securities market (that part of the asset market most profoundly impacted by defaulting sub-prime loans crashing MBS values). There was also an expected flow through from the MBS market to the housing market to lift house prices and, with house price inflation, reduce the number of households in negative equity (i.e., at risk of default). By QE2, the Fed's argument broadened from housing, morphing into the proposition that the capital-market benefits of QE would spread across all asset classes. The argument here was that as the prices of MBS rise, and so the yield falls, investors will shift to other, more profitable assets, pushing their prices up: a financial version of the rising-tide-lifting-all-boats catchphrase. The effect across capital markets was that the state was now, in effect, selling call options, enabling a protected exposure to the up-side of financial assets. Again, the "price" of these options was that capital markets had to secure liquidity and keep investing.

This derivative logic represents a profound shift in the framing of monetary policy. Liquidity was once provided directly into the debt market by central-bank adjustments in interest rates and/or the quantity of money in circulation. But in the era when liquidity (and crises of illiquidity) shifts from the banking sector to leveraged derivative markets, so the state's monetary policy has to shift to leveraged derivative interventions.

"Too Big to Fail": State Deposit and Bank Liquidity Guarantees

During the global financial crisis, and indeed before (prompted by earlier bank liquidity scares), many nation-states made undertakings—sometimes formal, sometimes by precedent—to underwrite the viability of financial institutions. The formal undertakings in many contexts relate to guarantees to citizens regarding the underwriting of certain levels of their bank savings. The informal undertakings, which manifestly arose in 2007 and 2008 in the midst of bank insolvencies, are captured by the popular expression "too big to fail." They involve the recognition that states cannot let large financial institutions collapse because of the high levels of collateral damage, and the overall loss of market liquidity, that would predictably follow. Federal Reserve chair Ben Bernanke's reputed advocacy of emergency bailouts, in the context of the Friday, September 28, 2008 stock market crash, famously captured the essence of the dilemma: "If we don't do this, we may not have an economy on Monday."[4]

The underwriting of financial assets, by asset purchase or some other method, has been a prevalent response of many states to the financial crisis. It is already well-recognized that financial institutions secured special treatment because of their pivotal economic position as providers (and deniers) of market liquidity. Beyond this, the interesting dimension of such underwriting is that these various forms of support are rarely formally costed. They are given at no stated charge and with no record on the state's fiscal balance sheet.

Robert Merton, famous for the Black-Scholes-Merton options pricing model, made a back-of-the-envelope calculation that, in 2013, the United States had explicitly and implicitly underwritten the value of financial assets totaling about US$17 trillion:

> U.S. Treasury debt held by the public was $9 trillion in 2010; that debt is probably closer to $11 trillion today. [There are further] U.S. government guarantees that are not on the balance sheet. To begin, there is about $1.9 trillion in guaranteed loan financing. Fannie Mae and Freddie Mac are both in receivership; the guarantees relating to Fannie and Freddie are just over $5 trillion. Finally, the off-balance-sheet guarantees of the Federal Deposit Insurance Corporation (FDIC), home loan banks, the Fed itself, and many other federal institutions are estimated at about $10 trillion. In sum, there is about $17 trillion in U.S. government off-balance-sheet guarantees. Note that the $17 trillion represents the amounts being guaranteed, not the actual value of the guarantees. The value of these guarantees, however, can be enormous, particularly in times of stress. (Merton et al., 2013: 22–23)

But, Merton noted, the cost of this underwriting has never appeared as a liability on the state's balance sheet, because it has (as yet) involved no "actual" expenditure.

The implicit promise to back the liabilities of banks involves the state in potential future expenditures should a crisis of bank illiquidity arises. Hence, contended Merton, such underwriting should be priced like other contingent claims: in this case, like a call option. The value of the option changes as the probability of its triggering changes. Underwriting has a low price during a boom, where it is unlikely to be called on by banks, but it has an extremely high price in a downturn, where the state's guarantees are increasingly likely to be called on.

In effect, the state is selling, at token price, call options on the provision of liquidity, but is not recording the contingent claims that this derivative position involves.

"Safe" Assets

The standard conception of a "risk-free" financial asset has been a Treasury bond (T-bond). Like the state's money (fiat currency), T-bonds are guaranteed by the state, and hence (nominally) face no default risk. No doubt there will be, for the foreseeable future, a large demand for Treasury bonds, especially US T-bonds, and many will argue that there is no real, "safe" alternative (He et al., 2016).[5]

But things are changing in the wake of the global financial crisis. Many nation-states pledged their government tax bases to rescue the banking system; many others used aggressive monetary policy easing, especially QE and interest rate cuts, to reflate asset markets and stimulate economic activity. A consequence was near zero and even negative real interest rates, with a recent estimate putting the global stock of negative-yielding bonds at US$10 trillion (Gutscher, 2019).

Further, yields became not just negative, but also volatile. As a central plank of QE, the US Federal Reserve started to purchase much of the supply of five to ten year T-bonds. Concurrently, long-term uncertainty reduced demand for longer-term (up to 30 year) T-bonds. That left public demand accessing shorter-term T-bonds, where prices are more volatile, and yields are directly influenced by short-term central-bank interest rate policy (Rogoff, 2019).

In this context, the aspiration of "safe" assets to anchor an asset portfolio is being re-thought. There is evidence showing renewed focus on a conception not of "risk free" assets (for bonds with negative yield are not "risk free") but of "safe" assets. Within this policy momentum, there is also an increasing focus on privately issued "quasi-safe assets." As we have argued elsewhere, with not enough "born safe" assets in supply, central banks and financial markets have been attempting to find ways to "make" some assets safe (Bryan et al., 2016). Caballero et al. (2017) depict the safe assets "conundrum":

> In the short- and medium-term, the quantity of safe assets may increase via stronger exchange rates in the safe asset issuers, and via public debt issuance in those countries. Over time, a lasting solution to the shortage of safe assets will require a combination of finding alternative sources of safe asset supply and a reduction in demand.

The depiction of T-bonds as inherently and uniquely "safe" now comes with caveats (Golec & Perotti, 2017; Gorton, 2016). T-bonds may be safe from formal default, but they are not always safe in terms of yield, or the option to renegotiate. This can be seen in the spread in yields between Eurobonds issued by Eurozone countries. Indeed, with QE, T-bonds and their quantities, prices and yields have been used as key tools of government policy. Over the past decade, in some leading industrial economies—Germany and Japan, for instance—government debt has been generating negative yields. When there is a widespread fear of market downturn, traders bid up the prices of these safe assets, turning their yields negative, just as some states were issuing bonds at negative real interest rates.

But in the United States, there is a further and countering agenda. As part of its QE policy, the US Federal Reserve repeatedly stated a longer-term commitment to reduce the holdings of Treasury bonds and mortgage-backed securities after markets stabilized: a process it describes as "normalizing" its balance sheet. This process of "normalization" was initiated in October 2017. The Fed allowed US$30 billion in Treasury proceeds and $20 billion from mortgage-backed securities to roll off its books each month. All other expiring assets would be rolled over (reinvested). Via these monthly releases, there was to be a long, steady winding-back of the Federal Reserve's balance sheet. But the process was paused, i.e., effectively terminated, in May 2019, amidst fears for the stability of the bond market. The effect is that the price of, and hence yield on, Treasury bonds has become volatile, especially since they are seen to have become a permanent tool of discretionary, short-term central-bank policy (e.g., Rocco & Henderson, 2019).

There is a critical sense in which T-bonds, once themselves the safe asset, are becoming a derivative position—in the sense that they are the liquid hedge on the portfolio, not simply its stable part. This is because there is now a range of assets in which there are calculable probabilities of safety (indeed variable forms of state backing), which can sit alongside Treasury bonds in asset portfolios. In this scenario, it is worth considering what might fill the "safe" end of a pension or sovereign wealth fund portfolio if government debt is evolving to the derivative position.

Safe assets are most likely to attach in some way to the nation-state—for states can guarantee against default risk in a way no private organization can—but the form of that state guarantee can change. The critical issue is that safety is not innate to an asset: the conditions (and degrees) of safety can be created (or withdrawn) by nation-state policy. States don't need necessarily to be the direct suppliers of safe assets; they simply need to be the guarantors of safety (the state's leveraged position).

One area of growing interest in this context is infrastructure bonds: bonds issued to fund the construction or operation of roads, railways and tunnels, power stations and power services, telecommunications, hospitals, and so on. Critical to this development has been the process of privatization of once-state-owned assets and the state's role as underwriter in public-private partnerships. The contractual terms are instructive for here we discover the ways in which states may provide forms of safety. States may underwrite revenue streams by guaranteeing patronage, embedding market rates of return into regulated pricing structures, and so on. Here arises the allure of both safety and yield.

The connection to potential financial volatility that comes with this development is made clear in a 2014 OECD report on investment in infrastructure:

> The massive liquidity injections that Central Banks have carried out between 2009 and 2012 in response to the Lehman Brothers and European sovereign debt crises have led to a compression of the yields of debt capital market instruments. The search for yields by institutional investors has found a possible solution in the investment in alternative asset classes like infrastructure [...]

In this sense, the report outlines the typical characteristics of infrastructure as an alternative asset class for private investors and focuses on the riskiness of infrastructure projects from a financial investor's standpoint. When an acceptable risk/return profile cannot be reached, some form of public intervention is needed to leverage private capital intervention. This public intervention refers obviously, but is not limited to, provision of financial back up and support that can take many alternative forms. (OECD, 2014: 6–7)

Currently infrastructure bonds are issued in Anglo countries and some emerging markets,[6] so the innovation here should not be depicted as yet widespread. But significant here is that the state's underwriting of revenue streams on privatized assets creates possibilities for (close to) AAA-rated securitization, generating "safe" bond-like assets with many of the financial attributes of Treasury bonds. With guarantees of inflation-linked revenue, for example, they may even have more stable prices and positive yields than T-bonds, especially if their financial structures are not, in turn, leveraged. Demand has grown accordingly from both pension funds and sovereign wealth funds (Alonso et al., 2015; Arezki et al., 2016).[7]

Financially, therefore, the state can be seen as meeting market demand for safe assets without having to produce the safe assets itself: it is leveraging its balance sheet not by issuing public debt per se, but by selling a put option to private developers, with a strike price determined by the conditions of profitability of the infrastructure developer.

Fiscal Contraction and Community Development

The debates about the merits of QE, and the general bailout strategies by central banks in the wake of the financial crisis, are extensive: they are not for review in this context (on central-bank responses to the crisis, see instead Fontan & Larue's chapter in this *Handbook*). But it does bear noting, because this has not been subject to nearly the same scrutiny, that the objective and logic of QE has been the security of financial market liquidity; not the well-being of households per se.

While, in the aftermath of the global financial crisis, financial institutions were "bailed out" and underwritten in return for sustaining market liquidity, households received no such support. Instead, they have faced policy positions described as "austerity." While banks are constitutionally incapable of securing their own liquidity (they cannot, e.g., trade while insolvent), households are different, for they will tend to pursue subsistence by any means in most circumstances. Not only will they choose to trade while insolvent, but social policy also generally expects them to do so: a process of "responsibilization" of householders to ensure they comply with their debt commitments (Beggs et al., 2014). The effect is that households could face state policies to create intentional household illiquidity, and nonetheless stay viable, or at least on payment.

While corporations pursue profitability, in recent decades households have faced policy agendas designed to force them to run to principles of "responsibility" and "rationality." The application of behavioral economics (the "nudge" agenda that links psychological postulates to financial incentives and compulsion) sees welfare policies themselves used as a form of state leverage to prompt people to act "rationally." Central has been the withdrawal of many forms of state provisioning, requiring households to manage their own risks by trading in call options (insurance) to replace many services formerly part of social policy. Health insurance is a clear illustration, but so too is the escalation of education fees, as students are encouraged to buy put options on their income-earning futures. In effect, the state has been requiring that households leverage themselves so as to manage their austerity-driven illiquidity.

The history of the England and Wales's fees-and-debt regime of university finance is politically interesting here.[8] Student loans can be considered a put option because if the value of the underlying asset—the graduate's future earnings—falls, then annual debt repayments also fall; and because, in the British system, any outstanding debt is canceled 30 years after graduation, a large proportion of student debt will never be repaid. This feature of the model has been emphasized by its defenders, who insist (with some justification) that it shares many characteristics with a graduate tax—a means of funding higher education that commands far higher public backing. By contrast, the present regime is widely reviled. Its introduction in 2010, when parliament voted to triple student fees, sparked a mass student movement, involving demonstrations and the occupations of the ruling Conservative Party's headquarters, and of dozens of university campuses. Indeed, these student activists have been credited by some as forming the basis of the movement that elected the socialist Jeremy Corbyn as leader of the Labour Party in 2015 (Chessum, 2015; Myers, 2017). The government opted for the fees-and-debt scheme—rather than the less contentious graduate tax—for a competing reason of political expediency and, in fact, a derivative-like, off-balance-sheet reason: controlling the headline public debt. In an era in which the Conservative-Liberal-Democrat coalition government had pledged to "fix the deficit" (and was blaming the previous Labour administration for its fiscal "profligacy"), a politically attractive feature of the model was that loans granted to students for tuition and maintenance, although backed by the state, would not be included in the current accounts and therefore would not make up part of the Treasury's public-sector net borrowing. In 2018, however, the Office for Budget Responsibility suggested that this method of accounting for student debt creates a "fiscal illusion"; and the Office for National Statistics has decided instead to treat student loans issued by the state as a mixture of financial transaction (the portion of the loan that is expected to be repaid) and government expenditure (that portion that will likely not be paid) (ONS, 2018; see also Adams, 2018).

The sorts of changes mentioned above have had a significant impact, especially on lower- and middle-income and young households. But the further effect of derivative austerity was that the once-standard Keynesian counter-cyclical fiscal measures (essentially greater state welfare expenditure triggered by an economic downturn) were not enacted, or at least not to the extent that happened in the twentieth century.

It is, therefore, an interesting twist to see in the United States that the Federal Reserve, in addition to QE which Kenneth Rogoff (2019) called a "trespass into fiscal policy" is also now pursuing a range of agendas of employment creation and urban renewal. These agendas are being advanced not primarily in the name of redressing growing social and economic inequality, but rather in the name of social order and financial stability—"community development." In the process, what is framed as "excessive" expenditure from a social distribution (fiscal) agenda is re-appearing as a foundational requirement of future financial (and monetary) stability. In effect, in the hands of the Federal Reserve, "community development" becomes a path to financial liquidity, and the strategy is to leverage that "development" activity on the smallest possible amount of state expenditure.

For instance, the Federal Reserve's Boston division has developed a Working Cities Challenge (WCC), an outcome of research into 25 cities that had experienced forms of de-industrialization and financial stress. This research found that common to those cities that had been able to stabilize or turn around their fortunes was the development of forms of trusteeship: "the ability of leaders in those cities to collaborate across sectors" (n.d.). As the WCC noted, this led to the question, "is there something the Boson Fed can do to help cities strengthen it in a way that extends growth to residents struggling most?"[9] In a rural context, the Federal Reserve Bank of Richmond has a community development section which has as a goal of understanding and developing:

> economic issues and community development tools to strengthen low- and moderate-income communities across the Fifth District through sharing data-supported community investment strategies that promote economic mobility, improve access to credit and information, and support innovations that lead to economic growth. (n.d.)

The interventions funded and developed by WCC/community development-like projects include labor market initiatives, education and training, and infrastructure projects—all initiatives that have clear fiscal policy-like attributes.

The derivative-like position here is as follows. The agenda of central banking in community stability and development is not directly targeting national aggregates (broad national monetary stability, or even GDP growth). Rather, it is those communities that are most financially risky: the communities in the lower tranches of financial stability; the "at risk." This is a pre-emptive intervention designed to prevent the conditions that might generate further financial (and social) instability (contagion). Second, the approach targets the small outliers, and is supplemented with policy instruments that are said to "leverage small investments," by combining them with charitable and foundation funds, and using local leadership to act as trustees for community development projects.[10] Finally, the effects of these derivative-like interventions are carefully monitored, measured, and compared in a process of innovation, experimentation, and commensuration.

Social Impact Bonds

At the same time as certain forms of assets (especially infrastructure) are being re-invented or re-engineered as quasi-safe assets, states have been inventing new, riskier assets in policy domains where bond finance once was absent. The new assets are known as social impact bonds (SIB) (in Australia, they are called Social Benefit Bonds). The SIB is one of a raft of "innovative" new financial instruments, part of an even broader field of "social finance," designed to bring the supposed benefits of financial markets and financial logic to help solve some of society's "most intractable problems" (Social Finance, 2009: 4). Besides the SIB, other examples of the same stable include development impact bonds, climate bonds, and conservation bonds. As with "community development," discussed above, the social impact bond blurs the boundaries between the state, civil society, and (financial) markets.

The social-investment model involves the state commissioning non-state organizations (whether for-profit or not-for-profit) to intervene in areas that were once, at least in the post-war welfare-state era, seen primarily as the responsibility of the state. Examples include probation services, interventions targeting homelessness, foster care, school truancy, and "employability." While the state defines desirable outcomes, service-providers are supposedly free to design innovative interventions. Funding for the intervention comes from financial investors. The SIB is designed to align the interests of these three actors—commissioner, service-provider, and financial investor. If the intervention is successful, to the extent that the social outcomes meet or exceed a pre-specified target, then investors receive a financial return; if targets are not met then investors receive no return and may lose the value of their initial investment. In this way, the state only funds successful interventions and, thus, (nominally) shifts risk onto private investors.

There is now a growing critical literature on SIBs (see, e.g., Harvie, 2019; Harvie & Ogman, 2019). Rather than attempting to summarize that literature we draw out the extent to which SIBs can be situated in a world dominated by a social derivative logic (Harvie et al., 2019).

First, despite its name, the SIB is not in fact a bond, at least not in the conventional sense. Rather it is much more accurately described as a social derivative—an option on the performance of some social intervention. Although the actual intervention or service might be funded by the financial investor's capital (as with a conventional bond), the value of the SIB in fact derives from the performance of an "underlying" variable or asset, namely, the performance of the service-provider against a set of metrics that measure the success of the invention. Moreover, in the event of an unsuccessful intervention, the SIB's holder has no claim on the assets of the failing/failed service-provider (as would be the case with equity or a conventional bond). The critical issue is that the owner of a SIB has a stake only in the performance of the service-providing organization, not in the organization itself.

Of course, the state—the commissioner of the intervention—is also a "stake-holder"; it too desires the social outcomes it has specified to be achieved. But instead of investing all of the funds for an outcome, it has issued a contingent claim to the SIB investor. To the extent that targets are met or exceeded, the value of the SIB will change, and the "debt" to the SIB investor will rise or fall. Moreover, the bond is structured as a contingent claim: the state only pays a "dividend" to investors if these targets are achieved.

Thus, we can understand the SIB as a call option held by the state, where the underlying "asset" is (the value of) the desirable social outcome, where the strike "price" is actually not a monetary price, but an intervention performance metric. We might also understand the relationship between state and financial investors as akin to a swap (a rolling series of options). In the world of the welfare state, the state was liable for fixed financial payments necessary to maintain a social service, but in the neoliberal world of the social-investment state, it has exchanged—or swapped—these fixed liabilities with financial investors, to whom it pays a floating (or variable) stream of dividends, depending on performance against a metric.

Finally, and more generally, we can understand social impact bonds as facilitating a making-commensurable of heterogeneous activities in the "social sphere." By means of SIBs traded in the social-investment market, the productive performance, the labor, of a probation officer, say, might be measured against that of a youth worker—or indeed against that of their "clients." And since there is no firewall between "social" investments and other financial markets, then the labor, both waged and voluntary, of such "social" workers can be integrated into the world of "capitalism with derivatives" (Bryan & Rafferty, 2006; Harvie, 2019).

Conclusion

The growing incorporation of a financial derivative logic into state policy since the global financial crisis is changing the way many state activities are conceived, financially structured, and organized. The chapter developed this proposition through five broad examples or cases: the policy of Quantitative Easing; bank underwriting and "too-big-to-fail"; the problem of "safe assets"; central-bank incorporation of social policy into financial stability; and "social investment" bonds designed to turn welfare provision into a financial asset.

This sample of policy change does not sum to a totalized claim that the state is to be depicted somehow as different from what it was before. It is the claim simply that we can see evidence that the techniques of finance—the social logic of the derivative—are being increasingly incorporated into the design of state intervention. It is not, in any verifiable way, a strategic plan to do so: it is simply the playing out of a financial logic that keeps being "revealed" in policy innovation.

The policy expression of this logic is that, because the state seeks to secure as much impact as it can out of its expenditures and interventions, it will utilize the techniques of leverage to give access to that impact. But leverage always leads to a vulnerability: it can accentuate not only benefits, but also costs. In particular, it requires a liquid market for the financial products it creates.

So the state must build liquidity guarantees into its strategy. In some contexts, these liquidity guarantees are virtually gifts, because the state has lost direct control over liquidity. QE and the underwriting of financial institutions are stark cases, because of the capacity of banks to withhold liquidity and thereby threaten the viability of capitalist financial markets. In other contexts, the state must build alternative platforms of liquidity, such as the conditions for quasi-safe assets and community development programs designed by central banks.

But the creation of liquidity in social-investment bonds—the opening up of a secondary market where these bonds can be traded as financial assets, giving them a current market value—is perhaps the most telling of all. This secondary market is not only generating real-time pricing on provider performance in what is traditionally called the "social safety net" of "the welfare state," but it also opens the potential for derivative positions on SIBs. Perhaps we are looking to a future where taking short positions on the welfare state (betting on the failure of SIBs) becomes a high-yielding financial asset or investment strategy.[11]

Notes

1 Most definitions of leverage focus on the increasing levels of debt, including state debt, as a means amplify the profit (or loss) on a financial position.
2 Liquidity here refers to the ease with which one can trade into, or out of, an asset, usually by reference to the transaction cost, or spread between the buy and sell price (see also Ortiz's chapter in this *Handbook*).
3 Imagine a racehorse worth $2 million. You will stand to win far more from the horse winning a race if you bet $2 million on a race than if you own the horse and collect the prize money. But if the horse loses, the gambler has lost the $2 million wager; the owner still has a $2 million horse.
4 The statement was said to have been made in the office of the then House Speaker Nancy Pelosi. See, for example, Ross Sorkin et al. (2008).
5 Helleiner (2014: 241) cites a Chinese official in 2009 making essentially the same point in explaining why China kept buying US Treasury bonds during the crisis: "Except for US Treasuries, what can you hold? [...] US Treasuries are the safe haven."
6 See Firzli (2016) for a brief review. To date, the main sites of state-backed infrastructure bonds are municipalities in the United States, the World Bank in Brazil, and the national governments of Britain, Canada, and Australia. For example, the British state has been toying with the possibility of issuing "infrastructure bonds" rather than T-bonds, essentially because the former are seen to be backed by "real"

assets; the latter just by state reputation. See, for example, Thorpe (2016) and Pickard et al. (2016).

7 OECD (2018) confirms the concentration of these investments in Anglo countries.
8 The funding models are different in Scotland and Northern Ireland.
9 This led the Boston Fed to a collaboration with Living Cities, a foundation that says it is "an innovative philanthropic collaborative of the world's largest foundations and financial institutions working together to dramatically improve the economic well-being of low-income people in cities." Notable for the propositions we are making about state and markets and leverage, Living Cities operates a Catalyst Fund which, "by providing loans that are combined with loans from other Living Cities members to enable the *creative use of debt to further program activities and leverage grant and private sector loan funds.*" The WCC is an adaptation of the Integration Initiative for the context of smaller cities; it was designed in partnership with the Boston Fed's own network of cross-sector collaborators, which takes the form of a Steering Committee comprised of leaders from the public, private, and philanthropic sectors who continually inform the WCCs approach with their knowledge of these cities and the field.
10 These interventions also blur the boundaries between the state, civil society, and markets.
11 We acknowledge Bob Meister who first posed to us this dark potential.

References

Adams, R. (2018, December 16). Change in student loan accounting could add £10bn to UK budget deficit. *The Guardian.* Retrieved from https://www.theguardian.com/education/2018/dec/16/change-in-student-loan-accounting-could-add-10bn-to-national-debt.

Alonso, J., Arellano, A., & Tuesta, D. (2015). *Pension Fund Investment in Infrastructure and Global Financial Regulation.* Pension Research Council Working Paper PRC WP2015-22, The Wharton School, University of Pennsylvania.

Arezki, R., Bolton, P., Peters, S., Samama, F., & Stiglitz, J. (2016). *From Global Savings Glut to Financing Infrastructure: The Advent of Investment Platforms.* IMF Working Paper Research Department.WP86/18. Retrieved from https://www.imf.org/external/pubs/ft/wp/2016/wp1618.pdf

Beggs, M., Bryan, D., & Rafferty, M. (2014). "Shoplifters of the World Unite! Law and culture in financialized times," *Cultural Studies* 28(5–6): 976–996.

Bryan, D., & Rafferty, M. (2006). *Capitalism with Derivatives: A Political Economy of Financial Derivatives, Capital and Class.* Basingstoke: Palgrave.

Bryan, D., & Rafferty, M. (2014). "Financial derivatives as social policy beyond crisis," *Sociology* 48(5): 887–903.

Bryan, D., & Rafferty, M. (2017). "Financialization," in D. M. Brennan, D. Kristjanson-Gural, C. P. Mulder, and E. K. Olsen (eds.), *Routledge Handbook of Marxian Economics.* New York, NY: Routledge.

Bryan, D., & Rafferty, M. (2018). *Risking Together: How Finance Is Dominating Everyday Life in Australia.* Sydney: Sydney University Press.

Bryan, D., Rafferty, M., & Tinel, B. (2016). "Households at the frontiers of monetary development," *Behemoth: A Journal on Civilisation* 9(2): 46–58.

Caballero, R., Farhi, E., & Gourinchas, P.-O. (2017). "The safe assets shortage conundrum," *Journal of Economic Perspectives* 31(3): 29–46.

Chessum, M. (2015, October 2). How the student protestors of 2010 became the Corbyn generation. *The Guardian.* Retrieved from https://www.theguardian.com/commentisfree/2015/oct/02/student-protesters-2010-jeremy-corbyn-election-labour-party.

Federal Reserve Bank of Richmond (n.d.). *About Community Development*. Retrieved from https://www.richmondfed.org/community_development/about_commaff

Firzli, M. N. J. (2016, May 24). *Pension Investment in Infrastructure Debt: A New Source of Capital for Project Finance*. Retrieved from http://blogs.worldbank.org/ppps/pension-investment-infrastructure-debt-new-source-capital-project-finance.

Golec, P., & Perotti, E. (2017). *Safe Assets: A Review*. European Central Bank Working Paper Series No. 2035. Retrieved from https://www.ecb.europa.eu/pub/pdf/scpwps/ecbwp2035.en.pdf.

Gorton, G. (2016, April). *The History and Economics of Safe Assets*. NBER Working Paper No. 22210. Retrieved from https://www.nber.org/papers/w22210.

Gutscher, C. (2019, March 25). "The $10 trillion pool of negative debt is a late-cycle reckoning." *Bloomberg News*. Retrieved from https://www.bloomberg.com/news/articles/2019-03-25/the-10-trillion-pool-of-negative-debt-is-a-late-cycle-reckoning.

Harvie, D. (2019). "(Big) society and (market) discipline: The financialisation of social reproduction," *Historical Materialism* 27(1): 92–124.

Harvie, D., Lightfoot, G., Lilley, S., & Weir, K. (2019). "Using derivative logic to speculate on the future of the social investment market," *Journal of Urban Affairs*. doi: 10.1080/07352166.2019.1584529.

Harvie, D., & Ogman, R. (2019). "The broken promises of social investment," *Environment and Planning A: Economy and Space* 51(4): 980–1004.

He, Z., Krishnamurthy, A., & Milbradt, K. (2016). *What Makes US Government Bonds Safe Assets?* NBER Working Paper No. 22017. Retrieved from https://www.nber.org/papers/w22017

Helleiner, E. (2014). *The Status Quo Crisis: Global Financial Governance after the 2008 Meltdown*. Oxford: Oxford University Press.

Martin, R. (2002). *Finacialization of Daily Life*. Philadelphia, PA: Temple University Press.

Martin, R. (2014). "What difference do derivatives make?" *Culture Unbound* 6: 189–210.

Martin, R. (2015). *Knowledge LTD: Towards a Social Logic of the Derivative*. Philadelphia, PA: Temple University Press.

Merton, R. C., Billio, M., Getmansky, M., Gray, D., Lo, A. W., & Pelizzon, L. (2013). "On a new approach for analysing and managing macrofinancial risks," *Financial Analysts Journal* 69(2): 22–33.

Myers, M. (2017). *Student Revolt: Voices of the Austerity Generation*. London: Pluto.

OECD (2014, September). *Private Financing and Government Support to Promote Long Term Investments in Infrastructure*. Financial Affairs Division. Retrieved from https://www.oecd.org/daf/fin/private-pensions/Private-financing-and-government-support-to-promote-LTI-in-infrastructure.pdf.

OECD (2018). *Survey of Large Pension Funds and Public Pension Reserve Funds, 2016*. Retrieved from http://www.oecd.org/daf/fin/private-pensions/2016-Large-Pension-Funds-Survey.pdf.

ONS (2018, December 17). *New Treatment of Student Loans in the Public Sector Finances and National Accounts*. Retrieved from https://www.ons.gov.uk/economy/governmentpublicsectorandtaxes/publicsectorfinance/articles/newtreatmentofstudentloansinthepublicsectorfinancesandnationalaccounts/2018-12-17.

Pickard, J., Plimmer, G., & Rovnick, N. (2016, November 15). UK drawing up plans for infrastructure bonds for large projects: Chancellor Philip Hammond interested in proposals despite resistance. *Financial Times*.

Rocco, M., & Henderson, R. (2019, April 1). US Treasuries suffer largest sell-off since January. *Financial Times*.

Rogoff, K. (2019, May 31). How Central-Bank Independence Dies. *Project Syndicate*. Retrieved from https://www.project-syndicate.org/.

Ross Sorkin, A., Henriques, D. B., Andrews, E. L., & Nocera, J. (2008, October 1). As Credit Crisis Spiraled, Alarm Led to Action. *New York Times*.

Social Finance (2009). *Rethinking Finance for Social Outcomes*. London: Social Finance. Retrieved from https://www.socialfinance.org.uk/sites/default/files/publications/sib_report_web.pdf.

Thorpe, D. (2016, November 17). "Government infrastructure bonds can be 'excellent investments'." *WhatInvestment*. Retrieved from http://www.whatinvestment.co.uk/uk-government-infrastructure-bonds-excellent-investment.

Working Cities Challenge (n.d.) *Overview*. Retrieved from https://www.bostonfed.org/workingcities/about/index.htm.

14

THE FINANCIALIZATION OF EVERYDAY LIFE

Léna Pellandini-Simányi

Introduction

The term "financialization of daily life" was coined by Marxist sociologist Randy Martin in the identically titled book (Martin, 2002). The book's main focus was growing indebtedness; however, since its publication, the terms "financialization of daily life" and "financialization of everyday life" have inspired studies looking at subjects ranging from everyday investment to pensions, insurance, and the financialization of biological life itself. As it is often the case with terms that become buzzwords overnight, the financialization of everyday life literature is informed by different conceptual uses, theoretical traditions, and critical angles. This chapter provides an overview of this dynamic field.

The first part looks at *what is* the financialization of everyday life, contrasting three main uses of the term. The second part summarizes the socio-economic processes, associated with neoliberalism, that provide the common starting points of all approaches to the financialization of everyday life (FoEL thereafter). The third part, in turn, discusses the main theoretical traditions as part of which the FoEL has been studied: (1) Foucauldian governmentality approaches that undoubtedly had the biggest impact on the field; (2) (cultural) economic sociology in a Weberian and Zelizerian tradition, (3) social studies of finance; and (4) the sociological study of inequality. This part looks at the longer traditions as part of which FoEL arguments have been proposed in each area and maps the key debates. The fourth part discusses the critical angles used by each tradition. The chapter concludes by considering the ways in which the FoEL lens enables constructive criticism of contemporary finance.

What Is the Financialization of Daily/Everyday Life?

Natasha van der Zwan (2014), in her review of the financialization literature, identifies three uses of the term "financialization": financialization at the macro level of the economy, financialization at the meso level of firms, and finally, financialization at the micro level of households (see also Davis & Kim, 2015). To refer to the household level, contrary to Randy Martin's use of financialization of "daily" life—a term with little theoretical tradition—she uses the term financialization of "everyday life." This terminology connects the concept to longer traditions in cultural studies, anthropology, and sociology that considered the everyday as a site where larger (cultural, social, economic, and political) structures are reproduced through routines, but where they can also be challenged and changed (De Certeau, 1984; Slater, 2009; Trentmann, 2012). To invoke this connection, most current studies use the term financialization of *everyday life*, rather than financialization of daily life (see Hall, 2012; Lai, 2017b; Langley, 2008a; Pellandini-Simányi et al., 2015).

The term "financialization of everyday life" is used in three main senses in the literature. The first refers to businesses capitalizing on everyday activities, for example, by reselling home mortgage obligations as mortgage-backed securities (Aalbers, 2008; Hacker, 2004; Montgomerie, 2009). Recently, this use has been expanded to include "bio-financialization," referring to the financialization of biological life itself (Langley, 2019; Lilley & Papadopoulos, 2014). For example, an annuity-based pension plan offered specifically for smokers is a case of financialization of everyday life in this sense because it allows firms to capitalize the "morbidity and the residual vital capacities of life" (French & Kneale, 2012: 391).

The second use of the term "financialization of everyday life" refers to the financial *behavior* of households. Here the FoEL denotes households' use of financial products that either carry some form of risk, or enable the active management of risks. To capture this aspect, Lazarus and Luzzi (2015) introduce the distinction between "bankarization," referring to the use of basic financial services, such as a bank account, vs "financialization" referring to risk-bearing or risk-managing financial products. The financial product uses most widely analyzed, as indicators of FoEL in this sense are (1) investment products that can be acquired by ordinary people, such as stocks, mutual funds (Davis, 2008; Fligstein & Goldstein, 2015), and capital-funded pension plans (Davis, 2009; Dixon, 2008; Langley, 2004); (2) investing in real estate ("house flipping") (Engelen et al., 2010; Fligstein & Goldstein, 2015; Lai, 2016; Roscoe & Howorth, 2009); (3) credit products, such as credit card overdrafts, consumer loans, home equity, and mortgages (Fligstein & Goldstein, 2015; Gonzalez, 2015; Langley, 2008c; Martin, 2002); and (4) insurance products, in particular health, life, and property insurance (Lehtonen, 2017; Leyshon et al., 2004; McFall, 2014).

The third, and by far the most common use of the FoEL term (adopted in this chapter), refers to a cultural shift: the adoption of "financialized" subjectivities in everyday life. This use also considers financial practices, yet unlike the second approach, here these are analyzed from the point of view of the financial subjectivities that they purport or express. The cultural shift associated with the FoEL encompasses various aspects: that people seek and willingly embrace financial risk (Aalbers, 2008; Davis & Kim, 2015; Fligstein & Goldstein, 2015; Lai, 2017; Langley, 2007, 2008a; Martin, 2002); are open to taking credit, particularly if it is for funding new investment (Aalbers, 2008; Fligstein & Goldstein, 2015; Langley, 2008c; Martin, 2002); constantly look for opportunities to invest their money (Fligstein & Goldstein, 2015; Langley, 2008a; Martin, 2002); are happy to take control and assume individual responsibility for their future financial welfare (as opposed to, e.g., participating in state pension plans) (Davis, 2009; Davis & Kim, 2015; Fligstein & Goldstein, 2015; French & Kneale, 2009; Lai, 2017; Langley, 2008a; van der Zwan, 2014; Watson, 2009); engage in rational financial calculations—involving a calculative, rather than emotional stances and exercising self-discipline—may it be for investment or for managing revolving credit (Aalbers, 2008; Davis & Kim, 2015; Langley, 2008a); and that they consider financial choices easy and enjoyable (Arthur, 2012; Greenfield & Williams, 2007; Martin, 2002). Taken together, the adoption of these ideas amounts to a change in "outlook from being passive to proactive financial subjects [...] [and] to learn to think like financial economists in order to manage their consumption, investments and debts" (Fligstein & Goldstein, 2015: 7).

Beyond a more eager engagement with finance proper, this understanding of the FoEL is also used to describe the penetration of the financial, speculative logic in more and more fields of everyday life (e.g., Adkins, 2018; Martin, 2002). For example, when families assess a new house primarily from the point of view of its qualities as an investment rather than based on how it would function as a home, financial considerations dominate a decision connected to the home and family (Davis, 2009; Langley, 2008a; Martin, 2002). People factoring in governmental mortgage subsidies linked to the number of children in their child-bearing choices introduce financial rationality into an otherwise non-financial decision. When an insurance company charges lower fees for people who exercise, going to the gym—an otherwise non-financial activity—becomes infused with monetary value. Approached from a different angle, assessing people's worth and establishing one's self-worth based on financial success is another instance of the financial logic conquering everyday life in a similar sense (Martin, 2002).

As this brief overview of the different uses illustrates, the empirical phenomena classified under the "financialization of everyday life" heading are very diverse. They range from households entering "high finance" proper, for example, when ordinary people become day traders and active in the stock exchange; to cases that do not even involve "finance" in the traditional sense of the word—for example, when households factor in the future re-sale value of the house when purchasing their home.

Neoliberalism and the FoEL: Common Starting Points

Different theoretical traditions interrogate the FoEL from different angles, as we will discuss in the next section. However, common to all strands is that they consider the FoEL as related to a set of economic and political trends, which characterized the United States and the United Kingdom—the two countries where the FoEL arguments were originally developed—since the 1970s. These included, first and foremost, the expansion of neoliberalism, associated, at a general level, with submitting more and more areas of social life to a financial, market-based logic. This involved the retrenchment of the welfare state, the privatization of state services—for example, pensions, healthcare, education—and the replacement of collective, solidarity-based insurance schemes with voluntary, individual schemes. These changes brought about a "risk shift" (Hacker, 2008) from the state and institutions to the individual: the individual is expected to handle risks by making arrangements to secure against unemployment, illness, and even financial crises. These changes, which ultimately delegated increasing costs and responsibilities to the individual, were aggravated by stagnating real wages, particularly in the United States, growing inequalities and the rise of precarious work (Brenner et al., 2009; Crouch, 2009; Ferguson, 2010; Harvey, 2005; Kalleberg, 2009; Springer et al., 2016).

The FoEL literature considers the adoption of financialized subjectivities and the increasing use of financial products as the micro-level consequences of these macro-level changes. Indeed, the empirical phenomena analyzed by the FoEL field, discussed above, can be grouped into two main categories— investment and debt—which correspond to the two main ways in which households manage these macro changes.

First, these changes responsibilize households and compel them to make individual arrangements for their future financial welfare. The adoption of investorial-entrepreneurial subjectivities, such as entrepreneurial, risk-tolerant, self-responsible attitudes and the increasing use of investment and insurance products, is analyzed as part of these responsibilization processes.

Second, stagnating real wages and the growing cost of privatized services make households worse off, forcing them to take on credit to maintain their living standard. The adoption of lenient attitudes to debt and the increasing use of credit products are customarily analyzed in the FoEL literature as part of this compensation process. This argument draws heavily on Colin Crouch's (2009) thesis on "privatized Keynesianism." According to this thesis, whereas the original Keynesian economic policy proposed to increase state spending to boost the economy even at the expense of growing sovereign debt, in the new era of financialization, households themselves fund the spending boost, incurring private, rather than state debt. Growing household debt thus acts as a privatized form of the economic boost package. Recent studies (dal Maso, 2015; Fligstein & Goldstein, 2015; Fridman, 2017; Langley, 2007) connect the two areas, showing how investment is becoming positioned as a way out of poverty and a way to compensate for declining real wages.

While the trends seen as the main driving forces of the FoEL originated in the United Kingdom and the United States they also appeared, consistently with the variegated neoliberalism argument (Brenner et al., 2009), partially or fully, in different forms across the globe. Giulia del Maso's (2015) research on financialization in China shows similar tendencies even in a self-proclaimed socialist state. When Deng Xiaoping introduced economic reforms that cut the welfare state and dismantled the communist collective work units that provided secure revenue, the state actively encouraged ordinary people's participation in the stock market as a way to compensate for their decreasing income and to build an individual form of financial security (on China, see also Wang's chapter in this *Handbook*). These similar tendencies across different countries have made it possible for the FoEL research to provide a platform of dialog beyond the original US/UK context.

Financialization of Everyday Life: A Longue Durée View

It is worth noting here that while nearly all studies of the FoEL associate the emergence of financialized subjectivities with these relatively recent developments, the link is far from straightforward. As Brett Christophers (2015) points out, key features of the financialized subjectivities associated with the FoEL today have already been present in nineteenth and early twentieth centuries. Indeed, historical work on everyday forms of investment (e.g., Perrotta, 2004) and debt (e.g., Graeber, 2011) suggest an even longer history of the "financialized" mindset and of the enduring presence of the financial logic in non-financial realms.

For example, before the nineteenth century, clothes and furniture maintained their value over time, which allowed them to function simultaneously as a consumer good and as a form of saving, akin to houses today. People purchased them with an eye on their long-term resell value (McCracken, 1988; Nenadic, 1994), which, read through a FoEL lens, would count as an instance of the penetration of the financial logic into a non-financial realm. In fact, it is only due to the rise of cheap mass production and shorter fashion cycles that people *no longer* apply a calculative, investorial logic, but a purely hedonistic or aesthetic one to these goods today.

This means that in the past, everyday life may have been more, rather than less financialized. Against the financialization of everyday life being a brand-new phenomenon, these examples point to a longer genealogy. This does not mean that there is nothing new about contemporary forms of the FoEL; but that they may be better understood as shifts in the modalities and areas of financial logics that have cross-cut everyday life well before neoliberalism, rather than being brand-new phenomena.

Theoretical Frameworks and Angles of Critique

The previous part lumped together different, often competing theoretical approaches to give a general sense of the FoEL field. This section, in turn, discusses the differences between the academic traditions as part of which the FoEL has been analyzed.

Empirical topics are rarely considered interesting in their own right in social sciences, but they gather interest by shedding new light on long-standing theoretical debates. The topic of the financialization of everyday life is no different. This section looks at the four main academic debates in which the FoEL became interesting by shedding new light to them: (1) post-structuralist, Foucauldian approaches interested in forms of governance; (2) (cultural) economic sociology approaches in the Weberian and Zelizerian tradition interested in the growing rationalization of life and the mutually shaping relations between culture and the economy; (3) social studies of finance interested in the making of markets and calculative agencies; and (4) sociology approaches interested in inequality dynamics. Most current studies use a combination of the above approaches; however, to understand the field, it is important to separate analytically these traditions. The aim of this section is to give an overview, in the case of each of the four traditions, of (a) the analytical angles and key questions from which they examine the FoEL; (b) the main processes driving the FoEL, with particular attention paid to the role of subjectivity, identified by them; (c) key debates animating these fields; and (d) the normative angles from which they exert their criticism (see Table 14.1).

Marxist and Foucauldian Analysis: FoEL as a Mechanism of Governmentality

How finance shapes everyday life and how people make financial decisions are topics that have been studied by the social sciences for more than a century. Finance, behavioral economics (e.g., Kahneman & Tversky, 1979), and the positivist branch of consumer behavior (e.g., Raghubir & Das, 2010) have long been researching individual financial decision-making, inquiring into the modalities and conditions of rational financial choices. Anthropology has a long tradition of examining the mutually constitutive relations between economic transactions and social ties (e.g., Appadurai, 1986), with a vibrant contemporary research area dedicated to the anthropological study of money, debt, and credit (e.g., Mauer, 2006; Maurer et al., 2017). In sociology, Weber and Simmel paved the way for studies looking at the increasing rationalization of various areas of life in capitalist modernity, while Viviana Zelizer's (1997, 2005, 2011) work on the way the economy is intertwined with intimate relationships informed an entire subfield of economic sociology research.

All of these fields have a lot to say about how finance shapes everyday life. Research on the financialization of everyday life, however, did not emerge from these fields, but from Marxist sociology and from post-structuralist, Foucauldian-inspired political economy and economic geography. Initially, it entered into very little conversion with the above fields, even though its core concern, at least on the face of it, was the connection between finance and the everyday. The reason for this curious case is that initially, FoEL research was less interested in how financial decisions are actually made and in how they

Table 14.1 The Four Main Traditions Informing the FoEL Field

	Marxist and Foucauldian Analysis	(Cultural) Economic Sociology	Social Studies of Finance	Sociology of Inequality
Key research questions/ analytical angles	Why do people accept and willingly participate in neoliberalism? How are people governed in neoliberal regimes?	What happens to culture and social relations in a financialized capitalist society?	What are the concrete processes through which markets and the calculative *homo economicus* are assembled?	How does financialization affect social inequalities?
Main process of the FoEL	Discourses and practices of the state and organizations that assume and call forth financialized subjects	Financial logics interact with social and cultural logics (concepts: embeddedness, domestication, relational work)	Material devices and agencements that equip people to act rationally and in a calculative fashion	The different access and uses of financial products across social groups shape inequalities
Financial subjects	People are encouraged to adopt financialized subjectivities (although there is room for resistance)	Financial and non-financial subjectivities are intertwined	Financial subjectivity may arise through agencements, but people may act in a financialized manner even if they do not hold financialized subjectivities	Focus is on behavior; subjectivity is rarely addressed
Critical angle	Whether people are constrained in their ability to contest power structures that make them poorer (in Marxist analysis) or less autonomous (in Foucauldian analysis)	Whether finance erodes social ties and culture and provides less opportunities for real happiness	No single critical angle, but tools to unpack the operations of power and the making of inequalities	Whether inequalities and social exclusion increase

affect the everyday. Rather, it started as study of new forms of governmental mechanisms under neoliberalism. From this angle, financialized subjectivities became important not in their own right, but through the role they played in governmentality.

These first FoEL studies were primarily interested in how people are made to accept and willingly play their part in the large-scale neoliberalization processes described in the previous section. In the Marxist reading, the cultural shift associated with the financialization of everyday life serves as an ideology of neoliberalism. Neoliberalism needs subjects who take over tasks previously done by the state—and do so willingly, thereby maintaining the legitimacy of the system. According to this reading, by believing that finance is fun, thinking of their home as an asset, adopting risk-seeking and investorial attitudes, and experiencing the withdrawal of state services as a new freedom, people buy into neoliberalism, and become willing agents of financialization. Adopting more lenient attitudes to debt is interpreted in a similar way. Debt fills the gap left by declining/stagnating wages; thus, without debt, the problems of the system would become quickly apparent and would likely trigger opposition. Debt-tolerant attitudes thus have an ideological function: they allow the system to mask its faults and to maintain its legitimacy (Martin, 2002).

These points were central to Randy Martin's (2002) pioneering book, the *Financialization of Daily Life*. While the book did not contain references to Foucault, its focus on non-coercive, soft forms of power lent its themes to Foucauldian analysis, which has become the most prominent line of scholarly literature on the FoEL. Foucauldian scholars were interested in the FoEL as an instance of governmentality (Hillig, 2019; Knights, 1997; Langley, 2007, 2008b, 2008c, 2009; Langley & Leaver, 2012; Roscoe, 2015). Empirically, they focused on processes through which neoliberal subjects—investors, debtors, insurance subjects—exhibiting the financialized subjectivities discussed in the first section are produced. These processes include discourses, such as marketing, popular finance, and policy discourses (Greenfield & Williams, 2007; Langley, 2007; Martin, 2002; Mulcahy, 2017); and practices of particular institutions, such as credit scoring systems, new financial products, regulation itself (Arthur, 2012; Davis, 2009; Leyshon et al., 2004; Leyshon & Thrift, 1999; Martin, 2002), and financial literacy programs (Arthur, 2012; Clarke, 2015; Lazarus, 2016) that assume, address, and call forth people as entrepreneurial, risk-taking, responsible subjects.

The core question driving this inquiry is not an interest in subject formation per se, but in what these processes reveal about forms of governmental power under neoliberalism, a regime whose self-declared foundation is personal freedom (Burchell, 1996; Miller & Rose, 1990, 2008). The central argument is that the financialization of everyday life enables neoliberal governmentality, exerting power through self-governance (Aitken, 2007; Knights, 1997; Langley, 2006, 2007). As Langley (2008a: 91) explains:

> On the one hand, (neo)liberal government respects the formal freedom and autonomy of subjects. On the other hand, it governs within and through those independent actions by promoting the very disciplinary technologies deemed necessary for a successful autonomous life.

By engaging in the careful planning of risks and investments or in the rational management of debt obligations, people exercise the rational self-discipline required from them by neoliberal regimes. At the same time, as the quote above suggests, people experience these activities as means of achieving individual freedom, autonomy, and security, confirming the paradoxical logic of Foucault's argument of governance *through* freedom.

Looking at how people come to adopt these self-disciplining mechanisms, authors of this line of research (e.g., Fridman, 2017; Langley, 2019) have used Foucault's concept of "technologies of the self." The concept refers to people's "operations on their own bodies and souls, thoughts, conduct, and way of being" to reach specific versions of desired states, such as happiness of wisdom (Foucault, 1988b: 18). Applied to the terrain of financialization, successfully managing money, acquiring enough wealth to not having to work anymore, having successful investments, or being in control of one's finances are seen as essential for having a full and autonomous life, free from fears and limitations (Fridman, 2017; Langley, 2008a). This way, neoliberal governance operates through the technologies of the self; through the very practices through which people thrive to be a better person and to achieve an autonomous life.

While these analyses convincingly show that discourses and practices do assume and call forth self-governing neoliberal subjects, criticism of this line of research has pointed out that less empirical attention has been paid to understand if people themselves adopt these self-governing mechanisms (Langley, 2014; Pellandini-Simányi et al., 2015). Recent studies looking at actual subjects of financialization show a more nuanced and contradictory picture than the one pained by studies looking only at discourses. On the one hand, they do document elements of the self-governing mechanisms at work in everyday life. For example, Daniel Fridman's (2017) ethnographic work on financial self-help groups in New York and Santiago de Chile, organized around the work of best-seller financial guru Robert Kiyosaki's advice, provides one of the most in-depth analyses of how neoliberal ideals and self-governing mechanism are adopted. Fridman shows that developing financial and calculative skills and becoming an entrepreneurial-investorial subject are embedded in a broader moral project of transforming oneself to acquire personal freedom and control over one's life.

On the other hand, studies highlight contradictions, resistance, and different outcomes of financialization (Coppock, 2013; Di Feliciantonio, 2016; Fields, 2017; Hillig, 2019; Lai, 2017a). One source of resistance stems from the fact that governance discourses themselves are multiple, calling forth competing, often irreconcilable subject positions. For example, people are simultaneously expected to enterprise, to invest, to make arrangements for their pension, and to consume (Langley, 2007). Other sources include social movements, such as debt resistance and debt audits (Di Feliciantonio, 2016; Montgomerie & Tepe-Belfrage, 2019). Yet probably the most important source of resistance is everyday life itself; its existing moral economies, beliefs, and social relations, which subvert financialization in less visible, implicit ways. Hadas Weiss's (2015) study of Israeli pension insurance highlights one example of this invisible, yet widespread form of resistance to the self-governing responsibilization discourse. Insurers and regulators often complain of people's irrationality: the fact that they do not make complex, forward-looking calculations when choosing a financial product. She suggests that the root of this seeming irrationality is people's unwillingness to turn themselves into those responsible, calculative, self-governing subjects that insurers and regulators expect them to become. By using simple heuristics and expecting "to be protected insofar as they act responsibly as savers and citizens," people, even if unconsciously and unsuccessfully, try to resist the risks that they are forced to bear (Weiss, 2015: 506).

(Cultural) Economic Sociology: FoEL as a Mechanism of Cultural Dynamics

Foucauldian analysis of the FoEL is interested primarily in how subjects are governed under neoliberalism. However, to make their points on governmentality, authors of this line of research also made strong claims about how finance enters everyday life. By making these claims, they inadvertently stepped into the territory of the cultural theory branch of economic sociology, with a long tradition of research on how economic relations interact with subjectivities in everyday life. This led to an entry of these scholars into the FoEL field. Their analysis, however, was less interested in neoliberal governance, and more in how and to what extent people's subjectivities and relationships are "financialized."

People making economic calculations in their everyday life is not a recent phenomenon. Work on money, the economy, and everyday life, conducted at the intersection of cultural theory and economic sociology, originates in the nineteenth and early twentieth centuries with major sociologists dedicating some of their key texts to understanding how capitalism infuses everyday life with rationality and calculative logics. Weber's (1905/2003) *The Protestant Ethic and the Spirit of Capitalism* focused specifically on the emergence of the rational, calculative, entrepreneurial spirit, which he traced to the moral-religious legitimation of the pursuit of monetary gain by Protestantism. Simmel (1978/2004, 1991) wrote extensively on how the money economy transforms everyday life, infusing it with a calculative character and making social action increasingly calculated rather than emotional. Polanyi (1957) argued that the economy has been embedded in society and its institutions throughout history and analyzed how the market economy acted as a disembedding force, producing new subjectivities suited to its individualistic logic. Later work in cultural and economic sociology showed how market relations are intertwined with specific social relations (Zelizer, 2005, 2011).

These authors wrote about economic/capitalistic logics rather than about finance in most cases. However, as noted above, the FoEL literature does not only focus on finance, but encompasses a more broadly conceived financial logic in everyday life. This financial logic—understood as a calculative, rational, investorial stance—on closer look is a potentially new variant of the very same phenomena that these earlier studies analyzed. Cultural/economic sociology authors thus read FoEL texts as contributions to their own field of study and drew the much-needed connection between the contemporary stage of financialization of everyday life and its antecedents.

Read through the lens of cultural/economic sociology traditions, the argument that macro- and meso-level financialization leads to the "financialization" of subjectivities sounded rather crude. Even worse, it was easily read as a return to the account that saw finance and culture/society as separate, antagonistic realms—an account that Viviana Zelizer and her followers have spent decades refuting. This is why, initially, most of the engagement of (cultural) economic sociologists with the FoEL literature had been that of a critique. At the same time, the FoEL provided new impetus for economic sociologists to examine what, if anything, is new in the way ordinary people engage with contemporary finance. Illustratively, recent years have seen a growth of ethnographic, interview-based and survey research on "low finance."

In these works, the key question is not centered on governmentality but on how finance reshapes everyday culture, subjectivity, and relationships. A key line of research demonstrated that people do not simply adopt financial logics in their everyday life, let alone in such a way that these financial logics would overwrite other logics—such as logics of care of domestic relations, moral logics, and so on (Lai, 2017a). Rather, finance is "domesticated" (Pellandini-Simányi et al., 2015)—appropriated and reinterpreted according to existing subjectivities and social ties and re-articulated as part of moral economies. This is not a one-way process, however: through the interaction, subjectivities and social ties are also shifted into new directions (Čada & Ptáčková, 2017; Wilkis, 2015).

An even stronger critical point has been made by studies suggesting that the financial subjectivities described by the FoEL studies do not, or only partially, characterize people's subjectivities and financial behaviors, neither in core financialized countries like the United States and in the United Kingdom (Fligstein & Goldstein, 2015) nor outside of them (Gonzalez, 2015; Kutz, 2018; Lazarus, 2017; Naumanen & Ruonavaara, 2016; Toussaint & Elsinga, 2009).

At the same time, other studies demonstrated that in some contexts, people do become akin to the calculative, rational everyday economist described above (Fridman, 2017; Hillig, 2019; Roscoe, 2015). While these findings can be read in oppositional terms—that finance overwrites culture and social ties in these cases—what most of these studies show is that financialized subjectivities themselves rely on culture. Financialized subjectivities emerge through the moralization of financial success and skills (Fridman, 2017) and even the self-interested, atomistic relations observed, for instance, among lay traders, rely on "complex moral and reflexive sense-making processes" (Ailon, 2019: 927). This is where Max Weber's points meet the Foucauldian argument of investment being a technology of the self: in both cases, finance, rather than appearing as an antagonistic logic to culture, is translated into cultural-moral imperatives.

Social Studies of Finance: FoEL as a Mechanism of Marketization

The third theoretical context of the FoEL field is the social studies of finance. Unlike economic sociology that stressed the enduring embeddedness of the economy in society and culture and confronted economic models of rational action, this line of research started from the opposite assumption. It suggested that markets and calculative actors, described by economic textbooks, do exist—the question is what makes them possible. A key area of research, drawing on Austin's performativity theory, formulated as an explicit research program on marketization, focused on the making of the *homo economicus*, the rational, calculating subject of economics (Çalışkan & Callon, 2009, 2010; Callon, 2008, 1998b). This focus created a connection between the social studies of finance and the FoEL, with increasing dialog in recent years.

Unlike Foucauldian analysis and economic sociology approaches discussed above, the social studies of finance were primarily interested in how exactly markets and calculative, rational action are assembled in practice. Informed by Science and Technology Studies (STS) and Actor-Network Theory (ANT) (Callon, 1999; Latour, 2005), they stressed the role of non-human actors in the making of calculative agents. Callon's (1998a) influential introduction to the *Laws of the Markets* argued that for rational, calculative action to take place, people do not need to be rational and calculative. Rather, they need "prosthesis," material devices that enable, or even accomplish calculation and rational choices for them. Think of a mortgage comparison website: after answering a few basic question, the website's algorithm calculates the best choice for you. You are able to make a rational, calculative choice without being rational or able to perform the calculations yourself.

These processes differ in a key respect from the Foucauldian line of research. While there the question is how people willingly embrace neoliberal, calculative subjectivities, here the key point is that such willing embracement is not necessary. People can exhibit all the traits of the financialized subject, without possessing a conscious financialized subjectivity. This idea has been much more refined since the *Laws of the Markets* 1998 publication, with ample studies looking at the ways material market devices act as agencements—facilitators of the emergence of particular rational agents, often in the absence of rational subjectivities (e.g., Callon et al., 2007; Cochoy et al., 2017; McFall, 2014).

The entry of social studies of finance scholars into the FoEL debate enriched the field by shifting the focus to the practical, material making of financialized subjectivities and practices that were less developed in the Foucauldian and in the economic sociology frameworks discussed until now. Drawing on previous work on financial intermediation that showed how selling devices "agence" people to act according to particular rationalities and to assume risks (Vargha, 2011), STS-inspired FoEL research traced the role of financial devices in the making of financialized subjects and behaviors associated with the FoEL (Lai, 2016, 2017; Pellandini-Simányi et al., 2015). Others used the social studies of finance tools to better understand how Foucauldian governmentality works through devices and embodied experiences (Fridman, 2017; Lai, 2017). Similarly, economic sociologists incorporated these theoretical tools used to unpack the concrete, material assembly of moral economies, combining social, moral, and economic dimensions (Ailon, 2019; Lehtonen, 2017; Samec, 2016).

Sociology of Inequalities: FoEL as a Mechanism Deepening Inequality

The fourth and final key line of research in the FoEL field uses the term to understand changing patterns of inequalities. The key argument here is that financial markets became a new structuring force in society, reproducing, depending, or even reversing existing inequalities; and, at times, producing novel forms of inequalities. Most of this literature uses the term "financialization of everyday life" (or household financialization) in the sense of behavior (ownership of particular products and financial behaviors) or in the sense of firms financializing everyday activities, rather than to denote specific subjectivities (see the discussion of definitions of the FoEL above). Their starting point is that certain financial products and practices allow households to accumulate wealth, while others have the opposite effect. For example, predatory loans tend to lead to a debt trap, eating up one's assets and savings. In contrast, pension savings, low-cost mortgages, and lucrative investments allow for increasing one's wealth. Consequently, financial behaviors can be a vehicle both for social mobility and for decline, affecting social inequalities.

The central question of this line of research thus has been how differences in financial market participation affect social inequalities. While financialization has, in theory, the potential to reduce inequalities—which forms the basis of micro-credit programs and the financial inclusion agenda—the overwhelming majority of research documents its effects on deepening income, racial, and geographical inequalities (Fligstein & Goldstein, 2015; Kornrich & Hicks, 2015; Montgomerie, 2009; Tomaskovic-Devey & Lin, 2011; for a review of studies conducted in the United States, see Dwyer, 2018).

Research establishing these points has focused on two main, interrelated mechanisms. The first shows how differences in social groups' uses of financial products deepen inequalities. For example, Joanne Montgomerie (2009) studied the financialization of US households and showed that unsecured debt in the middle class produced inequalities between those participating in the credit boom and those who did not.

The second focuses on the different—more or less favorable—conditions under which different social groups get the same financial product, for example, a mortgage. This line of research is closely connected to the longer tradition of studies on discrimination in financial markets, such as red-lining. These studies showed how the poor, and applicants from neighborhoods inhabited by minorities, are granted more expensive loans than the rich are, or are being denied a loan altogether (Aalbers, 2011; Dwyer, 2018; Squires, 2004). Economic geography scholars (Dymski & Veitch, 1996; Leyshon et al., 2004, 2008), in turn, highlighted geographical inequalities: similarly to food deserts, poor areas with scarce financial services have no other option than to use the limited and pricy services of the existing offers. Extending the argument of finance's role in the deepening of inequalities, Fourcade and Healy argued that different scoring techniques, principally, credit scoring, have become a new structuring force of class, constituting a new form of "übercapital." Scoring sorts people into different classes and structures their life chances accordingly, be it through differently priced credit, insurance, or access to positions in the job market (Fourcade & Healy, 2013, 2017).

So far, this line of research entered into little dialog with the above approaches to the FoEL, despite the shared terminology of financialization. Important exceptions include Fourcade and Healy's (2013) and Fligstein and Goldstein's (2015). The latter examined both financial product use and subjectivities, treating them as different aspects of finance culture. It showed that in the United States, financialization benefited the upper income echelons of society, who embraced financialized mindsets and exploited new investment opportunities to increase their assets. By contrast, the lower income echelons of society used financialization as a defense strategy to combat declining income, by getting into debt.

Taking Stock: Critical Angles in the Financialization of Everyday Life Field

The previous section looked at the main analytical angles and debates in the four main traditions present in the FoEL field. This section revisits these four traditions through a different question, central to critical finance studies: to what extent and along which normative angles are studies of the financialization of everyday life field critical?

The only strand of the FoEL with a well-defined critical-normative angle is the last one, focused on inequalities. It evaluates financialization processes from the point of view of whether they deepen or even out inequalities—particularly income, racial, and gender inequalities. Other lines of research are also critical, yet their normative angles are less straightforward.

Growing inequalities are also central to the Marxist line of analysis of the FoEL (e.g., Martin, 2002), yet here the main basis of the criticism is that neoliberal policy makes the majority of the people worse off financially and exposes them to unprecedented financial risks. They are put in the peril of losing their home, ending up without a pension and healthcare and being unable to afford basic services. For Marxist analysts, the FoEL is problematic because it silences potentially dissenting voices by inviting people to regard these developments as advancements to their freedom.

A related critical angle applied to the FoEL suggests that neoliberalism delegates risks to the individual level that are systemic in nature and cannot be adequately handled at an individual level (e.g., Clarke, 2015). No matter how docile a neoliberal subject one becomes, he or she will still be ill-equipped to manage the risks posed by financial meltdown. According to this critique, by responsibilizing individuals, neoliberalism fails to address the root cause of systemic problems and is thus unable to solve them. Instead, it makes this failure appear as individual (moral) failings (Shamir, 2008).

Unlike some of the Marxist analyses, the Foucauldian line of critique does not assume powerful groups devising a specific ideology to purport their own interests (see Langley, 2019). While it is strongly critical tradition, its normative angle is difficult to pin down because it does not believe in an objective point of truth or justice from which particular arrangements can be criticized. It is nevertheless informed by a pursuit of liberation and autonomy. By showing how our conceptions of the self and happiness are shaped by powerful discourses, it invites us to think of alternative selves and forms of happiness, and of alternative social and economic arrangements (see also Borch's introductory chapter in this *Handbook*).

Similarly to Foucauldian studies, most (cultural) economic sociology research is critical, yet without an explicitly stated normative standpoint. Tentatively, I would propose that the implicit normative angle is informed by critical theory and older debates on the potentially corrosive effect of the economy on culture (Slater, 1997). The core concern is whether people are able to develop meaningful social relations and subjectivities that allow them to live meaningful lives; or, on the contrary, society becomes atomized and people's subjective lives becomes more and more impoverished.

While all above strands of the FoEL have an obvious critical orientation (even if its exact direction is sometimes unclear), the social studies of finance have often been accused of not being critical enough, providing merely descriptions (Mirowski & Nik-Khah, 2007; Winner, 1993). Albeit this is certainly the case with many social studies of finance, it is not inherent in its theoretical tools. These studies build on ANT, which, according to Latour's (2005) foundational book, *Reassembling the Social*, was originally meant to allow for a better understanding of how exactly power operates. Description is thus not the aim, but a tool for understanding and analyzing power for Latour. Similarly, Çalışkan and Callon (2010) stress that people have different calculative capacities, stemming from the different calculative devices that equip them. They consider these as a key source of domination and of power inequalities and suggest that the marketization research program is well suited to expose these dynamics. Callon's (2007) notion of "performation struggle," referring to the power struggle between competing socio-technical agencements, also makes the aspect of power evident in the creation of specific calculative agencies.

These theoretical possibilities for a critical social studies of finance are increasingly used by studies applying the ANT/STS/performativity toolbox to uncover and criticize hidden relations of power, particularly in combination with more openly critical approaches—such as Foucauldian analysis (e.g., Lai, 2017).

Conclusion

This chapter provided an overview of the different uses of the term "financialization of everyday life" and identified four theoretical traditions as part of which the FoEL emerged as an important analytical term. All four reflected on how meso- and macro-level financialization of the economy shapes and is shaped by the everyday life of households, yet focused on different questions. Foucauldian analysis has sought to understand mechanisms of neoliberal governance; economic sociology has focused on how everyday culture is being transformed; social studies of finance have been interested in the material-practical making of the *homo economicus*, while the fourth line analyzed the FoEL from the point of view of its impact on inequalities.

The chapter traced key debates across these diverse fields and showed how they entered into often critical, yet productive dialogs with each other through the FoEL field. Many of the current studies in the FoEL draw on more than one of these traditions. Indeed, probably the key attraction of the field is that it is an interdisciplinary space between political economists, economic geographers, sociologists, and cultural studies scholars.

The review's caveat is that it only included fields that explicitly use the concept of "financialization." For example, economic anthropology research on money, debt, and credit, or consumer culture theory scholarship on responsibilization and financial consumption was not covered here because they do not engage with the FoEL literature—even if they deal with topics clearly relevant for the FoEL.

In these closing remarks, I would like to reflect on the critical dimensions of the FoEL and to propose a few programmatic points. As discussed above, apart from studies looking at social inequalities, all lines of the FoEL research use a largely implicit critical angle. Further, nearly all studies stop at highlighting problems without proposing alternatives. There are several reasons for this. For the Foucauldian line of research, it is inherent in its post-structuralist, relativist theoretical stance. A further reason is the prevalent implicit assumption that those in power will not listen anyway, so it is pointless to propose solutions. Finally, proposing solutions is considered a somewhat lowly intellectual endeavor compared to theoretical analysis, and as such, it earns lower symbolic profits in academia, particularly in Europe, where the FoEL research has flourished the most. This does not only apply to concrete policy solutions, but even for offering broad outlines of how such a solution would look like.

At the same time, the 2007–2008 financial meltdown, growing household indebtedness, and collapsing pension systems put the topics addressed by the FoEL high on the policy agenda and made policy-makers more open to voices that are critical of standard economics. The assumption that policy-makers will not listen anyway is no longer true (even if it would be, all the more reason to talk louder). While most FoEL scholars are reluctant to offer explicit critique and steps toward a solution of the problems identified, other disciplines are not only willing, but are actively working on making their voices heard and be implemented by policy-makers, firms, and the media. Finance has a whole field dedicated to "household finance," marketing has a critical "marketing and public policy" branch, with active dialog with policy-maker and think tanks. Behavioral economists, testing and bringing mostly old sociology and social psychology theories into the attention of the wider public and policy, have become the go-to experts for policy-makers and companies. The FoEL field would have a lot to contribute to these policy-debates—a potential that so far has hardly been realized.

There are positive developments, however. For example, Ash and collaborators' (2018) research on payday loan apps involved policy-makers and used its findings to further both the academic and the policy debate. Recent research on financial citizenship aims to bring ordinary people's voices to bear on financial policy-making in central banks and debt policy, through collaborative projects (e.g., Riles, 2018; Wherry, 2019). However, much more could and should be done. For that, we need to work toward normative frameworks that allow us to take a stand even if we are using a deconstructivist relativist theory, and we need to change our own perception that proposing solutions somehow devalues our academic arguments.

Funding

This work was supported by the Swiss National Science Foundation grant "Driving forces of the financialization of everyday life" (grant number 171351).

References

Aalbers, M. B. (2008). "The financialization of home and the mortgage market crisis," *Competition & Change* 12(2): 148–166.

Aalbers, M. B. (2011). *Place, Exclusion and Mortgage Markets*. Malden, MA and Oxford: Blackwell.

Adkins L. (2018). *The Time of Money*. Stanford, CA: Stanford University Press.

Ailon, G. (2019). "'No one to trust': The cultural embedding of atomism in financial markets," *British Journal of Sociology* 70(3): 927–947.

Aitken R. (2007). *Performing Capital: Toward a Cultural Economy of Popular and Global Finance*. Basingstoke: Palgrave MacMillan.

Appadurai, A. (1986). "Introduction: Commodities and the politics of value," in A. Appadurai (ed.), *The Social Life of Things: Commodities in Cultural Perspective* (pp. 3–63). Cambridge: Cambridge University Press.

Arthur, C. (2012). *Financial Literacy Education: Neoliberalism, the Consumer and the Citizen.* Rotterdam: Sense.

Ash, J., Anderson, B., Gordon, R., & Langley, P. (2018). "Digital interface design and power: Friction, threshold, transition," *Environment and Planning D: Society and Space* 36(3): 1136–1153.

Brenner, N., Peck, J., & Theodore, N. (2009). "Variegated neoliberalisation: Geographies, modalities, pathways," *Global Networks* 10(2): 1–41.

Burchell, G. (1996). "Liberal government and techniques of the self," in A. Barry, T. Osborne, and N. Rose (eds.), *Foucault and Political Reason: Liberalism, Neo-Liberalism, and Rationalities of Government* (pp. 19–36). Chicago, IL: University of Chicago Press.

Čada, K., & Ptáčková, K. (2017). "The domestication of financial objects: Narrativisation, appropriation and affectivation," *Czech Sociological Review* 53(6): 857.

Çalışkan, K and Callon, M. (2009). "Economization, part 1: Shifting attention from the economy towards processes of economization," *Economy and Society* 38(3): 369–398.

Çalışkan, K., & Callon, M. (2010). "Economization, part 2: A research programme for the study of markets," *Economy and Society* 39(1): 1–32.

Callon, M. (1998a). "Introduction: The embeddedness of economic markets in economics," in M. Callon (ed.), *The Laws of the Markets.* Oxford and Malden, MA: Blackwell.

Callon, M. (1998b). *The Laws of the Markets.* Oxford and Malden, MA: Blackwell.

Callon, M. (1999). "Actor-network theory—The market test," *Sociological Review* 47(1): 181–195.

Callon, M. (2007). "What does it mean to say that economics is performative?" in D. MacKenzie, F. Muniesa, and L. Siu (eds.), *Do Economists Make Markets? On the Performativity of Economics* (pp. 311–357). Princeton, NJ: Princeton University Press.

Callon, M. (2008). "Economic markets and the rise of interactive agencements: From prosthetic agencies to habilitated agencies," in T. Pinch and R. Swedberg (eds.), *Living in a Material World: Economic Sociology Meets Science and Technology Studies* (pp. 29–56). Cambridge, MA and London: MIT Press.

Callon, M., Millo, Y., & Muniesa F. (2007). *Market Devices.* Malden, MA and Oxford: Blackwell Pub./The Sociological Review.

Christophers, B. (2015). "The limits to financialization," *Dialogues in Human Geography* 5(2): 183–200.

Clarke, C. (2015). "Learning to fail: Resilience and the empty promise of financial literacy education," *Consumption Markets & Culture* 18(3): 257–276.

Cochoy, F., Deville, J., & McFall, L. (2017). *Markets and the Arts of Attachment.* London: Routledge.

Coppock, S. (2013). "The everyday geographies of financialisation: Impacts, subjects and alternatives," *Regions, Economy and Society* 6(3): 479–500.

Crouch, C. (2009). "Privatised keynesianism: An unacknowledged policy regime," *The British Journal of Politics & International Relations* 11(3): 382–399.

Dal Maso, G. (2015). "The financialization rush: Responding to precarious labor and social security by investing in the Chinese stock market," *South Atlantic Quarterly* 114(1): 47–64.

Davis, G. F. (2008). "A new finance capitalism? Mutual funds and ownership re-concentration in the United States," *European Management Review* 5(1): 11–21.

Davis, G. F. (2009). *Managed by the Markets: How Finance Reshaped America.* New York, NY: Oxford University Press.

Davis, G. F., & Kim, S. (2015). "Financialization of the economy," *Annual Review of Sociology* 41: 203–221.

De Certeau, M. (1984). *The Practice of Everyday Life.* Berkeley: University of California Press.

Del Maso, G. (2015). "The financialization rush: Responding to precarious labor and social security by investing in the Chinese stock market," *South Atlantic Quarterly* 114(1): 47–64.

Di Feliciantonio, C. (2016). "Subjectification in times of indebtedness and neoliberal/ austerity urbanism," *Antipode* 48(5): 1206–1227.

Dixon, A. D. (2008). "The rise of pension fund capitalism in Europe: An unseen revolution?" *New Political Economy* 13(3): 249–270.

Dwyer, R. E. (2018). "Credit, debt, and inequality," *Annual Review of Sociology* 44: 237–261.

Dymski, G. A., & Veitch, J. M. (1996). "Financial transformation and the metropolis: Booms, busts, and banking in Los Angeles," *Environment and Planning A: Economy and Space* 28(7): 1233–1260.

Engelen, E., Konings, M., & Fernandez, R. (2010). "Geographies of financialization in disarray: The Dutch case in comparative perspective," *Economic Geography* 86(1): 53–73.

Ferguson, J. (2010). "The uses of neoliberalism," *Antipode* 41(s1): 166–184.

Fields, D. (2017). "Unwilling subjects of financialization," *International Journal of Urban and Regional Research* 41: 588–603.

Fligstein, N., & Goldstein, A. (2015). "The emergence of a finance culture in American households, 1989–2007," *Socio-Economic Review* 13(3): 575–601.

Foucault, M. (1988). "Technologies of the self," in L. Martin, H. Gutman, & P. Hulton (eds.), *A Seminar with Michel Foucault* (pp. 16–49). London: Tavistock.

Fourcade, M., & Healy, K. (2013). "Classification situations: Life-chances in the neoliberal era," *Accounting, Organizations, and Society* 38: 559–572.

Fourcade, M., & Healy, K. (2017). "Seeing like a market," *Socio-Economic Review* 15(1): 9–29.

French, S., & Kneale, J. (2009). "Excessive financialisation: Insuring lifestyles, enlivening subjects, and everyday spaces of biosocial excess," *Environment and Planning D: Society and Space* 27(6): 1030–1053.

French, S., & Kneale, J. (2012). "Speculating on careless lives: Annuitising the biofinancial subject," *Journal of Cultural Economy* 5(4): 391–406.

Fridman, D. (2017). *Freedom from Work: Embracing Financial Self-Help in the United States and Argentina*. Redwood City, CA: Stanford University Press.

Gonzalez, F. (2015). "Where are the consumers?: 'Real households' and the financialization of consumption," *Cultural Studies* 29(5–6): 781–806.

Graeber, D. (2011). *Debt: The First 5000 Years*. New York, NY: Melville House.

Greenfield, C., & Williams, P. (2007). "Financialization, finance rationality and the role of media in Australia," *Media Culture & Society* 29(3): 415–433.

Hacker, J. S. (2004). "Privatizing risk without privatizing the welfare state: The hidden politics of social policy retrenchment in the United States," *American Political Science Review* 98(2): 243–260.

Hacker, J. S. (2008). *The Great Risk Shift: The New Economic Insecurity and the Decline of the American Dream*. New York, NY and Oxford: Oxford University Press.

Hall, S. (2012). "Geographies of money and finance II: Financialization and financial subjects," *Progress in Human Geography* 36(3): 403–411.

Harvey, D. (2005). *A Brief History of Neoliberalism*. Oxford: Oxford University Press.

Hillig, A. (2019). "Everyday financialization: The case of UK households," *Environment and Planning A: Economy and Space*. Preprint at doi: 10.1177/0308518X19843920.

Kahneman, D., & Tversky, A. (1979). "Prospect theory: An analysis of decision under risk," *Econometrica* 47(2): 263–291.

Kalleberg, A. L. (2009). "Precarious work, insecure workers: Employment relations in transition," *American Sociological Review* 74 (1): 1–22.

Knights, D. (1997). "Governmentality and financial services: Welfare crises and the financially self-disciplined subject," in G. Morgan and D. Knights (eds.), *Regulation and Deregulation in European Financial Services* (pp. 216–236). Basingstoke: Palgrave Macmillan.

Kornrich, S., & Hicks, A. (2015). "The rise of finance: Causes and consequences of financialization," *Socio-Economic Review* 13(3): 411–415.

Kutz, W. (2018). "Financialization interrupted: Unwilling subjects of housing reform in Morocco," *City* 22(4): 568–583.

Lai, K. P. Y. (2016). "Financial advisors, financial ecologies and the variegated financialisation of everyday investors," *Transactions of the Institute of British Geographers* 41(1): 27–40.

Lai, K. P. Y. (2017a). "Unpacking financial subjectivities: Intimacies, governance and socioeconomic practices in financialisation," *Environment and Planning D* 35(5): 913–932.

Lai, K. P. Y. (2017b). "Financialisation of everyday life," in G. L. Clark, M. P. Feldmann, M. S. Gertler, and D. Wojcik (eds.), *New Oxford Handbook of Economic Geography*. Oxford: Oxford University Press.

Langley, P. (2004). "In the eye of the 'perfect storm': The final salary pension crisis and financialisation of Anglo-American capitalism," *New Political Economy* 9(4): 539–558.

Langley, P. (2006). "The making of investor subjects in Anglo-American pensions," *Environment and Planning D: Society and Space* 24: 919–934.

Langley, P. (2007). "Uncertain subjects of Anglo-American financialization," *Cultural Critique* 65(Fall): 67–91.

Langley, P. (2008a). *The Everyday Life of Global Finance: Saving and borrowing in Anglo-America.* Oxford: Oxford University Press.

Langley, P. (2008b). "Financialization and the consumer credit boom," *Competition & Change* 12(2): 133–147.

Langley, P. (2008c). "Sub-prime mortgage lending: A cultural economy," *Economy and Society* 37(4): 469–494.

Langley, P. (2009). "Consumer credit, self-discipline, and risk management," in G. L. Clark, A. D. Dixon and A. H. Monk (eds.), *Managing Financial Risks, From Global to Local* (pp. 282–302). Oxford: Oxford University Press.

Langley, P. (2014). "Consuming credit," *Consumption Markets & Culture* 17(5): 417–428.

Langley, P. (2019). "The financialization of life," in V. Zwan, P. Mader, and D. Mertens (eds.), *International Handbook of Financialization.* Abingdon: Routledge.

Langley, P., & Leaver, A. (2012). "Remaking retirement investors: Behavioural economics and occupational pension funds in the UK and USA," *Journal of Cultural Economy* 5(4): 473–488.

Latour, B. (2005). *Reassembling the Social: An Introduction to Actor-Network-Theory.* Oxford and New York, NY: Oxford University Press.

Lazarus, J. (2016). "The issue of financial literacy: Low finance between risk and morality," *Economic Sociology_The European Electronic Newsletter* 17(3): 27–34.

Lazarus, J. (2017). "About the universality of a concept. Is there a financialization of daily life in France?," *Civitas* 17(1): 26–42.

Lazarus, J., & Luzzi, M. (2015). "Les pratiques monétaires des ménages au prisme de la financiarisation," *Critique Internationale* 69(4): 9–16.

Lehtonen, T-K. (2017). "Domesticating insurance, financializing family lives: The case of private health insurance for children in Finland," *Cultural Studies* 31(5): 685–711.

Leyshon, A., Burton, D., & Knights, D. (2004). "Towards an ecology of retail financial services: understanding the persistence of door-to-door credit and insurance providers," *Environment and Planning A* 36(4): 625–645.

Leyshon, A., French, S., & Signoretta, P. (2008). "Financial exclusion and the geography of bank and building society branch closure in Britain," *Transactions of the Institute of British Geographers* 33(4): 447–465.

Leyshon, A., & Thrift, N. (1999). "Lists come alive: Electronic systems of knowledge and the rise of credit-scoring in retail banking," *Economy and Society* 28(3): 434–466.

Lilley, S., & Papadopoulos, D. (2014). "Material returns: Cultures of valuation, biofinancialisation and the autonomy of politics," *Sociology* 48(5): 972–988.

Martin, R. (2002). *Financialization of Daily Life*. Philadephia, PA: Temple University Press.

Mauer, B. (2006). "The anthropology of money," *Annual Review of Anthropology* 35: 15–36.

Maurer, B., Musaraj, S., & Small, L. (2017). *Money at the Margins: Global Perspectives on Technology, Financial Inclusion and Design*. New York, NY and Oxford: Berghahn.

McCracken, G. (1988). *Culture and Consumption: New Approaches to the Symbolic Character of Consumer Goods and Activities*. Bloomington: Indiana University Press.

McFall, L. (2014). *Devising Consumption: Cultural Economies of Insurance, Credit and Spending*. New York, NY and London: Routledge.

Miller, P., & Rose, N. (1990). "Governing economic life," *Economy and Society* 19(1): 1–31.

Miller, P., & Rose, N. (2008). *Governing the Present: Administering Economic, Social and Personal Life*. Cambridge: Polity.

Mirowski, P., & Nik-Khah, E. (2007). "Markets made flesh: Performativity, and a problem in science studies, augmented with consideration of the FCC auctions," in D. MacKenzie, F. Munies, and L. Siu (eds.), *Do Economists Make Markets? On the Performativity of Economics* (pp. 190–254). Princeton, NJ: Princeton University Press.

Montgomerie, J. (2009). "The pursuit of (past) happiness? Middle-class indebtedness and American financialisation," *New Political Economy* 14(1): 1–24.

Montgomerie, J., & Tepe-Belfrage, D. (2019). "Spaces of debt resistance and the contemporary politics of financialised capitalism," *Geoforum* 98: 309–317.

Mulcahy, N. (2017). "Entrepreneurial subjectivity and the political economy of daily life in the time of finance," *European Journal of Social Theory* 20(2): 216–235.

Naumanen, P., & Ruonavaara, H. (2016). "Why not cash out home equity? Reflections on the Finnish case," *Housing, Theory and Society* 33(2): 162–177.

Nenadic, S. (1994). "Middle-rank consumers and domestic culture in Edinburgh and Glasgow 1720–1840," *Past & Present* 145(1): 122–156.

Pellandini-Simányi, L., Hammer, F., & Vargha, Z. (2015). "The financialization of everyday life or the domestication of finance? How mortgages shape borrowers' temporal horizons, relationships and rationality in Hungary," *Cultural Studies* 5(6): 733–759.

Pellandini-Simányi, L., & Vargha, Z. (2019). "How risky debt became ordinary: A practice theoretical approach," *Journal of Consumer Culture* 20(2): 235–254.

Perrotta, C. (2004). *Consumption as an Investment: The Fear of Goods from Hesiod to Adam Smith*. London: Routledge.

Polanyi, K. (1957). *The Great Transformation: The Political and Economic Origins of Our Time*. Boston, MA: Beacon Press.

Raghubir, P., & Das, S. R. (2010). "The long and short of it: Why are stocks with shorter runs preferred?," *Journal of Consumer Research* 36(6): 964–982.

Riles, A. (2018). *Financial Citizenship: Experts, Publics, and the Politics of Central Banking*. Ithaca, NY; London: Cornell University Press.

Roscoe, P. (2015). "'Elephants can't gallop': Performativity, knowledge and power in the market for lay-investing," *Journal of Marketing Management* 31(1–2): 193–218.

Roscoe, P., & Howorth, C. (2009). "Identification through technical analysis: A study of charting and UK non-professional investors," *Accounting Organizations and Society* 34(2): 206–221.

Samec, T. (2016). "Performing housing debt attachments: Forming semi-financialised subjects," *Journal of Cultural Economy* 11(6): 549–564.

Shamir, R. (2008). "The age of responsibilization: On market-embedded morality," *Economy and Society* 37(1): 1–19.

Simmel, G. (1978/2004). *The Philosophy of Money*. London: Routledge.

Simmel, G. (1991). "Money in modern culture," *Theory, Culture & Society* 8: 17–31.

Slater, D. (1997). *Consumer Culture and Modernity*. Cambridge: Polity Press.

Slater, D. (2009). "The ethics of routine: Consciousness, tedium and value," in E. Shove, F. Trentmann, and R. Wilk (eds.), *Time, Consumption and Everyday Life: Practice, Materiality and Culture* (pp. 217–230). Oxford: Berg.

Springer, S., Birch, K., & MacLeavy, J. (2016). *Handbook of Neoliberalism*. London: Routledge.

Squires G. D. (2004). *Why the Poor Pay More: How to Stop Predatory Lending*. Wesport: Greenwood Publishing Group.

Tomaskovic-Devey, D., & Lin, K. H. (2011). "Income dynamics, economic rents, and the financialization of the U.S. economy," *American Sociological Review* 76(4): 538–559.

Toussaint, J., & Elsinga, M. (2009). "Exploring 'housing asset-based welfare'. Can the UK be held up as an example for Europe?," *Housing Studies* 24(5): 669–692.

Trentmann, F. (2012). "The politics of everyday life," in F. Trentmann (ed.), *The Oxford Handbook of the History of Consumption* (pp. 521–547). Oxford: Oxford University Press.

van der Zwan, N. (2014). "Making sense of financialization," *Socio-Economic Review* 12: 99–129.

Vargha, Z. (2011). "From long-term savings to instant mortgages: Financial demonstration and the role of interaction in markets," *Organization* 18(2): 215–235.

Watson, M. (2009). "Planning for a future of asset-based welfare? New labour, financialized economic agency and the housing market," *Planning, Practice and Research* 24(1): 41–56.

Weber, M. (2003). *The Protestant Ethic and the Spirit of Capitalism*. Mineola, NY: Dover Publications.

Weiss, H. (2015). "Financialization and its discontents: Israelis negotiating pensions," *American Anthropologis* 117(3): 506–518.

Wherry, F. F., Seefeldt, K. S., & Alvarez, A. S. (2019). *Credit Where It's Due: Rethinking Financial Citizenship*. New York: Russell Sage Foundation.

Wilkis, A. (2015). "The moral performativity of credit and debt in the slums of Buenos Aires," *Cultural Studies* 29(5–6): 760–780.

Winner, L. (1993). "Upon opening the black box and finding it empty: Social constructivism and the philosophy of technology," *Science Technology Human Values* 18(3): 362–378.

Zelizer, V. A. (1997). *The Social Meaning of Money: Pin Money, Paychecks, Poor Relief, and Other Currencies*. Princeton, NJ: Princeton University Press.

Zelizer, V. A. (2005). *The Purchase of Intimacy*. Princeton, NJ: Princeton University Press.

Zelizer, V. A. (2011). *Economic Lives: How Culture Shapes the Economy*. Princeton, NJ: Princeton University Press.

15

CONSUMER CREDIT AND CREDIT ASSESSMENT

José Ossandón

Introduction: A Pragmatic Sociology of Credit

Sociologist Viviana Zelizer (2010) explains that when social scientists approach financial issues—for instance money, insurance, or credit—they normally start from one of two opposing perspectives. The first perspective, which Zelizer labels "hostile worlds," assumes that finance and financial instruments are inherently contraposed to social life. The social scientist's job, from this position, is to describe and denounce how intimacy, morality, love, or religious belief are *threatened* and *contaminated* when finance expands to their domains. Zelizer names the second perspective as "nothing-but." From this point of view, the assumption is that financial life and life in other social domains, for instance, family, education, or art, respond to a similar logic. As neo-classical economists often assume, people will always act as expected in the model of the *homo economicus*, or, as sometimes assumed by sociologists, no matter the context, people are always involved in struggles for their relative position in "social fields." The perspective introduced in this chapter is different from these two approaches.

The point is certainly not to make a strawman of a huge amount of certainly valuable research. Zelizer's contraposition is useful to set a boundary of what the type of work presented here does not *attempt* to do. But, what does it do? This chapter introduces what I call a "pragmatic sociology of credit."[1] The main proposition is that this work covers a relatively novel area of empirical inquiry in sociology, and it develops a distinctive angle to the study of finance and society. This chapter's main aim is to formulate and illustrate this approach.

The object of study of a pragmatic sociology of credit are financial practices. These practices include the work of those whose work is normally seen as "technical" as well as the activities of those who use financial products as part of their everyday life. A pragmatic sociology of credit, in this sense, does not need—as research in the "social studies of finance" tradition often tends to do—to limit itself to the study of practitioners or "experts"—or, as anthropologists of household economies sometimes do, to limit itself to the *lay* uses of credit (Ossandón et al., 2018). In the last decade, ethnographic and descriptive studies of activities involving commercial products that target households and the set of actors and institutions involved in them have proliferated. The following pages do not need to explore all this literature in detail.[2] This chapter has a different goal. The aim is to illustrate how the analysis of practices of consumer credit opens a new type of question in the study of finance and society. The new question is how financial practices help to assemble new social formations. In order to do that, I have chosen to focus the review in this chapter to research on a particular type of practice, namely, credit assessment.

There are different reasons why credit assessment is a good pick. First, it is an operation that has received wide attention in recent sociological research. Second, this research crosses different sites and areas of the world. Third, credit assessment has been inspected not only as a relevant financial practice but also in terms of how it helps to produce new social configurations.

The argument unfolds in four main parts. In the first section, I explain what the label "pragmatic sociology" entails. The second section reviews recent sociological studies on consumer credit, with a focus on work on credit assessment. The third section discusses how the study of the practices of credit assessment provides access to the assembling, or knitting, of new social formations. The chapter closes with a brief discussion on how the label "critical studies of finance" and the work here introduced pair.

Pragmatic Sociology

The term "pragmatic sociology" marks, in this chapter, a particular sociological angle to the study of credit. Two aspects characterize this particular perspective, first, a specific object of study, and, second, a particular stance in relation to the social. These two elements, in turn, can be connected with two moments in sociology that are associated with the label pragmatic. While the former can be traced back to the sociology inspired by pragmatist philosophy developed in Chicago, the second aspect has been more clearly put forward in the context of what is today often referred to as "French pragmatic sociology."

Practices as the Object of Study

In its more traditional sense, for instance in the sociology developed in the tradition of Chicago by the likes of Hughes (1984) or Becker (2008), pragmatic sociology refers to a type of research that makes *how people do things*, their practices and techniques, their object of study. Unlike the "hostile worlds" perspective, to use Zelizer's distinction again, this approach does not assume a large divide between domains or spheres. From this point of view, practices conducted at sites such as banks, regulatory bodies, or rating agencies are as valuable an object for social research as activities carried out in people's households or in church. Unlike the "nothing but approach," pragmatic sociology does not start from the assumption that the analyst knows in advance the logics that these different practices follow. As Bowker and Leigh Star put it:

> The most radical turn taken by pragmatist philosophers such as Dewey and Bentley, and closely followed by Chicago School sociologists such as Thomas and Hughes, is perhaps the least understood. [...] What matters about an argument is who, under what conditions, takes it to be true. Carried over into sociology, Thomas used it (as Becker would some decades later) to argue against essentialism in examining so-called deviants or problem children. If as a social scientist you do not understand people's definition of a situation, you do not understand it at all. (Bowker & Star, 2000: 152)

It is in this context that notions such as those in Zelizer's "hostile worlds" approach can re-enter the analysis. A view that sees finance as polluting intimacy, for instance, does not merely work as a sociological approach, it might also be part of the repertoires those whose practices are studied use to define their own financial situations. This is precisely what Zelizer (2009) shows, for instance, in her studies of controversies regarding payments and pricing. People spend a great deal of time and energy delimiting when specific payments are or are not acceptable, setting moral and material boundaries to prevent the wrong money moving to the wrong places.

The Social as Outcome

As Bruno Latour (2005) explains, sociologists normally take the social as the *independent* variable. The most various outcomes—for instance, scientific theories, art styles or music tastes—are analyzed as fully or partially dependent upon social variables such as "cultural capital," "class domination," or "culture." This is in fact what the phrase "the social construction" of something normally implies. It is such an approach, in fact, which has characterized an important proportion of sociological studies of finance, in particular in the tradition of the "new economic sociology." Here the social, represented for instance in structural patterns of social networks, is studied as a variable that explains partially economic outcomes such as price volatility (Baker, 1984) or access to credit (Uzzi, 1999).

With ethnomethodology, Latour adds, a different approach to the social was initiated. From this perspective, it is not only sociologists who produce scientific categories and variables to explain and organize the social world, sociologists study also the work of constructing social categories. In Lucy Suchman's words:

> Within recent social science, in particular ethnomethodology this tra-
> dition [traditional approach in sociology] has been challenged through a
> conceptually simple but consequentially complex inversion of the status of
> categorization devices as analytical resources. Briefly, categorization has
> been taken up not just as a resource for analysts but as a part of their topic
> or subject matter, that is, as a fundamental device by which all members of
> any society constitute their social order. (Suchman, 1993: 181)

Sociologists, to use Garfinkel's (1967) terms, make "practical sociological reasoning" their object of analysis. In the context of what has been labeled as
"French pragmatic sociology" (Bénatouïl, 1999) the approach initiated with
ethnomethodology has been importantly expanded. For instance, in his study
on the formation of the category of the *Cadres*, Luc Boltanski (1984) shows how
the statistical classifications of labor categories are historically linked with the
formation of socially recognized classes and other forms of collective representation (see also, Boltanski & Thévenot, 2006; Thévenot, 1984). The study of
native forms of categorization is linked with the analysis of how new forms of
assembling collectives are made. Another author normally included under the
French Pragmatic Sociology label, Michel Callon (2007), initiated a related
development, which, in turn, is also inspired by the revision of political ideas
regarding issue formation and the constitution of "publics" that comes from
Dewey's pragmatist philosophy (Marres, 2007). Like Boltanski and colleagues,
Callon defends the importance of studying the emergence of new collectives.
His emphasis, however, is not on the performative effect of sociological classifications but on what he terms "the proliferation of the social" (Callon, 2007).[3]
From Callon's perspective, the sociological study of markets should not only
focus on how existing social formations are threatened but on how the practical
construction of markets and the knowledge and devices used in this process
might trigger the emergence of new collective formations.

To sum up, from a pragmatist perspective, social research does not study
the social construction of other *things*, it studies, instead, how *collectives* are
made up. This implies a particular understanding of the social. One way to
put it is that the social in this context encompasses the two different uses
of the term social solidarity in everyday language (Ossandón, 2014a). The
social can refer to collectives of actors that recognize each other and might
share emotional attachments and beliefs, like for instance in Callon's affected
groups. It can also refer to the notion of solidarity used in insurance, in the
sense of a collective whose members do not know each other but are connected because of their participation in statistically assembled populations,
like in an occupational category. The social is therefore not necessarily a

normatively positive adjective, in this context. The stance here is not to defend the social, nor to understand how solidarity explains something else (for instance, patterns of suicides in Durkheim's (1951) classic study nor how existing solidarity is threatened). These, of course, are relevant questions, but they relate to other agendas of research. Pragmatic sociology asks instead how *solid-ties*, in the form of new ways of grouping previously unconnected actors, are empirically assembled (Latour, 2005).

The Sociology of Credit Assessment

In 1986, photographer and art theorist Allan Sekula (1986) published an article titled "The body and the archive." It analyzed how a diverse array of issues (developments in statistics and new disciplines such as criminology, elements of evolutionary theory and eugenics, new modes of visualizations—such as the "normal curve" and the construction of archives to organize files and images) coalesced in the second half of the nineteenth century in new forms of classifying, surveilling, and predicting criminality. The interest of an artist in these otherwise quite technical developments has to do with the fact that Sekula understood that the history of photography is not only a history of artistic images. The history of photography is also about its applied developments, among those the criminal file archiving technology. The relation between sociology and consumer credit assessment and reporting is not that dissimilar.

Consumer credit takes many forms: informal lending in local stores, for instance, when shop owners keep a record of purchases to be paid at the end of the month; purchases in installments, when expensive or large items—for example, sewing machines, cars, or today a smart phone—are paid in monthly payments plus added fees and interests; credit cards and credit accounts issued in department stores and other large retailers such as supermarkets; revolving credit cards and loans in cash produced in banks or other financial agencies like "payday lenders." Sociological interest in the practices conducted in these institutions has paid special attention to "credit assessment": the work involved in valuing borrowers. Credit assessment is conducted in many ways. However, what credit assessment always shows is that—from its more basic (for instance, a shop owner's book) to its most sophisticated forms (for instance, automatized algorithmic decision systems that select potential customers of mass lenders like retail banks today)—it goes hand in hand with the production of archives and techniques to record and predict consumer behavior. To study consumer credit assessment is to study "*ethno-sociologies*," to paraphrase Garfinkel, i.e., practices, techniques, and expertise oriented at organizing, classifying, and predicting human behavior.

The following sections introduce recent sociological research inspecting credit assessment. The review is split into three parts: studies of quantitative credit evaluations, studies inspecting the construction of credit infrastructure, and studies of assessment in "other" forms of lending.

The Comparative Study of Credit Evaluation

French sociologist Jeanne Lazarus (2009) argues that credit assessment is a "test." Like a school exam, credit evaluation often involves a complicated combination of quantitative scales, face-to-face judgment, and socio-material instruments. Like school exams, too, it is a test with important consequences for those assessed. Obviously, the evaluation defines whether a customer can access or not a particular loan. In many cases, the credit limit and interest rates customers face are also variable. Like in insurance, more "risky" customers are often made to pay higher amounts for similar loans. In some places, like in the United States, a person's "credit score" does not only affect the access to lending, but is inscribed in other socially relevant evaluations, for instance in hiring decisions (Kiviat, 2017). It is in this sense that Fourcade and Healy (2013) speak of consumer credit as a case of what they term "classification situations," situations of sorting people out that, in turn, open or close future possibilities in other areas of social life. Recent research has made the test of consumer credit an object of sociological inquiry.

Alya Guseva and Akos Rona-Tas (2001) developed an early and influential sociological approach to credit evaluation. Based on information collected from documents and interviews with practitioners, they inspected how issuers of bank credit cards in different countries deal with the uncertainty of lending. Guseva and Rona-Tas compared the consolidated US credit card industry with the, at that time, newly developed Russian market. They found that the mode of sorting and selecting potential consumers varied. While in the United States the selection of new customers relied on statistical models and credit scores, in Russia credit cards were given mostly to specific individual customers, people that would be easy to track in case of default. The authors generalized this finding distinguishing two types of credit decisions: decisions in which the uncertainty of lending is *made* into a statistical risk and decisions in which uncertainty is processed as "personalized" trust. In later work, which compared consumer credit evaluation and risk assessment of firms and bonds, Rona-Tas and Hiss (2010) identified a third type of evaluation: credit screenings that are based on case-to-case formal evaluations. In this type of decisions, uncertainty reduction depends less on trust and statistical models, and more on the credit officers' expert judgment.

In the last decade, studies of consumer credit evaluation have been conducted in different countries. A particularly large number was carried out in France (see Lazarus & Lacan, 2018 for a detailed review). For instance, in their work Ducourant (2009) and Lazarus (2009) combined interviews and observations to inspect the specific interaction between customers and practitioners in institutions that lend money to consumers. Ducourant studied specialized credit lending institutions—for instance, Cetelem—and followed the process of automation of credit decisions. Lazarus analyzed banks, in particular how decisions to grant loans were justified. In the United Kingdom, Deville and

van der Velden (2015) developed a method to reconstruct how recently popular online payday lenders assess customers. What they did was to ask people
to use these companies' webpages and then analyzed the *cookies* used in the
webpages. What they found was that payday lenders' algorithmic assessments
collect quickly available information (for instance, the type of device used to
access their webpage, or, the location of the IP) to screen customers and define
their credit limits.

I can, finally, mention some of my work carried out in Chile (Ossandón,
2014b). Based on interviews with risk analysts in banks and department stores
that issue their own credit cards, I found two distinctive forms of justifying
statistically based credit decisions. Banks assessed the risk of their potential
customers mostly in terms of their available resources, what in the banking
industry is known as "collateral." They constructed scores that assigned quantitative values to variables like properties, level of education, jobs, and previous
defaults. Risk analysts in stores, however, relied heavily on a particular type of
behavioral scoring. Stores in Chile tend to grant cards to borrowers that would
have been deemed too risky for banks, but these customers will start with only
tiny credit limits. If the card is used and the debt associated with it is paid on
time, the credit limit will grow. "Sowing" is the term the risk managers I spoke
with used to refer to this particular management technique.

The Historic Sociology of the Credit Assessment Infrastructure

As Laferté (2010) points out, credit assessment has become something like the
economic counterpart of state identification. Each credit card, each account, is
tied to a file and the file is a record of all the card's transactions. Besides that,
lenders and credit bureaus routinely add extra information to these files, expecting that it will help future decisions. Like the police archive of the nineteenth
century discussed by Sekula, the consumer credit industry builds archives with
individualized and detailed files collecting records of millions of individuals.
A second area of research has inspected the work invested in building the consumer credit assessment data infrastructure.

Credit information is, like payment, a complex socio-technical infrastructure that connects multiple organizations and actors.[4] Actors include not only
those who work in companies that lend money, but also agents in specialized
firms providing software and systems to optimize decisions, credit bureaus, and
a variety of organizations involved in regulating financial information sharing.
Particularly relevant in this context is the work by Martha Poon (2009, 2011)
on the history of *Fair, Isaac & Company*. Poon shows how this firm transitioned
from providing specialized and customized engineering services—systems that
helped other firms to optimize credit decisions—to become the producer of
the main score in the US consumer credit industry. Besides providing an excellent detailed history, Poon's work is important because it shows how two

initially distant types of credit evaluations—those performed by consumer credit issuers, like banks, and the risk pricing of financial derivatives, in particular asset-backed securities, performed by investment banks and bond rating agencies—became empirically entangled. The FICO score, the score created by Fair Isaac Corporation, originally used to sum up the risk of specific customers, was inscribed into the formulas used to assess the risk of bonds that package the expected future streams of thousands of individual loans. The score became one of the infrastructural bridges that couple pre-crisis low and high finance.

Another issue that has been inspected is the consolidation of the profession of "the credit man." Like actuaries and accountants in Porter's (1996) influential account, Jeacle and Walsh (2002) showed how the practice of credit evaluation started to be associated with professional rules of conduct and with the inter-organizational proliferation of techniques of archiving, sorting, and screening customers. Other studies focus on the technological devices needed to process the increasing amount of data collected *in-house* by lenders, like banks and department stores, and the increasingly important credit bureaus. As Lauer (2018) documents in detail, the consolidation of technologies of sorting, standardizing, and classifying data—particularly, the Kardex file system in the early twentieth century and the computer database since the mid-twentieth century—are central components in the history of credit assessment. Lauer also shows how the data used changed in this process. Massive data collection in the pre-digital period was certainly shaped by its formats (the size of the file card, for instance), but it enabled collecting a much richer variety of information. For instance, newspaper articles and photos could simply be clipped to the file. The computerized apparatus can only process information that is formatted for databases. Data collection transformed from constructing individuals' files as rich as possible to constructing databases that assemble as many statistical sources as possible (for instance, combining Census and geo-referential data).

The studies just mentioned focus mostly on the United States. There is, however, work inspecting parallel developments in other countries. Orsi Husz (2020) has inspected the history behind Sweden becoming an exemplary case of a "cashless" society. Finally, in their more recent work, Rona-Tas and Guseva (2014) conducted an impressive comparative analysis based on the construction of detailed case studies of the institutionalization of payment and credit data sharing mechanisms in different post-socialist countries.

The Sociology of "Other" Forms of Credit Assessment

A trend often highlighted in the literature (Langley, 2008; Leyshon & Thrift, 1999; Marron, 2007) is that the assessment of consumer credit increasingly relies on the identification of statistical risks and algorithmic automated decision-making. But, as researchers in different countries have pointed out too, the quantification and automation of mass credit has not meant the disappearance of consumer lending that relies on other forms of evaluation. Degenshein (2017), for instance, observed the everyday operation of the very much present "pawn shops" in the city of Chicago, where consumer lending decisions are based on the specific item that is pawned. In his study of financial practices in a poor area of Buenos Aires in Argentina, Wilkis (2015) found retailers who evaluate their customers' creditworthiness by paying a visit to look, literally, at their home.

Studies, like those of Wilkis, which start from household financial activities, not only show that there is a plurality of forms of evaluations. These studies demonstrate too that the line between lending and borrowing, and accordingly between assessor and assesse, can be porous. For example, the people Wilkis (2015) studied normally used ROSCAS, rotating savings and credit associations.[5] This means that they normally shift back and forth the roles of borrower and lender. Accordingly, they collectively have to deal with the problem of assessment and to define who can or cannot join a group and the consequences in case someone does not follow the rules. The following quotation is from Müller's study of the practices of women with recent access to banking in Brazil:

> Whenever necessary, Elvira and other family members turn to her sister who, due to her regular widow's pension, has a bank credit limit higher than the others, as well as access to credit with lower interest rates through the payroll loan system. (Müller, 2014: 205)

Elvira's sister has a widow pension. This means that she has a source of regular income, which, in turn, makes her better assessed by banks or other consumer lenders. She has a better credit access and higher credit limit than her relatives. This also means that her relatives can, in certain situations, access her access to credit, making her a financial intermediary and a lender.

A similar dynamic became the main object of attention in a study my colleagues and I conducted on uses of department store cards by low-income families in Chile (Ossandón, 2017; Ossandón et al., 2018). In this context, most people have or have had access to department store credit cards and many had cards from several stores. However, their credit limit varied (depending on their scores and card payment behavior) and some do not have access to credit anymore because they couldn't repay past debts. Even though cards refer, and are legally bound, to single individuals, they were used in complex networks of cross lending. For example, teenagers would use their mom's card, someone would use their friend's, a husband his wife's, or a daughter-in-law her parents-in-law's. As the interviewees explained, lending of credit limit was not always easy. Users of cards in Chile do not only have to manage the debts.[6] They also have to learn to asses who should pay what (for instance, the administration fees), and, more generally, when it is accepted or not to use someone else's cards or to try to collect delayed payments.

More generally, what these different studies show is that these alternative forms of credit assessment are not simply archeological relics, remains of primitive forms of credit, but practices that grow together with automatized forms of credit assessment and payment.

How Does Credit Assessment Knit New Social Formations?

As Krippner put it recently: "Credit scores, like other actuarial techniques place individuals in groups constructed from a seemingly arbitrary confirmation of characteristics, rendering invisible structural categories such as race or gender that stratify access to resources in our societies" (Krippner, 2017: 10–11). As Krippner's historical analysis of the United States in the 1970s demonstrates, social controversies regarding credit have helped to make visible how existing forms of categorizing people, like race and gender stereotypes, are relevant at the moment of granting credit. What Krippner does not inspect is how credit assessment does not only hide the part played by existing social categories but it also produces new forms of segmentation. The previous section reviewed recent sociological literature that has studied the practices of credit assessment. This section hints at how the study of these practices provides access to the knitting of new social formations. I distinguish three different types of collectives: statistical populations that emerge with risk pooling in quantified credit evaluations; "bonds" that emerge with the connection between the assessment of consumer debt and aggregated financial instruments; and, commercial circuits.

As mentioned already, Lazarus (2009) saw credit evaluation as a test. She borrows this concept from Boltanski and Thévenot's (2006) study of different forms of attributing worth. As Lazarus points out, credit assessment does not simply imply the evaluation of individuals in relation to existing categories; assessing "creditworthiness" requires continuous categorizing and classification of cases, which, in turn, creates new forms of grouping people. This *creativity* results particularly manifest in quantified credit assessment. Since the 1970s, consumer credit evaluation increasingly resembles insurance and the way in which actuarial techniques construct statistical populations.[7] Private insurance and risk screening in consumer credit continuously search for new variables and correlations to use them to construct increasingly detailed and smaller pools. Lauer illustrates this point with the following example: "Experian, for instance, offers 'consumer classification solutions' that segments households into seventy-one distinct categories" (Lauer, 2018: 274). Quantification does not only allow massive data collection, but also allow new forms of connecting. Risk screening and assessment is not about setting a number, a score that cuts who can or cannot access credit, but about constructing matrixes with increasingly detailed categories. Each category defines groups with their own expected credit behavior. In these categorizations, credit cards and consumers are not taken as individuals, but rather as part of populations, and it is the collective behavior of this emergent population that risk management manages. It is in this context that the metaphor of "sowing" used by Chilean risk managers acquires full sense (Ossandón, 2014b). The files of credit cards are not isolated, but, like in a garden, connected, and these connections are not mere statistical abstractions, but technically knitted collectives, and the specific way in which these collectives are assembled have strong consequences for those that become connected with them. The study of the practices of assessment provides a privileged access to this process of social segmentation.

A second form of knitting collectives connects with the notion of "derivation." As Vincent Lépinay explains:

> A derivative product [...] creates value from the existing values of underlying assets, such as securities or indices. It is tied to outstanding products but simultaneously derives its specificity and its value from the lack of any prior integration between these carefully picked underlyings. (Lépinay, 2011: 224)

To understand derivatives, Lépinay uses the anthropological work on conversion between different units conducted by Jane Guyer in Nigeria. Derivation is the work in which financial practitioners construct products that connect heterogeneous goods while keeping a distance between the different layers that are assembled. Formulae, in this context, do not simply represent the value of underlying assets, these are also mechanisms that translate and assemble previously scattered elements. A similar process is what Poon's (2009) work shows for the case of consumer credit. Asset-backed securities are bonds that collect the future streams of receivable income, for instance, from mortgage or credit cards. Credit scores, in this context, Poon shows, are inscribed in the formulae used to assess these instruments. The risk of particular credit debts are assembled into pools of a different level of abstraction and magnitude. This process is not only relevant in terms of the technological infrastructure they entail and produce, but it is also relevant because it actually *bonds*—connects, ties, associates—the financial resources and future lives of thousands of households. In this sense, studies of credit assessment are also a unique entry point to how financial practices *bond* social formations.

Often credit and debt are seen as parasites, economic activities that are built and benefit from existing social and economic operations. Credit uses, captures, and many times exploits existing social dynamics (Elyachar, 2010). Less attention has been paid to formations that emerge with or after credit and debt. The networks of credit card lending in Chile are an example; here the parasite is parasitized so to say (Ossandón, 2017). A suitable concept for this emergent type of social formation is the notion of "commercial circuit" proposed by Zelizer. As Zelizer explains:

> To identify a circuit, look for the following elements:—a distinctive set of social relations among specific individuals;—shared economic activities carried on by means of those relations;—common accounting systems for evaluation of economic exchanges, for example, special

forms of monies;—shared meanings that people attach to their economic activities;—a well-defined boundary separating members of
the circuit from non-members, with some control over transactions
crossing the boundary. (Zelizer, 2010: 348)

Each network of credit card lending functions as a commercial circuit. These
collectives are embedded both in existing social relations and in the particular
calculative practices that made the credit limit of these cards vary. They are
also a new type of collective, with its norms of inclusion and exclusion and
accounting and its own special medium. The circuits are constructed from a
transformation of credit limit. People in Chile use the word *cupo*—a word that
can be translated as quota and also has a more material meaning relating to the
verb *caber*, to fit, like a space that needs to be filled—to refer to credit limit. The
circuits of card lending transform an abstract technical calculation, which is an
outcome of statistical analysis, into a tangible resource, a medium of a different
economy, an economy of the quota. A different type of derivation, it could be
said. The study of practices of card lending provides access to how these new
collectives are knitted.

Concluding Remarks: Is a Pragmatic Sociology of Credit *Critical*?

Two points summarize this chapter's intentions. First, it reviews pragmatic sociology, research which has made the practices of consumer credit its object of study.
Second, it shows that by studying consumer credit practices, pragmatic sociology
provides an angle that opens a new research agenda, how consumer credit knits
new collective formations. The example of credit assessment has been used in this
chapter to illustrate these points. The review focused on three types of practices:
studies of quantitative credit assessment, studies that inspect the construction
of credit data infrastructure, and studies of non-quantitative credit evaluations.
Likewise, each of these practices provides access to the study of three different
forms of knitting social formations: pooling populations, bonding derivatives,
and commercial circuits. To close, and in the context of this *Handbook*, it is worth
asking what kind of critical gesture a pragmatic sociology of credit entails. Is the
pragmatic sociology here presented critical? The answer is: it depends.

In a broad sense, the label "critical studies of finance" could be used to refer
to research that inspects finance from an alternative analytical angle. Critical
would be studies that do not follow the approaches that dominate the industry
and regulatory literature. The pragmatic sociology of credit presented here is
a critical approach, as it is clearly not influenced by approaches such as the
"principal-agent theory" or behavioral economics that dominate the expert
discussion on finance.

In a more specific sense, the adjective critical might refer to a particular
stance, a specific form of relating to the object of analysis. Critical are studies

that criticize finance, for instance, analyses that inspect how finance contaminates other areas of social life or how it generates exploitation. These are, of course, essential and important issues. Finance does certainly capture existing social dynamics, and it is full of unfair exploitation. The pragmatic sociology here presented, however, does not take such a stance. To use Boltanski and Thévenot's (1999) formulation, what is done here is closer to a sociology of critique than to a critical sociology, or in Latour's terms (2005), a sociology of associations rather than a sociology of the social. The stance taken here assumes that its main obligation is to describe the work of those involved and not to criticize what they do.

Critical, finally, could be seen as an angle that helps to see what has been kept hidden or invisible in previous research. It is in this sense, for instance, that feminist scholars critically approach the economy (Bear et al., 2015). Economics and sociological accounts of the economy tend to associate economy with a small fraction of economic life, for instance, what happens in firms' management and market trading. The point feminist scholars have made is that these accounts help to hide activities conducted elsewhere, for instance, at home or in outsourced places in "distant" countries, which are equally part of the economy. It is in a similar sense that the work presented here can be seen as critical. Social studies of finance have tended to equate finance with a minuscule part of finance. Financial are all practices of savings, lending, renting, and investing, but both economists and sociologists have tended to assimilate finance with what happens in the "financial industry," in commercial firms and on trading floors. The research presented here, a point that is developed further in Ossandón et al. (2020), is critical in the sense that it questions this assumption. It attempts to develop an angle of the study of finance that helps to make financial practices visible that tend to remain invisible and to develop methods to connect the practices to the different areas of financial life, which have remained analytically isolated.

Notes

1 This chapter re-uses and revises materials from two previous projects. It updates and continues a review of social studies literature on consumer credit published, in French, some time ago (Ossandón, 2012). I also use elements from a more ambitious collaboration with Joe Deville, Jeanne Lazarus, and Mariana Luzzi (the current version is Ossandón et al., 2020).
2 Elsewhere (Ossandón et al., 2020), my co-authors and I organized the large body of recent ethnographic literature in studies of seven different operations or bundles of practices (the notion of "bundle" comes from recent sociology of domestic practices, see for instance, Shove & Walker, 2014). The first bundle of activities is *attaching* and refers to the practices financial organizations conduct in order to attract customers and keep them affectively attached to their financial products. An example is Deville's (2015) study of the strategies and devices debt collectors use to keep their users connected to their debts. The second bundle is *budgeting*. It refers to how people represent and manage the accounts of their domestic financial economies. An example of research on budgeting is Halawa and Olcoń-Kubicka's (2018) study of how young couples in Poland

use spreadsheet software to represent and control, with varying success, their domestic expenses and debts. The third bundle of practices is *educating*. It refers to the work conducted at various governmental and non-governmental institutions to steer households' financial practices, as studied, for instance, in Lazarus's (2016) analysis of financial literacy programs in France. The third set of practices is *evaluating* and corresponds to activities and devices actors use to assess potential borrowers, for example, Guseva and Rona-Tas's (2001) study on credit cards' risk assessment. The fourth bundle of activities refers to the work of constructing the socio-material and socio-legal infrastructures that connect different types of financial institutions and actors, as shown, for instance, in Lauer's (2018) cultural history of credit registry in the United States. We call this set of activities *infrastructuring*. The fifth set of practices is *juggling,* which is the metaphor Villarreal and colleagues (2018) use in their ethnographic work, for instance, their analysis of financial domestic life of people that live on the border between Mexico and the United States, to name how people manage the transactions across multiple financial instruments, currencies, and types of debts and obligations. Finally, we term *politicizing*, activities involved in organizing political movements that respond to controversies regarding domestic finance. For instance, Luzzi's (2008) study of how *los ahorristas* (savers, bank account holders) became a strong political voice in the last financial crisis in Argentina.

3 An example is what Callon (2007) calls "affected groups." These are collectives that emerge in response to particular socio-technical controversies regarding marketization, for instance, an association whose members share having been affected by the pollution produced by a specific industrial commodity.

4 The growing payment literature (see Batiz-Lazo & Efthymiou, 2016) is not reviewed in this chapter, which focuses mostly on consumer credit. The two areas, as the studies by Husz and Guseva and Rona-Tas mentioned below show, have of course many elements in common. Payment and credit are complex social infrastructures and they are empirically entangled. For example, plastic cards are both instruments of credit and of payment. Some recent work in this context is asking similar questions to those asked here. Nelms et al. (2018), for instance, discuss how the social is conceptualized and configured with recent developments in the payment industry.

5 ROSCAS have been found in many countries in the world (Biggart, 2001). ROSCAS normally work like associations. For instance, an association can have ten members, where each member gives US$10 per week and every week a different member will take US$100. In this type of situation, members are both lenders and borrowers.

6 The following quotation is one example among many: "Luisa: Flor, my neighbor, was slow to pay, so now I don't lend them [cards] to her, because then she takes a long time to pay and I have to pay everything myself. And afterwards, they screw you over with the card" (cited in Ossandón et al., 2018: 209).

7 Other related literature not covered here, including research on social studies of insurance (for instance, Ewald, 1991; Lehtonen & Liukko, 2012; Ossandón, 2014a; Van Hoyweghen, 2010), has paid special attention to how actuarial techniques construct new forms of classifying and assembling the social.

References

Baker, W. E. (1984). "The social structure of a national securities market," *American Journal of Sociology* 89(4): 775–811.

Batiz-Lazo, B., & Efthymiou, L. (eds.). (2016). *The Book of Payments: Historical and Contemporary Views on the Cashless Society*. London: Springer.

Bear, L., Ho, K., Tsing, A., & Yanagisako, S. (2015, March 30). *Gens: A Feminist Manifesto for the Study of Capitalism.* Retrieved from https://culanth.org/fieldsights/652-gens-a-feminist-manifesto-for-the-study-of-capitalism.

Becker, H. S. (2008). *Tricks of the Trade: How to Think about Your Research While You're Doing It.* Chicago, IL: University of Chicago Press.

Bénatouïl, T. (1999). "A tale of two sociologies: The critical and the pragmatic stance in contemporary French sociology," *European Journal of Social Theory* 2(3): 379–396.

Biggart, N. (2001). "Banking on each other: The situational logic of rotating savings and credit associations," *Advances in Qualitative Organization Research* 3: 129–153.

Boltanski, L. (1984). "How a social group objectified itself: 'Cadres' in France, 1936–45," *Social Science Information* 23(3): 469–491.

Boltanski, L., & Thévenot, L. (1999). "The sociology of critical capacity," *European Journal of Social Theory* 2(3): 359–377.

Boltanski, L., & Thévenot, L. (2006). *On Justification: Economies of Worth.* Princeton, NJ: Princeton University Press.

Bowker, G. C., & Star, S. L. (2000). "Invisible mediators of action: Classification and the ubiquity of standards," *Mind, Culture, and Activity* 7(1–2): 147–163.

Callon, M. (2007). "An essay on the growing contribution of economic markets to the proliferation of the social," *Theory, Culture & Society* 24(7–8): 139–163.

Degenshein, A. (2017). "Strategies of valuation: Repertoires of worth at the financial margins," *Theory and Society* 46(5): 387–409.

Deville, J. (2015). *Lived Economies of Default: Consumer Credit, Debt Collection and the Capture of Affect.* London: Routledge.

Deville, J., & van der Velden, L. (2015). "Seeing the invisible algorithm: The practical politics of tracking the credit trackers," in L. Amoore and V. Piotukh (eds.) *Algorithmic Life: Calculative Devices in the Age of Big Data.* London: Routledge.

Ducourant, H. (2009). "Le crédit revolving, un succès populaire," *Sociétés Contemporaines* 4(76): 41–65.

Durkheim, E. (1951). *Suicide.* London: Routledge.

Elyachar, J. (2010). "Phatic labor, infrastructure, and the question of empowerment in Cairo," *American Ethnologist* 37(3): 452–464.

Ewald, F. (1991). "Insurance and risks," in G. Burchell and P. Miller (eds.) *The Foucault Effect: Studies in Governmentality* (pp. 197–210). London: Harvester Wheatsheaf.

Fourcade, M., & Healy, K. (2013). "Classification situations: Life-chances in the neoliberal era," *Accounting, Organizations and Society* 38(8): 559–572.

Garfinkel, H. (1967). *Studies in Ethnomethodology.* Cambridge: Polity Press.

Guseva, A., & Rona-Tas, A. (2001). "Uncertainty, risk, and trust: Russian and American credit card markets compared," *American Sociological Review* 66(5): 623–646.

Halawa, M., & Olcoń-Kubicka, M. (2018). "Digital householding: Calculating and moralizing domestic life through homemade spreadsheets," *Journal of Cultural Economy* 11(6): 514–534.

Hughes, E. C. (1984). *The Sociological Eye: Selected Papers.* Piscataway, NJ: Transaction Publishers.

Husz, O. (2020). "Money cards and identity cards: De-vicing consumer credit in postwar Sweden," *Journal of Cultural Economy*, online first, 1–20.

Jeacle, I., & Walsh, E. J. (2002). "From moral evaluation to rationalization: Accounting and the shifting technologies of credit," *Accounting, Organizations and Society* 27(8): 737–761.

Kiviat, B. (2017). "The art of deciding with data: Evidence from how employers translate credit reports into hiring decisions," *Socio-Economic Review* 17(2): 283–309.

Krippner, G. R. (2017). "Democracy of credit: Ownership and the politics of credit access in late twentieth-century America," *American Journal of Sociology* 123(1): 1–47.

Laferté, G. (2010). "L'identification économique," *Genèses* 79(2): 2–5.

Langley, P. (2008). *The Everyday Life of Global Finance: Saving and Borrowing in America.* Oxford: Oxford University Press.

Latour, B. (2005). *Reassembling the Social: An Introduction to Actor-Network-Theory.* Oxford: Oxford University Press.

Lauer, J. (2018). *Creditworthy: A History of Consumer Surveillance and Financial Identity in America.* New York, NY: Columbia University Press.

Lazarus, J. (2009). "L'épreuve du crédit," *Sociétés contemporaines* 4(76): 17–39.

Lazarus, J. (2016). "Gouverner les conduites par l'éducation financière," in S. Dubuisson-Quellier (ed.), *Gouverner les conduits* (pp. 98–128). Paris: Presses de Sciences Po.

Lazarus, J., & Lacan, L. (2018). "Toward a relational sociology of credit: An exploration of the French literature," *Socio-Economic Review*, 1–23.

Lehtonen, T., & Liukko, J. (2012). "The forms and limits of insurance solidarity," *Journal of Business Ethics* 103(S1): 33–44.

Lépinay, V. A. (2011). *Codes of Finance: Engineering Derivatives in a Global Bank.* Princeton, NJ: Princeton University Press.

Leyshon, A., & Thrift, N. (1999). "Lists come alive: Electronic systems of knowledge and the rise of credit-scoring in retail banking," *Economy and Society* 28(2): 434–466.

Luzzi, M. (2008). "La institución bancaria cuestionada. Actitudes y representaciones de los ahorristas frente a los bancos en el contexto de la crisis del 2001 en Argentina," *Revista Crítica en Desarrollo* 2: 173–190.

Marres, N. (2007). "The issues deserve more credit: Pragmatist contributions to the study of public involvement in controversy," *Social Studies of Science* 37(5): 759–780.

Marron, D. (2007). "'Lending by numbers': Credit scoring and the constitution of risk within American consumer credit," *Economy and Society* 36(1): 103–133.

Müller, L. (2014). "Negotiating debts and gifts: Financialization policies and the economic experiences of low-income social groups in Brazil," *Vibrant—Virtual Brazilian Anthropology* 11(1): 191–221.

Nelms, T. C., Maurer, B., Swartz, L., & Mainwaring, S. (2018). "Social payments: Innovation, trust, Bitcoin, and the sharing economy," *Theory, Culture & Society* 35(3): 13–33.

Ossandón, J. (2012). "Quand le crédit à la consommation classe les gens et les choses. Une revue de littérature et un programme de recherche," *Revue française de socio-economie* 9(1): 83–100.

Ossandón, J. (2014a). "Reassembling and cutting the social with health insurance," *Journal of Cultural Economy* 7(3): 291–307.

Ossandón, J. (2014b). "Sowing consumers in the garden of mass retailing in Chile," *Consumption Markets & Culture* 17(5): 429–447.

Ossandón, J. (2017). "My story has no strings attached: Credit cards, market devices and a stone guest," In F. Cochoy, J. Deville, and L. McFall (eds.), *Markets and the Arts of Attachment* (pp. 132–146). London: Routledge.

Ossandón, J., Ariztía, T., Barros, M., & Peralta, C. (2018). "Accounting in the margin: Financial ecologies in between big and small data," in B. Maurer, S. Musaraj, and I. Small (eds.), *Money at the Margins: Global Perspectives on Technology, Financial Inclusion, and Design* (pp. 200–219). New York, NY: Berghahn Books.

Ossandón, J., Deville, J., Lazarus, J., & Luzzi, M. (2020). "Financial oikonomization: the financial management and government of the household", submitted manuscript.

Poon, M. (2009). "From new deal institutions to capital markets: Commercial consumer risk scores and the making of subprime mortgage finance," *Accounting, Organizations and Society* 34(5): 654–674.

Poon, M. (2011). "Historicizing consumer credit risk calculations: The fair Isaac system of commercial scorecard manufacture, 1957–circa 1980," in B. Bátiz-Lazo, J. Carles Maixé-Altés, and P. Thomes (eds.) *Technological Innovation in Retail Finance: International Historical Perspectives* (pp. 221–245). New York, NY: Routledge.

Porter, T. M. (1996). *Trust in Numbers: The Pursuit of Objectivity in Science and Public Life.* Princeton, NJ: Princeton University Press.

Rona-Tas, A., & Guseva, A. (2014). *Plastic Money: Constructing Markets for Credit Cards in Eight Postcommunist Countries.* Stanford, CA: Stanford University Press.

Rona-Tas, A., & Hiss, S. (2010). "The role of ratings in the subprime mortgage crisis: The art of corporate and the science of consumer credit ratings," in M. Lounsbury and P. M. Hirsch (eds.), *Markets on Trial: The Economic Sociology of the U.S. Financial Crisis* (pp. 115–155). Bingley: Emerald Group Publishing.

Sekula, A. (1986). "The body and the archive," *October* 39(Winter): 3–64.

Shove, E., & Walker, G. (2014). "What is energy for? Social practice and energy demand," *Theory, Culture & Society* 31(5): 41–58.

Suchman, L. (1993). "Do categories have politics? The language/action perspective reconsidered," *Computer Supported Cooperative Work* 2(3): 177–190.

Thévenot, L. (1984). "Rules and implements: Investment in forms," *Social Science Information* 23(1): 1–45.

Uzzi, B. (1999). "Embeddedness in the making of financial capital: How social relations and networks benefit firms seeking financing," *American Sociological Review* 64(4): 481–505.

Van Hoyweghen, I. (2010). "Taming the wild life of genes by law? Genes reconfiguring solidarity in private insurance," *New Genetics and Society* 29(4): 431–455.

Villarreal, M., Guérin, I., & Kumar, K. S. S. (2018). "Carola and Saraswathi: Juggling wealth in India and Mexico," in B. Maurer, S. Musaraj, and I. Small (eds.), *Money at the Margins: Global Perspectives on Technology, Financial Inclusion, and Design* (pp. 128–149). New York, NY: Berghahn Books.

Wilkis, A. (2015). "The moral performativity of credit and debt in the slums of Buenos Aires," *Cultural Studies* 29(5–6): 760–780.

Zelizer, V. A. (2009). *The Purchase of Intimacy.* Princeton, NJ: Princeton University Press.

Zelizer, V. A. (2010). *Economic lives: How Culture Shapes the Economy.* Princeton, NJ: Princeton University Press.

16

CRITICAL FINANCIAL GEOGRAPHY

Julian Hartman and Mark Kear

Introduction

Financial relations are temporal relations. This goes almost without saying: interest is the time cost of money; debt is present consumption bought with future earnings; and most financial products exist to hedge risk and speculate on uncertain futures. Financial relations are spatial, too (Harker, 2017). While this statement may seem banal—of course all human relations occur in space— the ways that space matters for finance are rarely explicitly considered outside of Geography. Most scholarship on finance—critical or not—still assumes a pre-Einsteinian universe where space and time are independent, at least to the extent that one dimension, time, is clearly more "special" than the other when it comes to the operation of financial markets. The reduction of space to a passive container in which financial relations happen to unfold is perhaps not surprising given the reputation of financial markets as the most "autopoietic" of economic domains, where "whatever goes on in their environment matters only *indirectly* to them—namely, only as filtered through their own internal log- ics" (see Borch's introduction to this *Handbook*, emphasis added). In this chap- ter we (i) review some of the ways that geography and spatial context matter *directly* to finance and financial markets, (ii) argue for a co-constitutive under- standing of spatial, temporal, and financial relations (Christophers, 2013), and (iii) demonstrate the importance of a geographically informed critical financial studies by drawing on recent scholarship on the financialization of nature, cit- ies, and everyday life. The chapter concludes by outlining an empirical agenda for research on processes of bordering (Mezzadra & Neilson, 2013), financial borderscapes, and the objects that occupy these growing spaces.

Co-Production of Space and Finance

In the *Philosophy of Money*, Simmel devotes considerable attention to "distance" in his theorization of money, value, and economic activity. According to Simmel, economic value results from "establishing distance between the consuming subject and the object" of consumption, and "economic activity establishes distances and overcomes them" (Simmel, 2004: 62–72). While his conceptualization of "distance" is metaphorical, not necessarily spatial, and rarely discussed by geographers, Simmel's treatment of distance—measured absolutely, relatively, or perceptually—as constitutive of, rather than incidental to, economic activity, is as close to canon as it gets in economic geography. From this distance-centered perspective on exchange, money, and value, finance can be seen as an ever-expanding set of techniques and arrangements (loans, bonds, stocks, derivatives, insurance, securities, etc.) for coping with and closing distances between the near and far, the present and future, the trusted and doubted, the speculative and realized, the certain and uncertain—all of these together and more. Financial geography, then, at its most basic, is about how "distances" are established and overcome through flows of money, investment, credit, and debt; and, in turn, how flows of money, investment, credit, and debt create, reinforce, destabilize, overcome, and remake spatial relationships.

This co-constitutive conceptualization of the relation between space and finance is, we argue, one of the distinguishing features of "critical" approaches to financial geography. It is an approach to space and finance that draws on many sources, yet is most deeply rooted in the work of Marxist philosopher Henri Lefebvre, and more specifically his thesis that space, rather than a presocial surface or container in which things are made and history unfolds, is itself produced. For Lefebvre, "every society—and hence every mode of production [...] produces a space, its own space" (Lefebvre, 1991: 31). This constructivist ontology of space as a social product inseparable from its economic and historical context creates profound epistemological challenges. For geographers, it inaugurates, in Lefebvre's words, a shift from the study of "things in space to the production of space" (Lefebvre, 1991: 34). In other words, the task of the financial geographer is not merely to map and analyze the distribution of financial activities, centers, peripheries, networks, borders, exclusions, inclusions, etc., but to do so with the pieces arranged on a board that is alive, multiple, layered, intersecting, patterned, folded, contoured, cracked, and dynamic.[1] In the remainder of this chapter, we hope to show that attempting this maneuver is more than just an intellectual exercise. Rather, in keeping with the goals of this *Handbook*, attending to the co-constitutive entanglements of finance and geography contributes to the "critical" task of bringing financial markets "down to earth," to contextualize the overflows, excesses, and injustice they create in order to produce knowledge applicable to everyday life—knowledge that is of "practical usefulness in changing the world for the better" (Soja, 2000: xiv cited in the introduction to this *Handbook*).

The Qualities of Financial Space

The economic sociologist Viviana Zelizer is perhaps best known for challenging dominant conceptions of money as a "frightful leveler [that] hollows out the core of things their peculiarities their specific values and their uniqueness and incomparability" (Simmel, 2004: 14). Rather than reducing all quality to quantity, Zelizer showed how various cultural practices and social structures "mark the quality of money by institutionalizing controls, restrictions, and distinctions in the sources, uses, modes of allocation, and even the quantity of money" (Zelizer, 1989: 342). Nowhere is the quality of money more clearly marked than in space. This is very clearly the case with territorial currencies (Gilbert & Helleiner, 1999), but where money and capital flow easily across national boundaries, they do not flow outward in concentric rings from their sources to global peripheries like liquids poured on a flat surface. The physical space over which money and capital flow has friction; space is differentially smoothed by communications technologies, carved up by states, slowed and stemmed by regulations, risk and uncertainty, networked and contoured by personal, proprietary, and cultural connections, and so on. In sum, financial activity is impossible to decipher without attention to the seismically wild spaces of peaks, valleys, and deserts—created by hegemony and inter-state rivalries (Arrighi, 1994), colonialism and imperialism (Harvey, 2005), overaccumulation and crisis (Harvey, 2018; Smith, 2010), discourses of productiveness (Christophers, 2013), racism (Aalbers, 2014), policy (Immergluck, 2016; Rothstein, 2017; Walker, 2019), and practice(s) (Stenning et al., 2010), among myriad other. While attending to all the ways that geographers have sought to understand financial space is beyond the scope of this chapter, there are four features that we believe characterize "critical" approaches to the study of financial space.

Before outlining these, it is important to observe that there are no well-defined borders at the edges of the constellation of critical financial geography, or even critical geography more generally (Raju & Jeffrey, 2016); it is a (post-disciplinary) subfield composed of bodies of work that overlap with other approaches and disciplines. Such heterogeneity has sometimes occasioned agonized reflection over how to build a "critical" alternative to hegemonic institutional thought and whether that is the role of critique in the first place (see Amin & Thrift, 2005, 2007; Harvey, 2006; Smith, 2005 for one strand of this debate). Regardless, there is some practical agreement that critical geography operates within broad values of political engagement, power-critique, and reflexivity.

First, as already described, critical financial geography is reflexive, i.e., space is understood as both produced by financial relations and productive of them. Second, critical approaches to financial geography work to understand the co-constitution of finance and space by contextualizing these relations within macro-structural dynamics: capital accumulation, colonialism, white supremacy, hegemony, etc. Third, the relations through which finance produces space and space produces finance are not restricted to "the social" (Latour, 2007)—space and finance are entangled within arrangements of heterogeneous elements, both human and non-human, from equations and customs to endangered species and carbon credits (see "Geographies of 'Financialization'"). Finally, critical approaches to financial geography are often motivated by an explicit interest in the social and environmental justice implications of finance's operations, i.e., its role in distributing resources unevenly across race, class, gender, and generations, as well as its entanglements with processes of exploitation, domination, and subjectivization.

In the next section, we review recent efforts to map and taxonomize financial space, before considering how these uneven geographies are shaped by law.

Finance Is Uneven

No matter how finance's presence is measured—profits, assets, firms and institutions, transactions, debt, etc.—there is a tendency for financial activity to concentrate in particular places, flow away from some, and bypass others entirely; financial space is lumpy, pocked, and covered in spikes. In this way, financial activity reflects broader tendencies in the capitalist space economy to inundate areas deemed profitable with capital until they no longer are, while simultaneously eschewing and "underdeveloping" others. This "territorial see-saw" (Smith, 2010) can be observed, to varying degrees, at every level of scalar resolution, from the level of the city to the nation and the globe.

Critical accounts of financial unevenness often go beyond such empirical observations, linking simple "spatial facts"—where financial centers are located, and how they are connected—to broader historico-geographic dynamics of hegemony, colonialism, imperialism, and capitalism. Harvey (e.g. 2018/1982) has perhaps done more than anyone to initiate these conversations through his efforts to spatialize Marxist political economy. The many scholars who have contributed substantially to the development of critical approaches to the geography of financial centers have been influenced by a wide variety of literatures, including regulation theory, world systems theory, global production networks, and others. A common thread in many critical geographical characterizations of finance portrays finance as a moment in the circulation of capital. Whether finance is characterized as a mechanism for the equalization of the rate of profit as interest-bearing capital flows "in response to profit rate differentials" (Harvey, 2010/1982: 270), or the "sign of autumn" of a hegemonic capitalist power reallocating rents instead of producing goods (Arrighi, 1994), finance capital is seen as essentially relational: the manner in which capital relates to itself.

While on the surface, such formulations sound similar to theories of perfect markets which predict that money will flow like water to capital-scarce locales, it is important to note the role of various countertendencies in the geography of financial centers. For example, because opportunities and knowledge of risk are largely constructed in particular centers, money flows not on the basis of universal knowledge but rather local knowledge of the global economy that purports to be universal. Determined by cultural factors and pre-existing connections, money pools unevenly around nodes of knowledge agglomeration and financial economies of scale, flowing in torrents from one imagined opportunity to another rather than spreading out on a flat surface, less like water than like mercury (Clark, 2005; Hall, 2011).

Building on the foundational work of Sassen (1991), Friedmann (1986), and others, scholars have begun to more explicitly connect finance with the production of world city (Meeteren & Bassens, 2016) and global production networks (Coe et al., 2014). In this vein, Bassens and van Meeteren (2015) connect the World City Network (WCN) and its advanced producer services (APS) to scholarship on international financial centers (IFCs). They argue that APS—including services like accounting, law, and management consulting—mediate the relationship between financial and industrial capital. While all capitalist investment is ultimately speculative, APS firms construct and evaluate investment opportunities, turning uncertainty into risk and charging for information on relatively secure investment opportunities. Thus, a wider archipelago of global cities draws rent from constructing investments for and providing services to a more limited number of IFCs. The "island nodes" of the world city archipelago have each been shaped by unique historical, political, and geographical factors which determine their specializations and comparative advantages within the archipelago (Dörry, 2015; Jacobs et al., 2010). For example, Hong Kong, Shanghai, and Beijing function as centers of offshore finance, commercial activity, and political activity respectively (Lai, 2011); the Globalization and World Cities Network (GaWC) and other researchers have done substantial work in cataloging and ranking these world cities (Taylor et al., 2014).

Tax havens are a category of financial center that has received special attention recently, in part due to high-profile leaks (e.g., the Panama Papers and Paradise Papers) that have exposed the scale and scope of the practices used by corporations and the wealthy to shelter their assets from taxes, creditors, and other liabilities. In his recent review of work on financial geographies of tax, Aalbers, drawing on the work of several authors, offers a conceptual schema of overlapping networks, each comprised of a central node—a financial "supercenter," such as London or New York, that facilitates tax avoidance—that is surrounded by "inner" and "outer rings" composed of traditional tax havens, oftentimes island nations, as well as independent jurisdictions through which large volumes of capital flow. These latter centers often have legal systems which facilitate capital flows, for example former British colonies, or subnational jurisdictions like Delaware with special provisions encouraging corporate location (Aalbers, 2018).

Spatializing the "Code of Capital"

Underlying the present global geography of financial centers is law. Indeed, the broader role of law in the production of financial space has developed into a subfield of its own—legal financial geography (Ashton, 2014; Kay, 2016; Knuth & Potts, 2016; Valverde, 2009). From this subfield has emerged three provocative maxims (Potts, 2019): law constitutes all finance (Pistor, 2019); law is always spatial (Blomley, 1989); and, law is always anchored in state power (Potts, 2019).[2] In this section, we expand on each of these maxims before combining them to show how the global reterritorialization of finance and law are related to processes of "financialization."

In *The Code of Capital* (2019), Pistor contends that "capital is made of two ingredients: assets and the legal code." Just about anything can be an asset according to Pistor—an object, claim, skill, or idea. But, unlike land and nature, which produce something regardless of how they are treated in law, financial instruments exist only in law (Pistor, 2019: 3). In other words, law (e.g., contract, property, collateral) constitutes all finance (Potts, 2019). As Knuth and Potts put it, because financial property is comparatively removed from physical constraints, it "is close to a purely socio-legal construct" (2016: 461). Importantly, this does not mean that the financial "world is flat" (Friedman, 2005) and materially unconstrained, rather it means that "all financial processes are constituted in and through differentiated, overlapping, often competing, and frequently contradictory geographies of legal space" (Knuth & Potts, 2016: 458).

It follows from this relationship between law and finance that the characteristics of financial accumulation in a given time and place will articulate with and reflect the legal regimes established to protect intangible forms of property in those territories. Moreover, to the extent that the law has many sources (e.g., custom, common law, civil law, religious law) and is actively (re)constructed through the "the difficult accommodation of [...] tensions between power and reason, science and craft, and tradition and progress" (Dagan, 2013: 187), we should expect global and national legal landscapes to be highly differentiated and variegated.

Put more succinctly, law is always spatial (Blomley, 1989; Valverde, 2009). Bringing legal order to the world necessarily entails the construction of legal spaces (see Blomley & Bakan, 1992). Legal boundaries are spatially delimited, for example, by differentiating public and private space (Mitchell & Staeheli, 2006), defining governmental jurisdictions, and zones of personal mobility. Moreover, legal concepts from crime to property, contract, statute, and so on, all construct and order space—especially financial space—in various ways. These legal spaces promote, in often counterintuitive ways, the formation of distinct financial geographies. This can be seen in how prohibitions on *riba* (interest) in Islamic law have created a global ecosystem of *shari'a* compliant financial services (Pollard & Samers, 2007; Rudnyckyj, 2018). It can also be seen in the way that differences in consumer protection law affect the types of credit available in different places, and, within those places, who has access to loans and at what cost—not to mention redlining, greenlining, predatory lending, and many other inclusionary and exclusionary financial practices (Caplovitz, 1968; Dymski, 2006; Graves, 2003; Leyshon & Thrift, 1995; Pollard, 1996).

Behind the legal-financial-spatial order is the state and sovereignty. But the way that law, state power, and territory map onto each other no longer matches Westphalian congruence between financial systems and territorial nation states (if it ever did). Some (non-geographers) have gone so far as to suggest the obsolescence of territorial sovereignty or the de-territorialization/de-spatialization of sovereignty. While it is true that today many financial contracts "have little or no significant connection to the jurisdictions that govern them" (Potts, 2016), this "de-territorialization" has occurred unevenly. What has occurred is better described as a reterritorialization in which particular states structure financial activity beyond their borders.

As Potts (2016, 2017a) has shown in her work on sovereign debt, "vulture" funds,[3] and choice of law contracts, reterritorialization has "reduc[ed] the authority of most countries over their own economic decisions while expanding the judicial reach of a few" (Potts, 2017b: 2), especially certain jurisdictions in the United States (e.g., New York and Delaware) and the United Kingdom. Focusing on the Argentine sovereign debt crisis, Potts provides a detailed account of how purchasers of distressed Argentinian debt were able to sue the Argentinian government in a New York court, forcing this sovereign nation to show up in New York and abide by the rulings of a foreign judge. The legal device that ties this strange financial geography together is the choice of law contract. A choice of law clause in a contract specifies that any dispute arising among counterparties be resolved in accordance with the law of a particular jurisdiction. Potts shows that the jurisdictions chosen by counterparties, especially with financial contracts, increasingly have little to do with the geographic origins of the parties themselves, having more to do with the geoeconomic power and financial hegemony of certain jurisdictions and their friendliness to corporations and creditors. Why would a sovereign nation agree to have disputes settled in New York? Why would a sovereign nation show up to court in New York? Because, within the current geopolitical order, it, in some sense, "needs" Wall Street, and to eschew Wall Street would expose it to painful capital market discipline with harsh consequences for politicians and people's livelihoods. While this dynamic nominally extends the reach of capital-friendly jurisdictions like New York, it also constrains them. In order to fend off competition from Singapore, Hong Kong, and London, the "NYSBA [the New York State Bar Association] [urges] all interested parties to promote New York City as the best choice for governing law and forum" (Potts, 2016: 535). If legal conditions become unfavorable, companies can switch jurisdictions.

We can draw two extrapolations from Pott's work on choice of law in sovereign debt markets: (i) that law is anchored in state power (as already discussed), but also, (ii) that in an era when "financial motives, financial markets, financial actors and financial institutions" (Epstein, 2005: 3) are ascendant in the operation of the domestic and international economies, certain states and their laws bend financial space much more than others, and they are doing so in ways that confound traditional conceptions of how the state, sovereignty, territory, law, and the economy overlap. The law is far from the only terrain where "financialization" is reshaping the geographies investment, speculation, credit, debt, and so on. This topic of how geographers have responded to the "rise of finance" and deployed the concept of financialization is the focus of the next section.

Geographies of "Financialization"

In 2010, Brenner, Peck and Theodore described neoliberalism as "rascal concept" for being "promiscuously pervasive, yet inconsistently defined, empirically imprecise and frequently contested" (2010: 182, 184). A decade later, the label adheres just as well to financialization. This "rascal" status is among the many reasons that we have decided to sidestep debates about financialization and its limits (these are better dealt with elsewhere, see Christophers, 2015; see also the chapter by Bryan et al. in this *Handbook*), and instead provide brief reflections on how geographers have explored the growing role financial instruments, logics, and practices in shaping three areas within the ever-growing body of work on the "financialization of X" (Davis, 2018; Kear, 2015): specifically, nature, cities, and daily life/social reproduction.

The Financialization of Nature

Geographers working within a political ecology tradition, influenced especially by Marx and Polanyi (1944), have long been interested in the economic metabolization of nature (Ekers & Prudham, 2017; Swyngedouw, 2006), and the social and political struggles that arise when land and nature are regarded as "real" as opposed to "fictitious" commodities (see Mann, 2006 for a critique; Polanyi, 1944; Prudham, 2012). In other words, critical geographers have been concerned with the social construction of environmental problems as matters of market failure (Demeritt, 2002), and the impacts (both social and ecological) of efforts to address these "failures" through the marketization (McAfee, 2012) and commodification (Bakker, 2005; Castree, 2003; Heynen et al., 2007; Smith, 2007) of unruly natures. Increasingly, the marketization and commodification of nature has involved some degree of financial engineering.

Over the course of more than a decade of scholarship on the production of "neoliberal natures" (Bigger et al., 2018), geographers have devoted increasing attention to the role of the financial sector. Financialization "makes sense" in an era when, to paraphrase McAfee (1999), to save nature, you have to sell it; after all, biodiversity (McAfee, 2016), carbon (Bigger, 2015), ecosystems (Osborne, 2016), catastrophes (Johnson, 2013), and so on, cannot be bought and sold like other commodities, and therefore bringing nature to market is a technological achievement that recruits myriad financial actors as well as liquidity from global capital markets. This opening of environmental conservation as a frontier of speculative investment requires a rearticulation of the environment in terms of finance, involving the reconceptualization of natural stocks in banking terms and the creation of indicators to quantify conservation: what Sian Sullivan called "nature work" and "nature banking". Only then, can firms offer financial products with purported conservation benefits, or turn the possibility of natural loss into speculative opportunity through wagers (e.g., "nature derivatives," see Sullivan, 2012).

Recent trends in financialization have also intensified the sale and purchase of financial instruments related to food commodities. Jennifer Clapp argues that financialization of food commodities contributes to distancing in two ways that are similar to financialization in other contexts: both by increasing the number of actors involved, especially in intermediation, and by abstracting food into a homogenized form to traders. This financial distance obscures the causes of, for example, ecological damage, allowing companies to cloak their complicity and externalize costs while minimizing negative reputational effects (Clapp, 2014).

While the intensity with which new entanglements between the "natural world" and financial markets are being engineered today is perhaps novel, finance and nature have been tied together since well before the neoliberal era. For example, grain futures markets have been around since at least the mid-nineteenth century. As Cronon (2009/1991) famously showed in *Nature's Metropolis*, this entanglement had profound geographical implications, affecting the relationship between the country and city, between farmers, their buyers and their land, etc. It is important to note, then, that work on the financialization of nature in geography is about more than pointing out that the entanglement of finance with nature has deepened and widened with the rise of the financial sector's role in the economy. Indeed, Dempsey and Suarez (2016: 1) point out that despite the rhetoric around the growing role of finance in creating markets for conservation initiatives "the capital flowing into market-based conservation remains small, illiquid, and geographically constrained." Notwithstanding this gap between the rhetoric and reality of the financialization of nature, efforts to forge ties between nature and the market through finance are ongoing (see Kay, 2018), producing new socionatures, encountering resistance (Ouma et al., 2018), and having material effects that are uneven across space, race, class and gender.

There is arguably no issue for which the stakes of this entanglement are higher than with climate change, where green bonds (Bigger, 2017), insurance products (Knudson, 2018), trading schemes, and other financial instruments are foundational to many mainstream approaches to emissions reduction, mitigation, and adaptation. At a moment when international political will to acknowledge, let alone meaningfully address the climate crisis is severely lacking, an "all-hands-on-deck" approach that includes market makers and financial engineers may seem beyond dispute. However, some have questioned the capacity of market mechanisms to reduce emissions fast enough, and, more concerning, that reformist, market-based approaches are dangerous to the extent that they perpetuate liberal fantasies that the climate crisis can be resolved while preserving the status quo (see Wainwright & Mann, 2018). A bleaker position still views the climate crisis as financially manageable; in other words, that a global climate catastrophe, if properly hedged, need not be catastrophic for "the economy" or at least the financial sector. Instead, the uncertainties generated by climate change are reformulated and domesticated as tractable risks (Knight, 2012/1921), with the help of weather indexes, global circulation models, and other technologies. Here, uncertainty, reformulated as risk, can be financially managed and profitably exploited—at least by a few (e.g., Taylor, 2020 with respect to real estate climate risk in Florida). Finance is depicted with a Janus-faced capacity to perpetuate crisis and as necessary to the (status-quo-neutral) resolution of crisis. While this may strike the reader as a rather cynical take on the relationship between finance and nature, the idea that crisis affords opportunities for financial accumulation is common in Marxist political economy. The theorization of capitalism as both a "crisis-ridden and crisis dependent system" (O'Connor, 1998: 167) has also been influential in geographical thinking about the relationship between finance and cities.

Financialization of the City

Geographers have been interested in the relationship between finance and cities at least since the 1970s, when David Harvey argued that finance capital had supplanted industrial capital as the dominant organizing force of urban space (Harvey, 1974). In Harvey's account (1985) of the "urbanization of capital," the financial system acts as a conduit for rechanneling over-accumulated capital (in the primary circuit) into the built environment (secondary circuit) in order to manage and defer crises (see also Christophers, 2011). Since Harvey's foundational work, critical geographers have unpacked the relationship between finance and urban spaces in a variety of domains including real estate, housing, infrastructure, governance, and the relationship between these overlapping categories, some of which we highlight below.

There are several macro-level drivers that have led cities to deepen their connections to financial institutions, rationales, markets, and metrics. First among these is the urban austerity that accompanied the transition from Keynesian managerialism to neoliberal urban entrepreneurialism (Harvey, 1989; Leitner, 1990). Beginning in the 1970s, as higher levels of government began to "roll back" funding for urban development (Peck, 2012), cities increasingly required private (often mobile) capital to fund urban infrastructure and redevelopment projects. Along with the rise of inter-urban competition for footloose capital came a tremendous growth in municipal bond issuances. In 1981, there was $361 billion in municipal debt outstanding in the United States; by 2012 that number had climbed by an order of ten, to $3.7 trillion (Securities and Exchange Commission, 2012). The debt commitments resulting from this turn to bond markets has intensified local governments' exposure to various forms of financial market discipline. These pressures have induced a wide variety of responses up and down the urban hierarchy producing a diverse terrain of struggle, improvisation, and experimentation well described by Weber (2010: 210) as "the politics of financialization at the local level." In Black-majority US cities, financialization has intensified racialized patterns of urban development (Ponder, 2017). In cities under austerity and credit constraint (Lagna, 2016), financialization is associated with the reinvention of city assets and revenue streams as financial products for extra-local investors, including everything from property taxes (Kirkpatrick & Smith, 2011; Weber, 2010), sales taxes, tax credits (Tapp, 2019) and tolls to parking meter receipts (Farmer, 2014), stadium rental payments, and utility payments.[4] In cities at the top end of the urban hierarchy, financialization has inflated asset prices and transformed global cities like London, New York, and others into "safe deposit boxes" for the global elite (Fernandez et al., 2016).

Financial technology (fin-tech) companies and digital platforms have also transformed the ability of investors to extract rents from urban space. Stehlin (2018) evocatively describes how urban platforms like Airbnb, and Uber "create a shadow rent gradient—a contour of locational advantage—realized within physical urban space." These new relationships among finance, technology, and urban space have affected the dynamics of neighborhood change and motivated geographers to reconsider how gaps between actual and potential ground rent (i.e., "rent gaps," Smith, 1982) are opened and closed (Teresa, 2019). Slater (2017: 132) argues that by expanding the capital available to bid up real estate prices, financialization has increased "expectations of what can be extracted from legally enforced rights to land" in cities around the world. Wachsmuth and Weisler (2018; see also Grisdale, 2019; Yrigoy, 2018) show that digital platform technologies like Airbnb, by enabling tenantless apartments to earn income, are helping to pry open rent gaps and crowd out long-term rental units, along with their current (and potential future) lower-income occupants. These dynamics are (i) unfolding in neighborhoods not experiencing periods of disinvestment and decreases in capitalized rent, which have traditionally been associated with gentrification (Teresa, 2019) and (ii) especially pronounced in internationally recognizable neighborhoods and tourist destinations (Cocola-Gant & Gago, 2019).

This convergence of finance and digital technologies is reshaping housing dynamics outside world cities and tourism centers, as well. Fields (2018) demonstrates how in the aftermath of the 2008 crisis, foreclosed suburban houses were transformed into rental properties managed by large institutional investors. Fields argues that this new single-family rental (SFR) "asset class" (Fields, 2018) was made possible by an assemblage of heterogeneous elements (Callon, 2006), undergirded by various analytic, mobile, and cloud technologies that facilitated tenant discipline, rent collection, and maintenance at a scale and distance that was previously impractical (Fields, 2019).

As infrastructural networks are "constitutive parts of the urban" (Kaika & Swyngedouw, 2000), how infrastructure is altered through processes of financialization has also been explored by geographers: what gets built and what does not, how it is funded and who owns it, etc.? The logic of infrastructure finan-cialization echoes that of real estate (Moreno, 2014), in which steady streams of cash payments, whether for parking meters or water infrastructure, are made commensurable with other asset classes through securitization (O'Neill, 2019).

As Moreno argues, contemporary rent extraction—whether through infra-structure privatization, the development of new neighborhoods, the construc-tion of an SFR market, or something else—is very different from that of the late nineteenth and early twentieth centuries. Today, rent extraction requires a whole infrastructure of calculation and commensuration employing cadres of financiers, consultants, and data analysts who maintain power not through ownership of capital, but proximity to loanable funds, and the ability to direct their flow. This echoes Bassens and van Meeterens's (2015) argument above that advanced service providers can charge rent on information related to invest-ment risk, or even the construction of investment opportunity.

Finally, it is important to recognize that urban space is not financialized without struggle. Paralleling Simmel (quoted above), Fields argues that finan-cialization adds layers of distance—whether abstract distance, physical distance, or both—between owners and users, occluding the connections between own-ers and the lives of urban residents. Contestation, then, happens by collapsing the distance that finance creates in order to expose injustices in the emerging digital order of things. Yet, how best to contest such injustices, and support such contestation, is not always clear (Fields, 2017). García-Lemarca and Kaika (2016) argue that this requires more attention to how land-related capital flows at the scale of the city also affect processes of social reproduction. This connec-tion between financialization, daily life, and subject formation is what we turn to now (see also the chapter by Pellandini-Simányi in this *Handbook*).

The Financialization of Daily Life

The social reproduction of the household is increasingly intermediated by fi-nancial products and institutions: renting an apartment, or buying a home, car, or cellphone are all affected by credit score; the ability to retire, or attend col-lege depends on one's "portfolio" (see Ascher, 2016; e.g., in the US 401Ks, 529 "savings" plans, and other popular investment vehicles). These more inti-mate connections between the financial system and people's daily lives (Martin, 2002) have motivated Langley (2008) and others (e.g., Baker et al., 2019; Kear, 2016; Lai, 2016; Loomis, 2018; Rosenman, 2019) to explore the "intersection between changes in the capital markets, on the one hand, and transformations in everyday spaces, practices and identities, on the other" (Langley, 2008: 7). Moreover, just as life and the life course have come to depend more on finan-cial products, so too financial "literacy" (Clark, 2014) and "capability" have become objects of concern for the state and finance capital. As Bryan and Raf-ferty (2017: 13) emphasize, people's lives are now the raw materials—quotidian risks and payment streams for debts and a range of other goods and services—to be "engineered" into securities, (re)packaged, and potentially sold to investors anywhere in the world (Bryan & Rafferty, 2017: 13). In other words, the reallocation of risk from collective institutions and employers to individuals has made access to finance a necessity for households at the same time as access to households (more of them, including the poorer of them) has become necessary to satisfy the financial services industry's "appetite for yield" (Ashton, 2009). This arrangement, wherein people need finance to reproduce themselves and financial markets need more tractably risky subjects in order to profitably expand, has created new regulatory imperatives for the state, namely, the production of "good" financial consumer-citizens.

The implications of this financialized co-dependency between financial markets and individual subjects are far-reaching for the way geographers think about economic rights, poverty regulation, and financial subjectivities (see Hall, 2011; Kutz, 2018). For Kear (2013), it challenges dominant framings of the relationship between financially marginalized groups and the financial system as one of either discriminatory exclusion or usurious inclusion. Instead, Kear treats financial exclusion as a problem of financial government—i.e., of how to regulate the conduct of "risky" populations—the financial other—through the sale of financial products and services. To overcome this problem, the financial other has become a site of education and reform: the target of an effort to produce "self-sufficient" citizen-subjects (i.e., those who do not receive state assistance). The result is that a variety of state and non-state actors are today dedicated to developing products to "better serve" the "financial needs" of the "underbanked," and to cultivate citizens with the financial capability to use these products to improve themselves and their communities. Viewing financial exclusion as a problem of (neoliberal) financial government (Foucault, 2007) neutralizes the positive valence often unquestioningly ascribed to efforts to financially include and educate.

While such efforts to financially "include" and "empower" are often driven by national-level policy, this financial mode of social regulation intersects with people's lives in a diverse array of local settings. Here, Loomis's (2018) work on "financial coaching and the pedagogical spaces of financial inclusion" is particularly insightful. Loomis's ethnographic account of the "coaching turn" in financial education reveals how "clients" are motivated "to take control of their lives, feel empowered, and move past personal barriers to achieve their financial dreams" (Loomis, 2018: 146) by internalizing an etiology of poverty that obviates structural and historical factors beyond an individual's control. Here "the solution to poverty is discipline, agency and access to credit, rather than a living wage, adequate social support or reparations to address centuries of racialized wealth dispossession" (Loomis, 2018: 150).

Loomis's research also highlights the role of credit score in orienting financial inclusion initiatives and constructing connections between social reproduction and consumer financial markets (on credit assessment, see also Ossandón's chapter in this *Handbook*). Despite myriad well-documented blind spots, biases, and other shortcomings, credit score has endured as a central technology for objectifying the risks of ordinary consumers and, in so doing, making those risks priceable and "investible" (Baker et al., 2019). What makes credit score, and other similar metrics, indispensable to financial markets is that they replace an uncertain future with an automatically calculated, easily understood number, which helps markets to function *as if* the future were known, and, in theory, that means more efficiently and more competitively (see Ashton & Christophers, 2015; Kear, 2017 on legal technologies of arbitration).

In recent years many more measures and metrics have been developed in the service of bringing social problems to market and transforming them into investment opportunities (see Leyshon & Thrift, 1999). Often collapsed under the rubric of "social finance" (Rosenman, 2019), this expansive arena of experimentation encompasses impact investing (Kish & Fairbairn, 2018), social impact bonds (Berndt & Wirth, 2018; Harvie & Ogman, 2019; see also Bryan et al.'s chapter in this *Handbook*), mission-lead investing, and even microfinance (Rankin, 2013; Roy, 2010). As Rosenman points out, the geography that has emerged from this experimentation is highly uneven. More specifically, it is "the poor people and disinvested localities at the losing end of capitalism's uneven geographies [that] are to be converted into an investment opportunity" (Rosenman, 2019: 1–2).

As credit has become a substitute for wage income (Krippner, 2017), and the role of finance in meting out access to the necessities of life has grown, struggles over equity, wellness, housing, and many other things are increasingly being fought within the financial system—rather than against it. Rights and distributional claims are often (re)articulated in a financial idiom. Consumer financial markets, then, are key sites of contemporary distributional struggle. But where are these struggles? What are their geographies? How are financial markets spatially constituted (Alvarez León et al., 2018)? Here there is notable emerging scholarship on the "spatiality of debt" (Harker, 2017). How do "housing cooperatives make up a geography of spaces that are opaque to the creditor" in Uruguay (Vidal, 2018)? How is the "social unit of debt" (Schuster, 2014) variously constituted and spatialized from place to place? How do finance and debt obligations weave among il/licit spaces and practices (Johnson & Woodhouse, 2018)? This wide body of scholarship, while grappling with the variety of ways that finance intersects differentially with place, race, class, and gender around the world, is also sensitive to new battlegrounds created by the digital intermediation of financial life. Here markets are socio-technical "agencement" (read assemblages, Berndt & Boeckler, 2012; Callon, 2006) and agency is distributed (Callon & Muniesa, 2005) among a variety of heterogeneous elements that "hang together" (Woodward et al., 2010: 274) at particular moments in time and space (Kear, 2018) created by, for example, novel payment systems (Nelms et al., 2018; Swartz, 2014) and other digital interfaces (Ash et al., 2018).

We close this section on the financialization of everyday life with a brief mention of assemblages, "open-ended groupings of material and semiotic elements that do not form a coherent whole" (Sohn, 2016), because such re-lational approaches to financial markets complicate the categories of "nature," "cities," and "everyday life" that we have used to organize this review of the "financialization of X." While these have become common labels for the strands of scholarship within financial geography, the relationship between finance and its "outsides" does not fit neatly into these categories (or categories at all). In the next section we highlight a few examples of research on "boundary objects" that defy easy categorization and tie these strands together.

Borderscapes of Financialization

In their formative work on the derivative, LiPuma and Lee argue that deriv-atives enable a "plurality of incommensurable types of risk [to be] reduced to a singularity: risk in the abstract" (2005: 414). The story they tell about the derivative is about the commodification of risk, wherein qualitatively distinct risks are abstracted and detached from the social contexts in which they were created, so that they can be quantified, rendered equivalent, and tradable. As a tool of commensuration, the derivative is perhaps the highest example of finance's capacity to act as Simmel's "frightful leveler." Writing in a similar vein about the capacity of derivatives to reduce quality to quantity, Bryan and Rafferty note that "with derivatives, one trades in the performance (shift in the quantum) of an attribute of a thing, but without necessarily trading in the 'thing' itself" (Bryan & Rafferty, 2014: 892).

Paradoxically, this "leveled" world, where "quanta" matter more than the things from which they emanate, is one where borders—qualitative distinctions between people, places, and events—are proliferating. The drive to squeeze more "quanta" from more attributes of more things has succeeded in creating data on such a "big" scale that "it exceeds [...] human capacities to read and make sense of [it]" (Amoore & Piotukh, 2015: 343), and moved markets to learn "new ways of seeing" (Fourcade & Healy, 2017). More specifically, mar-kets have learned to "see" with algorithms that mine data for otherwise invis-ible correlations that can be used to erect probabilistic borders around credit, jobs, insurance, social assistance, in addition to territory and many other things (Eubanks, 2018; Moor & Lury, 2018; O'Neil, 2016).

The contradictory tendency of financialization to reduce and level, on the one hand, and border and order ("b/order," Berndt, 2013), on the other hand, disrupts traditional geographical and territorial understandings of boundaries. Following Mezzadra and Neilson (2013), the term "borderscape"[5] captures these tensions between finance and borders well. A borderscape is dynamic, a "shifting and conflictual zone" (Perera, 2007: 206) in which "the border" is a set of "practices and discourses that 'spread' into the whole of society" (Paasi, 1999: 670, cited in Mezzadra & Neilson, 2013: 13). Financial border-scapes, then, are market peripheries: growing zones of indistinction where new risks and uncertainties are managed through improvised repertoires of financial products and practices that overflow framings of nature, production, consumption, and reproduction, and map poorly onto binaries of "mainstream" and "fringe," "formal" and "informal," and "public" and "private."

To give this abstract discussion of the financial borderscape more concrete expression, we turn now to examples of research in financial geography whose objects do not fit within the "financialization of X," but rather, undermine and multiply borders. A necessary caveat is that these examples represent a far-too-narrow sample of the research in financial geography that crosses aforementioned boundaries in revealing ways.

Dempsey and Bigger, in their value-chain analysis of for-profit conservation finance, find that connecting a New York investment firm to a Kenyan conservation NGO is about more than accumulation and commodification. "Rendering biodiversity conservation investable" (2019: 519) involves far more than the one-way imposition of market rationality on a pliable nature. In their account, the financialization of nature is a messy process, unfolding across more than just the border between nature and the market, but among NGOs, grass, cattle, the practices of pastoralists, etc. Making the conservation of Kenyan grasslands valuable to distant "social" investors requires what they call "intimate mediations," drawing on "other-than-capitalist-social relations" to direct the conduct of institutions, people and animals toward the ideals of "*NGO economicus, homo economicus* plus, and *bos Taurus economicus*" (Dempsey & Bigger, 2019: 517). The story they tell is not just about the transformation of the environment, but a process of institutional capacity building and subject formation.

Lally et al. (2019) similarly seek to map how "value flows out of the landscape, through local communities, and toward sites of accumulation far away" (Robbins, 2011: 88, cited in Lally et al., 2019) using the example of bitcoin mining on the Columbia River. Although the authors do not identify as financial geographers, they provide a dramatic illustration of a financial borderscape taking form at the intersection of the digital and the physical. Part of bitcoin's ideological appeal (and the appeal of "digital metalism," more generally) is its ostensible potential to selectively decouple from the material constraints of physical currency while retaining its scarcity and preciousness—to act as a sort of non-metal metal. As the authors point out, the computationally taxing process of "mining" makes the production of cryptocurrency very energy intensive. These energy needs "anchor [bitcoin miners] to particular places" where electricity can be obtained at low cost, making bitcoin's geography "highly uneven and intertwined with the infrastructural and ecological structures on which it depends" (Lally et al., 2019). For the purposes of this chapter, the message we draw from their account is that no matter how autopoietic money and finance are imagined or desired to be, they are always already embedded in political, social, and ecological relations.

Working in an urban context, Akers et al. (2019) document how in the aftermath of the financial crisis shrinking parts of Cleveland were rehabilitated as sites of accumulation through a complementary process of demolition and greening. This "techno-green fix" has accelerated displacement in communities of color and exacerbated existing racialized patterns of urban inequality. Here, nature and processes of racialization combine in a post-financial-crisis urban landscape to create new investment opportunities.

The financial geographies taking shape in post-financial-crisis US cities, as well as most other contexts, cannot be understood without eschewing the siloed view of the "financialization of X." This siloed view is not one that attracts many adherents, and few (if any) true believers, but conversations across subgenres of financial geography are still too few. The three pieces we highlight above offer reason for hope, and there are many more examples. Other recent examples include Horton's investigation of how turning to debt markets to fund UK care homes transforms labor processes and imposes financial discipline on the everyday lives of their mostly female workforce. Financialization, she argues, "must be understood as constituted not only by financial practices [...] but also by specific forms of labour" (Horton, 2019: 1). Seymour and Akers (2019), again, cut across categories to connect foreclosure, speculation, and eviction to everyday life in spaces of decline. Our own recent work on manufactured housing (Kear et al., 2019) shows that to understand how this crucial form of housing has become the nexus of a variety of environmental, social, and financial vulnerabilities, it is necessary to connect fiscal geographies to consumer credit markets to the speculative practices of investors both big and small.

Where Is Finance?

What is finance? This is a question that has the awkward quality of being both too obvious to ask, but also rather hard to answer. What this "simple" question is really asking is, to borrow from Christophers (2015), how do things that "we identify as finance come to acquire that status"? Because such questions are rarely asked or answered, "finance" itself (with many notable exceptions) is a black box (see Ouma, 2015; Poovey, 2015) in most putative financial research. With tacit agreement to leave finance in its box, discussion can move on from what finance *is* to what finance *does* to nature, people, cities, etc. These effects are important to explore and dominate the financialization literature, yet opening this black box remains an important part of "critical financial studies."

Geography contributes to this endeavor by asking "where is finance?" Asking where something is implies that that something is material and can be studied in particular places. Answering the "where" question requires, in Ouma's (2015) words, "getting in between the M and M'[prime]"; in other words, to consider how this abstract time and space between investment (M) and realization (M') is lived in the concrete spaces of everyday life. Spatializing finance precludes its investigation as an autopoietic abstraction, free of context. Here we return to where we started the chapter: the co-constitution of finance and space. If finance cannot be studied outside of its context, then it always already contains space, and, as we have discussed at length, banks, lenders, products, scores, and so on, are always creating, breaking, and reformatting spatial relations.

This reflexive attention to the co-constitutive characteristics of space and finance is part of what defines critical financial geography (with all the pitfalls, provisos, and limits inherent in such a definitional exercise, notwithstanding). Another element of critical financial geography is the construction of "chain of explanations"[6] linking local, micro financial practices to macro-level process, and back again; for example, from global debt markets to labor practices, from farmers to global reinsurance giants, and many more. Moreover, in piecing together these chains of explanation no *a priori* restrictions are placed on the types of actors, both human and nonhuman, that can participate in the assemblages that (re)produce financial space. Regardless of who or what participates in the production of financial space, the results are uneven; uneven from place to place, but space is also gendered, classed, and racialized, and so uneven along many axes of difference. This gives critical financial geography a sensitivity to distributional justice (social, economic, and environmental), and the contemporary and historical drivers of injustice: colonialism, imperialism, patriarchy, racism, and the processes of exploitation, domination, and subjectivization through which they are enacted.

Notes

1 Lefebvre (1991) describes socially produced space using the culinary metaphor of the *mille-feuille* pastry—a layered, powdery French dessert whose name directly translates as "a thousand leaves" (Brenner, 2008).
2 While each of the maxims can be attributed to a variety of sources, Potts (2019; see also Knuth & Potts, 2016) brings them together systematically.
3 Hedge funds or private equity funds that purchase distressed debt at a large discount with the goal of forcing debtors to repay the full value of the original loan.
4 Work on urban finance overlaps substantially with an emerging literature on fiscal geographies (Tapp & Kay, 2019).
5 Mazzadra and Neilson (2013) attribute the term to Perera (2007).
6 A phrase strongly associated with political ecology and attributed to Blaikie (2016).

References

Aalbers, M. B. (2014). "Do maps make geography? Part 1: redlining, planned shrinkage, and the places of decline," *ACME: An International E-Journal for Critical Geographies* 13(4): 525–556.

Aalbers, M. B. (2018). "Financial geography I: Geographies of tax," *Progress in Human Geography* 42(6): 916–927.

Akers, J., Béal, V., & Rousseau, M. (2019). "Redefining the city and demolishing the rest: The techno-green fix in postcrash Cleveland, Ohio," *Environment and Planning E: Nature and Space*. doi: 10.1177/2514848619854371.

Alvarez León, L. F., Yu, L., & Christophers, B. (2018). "Introduction: The spatial constitution of markets," *Economic Geography* 94(3): 211–216.

Amin, A., & Thrift, N. (2005). "What's left? Just the future," *Antipode* 37(2): 220–238.

Amin, A., & Thrift, N. (2007). "On being political," *Transactions of the Institute of British Geographers* 32(1): 112–115.

Amoore, L., & Piotukh, V. (2015). "Life beyond big data: Governing with little analytics," *Economy and Society* 44(3). 341–366.

Arrighi, G. (1994). *The Long Twentieth Century: Money, Power, and the Origins of Our Times*. London: Verso.

Ascher, I. (2016). *Portfolio Society: On the Capitalist Mode of Prediction*. Cambridge, MA: MIT Press.

Ash, J., Anderson, B., Gordon, R., & Langley, P. (2018). "Digital interface design and power: Friction, threshold, transition," *Environment and Planning D: Society and Space* 36(6): 1136–1153.

Ashton, P. (2009). "An appetite for yield: The anatomy of the subprime mortgage crisis," *Environment and Planning A* 41(6): 1420–1441.

Ashton, P. (2014). "The evolving juridical space of harm/value: Remedial powers in the subprime mortgage crisis," *Journal of Economic Issues* 48(4): 959–979.

Ashton, P., & Christophers, B. (2015). "On arbitration, arbitrage and arbitrariness in financial markets and their governance: Unpacking LIBOR and the LIBOR scandal," *Economy and Society* 44(2): 188–217.

Baker, T., Evans, J., & Hennigan, B. (2019). "Investable poverty: Social investment states and the geographies of poverty management," *Progress in Human Geography*. doi: 10.1177/0309132519849288.

Bakker, K. (2005). "Neoliberalizing nature? Market environmentalism in water supply in England and Wales," *Annals of the Association of American Geographers* 95(3): 542–565.

Bassens, D., & van Meeteren, M. (2015). "World cities under conditions of financialized globalization: Towards an augmented world city hypothesis," *Progress in Human Geography* 39(6): 752–775.

Berndt, C. (2013). "Assembling market B/orders: Violence, dispossession, and economic development in ciudad juárez, mexico," *Environment and Planning A: Economy and Space* 45(11): 2646–2662.

Berndt, C., & Boeckler, M. (2012). "Geographies of marketization," in T. Barnes, J. Peck, and E. Sheppard (eds.), *The Wiley-Blackwell Companion to Economic Geography* (pp. 199–212). Malden, MA: Blackwell Publishing Ltd.

Berndt, C., & Wirth, M. (2018). "Market, metrics, morals: The social impact bond as an emerging social policy instrument," *Geoforum* 90: 27–35.

Bigger, P. (2017). "Measurement and the circulation of risk in green bonds," *Journal of Environmental Investing* 8: 273–287.

Bigger, P., Dempsey, J., Asiyanbi, A. P., Kay, K., Lave, R., Mansfield, B., Osborne, T., Robertson, M., & Simon, G. (2018). "Reflecting on neoliberal natures: An exchange: The ins and outs of Neoliberal natures," *Environment and Planning E: Nature and Space* 1(1–2): 25–75.

Bigger, P. M. (2015). "Environmental governance in the carbon economy: Regulating greenhouse gas emissions in California's cap-and-trade program," Theses and Dissertations– *Geography* 32. Retrieved from https://uknowledge.uky.edu/geography_etds/32/.

Blaikie, P. (2016). *The Political Economy of Soil Erosion in Developing Countries*. London: Routledge.

Blomley, N. K. (1989). "Text and context: Rethinking the law-space nexus," *Progress in Human Geography* 13(4): 512–534.

Blomley, N. K., & Bakan, J. C. (1992). "Spacing out: Towards a critical geography of law," *Osgoode Hall Law Journal* 30: 661–690.

Brenner, N. (2008). "Henri Lefebvre's critique of state productivism," in C. Schmid, K. Goonewardena, R. Milgrom, and S. Kipfer (eds.), *Space, Difference, Everyday Life* (pp. 245–263). New York, NY: Routledge.

Brenner, N., Peck, J., & Theodore, N. (2010). "Variegated neoliberalization: Geographies, modalities, pathways," *Global Networks* 10(2): 182–222.

Bryan, D., & Rafferty, M. (2014). "Financial derivatives as social policy beyond crisis," *Sociology* 48(5): 887–903.

Bryan, D., & Rafferty, M. (2017). "Reframing austerity: financial morality, savings and securitization," *Journal of Cultural Economy* 10(4): 339–355.

Callon, M. (2006). *What Does It Mean to Say that Economics Is Performative?* Centre de Sociologie de l'Innovation (CSI), Mines ParisTech. Retrieved from https://EconPapers. repec.org/RePEc:emn:wpaper:005.

Callon, M., & Muniesa, F. (2005). "Peripheral vision: Economic markets as calculative collective devices," *Organization Studies* 26(8): 1229–1250.

Caplovitz, D. (1968). *The Poor Pay More: Consumer Practices of Low-Income Families*. New York, NY: Free Press.

Castree, N. (2003). "Commodifying what nature?," *Progress in Human Geography* 27(3): 273–297.

Christophers, B. (2011). "Revisiting the urbanization of capital," *Annals of the Association of American Geographers* 101(6): 1347–1364.

Christophers, B. (2013). *Banking across Boundaries: Placing Finance in Capitalism*. Malden, MA: John Wiley & Sons.

Christophers, B. (2015). "The limits to financialization," *Dialogues in Human Geography* 5(2): 183–200.

Clapp, J. (2014). "Financialization, distance and global food politics," *The Journal of Peasant Studies* 41(5): 797–814.

Clark, G. L. (2005). "Money flows like mercury: The geography of global finance," *Geografiska Annaler: Series B, Human Geography* 87(2): 99–112.

Clark, G. L. (2014). "Roepke lecture in economic geography—Financial literacy in context," *Economic Geography* 90(1): 1–23.

Cocola-Gant, A., & Gago, A. (2019). "Airbnb, buy-to-let investment and tourism-driven displacement: A case study in Lisbon," *Environment and Planning A: Economy and Space.* doi: 10.1177/0308518X19869012.

Coe, N. M., Lai, K. P. Y., & Wójcik, D. (2014). "Integrating finance into global production networks," *Regional Studies* 48(5): 761–777.

Cronon, W. (2009). *Nature's Metropolis: Chicago and the Great West*. New York, NY: WW Norton & Company.

Dagan, H. (2013). "Lawmaking for legal realists," *The Theory and Practice of Legislation* 1(1): 187–204.

Davis, O. (2018, October 16). "All roads lead to wall street," *Dissent.* Retrieved from https://www.dissentmagazine.org/online_articles/working-class-shareholder-labor-activism-finance.

Demeritt, D. (2002). "What is the 'social construction of nature'? A typology and sympathetic critique," *Progress in Human Geography* 26(6): 767–790.

Dempsey, J., & Bigger, P. (2019). "Intimate mediations of for-profit conservation finance: Waste, improvement, and accumulation," *Antipode* 51(2): 517–538.

Dempsey, J., & Suarez, D. C. (2016). "Arrested development? The promises and paradoxes of 'selling nature to save it'," *Annals of the American Association of Geographers* 106(3): 653–671.

Dörry, S. (2015). "Strategic nodes in investment fund global production networks: The example of the financial centre Luxembourg," *Journal of Economic Geography* 15(4): 797–814.

Dymski, G. A. (2006). "Targets of opportunity in two landscapes of financial globalization," *Geoforum* 37(3): 307–311.

Ekers, M., & Prudham, S. (2017). "The metabolism of socioecological fixes: Capital switching, spatial fixes, and the production of nature," *Annals of the American Association of Geographers* 107(6): 1370–1388.

Epstein, G. A. (2005). *Financialization and the World Economy*. Cheltenham and Northampton, MA: Edward Elgar Publishing.

Eubanks, V. (2018). *Automating Inequality: How High-Tech Tools Profile, Police, And Punish The Poor*. New York, NY: St. Martin's Press.

Farmer, S. (2014). "Cities as risk managers: The impact of Chicago's parking meter p3 on municipal governance and transportation planning," *Environment and Planning A: Economy and Space* 46(9): 2160–2174.

Fernandez, R., Hofman, A., & Aalbers, M. B. (2016). "London and New York as a safe deposit box for the transnational wealth elite," *Environment and Planning A: Economy and Space* 48(12): 2443–2461.

Fields, D. (2017). "Urban struggles with financialization," *Geography Compass* 11(11). doi: 10.1111/gec3.12334.

Fields, D. (2018). "Constructing a new asset class: Property-led financial accumulation after the crisis," *Economic Geography* 94(2): 118–140.

Fields, D. (2019). "Automated landlord: Digital technologies and post-crisis financial accumulation," *Environment and Planning A: Economy and Space*. doi: 10.1177/0308518X19846514.

Foucault, M. (2007). *Security, Territory, Population: Lectures at the Collège De France, 1977–78*, trans. Graham Burchell. London: Palgrave Macmillan, UK.

Fourcade, M., & Healy, K. (2017). "Seeing like a market," *Socio-Economic Review* 15(1): 9–29.

Friedman, T. L. (2005). *The World Is Flat: A Brief History of the Twenty-First Century*. New York, NY: Macmillan Publishers.

Friedmann, J. (1986). "The world city hypothesis," *Development and Change* 17(1): 69–83.

García-Lamarca, M., & Kaika, M. (2016). "'Mortgaged lives': The biopolitics of debt and housing financialisation," *Transactions of the Institute of British Geographers* 41(3): 313–327.

Gilbert, E., & Helleiner, E. (1999). *Nation-States and Money: The Past, Present and Future of National Currencies*. London and New York, NY: Routledge.

Graves, S. M. (2003). "Landscapes of predation, landscapes of neglect: A location analysis of payday lenders and banks," *The Professional Geographer* 55(3): 303–317.

Grisdale, S. (2019). "Displacement by disruption: Short-term rentals and the political economy of "belonging anywhere" in Toronto," *Urban Geography* 0(0): 1–27.

Hall, S. (2011). "Geographies of money and finance I: Cultural economy, politics and place," *Progress in Human Geography* 35(2): 234–245.

Harker, C. (2017). "Debt space: Topologies, ecologies and Ramallah, Palestine," *Environment and Planning D: Society and Space* 35(4): 600–619.

Harvey, D. (1974). "Class-monopoly rent, finance capital and the urban revolution," *Regional Studies* 8(3–4): 239–255.

Harvey, D. (1985). *The Urbanization of Capital: Studies in the History and Theory of Capitalist Urbanization*. Baltimore, MD: The Johns Hopkins University Press.

Harvey, D. (1989). "From managerialism to entrepreneurialism: The transformation in urban governance in late capitalism," *Geografiska Annaler: Series B, Human Geography* 71(1): 3–17.

Harvey, D. (2005). *The New Imperialism*. Oxford: Oxford University Press.

Harvey, D. (2006). "Editorial: The geographies of critical geography," *Transactions of the Institute of British Geographers* 31(4): 409–412.

Harvey, D. (2018). *The Limits to Capital*. London: Verso.

Harvie, D., & Ogman, R. (2019). "The broken promises of the social investment market," *Environment and Planning A: Economy and Space* 51(4): 980–1004.

Heynen, N., McCarthy, J., Prudham, S., & Robbins, P. (2007). *Neoliberal Environments: False Promises and Unnatural Consequences*. New York, NY: Routledge.

Horton, A. (2019). "Financialization and non-disposable women: Real estate, debt and labor in UK care homes," *Environment and Planning A: Economy and Space*: 0308518X19862580.

Immergluck, D. (2016). *Credit to the Community: Community Reinvestment and Fair Lending Policy in the United.* London and New York, NY: Routledge.

Jacobs, W., Ducruet, C., & Langen, P. D. (2010). "Integrating world cities into production networks: The case of port cities," *Global Networks* 10(1): 92–113.

Johnson, L. (2013). "Catastrophe bonds and financial risk: Securing capital and rule through contingency," *Geoforum* 45: 30–40.

Johnson, R. L., & Woodhouse, M. (2018). "Securing the return: how enhanced US border enforcement fuels cycles of debt migration," *Antipode* 50(4): 976–996.

Kaika, M., & Swyngedouw, E. (2000). "Fetishizing the modern city: The phantasmagoria of urban technological networks," *International Journal of Urban and Regional Research* 24(1): 120–138.

Kay, K. (2016). "Breaking the bundle of rights: Conservation easements and the legal geographies of individuating nature," *Environment and Planning A: Economy and Space* 48(3): 504–522.

Kay, K. (2018). "A hostile takeover of nature? Placing value in conservation finance," *Antipode* 50(1): 164–183.

Kear, M. (2013). "Governing homo subprimicus: Beyond financial citizenship, exclusion, and rights," *Antipode* 45(4): 926–946.

Kear, M. (2016). "Peer lending and the subsumption of the informal," *Journal of Cultural Economy* 9(3): 261–276.

Kear, M. (2017). "Playing the credit score game: Algorithms, 'positive' data and the personification of financial objects," *Economy and Society* 46(3–4): 346–368.

Kear, M. (2018). "The marketsite: A new conceptualization of market spatiality," *Economic Geography* 94(3): 299–320.

Kear, M. (2015). *Governing Homo Subprimicus: Essays on the Financial Regulation of Poverty After the Subprime Crisis* (doctoral dissertation). British Columbia: Simon Frasier University.

Kear, M., Handschuh, T., Launius, S., Hartman, J., & Christopherson, G. (2019). *"The 'Manufactured Housing Gap' in Tucson and Pima County."* Tucson, Arizona: Economic and Business Research Center, Eller College, University of Arizona.

Kirkpatrick, L. O., & Smith, M. P. (2011). "The infrastructural limits to growth: Rethinking the urban growth machine in times of fiscal crisis," *International Journal of Urban and Regional Research* 35(3): 477–503.

Kish, Z., & Fairbairn, M. (2018). "Investing for profit, investing for impact: Moral performances in agricultural investment projects," *Environment and Planning A: Economy and Space* 50(3): 569–588.

Knight, F. H. (1921). *Risk, Uncertainty and Profit.* Boston, MA: Hart, Schaffner & Marx.

Knudson, C. (2018). "One size does not fit all: Universal livelihood insurance in St. Lucia," *Geoforum* 95: 78–86.

Knuth, S., & Potts, S. (2016). "Legal geographies of finance Editors' Introduction," *Environment and Planning A: Economy and Space* 48(3): 458–464.

Krippner, G. R. (2017). "Democracy of credit: Ownership and the politics of credit access in late twentieth-century America," *American Journal of Sociology* 123(1): 1–47.

Kutz, W. (2018). "Financialization interrupted: Unwilling subjects of housing reform in Morocco," *City* 22(4): 568–583.

Lagna, A. (2016). "Derivatives and the financialisation of the Italian state," *New Political Economy* 21(2): 167–186.

Lai, K. (2011). "Differentiated markets: Shanghai, Beijing and Hong Kong in China's financial centre network," *Urban Studies* 49(6): 1275–1296.

Lai, K. (2016). "Financial advisors, financial ecologies and the variegated financialisation of everyday investors," *Transactions of the Institute of British Geographers* 41(1): 27–40.

Lally, N., Kay, K., & Thatcher, J. (2019). "Computational parasites and hydropower: A political ecology of Bitcoin mining on the Columbia River," *Environment and Planning E: Nature and Space*. doi: 10.1177/2514848619867608.

Langley, P. (2008). *The Everyday Life of Global Finance: Saving and Borrowing in Anglo-America*. Oxford: Oxford University Press.

Latour, B. (2007). *Reassembling the Social: An Introduction to Actor-Network-Theory*. Oxford, New York, NY: Oxford University Press.

Lefebvre, H. (1991). *The Production of Space* (Vol. 142). Oxford: Blackwell.

Leitner, H. (1990). "Cities in pursuit of economic growth: The local state as entrepreneur," *Political Geography Quarterly* 9(2): 146–170.

Leyshon, A., & Thrift, N. (1995). "Geographies of financial exclusion: Financial abandonment in Britain and the United States," *Transactions of the Institute of British Geographers* 20(3): 312–341.

Leyshon, A., & Thrift, N. (1999). "Lists come alive: Electronic systems of knowledge and the rise of credit-scoring in retail banking," *Economy and Society* 28(3): 434–466.

LiPuma, E., & Lee, B. (2005). "Financial derivatives and the rise of circulation," *Economy and Society* 34(3): 404–427.

Loomis, J. M. (2018). "Rescaling and reframing poverty: Financial coaching and the pedagogical spaces of financial inclusion in Boston, Massachusetts," *Geoforum* 95: 143–152.

Mann, G. (2006). "Reflections on Scott Prudham's knock on wood: Is labor-power a fictitious commodity?," *Antipode* 38(5): 1069–1072.

Martin, R. (2002). *Financialization of Daily Life*. Philadelphia, PA: Temple University Press.

McAfee, K. (1999). "Selling nature to save it? Biodiversity and Green Developmentalism," *Environment and Planning D: Society and Space* 17(2): 133–154.

McAfee, K. (2012). "The contradictory logic of global ecosystem services markets," *Development and Change* 43(1): 105–131.

McAfee, K. (2016). "Green economy and carbon markets for conservation and development: A critical view," *International Environmental Agreements: Politics, Law and Economics* 16(3): 333–353.

Meeteren, M. V., & Bassens, D. (2016). "World cities and the uneven geographies of financialization: Unveiling stratification and hierarchy in the world city archipelago," *International Journal of Urban and Regional Research* 40(1): 62–81.

Mezzadra, S., & Neilson, B. (2013). *Border as Method, or, the Multiplication of Labor*. Durham and London: Duke University Press.

Mitchell, D., & Staeheli, L. A. (2006). "Clean and safe? Property redevelopment, public space, and homelessness in downtown San Diego," *The Politics of Public Space* 2006: 143–175.

Moor, L., & Lury, C. (2018). "Price and the person: Markets, discrimination, and personhood," *Journal of Cultural Economy* 11(6): 501–513.

Moreno, L. (2014). "The urban process under financialised capitalism," *City* 18(3): 244–268.

Nelms, T. C., Maurer, B., Swartz, L., & Mainwaring, S. (2018). "Social payments: Innovation, trust, bitcoin, and the sharing economy," *Theory, Culture & Society* 35(3): 13–33.

O'Connor, J. R. (1998). *Natural Causes: Essays in Ecological Marxism*. New York, NY: Guilford Press.

O'Neil, C. (2016). *Weapons of Math Destruction: How Big Data Increases Inequality and Threatens Democracy*. New York, NY: Broadway Books.

O'Neill, P. (2019). "The financialisation of urban infrastructure: A framework of analysis," *Urban Studies* 56(7): 1304–1325.

Osborne, T. (2016). "State forestry incentives and community stewardship: A political ecology of payments and compensation for ecosystem services in Guatemala's highlands," *Journal of Latin American Geography* 15(1): 83–110.

Ouma, S. (2015). "Getting in between M and M' or: How farmland further debunks financialization," *Dialogues in Human Geography* 5(2): 225–228.

Ouma, S., Johnson, L., & Bigger, P. (2018). "Rethinking the financialization of 'nature'," *Environment and Planning A: Economy and Space* 50(3): 500–511.

Paasi, A. (1999). "Boundaries as social practice and discourse: The Finnish-Russian border," *Regional Studies* 33(7): 669–680.

Peck, J. (2012). "Austerity urbanism: American cities under extreme economy," *City* 16(6): 626–655.

Perera, S. (2007). "A pacific zone? (In)Security, sovereignty, and stories of the pacific borderscape," in P. Rajaram and C. Grundy-Warr (eds.), *Borderscapes: Hidden Geographies and Politics and Territory's Edge* (pp. 201–227). Minneapolis: University of Minnesota Press.

Pistor, K. (2019). *The Code of Capital: How the Law Creates Wealth and Inequality*. Princeton, NJ: Princeton University Press.

Polanyi, K. (1944). *The Great Transformation*. Toronto and New York, NY: Farrar & Rinehart, Inc.

Pollard, J., & Samers, M. (2007). "Islamic banking and finance: Postcolonial political economy and the decentring of economic geography," *Transactions of the Institute of British Geographers* 32(3): 313–330.

Pollard, J. S. (1996). "Banking at the margins: A geography of financial exclusion in Los Angeles," *Environment and Planning A* 28(7): 1209–1232.

Ponder, C. S. (2017). *The Life and Debt of Great American Cities: Urban Reproduction in the Time of Financialization* (doctoral dissertation). British Colombia, Canada: University of British Colombia.

Poovey, M. (2015). "On 'the limits to financialization'," *Dialogues in Human Geography* 5(2): 220–224.

Potts, S. (2016). "Reterritorializing economic governance: Contracts, space, and law in transborder economic geographies," *Environment and Planning A: Economy and Space* 48(3): 523–539.

Potts, S. (2017a). "Deep finance: Sovereign debt crises and the secondary market 'fix'," *Economy and Society* 46(3–4): 452–475.

Potts, S. (2017b). *Displaced Sovereignty: U.S. Law and the Transformation of International Financial Space*. Berkley, CA: UC Berkeley.

Potts, S. (2019, April). *Beyond (De)regulation: Law and the Production of Financial Geographies*. Presented at the AAG, Washington, DC.

Prudham, W. S. (2012). *Knock on Wood: Nature as Commodity in Douglas-Fir Country*. New York, NY: Routledge.

Raju, S., & Jeffrey, A. (2016). "Critical geography," in D. Richardson (ed.), *International Encyclopedia of Geography: People, the Earth, Environment and Technology: People, the Earth, Environment and Technology* (pp. 1–7). Hoboken, NJ: Wiley-Blackwell.

Rankin, K. N. (2013). "A critical geography of poverty finance," *Third World Quarterly* 34(4): 547–568.

Robbins, P. (2011). *Political Ecology: A Critical Introduction* (Vol. 16). Malden, MA: John Wiley & Sons.

Rosenman, E. (2019). "The geographies of social finance: Poverty regulation through the "invisible heart' of markets," *Progress in Human Geography* 43(1): 141–162.

Rothstein, R. (2017). *The Color of Law: A Forgotten History of How Our Government Segregated America*. London and New York, NY: Liveright Publishing.

Roy, A. (2010). *Poverty Capital: Microfinance and the Making of Development*. New York, NY: Routledge.

Rudnyckyj, D. (2018). *Beyond Debt: Islamic Experiments in Global Finance*. Chicago, IL: University of Chicago Press.

Sassen, S. (1991). *The Global City: New York, London, Tokyo*. Princeton, NJ: Princeton University Press.

Schuster, C. E. (2014). "The social unit of debt: Gender and creditworthiness in Paraguayan microfinance," *American Ethnologist* 41(3): 563–578.

Securities and Exchange Commission. (2012). *Report on the Municipal Securities Market* (p. 165).

Seymor, E., & Akers, J. (2019). "Building the eviction economy: Speculation, precarity, and eviction in Detroit," Urban Affairs Review: https://doi.org/10.1177/1078087419853388

Simmel, G. (2004). *The Philosophy of Money*. New York, NY: Routledge.

Slater, T. (2017). "Planetary rent gaps," *Antipode* 49: 114–137.

Smith, N. (1982). "Gentrification and uneven development," *Economic Geography* 58(2): 139–155.

Smith, N. (2005). "Neo-critical geography, or, the flat pluralist world of business class," *Antipode* 37(5): 887–899.

Smith, N. (2007). "Nature as accumulation strategy," *Socialist Register* 43: 16–36.

Smith, N. (2010). *Uneven Development: Nature, Capital, and the Production of Space*. Athens: University of Georgia Press.

Sohn, C. (2016). "Navigating borders' multiplicity: The critical potential of assemblage," *Area* 48(2): 183–189.

Soja, E. W. (2000). *Postmetropolis: Critical Studies of Cities and Regions*. Oxford: Blackwell.

Stehlin, J. (2018, October 26). "Urban platforms, rent, and the digital built environment." Retrieved August 20, 2019, from Mediapolis website: https://www.mediapolisjournal.com/2018/10/urban-platforms-rent-and-the-digital-built-environment/.

Stenning, A., Smith, A., Rochovská, A., & Świątek, D. (2010). "Credit, debt, and everyday financial practices: Low-income households in two postsocialist cities," *Economic Geography* 86(2): 119–145.

Sullivan, S. (2012). "Banking nature? The spectacular financialisation of environmental conservation," *Antipode* 45(1): 198–217.

Swartz, L. (2014). "Gendered transactions: Identity and payment at midcentury," *WSQ: Women's Studies Quarterly* 42(1): 137–153.

Swyngedouw, E. (2006). "Metabolic urbanization: The making of cyborg cities," in M. Kaika, N. Heynen, and E. Swyngedouw (eds.), *In the Nature of Cities* (pp. 36–55). New York, NY: Routledge.

Tapp, R. (2019). "Layers of finance: Historic tax credits and the fiscal geographies of urban redevelopment," *Geoforum* 105: 13–22.

Tapp, R., & Kay, K. (2019). "Fiscal geographies: 'Placing' taxation in urban geography," *Urban Geography* 40(4): 573–581.

Taylor, Z. J. (2020). "The real estate risk fix: Residential insurance-linked securitization in the Florida metropolis," *Environment and Planning A: Economy and Space*, 0308518X19896579.

Taylor, P. J., Derudder, B., Faulconbridge, J. R., Hoyler, M., & Ni, P. (2014). "Advanced producer service firms as strategic networks, global cities as strategic places," *Economic Geography* 90(3): 267–291.

Teresa, B. F. (2019). "New dynamics of rent gap formation in New York city rent-regulated housing: Privatization, financialization, and uneven development," *Urban Geography* 0(0): 1–23.

Valverde, M. (2009). *Law's Dream of a Common Knowledge*. Princeton, NJ: Princeton University Press.

Vidal, L. (2018). "The politics of creditor–debtor relations and mortgage payment strikes: The case of the Uruguayan federation of mutual-aid housing cooperatives," *Environment and Planning A: Economy and Space* 50(6): 1189–1208.

Wachsmuth, D., & Weisler, A. (2018). "Airbnb and the rent gap: Gentrification through the sharing economy," *Environment and Planning A: Economy and Space* 50(6): 1147–1170.

Wainwright, J., & Mann, G. (2018). *Climate Leviathan: A Political Theory of Our Planetary Future*. London and New York, NY: Verso Books.

Walker, R. (2019, June). The New Deal Didn't Create Segregation. *Jacobin*. Retrieved from https://jacobinmag.com/2019/06/the-color-of-law-richard-rothstein-review.

Weber, R. (2010). "Selling city futures: The financialization of urban redevelopment policy," *Economic Geography* 86(3): 251–274.

Woodward, K., Jones III, J. P., & Marston, S. A. (2010). "Of eagles and flies: Orientations toward the site," *Area* 42(3): 271–280.

Yrigoy, I. (2018). "Rent gap reloaded: Airbnb and the shift from residential to touristic rental housing in the Palma old quarter in Mallorca, Spain," *Urban Studies* 56(13): 2709–2726.

Zelizer, V. A. (1989). "The social meaning of money: Special monies," *American Journal of Sociology* 95(2): 342–377.

17

FIN-TECH

Jing Wang

Introduction

Digital financial technologies or so-called fin-techs have reshaped the financial practices worldwide. Around the year 2014 when fin-tech just came into shape and was primarily run by IT corporations or start-ups, it was normally considered "alternative finance"—the non-mainstream, or the supplement to the traditional finance managed by banks (e.g., Agnew, 2015). While banks run as the dominant entities in traditional finance and get financial licenses from the government, the regulators often consider fin-tech companies as informational agencies rather than financial intermediaries (Wang, 2018a). However, in less than five years, almost all the major banks have set up a department or business sector to develop their fin-tech businesses (Deloitte, 2019). In the meantime, some of the leading fin-tech companies, (e.g., Ant Financial) are considered the most valuable companies in the world (Reuters, 2018). How have digital technologies played a transforming role in the financial domain? In addition to enhancing efficiency and innovation, what are the social and cultural consequences that are often ignored amid academic and public discussions?

This chapter sets its foundation in these two questions and studies fin-techs through a critical lens. Rather than finding fault with the established scholarly thoughts, it takes critique as a way of alternative thinking, which has three specific prongs. First, it invites the researchers in economics and finance studies to shift their focus from theorization and modeling to the social contexts in which these theories and models are applicable, and thus enables the conversations between the classic literature and the interdisciplinary studies. Second, it invites financial practitioners to alter their focus. In addition to drilling on the returns of specific financial products, they need to understand the social, political, and cultural settings of financial industries. This switch will help them to

343

develop more sustainable financial products and services. Last but not least, the critical lens aims at showing the large public the pitfalls of corporate-dominated finance which has seldom been discussed in the popular business and financial news.

Specifically, this chapter critically examines the performative nature of fin-techs. Based on a case study of Yu'ebao, a popular consumer investment app rolled out by Ant Financial in 2013 and has accumulated the largest money market fund in the world, this chapter analyzes how the political economic and cultural conditions have engendered the rise of financial technologies in China. Empirically, the analyses of the structures and mechanisms of fin-techs in China allows the readers to understand how Chinese fin-techs have enhanced capital liquidity using technological resources. Theoretically, drawing on the literature on performativity, this chapter introduces the idea of *performative technology* which emphasizes the social settings that enable the affordance of technological advancements.

China, a beginner in financial marketization but also a leader of the global fin-techs, has drawn attention from academic and industry observers. On the one hand, the official marketization began only three decades ago (Zhou, 2015), lagging far behind its counterparts in the West. On the other hand, the growing sector of alternative finance in China—the non-banking institutions which provide clearance, settlements, and investment products and services to individuals of all social strata—has been widely taken as the innovative leader of the global fin-techs (Pinter & Bago, 2019). Among all the top-valued Chinese fin-tech companies, Ant Financial has been the largest surprise for the global investment banking industry when its valuation reached $150 billion (Reuters, 2018). Ant Financial is also the most popular brand in consumer finance with more than 300 million individual/lay investors constituting the largest money market fund in the world (Mu, 2014). Beginning investors can start with as little as one Chinese yuan on Yu'ebao, a very user-friendly app, without paying Ant Financial any agency fee or commission. Based on technological advancement, fin-tech investment was in fashion among urban retirees, college students, and office workers, who conveniently turned their savings, pensions, and pocket money into financial investments such as stock trading, wealth management funds, and P2P lending through the Internet and various mobile apps (Wang, 2018a). While financialization in China has taken on some unique forms in the past decade (Wang, 2017), the socialization of digital financial technologies—increasingly more people have been attracted to the financial arena and turned themselves as lay investors using fin-tech apps—has certainly added a digital dynamic.

Since their advent, digital technologies have had significant economic, political, and cultural implications at the domestic and global level. Drawing on the idea of performative agency in the cultural economy (e.g., Butler, 2010; Callon, 2006, 2007), this chapter discusses the dynamics and consequences of digital technologies in the development of Chinese fin-tech industries. Based on the case study of Yu'ebao, it identifies the performative nature of digital financial technologies and takes fin-techs as a form of *performative technology*. While most research on fin-techs has focused on the affordance of digital technologies and considers that technological advancement is pivotal for financial innovation, this chapter asserts that it is the adoption and promotion of digital technologies by the stakeholders for their own ends that engineered the advancement of Chinese fin-techs, not the other way around. The key players include the state, oligopoly Internet corporations, and the massive numbers of lay investors. In other words, the powerfulness of digital technologies in financial innovation is highly performative rather than being functional or practical, and it has been engendered by the intentions and actions of the key political and corporate actors. In this vein, understanding the structures and motivations of pro-fin-tech actors is crucial to identify what determines fin-tech's success.

Combining policy research, analyses of market research data, ethnographic work, and media content analyses, this chapter articulates fin-tech research with performativity theory in critical economics (e.g., Callon, 2010; MacKenzie, 2004; MacKenzie & Millo, 2003; see also the detailed review in Cochoy et al., 2010). As Callon asserts, "economics does not describe an existing external economy, but brings that economy into being" (Callon, 2010: 164). If the manipulation, testification, and applications of economics models and formulas (e.g., Black, 1989; Derman, 2011) embody the performative agency in the traditional finance sector, the design, use, dissemination, and social understanding of digital affordances constitute the performative power of fin-techs. Moreover, this chapter enriches studies on technology and development by bridging the structural dynamics at the state and corporation level with the cultural forces at the individual level. The latter provides a thick description of the digital cultures of finance, whereas the former unravels the shifting conditions within which the cultural discourses are at play. The connection between the structural and the cultural can create a more rigorous and grounded understanding of the politics of fin-techs without rejecting the capabilities of technological advancement.

Performative Agency and Digital Financial Technologies

Performative theory, at its very origin, addresses the capacity of speech and language-mediated communication (Austin, 1962). Performativity refers to the consequences of speech as not only conveying certain words or sentences, but more importantly, as acting or consummating an action or constructing and performing an identity. A classic example is that the announcement by a husband "I hereby marry you as my wife" has formally defined the social and legal relations between the speaker and the other person in the marriage.

Performative powers are also found on many other non-verbal occasions, such as gift-exchange, a promise in which sending a gift legitimizes the expectation of receiving a gift in return (Mauss, 1954/1990), arranged orders of display in stores that defines the popularity of some commodities over the others (Cochoy, 2010), linguistic models in social scientific writing, a framing technique that sustains belief in the connections between financial investment and personal enrichment (La Berge, 2015), as well as financial derivatives, a new category of financial products that exploit the linguistic power of promise through the contracts between product issuers and investors (Appadurai, 2015). Just as Butler (2010) suggests, the uses of performativity theory are not limited within speech-related contexts; performative discourse does not have to take the form of discrete verbal enunciation. Other practices exercising performative power include the mundane and repeated acts of delimitation that "seek to maintain a separation among economic, social and political spheres, and the organizations of human and non-human networks, including technology, that enter into specific economic activities" (Butler, 2010: 150). In discussing the features of capitalism in the financial era, Butler's kernel question is:

> while the autonomy of the market is presumed as a necessity and a banality, we can still ask how that necessity and banality are established (performatively) through time, and how we understand the spatially distributed and temporally reiterative processes that characterize the performative agency of various institutions. (Butler, 2010: 149)

While a variety of economic practices have been related to performativity, fin-techs have seldom been put under the performative lens. Fin-tech, the portmanteau of finance and technology, often refers to the industries that use digital technologies to provide financial products and services (Chishti & Barberis, 2016). It is considered an innovative business sector not only because it is based on high technologies but also for its disruption to the existing structures of the traditional financial industries (Kshetri, 2016; Wang, 2018a). In the development of digital financial technologies, the design, diffusion, and institutionalization of technologies at the structural/market level are intertwined with the routinization of the everyday use of fin-techs at the company or consumer level. The market, banking industries, fin-tech companies, as well as millions of fin-tech users form a network in which technology performatively transformed financial practices. In addition, performative agency not only comes from a series of special arrangements by the above actors, it is also shaped by an ensemble of socio-technical and cultural forces. The formation of performative agency is a process constructed by various social actors, taking on various forms at a given time and space. Taking Chinese fin-techs as a case study, this chapter examines the cultural and political economic settings that enabled the performative power of digital financial technologies and how they contribute to the rise of Chinese fin-tech industries.

Cultural Settings: Yu'ebao, A "Paypal" That Can Make Money for You

Among the many online investment apps, Yu'ebao perhaps was the most successful in terms of drawing lay investors' attention, loyalty, and cash to the financial market. In the year 2013, the famous media slogan "Yu'ebao—the 'PayPal' that can make money for you" covered the outdoor media in metropolitan areas and many tier-one cities in China. Ant Financial and the affiliated marketers invested in LEDs and billboards along the busiest subway lines, the major commuting routes for office workers and college students, who comprise the targeted potential lay investors.

The slogan sounds simple but embodies rich meanings in the Chinese context. "Yu'e" in Chinese means remnant money, or the left over when expenses have been met and bills have been paid. The slogan reminds the (prospective) investors that they may have some money sitting in their bank accounts and can be activated, even if it is just a small amount. Second, remnant money normally would not affect one's wealth status, but this "Yu'ebao" slogan promises that putting the remnant money into a "PayPal" account will enlarge its value, and ultimately increase the investors' personal wealth. Lastly, "bao" in Chinese means treasure, often meaning something that people cherish, but that is not necessarily expensive. For example, an album by Professor Proton may be a "bao" (treasure) for Sheldon in the *Big Bang Theory*, even though it is not intrinsically valuable. Further, "bao" is also a less formal expression used to refer to family members, particularly younger ones that are often delightful but also need extra care. In many cases, Chinese people call their children "baobao" or "baobei," like calling a child "sweetheart" or "baby" in the American context. The advertising and marketing campaigns have constructed a discourse in which "Yu'ebao" is not only a specific financial product but also represents a new lifestyle that encourages the Alipay users to take care of the remnant cash in their digital payment accounts, no matter how small the amount. Moreover, the Yu'ebao investment is not stressful since investing with petty cash is different from a significant gamble in the stock market, and all you have to do is to relocate the money from a payment account, Alipay, to an investment account, Yu'ebao, both provided by Ant Financial.

Digital technologies are a vital part of this easy-and-fun discourse, and it helps to make complicated things easier. Because of this user-friendly feature, Yu'ebao lowers the barrier to financial investment and includes more people in small investment practices. In practice, the interface is designed to be very simple and easy to use: it shows the accumulative return as of today listed on top of the return rate. On the bottom of the interface sit two buttons, one for "transfer in" and the other "transfer out." Users can make their decisions and wire the money based on their estimate of the potential return on investment. The investor's focus has been directed to the return (rate), the only metrics shown on the interface. In this context, the investors' decision-making process has been considerably simplified compared to the processes involved in the stock market or investment with banks.

Yu'ebao's marketing slogan and the interface design collectively reflect a value-making process that combines cultural and technological elements. In Weber's (1905/2002) analysis of the Protestant ethic of capitalism, one needs to keep working hard and saving money to increase one's wealth through a long-term accumulation. Yu'ebao maintains the "saving" discourse but turns the elements of "hard-working" and "accumulation" into a fun and easy process that can be facilitated and fulfilled by an online application. This discourse has proliferated and engendered the moral imperative of not letting one's money sit idle, for instance, in a savings account, but looking for the highest investment returns. The unique value of Yu'ebao has been represented as helping to increase the value of personal wealth. This meaning complex is associated with multiple factors including the media discourses constructed by advertisements, digital technologies, and the interface effect of the Yu'ebao app.

In addition to the massive advertising and media exposure, Yu'ebao's corporate background also helps to attract and sustain a large number of lay investors. As part of the multi-sided platform constructed by Alibaba, Yu'ebao was brought to the market almost a decade after the operation of the digital payment tool Alipay and the e-commerce site, Taobao (Wang & Doan, 2018). Upon the launch of Yu'ebao, millions of e-shoppers had already been gathered on Alibaba's e-commerce and payment platform. E-consumers have billions of dormant cash parking in their Alipay accounts and trust Alibaba with their money. Moreover, Alibaba does not charge any agency fee or commission for transactions and does not set the lowest investment amount. This low-bar strategy is another factor that boosted the growth of Yu'ebao investors.

In "The Ghost in the Financial Machine" (2011), Appadurai interprets the mechanisms of value-making in contemporary financial practices through three key concepts: return, uncertainty, and calculation, and the Weberian idea of "spirit" is the major thread running through these concepts and linking them together. The individual investors' spiritual forces comprise the vital part of the modern financial systems, and the notion of a "return" is more about a moral expectation than the economic interests rewarded from certain labor or capital inputs. Investors normally expect monetary returns, just as someone expects positive feedback (material or not) from sending a gift to another person. Marcel Mauss (1954/1990) noted this kind of moral force as a combination of contracting elements both voluntary and compulsory, disinterested but also self-serving. Investing in the financial market is voluntary and always inspired by the potential returns in imagination which in fact is not always guaranteed in reality.

The problem of uncertainty underpins the paradoxical nature of "return." Investors can control their participation in financial investments but cannot control the expected return. In Weber's (1905/2002) account of the Calvinist ethos, this sort of uncertainty is arranged and can only be diminished by God. For empirical economists, such as Adam Smith (1776/1991), such uncertainties have been controlled by an invisible hand, the market economy. In both explanations, uncertainty is inherent in the investment process and beyond the subjective control of the investors themselves. Thus, if investors cannot stop themselves from investing (for many reasons), all they can do is to calculate the likelihood of getting the return, or, to speculate and minimize the risks of losing their investment. For Weber, these calculations are driven by irrational power that is related to religion or certain ethical beliefs. Foucault (1989), however, rationalizes the calculation as a sort of self-examination. In Foucault's *Technologies of the Self,* the calculation is indispensable in one's daily routines.

> In the morning we must take account of our expenses, and in the evening, we must ask ourselves to render an account of our conduct of ourselves, to examine what is to our advantage and what is prejudicial against us. (1989: 44)

The calculation of returns and losses thus contains both the technique of calculating and the subjective feeling that one must keep calculating and engaging with the information and technologies essential for such calculations.

Political Economy: The Rise of the Wealth Management Community in China

If investing the remnant cash has been promoted as part of China's financial culture via Yu'ebao and other similar apps, this culture's political-economic foundation was laid in the early 1990s. Everyday finance (Langley, 2008) is not new in post-socialist China, and the formation of the lay investors market started as early as the 1989 inauguration of the Chinese stock market in Shanghai. The Chinese government's first unambiguous signals in favor of popular participation in the stock market resulted in the intensive "stock fever" which China had never experienced since the Republican era (Hertz, 1998). Since the early 1990s, the institutional reform (Harvey, 2005; Ong, 2006; Wang & Huters, 2003) has remarkably increased people's disposable income at the cost of decreased state benefits, pensions, and insurance. Specifically, benefits which were indirect income maintained and managed by the state were turned into cash income in their checking accounts. Also, inflation seemed an inevitable consequence of China's stimulus approach to economic reform (Bowles & White, 1989). As such, those increased cash incomes did not necessarily make much of a difference to mid-to-low income families. The Chinese central bank issued billions of additional currency notes in 2008 during the global financial crisis, and the resulting inflation has significantly reduced the value of people's increased incomes. Consequentially, people do have some extra cash, but they do not know how to secure the value of this money, and thus to secure their future after retirement. This dilemma motivated Chinese people to chase after all kinds of emerging financial investments. The long-lasting belief of "no pay, no gain" has been replaced by "if you don't care for your money, your money won't care for you" (Chumley & Wang, 2013).

In December 1990, Shanghai Mayor Zhu Rongji announced the establishment of the Shanghai Stock Exchange, the first official stock trading company in socialist China (Thomas, 2001). In the 1990s, about 300,000 people, mostly from the coastal areas of Shanghai and Shenzhen, took advantage of the opportunity to invest in the stock market. The average return on investment was around 20%, and many stock players turned into *wanyuan hu*—people with assets of more than 10,000 yuan (which was a phenomenal figure in the early 1990s). Some of them resigned from their jobs and became lay investors. The novel opportunities of re-making one's social and economic identity through investing in stocks attracted thousands of Chinese people to enthusiastically participate in the new occupation of "stir-frying stocks" (*chaogu*) (Shao, 2007). The stock fever lasted for almost a decade until the Asian Financial Crisis taught Chinese investors a lesson that the stock market has risks, and one needs to be cautious.

A decade later, wealth management (*licai*) became the most popular investment form, particularly after the stock plunge in 2008. Unlike bank savings with flexible but meager interest (usually around 0.3%), *licai* products offer higher interest rates (around 4%) but require a minimum deposit (usually above RMB 50,000 or US$8,000) and a fixed deposit term (usually more than three months). In 2010, all the major banks in China began the relentless promotion of *licai* products and services. According to the Fitch Ratings report in July 2013, the total wealth management products offered by Chinese banks had tripled compared to the supply in 2010 and amounted to more than 1.5 trillion dollars. During these years, foreign banks and capital investment companies also boosted their investment in Chinese wealth management products and services (Asian Investor, 2014). Along with the diversified wealth management market constructed by the formal financial sector, shadow banking (Hsu, 2017) and other non-sanctioned capital transactions (such as small loan companies and rotating savings and credit associations (Li & Hsu, 2009) constituted the increasingly vibrant informal finance sector in China, a unique financial channel for a specific social group, particularly small or micro business owners (Tsai, 2002; on shadow banking, see also the chapter by Wigger & Fernandez in this *Handbook*).

It was against this exponentially marketized financial background that the Chinese investing public became eager to try the new categories of financial investment, particularly those involving digital financial products and services. Thanks to the universal digital infrastructure, by the year 2017, more than 730 million Chinese people had access to the Internet or mobile network (CNNIC, 2018). At the same time, digital technology has become widely regarded as a new dynamic for financial innovation after Chinese Premier Li Keqiang announced the "Internet Plus" initiative in the year 2013. Both technological progress and positive political discourse boosted Chinese investors' confidence and enthusiasm for digital financial technologies, a convenient and also novel intermediary enabling investors to access this technology for everyday financial practices. In addition, news reports and magazines celebrated internet finance as the democratization of investing, and thus another rags-to-riches opportunity (Wang, 2017).

In this context, Alibaba, Tencent, and many other Internet companies turned to the so-called long tail market (Anderson, 2006)—a strategy targeting niche markets which are low-end but yield greater numbers of consumers/lay investors, and their pursuit of financial businesses was supported by policy changes in the oversight of Internet finance. In 2012, Chinese Premier Li Keqiang endorsed the prospects of Internet finance (*hulianwang jinrong*) whereby traditional financial industries (e.g., banks, insurance companies) and Internet companies collaborate to provide financial products or services, including online payments, person-to-person (P2P) transactions, online loans, crowdfunding, insurance, or to sell trusts and funds to individual investors, consumers, or small enterprises (*People's Daily*, 2015). It is unprecedented that the state has recognized the Internet's role as an intermediary and included more categories of actors in China's increasingly financialized economy. Since 2013, the prevalence of fin-techs has made significant changes in Chinese attitudes toward financial investment and engendered a growing investing public that cut across all social strata. Most fin-tech products and services yield a much higher return rate than the interest from regular savings accounts (which often is almost zero). Retirees, office or factory workers, college students, and even rural populations joined the trend of wealth management, relocating their savings to investment accounts. Investing in funds, stocks and various derivative products has become a way for the Chinese mid-to-low-income families to achieve some financial autonomy and manage their financial future. In this context digital technologies constitute a convenient and virtually indispensable platform for their economic lives.

Discussions: Digital Technologies and Financialization in China

The trend toward digital finance has been driven by a wide range of actors, including the state, Internet corporations, as well as individual lay investors, each with different goals. The collective efforts of these actors have led to a deepening financialization in Chinese society. The broader definition of financialization, referring in general to the growing weight and power of the financial sector in the overall economy (see detailed review in van der Zwan, 2014), is not constrained within a capitalist structure. Financialization in non-capitalist economies may carry the characteristics of the same process in other economies and also has distinctive forms underpinned by the unique political system and cultural circumstances.

In the past decade, the employment by the finance sector in China has more than doubled. According to the data from National Bureau of Statistics, in 2014, more than 5.6 million Chinese people worked for the finance industries. The number of financial workers (*gaojinrong de*) equaled 5–6% of the working population. In Chinese universities, majoring in finance and related fields has become very popular, and graduates with international degrees from the United States or United Kingdom are highly desired. The large demand for financial professionals is due to the vigorous growth of Chinese financial industries. In 2015, the contribution of the finance sector to the overall GDP had grown to 5.9%, and non-financial enterprises have gained almost 20% profits from financial channels (investments) as opposed to 3% ten years ago. Contributing to this is the fact that China's top 500 manufacturing companies registered a profit of 2.7% in 2014, far lower than the world average. Such a low return rate induces investment capital to flow to the more lucrative financial industries, turning the economy in the direction of the financial sector (Zhang, 2016).

The expansion of financial capital was not limited to financial industries. In the past decade, financial capital has increasingly controlled multiple areas of the domestic economy, including state asset management (Wang, 2015), goods and commodities (Zhao, 2014), home ownership (Forrest, 2015), etc. The majority of this capital is state-owned; private and international capital make up only minor percentages, the specific numbers of which vary across different industries. At the same time, China's non-financial industry has also garnered more profits from financial investments, with an increase from 3.3% to 19.6% in terms of their net profit level accounting for their entire profit in the last ten years. That means that nearly 20% of the overall profit of those manufacturers, agriculture producers, and real estate and property companies are from financial investments, a remarkable achievement. In my conversations with several small entrepreneurs in Beijing and Shanxi, "*laiqian kuai*" (getting returns faster) seemed to be the superpower of finance for these businessmen who often regretted that they did not start investing in the financial sector earlier. "If I had known how finance works earlier, I didn't have to work that hard on my traditional businesses!" Investing in commercial buildings or lending the money at a high interest rate often brings them a much higher return (usually around 8%) compared to what they get from the traditional businesses (4%, nothing, or even a negative balance).

An even stronger devotion to finance is reflected in the notion of "*shangshi*" (to be listed in stock markets, or so-called initial public offerings) among the owners of small to medium enterprises. Listing a company in the stock market has been a tempting approach to accumulating a significant amount of capital, whereas putting an investment of effort as well as money in products and services is perceived as very inefficient. This allegiance is underpinned by the increasing deregulation of the state regarding listings, the promotion of the industry by investment banks, and a trend to list overseas that has been welcomed by stock exchanges in the United States and Hong Kong. In 2015, the China Securities Regulatory Commission significantly shortened the number of documents required for the approval of listing by removing 27 items from the 68-item list announced in 2012 at the beginning of the Xi Administration. In this context, investment bankers relentlessly sought domestic companies and promoted the idea of making a fortune through listing on the stock market, providing technical and financial support to prospective companies. This promotion serves the banks' interests since injecting capital in a company is conditional on getting returns when the company is listed. Finally, at the same time as domestic listings were being made easier through deregulation, the state also opened up the avenue for Chinese companies to list in overseas markets. According to the 2016 statistics from Deloitte, Chinese enterprises have accounted for 23% of global public offerings, which makes China own the largest amount of capital from the global stock market. Actively adapting themselves to the global capitalist system, Chinese companies, particularly those small to medium companies, are pursuing business expansion by attracting financial capital rather than value-making through production or services.

In addition to the promotion of traditional financial businesses, the Chinese government has put increasing efforts to develop "alternative finance" to offset the economic slowdown. National financial policy-making has been centered on marketizing the financial industry and promoting "inclusive finance" (*puhui jinrong*) (Xie & Zou, 2012), meaning enhancing access to financial services and capital for individuals and small enterprises who had been locked out of the conventional banking system due to their low income or high risk of default. "Finance going to the rural" (*jinrong xiaxiang*), a policy announced in 2015, indicates that rural areas have been assigned as the next market for the lending and investment business, and efforts to popularize financial endeavors with the general population of these regions are underway. ICTs (information and communications technologies) have been extremely instrumental for the Chinese state to expand its financial domain in the overall economy.

Conclusion

The performative nature of fin-techs is both a cause and corollary of China's dual process of digitization of finance and the financialization of the Internet. Chinese economic reform since the 1990s set up the conditions for this process. Structural changes both in technology and in governmental oversight have contributed to the unprecedented financialization of Chinese society. The Yu'ebao case is particularly useful in understanding the complex financial context in which digital technology was adopted as an institution to establish a performative domain for a new financial market comprised of emerging small fin-tech investors and fin-tech companies. In line with the stratified analytical approach (Wullweber, 2016), we can also understand the performativity of Chinese fin-techs at three levels. At the micro-level, this chapter maps out how a belief in the connections between digital technology and personal enrichment was sustained through a set of advertising and marketing campaigns, as well as the linguistic and symbolic paradigms woven into these promotional practices.

While fin-techs have been adopted as part of their economic routines, fin-tech users are employing the apps to manage their savings, govern their emotions, and adapt to the contingencies embedded in everyday economic life.

At the meso-level, leading Chinese Internet corporations have used digital financial technologies to expand the reach of their businesses into the finance sector. In the past decade, the increasingly globalized financial market has allowed Chinese Internet corporations to proactively adapt to the global capitalist system. In particular, oligopolistic IT companies in China such as Baidu, Tencent, and Alibaba are expediting growth through financial capital as opposed to profiting from products or services. In the meantime, these companies have used digital financial technologies to generate new forms of commodities—fin-tech products and services—and to promote fin-techs to users from their traditional IT businesses.

At the macro-level, the development of Chinese fin-techs has been driven by the Chinese government's pursuit of digitization of the overall economy, and digital technologies have been in the vanguard, especially since 2012 when the central government announced the "Internet plus" initiative and the direction of "Internet thinking" as a way to stimulate economic development. In addition, reform of the financial system has always been central to China's economic transformation since the Deng Xiaoping era, and market-oriented institutional shifts have gained velocity since the early 2000s (Calomiris, 2007). Fin-techs, in this context, have been considered a new form of financial intermediary which enables the competition between traditional banks and alternative financial companies. Such a competition has been endorsed by the state to deepen the marketization of financial industries.

On each of the three levels, digital financial technologies embody the agency that organizes human or non-human networks through which different actors maintain or create certain spheres. Specifically, the nation-state has promoted the "Internet Plus" action plan and "Internet thinking" in order to stimulate the development of financial sectors. Fin-techs in this context are a new form of financial intermediary which legitimized competition between traditional banks and emerging financial companies and facilitated the increased marketization of Chinese financial industries (on financial intermediaries, see also the chapter by Tadjeddine in this *Handbook*). In the meantime, fin-techs sanctioned the inclusion of Internet corporations when the state granted licenses and permits authorizing these non-financial companies to venture into financial industries. Finally, for many individual investors who were locked out by the high threshold of bank-provided investment products and services, fin-techs provided access to a financial world which had been visible but untouchable. To most of the investing-for-fun people, fin-tech apps are not only a platform for them to practice investment but also the ways in which they make "managing wealth" as part of their daily routine.

The various forms of agency reflected in Chinese fin-techs share a performative nature. By announcing and promoting the pivotal role of digital technologies in economic rejuvenation and financial transformation, the Chinese state took a marketized approach to reforming its financial sector which they believe contributes to sustainable development in the post-crisis era. After making fin-tech apps available to the individual investors market, the major Internet corporations in China jumped into the global capitalist system in which finance is the primary approach to business innovation and continuous growth. Lastly, by adopting digital technologies in their financial practices, the growing investing public tended to abandon traditional modes of wealth accumulation and strove for an investor's identity during their struggles with currency (renminbi) inflation and the increasing unemployment in the context of marketization and privatization of state-owned enterprises since the 1990s.

It is noteworthy that the performative agency embodied at the state, corporate, and individual levels are not running on separate tracks. Instead, these levels are always interacting with each other, which creates the symbiosis and tensions among the various actors. Considering such relations helps to sort out the paradox of a process that achieves its effects in both regenerative and accumulative ways, thus contributing to theorizing the idea of performative agency in the financial context. The emerging fin-tech cultures are not the utterance of single subjects; they rely on broad networks of social relations and institutionalized practices, which have been organized by the highly performative fin-techs themselves. While most of research and media reports about fin-tech development have centered primarily on its innovative and technological advancement, this chapter sheds light on the performative nature of financial technologies and draws attention to the ensemble of cultural and structural forces that define the future of global fin-techs.

References

Agnew, H. (2015, February 23). *European Market for Online Alternative Finance Surges.* FT.com.

Anderson, C. (2006). *The Long Tail: Why the Future of Business Is Selling Less of More.* New York, NY: Hyperion.

Appadurai, A. (2011). "The ghost in the financial machine," *Public Culture* 23(3): 517–539.

Appadurai, A. (2015). *Banking on Words: The Failure of Language in the Age of Derivative Finance.* Chicago, IL: The University of Chicago Press.

Asian Investor. (2014, Feb.). RBC Wealth Management adds Greater China heads. *Asian Investor,* 25.

Austin, J. L. (1962). *How to Do Things with Words: The William James Lectures Delivered at Harvard University in 1955.* Oxford: Clarendon Press.

Black, F. (1989). "How we came up with the option formula," *Journal of Portfolio Management* 15(2): 4–8.

Bowles, P., & White, G. (1989). "Contradictions in China's financial reforms: The relationship between banks and enterprises," *Cambridge Journal of Economies* 13: 481–495.

Butler, J. (2010). "Performative agency," *Journal of Cultural Economy* 3(2): 147–161.

Callon, M. (2006). "What does it mean to say that economics is performative?" in D. MaccKenzie, F. Muniesa, and L. Siu (eds.), *Do Economists Make Markets? On the Performativity of Economics.* Princeton, NJ: Princeton University Press.

Callon, M. (2007). "An essay on the growing contribution of economic markets to the proliferation of the social," *Theory, Culture & Society* 24(7): 139–163.

Callon, M. (2010). "Performativity, misfires and politics," *Journal of Cultural Economy* 3(2): 163–169.

Calomiris, C. (2007). *China's Financial Transition at a Crossroads.* New York, NY: Columbia University Press.

Center, C. I. N. I. (2018). 第41次《中国互联网络发展状况统计报告》 "The 41st Statistical Report on Internet Development in China". Retrieved from http://www.cnnic.net.cn/hlwfzyj/hlwxzbg/hlwtjbg/201803/t20180305_70249.htm

Chishti, S., & Barberis, J. (2016). *The FinTech Book: The Financial Technology Handbook for Investors, Entrepreneurs, and Visionaries.* Hoboken, NJ: Wiley.

Chumley, L., & Wang, J. (2013). "'If you don't care for your money, it won't care for you': Chronotypes of risk and return in Chinese wealth management" in P. L. Cassidy (ed.), *Qualitative Research in Gambling: Exploring the Production and Consumption of Risk* (pp. 202–217). London and New York, NY: Routledge.

Cochoy, F. (2010). "How to build displays that sell: The politics of performativity in American grocery stores (Progressive Grocer, 1929–1946)," *Journal of Cultural Economy* 3(2): 299–315.

Cochoy, F., Giraudeau, M., & McFall, L. (2010). "Performativity, economics, and politics," *Journal of Cultural Economy* 3(2): 139–146.

Deloitte. (2019). *Banking Industry Outlook.* Retrieved from https://www2.deloitte.com/global/en/pages/financial-services/articles/gx-banking-industry-outlook.html

Derman, E. (2011). *Models Behaving. Badly: Why Confusing Illusion with Reality Can Lead to Disaster, on Wall Street and in Life.* New York, NY: Free Press.

Forrest, R. (2015). "The ongoing financialisation of home ownership – new times, new contexts," *International Journal of Housing Policy* 15(1): 1–5.

Foucault, M. (1989). In L. H. Martin, H. Guman, and P. H. Hutton (eds.), *Technologies of the Self* (pp. 16–49). University of Massachusetts Press.

Harvey, D. (2005). *A Brief History of Neoliberalism.* Oxford: Oxford University Press.

Hertz, E. (1998). *The Trading Crowd: An Ethnography of the Shanghai Stock Market.* Cambridge: Cambridge University Press.

Hsu, S. (2017). "Shadow banking in China," *China Quarterly* 229: 232–233.

Kshetri, N. (2016). "Big data's role in expanding access to financial services in China," *International Journal of Information Management* 36: 297–308.

La Berge, L. (2015). "How to make money with words: Finance, performativity, language," *Journal of Cultural Economy* 9(1): 43–62.

Langley, P. (2008). *The Everyday Life of Global Finance: Saving and Borrowing in Anglo-America.* Oxford: Oxford University Press.

Li, J., & Hsu, S. (2009). *Informal Finance in China American and Chinese Perspectives.* Oxford: Oxford University Press.

MacKenzie, D. (2004). "The big, bad wolf and the rational market: Portfolio insurance, the 1987 crash and the performativity of economics," *Economy and Society* 33(3): 303–334.

MacKenzie, D., & Millo, Y. (2003). "Constructing a market, performing theory: The historical sociology of a financial derivatives exchange," *American Journal of Sociology* 109(1): 107–145.

Mauss, M. (1954/1990). *The Gift: The Form and Reason for Exchange in Archaic Society.* New York, NY: W.W. Norton.

Mu, E. (2014, May 18). "Yu'ebao: A brief history of Chinese Internet financing upstart," *Forbes.*

Ong, A. (2006). *Neoliberalism as Exception: Mutations in Citizenship and Sovereignty.* Durham: Duke University Press.

People's Daily. (2015, January 4). Chinese Premier Li Keqiang visit the inauguration of Webank. http://politics.people.com.cn/n/2015/0104/c1001-26322036.html

Pinter, E., & Bago, P. (2019). *Smart Asian Fintech: Hungarian Project Conference Paper 2019*. University of Obuda. Retrieved from https://ssrn.com/abstract=3410467.

Reuters. (2018). Explainer: Ant Financial's $150 Billion Valuation, and the Big Recent Bump-Up. April 18, 2018. *Reuters Technology News*.

Shao, Q. (2007). "A community of the dispersed: The culture of Shanghai's neighborhood stock markets," *The Chinese Historical Review* 14(2): 212–239.

Smith, A. (1776/1991). *The Wealth of Nations*. New York, NY: Knopf.

Thomas, W. A. (2001). *Western Capitalism in China: A History of the Shanghai Stock Exchange*. Aldershot: Ashgate.

Tsai, K. S. (2002). *Back-Alley Banking: Private Entrepreneurs in China*. Ithaca, NY: Cornell University Press.

Van Der Zwan, N. (2014). "Making sense of financialization," *Socio-Economic Review* 12(1): 99–129.

Wang, H., & Huters, T. (2003). *China's New Order: Society, Politics, and Economy in Transition*. Cambridge, MA and London: Harvard University Press.

Wang, J. (2017). "'Stir-frying' Internet finance: Financialization and the institutional role of business and financial news in China," *International Journal of Communication* 11: 581–602.

Wang, J. (2018a). "Inclusion or expulsion: Digital financial technologies and socio-technical formations in China's Internet finance," *Communication and the Public* 3(1): 34–45.

Wang, J., & Doan, M. (2018). "The Ant empire: Fintech media and corporate convergence within and beyond Alibaba," *The Political Economy of Communication* 6(2): 25–37.

Wang, Y. (2015). "The rise of the 'shareholding state': financialization of economic management in China," *Socio-Economic Review* 13(3): 603–625.

Weber, M. (1905/2002). *The Protestant Ethic and the Spirit of Capitalism*, trans. S. Kalberg. Los Angeles, CA: Roxbury Publishing Company.

Wullweber, J. (2016). "Performative global finance: bridging micro and macro approaches with a stratified perspective," *New Political Economy* 21(3): 305–321.

Xie, P., & Zou, C. W. (2012). "Research of internet financial pattern," *Financial Research* 12: 11–22.

Zhang, C. (2016). "Dangers of 'excessive financialization' in Chinese economy." Retrieved from http://www.china.org.cn/opinion/2016-01/01/content_37433275.htm.

Zhao, C. (2014). "Goods financialization and inflation in China," *Economic Research Journal* 49(1): 140–154.

Zhou, X. (2015). "Jinrong gaige fazhan jiqi neizai luoji" [Financial reform and development and its internal logics]. 金融改革与发展的内在逻辑 *China Finance* 19. Retrieved from http://www.cnfinance.cn/magzi/2015-10/08-22509_1.html.

18

FINANCE FICTION

Torsten Andreasen, Mikkel Krause Frantzen
and Frederik Tygstrup

Introduction

In the wake of the global financial crisis that broke out more than a decade ago, the otherwise discreet and arcane world of banking and investment has been subject to intense public interest. The crisis suddenly made it clear that the new order of the financial sector—with its plethora of shrewd products and complex digital technologies—had immense and immediate consequences for the lives of ordinary citizens. One token of this new interest is the advent of what is becoming increasingly recognizable as a new literary genre: finance fiction. Novels and documentary accounts alike (by authors such as Robert Harris, Sebastian Faulks, Carolina Neurath, Daniel Kehlmann, Adam Haslet, Phillippe Sollers, and Justin Cartwright; and Michael Hirsch, Scott Patterson, Michael Lewis, and Joris Luydendijk, respectively), as well as numerous films and television series (like *Too Big to Fail*, *Margin Call*, *The Wolf of Wall Street*, *The Big Short*, *Billions*) have concurred in trying to describe the working of present-day financial activity and its influence on the way we live now.

In tandem with the broader field of critical finance studies, finance fictions thus contribute to *understanding* finance and financialization. Understanding, here, is not about getting one's head around that particular scientific object constructed by economists, but about properly envisaging finance as a matter that reverberates in social life at large, not only setting the conditions for what we can and cannot do—as individuals, societies, and nation states—but also increasingly impregnating the imaginaries, emotions, and propensities of our social and individual lives.

The impact of contemporary finance, however, reaches well beyond the financiers and their doings, and the term "financialization" now increasingly designates how values, mindsets, and modes of agency are becoming invested with rationales and motifs that derive from the world of finance and thus how still more areas of contemporary life are being subsumed under the aegis of finance (Haiven, 2014; Martin, 2002). Consequently, literature's attempt to understand finance also involves finding traces and instantiations of the logic of finance where one would not have searched for them in the first place, and it is a seminal task for the study of finance fictions to unearth how the repercussions of financialization in the lives of our contemporaries are minutely and imaginatively recorded in literary writing.

In this chapter, we first sketch an overview of literature's engagement with money and finance in a long historical perspective and according to different modalities (the first two sections). The third section attempts to give a horizon scan of the different approaches and main insights in the presently quite burgeoning field of finance fiction studies. After suggesting some main directions for further studies of finance fiction based on some of the most prominent problematics in the field, the fourth section provides three short examples of analyses of finance fiction and indicates their import for the larger field of critical finance studies.

Finance and Fiction: Historical Encounters

Literature has a long history of taking an interest in economic and financial matters. One of the most played comedies from the French classicist tradition, Molière's *The Miser* from 1724, is about the obstinate avariciousness of M. Harpagon, whose countless and highly inventive attempts to find ways of *not* opening his chest of gold have all become proverbial. A bit more than a century before that, in 1595, Shakespeare wrote what has become the foundational text in the Western canon about the vicissitudes of indebtedness, *The Merchant of Venice*, where Bassanio takes money from Shylock, guaranteed by Antonio, who however does not actually hold any wealth, but waits for it to materialize from his overseas ventures, terminating in the cruel scene of bankruptcy where Shylock eventually claims the famous "pound of flesh." A century after Molière, Goethe's *Faust II* (1832) seems to offer a remedy to the conundrums of the two earlier works: too much money stacked up in one place and too much dangerously outstanding debt in another. At some point, Mephistopheles proposes to the prince, in distress over the state finances, that he simply issue paper money, guaranteed with nothing but his royal signature:

> And thus the paper debt's at once paid up / And all the mocking sceptics put to shame. / Everyone's used to this, they want the same / System continued; thus the Empire far and wide / With jewels, gold, and paper now is well supplied. (Goethe, 1994: 6126–6130)

Three works, then, arguably all belonging in the top tier of any canonical list of consecrated classics, that can teach us more or less everything we need to know about circulating capital: about asset accumulation, about securities, and about liquidity. Nice as it is to have literary examples at hand to demonstrate particular economic phenomena, literature's proclivity for matters of money (and Shakespeare, Molière, and Goethe are but three of many instances) nonetheless also rests on a more profound kinship between literature and money, a kinship indicated in different ways in these three classics.

When stacking up wealth is no longer a matter of securing the means for useful exchange but becomes a goal in its own right, we leave the realm of economy proper and enter the domain of the imaginary. This leap is probably as ancient as economy itself (Aristotle named it *chrematism*), just as it is indeed a predominant motif in the economic realm today. But it is also a somewhat irrational attitude to come across at the very heart of economics, because the imagery of accumulation is invested with all kinds of feelings and affective reactions. This is what Molière has pinpointed with durable effect, thereby indicating a first point of encounter between money and literature: they both unbind the imaginary and the affects it nurtures to operate well beyond the realm of strict necessities.

A second point is magisterially identified by Shakespeare: namely, that dramatic storytelling and the making of debt share a profound common structure, that of hypothesizing future outcomes of present situations. The financial actors in *The Merchant of Venice*, Bassanio, Antonio, and Shylock, are each confecting their particular plots—temporal models of how one situation might transform into another—leaving the master plotter, the dramatic author himself, to simply organize and orchestrate the competition between the different plotmakers. Success, for writers and financiers alike, is about devising the best plot, the shrewdest way of imagining how a future state of things can be achieved through actions performed in the present.

The third point of encounter between the realms of finance and of literature, represented by Mephistopheles's machinations in *Faust*, concerns the very idea of fictionality. When Goethe was preparing his second Faust-drama, he studied the (failed) French money reforms of the 1720s inspired by John Law, and he was obviously fascinated by the mundane magic of money they elicited. On the one hand, Mephistopheles's proposition highlights the fictitiousness of finance in the form of paper money while, on the other, insisting that fictitious claims might indeed have factual, and perhaps even beneficial, effects. We are reminded, thus, that both fiction and money are fueled by Western modernity's characteristic propensity for speculation. Fictions are imaginary tales with no real referent in the world, but they nonetheless retain interest by presenting events that might arguably have been, once one had willingly suspended one's disbelief. And although paper money has no intrinsic value whatsoever, it nonetheless possesses the practical quality of being a measure of relative value, if backed by a belief in their ultimate convertibility by the state. Both fiction and money make a speculative leap into a universe of conjecture, and they both come with the caveat that this leap is only warranted if we don't take the speculative face of fiction for something real (in the first case), and if we don't take the speculative face of money as something unreal (in the second). As long as we believe firmly enough in fiction *not having* an actual referent, and in money *having* an actual value, we are able to maneuver these otherwise slippery media that diligently blend extravagant speculation and practical usefulness (on speculation, see also Konings's chapter in this *Handbook*).

Finance might not recognize itself in literature, but literature obviously appreciates the kinship and sees resemblances that put it in an intimate (if only unilaterally recognized) relationship with the world of money. Through the lens of literature, economy does not simply appear as a matter of prudence, rational calculation, and transparent mediation, but also, and perhaps more importantly, as a sphere of emotion-driven imagination, of telling tales about the future, and of manipulation of what appears real by way of speculative fiction. Literature is drawn to the world of money, hence, because they share a crucial epistemic feature, in Mary Poovey's words: "What economic writing and Literary writing share, both historically and theoretically, is an engagement with the problematic of representation" (Poovey, 2008: 5). And representation, to be sure, is far from being a neutral or transparent process; with representation come distortions, conjectures, and speculative inferences. This might not be deeply ingrained in the self-consciousness of economic actors, but it is acutely present in the minds of those engaged with literature. And this seems to be the reason why it should be bestowed on literature to recognize and indeed to brandish the stirred feelings, the fantasized futures, and the fictitious claims that invariably accompany finance as an irradicable shadow.

Literary Form and Financial Form

Literature has indeed shown a remarkable sensitivity toward the historical transformations of capitalism. Throughout the nineteenth century, the proud tradition of realist literature has documented and glossed the booms and the crises, the fortunes and the losses, of the burgeoning industrial revolution. It has described the projection of railways and the building of boulevards, and behind them, the stocks and bonds, the credit negotiations, and the lineages of debt. It has pinpointed the characters populating this world, the usurers and the idealists, the industrialists and the bankers, the splendor of the rentiers and the poverty of the dispossessed. Charles Dickens's Ebenezer Scrooge, Honoré de Balzac's baron Nucingen, Anthony Trollope's Augustus Malmotte, and Émile Zola's David Séchard all come across as innovative concatenations of Harpagon, Shylock, and Mephistopheles, painting the ever-morphing archetypes of the new financial world.

In the late nineteenth and early twentieth centuries, where the momentum of capitalist accumulation moves from Europe to the United States, American fictions of finance similarly come to abound, with Henry James, Frank Norris, Theodore Dreiser, Scott Fitzgerald, and John Dos Passos as important proponents, and with an acute attention toward the locus of money handling and financial speculation, epitomized in the name of Wall Street. Characteristically, and somehow in distinction to the European predecessors, industry and empire slightly move out of focus in favor of the fascination with finance and speculation themselves—a change that can of course also be detected in European literature around the turn of the century, in Thomas Mann's *Buddenbrooks* (1901) for instance, that charts the transition from merchant capital to investment capital and the generational conflicts it entails, or in Fernando Pessoa's *The Anarchist Banker* from 1922 where the conversations between the anarchist turned banker and his interlocutor revolve around the question of money as "social fictions" as it is called in the Portuguese author's short story.

If the narrative mode of realist novels is a literary counterpart to the form of interest-bearing capital in the nineteenth century, it can similarly be argued that the narrative mode of the modernist novel expresses the financial regime of intensified capital accumulation with huge and opaque monopolistic corporations and equally, devastatingly, huge crises of a global scale. A suitable proponent of this could be John Dos Passos's *The Big Money* from 1936, where the linear narrative of individual destinies is replaced by a kaleidoscopic montage of life fragments, some taken from real persons like Frederick Taylor, the founder of modern scientific management, or Thorstein Veblen, the sociologist of consumption, others portraying invented characters and fragments of their different struggles in a crisis-ridden contemporary landscape. These glimpses into an array of juxtaposed real and invented lives are then interspersed by sections citing anonymous sensations in a disorganized *stream-of-consciousness*, and striking assemblages of newspaper-headlines and advertising slogans. No longer a form that mimics the alignment of life trajectories with returns on interest, but rather one that stages a new sense of distress corresponding to, as it is put at one point, "the sabotage of production by business, the sabotage of life by blind need for money profits" (Dos Passos, 2013: 81).

The problematic respective relations of fiction and finance to material reality, the narrative attempts to resolve the real contradictions of economic conditions, are further expressed by the relative absence of literary works engaging with the world of finance during the historic anomaly of the post-war boom, *Les trente glorieuses*. Only as the economic expansion wanes do we see a new surge within finance fiction. In 1973, the year of the oil crisis and the definitive abolition of the Bretton Woods System, former banker Paul Erdman invented the genre of the finance thriller with the book *The Billion Dollar Sure Thing*, and soon other writers—and financiers turned writers—followed in his wake. Arthur Hailey (*The Moneychangers* from 1975) and Michael M. Thomas (*Green Monday* from 1980) are but two examples. In the 1980s and 1990s Tom Wolfe and Bret Easton Ellis wrote their famous renditions of financial fantasy and psychosis, *The Bonfire of the Vanities* (1987) and *American Psycho* (1991), Don DeLillo described the financial desire for immateriality in *Cosmopolis* (2003) and after the financial crisis of 2007–2008 there has been an explosion of books negotiating the crisis and its aftermaths. We will revert to some of these concrete finance fictions at the end of this chapter.

Based on this brief historical sketch, it would be tempting to envisage a full history of literature based on the history of money and of capital in all its forms. Such an undertaking, however, indeed one within the scope of contemporary studies of finance fiction, would have to move beyond both the interest in money and finance as a prominent *motive* in literature and literature's epistemic kinship with money, what one could call an *allegorical* relationship between literature and money. What importantly needs to be done, and what is being done at present, as will be fleshed in more detail below, is to gauge the way in which literary *form* is mobilized to emulate—and thus make intelligible—the forms of financial agency that take part in the ongoing modification of the world we live in.

The Merchant of Venice can serve as a case in point; what Shakespeare found here was nothing less than an ideal driver of a plot: the maturation of debt. The sense of an ending is where the debt is due. Necessity, fatality, intransigence—it all follows from the signature on a credit note. This narrative device was taken to the highest degree of refinement in the prose fiction of the nineteenth century. The tradition of the realist and Victorian novel is known for its application of a strict and efficient plot-line, distinct from the more vagarious plots of multifarious lives and voyages in earlier novels. This streamlining of narrative fiction—which has remained an unspoken ideal (and a popular requirement) for good storytelling—was also, however, contextually motivated as a narrative mode that quintessentially expressed how economic and financial prerogatives weighed down on the conduct of modern nineteenth-century lives. Moreover, as Anna Kornbluh has shown, Dicken's use of narrative voice and perspective were a *formal* rendition of the world of finance in the Victorian age (2014: 51–53).

So, if the history of capitalism, money, and finance can be illuminated by the history of literature, it is not because literature is a mere reflection, conditioned by a determining economic base. Raymond Williams has remarked that the relation between literature and the economy "is not a relation between, on the one hand, various individual works and, on the other hand, various empirical facts. The real relation is within a totality of consciousness" (1980: 22). This totality of consciousness involves what Williams also calls changing structures of feeling that often "precede those more recognizable changes of formal idea and belief which make up the ordinary history of consciousness" (1980: 25). In this sense, literature becomes a sort of social laboratory which can articulate both emergent and residual social relations within a given historical period (see also Bernes, 2017: 33).

Literature, then, does more than identifying or presenting problems in the real world; it responds to or mediates them, and transforms them in the process, a process that is both material *and* imaginative. As stated above, it is crucial to recognize that this *modus operandi* is not merely a question of content but also and above all a question of literary *form*. Since the "reality of capital is poetic, unreal, and fictitious," the aforementioned Kornbluh writes, "realist depiction of it must therefore involve feigning and forming" (2014: 12). It is thus *as fiction*—more than as documentary evidence, representational image, referential machine, or homological procedure—that literature is able to access, process, and, potentially, criticize what goes on in the financial world (2014: 4).

While the relevance of the concepts of form and fiction cannot be overstated, another, yet related, way of probing the relation between capitalism and culture, finance and literature, is to scrutinize the relation between financial event and literary *genre*. Combining Williams's concept of structures of feelings with queer theory, Lauren Berlant thus speaks of "temporal genres of the stretched-out present," and "genres of the emerging event" (2011: 5). The question, then, becomes which literary and non-literary genres emerge and respond to specific historical and financial events. We will return to and elaborate on this in greater detail below. First, however, we would like to anatomize the contemporary landscape of finance studies within the field of cultural and literary studies.[1]

Cultural Approaches to Finance

Since the beginning of the 1970s and, in particular, since the financial crisis of 2007–2008, there has been a remarkable upsurge of literary and other cultural works and artifacts that confront the new financial reality. The same historical period, and again especially the last decade or so, has also witnessed a plethora of critical finance studies, drawing on insights from sociology, anthropology, and history, disciplines that have not traditionally fallen within the purview of modern economics. These approaches have contributed to the understanding of how financial capitalism mediates power relations and social distributions, how it operates through specific modes of interaction and agency, and how it is inscribed in historical modes of production and the social forms they entail. In addition to—and in dialogue with—these emerging critical approaches to and renditions of financialization, the financial crisis of 2007–2008 has also instigated an increased interest in finance capital within the humanities. As literary scholars Paul Crosthwaite, Peter Knight, and Nicky Marsh write, "there has been a growing recognition among scholars that economic discourses, narratives, visualizations, and other forms of cultural mediation actively constitute what we call 'the economy' in the process of representing it" (2019: 1).

The interest in the relation between literature and economics, between fiction and finance, is obviously not new. As a version of New Historicism's engagement with "the historicity of the text and the textuality of history" (Louis Montrose), New Economic Criticism flourished in the 1980s and 1990s and provided a swath of analyses of the language of economic transaction and the economic transactions of language with publications such as Walter Benn Michaels's *The Gold Standard and the Logic of Naturalism* (1987), Marc Shell's *Money, Language, and Thought* (1982), Jean-Joseph Goux's *The Coiners of Language*

(1984, English translation 1994), Jochen Hörisch's *Heads or Tails: The Poetics of Money* (1996, English translation 2000), and, of course, Martha Woodmansee and Mark Osteen's *The New Economic Criticism: Studies at the Interface of Literature and Economics* (1999). These scholars were particularly occupied with what they considered the homologies between and reciprocal constitutions of money and language, economic and linguistic systems.

This strain of thought was, in certain ways, related to French post-structuralist thought from the late 1960s to the 1980s where, for example, Michel Foucault had theorized the relation between discourse and power, and Gilles Deleuze and Félix Guattari had analyzed capitalism, producers, consumers, and the means of production as matters of code. This focus on the semiotic persists today in the work of thinkers such as Franco "Bifo" Berardi, Christian Marazzi, and Maurizio Lazzarato with their respective work on "semiocapitalism" where "economic production is increasingly tightly interwoven with processes of linguistic exchange" (Berardi, 2011: 106); language as a "means of production and circulation of goods" (Marazzi, 2008: 48); and contemporary capitalism as an operation between social subjection via signifying semiotics and machinic enslavement via a-signifying semiotics (Lazzarato, 2014: 39). In addition to the French post-structuralist tradition and the Italian post-workerist tradition, we also find a more anthropologically inflected focus on cultural and linguistic practices. Here, Arjun Appadurai's 2016 work *Banking on Words* stands out, in which he describes the 2008 crisis as a failure of language, i.e., a failure of the chain of promises that constitutes the derivatives market, as well as Benjamin Lee (2016) and Edward LiPuma's (2016) work on ritual and the gift as the historical bases for contemporary finance. Yet another important approach to the relation between language and the economy is Joseph Vogl's diptych *The Specter of Capital* and *The Ascendancy of Finance,* analyzing the fictions told by the market and its agents in order to legitimate their endeavors—the idylls and states of emergency that assure "the coherence of the economic universe" (2015: 14) and establish the financial industry as "an essential relay in the mediation between political and economic global organization" (2017: 11).

Since the crisis, however, the focus on language and semiotics, on subjectivity and performativity—whether in the guise of new economic criticism, post-autonomist, post-structuralist, or anthropological approaches or, finally, the history of knowledge—has been accompanied by more materialistic approaches with explicit reference to Marx. Often directly criticizing the focus on language and subjectivity in favor of a focus on the value theory of labor, crisis theory, and a critique of structural violence, these approaches tend to argue that both finance and the focus on language obscure the faltering production of surplus value via labor since the beginning of the 1970s. In this regard, Joshua Clover views finance as "a struggle over extant profits and a claim on future productive labor" (2012: 110), which temporarily reorders Marx's formula of capital M-C-M' as M-M'-[C] by deferring commodity production. Such a deferral is bound to express itself in crisis, where "fictitious capital" encounters reality in what Clover calls the "forcible realignment" of M-C-M', i.e., the violent bursting of the bubble. And just like the speculative value of finance, the notion of immaterial labor or language as a means of production is, to Clover, "neither cause nor solution for this problem but its veil" (2012: 112).

Similar analyses of the relation between fiction and the historical transformation from a production-based economy to a financialized economy of fictitious capital can be found in Annie McClanahan's *Dead Pledges: Debt, Crisis, and Twenty-First-Century Culture* (2017) and in Jasper Bernes's *The Work of Art in the Age of Deindustrialization* (2017). McClanahan, Clover, and Bernes all investigate the *formal* historical correlations between the economy and fiction. Clover discusses postmodernism and poetry as more or less adequate expressions of financialized experience, McClanahan works to "connect debt's cultural representations to its material and political consequences" (2017: 1), and Bernes examines the mediations between labor and art, where experiments with fictional forms in the 1960s and 1970s are considered as laboratories for the articulation of the transition from a production-based to a financialized economy.

The relation between finance and fiction is thus examined as the correlation between aesthetic strategies of fiction and the given dominant mode of capitalist accumulation, a matter often analyzed as an opposition between postmodernist and realist sensibilities. Such approaches usually reference Fredric Jameson's claim that the "classical or national market capitalism known to Marx, the moment of monopoly capital or the stage of imperialism (theorized by Lenin), and the permutation, finally after World War II, into a global form of multinational capitalism" corresponded to the "cultural moment of realism, modernism and postmodernism respectively" (Jameson, 2008: 71).

If, as Richard Godden would have it, "financialization stands at the structural core of the real" (2011: 415), which representative modes can then be adequate to this historical state of things? And if, as Anne Kornbluh argues in *Realizing Capital: Financial and Psychic Economies in Victorian Form*, we should not consider realism "as the determined reflection of established reality, but as the over-determined representation of unsolvable dilemmas that disrupt the integration of reality" (2014: 4), then perhaps she is right that the fundamental dichotomy is not that between real and unreal, but between real and fictitious (2014: 6). Or, as Arne de Boever proposes in *Finance Fictions: Realism and Psychosis in a Time of Economic Crisis* (2018), there is a fundamental tension between psychosis and realism as a result of the fictitious character of contemporary capital. Further, in *Scandals and Abstraction: Financial Fiction of the Long 1980s* (2015), Leigh Claire La Berge pinpoints the tension between postmodern and realist strategies as a means to capture the new relationship between abstraction and concrete form. Finally, in *The Financial Imaginary: Economic Mystification and the Limits of Realist Fiction*, Alison Shonkwiler analyzes how the novel attempts "to fill in the negative space of abstraction" produced by financialization, and she argues that new hybrid realist forms allow the imagining of the abstractions of finance capital and promise "to reveal more deeply the narrative structures of finance itself" (2017: 127).

Considering the heterogeneous field of research described above, it is no doubt beneficial to follow Crosthwaite's suggestion to approach "it as still emerging and in formation, and so aim to expand its boundaries and open it to new forms of critical inquiry" (2019: 7). Nonetheless, such transdisciplinary ventures remain in a nascent phase, as La Berge points out: "[O]ur hierarchies of disciplinary knowledge mean that cross-disciplinary traffic moves largely down a one-way street; humanities reads social science but social science does not read humanities" (2018: 203). We argue with La Berge that the cross-disciplinary traffic of social scientific material into the humanities ought to be bidirectional. Critical finance studies could benefit from an interdisciplinary inclusion of the literary scope, and learn, so our immodest claim goes, from literary history, theory, and analysis.[2] As La Berge also writes in the same text, for quite a while, "literary studies has investigated how time, narrative and the presumed indexicality of language all take new form in a financial era" (2018: 203). The German sociologist Jens Beckert agrees when pointing out the fundamental similarities between fiction and expectations regarding future economic outcomes: "Since literary theory is the academic discipline most specialized in the analysis of fiction, it is only natural to pursue the parallels observed between expectations under conditions of uncertainty and fiction by exploring this field" (Beckert, 2016: 62).

Recognizing that what is at stake is simultaneously the finance of fictions (i.e., literary mediations of finance) and the fictions of finance (i.e., the fictionality of finance itself), finance fiction studies necessarily entail a re-orientation toward the fictional dimensions of capitalism in its contemporary, financialized form.[3] And again, it is precisely its form and its status as fiction that enables literature to engage with the world of finance. Intended as a supplement to the field of finance and society studies, critical finance, and economic sociology, finance fiction studies contribute to critically analyze the intricate and intimate relation between capitalism and culture, finance and fiction. Below, we will sketch three examples, three historical constellations as it were. The purpose of each example is to offer a short and illustrative periodization of both financial capitalism and of the literary history of finance fiction, and to show, above all, how different—emergent and/or residual—literary forms and genres respond to the historical transformations in the increasingly financialized form of the economy.

Contemporary Finance Fiction

The 1970s, Paul Erdman, and the Birth of the Financial Thriller

It is uncontroversial to claim that the contemporary era of financialization and the current crisis date back to the beginning of the 1970s. The inaugural year is 1973, which saw the termination of the Bretton Woods agreement, the oil crisis, the founding of the Chicago Board Options Exchange, the invention of the Black–Scholes formula for pricing derivatives, the publication of *A Random Walk Down Wall Street* by Burton Malkiel (1973), a book that instantly popularized the random walk theory, etc. Scholars such as David Harvey, Robert Brenner, Giovanni Arrighi, and Joshua Clover all agree that 1973 is no ordinary year in the capitalist calendar of the twentieth century, nor is the 1970s just another decade. It was at this historical moment, after the three golden post-World War II-decades, that a post-Fordist, deindustrialized, and financialized world came into being, accompanied by stagnation, declining rates of profit (mainly in the manufacturing sector) and zero growth in real wages. It was the moment when capitalism moved its center of gravity, in Joshua Clover's words, from industrial to finance capital (2014: 11).[4]

It should come as no surprise, then, that the financial history of the 1970s has been blessed with an enormous amount of academic attention. What should surprise us, however, is that the literary history of the very same decade—that is to say, the literary history of works that in one way or another deal with the world of finance—has received scant scholarly attention. This is particularly astounding since the 1970s saw the rise of the financial thriller and a lot of other works to which the new financial reality seemed to necessitate literary interest: B.S. Johnson's avant-gardist comedy *Christie Malry's Own Double-Entry* (1973); Paul Erdman's series of novels *The Billion Dollar Sure Thing* (1973), *The Silver Bears* (1974), and *The Crash of '79* (1976); Arthur Hailey's melodramatic *The Moneychangers* (1975, turned into a mini TV-series by NBC in 1976), William Gaddis's encyclopedic and satirical *J R* (1975), which won him the National Book Award in 1976; Jocelyn Davey's (a pseudonym for Chaim Raphael) *A Treasury Alarm* (1976); Zachary Stone's *Paper Money* (1977, another pseudonym, its real author is Ken Follett); Don DeLillo's *Players* (1977); and Michael M. Thomas's *Green Monday* (1980).

As hinted at above, Lauren Berlant understands genres as something that "provide an affective expectation of the experience of watching something unfold, whether that thing is in life or in art" (2011: 6). Genres are thus not reducible to strictly literary genres and we can define genres more broadly as *formal structures of historically specific feelings*. Instead of tracking what has been called "the waning of affect," Berlant is interested in the waning of genre, in the disappearance (and re-appearance) of old genres, and the birth of new ones (2011: 6–9). In the vocabulary of Raymond Williams—on whose work Berlant draws—we can speak of both emerging and residual genres, and the financial thriller is a very clear case of an emerging genre in the 1970s.[5]

A system of representation is experienced as problematic only when it ceases to work, writes Mary Poovey in *Genres of the Credit Economy* (2008: 6), and the 1970s clearly demanded new systems of representation, new genres. The financial thriller was the predominant genre of finance fiction as a whole during the 1970s: a new intrigue based not on murder but on money, a new kind of character paradigmatically embodied by the speculator, a new type of crime, and, also, a new capitalist spirit or ethos. It was also a genre written exclusively, it would seem, by Anglo-Saxon white men, a lot of them being financiers turned writers.

Paul Erdman is generally credited with having invented the genre of the financial thriller. The former banker from Canada wrote his first novel, *The Billion Dollar Sure Thing* (1973)—this "supernovel about supermoney" as the original cover has it—while incarcerated in a Swiss prison, accused of fraud and gross mismanagement of the Salik Bank. Erdman's book takes place in what is presumably the fall of 1973, although no exact indications are given in the novel. Its overarching intrigue is foreign currency speculation on the geopolitical stage including the Americans, the Swiss, the Arabs, the Russians: "speculation in foreign exchange has become such a popular sport," says one character, "It's the best game in town" (Erdman, 1973: 135). The characters are all involved in what the novel itself refers to as a "double whammy." They go long on gold and short the dollar.

Of course, this plot does not come out of thin air. On August 15, 1971, President Nixon abolished the gold standard and thereby created a rather new financial system, especially with regard to currency speculation, now possible because of the floating and suddenly wildly fluctuating exchange rates (and the overall juridical tendency toward financial deregulation). In the universe of most financial thrillers of the decade, this is a thoroughly mythological and quintessential event. It gave rise to a new kind of plot, and "the emergence of a new kind of financial crime," as Nicky Marsh writes in *Money, Speculation and Finance in Contemporary British Fiction* (2007: 30).

What makes Erdman's book a *financial* thriller is the fact that the world of finance is absolutely central to its plot. And, also, that it deals with a new logic of speculation that accommodates the restructuring of the global economy. Almost every single financial thriller of the 1970s is about money (paper money, green money, petro-dollars, Eurodollars), gold, and oil. They constitute the holy trinity of the genre. As far as money is concerned, it is also at the center of Gaddis's *J R*, the first word of which is "Money" and where the titular protagonist, an 11-year-old boy, who speculates wildly—in junk bonds and penny stocks, hostile takeovers, anticipating in this manner the 1980s and the junk bond king Michael Milken—and builds up a vast "paper empire" as it is called in the novel (Gaddis, 1975: 651).

What makes it a financial *thriller* is not only the machinery of the plot but above all its affective atmosphere, its structure of feeling. The thriller is a genre about fear. Whereas a newer financial thriller like Robert Harris's *The Fear Index* from 2011 vividly describes the fear of algorithms becoming autonomous and monstrous, like Frankenstein's monster, the financial thrillers of the 1970s fear the consequences of *human* speculation and speculators. The critique that accompanies this kind of fear is not a critique of technology, of machines and algorithms gone rogue, nor is it a political critique, but rather a *moral* critique. It is perhaps *the* residual element in this, at the time, emerging genre.

In *The Billion Dollar Sure Thing* and in his money guide, *Paul Erdman's Money Guide*, Erdman is fully aware of what he calls, in the latter, the cyclical nature of capitalism (Erdman, 1985: 19). He mentions one crisis after the other—bankruptcies, bailouts, collapses—and has no rosy view of the future of capitalism. And yet, he consistently reduces the question of money to a question of morals. According to the financial thriller, the problem with the capitalist system of risky speculation and excessive borrowing that emerged in earnest after the demise of the gold standard is that it has, as Arthur Hailey puts in *Moneychangers*, "downgraded American morality" (Hailey, 1975: 78).

The question of morality entails a certain nostalgia for the good old days, with a flourishing manufacturing industry and a truly *"real"* economy based on the gold standard. A similar conflict runs through films such as *Wall Street* (1987), *Pretty Woman* (1990), and *Barbarians at the Gate* (1993), which depict various conflicts between, on the one hand, speculators, corporate raiders, junk bond traders, and firms that facilitate and profit from their dodgy operations. And on the other, industry and the manufacturing of ships (*Pretty Woman*) or airplanes (*Wall Street*), good old, blue-collar America. In these films, there is an obsession with real things, real money, and real people, instead, in the words of the character Forstmann in *Barbarians at the Gate*, of all this "phoney junk bond crap." We are real people with real money, he says, and together "we need to push the barbarians back from the city gates."

As a consequence, the genre of the financial thriller not only fails to see that the fictionality of finance post-Bretton Woods is an ideological fiction itself, and that the world of finance is not a world in itself, totally removed from the real economy and the world of production (cf. Finch, 2015: 731). It also risks succumbing to the seduction described aptly by Joshua Clover in the article "*Retcon*: Value and Temporality in Poetics": That one views finance, with its unreal acts of speculation and its endless extension of credit, as the cause of crisis. It would, as Clover points out with reference to the work of Giovanni Arrighi, be "just as true to say that crisis causes finance" and that at the end of the day "finance is crisis: crisis as regime, crisis as mode of capital" (2014: 26). This truth, the financial thriller cannot, or does not, want to face. At least not in the case of Erdman.

From the Golden Age of the 1980s to the Day the Music Died

The first explorations in the 1970s financial thriller of the new possibilities of global speculation and profit as embodied in the character of the speculator are followed in the 1980s by what has been called the Masters of the Universe (Tom Wolfe: *Bonfire of the Vanities*) and the Big Swinging Dicks of finance (Michael Lewis: *Liar's Poker*): "If he could make millions of dollars come out of those phones, he became that most revered of all species: a Big Swinging Dick" (Lewis, 2010: 56).

Limitless accumulation of capital through the technologically mediated and thus immediate exchange of paper, this is the fantasy of the masters of the universe. These masters are generally depicted as incorporations of hubris, they are figures of Icarus who, in their euphoria, fly too close to the sun and fall as a result of their moral transgressions. Sherman McCoy of *Bonfire* and Gordon Gekko of Oliver Stone's *Wall Street* are the stereotypes here.

Something happens in the beginning of the 1990s, however. In Ellis's *American Psycho* (1991), investment banker Patrick Bateman is the next-generation Master of the Universe, who is not much of a master at all. Euphoria has become psychosis. The masters' fantasy of a world of financial signs with immense exchange value but no material reality behind them to limit their instantaneous circulation has begun to crack and is becoming a source of extreme anxiety.

Similarly, in Don DeLillo's *Cosmopolis* (2003), the financier Eric Packer rides around in his limousine manifestation of the Big Swinging Dick fantasy of an immaterial connection to the market and the future as such. The limousine as both a vehicle of immaterial fantasy and the vehicle leading toward a material and emotional reality, a haircut from his childhood barber, incorporates the now haunted fantasy of high finance. Through the limousine sunroof, Packer contemplates an urban scene, focusing on the bank towers a bit further away. They are so abstract that he must concentrate to see them. The material world becomes the veil through which a glimpse of the abstraction of the "purer" realm of market information is possible. But when confronted with the televised images of a man in flames, reality beyond financial signifiers crack the surface of the spectacle of the market: "The market was not total. It could not claim this man or assimilate his act. Not such starkness and horror. This was a thing outside its reach" (DeLillo, 2003: 99–100).

A very different affective mode dominates the finance fiction from after the crisis of 2007–2008, however. Everywhere, we meet either financiers losing comprehension and control or regular people simply giving up on the ability to influence their own destinies. We are far from the 1980s fascination with the immoral yuppie and the psychotic violence of the super-rich in the 1990s and early naughts. In Sebastian Faulks's *A Week in December* (2009), Gary Shteyngart's *Lake Success* (2018), Joseph O'Neil's *Netherland* (2008), and Adam Haslett's *Union Atlantic* (2009), we find either complete emotional exhaustion and resignation or the elimination of any emotional bond with the world in order to maintain the fantasy of the magical self-sufficiency of financial circulation. To master the money, the masters must forego the world, while the numerous *others* are left to suffer the consequences.

This change of focus from depictions of morally bankrupt fantasies of profit, over the material world's threat of bursting the bubble of financial fantasy to the resignation of financial actors can be considered historically specific affective relations to the given possibilities of capital accumulation. Or, referencing once again Berlant's notion of "the waning of genre," we could say that the plot-structuring device of capital accumulation has undergone a historical transformation manifested as a transformation in the "affective expectation of the experience of watching something unfold" (Berlant, 2011: 6).

The fantasy of finance that superseded the production-based economic expansion of the postwar boom is, in Marxian terms, based on the belief that it is possible to cut out labor-exploiting commodity production from the equation, so that money is exchanged for more money with no value-adding labor required. This is what Marx, in *Capital* volume 3, called the "most superficial and fetishized form" of the capital relation, it is "fictitious capital" (Marx, 1981: 515–517). The fantasy of the Masters of the Universe and the Big Swinging Dicks of the 1980s springs from their belief in this fictitious relation. The structuring of affective expectation in 1980s fiction is here one of immediacy, immediate profit, only hindered by moral judgment.

This fantasy found its material underpinnings in the general slowdown in manufacturing profitability in the beginning of the 1970s, the subsequent high inflation peaking at 14.8% in March 1980, combatted by Fed Chair Paul Volcker by increasing the Fed funds rate to its peak of 20% in June 1981. Wall Street suffered immensely during this slowdown and over 150 firms disappeared as independent entities from 1968 to 1975. However, while the Volcker shock inaugurated a recession in the American economy (1979–1982), it also marked what Michael Lewis described as "the beginning of the golden age of the bond man" (Lewis, 2010: 43). The waning profitability of production and increased profitability of debt engendered the invention of the securitized mortgage loan and its repackaging in so-called CDOs (collateralized debt obligations) and "between 1977 and 1986, the holdings of mortgage bonds by American Savings and Loans grew from 12.6 billion dollars to 150 billion dollars" (Lewis, 2010: 142; on CDOs, see also the chapter by Hardin and Rottinghaus in this *Handbook*). The same conditions created an explosion in Junk bonds and the related debt-fueled hostile mergers and acquisitions. This massive expansion in debt also drove stocks toward new highs before the crash in 1987. The fantasy of immediate and immaterial economic expansion sprang from this bull market run-up to October 1987, which was to a large extent based on the invention of new financial instruments. Just as debt had been a structuring plot-device of the nineteenth century realist novel, new financial instruments and their resulting profit and takeovers came to structure the fictions of the 1980s. Sherman's attempted creation of the *Giscard* bond in *Bonfire* and Gekko's attempted takeover of *Bluestar Airlines* are cases in point.

While the Masters of the 1980s were hubristic because of their belief in the possibility to persistently short-circuit the law of capital accumulation by having profit without the realization of value in production, the psychotic acting out in the 1990s and early naughts is characterized by the *experience* of the complete separation of price and value. Bateman and Packer still subscribe to the fantasy of fictitious capital, but the feeling that the deferred materiality of production cannot be kept at bay forever is beginning to manifest itself as the approach of a psychotic breakdown. The haunting material character of both commodity and human flesh followed as the bull market of 1981–1987 came abruptly to a halt and what could, in the 1980s, be considered the immoral behavior of the dicks of Wall Street turned out to be a systemic negation of reality. Across the world, authorities slashed interest rates as a means to alleviate the collapse in equity prices and the market believed that governments would never allow it to drop. As described by Robert Brenner, the continued asset-price run-up in the late 1990s was effectively "the Stock market [...] climbing skyward without a ladder" (Brenner, 2009: 21).

In this perspective, the resignation of post-crisis literature of the last ten years is thus the affective correlate of the reassertion of the economic law of value: "The law of value asserted itself with savage clarity, fictitious capital was destroyed, jobs were annihilated, exported immiseration refluxing toward the economic cores" (Clover, 2012: 113). With the devastating bursting of the bubble, finance fiction lost one of the main driving forces of narrative development. Expecting to experience something unfold simply became much more difficult as concrete economic development proved that the plot-device of capital accumulation was nothing but an illusion.

Only after the crash of 2007–2008 did the fantasy of unlimited economic expansion within the financial sector become apparent as such and, thus, as the waning of the genre conventions "relating fantasy to ordinary life and whose depictions of the good life now appear to mark archaic expectations about having and building a life" (Berlant, 2011: 6). The at times violently haunted fantasy of omnipotence and pure profit finally gave way to resignation. As stated by Jeremy Irons's diabolic CEO in *Margin Call* when he is confronted with the imminent crisis:

> I am here for one reason and one reason alone. I am here to guess what the music might do a week, a month, a year from now. That's it, nothing more. Standing here tonight, I am afraid that I don't hear a thing. Just silence.

After the Crisis: Finance Epic

Amanda Craig's recent novel, *The Lie of the Land* (2017), opens by describing a divorce which is effective in every aspect but one: the partners keep living together, hoping that the market value of their house in London will rise sufficiently to pay for their future separate accommodations. A plot, in other words, which is somehow usurped by a bigger plot, not only one about pecuniary scarcity (the driver of so many plots in the history of literature), but one about the expectancy for future trading value of real estate, and thus a plot that follows a logic of financialization. In Craig's novel, the characters and events remain at the center of the narrative, but they are subject to coercive conditions that eventually tend to annul the meaningfulness of what takes place on the level of characters and events; instead, they point back to the big plot scintillating in the background, and they become interesting to the degree that they are linked to this plot as its subjects. This narrative template deviates from what we would normally identify as the properly novelistic qualities of "sovereign life unfolding from actions" (Berlant, 2011: 7) and comes closer to the traditional epic form, betoken to paint the big picture of trans individual destinies and historical processes. Narratives of the post-crisis era tend to revert from a *novelistic* focus on interesting individuals and their actions to an *epic* focus on the larger forces that determine the way of the world, and thus also the subjection of mundane lives to larger prerogatives.[6]

The distinction between epic and novel comes out of Romanticist aesthetics. Hegel, Schiller, and Humboldt contrasted the traditional epic of Homer and Vergil, where the heroic deeds would actually incarnate a coherent and integral world image, and the novel, which they considered to be a modern and essentially bourgeois form, constricted to a focus on the psychologically and sociologically particularized individual. The novel, in other words, belongs to a world where a divine totality is replaced by a mottled multiplicity of individual perspectives. To Georg Lukács, in his seminal *Theory of the Novel* from 1917, this dialectical tension between abstract totality and concrete particularity constitute the fundamental predicament of the novel: "the paradoxical fusion of heterogeneous and discrete components into an organic whole which is then abolished over and over again" (1971: 88).

While the novel bases its universe on the perspectives of its characters and what they can be imagined to do, think, and feel, epic narrative, then, relies less on the meaningfulness of literary characters and the symbolic pregnancy of individual life stories. It seeks beyond and above them and liberally allows digression, reflection, and compilation of all sorts of material that we would not otherwise have expected to find in a novelistic fiction. It does not dispel the use of character altogether, but the core of the narrative migrates away from their individual situations and propensities, and toward that "big canvas," now discernible as the universe in which the characters are embedded.

In the ancient epic, the question of "individuality" was not really an issue, because in the end destiny would prevail; and in modern epic, fiction writers become keen on trying out literary forms that might equally gauge those societal powers that effectively nullify the weight of individual agency rather than clinging to those vain aspirations. Craig's divorce-plot is a case in point, as if urging us to look beyond whatever motivates the characters in question, beyond the time of their domestic miseries, to see instead the intransigent temporality of finance to which they will eventually have to adapt. Accordingly, as pointed out by David Cunningham, the novel's

> ultimately impossible epic perspective of totality, has always had, in more or less intense a fashion, to negotiate the problem of its relation to the real and expanding totality of capitalism itself, and to the always already global space of the accumulation of value. (2010: 18)

When the prerogatives of finance increasingly dominate the entirety of social and individual life by turning dwellings into an interconnected system of reciprocally balanced assets, and the time of our lives into an instantiation of risk that can be algorithmically priced, it becomes still more necessary to invent literary forms that have the epic capability to foreground the spectral omnipresence of finance as a totality.

When incidents that take place in the first-person perspective of characters are subdued, as in Craig's novel, it also opens up the plot-structure. "The epic poet's purpose lies at every point along the way of his narrative," Friedrich Schiller said: "Thus, we do not rush impatiently toward a goal; rather, we tarry fondly at every step" (Staiger, 1991: 116). In keeping with this, the palette of sentiments and affects, no longer tied to the realization of a strict plot, becomes both broad and mottled, albeit also largely undetermined, like a huge archive of structures of feeling, in finance epics like Benjamin Markovits's *You Don't Have to Live Like This* (2015) or Virginie Despentes's extraordinary trilogy *Vernon Subutex* (2015–2017).

"Tarrying at every step" might also be an inroad to an epic representation of the bleak sense of futurity that haunts a financialized world, where the frenetic production of debt seems to pile up insurmountable future obligations, and where the future itself is becoming subject to relentless remodeling by forwards, swaps, futures, and options. If it is true, as the French critic Bernard Maris had it, that Michel Houellebecq is indeed an economist (Maris, 2014), it very much surfaces in his latest, desolate epic *Sérotonine* (2019), in which he meticulously elaborates a breath-taking (and breathtakingly boresome) exercise in contemplating an infinite present of non-promissory immanence. A similar gesture portraying the looming impossibility of imagining a future, albeit in a more humorous-grotesque fashion than in Houellebecq, can be found in Gary Stheyngart's recent *Lake Success* (2018) that follows a hedge fund manager in his hilariously futile quest for actually learning to want something.

The vicissitudes of fiction and fictionality also tend to come forward in epic formats. "Epic brings independent elements together," Emil Staiger notes (1991: 122), and thus necessarily tends to blur the fine line that separates what is part of a fictional universe and what is not. This is another quality of the epic that makes it an interesting formal tool for finance fiction. Partly because toying with fiction and fictionality can foreground the fictitious qualities of fiduciary finance itself, as in Daniel Kehlmann's *F* from 2013, where he playfully tries out the different correspondences between faith, forgery, finance, and family matters in a dizzying supernatural constellation of reflections and encounters. But partly, also, because the contemporary plethora of fiduciary formats can give rise to new ways of constructing fictional universes. An obvious case in point here would be Zia Haider Rahman's acclaimed first novel *In the Light of What We Know* from 2014, a long and circuitous story of the lives of two young southeast Asian men, both working in finance (like Rahman himself), following their ramified meanderings around the globe in the late 1990s and early 2000s through high society and migrant slum, through war zones and commercial centers, through capitals and shantytowns, and of course through all varieties of finance and its mathematics. This story is not only epic in its extreme latitude, but also in the slightly confusing way in which it maneuvers this landscape, where the voices of the protagonists tend to converge and blend almost to indistinction, where every small incident can lead on to any other based on the slightest of similarities; not only a truly labyrinthine discourse, but also a logical one in a world where everything is related and where everything can be effectively correlated; a derivative discourse, really, exploring the fiction-making power of our contemporary system of fiduciary contracts.

Conclusion

In this chapter, we have taken as our point of departure the claim made by Annie McClanahan, that "our understanding of the economy can be illuminated by culture" (2017: 2). Understanding finance through culture, and in this specific case through literature and literary fiction, provides images of the agents of finance, their ethos and shared prepositions, the institutions of finance and their societal encroachment, the interactions we all have with its many manifestations. Literature visits unfamiliar corners and cribs of a society and conveys a sense of the lifeforms they lodge, almost as an ancestral form of anthropology. Hence the upsurge, in recent years, of literary works that set out to explore and present this increasingly important abode of societal power.

As we have also shown, however, literature does not access the financial reality at a representational level alone, but also, and perhaps above all, at the level of literary form. This, in turn, necessitates inquiries into the question of genre and how different genres emerge and respond to varying financial events. In the last part of the chapter, we have thus offered, in a highly abbreviated form, three historical, and illustrative, renditions of the relation between finance and fiction in the 1970s, the 1980s and 1990s, and post-2008, respectively. Here, we have demonstrated how in each period, finance fiction incorporates various literary genres in its attempt to grapple with financialization: the thriller, the tension between realism and psychosis, and the epic, although a wide range of other genres could be included as well. Hopefully, this demonstration contributes to the still emerging and heterogeneous intersection of literary and (critical) finance studies as a field of cross- and transdisciplinary dialogue between the humanities and the social sciences.

Notes

1 It should be noted that although the present chapter analyzes the relation between literature and finance in terms of *narrative* form, this is, of course, not the only approach. As Joshua Clover argues in various texts, *poetic* form, or the genre of the lyric, may be considered to grasp the historical form of contemporary, financial capitalism in a more fundamental manner. In "*Retcon*: Value and Temporality in Poetics," he thus concludes that "while narrative fiction has been taken insistently as the relevant literary mode or genre for understanding the motion and particularly

the temporality of finance, poetry finally provides a better heuristic for such an understanding" (2014: 13; see also 2010: 321; 2011: 34).

2 Such bidirectional work does, of course, exist. In a concrete example of such work, Kristian Bondo Hansen's review essay on Robert Harris's *Fear Index* argues for the valuable sociological use of literary fiction as a source of data: "literary fiction has the ability to bring emotional, historical, social and political aspects to light which are unutterable and therefore invisible in the conventional finance discourse" (Hansen, 2015: 1085).

3 In addition to the countless monographs already mentioned, several academic journals have, in the last few years, made the relation between fiction and finance the topic of a special issue: "Fictions of Finance," *Journal of Cultural Economy,* 2013; "The Fictions of Finance," *Radical History Review,* 2014; "Fictions of Speculation," *Journal of American Studies,* 2015; and "Speculative Finance/Speculative Fiction," *CR: The New Centennial Review,* 2019. As a quick glance on the titles alone reveals, speculation and fiction are keywords here, an obvious reason being that speculation and fiction are at work and central to both the domain of finance and the domain of literature.

4 Of course, there were other significant events in the 1970s: the collapse of Penn Central in 1970; the international banking crisis of 1974 and the failure of the Franklin National Bank; the fiscal crisis of New York in 1975; and the Volcker shock in 1979—not to mention the Vietnam War and the coup d'état in Chile. But 1973 was arguably the most important year as far as the history of finance is concerned. In the words of Laura Finch, it was a year "replete with financial events" (2015: 731). See also Haiven (2018: 88).

5 In the article "The Un-real Deal: Financial Fiction, Fictional Finance, and the Financial Crisis," Laura Finch makes the case for taking genre and genre fiction seriously, intuiting that the revitalized genre of financial thrillers are "reacting to the genrelessness of crisis that Berlant identifies" (2015: 751).

6 See, for example, Shonkwiler (2017: 53–72), or Toral Gajarawala's text "The Fictions of Finance," in which she writes about how "[t]oday's fiction shifts from the register of the megalomaniacal to that of the mundane" (Gajarawala, 2015: n.p.).

References

Appadurai, A. (2016). *Banking on Words: The Failure of Language in the Age of Derivative Finance.* Chicago, IL: University of Chicago Press.

Beckert, J. (2016). *Imagined Futures: Fictional Expectations and Capitalist Dynamics.* Cambridge, MA: Harvard University Press.

Berardi, F. (2011). *After the Future.* Edinburgh: AK Press.

Berlant, L. (2011). *Cruel Optimism.* Durham and London: Duke University Press.

Bernes, J. (2017). *The Work of Art in the Age of Deindustrialization.* Stanford, CA: Stanford University Press.

Brenner, R. (2009, April). "What is good for goldman sachs is good for America: The origins of the current crisis." Retrieved from http://www.sscnet.ucla.edu/issr/cstch/papers/BrennerCrisisTodayOctober2009.pdf.

Clover, J. (2010). "'A form adequate to history': Toward a renewed Marxist poetics," *Paideuma: Modern and Contemporary Poetry and Poetics* 37: 321–348.

Clover, J. (2011). "Autumn of the system: Poetry and financial capital," *Journal of Narrative Theory* 41(1): 34–52.

Clover, J. (2012). "Value | theory | crisis," *PMLA* 127(1): 107–114.

Clover, J. (2014). "Retcon: Value and temporality in poetics," *Representations* 126: 9–30.

Craig, A. (2017). *The Lie of the Land.* London: Little, Brown Book Group.

Crosthwaite, P. (2019). *The Market Logics of Contemporary Fiction*. Cambridge: Cambridge University Press.

Crosthwaite, P., Knight, P., & Marsh, N. (2019). "The economic humanities and the history of financial advice," *American Literary History* 31(4): 1–26.

Cunningham, D. (2010). "Capitalist epics: Abstraction, totality and the theory of the novel," *Radical Philosophy* 163: 11–23.

Davey, J. (1976). *A Treasury Alarm*. London: Chatto & Windus.

De Boever, A. (2018). *Finance Fictions: Realism and Psychosis in a Time of Economic Crisis*. New York, NY: Fordham University Press.

DeLillo, D. (2003). *Cosmopolis*. New York, NY: Scribner.

DeLillo, D. (2016). *Players*. New York, NY: Picador.

Despentes, V. (2015–2017). *Vernon Subutex 1–3*. Paris: Grasset.

Dos Passos, J. (2013). *The Big Money*. Boston, MA: Houghton Mifflin.

Ellis, B. E. (1991). *American Psycho*. New York, NY: Vintage.

Erdman, P. (1973). *The Billion Dollar Sure Thing*. New York, NY: Charles Scribner's Sons.

Erdman, P. (1974). *The Silver Bears*. London: Hutchinson.

Erdman, P. (1976). *The Crash of '79*. New York, NY: Simon & Schuster.

Erdman, P. (1985). *Paul Erdman's Money Guide*. London: Sphere Books Ltd.

Finch, L. (2015). "The un-real deal: Financial fiction, fictional finance, and the financial crisis," *Journal of American Studies* 49(4): 731–753.

Follett, K. [Stone, Z.] (1996). *Paper Money*. London: Pan Books.

Gaddis, W. (1975). *J R*. New York, NY: Alfred A. Knopf.

Gajarawala, T. (2015). "The fictions of finance," *Dissent Magazine*. Retrieved from https://www.dissentmagazine.org/article/finance-novel-zia-haider-rahman-in-light-what-we-know.

Godden, R. (2011, March). "Labor, language, and finance capital," *PMLA* 126(2): 412–421.

Goethe, J. W. v. (1994). *Faust Part Two*. Oxford: Oxford University Press.

Goux, J. J. (1984). *The Coiners of Language*. Oklahoma City: University of Oklahoma Press.

Hailey, A. (1975). *The Moneychangers*. New York, NY: Bantam Books.

Haiven, M. (2014). *Cultures of Financialization: Fictitious Capital in Popular Culture and Everyday Life*. London: Palgrave MacMillan.

Haiven, M. (2018). *Art After Money, Money After Art: Creative Strategies against Financialization*. London: Pluto Press.

Hansen, K. B. (2015). "The politics of algorithmic finance," *Contexto Internacional* 37(3): 1081–1095.

Hörisch, J. (2000/1996). *Heads or Tails: The Poetics of Money*. Detroit, MI: Wayne State University Press.

Jameson, F. (2008). *The Ideologies of Theory*. London and New York, NY: Verso.

Johnson, B. S. (1973). *Christie Malry's Own Double-Entry*. London: William Collins Sons & Co. Ltd.

Kornbluh, A. (2014). *Realizing Capital: Financial and Psychic Economies in Victorian Form*. New York, NY: Fordham University Press.

La Berge, L. C. (2015). *Scandals and Abstraction: Financial Fiction of the Long 1980s*. Oxford: Oxford University Press.

La Berge, L. C. (2018). "Money is time: On the possibility of critique after neoliberalism," *Finance and Society* 2(4): 199–204.

Lazzarato, M. (2014). *Signs and Machines: Capitalism and the Production of Subjectivity*. Los Angeles, CA: Semiotext(e).

Lee, B. (2016). "From primitives to derivatives," in B. Lee and R. Martin (eds.), *Derivatives and the Wealth of Societies*. Chicago, IL: University of Chicago Press.

Lewis, M. (2010). *Liar's Poker*. New York, NY: W.W. Norton.

LiPuma, E. (2016). "Ritual in financial life," in B. Lee and R. Martin (eds.), *Derivatives and the Wealth of Societies*. Chicago, IL: University of Chicago Press.

Lukács, G. (1971). *Theory of the Novel*. Cambridge, MA: MIT Press.

Malkiel, B. (1973). *A Random Walk Down Wall Street*. New York, NY: W.W. Norton & Company.

Mann, T. (1901). *Buddenbrooks: Verfall einer Familie*. Frankfurt: Fischer Verlag.

Marazzi, C. (2002/2008). *Capital and Language: From the New Economy to the War Economy*. Cambridge, MA: Semiotext(e).

Markovitz, B. (2015). *You Don't Have to Live Like This*. London: Faber & Faber.

Maris, B. (2014). *Houellebecq économiste*. Paris: Flammarion.

Marsh, N. (2007). *Money, Speculation and Finance in Contemporary British Fiction*. London: Bloomsbury.

Martin, R. (2002). *Financialization Of Daily Life*. Philadelphia, PA: Temple University Press.

Marx, K. (1981). *Capital*, Volume III. London: Pelican Books.

McClanahan, A. (2017). *Dead Pledges: Debt, Crisis, and Twenty-First-Century Culture*. Stanford, CA: Stanford University Press.

Michaels, W. B. (1987). *The Gold Standard and the Logic of Naturalism: American Literature at the Turn of the Century*. Berkeley, CA: University of California Press.

Pessoa, F. (2018). *The Anarchist Banker*. Toronto: Guernica Editions.

Poovey, M. (2008). *Genres of the Credit Economy: Mediating Value in Eighteenth- and Nineteenth-Century Britain*. Chicago, IL: Chicago University Press.

Shell, M. (1982). *Money, Language and Thought: Literary and Philosophical Economies from the Medieval to the Modern Era*. Berkeley, CA: University of California Press.

Shonkwiler, A. (2017). *The Financial Imaginary*. Minneapolis: University of Minnesota Press.

Shteyngart, G. (2018). *Lake Success*. New York, NY: Random House.

Staiger, E. (1991). *Basic Concepts of Poetics*. University Park: Pennsylvania State University Press.

Thomas, M. M. (1981). *Green Monday*. New York, NY: Fawcett Crest Books.

Vogl, J. (2010/2015). *The Specter of Capital*. Stanford, CA: Stanford University Press.

Vogl, J. (2015/2017). *The Ascendancy of Finance*. Oxford: Polity.

Williams, R. (1980). *Culture and Materialism*. London: Verso.

Wolfe, T. (1987). *The Bonfire of the Vanities*. New York, NY: Picador.

Woodmansee, M., & Osteen, M. (1999). *The New Economic Criticism: Studies at the Intersection of Literature and Economics*. London: Routledge.

19

ART, MARKETS, AND FINANCE

Victoria Ivanova and Gerald Nestler

Critique, Speculation, and Infrastructural Projections: An Introduction

This chapter offers a critical overview of the approaches that inform theorizations and practical applications of art's relationship to finance. Rather than offering a comprehensive survey of artists engaged with finance, the text distils methodological lenses through a selection of relevant practices. Thus, it charts a landscape of methodologies that have been developed within the art field and at its interfaces with other fields, analyzing their contributions and limitations. The analysis limits itself historically to the post-World War II era, focusing on the institution of contemporary art and the global financial order, both of which may be said to represent the hegemonic forms of art and finance today. As such, contemporary art is approached as a unified paradigm for art production and dissemination at global scale mediated by a set of shared discursive, institutional, and economic practices (Velthuis & Baia Curioni, 2015: 1–2). As a genre of art, contemporary art emerges from the legacy of the conceptual turn of the 1960s (Osborne, 2013), while the practice of Marcel Duchamp from 1913 onwards when he created his first readymades is seen as a key historical precursor, if not straight out template, for both the logic and operational sensibility of contemporary art (de Duve, 2012, who dubs Duchamp "the witty financier who holds the secret of artistic exchange value"; Roberts, 2007). Meanwhile, the global consolidation of contemporary art's socio-institutional complex is typically associated with the post-1989 period (Augita et al., 2009; Osborne, 2013).

The sphere of modern finance follows a comparable historical periodization, emerging as a self-standing branch of the economic discipline and an independent sector of national and international economies in the aftermath of World War II. Through such institutions as the IMF and the World Bank, finance attained greater international reach in the 1970s. The collapse of the Bretton Woods agreement and the rise of derivative markets consolidated the financial sphere as the central system of governance within a globalized world in the 1990s.

The five key lenses through which the relationship between art and finance has been perceived are art theory, critical artistic practice, art institutional practice, sociological analysis, and a financial business perspective. The first part of the chapter focuses on the emergence and consolidation of the critical art paradigm as the dominant framework for understanding art's approach to finance in the sphere of contemporary art, outlining its historical emergence, philosophical commitments, and *de facto* constraints. It will be concluded that in the light of present-day dynamics within the spheres of art and finance, the critical art paradigm is not only highly constrained epistemologically but may in fact contribute to the perpetuation of the very conditions that it critiques. The second part of the chapter focuses on methodologies that take on a more post-disciplinary (Nestler, 2017) approach and strives to recode the relationship between critical understanding and the capacity to operationalize and influence. To this extent, the section explores historical practices such as those related to digital art, and emerging performative methodologies that cut across multiple fields and aim to produce infrastructurally significant feedback through their actions. Rather than departing from the premise that art and finance exist in two separate realms, the selected approaches harness the cross-cutting dynamics of our techno-financial societies, strategically identifying ways in which these dynamics may be manipulated and redeployed. While these exploratory approaches and hacks most often function as temporary systemic interjections, they nonetheless open up a realm of alternative epistemological and strategic possibilities for art as an expression of techno-financial ordering.

The evolutionary trajectories of contemporary art and finance, and the impact that their formative dynamics have had on theorizing their relationship, are of key importance in understanding the established approaches to art and finance today. Scholarly (primarily, sociological) identification of financialization arose in conjunction with discourses on the economic, geopolitical, and socio-cultural effects of globalization (Axford, 1995; Knorr Cetina & Preda, 2004; McNally, 2011; Sassen, 1998), while increasing attention to financialization as a phenomenon in its own right (Krippner, 2005) has been an influential factor in the formation of critical positions on the topic (Berardi, 2012; Lazzarato, 2012; Marazzi, 2009). Simultaneously, processes of contemporary art's financialization have led to the formation of specialist art business and finance knowledge, based on financial measures such as indexing and due diligence. Driven primarily by specialized art market actors and analysts (e.g., Mei Moses Art Indices, The European Fine Art Fair (TEFAF) Report), investment funds and larger financial institutions such as UBS and Deloitte, the financial expertise aimed at offering art as an alternative asset class to high-net-worth individuals (HNWIs) has been seized upon by art fairs such as Art Basel. Financialization of contemporary art spurred increasing critical responses from within the art field (Steyerl, 2017; Toscano & Kinkle, 2015). Both of these tendencies only intensified with the global financial crisis of 2008 as the complexity and power of the financial order became widely felt and at the same time better understood.

Sociological analysis and institutional practice offer a more systematic understanding and pose questions about the relationship between contemporary art and modern finance that neither the business perspective nor the established critical approaches are able to answer (Ivanova, 2016b; Malik & Nestler, 2016; Velthuis, 2007). A central question concerns the structural role of the art market system in the field of contemporary art: the institutional structures of the art fair and the biennial are on the one hand places of "collision" between business and critical approaches, and on the other fertile grounds for symbiosis insofar as critical art endows the market with value (Malik, 2008). While it is often argued that this dynamic attests to the all-encompassing reach of financialization (Martin, 2002), it equally points to the limitations of the critical approach in generating positions vis-à-vis finance that transcend the circular feedback between criticality and financialization as the two only possible ways of conceiving the relationship between art and finance, monopolizing our understanding of the functions that art and finance can have in society. Thus, the larger ambition of this text, outlined in the second part of the chapter, is to start sketching a progressive vision for art and finance that departs from the functions that they perform within today's dominant systems of governance.

Critical Art Paradigm and Its Discontents

Emergence and Consolidation of the Critical Art Paradigm

The 1950s and 1960s saw a shift in the logic of art history from a focus on chronological cataloguing of historical artists to selective interpretation and engagement with living artists (Meyer, 2013). The terms of analyzing art expanded from strictly formal and historical considerations to the assessment of the artwork's *critical* dimension, its potentiality for rupturing and displacing convention (Holmes, 2009), particularly in relationship to wider societal conditions. The shedding of disciplinary insularity in the name of greater socio-political awareness—both in theoretical terms and vis-à-vis co-temporary events of political nature—intersected with the intellectual sensibility that cut across academic and activist milieus of the time, articulated through the writings of thinkers that we now associate with the various waves of critical thought in the Euro-American contexts. The newfound critical disposition in art theory and practice can to a certain extent be aligned with the emergence of critical Marxist-inspired methods in approaching the legacy of modernity and its aesthetics and in addressing the contingent social and political structures imposed by industrial capitalism (Adorno & Horkheimer, 1997; Marcuse, 1964). Theorization of socio-political emancipation in terms of material reconstitution of societal conditions was emblematic of the general epistemological reorientation from art theory and practice as fields that dealt with representation to art theory and practice predicated on a self-reflexive approach to their historical positioning. A second wave of critical theory finds most proximate resonance with the modality of critique that formed the foundations of the critical art paradigm that contemporary art consequently inherited. In other words, while Marxist critical theory coalesces with the birth of art's co-temporary consciousness, it was post-structuralism's break from universalist assumptions and embrace of contextual probing of hegemonic norms in the name of producing antagonistic and difference-based models for social emancipation (Deleuze, 1994; Deleuze & Guattari, 1977, 1987; Derrida, 1978; Mouffe, 1992) that established the directional template for art's critical disposition.

Conceptual art of the post-war period abandoned modernism's formalism in search of different paradigms through which art could relate to reality (Alberro, 2000). For artists such as Adrian Piper, Hans Haacke, Robert Smithson, Vito Acconci, Art & Language, Joseph Kosuth, Mary Kelly, Martha Rosler, Barbara Kruger, Critical Art Ensemble, Marta Minujín, Cildo Meireles, and Bruce Nauman, the artwork became a conceptual prism that allowed a symbolic exploration of racial, gender, sexual, or socio-economic inequality, chiming with wider critical discourses on these subjects (Fanon, 2004; Ives, 2007). While many practices associated with the conceptual turn were invested in bringing out the subjective experience of oppressive structural conditions, others addressed more abstract aspects of the capitalist system and technological change. For example, artists associated with the first wave of institutional critique—most prominently, Haacke—adopted post-structuralism's deconstructive methodology to expose structural pathologies obfuscated in capitalist societies. The use of the artwork as a reference system (Weibel, 2008) composed of signs with the capacity to reveal what are generally obfuscated dovetails with the deconstructionist sensibility and post-structuralism's focus on the political dimension of semantics. The practices of such artists as Haacke, Robert Morris, or Lee Lozano, as well as those associated with institutional critique more generally, may be qualified as early attempts in formulating a methodological approach from within art practice to the relationship between art and finance (even though the latter term was not yet in use at the time). One of the most indicative works in this regard is *Shapolsky et al. Manhattan Real Estate Holdings, a Real Time Social System, as of May 1, 1971*, in which Haacke investigates and maps the connections between illicit real estate practices in New York City, "rogue" landlords and their integration into a large-scale business operation related to figures who sat on the Guggenheim's Board of Trustees.[1] The template, rooted in a conviction that art's critical potential is to be located in its ability to reveal what is obfuscated and signal potentialities would be expanded by the second wave of institutional critique. The latter is marked by the artist's self-inclusion in the artwork's semantic operation—from descriptive analysis of an external reality to an analysis that reflexively encapsulates the position of the describing subject position. Here, the work of artist Andrea Fraser is often taken to be exemplary. In *Untitled* (2003), Fraser arranged for her gallery Friedrich Petzel to negotiate a deal with a collector that would grant him a sexual encounter in a hotel room with the artist—an encounter that was videotaped, and the video consequently sold in the art market and "thus destined to circulate as a commodity" (in an interview with Praxis, 2004). *Untitled* manifests the central feature of second-wave institutional critique—the artist's performative self-reflexivity in engaging with the image of capital's total subsumption. Second-wave institutional critique shadows the critical positions explored by post-Fordist thinkers associated with the Autonomia Operaia movement (Berardi, 2009; Rancière, 2005; Virno & Hardt, 1996). It symbolically enacts art's compromised critical position when confronted with market forces and dynamics of commodification that make no distinction between material output as critical artwork in its object form and the immaterial labor that goes into producing and circulating critical discourse. Although not all critical artworks engaged with the latter subject matter fall under the rubric of institutional critique (as not all necessarily reflect on the complicity of art institutions and actors within those dynamics), the paradigm of revelation and critical reflexivity function as hegemonic tropes in the approaches taken by critical art practices to phenomena that connect art and finance since the 1960s.[2]

In "On Art Activism" (2014), Boris Groys argues that in contrast to "aestheticization" as a design strategy, which affirms, improves, and normalizes the neoliberal promise of human capital and value by way of usefulness and attraction, and in which the market serves as cure against alienated and alienating work, "artistic aestheticization means the defunctionalization of [a] tool, the violent annulation of its practical applicability and efficiency," which in his view serves as a foundation for a revolutionary project. The museum, in which "the aestheticized material corpse functions as a testimony to the impossibility of resurrection," is the central node for a transformation in which contemporary art "aestheticizes the present by turning it into the dead past." In contrast, by expanding on the undercurrents of financialization that reshape the museum, Brian Holmes (2006: 414) concludes that the museum (as well as the university) are "normalizing devices" that "frame art practice and lend it both meaning and value." The museum as an integrated infrastructure of financialization awakens the "dead" to a new, derivative form of life and monetary appreciation. The open question—and one might think here of Tino Sehgal's performative contracts that allow buying, selling, and repeating "situations" or the debate ensuing Marina Abramovic's work for a gala at the Museum of Contemporary Art in Los Angeles[3]—is whether contemporary art with its criticality protocol can act against financialization and wealth concentration (by defunctionalizing the total aestheticization of capital and its finance-based appreciation regime), or, whether it is prone to render its total subsumption to derivative capitalism as the symbolic-representational image of finance power, which speaks and acts performatively (Nestler et al., 2018: 136).

Critical Art Paradigm's Two Models

Given that, within the critical post-Marxist tradition, finance has been generally treated as a subset of the capitalist order, the construction of strong anti-capitalist languages through the critical art practice paradigm has been central in inform-ing theoretical and artistic approaches to finance more specifically. In tracing the historical emergence of artworks that deal with particular aspects of finance rather than with capitalist dynamics more generally, it is worth pointing out that the critique has tended to focus on finance's abstracting qualities (Lütticken, 2012) and the detrimental effects of the societal fetishization of money as the basic unit of exchange, the powers of which strive to extend into every domain of life (Diederichsen, 2008). Within this overarching agenda, there are two distinct methodological templates that, in many ways, mimic the distinction between first- and second-wave institutional critique as described above. The first follows the detached critical observer model, while the second presents a reflexive engagement with one's own position as part of the critical operation of the artwork.

The critical observer model is historically evidenced in such works as Kru-ger's *Untitled. Money Can Buy You Love* (1985), and more recently *Untitled (Money Money Money)* (2011). Other recent examples are Beate Geissler and Oliver Senn's *Volatility Smile* (2011), Melanie Gilligan's *Crisis in the Credit System* (2008), and Christian Jankowski's *Kunstmarkt TV* (2008). SuttonBeresCuller's *Distribution of Wealth* (2009)—"a stack of one-hundred $1 bills, sliced vertically into segments that correspond to the percentage of the work's sale price taken by the gallery, the dealer, and the artists themselves" (Haiven, 2015: 47)— is exemplary of the tongue-in-cheek aestheticization that often characterizes artworks within this rubric. Here the focus tends to be on the artwork as a representational and often investigative device that strives to communicate the experiential and affective dimensions of commodification and alienation.

Meanwhile, the performative reflexivity model is evident in works as early as Marcel Duchamp's *Tzanck Check* (1919), where the Dada-associated artist paid his dentist for services with a hand-drawn check, the value of which was correlated to the check as an artwork—and thus constitutes a speculation by the artist that the collector "instinctively recognized the speculative potential of the deal" (De Duve, 2012: 73)—rather than as the redeemable and fun-gible financial quantity specified on the fake bank note. The performative model became more pervasive with the normalization of post-formalist and post-medium specific art in the 1960s and 1970s—for example, Cildo Meire-les's *Insertions into Ideological Circuits: Cédula Project* (1970), where the Brazilian artist added messages on banknotes, after which he would put them back into circulation. In a similar vein, in 1984, J.S.G. Bogg started making payments with hand-drawn one-sided dollar notes, later offering collectors receipts for sale that allowed them to trace the original notes. Other examples include Lise Autogena and Joshua Portway's *Black Shoals Stock Market Planetarium* (2001) and

Michael Goldberg's *Catching a Falling Knife* (2002); more recently, Axel Stock-burger's *Quantitative Easing (for the street)* (2014), which randomly distributes Euro-coins publicly, as well as Sarah Meyohas's *BitchCoin* (2015-), in which the artist issued a digital currency backed by her photography at a fixed exchange rate of 1 BitchCoin to 25 square inches of photographic print, or Wong Kit Yi's *North Pole Futures* (2015) where patrons could buy future commissions, which the artist would create during her three-week trip to the North Pole with the money for the works used to fund her "residency."

The performative model coincides with an artistic strategy that the founder of the art journal *Texte zur Kunst*, Isabelle Graw (2009: 188), has termed "mar-ket reflexivity." Graw identifies artistic practices, from the modernist Gustav Courbet to Marcel Duchamp, Yves Klein, Robert Rauschenberg, Andy War-hol, Andrea Fraser, and Merlin Carpenter, which "[take] market activity as [their] material at the same time as opposing it." According to Graw (2009: 191), market reflexivity is the privileged form of artistic engagement within a financialized society—a position that not only allows critical art to accept its inclusion in the dynamics of capitalization and private wealth creation but also salvages Adorno and Horkheimer's dialectical vision for an art under capitalism, whereby "abandonment of an idealistic belief system does not mean that market and aesthetic autonomy are identical." Graw (2009: 191, 193) states that "rather than cancelling each other out, [the market's and art's] opposition is in fact the precondition of their constituting a unity." Graw's endorsement of market re-flexive critical practices as a method that allows the critical paradigm to have its cake and eat it, too, stands in sharp contrast to her disapproval of artistic prac-tices that in her judgment fall on the more affirmative side of market dynamics in their reflexive gestures. The paradigmatic examples within this category are Jeff Koons and Damien Hirst—artists whose practice came to the fore in the 1980s, a decade marked by significant expansion and commercialization of the art market toward embodying global finance (Horowitz, 2011; Malik & Phil-lips, 2012).

By demarcating a boundary between market-reflexive and market-affirmative practices, Graw reinforces the ideological assumption ingrained within the crit-ical art paradigm from the 1960s onwards that the value of art's epistemological and political contribution in capitalist societies lies precisely in its ability to generate critique that, in turn, generates *oppositional* discursive and intellectual positions *about* certain phenomena. Although the "postmodern turn" of the 1980s (Jameson, 1991) with its ironic celebration of glossy commercialization is often seen as a qualitative departure from the more intellectually earnest, directly critical and market-shy practices of the previous decade, it should not be treated as a steadfast rupture. As has been mentioned, artists "interpellated" market forces worldwide as early as Dada in the 1910s and 1920s, followed by those who emerged from conceptual circles of the 1950s and 1960s. Ac-cording to Graw's approach, such works present an element of subversion and/ or transgression that operates qualitatively differently to the strategies of blasé self-commodification and branding that are associated with names like Koons and Hirst in the 1980s and 1990s (Thompson, 2008).

However, instead of pitting the seemingly more nuanced and critical approaches of the earlier era—strategies that Graw (2009) categorizes as "market reflexive"—against those of the 1980s and 1990s—which capitalize on and mimic market dynamics in a much more direct way—we propose that these differences are not just innate to specific artistic dispositions but are telling of, coalesce with, and are impacted by wider shifts in the organization of national markets and the global economy that have arrived with policies of privatization, liberalization, and deregulation in the 1980s and 1990s. To this extent, the dualism of Graw's approach is problematic as it can only be sustained by an artificial boundary of ethical judgment, while underplaying the significance of wider infrastructural realities, against which such judgment must be calibrated. In other words, Warhol's factory is as much a child of the dawn of New York's financial hegemony where transition from industry-based to service-based economy was still in the process of being crystallized, as Koons's factory is a child of the 1980s when financial market innovations, deregulation (or, more appropriately, self-regulation), and control over cheap labor markets via any means possible, global trade, and aggressive merchandizing became the hallmarks of America's economic domination.

Equally, it was on the back of US-led global expansion under the banner of liberalism (politically, economically, and culturally) that the contemporary art paradigm nurtured by the critical fervor of the 1960s and 1970s attained a globally oriented and interconnected socio-institutional complex for the first time, which was further expanded and consolidated in the first decade of the twenty-first century. Thus, while the 1980s bore new artistic approaches to capitalist dynamics, the larger economic and geo-political conditions streamlined and directed the field infrastructurally. Although the 1980s and 1990s "art world" did for a while provide a stage for more spectacular art objects (Horowitz, 2011; Stallabrass, 2004), the structural significance of contemporary art's globalization lay in the proliferation of art fairs, biennials, and institutional spaces that lifted the critical art paradigm from a niche and localized phenomenon born out of post-World War II urban cosmopolitan centers across the world to the globally distributed hegemonic norm of artistic and theoretical disposition that represents contemporary art (Velthuis & Baia Curioni, 2015). Contemporary art attained a gatekeeping position via collecting for the inclusion into the global elite.[4]

The expansion of credit, leverage, income inequality, and capital accumulation in favor of a "transnational capitalist class" (Sklair, 2001), in combination with the fundamental turn in the online sector and the long tail economics of the Internet, brought about a sea change in economics from scarcity to abundance—for those who can profit from it. This condition is not jeopardized by boom-and-bust cycles, as the latter are rather a token of the shift and can thus present themselves as equally exploitable. While contemporary art remains bound to a logic of scarcity in the form of the rare commodity or event, it also caters to the notion of abundance, not in spite of but due to its criticality which constitutes art's inherent surplus value and therefore its unique feature for its incorporation as an asset class. Contemporary artists aim to produce artworks that stand out in similar ways as black swans, or, in financial terms, out-of-the-money options, which while still within the reach of probabilistic assessment (they do not exit the space of contemporary art) produce "fat tails," i.e., previously improbable horizons. Harvesting a slightly deferred perspective for looking back at the history of art (to paraphrase Walter Benjamin[5]), rather than opening toward new beginnings, they expand the possible *states* of a future-at-present that can be *backprojected*, i.e., priced. Even though a comparison of the two artists is hard to imagine, Fraser's *Untitled* is as much paradigmatic for this as is Koons's commercial porn *Balloon Venus*, a Dom Perignon Limited Edition bottle (both 2003).

This means that there is an under-acknowledged significance of institutional valorization and circulation enacted through the symbiotic relationship between systemic implications of financialization, infrastructural expansion of contemporary art, and the critical art paradigm. The integration of the market reflexive model into the institutional mainstream of contemporary art, reaffirmed by such valorizing publications as *October* and *Texte zur Kunst*, does not so much supplant the "dealer-critic model" (White & White, 1965) that functioned as the cornerstone of modern art's institutionalization in the late nineteenth century, but engendered a turn in the relationship between criticism and art practice, which through institutional circulation became the new ground zero for legitimizing templates of art's approach to societal systems and dynamics. In fact, the two models continue to exist side by side within a single ecology, although it would be more accurate to describe the older one as the "dealer-curator model." Artist such as Koons and Hirst, by advancing their institutional and market status, glaringly rely on the latter, which challenges the underlying politics of the critical art paradigm by pointing to their structural enmeshment. What becomes evident is that the relationship between the economic and the ethico-political value regimes in contemporary art is mediated via the infrastructural backbone of contemporary art, which, on the one hand, purports the value of their separation—or at least a claim to strive for their separation (as per Graw)—and, on the other hand, deploys art's claim to autonomy as a value-creating mechanism—culturally, socially, politically, and economically. Thus, the *de facto* integration of the value regimes and simultaneous claims to the need for their separation reflects a deeper structural imprint of the contemporary art field, namely the stark dissonance between the infrastructural realities inside the field (i.e., the reality of its operations and the nurturing effect of the market) and the discursive positions that are promoted at the field's "front-end"—whether in the form of mission statements, wall texts in galleries, artistic positions displayed in exhibition spaces, or contemporary art's various discursive fora (Ivanova, 2014). While the fact that significant actors within the socio-institutional complex of art (such as museums and critical publications) play an important role in the financial valuation of artworks by market actors is not new and may be traced as far back as the Renaissance (De Marchi & Van Miegrot, 2006; Parks, 2005; Velthuis & Coslor, 2012), what is novel is the particular way in which the dynamics of marketization and financialization in the globalizing art market post-1960s coalesce with the global trends of market liberalization and financialization (Malik, 2007; Stallabrass, 2004).

Contemporary Art as an Expression of the Global Financial Order

In this sense, the global push for "free trade" and "free art" (Stallabrass, 2004) has not been antithetical to one another, even if so much of "free art" openly critiques the forces of globalization and financialization. Rather, the two coalesce at the level of their overarching operative dynamics—expansion of institutional network with a global reach (via the creation of internationally interconnected institutional and market representatives, and collectors), institutional privatization in parts of the world where spaces for art were previously publicly funded, and the predominance of the "born private" model in countries where the sphere of contemporary art is just being developed or gentrified by a wealthy elite.[6] These dynamics resonate with the policies of privatization and deregulation, particularly in jurisdictions that came to depend on loans secured via the World Bank, International Monetary Fund, and European Bank for Reconstruction and Development, or directly from developed states, and the formation and consolidation of a mobile global elite. Indeed, cultural globalization in the form of contemporary art and economic globalization has not just been comparative at the level of their models but interlinked at the level of capital, such as the exorbitant amounts of liquidity held in private hands as a result of control over newly deregulated trade of natural resources, and the financial investment into the contemporary art scene through some of these funds (Velthuis, 2007).

Since the 1980s, art objects have not only been increasingly commodified as luxury goods and marketed to old and new financial elites worldwide, but increasingly financialized as an asset class. The emergence of art market reports such as TEFAF in 2000, Deloitte's Art & Finance annual report in 2011, and the Art Basel Market Report in partnership with UBS and cultural economist Claire McAndrew in 2017, as well as specialized services that lend against contemporary art either as a branch of existing art market activities (e.g., Sotheby's), as part of packaged financial services (e.g., Deutsche Bank), or as a boutique service (e.g., Athena Art Finance), is indicative of this shift in the supply chain toward a wealthy elite of art dealer-buyers and producers, contractors, and subcontractors (artists). Exploration of contemporary art's potential as an asset class had been stalled by lack of transparency at the level of price-setting and transactions (i.e., there are no explicit industry standards for setting prices for artworks, while primary market transactions are "over-the-counter" (OTC)—not publicly disclosed), protective business climate that had to keep up an impression that access cannot be granted to those who are simply interested in the financial value of an artwork, and relatively small sums involved in comparison to conventional securities.

The contemporary art market's resistance at the top end to following the steep downward market curve in the face of the 2008 financial crisis once again drew attention to contemporary art not only as a luxury commodity but also as an asset class with a low beta-coefficient, and hence a potentially useful tool for portfolio diversification. Consequently, the wealth management wings of global banks and financial institutions as well as their newly sprung boutique counterparts reinvested in their efforts of breaking contemporary art's barriers to financialization by pairing with such infrastructural actors as Art Basel (in the case of UBS) or by investigating the potential of data technology in making market transactions and prices traceable for investors (Deloitte, 2016), or trading and fractionalizing artworks through blockchain-based art fund and auction platforms (University of Oxford and The Alan Turing Institute, 2018). Thus, the approach of the financial sector—or equally, entities that structure themselves in line with the financial and fin-tech sector's operative dynamics (e.g., Athena Art Finance or Maecenas)—has been to bring the top market segment of contemporary art into its (digitized) operational scope (Arora & Vermeylen, 2013).

This trend also reveals a shadier dimension of contemporary art's financial credibility, namely its ability to lock in liquidity and to transport it across national borders without having to incur taxation that would be applied to capital transfer. Freeports such as Geneva Freeport, Luxembourg Freeport, and Le Freeport Singapore play a central role in this scheme (Ditzig et al., 2016). The internal dynamics of contemporary art's ecology have been conducive to this trend insofar as the last decade has seen the erosion of non-market based funding structures for the arts as well as the thinning out of smaller and midsized galleries and collectors that were typically associated with supporting local artists as well as younger practitioners whose position has not yet been affirmed by the market, and those artists whose future value trend was equally uncertain. The corporatization and monopolization of the global contemporary art market through a consolidation of a top segment of globally distributed galleries and collectors, and a global network of freeports as traffic hubs, signal that it has been in the process of restructuring with the top end segment pivoting toward the financial sector.

However, it would not be entirely accurate to isolate the "blue chip" segment of contemporary art from its more high-risk segments. For one, all segments of the market are unregulated and rely heavily on various forms of private interests and assets (a term that replaced "wealth" as it implies future profit) while circulation across the socio-institutional complex of contemporary art acts as a key parameter for financial and cultural valuation. Thus, the observation made in regard to the collision between the critical paradigm of art and its financialization at the outset of this section may be reframed as a general condition of the contemporary art sphere in terms of the relationship between the operational dynamics of its infrastructures and the operational norms of its epistemological positions. While the latter have the capacity to self-reflexively encapsulate and at times even mediate their subsumption within the financial conditions that they critique, they are incapable of transcending these conditions, both operationally and epistemologically. One might even take that argument further insofar as critique has become a vital component of the continual adaptation and reconfiguration that nurtures value creation within the current financial regime, from the macro level to the different tiers of the micro zone, in which all data and metadata become the "critical apparata" scrutinized for even the most miniscule profit opportunity.

Implications of a Systemic Approach

One approach that has attempted to rationalize the dynamic between the critical art paradigm and the reality of institutional functioning in contemporary art stems from the sphere of sociology. Pierre Bourdieu's analysis (1993, 1996, 2010) of the cultural sphere as a socio-institutional ecology where taste and value are defined in the struggle between its actors over symbolic capital that can, in turn, be translated into cultural and financial capital, leads to the conclusion that the epistemological potential of art is highly dependent on the possibilities offered by art's infrastructural conditions. To this extent, the work of Boltanski and Chiapello (2007), although not speaking on the matter directly, sheds further light on the compatibility of critical approaches to finance emerging from within art theory and practice with a financialized system of governance that prices all forms of value creation and privatizes its profits. The generation of critical discourse performs the liberal-capitalist definition of individual freedom, which, through institutional valorization and dearth of non-market-based options for material security, produces value for the overall ecology of the contemporary art sphere. The latter is, in turn, harnessed by a select number of participants. By the same token, the market institutional ecology is driven by the desire of actors to become part of the select circle, reinforcing an endemic culture of information asymmetry. Olav Velthuis's (2007) sociological analysis of the art market exposes market opacity as a mechanism for maintaining artificial scarcity and a highly coded power structure, which not only sets up barriers to entry but protects the critical correlation between symbolic value and financial value.

The sociological macro vision of the contemporary art field renders critical positions on finance emerging from within that field to be highly constrained by the conditions of their production, dissemination, and valuation. Whereas critical positions on finance within the paradigm described in this section often offer intellectually sound and aesthetically persuasive insights on finance, what is repressed infrastructurally is the possibility for art to relate *differently* to finance than within the established critical paradigm and its dependence on capital. In other words, there is an urgency for a shift to a new paradigm that builds on a concept and a contextualization of the nonlinearity, entanglement, and multiplicity of processes, to which we return below, for art to seek different modes of understanding and operationalizing its own financialized condition, and to harness new ways of acting as an interface with other processes. To this extent, the short-circuiting that is produced by the current closed loop of critical approaches to finance and contemporary art's financialized predicament is very much set on the self-perpetuation of its own condition, which, on the one hand, becomes further consolidated through ecological institutionalization, and, on the other hand, either absorbs or suppresses emerging/marginal tendencies.

In the meantime, technological transformations are continuing to reshape geopolitics and governance (Bratton, 2016). For these shifts, the technological "nature" of the financial sphere—an increasingly automated and algorithmic global platform—is the governing "kernel" that recalibrates volatility (i.e., the short-term risks that are either perceived as threats or opportunities) in a competitive environment in micro-time. In a world in which "states" (from corporate bodies to national states to social statuses, individual identities and probabilistic states of the world) are turning from at least theoretically autonomous devices within specific systems of relations into speculative ventures exposed to contingency, the ability to dynamically hedge exposure any time, externalize losses in no time, and leverage one's bets at high factor becomes the unifying—if not universal—methodology of governance in managing claims repetitively against one another.

Such "derivative condition" (Nestler, 2017) applies to market participants in general today, and as such also to the contemporary art market. Whether the condition is eschewed through critical distance of opposition or affirmed, in the sense that Catherine Malabou (2018) references Deleuze's differential repetition, decides how these shifts are confronted: "instead of thinking of repetition as the return of the same—that 'most abysmal thought' [i.e., critical position]—[one] learns to affirm what is repeated, thus transforming repetition itself." Since the stakes and the potentials are technopolitical,[7] they concern not only the ambition to surpass critique but also intelligent appropriation against increasingly performative technologies and media of power. We will below resort to artistic examples that take this approach, often deriving from a tradition that deviates from contemporary art.

Another major limitation of the critical paradigm lies in its inability to offer alternative approaches to art as a financial asset such as the ones that are currently advocated for by the financial realm and the top end segment of contemporary art. Here the shortcoming is the inability or unwillingness to recognize that art's financialization could take different routes and promote different sets of interests to the ones that are advocated for by wealth managers. This would mean looking at art's financialization as a testing ground for finance that is not driven by the neoliberal agenda, or, alternatively, as a platform for harnessing aesthetic, cultural, and social potentials from an activism that engages with finance and other black boxes from within.[8] And as the late sociologist, activist, and dancer Randy Martin (2015: 105) argued—against the misconception that neoliberalism simply means defunding the state in favor of privatization—"public and private are always constituted through a kind of interdependence, and the challenge is to understand what creates their mutual imbrications and differentiation, a problem to which the derivative logic provides some keys."

The historical overview of the critical art paradigm demonstrates that contemporary art is a historically and geopolitically specific formation—in its institutional, infrastructural, and ideological scopes. By contrasting critical aspiration with the field's infrastructural and institutional realities, we showed that this oppositional expectation cannot epistemologically or operationally transcend the parameters of the *status quo*. The artists João Enxuto and Erica Love argue that "while technology is intensifying the soft power of speculation, reputation, and the hype of networks, recent changes in technical infrastructure have done very little to shake the narrowly-defined and limited objectives of contemporary art" (2016: 173).[9] Contemporary art is therefore not verbatim for art of our time, but an ideological and institutional construct. As such, the term "contemporary art" relates to today's hegemonic order of art, intimately bound up with the hegemonic form of global finance. In order for art to advance in its ability to offer political and epistemological contributions to societal issues after financialization, it is necessary to break free from the position that contemporary art is the only possible paradigm within which such positions can be produced (Malik, 2013). In the case of critique grounded in another relationship than that of opposition, we will revisit certain art formations of the last three decades that germinated alternative approaches to finance, while developing new infrastructural parameters and protocols for art in its relationship to other spheres, which reconfigure the issues of autonomy and value within heterogenic and shifting postdisciplinary settings that can not only cope with but add to the complexity of the current condition.

Toward Speculative Horizons and Systemic Visions

Art in Search of Non-Art Repercussions

While the critical art paradigm and financialization are interlocked via the organizing logics of the contemporary art field, another direction was pursued within the same period by artists whose choice of tools and techniques was only marginally appreciated in the contemporary art world. New media, digital, electronic, and net art are terms for practices that evolved in the 1980s and 1990s following the initiation of the field in the late 1950s. Partly applied research and partly wild experimentation with new media and technologies, these approaches often radically interrogated the conditions of art and social reproduction. Highly politicized by a critical stance toward media and ICT, digital art not only attacked the new economy's sell out of the social potential of new information technologies but was also highly skeptical of how the art world operates. Instead of inscribing itself into the gallery and museum system—which in most cases was and is too inert and unskilled to deal with these new tools and concepts—digital art often either dismissed the art world or used it as an "attention tool" for wider aesthetic, activist, and political aims (Nestler, 2007).

In 1996, the media art theoretician Lev Manovich diagnosed that "the convergence between the contemporary art world and the computer art world [...] will NOT happen," jokingly differentiating between them as "Duchamp-land" and "Turing-land." Aware of the appropriation of Turing-land aesthetics by Duchamp-land art, he nevertheless recognizes "what we should not expect from Turing-land is art which will be accepted in Duchamp-land [since] Duchamp-land wants art, not research into new aesthetic possibilities of new media" (Manovich, 1996). One example of an artistic practice that complicates this verdict can be found in the work of Thomas Feuerstein whose artistic career began with media and net art in the early 1990s and whose work ranges across all aspects of the infosphere—or, as Tiziana Terranova conceptualized it, the "informational milieu" (2004: 8)—with a focus on rendering complex themes and issues. His collaborative project *Hausmusik. Network Installation for Real Data* (1993) is an early example of art addressing finance directly. *Hausmusik* used real-time stock market data provided by Reuters which was transformed to control a piano and a violin. Referring to the world as oikos, music was not produced by musicians but "by a collective of global consumers." Although in macro sense, "conceptual narration"—Feuerstein's method in which "confabulations [operate] like a mycellic network rather than causally and dually"[10]— may be categorized as representational and symbolic, it taps into the actual dynamics of algorithmic and biotechnological processes in order to expose their generative potential. In a similar vein, Sylvia Eckermann et al.'s *The Trend Is Your Friend!* (2009) constructs an automated and at the same time immersive market environment that mediates through moving image and sound the double auction market model. Viewers that enter the installation can affirm, negate, or amplify particular market dynamics that they are confronting by shifting their gaze as well as by voice. Here the artwork functions as a simulation that translates complex conditions that structure markets and trading dynamics into a participatory aesthetic experience. Raising the question of individual agency in complex and interrelated systems, the market as an abstraction attains an inherently social and affective character, of which it is generally deprived by both neoclassical economic theory (LiPuma, 2016) and standard contemporary art critique.

Before concepts like "post-media,"[11] and more recently "post-internet," liquidated into the contemporary art field's valuation regime (Connor, 2013) "by embracing the fluidity of the art object as it circulates, like a currency, through networks and markets alike" (Lotti, 2018: 98), digital art and its hacks constituted less of a genre of art but an attempt to re-invent both the art system and art practice for the twenty-first century and its technological edge. The explorative spirit behind these projects often exceeded the critical stance of contemporary art by its implicit desire to offer practical answers, however preliminary and contingent, to the question: "what is to be done?" Initially, much of digital art relied on its own institutional setting that it had been developing since the late 1970s, and which often depended on public funding. Its infrastructural backbone included festivals, conferences, zines, blogs, archives, and non-profit media art institutions and organizations. Especially in the 1990s and 2000s—i.e., at a time of economic and public funding crisis and subsequent renaissance of the commercial gallery system—there used to be little confluence between the worlds of contemporary art and digital art, except in countries where new media and new media art were adopted more quickly and widely as part of the global innovation paradigm in the development of capitalist markets and infrastructures.

Digital art practitioners were often less avid in defining themselves as artists in the usual connotation of the term, as this was seen as adhering to a reactionary interpretation of individuality instead of developing inclusive and common practices. Rather, many artists were affiliated with coding culture and digital counterculture. The field was and continues to be more engaged in open source than in "free art"; it is less invested in "breaking conventions" while remaining "snug in the market's lap" (Stallabrass, 2004) and instead focused on (artistic) forms of disruption, digital actionism, or hacker activism targeted at government agencies and policies, corporations, market structures, and Internet technologies, among others. Mainly emerging from Gen X, net artists constituted the first Internet generation but were still brought up in the "analogue" world. Hence, artists like Heath Bunting, Etoy, ®™ark or The Yes Men made use of art institutions as physical distribution spaces for the specific agenda or desire underlying their often highly political or anarchic work. The impact of a project could be extended and leveraged in the slipstream of art, yet the ultimate aim would be to produce an impact on the very forces that one was interrogating. Working with and through the volatilities in-between real life and cyberspace, artistic freedom and marketing strategies, open source and piracy,[12] research and playing it by ear, brought about new artistic and collaborative risk-tactics that countered capitalist claims with their own claims as to what the future should look like (mainly based on ideas and platforms of the commons). This involved methodologies that furthered a speculative attitude in order to performatively navigate the legal, economic, and other repercussions that these forms of intervention met as well as an anarcho-tactical disposition to obtain enough clout to perform within a rather capricious attention economy.

Such artistic methodologies are certainly performatively reflexive, however, rather than aiming to perform an oppositional stance to a certain state of affairs and to find discursive resonance in the sphere of contemporary art, a net art approach looks to elicit feedback within the targeted state of affairs through intervention. An earlier example in this vein is *Nike Ground* (2003) by Eva and

Franco Mattes (0100101110101101.ORG) in collaboration with Public Netbase/ t0 in Vienna. The intervention consisted of a massive Nike-swoosh made of "special steel covered with a revolutionary red resin made from recycled sneaker soles," a high-tech container as info box, a fake website, and an advertisement campaign based on the line "Karlsplatz, one of Vienna's main squares, is soon to be renamed Nikeplatz." *Nike Ground* mobilized massive reactions from the public and city officials. Nike corporation filed legal action "against the breach of copyright" but the Viennese Commercial Court "rejected Nike's plea for a provisional injunction on formal grounds"[13] and Nike decided to withdraw due to local and international criticism of being a spoilsport. (Corporations learnt their lesson quickly and integrated identity hacking into their marketing portfolios.)

This approach could be described as a form of affirmation-resistance by means of tactical media[14] escalation and identity hacking. Instead of reiterating older forms of critique, such projects—often collaboratively realized—appropriate the tools and language of power toward their breaking point, for example, by forging narratives between fact and fiction performatively and "recalibrating" the volatile course of events in real time. Another similar intervention is UBERMORGEN's *Voteauction. com* (initially conceived by James Baumgartner), which was initiated for the 2000 presidential election in the United States (Bush vs Gore) and offered an infrastructure to sell and buy votes via auction. With the subtitle "Bringing Democracy and Capitalism Closer Together," the project took a step from critique as performative representation toward a performative action based on the affirmation of a diverse set of conditions: financial capitalism as a global order; information technologies and media as the structure and networks of this order, also as regards politics; the admission that art was not a field beyond these confines or otherwise standing out from the more mundane forms of systemic violence. Other examples of hacking the financial and corporate system, in which UBERMORGEN collaborated with the artist Paolo Cirio and the editor and artist Alessandro Ludivico, are *Amazon Noir: The Big Book Crime* (2006) and *GWEI: Google Will Eat Itself* (2005). Addressing the issue of proprietary copyright protection, the media art performance *Amazon Noir* hacked Amazon's "Search Inside" service and freely distributed digital volumes of books: "The conceptual artwork integrated the criminalization of piracy with free circulation and access to knowledge, hence addressing copyright and fair use laws within the disrupted digital economy and information monopolies" (Amazon Noir, 2006).

While both the hacks of *Voteauction.com* and *Amazon Noir* resulted in spectacular media coverage (and in the latter case, Amazon's denial of the hack and of their vulnerability), lawsuits, and repercussions for the artists not unlike those experienced by whistleblowers,[15] *GWEI* shows more "stealth" characteristics with its conceptual elaboration of the parasite moving below the radar of law infringement in respect to brand, copyright, patent, etc.:

We generate money by serving Google text advertisements on a network of hidden Websites. With this money we automatically buy Google

shares. We buy Google via their own advertisement! Google eats itself—
but in the end "we" own it! By establishing this autocannibalistic model
we deconstruct the new global advertisement mechanisms by rendering
them into a surreal click-based economic model. (GWEI, 2005)

Even though the project parasitically exploits Google's money-generating algorithm through an act of infrastructural deconstruction (and here differing
from semantic deconstruction of post-conceptual art), it does so in a subtle
and positively inconsequential way, as it would take "202.345.117 Years until
GWEI would fully own Google." The number reminds us that Google the
data "para-site" exploits each and every click to a degree beyond imagination
without any redistribution effort except to owners and shareholders, a fact that
almost ridicules the debates about tax evasion and creative accounting. At the
same time, it hints at a fact already mentioned by Karl Marx in *Capital I*, but
neatly blanketed by neoliberals: that unchecked capitalism leads to monopoly
centralization. Here, artistic over-affirmation not only appropriates the models of mass media advertising, information technology, metadata, and financial
capitalism in an entertaining and timely fashion (and uses the art market to sell
all sorts of paraphernalia following from it); as early as 2005 and at a time when
Google was deemed digital savior rather than the data demon, it brought home
the "totalitarian power untouched" that the global data conglomerates of platform capitalism maintain today (*GWEI*, 2005). GWEI also demonstrates that
while art may actively intervene into wider infrastructures, the project-based
logics limits its potential for scalability. In this sense, art is still conceptualized
and actualized as a syncopated interjection.

Nevertheless, what many of these and other works have in common is an
explorative and constructive engagement with the powers, terms, and conditions that shape the world today. They are also characterized by "a new level
of awareness with regard to the extent to which market dynamics bleed into
the fabrics of the art milieu" (Lotti, 2018: 89). And in contrast to the critical
position in contemporary art, they signal an invigorated speculative inclination
and a strategic orientation pivoted beyond art world validation, even if the latter
is used as one of the avenues via which wider impact—and some income—is
achieved.

Affirmation in the Name of Speculative Exploration

Before speculative realism was inaugurated in philosophy (at a conference at
Goldsmiths, University of London, April 27, 2007), artists had already developed practices that incorporate technology, theoretical exploration, postdisciplinary research, and activist affiliation, and have since been engaged in acute
experiments with speculative hacks, direct interventions, forensic investigations, or precedent setting experiments.[16] This speculative thrust delineates a
positive or enduring attitude vis-à-vis the neoliberal conception of creativity

that not only privileges the objective to own and monopolize ideas, practices, and processes, but also seizes the notion of speculation as an intrinsically financial one. It recaptures speculation from the hegemonic "rationality" of economics and finance, which not only constrain speculative thought with its preference for quantitative analysis (which applies more to economics, as in finance speculation often runs wild by necessity) but also ethically and regarding its qualitative potentials (for a discussion of speculation, see also Konings's chapter in this *Handbook*). For a rather long time, speculation was yielded to capitalist ventures, leading to violent endeavors that are considered ethically unsound from a post-Marxist position but advocated by liberals, neoliberals, and libertarians alike who are partisan as to its foundational ethics of Western civilization. The distinguishing trait of these artistic works and practices is that they do not fall into the trap of this dichotomy. They speculate on speculation by using the technologies, materials, methodologies and narratives of—in our case—financial capitalism to confront the latter's "amoral" ambiguities—to quote the financial expert and whistleblower Haim Bodek (Nestler, 2012–15/2014–15: 39:30 min.)—and to explore avenues that contribute to reorienting the financial sphere. Such approaches activate art and post-disciplinary research toward envisioning and together crafting *other* narratives and imaginaries in favor of, for instance, "undercommon" (Harney & Moten, 2013) and common aims (Roio, 2018)—instead of simply rejecting finance as the epitome of capitalism and black box sovereignty. And instead of advocating "an insurrection of slowness, withdrawal, and exhaustion" like the theorist and activist Franco "Bifo" Berardi (2012: 68), it engages with forms of insurrection that attempt to recode access, flows, and protocols of finance (as well as other techno-prognostic operations). An example for a practice that makes use of the symbolic power of art and at the same time exceeds syncopated interjection is Paolo Cirio's *Loophole for All* (2013). Cirio hacked the company register of the Cayman Islands, promoting "the sale of real identities of anonymous Cayman companies at low cost to democratize the privileges of offshore businesses" (*Loophole for All*, 2013). The artistic intervention not only opened offshore schemes to "ordinary people to avoid taxation the same way as these companies do" (*Loophole for All*, 2013), but also cunningly exploited the asset of anonymity against those hiding behind it.

However, work initially delivered from such artistic research is frequently spiraled into contemporary art and its marketization, via critical reflexivity of opposition but in a derivative mode, once again seemingly fulfilling Manovich's paradigmatic divide between Duchamp-land and Turing-land. But what if this conceptual rift obscures rather than illuminates the post-media condition? What if another distinction, this time a philosophical one, would better describe the *tense relaxation* between art that tries to cut its way toward new aesthetics, materials, and distributions and art that the market can (and wants to) make use of? A distinction, in which the market trope is turned from "aestheticized" alienation to an engagement with its social and technological complexity, its processes, protocols, and criteria? We are thinking here of the proposition put forward by Steven Shaviro (2012: ix, xii) in his text *Without Criteria*: that we should not follow Heidegger's insistence on being, which he summarizes in the question "Why is there something, rather than nothing," but rather ask with Whitehead "how is it that there is always something new?" Shaviro argues that in contrast to Heidegger, Whitehead engages with the present and its challenges by appreciating repetition, recycling, and recalibration as possibilities for novelty. If thought is to become more Whiteheadian, we must turn away from the obsessive insistence on oppositional critique because our senses are telling us that "the world is *already* otherwise" (Shaviro, 2012: xii), which implies an opening toward "speculation, fabulation and invention" and thus toward nonlinearity, entanglement, and multiplicity as regards contingent becomings. Here lies a confluence between art and finance—at least when we give finance the credit of potentially exceeding the realms of capitalism and neoclassical economics and art the credit of exceeding symbolic enactment of opposition to a state of affairs that is by default already past.

The proposition to distinguish between a *Heidegger-time* and a *Whitehead-time*—in which temporality is not an instant of measurement but constructed in intensive experience—is also one that offers propositions, rather than judgments; metastable rather than stable states; potentiality rather than (absolute) truth, and in which relations—that seem derivative and therefore secondary, if not fictive—"are every bit as real as 'things' [...] because they are themselves 'experienced relations'" (Shaviro, 2012: 40–41). These formulations, implying nonlinearity, nonequilibrium, and contingency, neither sound alien to the post-media condition nor to the philosophy of finance, as exemplified by Elie Ayache (2010, 2015; Nestler, 2012) and Jon Roffe (2015). They reverberate in studies of the sociology of finance, most prominently in Knorr Cetina (2003) and Knorr Cetina and Preda (2007), and would probably be shared by many traders and quants who know the "uneconomic" *visceral feel* of being in the market all too well.

Even though Turing-land has been infiltrating Duchamp-land—such as in the eminent work of artists like Simon Denny and collectives like DIS—there is a lingering security-sensitive spirit, an asset allocative grasp in these works that signals an entrepreneurial animal spirit, as identified by Matteo Pasquinelli (2008).[17] It retro-exploits rather than forward-celebrates new media art, culture, and the commons—a concept that claims (rather than promises) acting "in solidarity of one world" (Shaviro, 2012, 108). In the specific instance of our concern here, this amounts to entanglements that reassemble revolutionary ethos, which got dispersed in the network assemblages of social media, within derivative practices that engender new optionalities also in the field of finance—an arguably utopian premise, but one deeply ingrained in the processual spirit of our time, grounded in wild bricolages and assemblages; (bio)materialities and codes; and the affective potentials of (bio)technopolitical hacking and (crypto) automation.

One example of these artistic approaches is *Terra0* by Paul Seidler, Paul Kolling, and Max Hampshire. The project uses a decentralized autonomous organization (DAO) on the Ethereum Blockchain to explore—by way of automated sustainable and resilient forestry—how a smart contract can sustain itself. A self-owned forest creates capital in which humans are not involved by selling licenses for the logging of its trees through automated processes, smart contracts, and blockchain technology.[18] The authors state that the art project "gives [them] the proper space for the speculative aspect [...] to set up a prototype of a self-utilizing piece of land" ("Introduction", n.d.) and examine a scenario whereby objects and natural systems appropriate and apply utilization mechanisms to themselves. Referencing this project among others, Laura Lotti (2018: 96) argues that the speculative consequences of peer-to-peer automated technologies are potentially far-reaching, as they expose "the multidimensionality of property rights as legal, economic, and social operators of subjectivation and power relations" and thus produce a hardcoded revolutionary ethos "in the very definition of agency and autonomy—in both artistic and economic terms [that challenges] received notions of ownership, personhood and autonomy in a post-blockchain near future." Thus, they illustrate the potentials of tokenization beyond the self-management of capital, "ultimately collapsing the boundaries between art, ecology, economy, and politics."

Here, the token can be described as a new vehicle for autonomy that (experimentally) outsources trust to automated processes but for the advantage of collectivizing and decentralizing systems in favor of stakeholders (also nonhuman ones). Such research orientation toward platforms may in fact point to an infrastructurally underexplored potential of art that exceeds the possibilities of individual artworks. There is a host of blockchain- and cryptofinance-related endeavors that are either co-developed by artists, in a close exchange with artists, or engaged between art and their fields of research. One example is ECSA (economic space agency), an offspring of Robin Hood Cooperative (or Robin Hood Asset Management), who self-describe as "a group of radical economists, finance theorists, software architects, game designers, artists, lawyers, peer production experts, and decentralized application engineers—exactly what is needed to reimagine what economy can be."[19] Another approach is taken by Denis "Jaromil" Roio who has been engaged in free software coding, hacker activism, and net art for over two decades. In 2002, he founded Dyne.org, a working platform of programmers, artists, and activists, which defines itself as a "non-profit free software foundry with more than 15 years of expertise in developing tools and narratives for community empowerment" and whose practice ranges from GNU/Linux-based operating systems (like Devuan) to privacy-aware tools and applications for complementary currency governance systems and direct democracy and economic empowerment (D-CENT), a social digital currency (Freecoin), an artistic research project "to contrast abstract value creation with new paradigms in distributed energy usage and value re-cycling" (*Entropical*) and a blockchain ecosystem for electronic cash and smart contracts based on energy-efficient Proof-of-Trust consensus algorithm (YETTA).

Quite recently, artistic-scientific research at the intersections of biology and technology has begun interrogating the consequences as well as potentials of finance as regards living organisms and biotechnology. An example for an art project experimenting with algorithmic engineering is *ADM XI* (2017) by the artist group RYBN.org. The platform hosts a collection of competing "heretic, irrational and experimental" trading algorithms which are not "driven by price [...] but by living organisms such as soil, plants, and bacteria" ("About ADM XI", n.d.). The project exploits "artist[s'] legendary vision and know-how, to create innovative and counter-intuitive strategies of investment and speculation." RYBN.org claims that "the uncanny strategies challenge the neo-classical economics dogma" by following:

> their own non-mercantile and obsessive logic: some attempt to produce a total and irreversible chaos, while others try to influence the market price to make it look like a given geometrical shape, while others try to saturate the market with non-human affects. ("About ADM XI", n.d.)

Another approach is taken by projects that engage with the *biosphere* by experimenting with biological structures and narrative streams. "Aliveness" is decoded along non-proprietary lines, challenging schemes indicated by terms like "Big Bio" and "Big Pharma." In *Metabolic Currencies* (2017), Lucie Strecker, Klaus Spiess, and collaborators from art and science explore whether experimental financial frameworks and currency systems can "negotiate value through their liveness when mediated by interfaces with consumers and their affective resources." This hybrid performance speculates on "how the invariances, the un-encodable and invaluable in biology and art could challenge economics' preference for perfect information acquisition and efficiency for prediction, to escape the capitalization of categorized life."

Within the notion of Whitehead-time, artistic experiments and realizations involved in the crypto- or biospheres not only pursue the explorative zeal of artistic research but also work toward a technology-inclusive affective orientation. As such, they at least circumscribe potential perspectives for contributing to a financial ecology after postcapitalism. There is an immanent necessity of work grounded in the potentiality of "decision"—a term with consequences in Whitehead's philosophy—from which all subsequent recalibrations are derivative of. These practices thus transform the affirmation of the derivative into new practices of being embodied (and not only incorporated) —which includes self-owned automation—in a way that reverberates in what Catherine Malabou (2018) conceptualizes as "plasticity"[20]—"the capacity to concurrently receive and bestow form." However, we are only half way into Whitehead-time because what is often missing in the speculative art forms—and not only there—is a positive conceptualization of novelty, contingency, volatility, and leverage;

and within a wider but crucial perspective, the protocols and platforms which performatively define, process and "switch" (Ayache, 2010) regimes of evaluation and decision-making.

Developing New Organizational Protocols

Financialization makes evident the pivotal role played by organizational protocols that structure the streamlining of value creation and distribution. As has already been identified, contemporary art's infrastructural functioning is largely downplayed in the assessment of art's epistemological and political potential. While this may be convenient for maintaining the status quo, the suppression of infrastructural realities and endeavors that seek to populate the field of art with new institutional models and missions is a major stumbling block for creating new art ecosystems that are capable of progressive operation in a technopolitical age. Thus, in many ways, the larger project of amplifying and scaling up the approaches to finance that are emphasized in this part of the chapter is tied in with a project that seeks to reform various organizational parameters shaping the institutional complex(es) of art. For example, currently, there are scarcely any institutional pathways available for institutional dissemination and the capacity to utilize knowledge generated through speculative artistic practices outside the exhibition/publication format. In many ways, the prototypical contemporary art institution still remains bound by a high modernist/late nineteenth-century conception of the museum (Bennett, 1995) as first and foremost an "interface" with "the public." To this extent, development of new organizational protocols that can reposition the art institution's existing capabilities to offer new interfaces with non-traditional stakeholders and partners still remains an open and much needed project. Development of such interfaces is in part dependent on a cultural shift from equating the field of art exclusively with art objects, events, and individual (i.e., fragmented) artistic expressions to understanding art from a systemic perspective.

As early as 1968, Jack Burnham's systems manifesto advocated for artistic approaches that shift from object-based to systems-based logics given that in technologically driven (and we may add, financialized) societies, "priorities revolve] around the problem of organization." Although Burnham has been largely taken up by the art field through artists who represent or fashion systems via their object-based works (Ivanova, 2017), there is another lineage of approaches that straddle art with the question of organization at a systemic scale. For example, Artist Placement Group—a UK-based collective that started operating in the 1970s—organized placements for artists in an attempt to develop new ways for art to interact with key industries. The model has been taken up by the world of tech start-ups where artists are frequently engaged as consultants (Salter, 2013) and even Google has launched a Cultural Institute—an art-driven R&D lab. What these developments indicate is that the ever open and synthesizing potential of art is a resource to be mined beyond the asset potential of contemporary art objects in a financialized economy. New organizational forms will yield novel articulations for the deployment of that resource with a potential to set systemic precedents, and there is thus an urgency to rethink the leverage that art institutions and actors within the art world already hold in pivoting toward modulated organizational formations.[21]

Another key access point for reforming the infrastructural constellation of the art field is its economic dimension. The advent of the online economy and availability of new tools such as blockchain has reawakened Seth Siegelaub and lawyer, Robert Projansky's *Artist's Reserved Rights Transfer and Sale Agreement* (1971) designed to provide artists agency over circulation of their work in a market economy.[22] Working Artists and Greater Economy (W.A.G.E.) is a New York-based lobbying agency and a self-appointed certification platform for institutions that agree to respect the agency's wage criteria in their work with artists. One of its new projects is a blockchain version of the Siegelaub contract, which will be integrated into an administrative platform that will allow wagents (artists) to manage their relationships with institutions and market actors. It utilizes the possibilities of digital platforms to coalesce administrative functionality with coalition building. While shortcomings may be identified in relation to projects such as W.A.G.E. and Artist Placement Group (APG)-inspired ventures, the main point here is that institutional reform cannot be overlooked in addressing the potential of art in "transforming repetition," especially in contrast to the often-exploitative subcontractor condition of the artist in the contemporary art supply chain.

Bestowing New Forms

While in the last decade, many more projects than can be mentioned took to accessing finance as a field of artistic research and infrastructural reform, the three strains that are emphasized here are artistic projects that take inroads into finance by entering into affiliations with financial experts to carve out new readings, narratives, and agencies; artistic interventions that hijack financial/capitalist operations and structures, and larger endeavors that develop new organizational forms and those that apply the blockchain technology as a way of reforming the infrastructural protocols of the art field. What is taken advantage of in all of these examples by way of acknowledgment is the fact that—as the editors of the special issue on art and finance in *Finance and Society*, Suhail Malik and Gerald Nestler (2014: 94–95), state—"by now, the interests of the art market [and we may add, by way of financialization] permeate all the way through the art system." This has profound repercussions for how actors—individual agents and organizations—conceive of their systemic function.

In the derivative paradigm and its operative market logic, world-producing and transgressive art of the past is conserved as pure financial wealth by deflating its former radical political clout in the purified citations offered by contemporary art, in which a political-emancipatory stance is prerequisite as a branding mechanism. This shift can be traced back to as early as 1984—to the height of financial deregulation policies—when Brian Wallis (1984: xii) observed that "[n]ow, not only is the avant-garde no longer radical, though its forms continue to be produced and simulated for an overextended art market, but in a final irony, modernism has become the official culture, the aesthetic haven of neo-conservatives." Modernist avant-garde has come to constitute "fundamental value" not in the sense of a politics of change, of radicality or of alterity, but as the underlying asset of a derivative speculation on future value transacted and recalibrated in the response chain with contemporary work (by way of dynamic hedging, to use a financial term). In contrast to the romantic notion of artistic value, art is either made productive (renders price) by entering circulation or it is nonproductive and as such externalized from the dynamic recalibration of pricing—it might hold value but in the most marginal and *unproductive* sense offered by the neoliberal ideology. Exposed to market forces, originality, trans-gression, and resistance—marks of quality of the liberal (modernist) conception of art—succumb to a relational "post-asset" and must not be "overemphasized" in the neoliberal "unleashing" of creativity. In this perspective, the derivative logics of new labels such as post-internet or street art (a derivative of the polit-ically controversial graffiti) and their artists' brands are akin to order types that allow the performative insertion of new speculative and shortcutting operations into the market for entering, exiting, or leveraging positions, not unlike those in high-frequency trading (on high-frequency trading, see also the chapter by Lange in this *Handbook*).[23] The derivative condition (Nestler, 2017) in which artists find themselves today is a highly volatile world (not only works but entire careers are market-performance related). Noise more often than not obscures information "productively" in order to leverage risk options. Here, the worlds of data, finance, and art coalesce: noise is the master of information (on noise, see the chapter by Preda in this *Handbook*).

Those art projects that tackle the black box constitution of informational and financial technocapitalism—and what Alberto G. Ramos (1981: 81) already in the early 1980s defined as the "deceitful cognitive politics […] peculiar to market centered societies"—are, as we have shown, aware of this incorporation. Moreover, they exceed the trope of market reflexivity as an anchor of critical art practice and do not stop at revealing the obfuscated nature of power dynamics under capitalism.[24] However, they are, not surprisingly, mostly at the margins of, or survive completely outside, the global art industry and its market-styled art assets, or they take activist positions that materialize at a variety of sites in-cluding the paradigmatic "white cube" and its asset-producing capital. In this case, however, their main source of funding and income is the increasingly neo-liberal "device" of the university, rather than the museum (Holmes, 2006), and thus—except in extant pockets of Western European welfare states—another highly financialized institution with a brutal debt/leverage ratio that signifies the crisis of the neoliberal regime based on probabilistic hypothesis in the face of contingency.

The derivative logics of the "art-finance complex" not only attempt to normalize art by financializing what it can capitalize on, it also externalizes resistant art practices it cannot co-opt easily, thus deflating art's emancipatory potentials. In the globalized art world, *differentiation* serves the flexible tastes of savvy collectors rather than the plasticity of art's "contestation" with reality. Historically, though, art has always reinvented itself with new questions, approaches, formats, and practices, thus averting attempts to homogenize the "culture of art," a fact that implies enormous losses on value investment, or, to the contrary, huge gains in profit and esteem for those few of the "leisure class" (Veblen, 1899) who took the risk to buy or finance art outside accepted categories of taste and esteem. And while new art has often been captured by the market after some time, it has also proven the "floating crap game" of the art "market" (Baumol, 1986) wrong many times by aiming at the *priceless truth value* (to adapt Hénaff, 2010) at the core of the condition of its time, its challenges, and bonds.

An approach that repoliticizes activist and artistic practices along the lines that can described as aesthetics in the field of consequences and which aims at enhancing resolution not for artistic means, but as an evidence-generating agency[25] is Forensic Architecture (FA), a London-based research collective that brings together architectural, artistic, and media research in order to "reverse the direction of the forensic gaze and to turn it back on those very state agencies—the police, military, or secret services—that otherwise use forensics (surveillance, tracking, and pattern analysis) to govern or control populations" ("Ground Truth", 2017). From an art theoretical perspective, this reversal constitutes a radical reformulation of new media art for the twenty-first century. The very antithesis to *l'art pour l'art*, FA's practice is situated in a realm of postdisciplinary research, which is operationalized within a number of contexts such as laws of court, NGO campaigns, and negotiations with governments, not to mention the extensive coverage received by mainstream media. In the light of Malabou's (2018) theorization of plasticity via repetition (and in contrast to ever "flexible" finance) what characterizes FA's radical counter-investigations is their deliberate intention—their agency—to "receive form" by way of acts of violence and "bestow form" by way of the event of forensic *reperformance* of these very acts. This *revolutionary* association of technology, theory, and research toward emancipatory, entangled, and encouraging agentorial interventions reverberates increasingly in art world corners that are seeking new conceptually, materially, and ethically consequential approaches for moving beyond the critical reflexivity paradigm.[26]

An aesthetics in the field of consequences engaging with finance directly is "aesthetics of resolution"—a project of one author of the present chapter (Nestler, 2014, 2015).[27] With transparency under extreme pressure as the paradigmatic model for governing sociality,[28] Nestler conceives the term resolution as a toolbox whose semantic field (spanning from perception to knowledge production to decision-making) offers an inroad for hacking[29] black box information and access asymmetry, and thus for *other* (political) sensibilities and relations. One of the artistic research outcomes was that despite of an existing array of (forensic) investigations, we are confronted with a secretive regime that only submits "substandard resolution, a ghost of an image"—to take Christiane Paul's observation (2015: 1–2) outside the art field. Hence, only someone from within the black box is essentially capable of making the black box speak. Nestler refers to this expert witness as the "figure of the renegade." Identified and denounced by the system as *traitor*, she—a whistleblower, hacker with "skin in the game" or "those with two names" (Brekke and Vickers, 2019: 63) —turns public *educator* (often in alliance with other experts). By producing knowledge against the proprietary logic of capitalism and the asymmetries manufactured by corporate or state actors,[30] she enhances resolution across all levels of the term. *Instanternity* is Nestler's collaborative effort with the high-frequency trader and whistleblower Haim Bodek and the artist Sylvia Eckermann to map automated finance not only techno-aesthetically but also legally, infrastructurally, and ethnographically. In experimental settings they refer the volatility and contingency of financial performance directly to the audience by constructing a space in which participation turns into a physical and affective disordering of concentration in order to create an awareness with which we can learn to *read* the performative speech of power (not unlike cultures deciphered representative power between physical experience and the abstractions of the mind). The artistic hypothesis is that we need to leverage the body's sensory and intuitive intelligence in its interaction with other *bodies* to build a new body politic on a common ecology. Projects like *Instanternity* and *Making the Black Box Speak* (2018),[31] which Nestler realized with Eckermann and other collaborators, engage with a conception of technology, agency, and solidarity in which the depth of resolution does not collapse into asymmetric leverage for the few. *Renegade agency* is affirmative in the sense that it enters into alliances with those who take the risk of confronting the system, and its non-transparency, from the inside. Rather than reiterating or recalibrating established frameworks of critique and transparency, resolution takes resistance to the level of insurrection.

Technocapitalist biopolitics rest on a volatile cohesion in which the promise of welfare for all is replaced by the automated exploitation of individualized affects. But *making sense* of the artistic, cultural, and financial potentials of the derivative, and volatility and leverage as constitutive forces, revalorizes the extensive capacities and temporalities to perceive and reorient deep (infra) structural changes—i.e., governmental in the Foucauldian sense—against behavioral and social normalization. New performative conceptions of the relations between art, data, and finance can contribute to a radical "arbitrage" that redistributes what today is the privilege of a tiny elite: the abundant wealth of the derivative condition. The notion of plasticity may serve as a lead as to how deep *re-form* ("receiving" and "bestowing form") can transform not only the mind but all bodies with dignity. Plasticity as a volatility practice is a *(self-) empirical process* in which bodies and minds perceive, shape, and leverage, each other—Whiteheadian aesthetics—but where confluences of bodies (human and nonhuman) take "random lead."

Notes

1 The Guggenheim canceled Haacke's solo exhibition, on the ground that the museum's policies "exclude active engagement toward social and political ends," and dismissed the curator, Edward Fry. See *New York Times*, April 7, 1971, online: https://www.nytimes.com/1971/04/07/archives/the-guggenheim-cancels-haackes-show.html (last accessed March 8, 2019).

2 This was not confined to the Western world, as instanced by *New Tendencies*, a movement initiated in non-aligned Yugoslavia in the early 1960s that spread across the Cold War divide (Medosch, 2016).

3 See: http://theperformanceclub.org/2011/11/yvonne-rainer-douglas-crimp-and-taisha-paggett-blast-marina-abramovic-and-moca-la/.

4 A central figure of art world dynamics is the collector (see, e.g., *Collecting Contemporary Art*, 2008). On the one hand, art-loving philanthropist and, on the other, savvy investor, he or she speculates on, hedges, and arbitrages aesthetic information and affective surplus, thus quantifying value into price.

5 Benjamin (1969), from *Theses on the Philosophy of History*, first published in English by Hannah Arendt.

6 In China, contemporary art museums are often part of real estate projects—the owner of K11 Art Malls, Adrian Cheng, explains that "[t]he point is to build a seamless ecosystem between art and retail" (Fan, 2017). Russia has seen strong international investments by the oligarch class. Latin America and the Caribbean region "boast" collector-institutions and Africa has seen its first art financialization controversy around the opening of the Zeitz Museum of Contemporary Art Africa in Cape Town.

7 The financial expert and philosopher Elie Ayache, for instance, defines derivative markets as "technology of the future" (2006).

8 Emily Rosamond (2016) points to the financialization of socially engaged art, which usually stands in opposition to the art market. With Michel Feher she argues (2016: 124):

> what is needed most from socially engaged art practices is that they experiment with their status as investees. This might involve not so much a futile attempt to shelter one's project from the logics of social investment, so much as embracing the double bottom line as an operational logic.

9 Examples sparking debates on automated art, human versa AI creativity, and fintech art market disruptions are Christie's $432,000 auction sale of a portrait generated by a "generative adversarial net" (GAN) algorithm and the Codex blockchain art auction at the Ethereal Summit 2018.

10 See http://www.myzel.net/Narration/vorwort_en.html.

11 The term was introduced in 1985 by Felix Guattari to designate mass media and was applied to aesthetics and art by theorists like Peter Weibel, Lev Manovich, Christiane Paul, or Matthew Fuller, and criticized by Rosalind Krauss. For a brief overview of the discussion, see: https://monoskop.org/Postmedia (last accessed March 8, 2019).

12 For example, *Kingdom of Piracy*, curated by Shu Lea Cheang, Armin Medosch, Yukiko Shikata as "an online, open workspace to explore the free sharing of digital content—often condemned as piracy—as the Net's ultimate art form." See, for example, http://www.medienkunstnetz.de/works/kingdom-of-piracy/.

13 See: http://www.t0.or.at/nikeground/pressreleases/en/003.
14 Tactical media (Garcia & Lovink, 1996) denotes radical activist/artistic interventions in the media sphere—the actual environment of such art practices, in contrast to the art world.
15 Apart from legal and political issues "[b]etrayal, blasphemy and pessimism finally split the gang of bad guys. The good guys (Amazon.com) won the showdown and drove off into the blistering sun with the beautiful femme fatale, the seductive and erotic massmedia" (GWEI, 2005).
16 This line of artistic experiments differs from the appropriation of speculative realism and object-oriented-ontology in the contemporary art sphere. For a critical interrogation of the latter, see *Speculative Aesthetics* (2014).
17 For an analysis in this vein, see also Zhang (2018).
18 See http://networkcultures.org/moneylab/2016/09/29/terra0-the-self-owning-augmented-forest/.
19 See: https://economicspace.agency/team.
20 Malabou argues against flexibility, which "only designates the capacity to be moulded or bent in all directions without resistance"—a similar assessment as Holmes' (2001) diagnosis of the "flexible personality" in neoliberal globalization.
21 Examples of artistic practices include Jubilee, which "functions as a cooperative structure that optimises the output of its members through joining efforts and equally distributing its collective assets and resources (economic, artistic and social)," and Primer, "a platform for artistic and organisational development" located in the headquarters of the biotech company Aquaporin.
22 For an updated version of the contract aimed at circulation of digital artworks, see Rafael Rozendaal's Art Website Sales Contract. In a similar vein, artists Jonas Lund and Harm van den Dorpel are using tokenization to control the financialization of their own practices. See https://jlt.ltd, and https://tokens.harmvandendorpel.com.
23 One ambiguous figure in this acceleration of leveraging speculative gains and arbitrage opportunities is the "art flipper" who produces market volatility (especially on social media platforms) to gain and exploit competitive advantage over established art market players. On this controversy, see, for example, Lotti (2016: 99), or, https://www.artsy.net/article/artsy-editorial-flippers-art-dealers.
24 Recent preeminent examples are The Sackler family and Whitney Biennial controversies.
25 In contrast to the "substandard resolution" of the "poor image" (Steyerl, 2009), which Paul (2015) views as an unsatisfactory but necessary mediation to "capture a certain condition of cultural and artistic practice in the early 21st century." On the poor image and the artwork as derivative, see Wark (2016).
26 A result of such art world demand is FA's shortlisting for the Turner Prize 2018, which highlights the ambivalence between politically and artistically relevant activist work and its contingent absorption into contemporary art. Eyal Weizman, director of FA, argues "we should rather insist, as counterintuitive as it may seem, on the evidentiary dimension of art and its truth value." Online: https://frieze.com/article/id-rather-lose-prizes-and-win-cases-interview-eyal-weizman-turner-prize-nominated-forensic.
27 Initially an artistic investigation of high-frequency trading and the Flash Crash 2010 in the context of the exhibition *Forensis* at the Haus der Kulturen der Welt in Berlin, 2014 (Forensic Architecture, 2015).
28 Transparency is commonly conceived as a prerequisite for resolution but under black box conditions this relation is ruptured, or, in fact "colonized by the logic of secrecy" (Pasquale, 2015: 2).

29 To quote the finance activist and anthropologist Brett Scott (2015, original emphasis), hacking "involves *queering*, deviating from established paths and making fluid the boundaries that are otherwise viewed as concrete and static."

30 Not confined to finance, this constitutes the social anesthetic of black box society (Pasquale, 2015).

31 See http://thefutureofdemonstration.net/passion/e03/index.html.

References

About ADM XI. (n.d.). Retrieved from http://www.rybn.org/ANTI/ADMXI/about/?ln=en.

Adorno, T. W., & Horkheimer, M. (1997). *Dialectic of Enlightenment*, trans. J. Cumming. London and New York: Verso Classics.

Alberro, A. (2000). "Reconsidering conceptual art, 1966–1977," in A. Alberro and B. Stimson (eds.), *Conceptual Art: A Critical Anthology* (pp. xvi–xxxvii). Cambridge, MA and London: The MIT Press.

Amazon Noir. (2006). Retrieved from http://paolocirio.net/work/amazon-noir

Arora, P., & Vermeylen, F. (2013). "Art markets," in R. Towse and C. Hanke (eds.), *Handbook of the Digital Creative Economy Cultural Economics* (pp. 322–329). Cheltenham: Edward Elgar Publishing.

Augita, L., Belluzo, A., Belting, H., & Buddensieg, A. (2009). *The Global Art World: Audiences, Markets, and Museums*. Berlin and Stuttgart: Hatje Cantz.

Axford, B. (1995). *The Global System: Economics, Politics and Culture*. New York, NY: St. Martin's Press.

Ayache, E. (2006). "Why 13 can only succeed to 11, or, the end of probability", *Wilmott*, July 2006: 30–38.

Ayache, E. (2010). *The Blank Swan: The End of Probability*. Hoboken, NJ: Wiley.

Ayache, E. (2015). *The Medium of Contingency: An Inverse View of the Market*. Basingstoke: Palgrave Macmillan.

Baumol, W. (1986). "Unnatural value: Or art investment as floating crap game," *American Economic Review*, 76(2): 10–14.

Benjamin, W. (1969). *Illuminations: Essays and Reflections*, ed. H. Arendt, trans. Harry Zohn. New York, NY: Schocken Books.

Bennett, T. (1995). *The Birth of the Museum. History, Theory, Politics*. London: Routledge.

Berardi, 'Bifo' F. (2009). *The Soul at Work: From Alienation to Autonomy*, trans. by Francesca Cadel and Giuseppina Mecchia. Los Angeles: Semiotext(e).

Berardi, 'Bifo' F. (2012). *The Uprising: On Poetry and Finance*. Los Angeles: Semiotext(e).

Boltanski, L., & Chiapello, E. (2007). *The New Spirit of Capitalism*, trans. by G. Elliott. London and New York: Verso.

Bourdieu, P. (1993). *The Field of Cultural Production*. Cambridge and Oxford: Polity Press.

Bourdieu, P. (1996). *The Rules of Art: Genesis and Structure of the Literary Field*, trans. Susan Emanuel. Cambridge and Maldon, MA: Polity Press.

Bourdieu, P. (2010). *Distinction*, trans. Richard Nice. Abingdon: Routledge.

Bratton, B. (2016). *The Stack: On Sovereignty and Software*. London and New York: Verso.

Brekke, J. K., & Vickers, B. (2019). *The White Paper by Satoshi Nakamoto*. London: Ignota Press.

Connor, M. (2013, November 1). "What's postinternet got to do with net art?," *Rhizome*. Retrieved from: http://rhizome.org/editorial/2013/nov/1/postinternet.

Deleuze, G. (1994). *Difference and Repetition*. New York, NY: Columbia University Press.

Deleuze, G., & Guattari, F. (1977). *Anti-Oedipus: Capitalism and Schizophrenia*, trans. R. Hurley, M. Seem, and H. R. Lane. New York, NY: Viking Penguin.

Deleuze, G., & Guattari, F. (1987). *A Thousand Plateaus: Capitalism and Schizophrenia*, trans. B. Massumi. Minneapolis: University of Minnesota Press.

De Duve, T. (2012). *Sewn in the Sweatshops of Marx*, trans. R. E. Krauss. Chicago, IL: University of Chicago Press.

De Marchi, N., & Van Miegrot, J. (2006). *Mapping Markets for Paintings in Europe, 1450–1750*. Turnhout: Brepols Publishers.

Deloitte. (2016). *Art & Finance Report 2016*. https://www2.deloitte.com/content/dam/Deloitte/global/Documents/Finance/gx-fsi-art-finance-report-2016.pdf

Derrida, J. (1978). *Writing and Difference*, trans. P. Patton. London and New York, NY: Routledge.

Diederichsen, D. (2008). *On (Surplus) Value in Art*. Berlin: Sternberg Press.

Ditzig, K., Lynch, R., & Ding, D. (2016). "Dynamic global infrastructure: The freeport as value chain," *Finance and Society* 2(2): 180–188. doi: 10.2218/finsoc.v2i2.1732.

Enxuto, J., & Love E. (2016). "The Institute for Southern Contemporary Art (ISCA)," *Finance and Society* 2(2): 173–174.

Fan, J. (2017, March 9). "Why Shanghai, China is the place to be for contemporary art," *Conde Nast Traveler*. Retrieved from https://www.cntraveler.com/story/why-shanghai-china-is-the-place-to-be-for-contemporary-art.

Fanon, F. (2004). *The Wretched If the Earth*, trans. R. Philcox. New York, NY: Grove Press.

Graw, I. (2009). *High Price: Art between the Market and Celebrity Culture*. Berlin: Sternberg Press.

Ground Truth: The al-Arabiq Museum of Struggle. (2017). *Forensic Architecture*. Retrieved from http://www.thefutureofdemonstration.net/e01/index.html.

Groys, B. (2014). "On art activism," *e-flux journal* 56. Retrieved from http://www.e-flux.com/journal/56/60343/on-art-activism/.

GWEI – Google Will Eat Itself. (2005). Retrieved from http://www.gwei.org/index.php.

Haiven, M. (2015). "Art and money: Three aesthetic strategies in an age of financialization," *Finance and Society* 1(1): 38–60.

Harney, S., & Moten, F. (2013). *The Undercommons: Fugitive Planning & Black Study*. New York, NY: Minor Compositions.

Hénaff, M. (2010). *The Price of Truth: Gift, Money and Philosophy*. Stanford, CA: Stanford University Press.

Holmes, B. (2001). "The flexible personality: For a new cultural critique," *transversal* 01/2006. https://transversal.at/transversal/1106/holmes/en?hl=

Holmes, B. (2006). "The artistic device, or, the articulation of collective speech," *ephemera* 6(4): 411–432.

Holmes, B. (2009). *Escape the Overcode: Activist Art in the Control Society*. Eindhoven: Van Abbe Museum Public Research #02.

Horowitz, N. (2011). *Contemporary Art in a Global Financial Market*. Princeton, NJ: Princeton University Press.

Introduction. (n.d.). Retrieved from https://www.gitbook.com/book/plsdlr/terra0/details.

Ivanova, V. (2016a). "Fractured mediations," in A. Avanessian and S. Malik (eds.), *The Time Complex. Post-Contemporary* (pp. 113–132). Miami: [NAME] publications.

Ivanova, V. (2016b). "Contemporary art and financialization: Two approaches," *Finance and Society* 2(2): 127–137.

Ives, K. (2007). *Cixous, Irigaray, Kristeva: The Jouissance of French Feminism*. Maidstone: Crescent Moon Publishing.

Jameson, F. (1991). *Postmodernism, or, The Cultural Logic of Late Capitalism*. Durham: Duke University Press.

Knorr Cetina, K. (2003). "From pipes to scopes: The flow architecture of financial markets," *Distinktion: Journal of Social Theory* 4(2): 7–23.
Knorr Cetina, K., & Preda, A. (2004). *The Sociology of Financial Markets*. Oxford: Oxford University Press.
Knorr Cetina, K., & Preda, A. (2007). "The temporalization of financial markets: From network to flow," *Theory, Culture & Society* 24(7–8): 116–138.
Krippner, G. R. (2005). "The financialization of the American economy," *Socio-Economic Review* 3: 173–208.
Lazzarato, M. (2012). *The Making of the Indebted Man*, trans. J. D. Jordan. Cambridge, MA and London: The MIT Press.
Loophole for All. (2013). Retrieved from https://paolocirio.net/work/loophole-for-all/.
Loophole for All. (2014). Retrieved from http://prix2014.aec.at/prixwinner/12143.
Lotti, L. (2016). "Contemporary art, capitalization and the blockchain: On the autonomy and automation of art's value," *Finance and Society* 2(2): 96–110.
Lotti, L. (2018). "Financialization as a medium: Speculative notes on post-blockchain art," in I. Gloerich, G. Lovink, and P. de Vries (eds.), *MoneyLab Reader: Overcoming the Hype*. Amsterdam: Institute of Network Cultures.
Lütticken, S. (2012). "Inside abstraction," *e-flux journal* 38. Retrieved from https://www.e-flux.com/journal/38/61196/inside-abstraction.
Mackay, R., Pendrell, L., & Trafford, J. (2014). *Speculative Aesthetics*. Falmouth: Urbanomic Press.
Malabou, C. (2018, September 21). "Repetition, revenge, plasticity," *e-flux architecture*. Retrieved from https://www.e-flux.com/architecture/superhumanity/179166/repetition-revenge-plasticity.
Malik, S. (2007, August 13). "A boom without end? Liquidity, critique and the art market," *Mute*. Retrieved from http://www.metamute.org/editorial/articles/boom-without-end-liquidity-critique-and-art-market.
Malik, S. (2008). "Critique as Alibi: Moral differentiation in the art market," *Journal of Visual Art Practice* 7(3): 283–295.
Malik, S. (2013). "Reason to destroy contemporary art," *Spike* 37. Retrieved from https://www.spikeartmagazine.com/en/articles/reason-destroy-contemporary-art.
Malik, S., & Nestler, G. (2016). "Introduction: Art and finance," *Finance and Society* 2(2): 94–95.
Malik, S., & Phillips, A. (2012). "Tainted love: Art's ethos and capitalization," in M. Lind and O. Velthuis (eds.), *Contemporary Art and Its Commercial Markets. A Report on Current Conditions and Future Scenarios* (pp. 209–240). Berlin: Sternberg Press.
Manovich. L. (1996, October 22). The Death of Computer Art. *Rhizome-blog*. Retrieved from http://rhizome.org/community/41703/
Marazzi, C. (2009). *The Violence of Financial Capitalism*, trans. K. Lebedeva. Cambridge, MA and London: The MIT Press.
Marcuse, H. (1964). *One-Dimensional Man: Studies in the Ideology of Advanced Industrial Society*. Boston, MA: Beacon Press.
Martin, R. (2002). *The Financialization of Daily Life*. Philadelphia, PN: Temple University Press.
Martin, R. (2015). *Knowledge LTD: Toward a Social Logic of the Derivative*. Philadelphia, PN: Temple University Press.
McNally, D. (2011). *Monsters of the Market: Zombies, Vampires and Global Capitalism*. Boston, MA: Brill.
Medosch, A. (2016). *New Tendencies. Art at the Threshold of the Information Revolution (1961—1978)*. Cambridge: MIT Press.
Meyer, R. (2013). *What Was Contemporary Art?* Cambridge, MA: The MIT Press.

Mouffe, C. (1992). *Dimensions of Radical Democracy: Pluralism, Citizenship, Community.* London and New York: Verso.

Nestler, G. (2007). *Yx. Fluid Taxonomies—Voided Dimensions—Enlitened Elevations—Human Derivatives—Vibrations in Hyperreal Econociety.* Vienna: Schlebrügge Editors.

Nestler, G. (2012–2015). *Portrait of a Philosophy Series: Contingent Claim. Elie Ayache* (2012); *Contingent Ethics. Haim Bodek* (2014–15); *Contingent Optionality. Randy Martin* (2014–15). 1-channel videos. Online: https://vimeo.com/channels/AoR.

Nestler, G. (2014). "Mayhem in Mahwah: The case of the flash crash; or, forensic re-performance in deep time," in Forensic Architecture (ed.), *Forensis.* Berlin: Sternberg Press.

Nestler, G. (2015). "Towards a poietics of resolution," *Journal for Research Cultures* 1. Online publication available at https://researchcultures.com/.

Nestler, G. (2017). *The Derivative Condition: A Present Inquiry into the History of Futures.* PhD thesis. Online: http://research.gold.ac.uk/20534/.

Nestler, G., Kloeckner, Ch., Mueller, S. (2018). "The derivative condition, an aesthetics of resolution, and the figure of the renegade: A conversation," *Finance and Society,* 4(1): 126–43.

Osborne, P. (2013). *Anywhere or Not at All: Philosophy of Contemporary Art.* London and New York: Verso.

Parks, T. (2005). *Medici Money: Banking, Metaphysics, and Art in Fifteenth-century Florence.* New York: W. W. Norton & Company.

Pasquale, F. (2015). *The Black Box Society. The Secret Algorithms That Control Money and Information.* Cambridge: Harvard University Press.

Pasquinelli, M. (2008). *Animal Spirits: A Bestiary of the Commons.* Rotterdam and Amsterdam: NAi Publishers/The Institute of Network Cultures.

Paul, C. (2015). "From immateriality to neomateriality: Art and the conditions of digital materiality," *Disruption.* Proceedings of the 21st International Symposium on Electronic Art (ISEA). Vancouver. Retrieved from http://isea2015.org/proceeding/submissions/ISEA2015_submission_154.pdf.

Praxis Bajo, D., & Carey, B. (2004, October 1). "In interview: Andrea Fraser," *Brooklyn Rail.* Retrieved from https://brooklynrail.org/2004/10/art/andrea-fraser.

Ramos, A. G. (1981). *The New Science of Organization: A Reconceptualization of the Wealth of Nations.* Toronto: University of Toronto Press.

Rancière, J. (2005). *The Politics of Aesthetics: The Distribution of the Sensible,* trans. G. Rockhill. London and New Delhi: Bloomsbury.

Roberts, J. (2007). *The Intangibilities of Form: Skill and Deskilling in Art after the Readymade.* London and New York, NY: Verso.

Roffe, J. (2015). *Abstract Market Theory.* Basingstoke: Palgrave Macmillan.

Roio, D. (2018). *Algorithmic Sovereignty.* PhD thesis. Retrieved from https://pearl.plymouth.ac.uk/handle/10026.1/11101.

Rosamond, E. (2016). "Shared stakes, distributed investment: Socially engaged art and the financialization of social impact," *Finance and Society* 2(2): 111–126.

Salter, C. (2013). *Enterprise Artworks, the Artist-Consultant, and Contemporary Attitudes of Ambivalence.* Master Thesis. MIT Archives.

Sassen, S. (1998). *Globalization and Its Discontent: Essays on the New Mobility of People and Money.* New York, NY: The New Press.

Scott, B. (2015). "Dark side anthropology & the art of financial culturehacking," in C. Wee and O. Arndt (eds.), *Supramarkt: How to Frack the Fatal Forces of the Capitalocene.* Nössemark: Irene Publishing.

Shaviro, S. (2012). *Without Criteria: Kant, Whitehead, Deleuze, and Aesthetics (Technologies of Lived Abstraction).* Cambridge, MA: The MIT Press.

Siegelaub, S., & Projansky, R. (1971). *The Artist's Reserved Rights Transfer and Sale Agreement.* Retrieved from http://www.primaryinformation.org/product/siegelaub-the-artists-reserved-rights-transfer-and-sale-agreement/.

Sklair, L. (2001). *The Transnational Capitalist Class.* Hoboken, NJ: Wiley-Blackwell.

Stallabrass, J. (2004). *Contemporary Art in a Neoliberal Climate.* Lecture notes. Retrieved from http://www.worldofart.org/aktualno/archives/131.

Steyerl, H. (2009). "In defense of the poor image," *e-flux* 10. Retrieved from https://www.e-flux.com/journal/10/61362/in-defense-of-the-poor-image.

Steyerl, H. (2017). *Duty Free Art: Art in the Age of Planetary Civil War.* London and Brooklyn, NY: Verso.

Terranova, T. (2004). *Network Culture: Politics for the Information Age.* New York, NY: Pluto Press.

Thompson, D. (2008). *The $12 Million Stuffed Shark.* New York, NY: Palgrave MacMillan.

Toscano, A., & Kinkle, J. (2015). *Cartographies of the Absolute.* Alresford: Zer0 Books.

University of Oxford and The Alan Turing Institute (2018). *The Market Report 2.0. Blockchain and Financialization in Visual Arts.* Retrieved from https://www.dacs.org.uk/DACSO/media/DACSDocs/Press%20releases/The-Art-Market-2-0-Blockchain-and-Financialization-in-Visual-Arts-2018.pdf.

Veblen, T. (1899). *The Theory of the Leisure Class: An Economic Study in the Evolution of Institution.* London: Macmillan.

Velthuis, O. (2007). *Talking Prices: Symbolic Meaning of Prices on the Market for Contemporary Art.* Princeton, NJ: Princeton University Press.

Velthuis, O., & Baia Curioni, S. (2015). *Cosmopolitan Canvases: The Globalization of Markets for Contemporary Art.* Oxford: Oxford University Press.

Velthuis, O., & Coslor, E. (2012). "The financialization of art," in K. Knorr Cetina and A. Preda (eds.), *The Oxford Handbook of the Sociology of Finance* (pp. 471–490). Oxford: Oxford University Press.

Virno, P., & Hardt, M. (1996). *Radical Thought in Italy: A Potential Politics.* Minneapolis: University of Minnesota Press.

Wallis, B. (1984). "What's wrong with this picture? An introduction," in B. Wallis *Art after Modernism: Rethinking Representation* (pp. xi–xviii). New York, NY and Boston, MA: The Museum of Contemporary Art/Godine.

Wark, M. (2016). "Digital provenance and the artwork as derivative," *e-flux* 77. Retrieved from https://www.e-flux.com/journal/77/77374/digital-provenance-and-the-artwork-as-derivative/.

Weibel, P. (2008). "Genealogy of media art," in F. Di'an and G. Zhang (eds.), *Synthetic Times* (pp. 112–143). Cambridge, MA and Beijing: The MIT Press.

White, H., & White, C. A. (1965). *Canvases and Careers, Institutional Change in the French Painting World.* New York, NY, London and Sydney: J. Wiley and Sons.

Zhang, G. (2018, September 24). "Art versus silicon valley: Are artists losing the conceptual advantage?" *Frieze.* Retrieved from https://frieze.com/article/art-versus-silicon-valley-are-artists-losing-conceptual-advantage?language=de%C2%AC.

INDEX

Note: Italic page numbers refer to figures and page numbers followed by "n" denote endnotes.

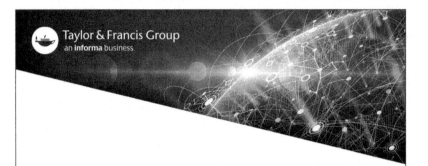

Printed in the United States
By Bookmasters